THE UNITED STATES NAVY AND THE VIETNAM CONFLICT

Volume II

From Military Assistance to Combat 1959-1965

by

EDWARD J. MAROLDA
OSCAR P. FITZGERALD

Naval Historical Center, Department of the Navy
Washington, D.C. 1986

Published by Books Express Publishing
Copyright © Books Express, 2011
ISBN 978-1-780390-28-4

Books Express publications are available from all good retail and online book outlets.
For publishing proposals and direct ordering please contact us at: info@books-express.com

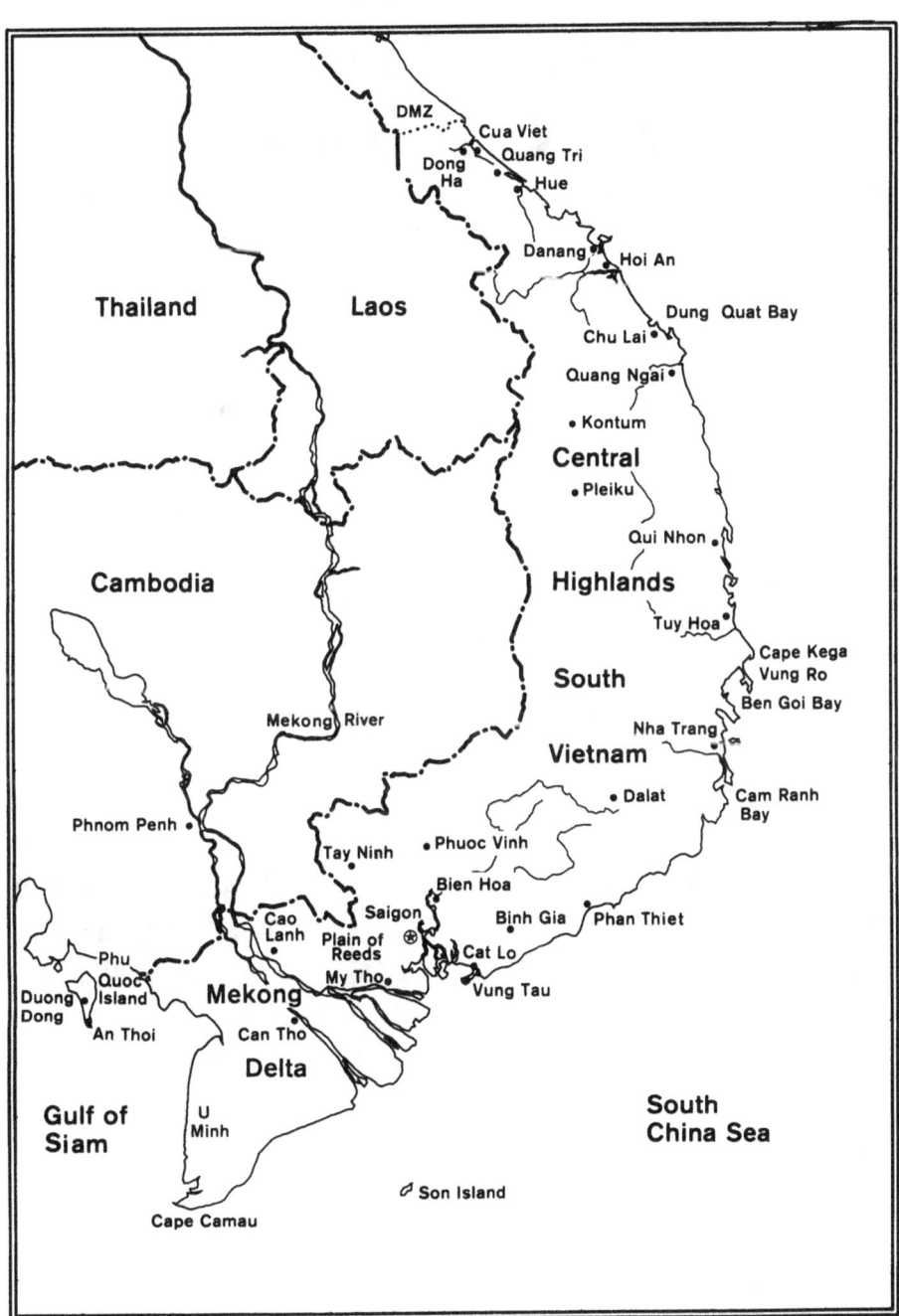

South Vietnam

Secretary of the Navy's Advisory Committee on Naval History

1984

Richard W. Leopold
(Chairman)

Arthur D. Baker, III
James A. Field, Jr.
John H. Kemble

Augustus P. Loring
Jon E. Mandaville
Forrest C. Pogue

Foreword

This second volume of the official history of the Vietnam War treats the period between 1959 and 1965, when the Navy's longstanding efforts to equip and train the South Vietnamese Navy began to be accompanied by unilateral operations in Southeast Asia on the part of U.S. naval forces. In addition to devoting considerable attention to the war in South and North Vietnam, this work details the Navy's actions in Laos, since developments in that country directly related to the defense of America's South Vietnamese allies.

As was true for the first volume in the series, *From Military Assistance to Combat* is primarily an operational account. In general terms this book analyzes the use of seapower to advance U.S. strategic interests in Southeast Asia. In addition to describing the Navy's continuing efforts to strengthen the South Vietnamese Navy through the Military Assistance Program, its authors discuss the operations of U.S. and South Vietnamese forces off the Indochinese coast, in the skies over Laos and North Vietnam, and on the serpentine inland waterways of South Vietnam. To provide background for these subjects, considerable attention is given to the development of strategic policy at the Washington, Honolulu, and Saigon levels, and to the development of American naval concepts and capabilities to undertake counterinsurgency and limited war operations.

This volume is based upon official naval records, to which the authors had full access, personal accounts by participants, and sources generated by other U.S. military services, joint commands, and governmental agencies. Nevertheless, the views expressed in this volume are those of the authors. Mr. Marolda and Dr. Fitzgerald do not necessarily speak for the Department of the Navy, nor have they attempted to present a consensus view of the war in Southeast Asia. The publication was reviewed and its contents declassified and cleared for release by relevant government agencies. Although the manuscript itself was declassified, some of the official sources cited in the volume remained classified at the time of publication.

In presenting this history, the Naval Historical Center hopes to enhance the knowledge by present and future generations of Americans of one aspect of the nation's prolonged involvement in Southeast Asia. We also seek to acknowledge the dedication, honor, and self-sacrifice of the naval officers and men who served their country in this conflict. Although future conditions can never exactly replicate those of the past, we hope that an understanding of this chapter in the Navy's long history will inspire and instruct naval personnel as they carry out their crucial responsibilities to defend the security of the United States.

JOHN D.H. KANE, JR.
Rear Admiral, USN (Ret.)
Director of Naval History

The Authors

Edward J. Marolda, an historian with the Naval Historical Center since 1971, heads the Historical and Writing Section of the Operational Archives Branch. A graduate of Pennsylvania Military College and Georgetown University, where he received the B.A. and M.A. degrees in History, Mr. Marolda currently is a doctoral candidate at The George Washington University. His military experience includes command of U.S. Army units in Vietnam during 1969 and 1970. Mr. Marolda is the coauthor, with G. Wesley Pryce, III, of *A Short History of the United States Navy and the Southeast Asian Conflict, 1950-1975* and he has published articles in the *Naval War College Review*, *Naval Institute Proceedings*, and other scholarly journals. At the present time, he is preparing Volume III in the official Vietnam history series.

Oscar P. Fitzgerald, who now is the Director of the Navy Memorial Museum, served as head of the Historical and Writing Section, Operational Archives, from 1966 to 1979, during which time he contributed to this volume. He received his B.A. degree from Vanderbilt University and the M.A. and Ph.D. degrees in History from Georgetown University. Dr. Fitzgerald coauthored, with Vice Admiral Edwin B. Hooper and Dr. Dean C. Allard, the first volume in the Navy's official Vietnam history series and has written articles for a number of historical journals, including the *Naval Institute Proceedings*.

Acknowledgements

The authors are grateful for the guidance and support provided throughout the preparation of this volume by Rear Admiral John D. H. Kane, Jr., the Director of Naval History. The project was under the immediate direction of Dr. Dean C. Allard, Head of the Operational Archives Branch. Dr. Allard's knowledge of naval history and keen literary sense greatly enhanced the manuscript. Mr. G. Wesley Pryce, III, and Ms. Nina F. Statum, also of the Operational Archives, assisted in editing the book's many drafts. We are especially grateful to Mrs. Katherine J. Huie and YNC Charles A. M. Maze for their extra effort to prepare the manuscript for publication and to Ms. Marianne Conte for the professional quality of her typing. Mr. Charles R. Haberlein, Jr., and Mrs. Agnes F. Hoover of the Curator Branch assisted with the location and reproduction of the work's photographs. The charts, designed by Mr. Marolda, were prepared for publication by Les Davis Designs, Inc. The staff of the Navy Department Library, in particular Mr. John E. Vajda, Ms. Barbara A. Lynch, and Mrs. Carolyn H. Chase, was especially helpful in locating and acquiring source materials. Captain Manuel B. Sousa, Deputy Director of Naval History; and Commander Stanley D. Clark and Mrs. Mary W. Edmison of the Center's Administrative Branch provided essential support in the preparation of the manuscript through the publication and funding process. Finally, we are grateful to many other members of the Naval Historical Center who encouraged and supported us in our work.

Special thanks must go to the distinguished reviewers of this volume, including Admiral Arleigh Burke and Admiral Harry D. Felt, who graciously read and commented on those chapters related to their terms as Chief of Naval Operations and Commander in Chief, Pacific, respectively. Admiral Horacio Rivero, former Vice Chief of Naval Operations, provided equally perceptive remarks on the chapters dealing with the Tonkin Gulf incidents. Vice Admiral Edwin B. Hooper, senior author of Volume I in the Vietnam series and former Director of Naval History, provided a thorough and insightful review of the entire manuscript for which the authors are deeply grateful. Captain William H. Hardcastle, a former Chief, Naval Advisory Group, Vietnam, thoughtfully commented on those chapters relating to the development of the Vietnamese Navy. Additionally, Dr. James A. Field, Jr., a distinguished scholar and member of the Secretary of the Navy's Advisory Committee on Naval History, prepared an invaluable critique of an earlier draft of this work. Captain Mitchell J. Karlowicz, Captain David A. Young, and Commander John C. Bruce, officers assigned to the Naval Historical Center, completed valuable research projects in support of the history. Colleagues in the historical offices of the other armed services, including Mr. Jack Shulimson, Dr. V. Keith Fleming, Jr., and Mr. Charles R. Smith of the Marine Corps Historical Center; Mr. Vincent H. Demma of the Army Center of Military History; and Mr. Warren A. Trest of the Office of Air Force History deserve our thanks for their pertinent comments on the narrative and consistent moral support of the authors on the long trail from conception to publication.

Grateful as we are for these reviews, the authors accept full responsibility for the conclusions drawn in this history and for any errors in fact.

Edward J. Marolda
Oscar P. Fitzgerald

Contents

Chapter	Title	Page
	Foreword	v
	Acknowledgements	ix
	Charts and Illustrations	xiii
I.	The Navy and the Evolution of U.S. Strategy, 1958-1960	1
II.	The Laotian Vortex, 1959-1960	22
III.	Confrontation Over Laos, 1961-1962	59
IV.	The Navy, Counterinsurgency, and the Growing Threat in South Vietnam, 1959-1961	88
V.	U.S. Military Assistance and the Vietnamese Navy	130
VI.	The Seventh Fleet's Contribution to the Limited Partnership, 1961-1963	164
VII.	The Navy Enters the Fight Against Communist Insurgency	189
VIII.	The Naval Advisory and Logistic Support Effort in Vietnam, 1961-1963	219
IX.	Perceptions of the Conflict in South Vietnam and the Diem Coup	264
X.	Readiness of the Fleet for Limited War, 1961-1964	277
XI.	The Advisory Program and the Vietnamese Navy in a Year of Turmoil, 1964	298
XII.	Naval Support to the Counterinsurgency Struggle	334
XIII.	Fleet Air Operations Over Laos	366
XIV.	Naval Engagements in the Gulf of Tonkin	393
XV.	The American Response to the Tonkin Gulf Attacks	437
XVI.	Preparations for an Expanded Conflict	463
XVII.	The Navy Begins Extended Combat Operations in Southeast Asia, 1965	494

Chapter	Title	Page
Appendix I.	Key U.S. Naval Leaders, 1959-1965	535
Appendix II.	Glossary of Abbreviations and Terms	537
Appendix III.	Larger Vessels of the South Vietnamese Navy, 1959-1965	545
	Bibliographic Note	549
	Index	561

Charts and Illustrations

(Illustrations identified by numbers preceded by USN, KN, or K are official U.S. Navy photographs and those preceded by NH are U.S. Naval Historical Center photographs.)

	Page
South Vietnam (chart)	frontispiece
Secretary of the Navy Gates and Admiral Burke	5
Marine helicopters land on board *Princeton*	12
Southeast Asia (chart)	16
Mainland Southeast Asia (chart)	19
Lexington steams for the South China Sea	32
Western Pacific (chart)	35
Joint Chiefs of Staff, 1960	48
Lieutenant John P. Sylva (CEC) meets Phoumi Nosavan	65
Kearsarge enters Subic Bay	67
Leaders of the national defense establishment, 1961	70
Admirals Burke and Hostvedt inspect a Nasty class MTB	92
Provinces of South Vietnam (chart)	105
Admiral Felt bids farewell to Vice President Johnson	110
U.S. naval officers call on Cambodian Defense Minister Lon Nol	119
U.S. Organizational Structure for Military Assistance	133
Organization of the South Vietnamese Navy, 1959-1963	136
Rear Admiral Alfred G. Ward and Commander Ho Tan Quyen	141
Vietnamese Navy LSIL *Long Dao*	144
Mekong Delta (chart)	153
17th Parallel Patrol (chart)	167
Ocean minesweeper *Pledge* on coastal patrol	170
Coastal Patrol in the Gulf of Siam (chart)	174
President Ngo Dinh Diem on board *Mahan*	181
EA-1F Skyraider at Cubi Point	186
SEAL on patrol in the Rung Sat	191
SEABEE Team Deployments in Central South Vietnam, (chart)	195
PTF-3 and PTF-4 off Hawaii	207
U.S. naval advisor observes training	222
Vietnamese Naval Zone Commands (chart)	226
Coastal Force junk patrol	235
Sea Force LSSL *Linh Kiem*	244
Rung Sat Swamp (chart)	246
Saigon (chart)	256

	Page
Aircraft carrier *Hancock*	271
Admirals Sharp and Moorer confer	274
Motor gunboat *Asheville*	290
F-4 Phantom II test fires a Sparrow III missile	296
U.S. naval advisors inspect Coastal Force quarters	300
American naval advisor and Vietnamese counterpart	307
Coastal Force Dispositions, January 1965 (chart)	315
Area of the An Xuyen Quarantine (chart)	321
Joint Operation at Ilo Ilo Island (chart)	328
River assault group craft	331
Coast of North Vietnam (chart)	336
Guided missile cruiser *Oklahoma City* visits Saigon	345
General Westmoreland on board *Princeton*	347
SEABEE Team Deployment Sites in South Vietnam, 1964-1965 (chart)	351
LST of Headquarters Support Activity, Saigon, loads supplies	360
Saigon Station Hospital nurses awarded Purple Hearts	362
Laotian Panhandle (chart)	374
Lieutenant Klusmann describes captivity to Admiral Johnson	383
Central Laos (chart)	387
RF-8A Crusader flies over *Ticonderoga*	390
Intended Track of the Desoto Patrol (chart)	401
Destroyer *Maddox*	403
Organization and Basing of North Vietnamese Naval Forces, 1964	408
Track of *Maddox*, 31 July-2 August 1964 (chart)	412
Captain Herrick and Commander Ogier	413
Naval Engagement of 2 August (chart)	416
North Vietnamese P-4 MTBs attack *Maddox*	418
Track of *Maddox* and *Turner Joy*, 3-5 August 1964 (chart)	423
Destroyer *Turner Joy*	428
Naval Action on the Night of 4 August (chart)	430
Area of U.S. Naval Operations in North Vietnam, 1964-1965 (chart)	439
A-4 Skyhawk launches from *Ticonderoga*	445
North Vietnamese naval craft under air attack	448
Enemy Swatow gunboat burns	450
Attack Squadron 146 Skyhawks fly over *Constellation*	458
Soviet-made MiG fighter	471
Ranger ordnancemen load bombs on a Skyraider	481
A-1 Skyraider launches from *Ranger*	499
Command Arrangements for Rolling Thunder	503
Task Force 77 at Yankee Station	508
F-4 Phantom II bombs Viet Cong positions	516
Market Time Patrol Areas (chart)	518
SP-2 Neptune patrol plane of Market Time	520

	Page
LCU 1476 transports Marine equipment ashore at Danang	528
Landing the Marines at Danang, 8 March 1965 (chart)	530

CHAPTER I

The Navy and the Evolution of U.S. Strategy, 1958-1960

The years from 1958 to 1960 witnessed a reorientation in strategic thinking that eventually contributed to a more extensive involvement by the United States Navy in the continuing Vietnam conflict. During the last years of the Eisenhower administration, the defense community gave greater attention to the theories of limited war and "flexible" or "graduated military response." Naval officers played a large role in refashioning military policies based on these concepts. The emerging strategic outlook influenced the composition and capabilities of the American fleet of the 1960s. As a result, the Navy of the Kennedy and Johnson administrations was different in many respects from that of the preceding administration.

Massive Retaliation

Until the latter part of President Dwight D. Eisenhower's second term in office, the "massive retaliation" doctrine, which was influenced by the deterrent effect of U.S. superiority in nuclear weaponry, was an important element of American strategic thinking. The concept was enunciated in January 1954 by Secretary of State John Foster Dulles and reflected the nation's experience during the Korean War. The heavy cost in American lives and material resources and the discontent resulting from that conflict's limited nature and inconclusive end led to the Eisenhower administration's "New Look" in defense policy. The program was influenced by the strategic perception that the overwhelming manpower superiority of the Communist powers could be countered realistically only through nuclear warfare. At the same time, the financial cost to the United

States of maintaining large tactical combat forces could be reduced correspondingly.

It was not long, however, before many academic theorists and retired military officers challenged the wisdom of this approach.[1] Even Secretary of State Dulles, who first detailed the massive retaliation doctrine, publicly qualified his support for it in October 1957. The fundamental precepts of U.S. defense policy were further questioned after the Soviet Union demonstrated its technological sophistication with the Sputnik launch and orbit that same month. It then became apparent that the Communists had the potential for developing long-range nuclear warhead delivery systems, challenging the U.S. monopoly in this field.

The following April, Dulles called for a serious review of strategic policy by the armed forces. The Secretary of State, at a meeting of the Armed Forces Policy Council on 7 April 1958, stated that "support for the present concept among our allies is diminishing rapidly" because the Soviet Union had also developed a lethal nuclear arsenal which would preclude resort to general war where "each side would wipe the other one out." The allies were concerned that the United States "would not invoke a massive retaliation under certain situations" such as limited conflicts or those where U.S. forces were not directly involved. Secretary Dulles went on to question, "are we prisoners of this retaliatory concept? Are our forces, our weapons and our strategy frozen to the use of general retaliation?" He was afraid that "perhaps our military establishment was getting unable to do anything but drop large nuclear weapons." The Secretary of Defense, Neil McElroy, replied that "the position and forces developed *do* [italics added] depend upon the strategic concept." Secretary of State Dulles called for "more flexibility than that concept alone will give us."[2]

---

[1] Henry Kissinger, *Nuclear Weapons and Foreign Policy* (New York: Harper and Brothers, 1957) and Matthew B. Ridgway, *Soldier: The Memoirs of Matthew B. Ridgway* (New York: Harper and Brothers, 1956). See also Paul R. Schratz, "The Military Services and the New Look, 1953-1961: The Navy" in David H. White, ed., *Proceedings of the Conference on War and Diplomacy* (Charleston, SC: The Citadel, 1976), pp. 140-43; Richard A. Aliano, *American Defense Policy from Eisenhower to Kennedy: The Politics of Changing Military Requirements, 1957-1961* (Athens, OH: Ohio Univ. Press, 1975), pp. 24-46; Edward J. Marolda, "The Influence of Burke's Boys on Limited War," *U.S. Naval Institute Proceedings* (hereafter USNIP), Aug 1981.

[2] CNO, memo for record, "Report of Meeting with Secretary of State on Concept of Retaliation," ser 000188-58 of 7 Apr 1958. See also John Foster Dulles, "Challenge and Response in United States Policy," *Foreign Affairs*, Vol. 36, No. 1 (Oct 1957), p. 31; OP-93, memo, ser 0007P93 of 30 Oct 1957; Arleigh A. Burke, transcript of interview with Richard Challener, John Foster Dulles Oral

Development of the Flexible Response Concept

The reanalysis of U.S. strategy within the national defense community already was underway, and it intensified in succeeding years. Advocates of a change in policy from one emphasizing nuclear retaliation to a more flexible system, using the full range of options available to the United States, included naval strategists and top-ranking officers. Present at the meeting with Dulles on 7 April was Admiral Arleigh A. Burke, Chief of Naval Operations (CNO), who stressed the need "to have the capability for deterring or fighting general nuclear war, for large local wars and for small local wars. We needed tactical nuclear weapons. We needed to have a capability for conventional weapons and plans to use them. We needed to be able to move fast."[3]

The following month, Admiral Burke, writing to Lord Louis Mountbatten, British First Sea Lord and Chief of Staff of the Royal Navy, expressed his concern that perhaps the concentration on nuclear war "has caused us to generate excessive forces for retaliation and not give enough thought to those forces useable in more limited situations." He added that "nuclear retaliatory forces will not solve the myriad other problems with which we are confronted." The Chief of Naval Operations, anticipating future crises, warned that "if we go too far on the megaton road we will, I think, have found that the free world will have been lost by erosion, and perhaps not even military erosion."[4]

Others in the defense community also argued that the United States should fashion its defense resources to meet all levels of potential enemy threats. Although nuclear weapons might form part of a response, conventional weapons and forces often were more appropriate. The

---

History Project, Princeton University, in Washington, D.C., 11 Jan 1966, pp. 4-5, 52-54; Aliano, *American Defense Policy*, pp. 47-60.

[3] CNO, memo for record, ser 000188-58 of 7 Apr 1958. See also OP-93, ltr, ser 0007P93 of 30 Oct 1957; OP-93, memo, ser 0008P93 of 3 Dec 1957; ltr, CNO to Flag and General Officers, of 22 Aug 1960, pp. 24-31; ltr, Burke to Stratton, of 14 Sep 1959; memo, OP-61 of SECNAV/CNO, ser 00195P61 of 8 Jun 1960; Anthony E. Sokol, "Sword and Shield in Our Power Structure," USNIP, Vol. 85 (Apr 1959), pp. 44-53; Brown Taylor, "The Lesser Deterrent," USNIP, Vol. 85 (Aug 1959), pp. 33-39; K.W. Simmons, "National Security in the Nuclear Age," USNIP, Vol. 86 (Jun 1960), pp. 83-91; Gordon B. Turner, "Air and Sea Power in Relation to National Power" in Gordon B. Turner and Richard D. Challener, eds., *National Security in the Nuclear Age: Basic Facts and Theories* (New York: Frederick A. Praeger, 1960), pp. 242-45; Schratz, "The Military Services and the New Look," p. 141; Aliano, *American Defense Policy*, pp. 116-19.

[4] Ltr, Burke to Mountbatten, of 15 May 1958.

concept of "flexible response," which gained wide currency following its elaboration in General Maxwell D. Taylor's work, *The Uncertain Trumpet*, published in 1960, represented the demand for a less restrictive strategy than that of assured nuclear retaliation.[5]

Naval policymakers had long stressed the multiplicity of the Navy's mission and its balanced capabilities. The Navy possessed a capacity for general retaliation throughout the 1950s in the form of nuclear armed carrier aviation, although the role of the aircraft carrier was seen as primarily tactical in nature. The acquisition of Polaris ballistic missile firing submarines, the first of which, *George Washington* (SSBN-598), entered the fleet on 30 December 1959, provided the Navy with its only major single-purpose strategic weapon system.[6] But the Navy also maintained a wide variety of conventional warfare weapons and forces, from ship and land-based aircraft, surface warships, and submarines, to amphibious ships and craft and deployed Marine units. The perceived advent of a period of mutual nuclear deterrence between the Soviet Union and the United States convinced many theorists that the ability of the Navy to deal with situations short of global war would become increasingly crucial.

As an alternative to general nuclear war, U.S. strategists developed a variety of limited war concepts which reflected the effort to restrict, localize, and shorten armed conflicts. This, it was reasoned, would enable the United States to combat less than total Communist aggression in such areas as Southeast Asia while decreasing the risk of all-out war. And many observers, including concerned naval leaders, believed that the most probable armed conflicts of the future would take the shape of limited objective or "brush-fire" wars.[7]

---

[5]The extent of General Taylor's later influence with the Kennedy administration is reflected in the fact that he was to serve as Special Military Representative to the President from 1961 to 1962 and as Chairman of the Joint Chiefs of Staff from 1962 to 1964. Maxwell D. Taylor, *The Uncertain Trumpet* (New York: Harper, 1960); memo, OP-90 to CNO, No. 427-58 of 4 Dec 1958.

[6]Lulejian and Associates, Inc., "Refining the Nuclear Attack Capability and Adapting It to a Mission (1952-1962)," pt. II of "US Aircraft Carriers in the Strategic Role," of study "History of the Strategic Arms Competition 1945-1972," Oct 1975, p. II-38.

[7]OP-93, ltr, ser 0008P93 of 3 Dec 1957; CNO, Annual Report, FY1958, pp. 1-3; Rand Corporation, "The Sierra Project: A Study of Limited Wars," Report No. R-317 of May 1958; Department of Defense Science Board, Task Group on Limited War, "Final Report," Vol. III, 1 Sep 1958; Arleigh Burke, "The Sea Carries Security on Its Back," *Navy - Magazine of Seapower*, Vol. 1, No.1 (May 1958), pp. 9-10; Malcolm W. Cagle, "Sea Power and Limited War," USNIP, Vol. 84, No. 7 (Jul 1958), pp. 23-27; George H. Miller, "Not for the Timid," USNIP, Vol. 85, No. 5 (May 1959), pp. 34-42; "Limited War: Where do they Stand," *Army, Navy, Air Force Register*, Vol. 80, No.

The Navy and the Evolution of U.S. Strategy 5

Admiral Arleigh Burke, the Chief of Naval Operations, confers with Secretary of the Navy Thomas S. Gates, Jr. in April 1959.

This new strategic emphasis soon was reflected in the contingency planning process. For instance, the basic plan from 1956 to 1958 for the defense of South Vietnam against Chinese or North Vietnamese attacks was the Commander in Chief, Pacific Operation Plan 46-56, the non-nuclear options of which were limited. Admiral Burke and other leaders questioned the current dependence on nuclear weapons in active plans. In January 1959 he proposed to the Joint Chiefs of Staff (JCS) that provision be made for major contingencies where conventional forces alone would have to be able to accomplish the mission. Gradually a consensus developed among the JCS in favor of this recommendation.[8]

Attuned to this new direction in strategic thinking, and indeed a persuasive advocate of it, Admiral Harry D. Felt, the Commander in Chief, Pacific (CINCPAC), explored changes to the plans relating to his theater. In this, he also was influenced by his experiences during the Taiwan Strait crisis of 1958, when he became aware of the lack of readiness for non-nuclear warfare. Early in 1959 he apprised Admiral Burke that "I have in mind the essential requirement for planners to think of and for operators to train with non-nuclear weapons."[9] Shortly afterward, Admiral Felt directed that all CINCPAC contingency plans to be prepared in 1959 provide for initial operations where atomic weapons would not be used.[10]

Under these circumstances, it is not surprising that, throughout the period, defense analysts and military leaders affirmed that additional conventional warfare resources were needed. As Admiral Burke stated in early 1959,

> situations requiring quick action and strong, capable forces will probably occur in the future. Crises such as Lebanon and Taiwan, occurring simultaneously and on opposite sides of the world, severely tax our

---

4146 (May 1959), pp. 24-25; CINCPAC, "CINCPAC's Evaluation of Capabilities and Major Deficiencies in His Command," (early) 1958; memo, DCNO (Plans and Policy) to ASD (ISA), ser 00099P60 of 19 Mar 1959.

[8]OP-60, briefing memo, No. 490-58 of 5 Jan 1959. See also memo, CNO to JCS, ser 0001P60 of Jan 1959; Ronald H. Spector, *Advice and Support: The Early Years, 1941-1960* in series *United States Army in Vietnam* (Washington: Center of Military History, U.S. Army, 1983), p. 358.

[9]Ltr, Felt to Burke, of 29 Jan 1959. See also Harry D. Felt, transcript of interview with John T. Mason, Jr., U.S. Naval Institute, in Makalapa, HA, Mar 1972, Vol. II, p. 396; NSC, OP-93, memo, ser 0007P93 of 30 Oct 1957; Lulejian, "U.S. Aircraft Carriers in the Strategic Role," pt. II, pp. 32-33; memo, OP-61 to OP-06, ser 00066P61 of 7 Jul 1959; ltr, CINCPACFLT to CINCPAC, ser 34/000322 of 20 Dec 1958.

[10]CINCPAC, Command History, 1959, p. 39.

limited war capabilities. We must have adequate and ready forces, in the right place at the right time and in sufficient strength to cope with what ever actions are required.[11]

This was indeed a tall order, because the Navy's worldwide responsibilities, in addition to the nuclear deterrence role, were many. During this period the Soviet-American confrontation required the constant deployment of the Sixth Fleet to the Mediterranean and other Atlantic Fleet forces throughout that ocean. Support for America's North Atlantic Treaty Organization allies, readiness to deter or limit war in the Middle East, and hindrance of Communist penetration of African and Latin American countries demanded a strong, mobile, and versatile fleet. Crises over Berlin, the Congo, and Cuba during this time emphasized that point.

The Pacific Fleet's mission was equally demanding and included readiness to protect vital sea lines of communication, deploy strong naval forces near contested areas, and project U.S. power ashore in support of allies. The Commander in Chief, U.S. Pacific Fleet (CINCPACFLT) acted under the direction of the Commander in Chief, Pacific, who, although traditionally a four-star admiral, was a unified commander exercising operational control of Army, Navy, and Air Force components. As the naval component, CINCPACFLT commanded the First Fleet in the Eastern Pacific and the Seventh Fleet in the Western Pacific. The latter naval force secured the waters stretching north to south, from Siberia to Australia and, west to east, from the Asian mainland to Hawaii, an area of thirty million square miles. This forward fleet was charged with the defense of Japan, South Korea, the Republic of China, the Philippines, and many of the non-Communist nations of Southeast Asia, in concert with their own forces. The Seventh Fleet faced the potentially hostile armed forces of the Soviet Union, the People's Republic of China, North Korea, and North Vietnam. As an example of its duties, Seventh Fleet units during 1960 deployed into the Sea of Japan, the Strait of Taiwan, and the South China Sea; conducted amphibious and antisubmarine warfare exercises with allied navies; carried Indonesian and Malayan troops to the Congo; rescued hundreds of aviators and mariners in distress; made an average of 300 port calls a month to friendly nations; and transported President Eisenhower during his historic visit to the Far East.

---

[11] Memo, Burke to All Flag Officers, of 4 Mar 1959.

The organization of the Navy's deployed fleets was well suited to the many diverse duties assigned to them. Each of the numbered fleets was composed of task forces oriented toward a specific operational function. For instance, the Seventh Fleet consisted of the Taiwan Patrol Force (Task Force 72), Mobile Logistic Support Force (Task Force 73), Amphibious Force (Task Force 76), Attack Carrier Striking Force (Task Force 77), and Fleet Marine Force (Task Force 79). These forces were further subdivided, according to mission requirements, into task groups, task units, and task elements. In addition, Commander Seventh Fleet controlled the separate antisubmarine Hunter-Killer Group (Task Group 70.4), Mine Group (Task Group 70.5), Cruiser-Destroyer Group (Task Group 70.8), Submarine Group (Task Group 70.9), and Amphibious Ready Group (Task Group 76.5)

Exclusive of operations, however, the Navy's surface vessel, submarine, and aircraft units were the responsibility of distinct "type commands" directly subordinated to area fleet commanders. For example, Commander in Chief, U.S. Pacific Fleet controlled a Cruiser-Destroyer Force, Naval Air Force, Submarine Force, Amphibious Force, Service Force, Mine Force, Fleet Marine Force, and Training Command. These commands ensured the personnel, material, and training support of the Navy's combat forces. In practice, Commander in Chief, U.S. Pacific Fleet, through his type commanders, assigned individual units to Commander Seventh Fleet or Commander First Fleet for operational missions. Still, this flexible and responsive organization, refined during World War II and the Korean conflict, required sufficient ships, weapons, and naval personnel to make it work.

Budgetary Constraints and Naval Conventional Forces

While the Eisenhower administration came to accept many of the theoretical assumptions of the flexible response concept, and endorsed a strengthening of U.S. non-nuclear weapons and forces, the austere defense budgets for the fiscal years from 1957 to 1960 did not generally reflect this new emphasis. Defense Department expenditures during these years ranged from $38.4 billion to $41.5 billion, and in the last two fiscal years expenditures remained virtually constant at just over $41 billion.[12] Almost half of these funds went to the Air Force, whose mission stressed the conduct of strategic nuclear warfare with long-range bombers and ballistic missiles. The Navy received about one-fourth of the budget and a significant percentage of that total went to the new strategic missile submarine force.[13]

The accent on strategic retaliation led to a reduction in the capacity of the conventional forces to perform all the roles assigned them in situations short of general war. While funds available to the Navy remained at a relatively constant level, labor, material, and other costs, especially those concerned with ship construction or modernization, rose significantly. Aggravating this problem was the fact that the majority of the ships in the fleet were of World War II origin, and were beginning to reach obsolescence en masse.

In an effort to improve fleet capabilities, ships incorporating the latest technology were designed, built, and introduced to the fleet, or existing vessels were converted and modernized. The new additions included nuclear-powered ships such as submarines of the *Skate* (SSN-578), *Skipjack* (SSN-585), *Triton* (SSN-586), and *Halibut* (SSGN-587) classes, as well as the conventionally powered aircraft carriers *Ranger* (CVA-61) and *Independence* (CVA-62). Guided missile ships such as *Dewey* (DLG-7), *Preble* (DLG-15), and submarine *Growler* (SSG-577) also entered fleet service during this period. Nonetheless, in the fiscal years from 1957 to 1960, fleet strength was reduced from 409 warships and 558 other combatants and auxiliaries to 376 warships and 436 other vessels. In 1959, the Secretary of the Navy, William B. Franke, noted that "only the ships at the very top of priority lists can be built, converted, or modernized" and that the quality of new ships was "excellent, but their number is insufficient to meet the replacement problem."[14]

---

[12]In contrast, in the first Kennedy administration budget, that of Fiscal Year 1962, expenditures totalled $46.8 billion. DOD, *Annual Report of the Secretary of Defense*, FY1960 (Washington: GPO,1961), p. 34. See also "Semiannual Report of the Secretary of the Navy" in DOD, *Semiannual Report of the Secretary of Defense*, 1 Jan to 30 Jun 1957 (Washington: GPO, 1958), p. 172; DOD, *Semiannual Report of the Secretary of Defense*, 1 Jan to 30 Jun 1958 (Washington: GPO, 1959), p. 17; DOD, *Annual Report of the Secretary of Defense*, FY1962 (Washington: GPO, 1963), p. 370.

[13]DOD, *Annual Report*, FY1960, p. 34; Robert F. Futrell, *Ideas, Concepts, Doctrine: A History of Basic Thinking in the United States Air Force, 1907-1964* (Maxwell AFB, AL: Air Univ., 1971), pp. 317-18, 322-29.

[14]"Annual Report of the Secretary of the Navy" in DOD, *Annual Report of the Secretary of Defense*, FY 1959 (Washington: GPO, 1960), pp. 244, 283. See also "Semiannual Report of the Secretary of the Navy" in DOD, *Semiannual Report*, Jan-Jun 1957, pp. 197, 231-33, 249; "Semiannual Report of the

The overall material condition of the fleet also had progressively worsened by the end of the decade. This resulted from the increasing age of the ships, heavy operating schedules during periodic international crises, and lack of sufficient funds for overhauls and maintenance. In 1959, 72 percent of the ships inspected by the Board of Inspection and Survey were found to be unsatisfactory. Measures were taken to alleviate this situation, which included institution of the Material Improvement Plan and the Fleet Rehabilitation and Modernization (FRAM) program. The former procedure gave priority in the allocation of funds to improvement of the fleet's striking power and its antisubmarine and antiaircraft systems. The FRAM program, introduced in 1959, sought to ameliorate the material deterioration of World War II ships, which then comprised over 80 percent of the active fleet, through a four-year reconditioning and modernization effort. Nonetheless, the following year Secretary of the Navy Franke reported that "the present material readiness of the Fleet is improved from a year ago but is still marginally low."[15]

The fleet's material problems were compounded by the yearly reduction in naval personnel. Between 30 June 1957 and 30 June 1960, the active duty strength of the Navy decreased by over 59,000 personnel, from 677,000 to 618,000. During Fiscal Year 1958, cuts in personnel, which previously had been absorbed by support activities, began to affect the combat forces. The following year, austere personnel allocations necessitated a manning level of 81 percent, which the Lebanon and Taiwan crises demonstrated was at least 4 percent below that deemed necessary for the operation of active ships. At the end of Fiscal Year 1960, the Secretary of the Navy cautioned:

> The pressure upon manpower resources continues to grow, and along with it the difficulty of meeting, within presently authorized limits, the increasing requirements of new ships and weapon programs. Coupled

---

Secretary of the Navy" in DOD, *Semiannual Report*, Jan-Jun 1958, pp. 240-42; "Annual Report of the Secretary of the Navy" in DOD, *Annual Report*, FY1959, pp. 31, 220, 241-42; "Annual Report of the Secretary of the Navy" in DOD, *Annual Report*, FY1960, pp. 249, 264-65.

[15]"Annual Report of the Secretary of the Navy" in DOD, *Annual Report*, FY1960, pp. 249, 270. See also "Semiannual Report of the Secretary of the Navy" in DOD, *Semiannual Report*, Jan-Jun 1957, p. 197; "Semiannual Report of the Secretary of the Navy" in DOD, *Semiannual Report*, Jan-Jun 1958, pp. 218, 221; "Annual Report of the Secretary of the Navy" in DOD, *Annual Report*, FY1959, pp. 221, 224, 244-45; memo, OP-09D to OP-90, ser 00614-58 of 17 Oct 1958.

with lowered manning levels in shore activities, these demands for naval personnel are creating the need for a higher authorized strength, or the alternative of further reductions in operating ships and aircraft.[16]

The degradation of the naval conventional warfare capabilities was especially pronounced in the amphibious forces. Most amphibious vessels in the fleet were of World War II construction, and as a result they suffered a high material casualty rate. Lacking the priority status of the submarine, air, and most other surface forces, the amphibious arm did not always have sufficient funds for proper maintenance and for replacement ships and craft.

The lack of funds especially hampered the development of the helicopter, whose potential for amphibious warfare long was recognized by officers of the Navy and the Marine Corps. For example, at the end of 1955 Admiral Burke concluded that "plans must be laid for a gradual transition from World War II concepts of landing entirely over the beaches to the ultimate goal of landing all the assault elements by [helicopter] transport aircraft."[17] New ships were needed to test these "vertical envelopment" techniques. But, before 1961 only the expedient of converting World War II aircraft carriers *Princeton* (CVS-37) and *Boxer* (CVS-21) and escort carrier *Thetis Bay* (CVE-90) to amphibious assault ships (LPH) enabled realistic exercises. In his final annual report, Secretary of the Navy Franke stated that "progress toward a strong helicopter-borne assault capability for the Marines continues to be limited by a lack of modern, specially configured ships."[18]

Resources for the traditional over-the-beach forces were even more strained. A small number of landing ships, tank (LST), landing ships, dock

---

[16]"Annual Report of the Secretary of the Navy" in DOD, *Annual Report*, FY1960, p. 259. See also "Semiannual Report of the Secretary of the Navy" in DOD, *Semiannual Report*, Jan-Jun 1957, pp. 4, 220; "Semiannual Report of the Secretary of the Navy" in DOD, *Semiannual Report*, Jan-Jun 1958, pp. 7, 226; "Annual Report of the Secretary of the Navy" in DOD, *Annual Report*, FY1959, pp. 9, 233.

[17]Quoted in Eugene W. Rawlins and William J. Sambito, *Marines and Helicopters, 1946-1962* (Washington: History and Museums Division, Headquarters USMC, 1976), p. 65.

[18]"Annual Report of the Secretary of the Navy" in DOD, *Annual Report*, FY1960, p. 242. See also "Semiannual Report of the Secretary of the Navy" in DOD, *Semiannual Report*, Jan-Jun 1957, pp. 182, 234-35; "Semiannual Report of the Secretary of the Navy" in DOD, *Semiannual Report*, Jan-Jun 1958, pp. 217, 223; "Annual Report of the Secretary of the Navy" in DOD, *Annual Report*, FY1959, pp. 219-20, 243, 283; ltr, CINCPACFLT to COMPHIBPAC and CGFMFPAC, ser 34/00419 of 12 May 1958; Norman Polmar, *Aircraft Carriers: A Graphic History of Carrier Aviation and Its Influence on World Events* (Garden City, NY: Doubleday and Co., 1969), pp. 609-12; Rawlins and Sambito, *Marines and Helicopters*, pp. 70-81, 87-89; William R. Fails, *Marines and Helicopters, 1962-1973* (Washington: History and Museums Division, Headquarters USMC, 1978), pp. 21-23.

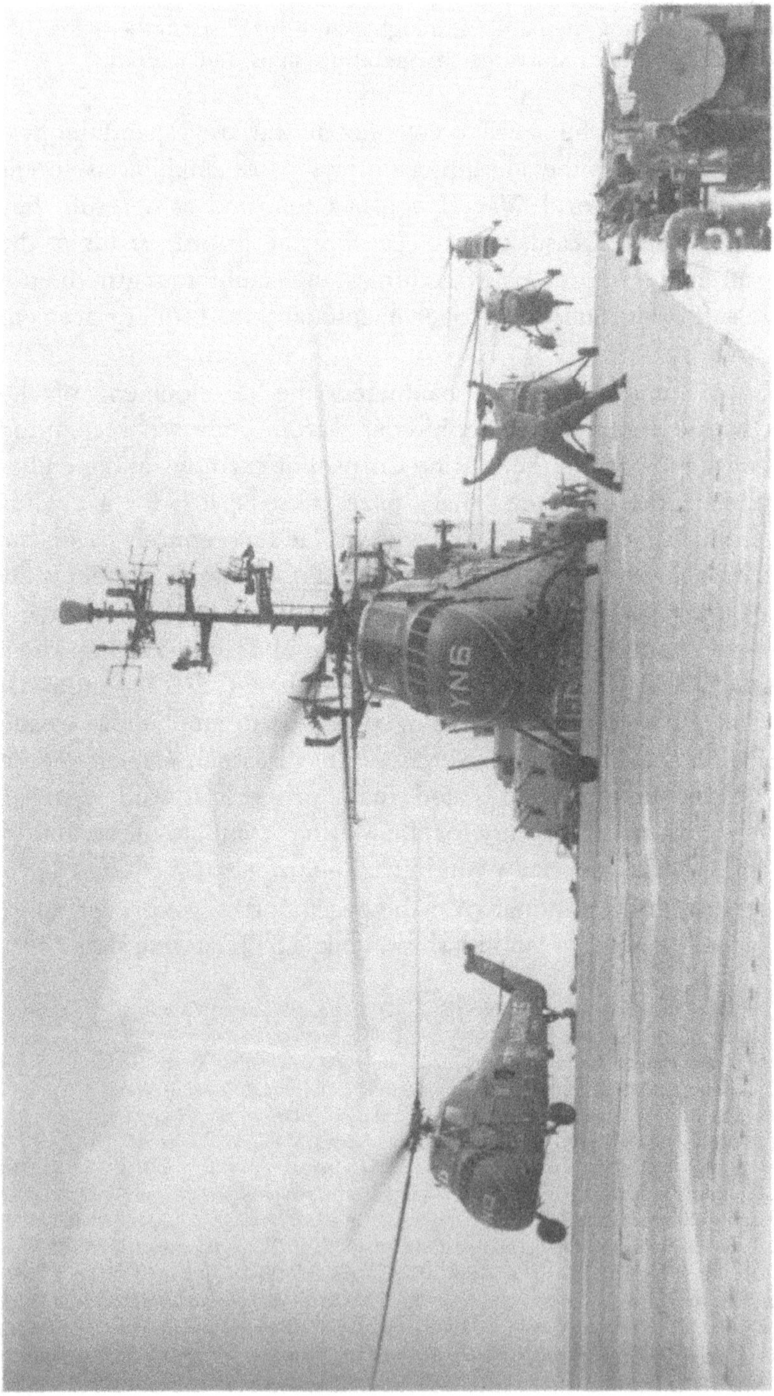

USN-1042924

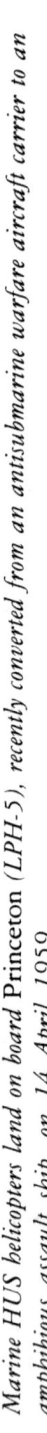

Marine HUS helicopters land on board Princeton *(LPH-5), recently converted from an antisubmarine warfare aircraft carrier to an amphibious assault ship, on 14 April 1959.*

(LSD), and other ships and craft entered fleet service in the 1957-1960 period, but this was more than offset by material deterioration and reductions resulting from obsolescence and lack of experienced manpower. Further, programmed construction of landing craft, mechanized (LCM), landing craft, personnel, large (LCPL) and landing craft, vehicle and personnel (LCVP), was curtailed in favor of other priority shipbuilding. In Fiscal Year 1959, the amphibious forces experienced difficulty in satisfying all operational requirements, and the following year, Secretary of the Navy Franke stated that "high shipbuilding costs and low annual replacement programs widen the gap between current modern amphibious shipping inventory and the minimum future goal."[19]

Another factor contributing to a decline in amphibious warfare capability was the continuous reduction of Marine Corps personnel. Between June 1956 and June 1959, Marine strength decreased from 201,000 to 171,000 active duty personnel. The cuts were absorbed, during Fiscal Years 1957 and 1958, by units of the Fleet Marine Force, and while combat readiness reportedly remained unimpaired, sustained combat would have taxed Marine resources. In 1959, however, the Secretary of the Navy noted that the continued decrease of Marine personnel resulted in

> reduction of some elements of the Fleet Marine Force to cadre status. Specifically, six battalion landing teams have been so reduced and Marine aviation elements were reduced by the equivalent of six squadrons. The net effect of this loss has been to decrease the combat effectiveness and staying power of each division and aircraft wing by about 20 percent.[20]

Pacific Naval Forces

The diminished capacity of the Navy's conventional warfare forces for conducting limited war was reflected in the status of Pacific naval forces. In early 1958, Admiral Felix B. Stump, CINCPAC, expressed his concern

---

[19] "Annual Report of the Secretary of the Navy" in DOD, *Annual Report*, FY1959, p. 219. See also "Semiannual Report of the Secretary of the Navy" in DOD, *Semiannual Report*, Jan-Jun 1957, p. 235.

[20] "Annual Report of the Secretary of the Navy" in DOD, *Annual Report*, FY1959, p. 227. See also "Semiannual Report of the Secretary of the Navy" in DOD, *Semiannual Report*, Jan-Jun 1957, pp. 4, 201; "Semiannual Report of the Secretary of the Navy" in DOD, *Semiannual Report*, Jan-Jun 1958, pp. 7, 223; DOD, *Annual Report*, FY1960, p. 9.

over the continued whittling away of U.S. military strength actually in place in the Pacific which is gradually reducing the capability of [Pacific Command] forces to meet the many emergency situations which may arise in limited war as well as the ever present threat of general war and which cannot entirely be compensated for by increased numbers of atomic weapons.[21]

The following year, in June, Admiral Felt, Admiral Stump's successor, stated that "the United States has no sustaining power in the Pacific for conventional war."[22] He noted the fact that his command possessed thousands of tons of World War II bombs that could not be effectively used with modern aircraft, and had other technical problems with antisubmarine torpedoes, depth charges, and low drag bombs. Furthermore, "replacement ammunition for conventional warfare has been cut out of our budgets for several years."[23]

Other naval leaders complained of an inadequate airlift and sealift capability, which hampered the mobility of Marine and Army forces and a decrease in the number of amphibious craft. The amount of conventional weapons and ammunition stored on board fleet carriers increasingly was reduced to accommodate nuclear devices. A U.S. government interdepartmental study group determined that, in the Pacific, the American ability to respond to conventional aggression was weakest in Southeast Asia, where only small stocks of supplies existed, and logistic support facilities, air bases, and communications facilities were inadequate for sustained operations. Admiral John H. Sides, CINCPACFLT, observed two months before President Eisenhower left office that "our limited war capability has decreased over the years."[24]

---

[21]CINCPAC, "CINCPAC's Evaluation of Capabilities," (early) 1958, p. 5.
[22]CNO, memo for record, ser 000300-59 of 29 Jun 1959.
[23]*Ibid.* See also memo, OP-90 to CNO, No. 427-58 of 4 Dec 1958.
[24]Ltr, Sides to Burke, of 14 Nov 1960. See also DOD, Science Board, "Final Report;" CINCPAC, "CINCPAC's Evaluation of Capabilities;" President's Science Advisory Committee, "Weapons Technology for Limited Warfare;" CINCPACFLT, Annual Report, FY1958, pp. 4, 23, 29-30; FY1959, pp. 3, 47; FY1960, pp. 4-5, 19, 24, 48; ltrs, Burke to Villiers, ser 00477P60 of 14 Oct 1958; Burke to Dowling, ser 00478P60 of 14 Oct 1958; CINCPACFLT to CNO, ser 45/00426 of 21 May 1959; CINCPACFLT to Chief, Bureau of Naval Weapons, ser 00754 of 1 Sep 1960; CNO, memo for record, ser 000300-59 of 29 Jun 1959; memos, DCNO (Plans and Policy) to ASD (ISA), ser 00099P60 of 19 Mar 1959; OP-405 to CNO, ser 005244P40 of 31 Dec 1960; msg, CPFLT 042155Z Nov 1959.

U.S. Policy Toward Southeast Asia

As strategic thinking underwent a reorientation in the last years of the Eisenhower administration, the U.S. perception of the Cold War, and its implications for Southeast Asia, was changing as well. Foreign affairs observers saw the Communist bloc as embarked on a new, more belligerent course of action in the effort to spread its influence to the developing nations of the world. Admiral Burke spoke for many in the defense and foreign policy establishments when he warned of the worldwide, unremitting threat of communism. Addressing the Senate Armed Services Committee on 24 January 1959, the CNO warned that "Moscow dominated Communism will continue to use political, economic, psychological, military and covert elements of Soviet Bloc power to achieve its aims" and that "attempts will be made to weaken Free World alliances — cause withdrawal of the United States from overseas bases — force disarmament agreement on Russian terms — and generally undermine the Free World's will to resist Communist penetration."[25] Soon afterward, Admiral Burke expressed alarm over the recent advances of the Soviet Union under the guidance of Premier Nikita Khrushchev: "He is winning. He is getting small nation by small nation under his control, a little bit at a time, like Egypt, Syria, and now maybe Iraq. He is working on Laos."[26]

Nowhere was the threat seen as great as in the Western Pacific. Following the Taiwan Strait confrontation in 1958, when Communist China exhibited great bellicosity, and that nation's involvement in Tibet and on the Indian border in 1959, U.S. policymakers anticipated further aggressive moves. Their fears were shared by military leaders familiar with the situation in Asia. In November 1959 Admiral Herbert G. Hopwood, the Commander in Chief, U.S. Pacific Fleet, intimated his fears for the future to Admiral Burke:

> I believe we are entering a new era of intensified cold and limited war in South and South East Asia.... The CHICOMS [previously] attempted to win friends and influence the many new and violently

---

[25]CNO, "Statement before the Senate Armed Services Committee, regarding the Military Posture of the United States Navy," of 24 Jan 1959. See also memo, CNO to Frankel, No. 89-59 of 2 Mar 1959; Naval Long Range Studies Project (Naval War College), "Long Range Estimate of the Situation," of 1 Aug 1960.

[26]Memo, Burke to Ward, of 30 May 1959.

Southeast Asia

nationalistic governments in this area.... In my opinion, they have now decided to use force and/or threat of [force] as a major instrument of policy for the predictable future.[27]

Policymakers and intelligence analysts in Washington shared this view. The Office of Naval Intelligence warned that "further development of the Chinese Communist hard line could lead to new emphasis on the development of indigenous Communist guerrilla capabilities in various parts of Southeast Asia, and possibly even to limited war adventures by Pciping."[28] Testifying before Congress, Admiral Burke forecast a continuation of Chinese Communist pressure and their utilization of tested methods: "They have made substantial gains in recent years by the use of tactics short of open warfare.... They will promote unrest in Burma, Laos, and Indonesia."[29]

The North Vietnamese also were seen to be demonstrating a growing inclination to use force to settle their dispute with President Ngo Dinh Diem's government of South Vietnam. During 1959 evidence increased that North Vietnam intended to support armed conflict in the South with cadre personnel, arms, and possibly troops. In fact, early in that year the Vietnamese Communist hierarchy in Hanoi decided on a change of tactics in the South. The Viet Cong were directed to complement their subversive efforts against the Diem government with outright military attacks. By the end of 1960, it was clear that the North Vietnamese were resolved to pursue the forceful unification of Vietnam. In December of that year the National Liberation Front of South Vietnam (NLF) was formed to prosecute the insurgency in the South. The strong influence and inspiration of Hanoi in the establishment of this political entity was evident to knowledgeable observers.[30]

---

[27]Msg, CPFLT 042155Z Nov 1959.

[28]ONI, "Status of the Cold War in Southeast Asia," *ONI Review*, Vol. 15, No. 1 (Jan 1960), pp. 29, 26-28. See also ONI, "Major Political/Economic Developments in the Sino-Soviet Bloc, 1959," *ONI Review*, Vol. 15, No. 4 (Apr 1960), pp. 212-13; ltr, Herter to Gates, of 1 Jul 1960 in memo, OP-61 to CNO, ser 00279P61 of 29 Jul 1960.

[29]CNO, "Testimony before Senate Armed Services Committee Regarding the Military Posture of the United States Navy," of 22 Jan 1960. See also JCS Paper 1992/643.

[30]Douglas Pike, *Viet Cong: The Organization and Techniques of the National Liberation Front of South Vietnam* (Cambridge, MA: MIT Press, 1966), pp. 74, 77-84; Guenter Lewy, *America in Vietnam* (New York: Oxford Univ. Press, 1978), pp. 15-18; King C. Chen, "Hanoi's Three Decisions and the Escalation of the Vietnam War," *Political Science Quarterly*, Vol. 90, No. 2 (Summer 1975); U.S. Defense Department, *United States-Vietnam Relations: 1945-1967* (Washington: GPO, 1971) (hereafter *U.S.-V.N. Relations*), bk. 2, pt. IVA. 5, tab 3, pp. 55-60; High-Level Military Institute, Socialist

The loss of the pro-Western, pro-American South Vietnam to the Communists was feared by American policymakers as the prelude to the inundation of all Southeast Asia. A basic tenet of American foreign policy held that the fall of any one Southeast Asian country would trigger the collapse of others in the area. It was believed that even a country's limited accommodation with the Communists would motivate others in the area to discard their anti-Communist positions. The takeover, or even neutralization, of Southeast Asia would in turn, it was feared, affect the credibility of U.S. alliances throughout the world. Although emphasizing his particular area of concern, Vice Admiral Roland N. Smoot, the Commander U.S. Taiwan Defense Command, spoke for many naval leaders when he stated that "not one more square inch of ground [should be] lost to the Communists by threat of force."[31]

But to make the U.S. commitment to pro-Western interests credible in the face of a perceived increase in Communist aggressiveness, highly visible measures were believed essential. In this vein, CINCPACFLT proposed the strengthening and forward deployment of U.S. limited war forces:

> It is obvious that the most important thing we can do for these countries during the next few years is to maintain a sufficiently high level of U.S. military power in the area as will enable these governments to review their foreign policies free of the awful threat of their 'powerful neighbor.' Our forces in the South East Asian area today are inadequate.... This is not just a plea for increased Pacific Fleet forces but a strong recommendation that there be a marked improvement in the overall U.S. capability to fight, and therefore to deter, limited war in this area.[32]

Other Pacific commanders also pressed for the adoption of a forward strategy. At a unified commanders conference at Norfolk, Virginia, in January 1960, Admiral Felt called for an increase in the "United States

---

Republic of Vietnam, *Vietnam: The Anti-U.S. Resistance War for National Salvation 1954-1975: Military Events* (Hanoi: Peoples Army Publishing House, 1980), translated by Foreign Broadcast Information Service, 1982, pp. 29-30, 43-44.

[31]Commander U.S. Taiwan Defense Command, memo for record, of 29 Dec 1959. See also *U.S.-V.N. Relations*, bk. 10, pp. 1082-83, 1087; JCS Paper 1992/652; Lewy, *America in Vietnam*, pp. 15-18; Dwight D. Eisenhower, *The White House Years: Waging Peace, 1956-1961* (New York: Doubleday and Co., 1965), p. 607.

[32]Msg, CPFLT 042155Z Nov 1959. See also OP-06, memo for record, of 3 Feb 1959; JCS Paper 1992/652.

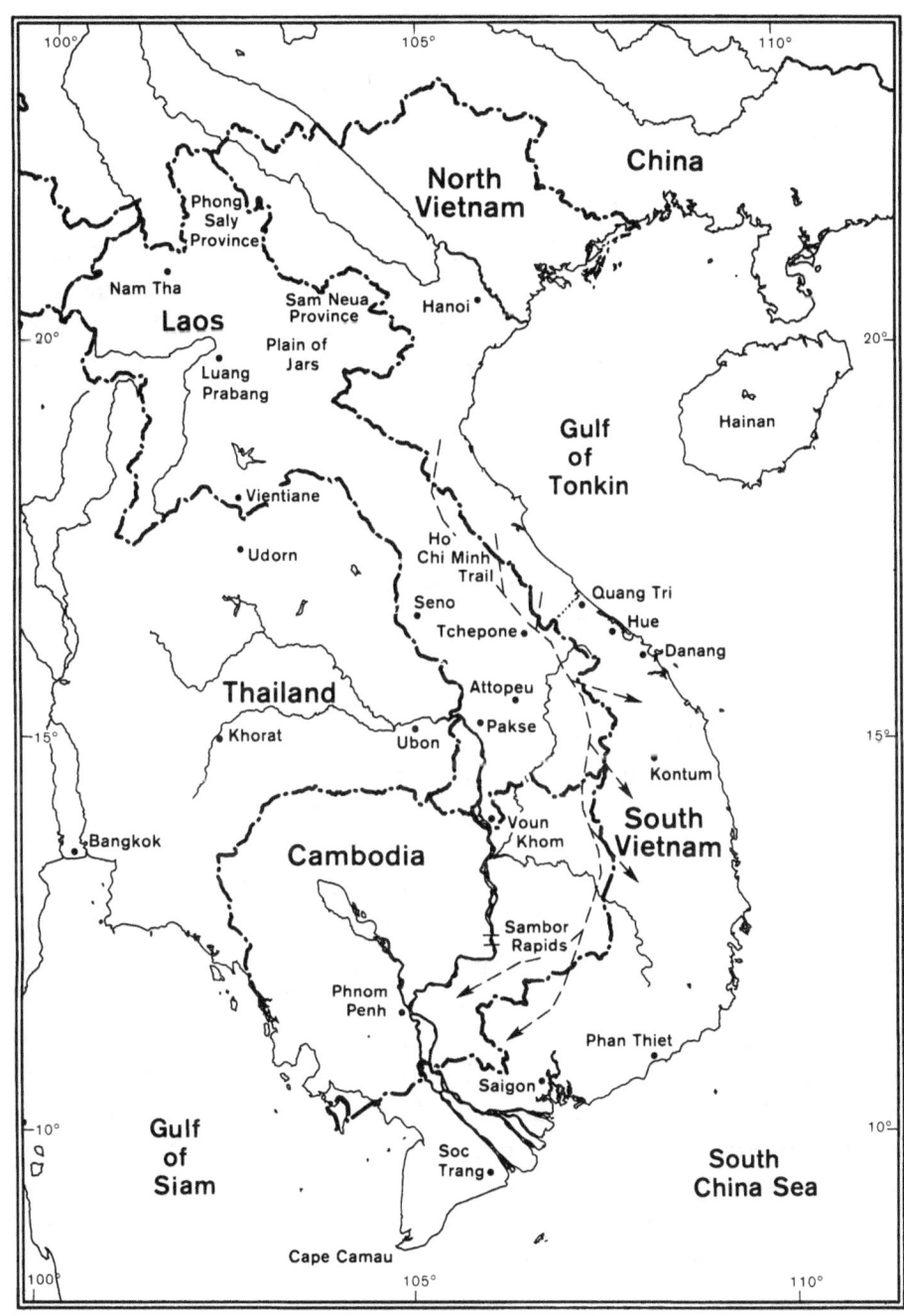

Mainland Southeast Asia

forces in the Southeast Asia area — forces ready to act. Forces a long way off in the United States do not do any good as far as the Southeast Asians are concerned."[33] Admiral Burke shared this perception and advocated "reasonably balanced and ready-to-go forces.... Forces in being are vital. A small force which can arrive on the scene early, before things get out of hand, will be decisive."[34]

These views reflected similar inclinations among foreign policymakers. In July 1960, the State Department apprised the Defense Department of the type of military forces and strategy required to support U.S. foreign policy. Needed was a force possessing mobility, substantial size, and flexibility. The first characteristic was essential so that "our allies and the Communists will realize that it can respond promptly to threats in any part of the world;" substantial size was necessary "so that our allies will appreciate our ability to help them meet attacks which might well involve the use of sizeable Communist" forces; and flexibility was important in order to "respond in each case with a use of force appropriate to the threat and so that we can achieve our military objectives with or without use of nuclear weapons, as the President may consider desirable." In addition to this armed strength so constituted, it was essential "to deploy these forces in accordance with a *forward strategy* [original italics], so as to present our allies and the Communists with tangible evidence of our capacity to resist aggression."[35]

During the years 1958 to 1960, U.S. strategic doctrine was in transition from emphasis on nuclear retaliation as a response to Communist aggression to adoption of a concept of flexible response, which held that the nature and seriousness of the threat should determine the solution. This ultimately resulted in stress on readiness for fighting limited wars with conventional military forces. The Navy, whose forces and weapons were suited for a wide range of missions and had traditionally supported a multi-role strategy, joined with the Army in pressing for this more versatile concept. But, in an era that saw continuing priority given to nuclear forces, combined with austere defense budgets, the readiness of conventional forces was impaired.

---

[33]As reported in CNO, memo for record, ser 0007-60 of 7 Jan 1960.
[34]Ltr, Burke to Campbell, of 29 Jul 1960.
[35]Ltr, Herter to Gates, of 1 Jul 1960 in memo, OP-61 to CNO, ser 00279P61 of 29 Jul 1960.

Developments in Asia during the last years of the Eisenhower administration gave impetus to the defense establishment's increasing interest in the U.S. capability to deter or prosecute limited war. Many foreign policymakers became convinced that the Communist bloc, chiefly North Vietnam and China, had initiated a new, more aggressive phase in the effort to absorb the non-Communist nations of Southeast Asia. In the face of this threat, U.S. civilian officials and military leaders pursued a policy of uncompromising determination to contain Communist military or political incursions. In the former sphere, this represented the use of forward deployed, mobile reaction forces. In the latter sphere, the U.S. response became one of wholeheartedly supporting anti-Communist elements in Southeast Asian countries facing insurgencies. The first manifestation of this activist foreign policy in the area occurred in the small kingdom of Laos.

CHAPTER II

The Laotian Vortex, 1959-1960

The growing perception that the future would bring more limited armed confrontations, such as had occurred during the Lebanon and Quemoy-Matsu crises of 1958, was strengthened by the outbreak of violence in Laos during the late summer of 1959. This development appeared to U.S. national and military leaders to fit the pattern of new Communist-inspired aggression. Laos itself was a minor factor in global political and military affairs. But the country was strategically located between Asian Communist powers and the Western-oriented nations of Southeast Asia. U.S. policymakers believed that actions in Laos would ultimately determine the course of events throughout the peninsula, since Laos was seen as the forward defense line for South Vietnam, as well as for Thailand, in the continuing Cold War struggle.

From the end of the French Indochina War in 1954, and the signing of the Geneva Agreement consummating that long and bitter struggle, Laos experienced much political instability. The Royal Laotian Government received its legitimacy and the country's independence from France. The continuity of Western political influence was indicated by the provision in the Geneva accord allowing as many as 1,500 French troops to remain in Laos to train the Laotian Armed Forces (FAR) at two bases. But, almost immediately, the central government's authority was challenged by the Pathet Lao, a Communist organization that had fought against the French and aligned itself with Ho Chi Minh's Viet Minh. While the government exercised its administration in the more populous Mekong River Valley, the Communists regrouped in the rural areas of two provinces bordering North Vietnam, Phong Saly and Sam Neua, and established a strong presence there.

In November 1957, Prime Minister Souvanna Phouma, in an effort to end the festering conflict in Laos, fostered the inclusion of the Pathet Lao, under the titular leadership of his half-brother Prince Souphanouvong, in a coalition government. This development in Laos alarmed and dismayed American policymakers in the Eisenhower administration who sought not only to contain Communist military expansion, but Communist ideology as well. Souvanna's action to integrate the Communists into the national political structure, while espousing a neutralist stance in foreign affairs, was perceived as naive and ultimately fatal. Hence, U.S. representatives were directed to oppose the new coalition.[1] Soon afterwards, elements on the right of the Laotian political spectrum, alarmed by the inclusion of Communists in the government and in the army, coalesced in opposition. Their campaign was encouraged by the Eisenhower administration. The U.S. government quickly terminated its financial support to the Laotian government, which was heavily dependent on American funding. In August 1958, the rightists, spearheaded by a nationalist group led by army officer Phoumi Nosavan, replaced Souvanna with Phoui Sanikone, damaging the coalition experiment. Phoui's government immediately enunciated a policy of opposition to Communist influence in Laos.[2]

In an effort to bolster this new government, the U.S. administration greatly increased its economic and military assistance to the mountain kingdom. Since 1955 the general U.S. aid program had been administered under the U.S. ambassador's direction, with the United States Operations Mission handling economic assistance and the Programs Evaluation Office (PEO) overseeing the military aspects. Because of the Geneva Agreement restrictions against a foreign military presence in Laos (other than the French), PEO Laos initially was staffed by civilians. But, beginning in 1959 the organization contained U.S. military personnel in civilian clothes.

Brigadier General John H. Heintges, USA, the prospective Chief, PEO Laos, concluded early in 1959 that the FAR was the only reasonably effective and truly anti-Communist arm of the government. But the army

---

[1] JCS Paper 1992/643, p. 1129; 1992/649; 1992/652; *U.S.-V.N. Relations*, bk. 10, p. 1092; Arthur J. Dommen, *Conflict in Laos: The Politics of Neutralization* (New York: Praeger, 1971), pp. 94-111; Hugh Toye, *Laos: Buffer State or Battleground* (New York: Oxford Univ. Press, 1968), pp. 104-16; Charles A. Stevenson, *The End of Nowhere: American Policy Toward Laos Since 1954* (Boston: Beacon Press, 1972), pp. 28-58; Sisouk Na Champassak, *Storm Over Laos: A Contemporary History* (New York: Praeger, 1961), pp. 51-74; Bernard B. Fall, *Anatomy of a Crisis: The Laotian Crisis of 1960-1961* (Garden City, NY: Doubleday, 1961), pp. 80-81, 162-72; Martin E. Goldstein, *American Policy Toward Laos* (Cranbury, NJ: Associated University Presses, 1973), pp. 122-41; Bernard B. Fall, "The Pathet Lao: A 'Liberation Party'" in Robert A. Scalapino, ed., *The Communist Revolution in Asia: Tactics, Goals, and Achievements* (Englewood Cliffs, NJ: Prentice Hall, 1965), pp. 173-94.

[2] CINCPAC, Command History, 1959, pp. 200-06; 1961, pt. II, pp. 1-12; Fall, *Anatomy of a Crisis*, pp. 82-89; Dommen, *Conflict in Laos*, pp. 115-16; Stevenson, *End of Nowhere*, pp. 59-68; Toye, *Laos*, pp. 119-23.

then was in poor material condition. The "Heintges Plan," named for its principal architect, sought to remedy this problem with a major strengthening and rejuvenation of the FAR. The plan was quickly endorsed by the Eisenhower administration and by mid-year significant amounts of weapons, clothing, communications equipment, ammunition, and other essential items were provided through the Military Assistance Program (MAP).

Of greater significance, U.S. military personnel began supplementing the work of the French training mission, which was seen as woefully inadequate by American observers. By the end of July 1959, Special Forces training teams were established in Laos and prepared to institute training in guerrilla warfare techniques and small unit tactics.[3]

In line with the general recommendations of the Heintges Plan and earlier country team plans to enhance the fighting capability of the Laotian military, measures were taken to improve lines of communication. The betterment of airfields and roads, which were militarily vital in a country lacking a significant number of either, was considered essential. A proposal was made to use U.S. personnel ideally suited to the Laotian environment — the Navy's construction battalion (SEABEE) units.

Since 1955, naval construction forces had operated on the Southeast Asian mainland under the Officer in Charge of Construction, Thailand, located in Bangkok. And, beginning in February 1956, the U.S. Navy was assigned responsibility for all Military Assistance Program construction in Southeast Asia by the Assistant Secretary of Defense (International Security Affairs). To this was later added control of all military construction in the area. However, the Bangkok office conducted no significant activities in Laos until early 1957 when engineering and planning assistance was provided the Laotians through the PEO. Then, at the end of 1958, CINCPAC directed his component commanders to provide the PEO and the FAR with skilled advisors in order to implement the needed construction program. The work to be accomplished included road, airfield, and bridge construction and repair, and the erection of two sawmills. In February 1959, Chief Warrant Officer T. M. Skates and a representative of Commander Naval Construction Forces, Pacific, visited Laos to make arrangements for the proposed project. On 14 March, a five-

---

[3]CINCPAC, Command History, 1961, pt. II, pp. 13-14, 18-20; JCS Paper 1992/652; Bernard B. Fall, *Street Without Joy* (Harrisburg, PA: Stackpole Co., 1961), pp. 299-300; "Anti-Communism: The Rationale for U.S. Aid" in Marvin Gettleman *et al.*, eds., *Conflict in Indo-China: A Reader on the Widening War in Laos and Cambodia* (New York: Random House, 1970), pp. 172-84.

man naval team, led by Skates, deployed to Laos. By then, however, the team's mission was reoriented toward more critical equipment repair work.

Following completion of their temporary tour of duty in September, the small team was relieved by a seventeen-man SEABEE detachment, which concentrated its work on air facilities, mainly at Wattay Airfield in Vientiane, and on the main roadways. The SEABEEs, although hampered by the rainy season and the primitive technological base of the country, greatly increased the operational capacity of the Vientiane airfield by constructing a new, 6,560-foot runway, taxiways, a drainage system, and a runway lighting system. By the end of the year, CINCPAC reported that approximately half of the airfield and road improvement project was completed.

Consideration also was given to providing the Laotians with SEABEE assistance in the construction of an all-weather road from Attopeu toward the South Vietnamese border at Kontum. The road improvement plan was supported wholeheartedly by President Diem of South Vietnam, who felt that it was needed to bring some measure of governmental control—both Laotian and South Vietnamese — to this area of Communist infiltration and subversion of the hill tribes. U.S. military planners also recognized the value of this shortest, most direct line of communication to Laos from the South China Sea, by way of the Central Highlands of Vietnam. The project reflected the growing belief among American officials that U.S. assistance to the Royal Laotian Government would increase. However, by the end of the year the project was shelved. At first enthusiastic about the plan to improve lines of communication on both sides of the border, President Diem withdrew his support. In October he expressed the opinion that it was already too late to impede Communist infiltration through the area. There was lessened U.S. interest, as well. Hence, the project did not come to fruition.[4]

---

[4]Msgs, AMEMB Saigon 7PM 17 Feb 1959; CP 260306Z Aug 1959; 272009Z; USARMVT 061655Z Sep; CPADMINO 020436Z Oct; JCS 052036Z; 012341Z Dec; CP 052230Z; DIRPAC-DOCS 052318Z; CINCPAC, Command History, 1959, pp. 130, 222, 224; 1960, p. 225; Richard Tregaskis, *Southeast Asia: Building the Bases: The History of Construction in Southeast Asia* (Washington: Naval Facilities Engineering Command/GPO, 1975), pp. 13-21; ltrs, COMNCFPAC to CINCPACFLT, ser 0031 of 9 Jun 1959; ASD (ISA) to Special Assistant for Mutual Security Coordination, Department of State, of 25 Aug 1959; John P. Sylva, transcript of interview with Edward J. Marolda and Oscar P. Fitzgerald, Naval Historical Center, in Washington, D.C., 3 Nov 1978.

The First Laos Crisis

In the spring of 1959, growing internal tension in Laos revolved around the government's efforts to eliminate the greater part of the Communist military arm in one bold stroke. Government forces surrounded the barracks of two Pathet Lao battalions and demanded their total integration into the armed forces of the coalition government. One battalion acceded to this pressure on 17 May, but the following night the other unit escaped and made its way into the jungle along the North Vietnamese border. Simultaneously, ten Pathet Lao political leaders, including Souphanouvong, the "Red Prince," were quickly arrested and imprisoned. The national coalition was thereby ended. Two months to the day later, on 18 July 1959, the Pathet Lao retaliated with an attack on a government outpost in Sam Neua Province, initiating overt conflict in Laos. With the Pathet Lao attacks increasing in intensity and scope during July and August, U.S. policymakers became alarmed at the threat to the Laotian government. U.S. officials in Washington generally accepted Laotian assertions that external Communist powers were fomenting the trouble and became concerned that the North Vietnamese soon would increase their involvement.[5]

The Pacific Command anticipated the deterioration of the situation in Laos and the possible need for an armed U.S. response. CINCPAC Operation Plan 32(L)-59, concerning unilateral U.S. military reaction to Communist insurgency in the country, was a component part of the still incomplete Operation Plan 32-59, which dealt with the overall defense of Southeast Asia. Admiral Felt issued the former plan separately on 16 June 1959 because he was concerned about the situation in Laos.[6]

The Laos plan was designed for U.S. military operations to insure the stability and friendly control of Laos in the event it was threatened by Communist insurgency.[7] The concept of operations entailed the rapid deployment and securing of air facilities and Mekong River crossings near

---

[5] Msgs, SECSTATE 10PM 7 Aug 1959; AMEMBVT 9PM 22 Aug; Stevenson, *End of Nowhere*, pp. 69-71; Fall, *Street Without Joy*, pp. 300-02; Fall, *Anatomy of a Crisis*, pp. 94-109; A. M. Halpern and H. B. Fredman, *Communist Strategy in Laos* (Santa Monica, CA: Rand Corp., 1960), pp. v-vii, 147-59.

[6] Ltr, Burke to Felt, ser 00301P60 of 11 Aug 1959; OP-60, briefing memo, No. 414-59 of 4 Sep 1959; msg, JCS 051736Z Sep 1959.

[7] A U.S. military reaction to an overt Chinese or North Vietnamese invasion was not seriously considered in the plan. That contingency was addressed in the parent plan. See OP-60, briefing memo, No. 414-59 of 4 Sep 1959.

Seno and Vientiane, the administrative capital of Laos, by Joint Task Force 116. The primary function of this force would be to "free the indigenous forces for counterinsurgency operations and to support and assist them in these operations as required." In recognition of the preponderant Marine contribution, Major General Carson Roberts, USMC, the Commanding General, 1st Marine Aircraft Wing, was designated Commander Joint Task Force 116. The force consisted of headquarters elements, one Marine regimental landing team of three battalions, one Marine aircraft group, support units, Army Special Forces and civil affairs teams, and elements of a SEABEE battalion.[8]

In the first of the plan's several phases, the task force headquarters elements, one of three battalion landing teams (BLT), and the support units would be airlifted to Vientiane. When this move was completed, the second BLT and some SEABEEs would be transported to Seno approximately five days later. These forces would be followed by the thirty helicopters and thirty-four fixed-wing aircraft of the Marine aircraft group and the last BLT. Although Laos is a land-locked country, Admiral Felt assigned major Marine formations to the operation. He based his decision on the proximity of Marine forces in Okinawa to Southeast Asia and their combat readiness, both essential for rapid reaction to fast-developing crises, and because the problem in Laos still was regarded as an insurgency rather than an overt conventional conflict requiring more heavily armed and equipped ground forces.[9]

In the wake of these first stages, other forces in the Pacific Command would be prepared, if the situation warranted, to deploy in support of Joint Task Force 116 or to replace the predominant Marine force. Command of the task force would be passed to an Army general once forces from that service relieved the Marine contingent. So far as the Navy was concerned, the Pacific Fleet was charged with deploying naval combat and support forces to Southeast Asia, conducting air support, air and sealift operations, and defending sea lines of communication. The fleet was specifically directed to provide the Joint Task Force 116 commander, once he was ashore, with command and staff personnel, personnel and equipment to operate a joint operations center, and naval and support

---

[8]*Ibid.*
[9]Msg, CP 152347Z Aug 1959; OP-06, memo for record, ser 000157P06 of 24 Aug 1959; OP-60, briefing memo, No. 414-59 of 4 Sep; OPNAV, memo for record, of 7 Sep; Spector, *Advice and Support*, pp. 359-60.

forces. One of the Navy's nucleus port crews also was responsible for communications support and for port operations in Bangkok, prior to relief by Army logistic units.

On 23 June CINCPACFLT issued his supporting plan and distributed it to his own component commands. In addition to detailing the Marine forces slated for the Laos operations, Admiral Herbert G. Hopwood directed that an attack carrier strike group be prepared to operate in the South China Sea "to deter overt Communist aggression and...to support COMJTF 116 operations as may be required."[10] In addition to preparing contingency instructions, on 15 August CINCPAC gathered the Joint Task Force 116 headquarters in Iwakuni, Japan. During the month, General Roberts and key members of his staff visited Laos and became familiar with the problems there. Admiral Felt reported that "although no one deprecates the magnitude of the tasks which may confront us should it become necessary to implement CINCPAC OPLAN 32(L)-59, the latter is judged to be a feasible plan."[11]

CINCPACFLT took other steps, including the postponement on 27 August of the scheduled departure of *Thetis Bay* (LPH-6) from the Western Pacific for the United States, and, beginning on 1 September, the deployment of one carrier task group to the South China Sea and another to the Taiwan area. This latter concentration was intended to deter hostile Chinese actions while retaining a readiness for general war in the Pacific.

On 24 August, while these preparations were underway for possible U.S. participation, the Secretary of State informed Ambassador Horace Smith that the State and Defense Departments decided jointly to support a temporary increase in Laotian paramilitary forces in order to restore the country's internal security. CINCPAC also was authorized to expedite the dispatch to Laos of material and equipment, including small arms, clothing, communications apparatus, and engineer items. From U.S. facilities throughout the Pacific, including the Naval Supply Depots at Yokosuka, Japan, and Guam, the required assistance was sent by air on a priority basis.[12]

Despite these steps, the armed conflict in Laos continued. In the early morning hours of 30 August, the Communists launched major, coordinat-

---

[10] CINCPACFLT OPLAN 32(L)-59 in CINCPACFLT Chief of Staff, memo, of 23 Jun 1959.
[11] Msg, CP 260229Z Aug 1959. See also msgs, CP 152347Z; CPFLT 271852Z; 280130Z.
[12] Msgs, AMEMBVT 4PM 24 Aug 1959; SECSTATE 10PM 24 Aug; AMEMBVT 1PM 25 Aug; CP 022325Z Sep; CPADMINO 162210Z.

ed attacks on FAR positions in Sam Neua Province, inspiring alarmed reports by the government of massive North Vietnamese aggression. While U.S. officials generally believed that reports of overt incursion by Hanoi's forces were exaggerated, the existence of North Vietnamese training, propaganda, material, and other assistance was amply supported. An effective Pathet Lao armed force that secured the western flank of North Vietnam, stretched U.S. resources, and diverted Western attention from South Vietnam was an obvious advantage to Hanoi. Hence, it was in the interest of the North Vietnamese to exploit, exacerbate, and sustain the growing conflict among Laotian factions, especially since this freed their forces for the primary goal — unification with the South.

The Laotian government, now firmly controlled by anti-Communist factions, attempted to bolster its position with outside support. On 3 September the Royal Laotian Government appealed to the United Nations (UN) to dispatch an "emergency force" to Laos, citing the intervention of Hanoi as an especially alarming development. This was followed by requests for troops and material assistance from the armed forces of South Vietnam and Thailand. And, before they were dissuaded by U.S. representatives from such action, the Laotians prepared to call for Southeast Asia Treaty Organization (SEATO) intervention. Most importantly, however, the Laotian government actively sought an actual and open U.S. commitment to the defense of the country.[13]

Evidence of North Vietnamese intervention was based primarily on Laotian reports, although the South Vietnamese provided some supporting intelligence.[14] Based largely on these sources, Ambassador Smith and General Heintges were convinced that Laos was in grave jeopardy. Ambassador Smith recommended that the North Vietnamese be warned against further actions, and if this were disregarded, U.S. forces be introduced into Laos. The ambassador expressed his "deepest personal conviction that unless we draw line now, we will have to draw it later when Laos may be partially or wholly lost along with entire U.S. position and prestige in SE Asia if not all Far-East. Like Quemoy or Berlin, I think

---

[13]Msgs, USARMA Laos 030500Z Jun 1959; AMEMBVT 2PM 4 Sep; AMEMB Saigon 040025Z; AMEMBVT 1PM 5 Sep; Chae-Jin Lee, *Communist China's Policy Toward Laos: A Case Study 1954-67* (Manhattan, KS: Center for East Asian Studies, Univ. of Kansas, 1970), pp. 55-56.

[14]Later in the month President Diem informed Admiral Felt that the North Vietnamese had introduced armor, artillery, and aircraft into Laos. See ltr, CINCPAC to JCS, ser 00642 of 17 Oct 1959.

the time is now come when we have to take our stand."[15] Admiral Felt concurred with Smith's conclusion, stating that "the time for decision and action is now, and that the leadership and inspiration of Communist aggression in Laos is located outside that country."[16] As the senior military officer in the Pacific, Admiral Felt's views on the Southeast Asian problem carried great weight, especially before the creation of the U.S. Military Assistance Command, Vietnam, in 1962.

The Chief of Naval Operations subsequently expressed many of these same views with regard to the early use of force in situations such as existed in Laos. In a letter to Congressman Samuel S. Stratton, Admiral Burke stated:

> Threats to our national welfare such as these must be localized and stamped out where they occur — that is, far from home.... The United States does have the strength and capability to help Laos without destroying their country — or their neighbor's country. We have strong mobile forces for handling this type of situation.... We have the power *now* [original italics] and stand ready to use it.[17]

The Chief of Naval Operations highlighted the fact that the United States Navy was well-suited to implement that policy:

> In these situations we must take advantage of the ocean highways to project the force necessary to eliminate the menace wherever it occurs. The Navy is more than a "first line" of defense. It frequently is and must be the spearhead of our military actions overseas. It is a "first line of impact" on many occasions.[18]

The Pacific Command Prepares for Military Action

Other officials of the Defense and State Departments in Washington were convinced that the situation was critical. The attack in Sam Neua Province was growing and believed to be supported either by North Vietnamese troops or artillery and supplies. At the same time, it was recognized that the SEATO powers were either apathetic to the threat or

---

[15] Msg, AMEMBVT No. 518 of 3 Sep from msg, CNO 041449Z Sep 1959. See also msg, CNO 041623Z.
[16] Msg, CP 050232Z Sep 1959.
[17] Ltr, Burke to Stratton, of 14 Sep 1959.
[18] *Ibid.* See also memo, VCNO to JCS, ser 000387P60 of 16 Oct 1959.

inclined to support UN rather than SEATO action. Accordingly, the JCS recommended authorizing CINCPAC to alert his forces for possible unilateral intervention while the United Nations attempted a negotiated solution to the crisis. This step would include the positioning of transport aircraft, embarkation of forces on board amphibious craft off Okinawa, and sailing of Seventh Fleet elements to the South China Sea. The following day, 4 September, President Eisenhower approved the proposed measures. Late that day CINCPAC issued an alerting directive, activated Joint Task Force 116, ordered the assembly of forces, and advised CINCPACFLT to stand by for immediate action.[19]

On 5 September, Admiral Felt took steps to prepare Joint Task Force 116 and supporting naval forces for deployment to Laos, in accordance with the provisions of his Operation Plan 32(L)-59. Marine units began embarking at all the designated ports in Okinawa and Japan; over 200 transport aircraft assembled at their respective airfields; naval amphibious ships and Military Sea Transportation Service (MSTS) shipping converged on the embarkation areas; and naval forces proceeded to supporting positions, all under the cover of routine training exercises and movements. By 9 September, almost all the ground units slated for amphibious lift were embarked. In Buckner Bay, Okinawa, the 2nd Battalion, 3rd Marines, a detachment of Marine Observation Squadron 2, and a logistic support detachment were in the final stages of loading on board 2 attack transports (APA), 2 attack cargo ships (AKA), 2 LSTs, and 1 LSD. *Henrico* (APA-45) was due in at Buckner Bay on 10 September. *Thetis Bay*, 1 LSD, and 2 LSTs had loaded Marine Aircraft Group (MAG) 16 with its thirty HU helicopters at Yokosuka, Japan, and were enroute to the Okinawa rendezvous with the other groups. At Iwakuni, Marine Air Base Squadron 12 and Marine Attack Squadron (VMA) 211 were loaded or loading on board 2 LSTs and 1 APA; and *Comstock* (LSD-19) was due to arrive there on 11 September.

Also by 9 September, combatant ships of the Seventh Fleet were deployed to waters adjacent to the critical areas of Southeast Asia, with logistic units standing by in support. In the South China Sea between Luzon and South Vietnam, a carrier task group composed of *Lexington*

---

[19]Msgs, COM7FLT 030920Z Sep 1959; CP 042235Z; CPFLT 020144Z; 040055Z; 050114Z; 050135Z; 050520Z; SECSTATE 050550Z 10PM 6 Sep; memos, CNO to ASD (ISA), ser 000486-59 of 4 Sep; Burke to Twining and Picher, ser 000487-59 of 4 Sep; Arleigh Burke, transcript of interview with John T. Mason, Jr., U.S. Naval Institute, in Annapolis, MD, 1963, p. 167.

Aircraft carrier Lexington (CVA-16) steams for the South China Sea during the Laos crisis of 1959.

(CVA-16), *Saint Paul* (CA-73), with Commander Seventh Fleet embarked, and escorting destroyers prepared to protect the air and sealift components of Task Force 116. At the same time, another group, formed around *Shangri La* (CVA-38), stood off Taiwan to deter aggressive activity by either the Chinese or the North Koreans. Destroyer Division 11 remained close at hand at Subic Bay to sortie into the South China Sea, and the oilers and ammunition ships of Task Force 73 were ready to provide needed logistic support. And, additional ships were deployed to the Western Pacific. *Hancock* (CVA-19) arrived in the operational area on 8 September and *Toledo* (CA-133) joined the assembled naval forces in Buckner Bay the following day. *Midway* (CVA-41) and four logistic support ships were all due within days.[20]

Measures also were taken to shorten the time needed to execute the Laos operation if the final order to place forces ashore was given. The Seventh Fleet commander proposed that when the LSTs finished loading at Okinawa they be immediately deployed forward to the Subic-Sangley area. Because of their slower speed (between 11 and 17 knots) and the distance to Bangkok, this gave the ships a three-day lead over the faster transports. CINCPACFLT endorsed this concept on 7 September and added to the group *Thetis Bay*, whose embarked helicopters would overfly South Vietnam enroute to Laos.[21]

With the strength of the assembled air, land, and naval forces growing daily, commanders gave greater consideration to the ramifications of the employment of these forces. Admiral Hopwood expressed dissatisfaction with the nature of the fleet's deployment. The admiral stated: "It seems to me that by remaining out of sight of land and attempting to disguise our intentions is not compatible with our objective of taking effective action to support [Royal Laotian Government]." Instead, he proposed an open "show of force" in the Hainan-Paracels area to impress the Chinese and "all concerned that we mean business."[22] CINCPACFLT also proposed,

---

[20]Msgs, COM7FLT 050620Z Sep 1959; 050702Z; CTF116 050817Z; 050820Z; CPFLT 051045Z; 052257Z; CP 060055Z; CPFLT 060310Z; CTF76 061115Z; COM7FLT 051400Z; 061630Z; 070600Z; 071725Z; 080542Z; 090450Z; CPFLT 092300Z; OPNAV, memo for record, of 7 Sep; OP-332E2, memo, of 8 Sep 1959; memo, CNO to SECDEF, ser 000490-59 of 8 Sep; memo, OP-40 to CNO, ser 0003104P40 of 11 Sep; memo, OP-333D to OP-33, of 15 Sep; ltr, COM7FLT to CNO, ser 002-002 of 2 Jan 1960.

[21]Msgs, COM7FLT 051620Z Sep 1959; 061716Z; CPFLT 072009Z; 072010Z; COM7FLT 080216Z; CP 082355Z; OP-332E2, memo, of 8 Sep 1959.

[22]Msg, CPFLT 062208Z Sep 1959.

should the Laos operation be ordered, a simultaneous feint by a high-speed carrier group toward the Chinese coast to divert Communist attention from the Task Force 116 airlift. Commander Seventh Fleet, Vice Admiral Frederick N. Kivette, however, feared that while the deception operation might succeed initially, the airlift would be left dangerously exposed without the air support of the carrier group. He felt that "we should put nothing less than our maximum effort into protection and defense of the landing team air lift."[23] Commander Seventh Fleet also cautioned that a show of force not be premature. Admiral Kivette expressed the

> hope [that] we don't make such a show of forces unless we are awfully certain we are going to follow it up if they call our hand. I think timing of a show of force is very important. It should not be undertaken [until] JTF116 is ready to move reasonably quickly if the other side calls our hand.[24]

Admiral Felt was even more dubious about publicizing the interjection of an overwhelming U.S. military presence into the area. He believed that, with a United Nations mediation effort in progress, the time had not come for a show of force. In this connection, the admiral stated:

> I have not yet taken full advantage of the authorization [to move large naval forces into the South China Sea] and do not intend to until situation develops to point where 32L-59 is executed or where it is desirable to attain an important effect in the diplomatic play now in progress.... [Seventh Fleet] strike elements are in good position. Let us not wear them down before their strength is needed.... In my opinion, [Seventh Fleet] strike forces should carry on normal routine but continue to keep center of gravity to the southward so as to be ready to cover JTF 116 when it puts down in Laos and be fresh enough to conduct sustained operations thereafter.[25]

CINCPAC additionally was concerned about the message that a major deployment of U.S. forces into Southeast Asia would send to the Chinese and North Vietnamese. Felt stated that a show of force to bluff the Communists into line "would be interpreted to mean far more than we

---

[23]Msg, COM7FLT 070638Z Sep 1959. See also msg, CPFLT 060445Z.
[24]Msg, COM7FLT 070820Z Sep 1959.
[25]Msg, CPFLT 081004Z Sep 1959.

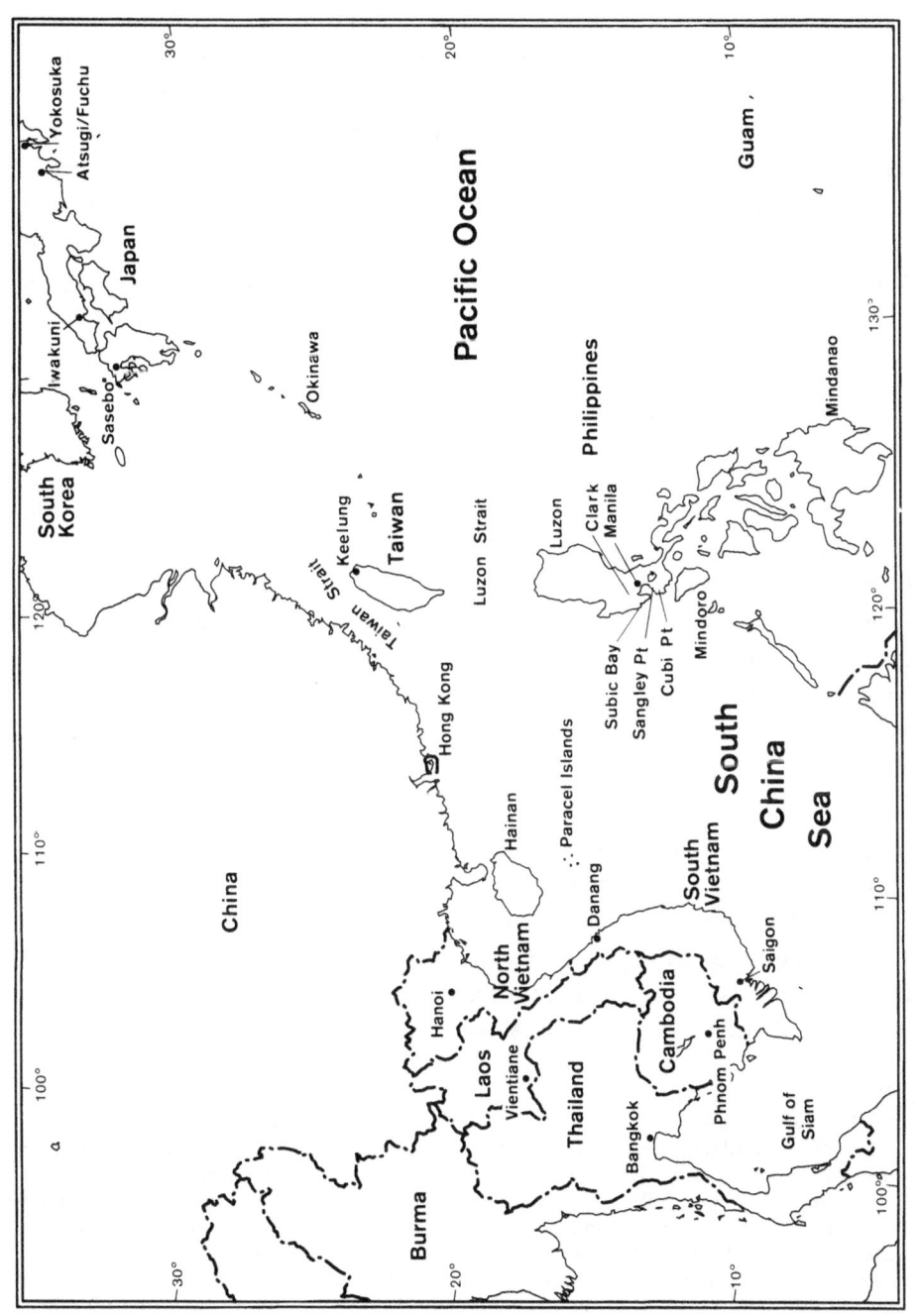

Western Pacific

intend to do even if we decide to move some military forces into Laos," for Operation Plan 32(L)-59 was designed primarily to cope with an insurgency. The U.S. forces introduced would be hard pressed to deal with more than a counterinsurgency operation. CINCPAC was concerned that the commitment of American forces to Laos would precipitate a limited war in all Southeast Asia. Admiral Felt concluded his dispatch on a cautionary note: Southeast Asia "is tough. I am trying to keep us from having the same kind of experience as the French during their catastrophic Indo China war when they won many a battle but lost the campaigns."[26]

Thetis Bay and Diplomatic Efforts to Resolve the Crisis

As the United States readied its Pacific forces for possible intervention in Laos, steps were taken on the diplomatic level to resolve the conflict. For the interested powers, the key issue was the nature and degree of external support for the Laotian Communists. Although there was evidence of North Vietnamese assistance to the Pathet Lao, the Royal Laotian Government's claim that the crisis resulted from overt North Vietnamese aggression was questioned, especially by America's Western allies.[27]

Many U.S. civilian officials and military leaders, however, saw the conflict in Laos as the most recent manifestation of the Communist bloc's design to probe for weak spots in the defenses of the "Free World." During a later period of tension in this extended confrontation over Laos, Admiral Felt, for example, expressed his conviction that the Pathet Lao were "organized, trained, directed and supported by Communist leaders in North Vietnam and possibly South China."[28] The commander of U.S.

---

[26]*Ibid*. See also msg, CP 130013Z.

[27]CINCPAC, Command History, 1959, pt. II, p. 16. Bernard Fall, who later achieved fame as an historian of the decades-long conflict in Southeast Asia, during this time conducted an extensive tour of Laotian government outposts on the North Vietnamese and Chinese borders. He concluded that the crisis resulted from the collapse of government authority and credibility and that this vacuum was filled by the Communists, who exploited the natural antipathy of the hill tribes for the lowland Lao people. Dr. Fall doubted that the North Vietnamese were serving in a combat or advisory capacity, but he concluded that external Communists were successfully proselytizing the mountain people. See msgs, USAIRA Bangkok 151605Z Sep 1959; AMEMB Manila 11AM 8 Sep; USARMVT 091800Z; AMEMBVT 081517Z; AMEMB Paris 7PM 9 Sep; USARMA Bangkok 110925Z; AMEMB Paris 2PM 12 Sep; CPFLT 122245Z; Goldstein, *American Policy Toward Laos*, pp. 164-71.

[28]CINCPAC, memo, ser 00209 of 25 Apr 1960. See also msg, CPFLT 060445Z Sep 1959.

Pacific forces denigrated the view that the Laotian conflict was solely an indigenous affair: "The threat is always posed as 'internal' and acceptance of this facade contributed to the loss of China to the Free World.... Laos today is a distinct military target of the Communist world."[29] Admiral Burke also evinced little doubt as to the nature of the struggle, noting that "the present Laos aggression is but another extension of the Soviet Union's continuous peripheral efforts."[30] During this same week of crisis, the Joint Chiefs of Staff proposed warning the "Soviet Bloc that the price for continued intervention in Laos will be higher than they are willing to pay."[31]

Although members of the U.S. country team in Laos, CINCPAC, and Defense and State Department officials in Washington expressed few doubts regarding North Vietnamese involvement, there was a lack of concrete evidence of organized combat units. Efforts to prod the Laotians to obtain conclusive information were unsuccessful, and a proposal by the country team to place covert U.S. investigators in the field was declined as too great a political risk. For these reasons, a thorough and speedy investigation by a UN subcommittee of Laotian allegations of North Vietnamese intervention was fully supported by the United States. While doubting that the group would turn up much hard evidence, U.S. leaders hoped that the UN presence in the combat area would at least deter Communist incursions and possibly cause the guerrillas to move into North Vietnam.

Because of the primitive state of the transportation system in Laos, the most expeditious method for searching the rugged border areas was by air. Accordingly, on 11 September CINCPAC alerted CINCPACFLT to prepare *Thetis Bay* for possible support of the UN subcommittee. Admiral Hopwood was specifically requested to ready eight of the ship's Marine helicopters by painting the craft white and stenciling them with blue UN initials. *Thetis Bay* already was deployed in the South China Sea, but on the evening of 13 September her commanding officer, Captain Norman C. Gillette, Jr., was directed to proceed to a point out of sight of land off

---

[29]CINCPAC, memo, ser 00209 of 25 Apr 1960.
[30]Ltr, Burke to Stratton, of 14 Sep 1959.
[31]Msg, JCS 111829Z Sep 1959. See also CIA, "The Situation in Laos," SNIE 68-2-59, of 18 Sep 1959; Halpern and Fredman, *Communist Strategy in Laos*, pp. 154-55; OP-612, memo for record, of 21 Aug 1959; msgs, AMEMBVT 080715Z; USARMA Bangkok 150905Z; 020850Z Oct; USARMAVT 151755Z.

Danang to await further instructions. Soon thereafter, Commander Seventh Fleet advised Captain Gillette that clearance for overflight of South Vietnam and Thailand, as well as emergency landing at Danang, had been granted by the respective governments. The helicopters would follow a route over Hue and Quang Tri before landing at Seno for fuel prior to continuing on to Vientiane. The subcommittee arrived in Vientiane on 15 September, but the offer of U.S. air support temporarily was declined.

At the end of the month, the advisability of using U.S. helicopters came into question. Secretary of State Christian Herter feared that the appearance in Laos of the Marine crews and maintenance personnel for the eight helicopters might highlight the U.S. military presence in the country to the UN subcommittee. Further, UN Secretary General Dag Hammarskjold recommended that the group not use helicopters supplied by Security Council members or by states bordering Laos. For lack of available aircraft, the subcommittee dropped the idea of a helicopter tour and instead conducted it in fixed-wing aircraft, which unfortunately restricted on-the-ground inspection to the immediate vicinity of the Sam Neua and Luang Prabang airstrips. On 28 September, Ambassador Smith suggested that the new situation hardly seemed to warrant the continued commitment of *Thetis Bay*. On 1 October, CINCPACFLT authorized Commander Seventh Fleet to relax *Thetis Bay*'s readiness, although the ship was to be prepared to respond to a UN request for helicopter support on forty-eight hours notice. Thus freed from the necessity to react immediately, *Thetis Bay* sailed for a port call in Hong Kong and then proceeded to Subic Bay on 9 October.[32]

The Seventh Fleet Relaxes Readiness as the Crisis Ebbs

The constant readiness but actual inaction of *Thetis Bay* was paralleled by the activities of other units of the Seventh Fleet and Joint Task force 116. On 9 September, Admiral Kivette, apprised by Admiral Hopwood

---

[32]Msgs, SECSTATE 8PM 4 Sep 1959; CP 090322Z; CPFLT 092038Z; CP 110150Z; COM7FLT 110612Z; THETIS BAY 120133Z; COM7FLT 130556Z; 131820Z; 140604Z; 160530Z; AMEMBVT 3PM 16 Sep; COM7FLT 190358Z; 200404Z; AMEMB Saigon 1200 23 Sep; CPADMINO 262228Z; COM7FLT 270546Z; 280153Z; AMEMB Saigon 281000Z; AMEMBVT 11AM 30 Sep; CPFLT 011958Z Oct; COM7FLT 050932Z; 070512Z; 071538Z; 090434Z; 130752Z; memo, OP-33D to OP-33, of 15 Sep 1959.

that the possibility of initiating Operation Plan 32(L)-59 was somewhat diminished, advised his subordinate Seventh Fleet commands that "the indefinite waiting and standby period commences." He further directed that "during this period it is my desire that operations be reduced to a slow pace and that advantage be taken of the lull to improve and increase your material readiness.... We may have a long haul ahead of us."[33]

Seventh Fleet naval forces and the embarked units of Joint Task Force 116 spent an arduous month at sea during which they evaded fierce Asian typhoons. Meanwhile, because of the presence in Laos of the UN investigating committee, the Communist threat subsided markedly. Finally, on 6 October, Admiral Felt authorized a gradual relaxation of readiness measures. This included the return to Guam from Okinawa of Naval Mobile Construction Battalion (NMCB) 5, offloading of equipment, return to duty of personnel from General Roberts's Joint Task Force 116 staff, and preparation for the offloading of Marine helicopter squadrons prior to *Thetis Bay*'s return to the United States. On 10 October, CINCPAC deactivated Joint Task Force 116, released *Thetis Bay* for relief by *Kearsarge* (CVS-33), and returned the Pacific Command to a normal alert condition.[34]

When the UN subcommittee completed its investigation on 12 October, conclusive evidence of external aggression had not been found. For lack of suitable aircraft, the group did not visit the areas of alleged aggression nearest the North Vietnamese-Laotian border and the government continued to produce insufficient material verification or prisoners. On 7 October, the U.S. country team lamented this fact and, less sure of Laotian allegations, stated that it was "imperative obtain best available info relative degree [Democratic Republic of Vietnam] participation and or support insurgency be it positive or negative [because] info [FAR] has obtained poorly documented and impression of exaggeration cannot be discounted."[35]

---

[33] Msg, COM7FLT 090900Z Sep 1959. See also msg, COM7FLT 091534Z.

[34] Msgs, COM7FLT 130738Z Sep 1959; CTF116 170544Z; COM7FLT 190848Z; CP 060245Z Oct; 102234Z; 102239Z; CPADMINO 262205Z; ADMIN CPFLT 282214Z; COM7FLT LAOS OPSUMS 9-34; memo, OP-33D to OP-33, of 15 Sep 1959; ltr, COM7FLT to CNO, ser 002-002 of 2 Jan 1960.

[35] Msg, USARMAVT 071315Z Oct 1959. Several accounts, such as Fall's *Anatomy of a Crisis*, pp. 122-56, and *Street Without Joy*, pp. 303-05, express doubts that North Vietnamese involvement in the fighting was significant. Others, such as Paul F. Langer and Joseph J. Zasloff in *North Vietnam and the Pathet Lao: Partners in the Struggle for Laos* (Cambridge, MA: Harvard Univ. Press, 1970), pp. 68-69

Whether for lack of sustaining power or the presence of the UN investigating committee in Laos, the still relatively modest Pathet Lao armed forces dispersed into the jungle at the end of 1959. Government forces soon filled the vacuum and, by March 1960, control was reestablished in almost half the districts lost to the Pathet Lao.

That the leaders of threatened Southeast Asian nations were favorably impressed with the U.S. actions in this instance was attested to by President Diem's response to the Laos crisis. The Vietnamese leader expressed satisfaction with U.S. moves to rush military aid to Laos and to alert the Seventh Fleet. Publicized accounts of Admiral Burke's support for possible U.S. armed intervention in that country were well received in Saigon. Rear Admiral John M. Lee, the Director, Politico-Military Policy Division in the Office of the Chief of Naval Operations, observed that, as in the Lebanon and Taiwan Strait confrontations of 1958, U.S. resolve in deterring Communist aggression was noted by leaders of threatened nations. He stated that "using President Diem's reaction as a barometer of SE Asian attitudes, the strong U.S. stand in the Laotian crisis has borne fruit in increased U.S. prestige in SE Asia, and a firmer conviction that the U.S. can be relied upon."[36]

Influence of the Laos Crisis on Fleet Readiness

The fleet's deployment in response to the flare-up of 1959 did much to reveal its value as an instrument of U.S. foreign policy, but also its deficiencies for supporting a large-scale military conflict in the area. Submitting force requirements in early 1960 for the fiscal year beginning in July 1961, both CINCPACFLT and Commander Seventh Fleet stressed the over extension of their resources. They found it possible to maintain three aircraft carriers on station in the Western Pacific for certain lengths of time, but only with deleterious effects on training, overhaul, and deployment schedules and bluejacket morale. In addition, the operational flexibility of one of the carriers was constrained by the necessity to remain

---

and the *U.S.-V.N. Relations*, bk. 2, pt. IV.A.5, tab 3, pp. 60-61, assert that regimental-size units, commanded from North Vietnam, took part.

[36]Memo, OP-61 to SECNAV, ser 022P61 of 15 Jan 1960. See also msg, USARMAVT 090215Z Apr 1960; memo, OP-61 to SECNAV, ser 00549P61 of 29 Dec 1959; OP-92, memo, ser 001426P92 of 31 Dec 1959; Stevenson, *End of Nowhere*, pp. 84-91; Toye, *Laos*, pp. 131-37; Dommen, *Conflict in Laos*, pp. 124-39; Fall, *Anatomy of a Crisis*, pp. 134-83.

off the Chinese mainland in readiness for general war retaliation. Admiral Kivette, as did Admiral Felt the previous year, concluded that three aircraft carriers continuously deployed to the Seventh Fleet was the absolute minimum needed for limited war and general war readiness. In July 1960 the JCS authorized an additional aircraft carrier for the Pacific Fleet, thereby enabling the permanent deployment to the Western Pacific of three such ships. At the same time, two more patrol squadrons were assigned to the naval air component slated to support operations in Laos.[37]

The most unsettling observations by these fleet commanders concerned the Pacific amphibious forces and the Fleet Marine Force. Commander Seventh Fleet was responsible for the sealift in some contingencies of a full Marine division and its supporting air wing. But, in actuality, only two-thirds of the 3rd Marine Division and two-thirds of the 1st Marine Aircraft Wing were in being. In addition, these Marine units were seriously undermanned and one of the two regimental landing teams (RLT) and one of the two Marine aircraft groups were stationed in Hawaii, 4,000 miles from the Western Pacific. The amphibious shipping in the Western Pacific was only capable of transporting the troops and combat-loaded cargo of one regimental landing team. Had the Laos deployment entailed the sealift from Hawaii of the second RLT and its accompanying MAG, Pacific shipping resources would have been strained and the actual movement of the force to Southeast Asia would have taken the better part of a month. For these reasons, Admiral Hopwood, shortly after the first Laos crisis subsided, recommended that additional transports and cargo ships be made available in the Western Pacific.

While Pacific Fleet naval and Marine commanders pressed for the long-term personnel and material augmentation and modernization of their forces, other interim measures were proposed as well. Admiral Kivette urged that the RLT and the MAG in Hawaii be deployed permanently with the rest of the 3rd Marine Division and the 1st Marine Aircraft Wing on Okinawa. Admiral Hopwood endorsed this recommendation, stressing the benefits of concentration and "unit integrity." However, during 1960 the deployment forward to Okinawa of Army units took precedence over a move of Marine forces.

---

[37]CINCPAC, Command History, 1960, pp. 7, 36-37, 52-53; msgs, CP 122133Z June 1960; COM7FLT 010730Z Jul; ADMIN CPFLT 150320Z; 150322Z; 160225Z; COM7FLT 180910Z; ADMIN CPFLT 220420Z; 232306Z; CINCPAC, Operation Plan 32-59, of 16 Dec 1959; Change No. 3 of 9 Aug 1960, pp. 13-5, C-II-1, C-III-1, F-1-A-1.

Another proposal made by Commander Seventh Fleet was to establish a permanent presence in his volatile area of responsibility of an alert amphibious task group. Previously, in response to a crisis, amphibious forces often had to be concentrated off Okinawa and Japan from widely separated locations throughout the Western Pacific before deploying to the trouble spot. But the permanent combination of a combat-ready Marine BLT, an assault helicopter squadron, a fast LSD, and a fast AKA to carry support personnel, equipment, and supplies, and the versatile LPH, would provide Admiral Kivette with an amphibious force prepared for immediate commitment. *Thetis Bay*'s potential for fast, decisive action was amply demonstrated during the Laos crisis of 1959.

Admiral Hopwood wholeheartedly supported this proposal and, aware of Army intentions to deploy an airborne battle group to Okinawa, recommended that the CNO concur "if the Marine Corps is to maintain its position as the nations alert force" and to "justify the use of the Marines by CINCPAC for the initial phase of any contingency."[38] He added later that the 1959 crises in Laos and elsewhere "highlighted the need for combat-loaded Marines ready for immediate commitment. A battalion, committed initially when needed, may be able to handle a situation which would require a regiment or division two or three weeks later."[39] Accordingly, in July 1960, an Amphibious Ready Group was formed under the Seventh Fleet's amphibious task force commander, Rear Admiral Charles C. Kirkpatrick.

In recognition of the fact that the helicopter provided commanders with greater operational range, more attention was given to identifying areas suitable for helicopter assaults. Of sixteen worldwide geographic areas surveyed during Fiscal Years 1958 through 1960, as part of the Amphibious Objective Studies Program, seven were located on the Southeast Asian mainland. Each study provided information pertinent to planning operations in an area comprising sixty to eighty miles of coastline and thirty to forty miles inland. These studies included identification of specific helicopter landing sites. Similar work was conducted in the Gulf of Siam by surveying ship *Maury* (AGS-16) during April and May of 1960. Captain Roger W. Luther's men produced valuable information on navigational aids, tides, and weather in the gulf and surrounding areas.[40]

---

[38]Ltr, CINCPACFLT to CNO, ser 6/00253 of 22 Mar 1960.
[39]Ltr, CINCPACFLT to CNO, ser 61/000131 of 29 Apr 1960, pp. VII-2.
[40]Ltrs, CNO to dist. list, ser 000197P60 of 1 Jun 1959; CINCPAC to JCS, ser 000116 of 11 Jun 1959; ACNO (General Planning) to CNO, ser 0070P90 of 10 Aug; CINCPACFLT to CNO, ser 33/

Other measures were taken to ready naval forces for anticipated Southeast Asian contingencies. On 2 January 1960, the Futema Air Facility was activated on Okinawa as part of a plan to base there eventually all Marine helicopter squadrons in the Western Pacific. And a CINCPAC study, initiated at the request of Admiral Burke, reaffirmed the great strategic value for Southeast Asian operations of the naval air facilities at Cubi Point and Sangley Point in the Philippines. This conclusion was reiterated by Rear Admiral Robert J. Stroh, of the CINCPAC staff, who conducted a tour of Southeast Asia in March. He found, however, that several facilities, especially those at Sangley Point, needed an "expensive 'shot in the arm' if we are going to stay on" there.[41] These and other concerns reflected the continuing focus on Southeast Asia.

The Mekong River Flotilla

In early 1960, as part of the continuing effort to bolster the Laotian armed forces, consideration was given to an increase in the strength of its miniscule river flotilla, which then comprised a motley assortment of river craft.[42] In January, Admiral Felt recommended that in addition to five landing craft, mechanized (LCM) intended for Laos in the Fiscal Year 1960 MAP budget, another five landing craft, vehicle and personnel (LCVP) be provided as military assistance. He proposed delivery of the craft via the Mekong River, in July, when snow runoff from the Tibetan mountains supplied the high water needed to navigate the waterway. CINCPAC further directed that the craft be assembled near Saigon or Phnom Penh, Cambodia, by late June.

This action set in motion urgent efforts to transport the craft to Southeast Asia, obtain requisite diplomatic clearances from the mutually

---

01977 of 16 Oct; CINCPACFLT to CNO, ser 61/00029 of 5 Feb 1960; CINCPACFLT to CNO, ser 61/000131 of 29 Apr; Felt to Burke, of 14 May; ACNO (General Planning) to CNO, ser 0060P90 of 31 Aug; *Maury*, Survey Report, ser 405 of 14 Jun 1960; Joshua W. Cooper, transcript of interview with John T. Mason, Jr., U.S. Naval Institute, in Alexandria, VA, 1973-1974, pp. 434-38; CINCPAC, Command History, 1960, pp. 23, 51, 256.

[41] "Memorandum Report by RADM Stroh of SEASIA Planning Trip 11-23 March," ser J50073-60 of 23 Mar 1960 in CINCPAC, Command History, 1960, app. C, p. 255.

[42] CINCPAC, Command History, 1960, pp. 129-33.

suspicious South Vietnamese, Cambodian, and Laotian governments, and assemble the U.S. Navy's crewmen for the mission. By early June the U.S. officials and military commanders assigned to oversee the mission completed the necessary preparations. Commander Clarence W. Westergaard, of Naval Beach Group 1, assigned to command the Mekong transit force, was joined by Lieutenant David Del Giudice and the ten men of his Underwater Demolition Team (UDT) 12, Mike Detachment at Yokosuka, Japan. There, the group reported on board *Okanogan* (APA-220) to prepare for the voyage to Saigon. The twelve officers and men of the group were joined by five boatswain's mates and enginemen from the ship's crew. The LCMs were tested and minor repairs made at the Ship Repair Facility. In the meantime, essential equipment, supplies, and spare parts were obtained from the Supply Depot and Naval Beach Group 1 stores. Finally, on 5 June, the five LCVPs arrived from the United States on board SS *Oregon Mail* and were transferred to *Okanogan*, where the LCMs already were loaded. That same day, the ship got underway for Southeast Asia.

After a week at sea, the attack transport arrived at Saigon for final preparations. On 12 June the Mekong Boat Flotilla was activated under the operational control of the Chief, Military Assistance Advisory Group (MAAG), Vietnam, and the LCMs, with the LCVPs secured on board, made ready for the trip upriver. Lieutenant (j.g.) John McAlister of the MAAG was attached as a translator and representative of Lieutenant General Samuel T. Williams, USA, the Chief, MAAG, Vietnam. The flotilla set out at 0700 on 14 June, escorted by *Tam Xet* (HQ-331), a landing ship, infantry, large (LSIL) of the Vietnamese Navy, and for the next two days labored upstream at 7 knots. Experiencing numerous mechanical troubles, the flotilla struggled into Phnom Penh at dusk on the 16th.

The sojourn in the Cambodian capital, which was expected to take no more than one day, actually lasted until the end of the month. Aside from needed repairs, other delays were caused by the refusal of the Cambodian pilots to navigate the river too early in the season. Further, Capitaine de Frégate Pierre Coedes, French Commandant of the Cambodian Navy, would not provide armed escort before his boats performed a ten-day reconnaissance of rapids upriver.[43] The Mekong Boat Flotilla finally

---

[43]French officers staffed the Cambodian Navy, much as they had in South Vietnam until 1955.

resumed its passage on 30 June, under the guidance of Capitaine de Corvette Sergé Dupuis, a French officer and experienced pilot of the Mekong. The river force proceeded without incident until reaching the treacherous Sambor Rapids on 2 July. At this point, forward progress became difficult. The following day, leaving behind the underpowered Cambodian LCVP escorts, the flotilla pressed ahead against an 8-knot current, at times making less than 1 knot forward. Several boats struck submerged obstacles, becoming temporarily hung up, but by 1315 the most dangerous section of rapids was traversed. At last, on the 4th of July, the Mekong Boat Flotilla crossed the Laotian border at Voun Khom, where the U.S. ensigns were ceremoniously hauled down and the boats turned over to the Laotians. Having successfully transited 430 miles of relatively uncharted, rapid-studded river to accomplish their mission, the eighteen officers and men of the flotilla boarded an aircraft at Pakse for the return flight to Saigon.[44]

The Kong Le Coup and the Outbreak of Civil War

In early 1960, with the military situation stabilized and the government increasingly taking on a pro-Western, anti-Communist character, many U.S. officials expressed guarded optimism for the future. For example, a Defense Department Special Survey Team concluded after their visit to Laos that "the results achieved to date in both the political and military fields are impressive.... Despite formidable obstacles, this previously split country has been to a large degree unified in the Western camp."[45] But, paralleling the consolidation of power by the U.S.-backed political element in the population centers was the buildup of the North Vietnamese-supported Pathet Lao in the highlands. Hanoi was strengthening its Laotian allies for another confrontation with the government.

[44]Ltr, Commander Naval Beach Group 1, WESTPAC Detachment to COM7FLT, ser 034 of 12 Jul 1960; NA Saigon, report, 150-60 of 16 Aug 1960; msgs, CP 162009Z Jan 1960; CHPEO Laos 180330Z Feb; COM7FLT 040257Z May; CHMAAGCAM 041030Z Jun; CP 062245Z; CNO 081813Z; CPFLT 110230Z; CP 110301Z; CPFLT 120350Z; CHMAAGVN 220533Z; CHMAAGCAM 280230Z; CHMAAGVN 051401Z Jul; ADMIN CPFLT 052144Z; COM7FLT 071052Z; CHMAAGVN SITREPS 5-8; CHMAAGCAM SITREPS 1-20.

[45]"DOD Spec Survey Team Report," of 25 Mar 1960, p. 2. See also CINCPAC, Command History, 1960, pp. 259-62; JCS Paper 1992/652.

On 9 August, Captain Kong Le, a paratroop commander, committed his battalion to open revolt against the government. Kong Le's force quickly gained control of Vientiane. That same day, the captain issued demands that Souvanna Phouma, who headed the government during the short-lived coalition in 1957 and 1958, be reinstalled and that Laos henceforth adhere to a policy of strict neutrality. On 16 August, the National Assembly, having already ended the tenure of the former government, voted Souvanna the new prime minister. The establishment of the essentially neutralist government brought together various formerly antagonistic political groups. However, General Phoumi, the leading figure in the staunch anti-Communist, pro-United States faction, who also controlled most of the armed forces outside Vientiane, opposed the coup from the start.

While the Eisenhower administration assessed the tangled internal situation in Laos to determine the best policy to pursue, the Seventh Fleet and its Marine forces continued to prepare for likely contingencies. On 11 August, shortly after the outbreak of the Kong Le coup, Admiral Felt authorized Major General Robert B. Luckey, USMC, to assemble Task Force 116 staff elements as a precautionary measure. And, on 18 August, after the Souvanna government was installed by the Laotian National Assembly, Pacific Fleet units deployed to the South China Sea off South Vietnam ready "to react swiftly should decision be taken to do so."[46] At this time, Admiral Hopwood directed Vice Admiral Charles D. Griffin, the new Seventh Fleet commander, to embark Marines in Japan on board *Lenawee* (APA-195) and *Thomaston* (LSD-28). The ships were then ostensibly to proceed to Okinawa for typhoon evasion, but actually to sail to Southeast Asian waters. *Hornet* (CVS-12) and the carrier task group's other ships also were ordered south to Buckner Bay in order to load a Marine transport helicopter squadron, HMR 162, before continuing on to the South China Sea. To provide carrier support, *Hancock*, in company with the other ships of Rear Admiral Francis D. Foley's carrier task group, consisting of Destroyer Division 152 and *Rogers* (DDR-876), was deployed from Guam to Subic Bay.[47] For the next three months, the ships and men of this Laos contingency force continued to operate in the South China Sea or close at hand in Subic Bay and off Taiwan. The force, formed

---

[46]Msg, ADMINO CP 180514Z Aug 1960. See also CP 102319Z Aug 1960.
[47]Msgs, CPFLT 182058Z Aug 1960; 182059Z; 182101Z; 182104Z; 182144Z; COM7FLT 190518Z; 190726Z.

around *Hancock*, *Hornet*, and the newly formed Amphibious Ready Group, was prepared to respond militarily, but its presence was designed primarily to deter the Communist powers from exploiting the Kong Le coup.

U.S. decisionmakers were divided over the optimum course of action in Laos. Admiral Felt saw Souvanna as leading a "government which is becoming the chosen instrument of Peking, Hanoi and [the Laotian Communists]. In my opinion Souvanna Phouma's appeasement policy toward the Pathet Lao is bound to fail eventually. Meantime it would render the [FAR] incapable of effective anti-Communist action."[48] But Phoumi's weaknesses also were recognized. The general displayed a lack of physical courage on occasion, proved less than brilliant in military operations, and sometimes showed himself impervious to U.S. advice. As Admiral Felt pointed out, "Phoumi is no George Washington. However, he is anti-communist which is what counts most in the sad Laos situation."[49] Admiral Burke believed "Phoumi is the only man who has the guts and willingness to support United States," but he amended this to include the Laotian king as well: "There are only two people in all Laos who are on our side: The King and Phoumi.... We must support [them] with all their faults" although "we must control them as much as we can."[50]

To bring the Souvanna government closer to the Western camp, the Eisenhower administration applied pressure by reducing the level of economic aid and finally, early in October, suspended all assistance. President Eisenhower stated emphatically that "Souvanna had to make up his mind between communism and the West. If he was not for us, we should support Phoumi."[51]

An important factor in this decision was the perceived need to demonstrate to South Vietnam and Thailand the firmness of American resolve to halt the drift of Laos and Southeast Asia as a whole to

---

[48]Msg, CP 180610Z Sep 1960. See also msg, CP 300310Z; OP-60, memo, of 9 Aug 1960.
[49]Msg, CP 022040Z Oct 1960.
[50]Msg, CNO 011943Z Oct 1960. Seven years later, Admiral Burke reiterated his conviction that "if you want to support a country, you have to support an individual... and you have to accept them for what they are." See Arleigh Burke, transcript of interview with Joseph E. O'Connor, John F. Kennedy Library, in Washington, D.C., 20 Jan 1967, pp 55-57.
[51]As reported in memo, OP-09 to CNO, of 12 Oct 1960. See also msgs, CP 070855Z; 072107Z Oct 1960; CNO 072107Z; 072125Z; OP-61, memo, of 9 Aug 1960; Stevenson, *End of Nowhere*, pp. 95-114; Dommen, *Conflict in Laos*, pp. 139-54; Fall, *Anatomy of a Crisis*, pp. 184-96; Goldstein, *American Policy Toward Laos*, pp. 209-15; Eisenhower, *Waging Peace*, pp. 607-12.

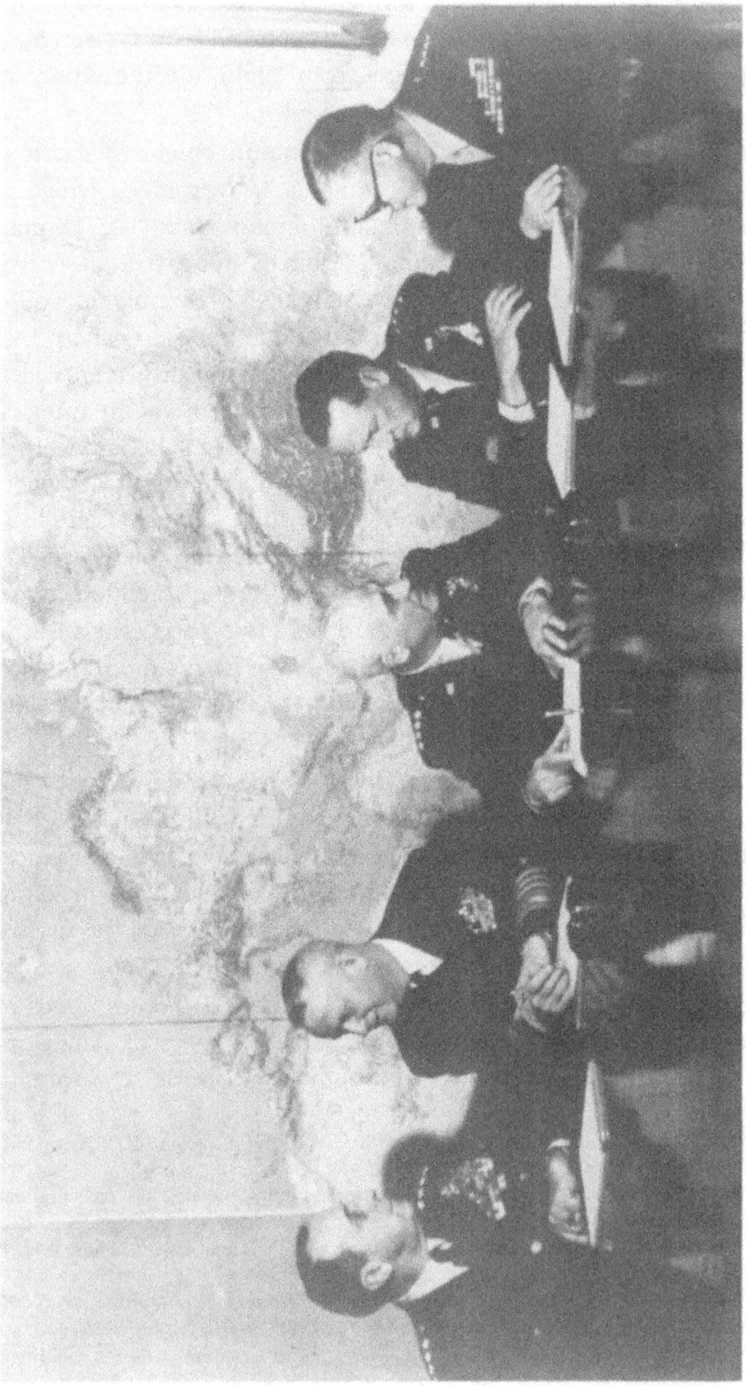

USN-1047895

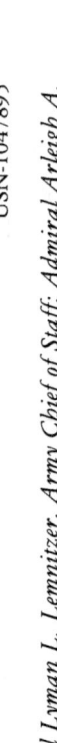

The Joint Chiefs of Staff in February 1960. From left to right, General Lyman L. Lemnitzer, Army Chief of Staff; Admiral Arleigh A. Burke, Chief of Naval Operations; Air Force General Nathan F. Twining, Chairman of the Joint Chiefs; General Thomas D. White, Air Force Chief of Staff; and General David M. Shoup, Commandant, U.S. Marine Corps.

communism or a left-leaning neutralism. There was a particular need to reassure South Vietnam's leaders on that score. An indication of the importance that U.S. leaders gave to commitments in Southeast Asia was the cruise of *Saint Paul*, flagship of the Seventh Fleet, with Vice Admiral Griffin embarked, to friendly nations in the area during October and November. As an important part of this Southeast Asian tour, Captain Frederick H. Schneider conned his ship up the Saigon River on 24 October to participate in the South Vietnamese Independence Day celebrations to be held on the 26th. Reflecting the great importance President Diem attached to the U.S. military presence in that part of Asia, the South Vietnamese head of state made an hour-long visit on board *Saint Paul*, which only four months earlier carried the President of the United States in his well-publicized Asian tour. Admiral Griffin was impressed with the port call to Saigon and subsequently expressed the view that "the pro-West regime in South Vietnam is fighting a good and continuous fight against Communism, sometimes against heavy odds. This deserves our support."[52]

At the same time in Laos, Souvanna Phouma continued to feel pressure from the United States. He reacted by urgently requesting, and quickly receiving, emergency military and economic assistance from the Soviet Union, which mounted an airlift into the mountain kingdom by way of North Vietnam.[53]

As a result, at the end of November the U.S. administration agreed to support the advance of Phoumi's forces from southern Laos and the seizure of Vientiane with material assistance and air transportation by Central Intelligence Agency (CIA) piloted aircraft of troops and supplies. On 28 November, General Phoumi launched the long awaited offensive. Souvanna Phouma declared Vientiane an open city on 9 December and fled to Phnom Penh. Soon afterward, the king dissolved the old government and installed the Phoumi faction in power under Prime Minister Boum Oum. Before the new government could be firmly established, however, the last of the opposition forces had to be eliminated. Kong Le, who initiated the rebellion in early August, continued to hold Vientiane with a force of about 2,000 of his

---

[52]Msg, COM7FLT 200914Z Oct 1960. See also COMCRUDIVONE, report, ser 358 of 31 Oct 1959; msg, 271220Z Oct 1960; *Saint Paul*, report, ser 068 of 27 Jun 1960; ltr, CPFLT to CP, ser 32/0259 of 13 Feb 1961.

[53]Msgs, SECSTATE 3PM 3 Oct 1960; AMEMBVT 7PM 3 Oct; 1PM 7 Oct; JCS 081653Z.

paratroopers. Between 13 and 16 December, before taking the city, Phoumi's forces engaged in heavy combat with Kong Le's forces, causing great destruction and loss of civilian life.[54]

The Seventh Fleet Prepares for Action

The fighting in Vientiane, during December 1960, endangered the American country team and threatened to instigate Communist countermoves. Hence, CINCPAC, on 14 December, ordered the units designated for Joint Task Force 116 into a higher state of readiness. Admiral Felt's prior decision to position major fleet units close at hand proved beneficial, because delays for deployment were minimal. A carrier task group, under the command of Captain Stockton B. Strong and composed of *Lexington* and Destroyer Division 171, already operated off Manila, while the 1st Battalion, 7th Marines, embarked in *Paul Revere* (APA-248) and *Monticello* (LSD-35), remained in Subic Bay. Also in Subic was Rear Admiral John W. Byng's antisubmarine Hunter-Killer Group comprising *Bennington* (CVS-20) in an LPH role with HMR 163 embarked. Destroyer Divisions 212 and 251 escorted the group.

The Seventh Fleet quickly and efficiently deployed to operational areas in the South China Sea fifty to eighty miles off Danang and Phan Thiet. By the following day, 15 December, the task force was concentrated in the designated areas and awaiting orders to implement CINCPAC Operation Plan 32(L)-59. Admiral John H. Sides, only recently placed in command of the Pacific Fleet, summarized the accomplishment for Admiral Burke and apprised him of the fact that "Navy forces will be in position well ahead of others." He added that the "combination of afloat BLT, CVS/LPH, and CVA air cover provides CINCPAC with versatile force whose influence can be projected well beyond the coastline of the South China Sea."[55]

---

[54]Stevenson, *End of Nowhere*, pp. 115-20; Toye, *Laos*, pp. 155-60; Dommen, *Conflict in Laos*, pp. 161-70; Fall, *Anatomy of a Crisis*, pp. 197-99; Champassak, *Storm Over Laos*, pp. 169-70; Earl H. Tilford, Jr., "Two Scorpions in a Cup: America and the Soviet Airlift to Laos," *Aerospace Historian* (Fall/Sep 1980), pp. 151-62.

[55]Msg, CPFLT 141906Z Dec 1960. See also msgs, COM7FLT 010620Z Dec 1960; 080826Z; CP 140029Z; CPFLT 140104Z; 140131Z; COM7FLT 140936Z; 140938Z; ltr, COM7FLT to CNO, ser 002-0027 of 10 Feb 1961.

In contrast to the previous crisis, the struggle in Laos during 1960 focused greater attention on the population centers. CINCPAC, in mid-October, stated that "we may have to fight our way into the airfields at Vientiane and Seno or Pakse in order [to] establish bases for further military operations."[56] Since this mission was the primary role of airborne units, the Army's 2nd Airborne Battle Group was designated the first element to enter Laos, a development that represented the Army's growing interest in and capability to provide mobile readiness forces for Southeast Asian contingencies.[57]

Preparations also were made to ensure that the fleet would be able to conduct aerial reconnaissance and photography of northern Vietnam and northern Laos, should U.S. forces be ordered to intervene in Laos. Consequently, on 14 December Admiral Griffin ordered a composite photographic squadron, VCP 63, to embark three F8U-1P Crusader aircraft in *Lexington*, while three additional F8U-1Ps and three A3D-2P Skywarriors of VCP 61 were directed to form the reserve at Cubi Point in the Philippines. Possessing no carrier-based aerial photographic aircraft, Commander Seventh Fleet had to bring the planes to the operational area from Naval Air Station, Agana, Guam, to Cubi Point. The first three F8U-1Ps arrived on board *Lexington* on 17 December.[58]

With the battle for Vientiane reaching a climax, Admiral Felt took additional steps to ready his forces. CINCPAC issued an alerting directive on 16 December to activate Joint Task Force 116, marshal airlift resources of the 315th Air Division, and begin the cargo loading of the amphibious force in Okinawa. Transports *Fort Marion* (LSD-22) and *Magoffin* (APA-199) were prepared to embark a second BLT at Buckner Bay. *Seminole* (AKA-104) and five LSTs of Task Force 76 already were assembled in Buckner Bay or enroute. Support ships *Pollux* (AKS-4) and *Firedrake* (AE-14) were also advised to anticipate operations in the South China Sea. The Seventh Fleet was poised and ready for action.[59]

---

[56] Msg, CP 180305Z Oct 1960.
[57] Msgs, CP 180305Z Oct 1960; CTF116 181320Z; CP 272245Z Nov; Spector, *Advice and Support*, pp. 359-60.
[58] Msgs, JCS 151455Z Dec 1960; COM7FLT 160048Z;160520Z; 160630Z; CTG77.7 170020Z; CG3MARDIV 170800Z; NASCUBIPT 190050Z; CNO 201555Z; COM7FLT 210806Z; VCP61 210927Z; CPFLT 240254Z.
[59] Msgs, CPFLT 170258Z Dec 1960; COM7FLT 160952Z;161422Z; CP 162357Z; COM7FLT 171502Z; 200204Z; OP-61 Laos Task Force, "U.S. Naval Forces," of 17 Dec 1960; ltr, COM7FLT to CNO, ser 002-0027 of 10 Feb 1961.

While the fleet assembled, other naval units engaged in special operations. At the request of the U.S. Ambassador to Thailand, U. Alexis Johnson, surveying ship *Maury* was directed to provide her one helicopter to American representatives in order to evacuate casualties from Vientiane. Sailing in the Gulf of Siam, *Maury* immediately dispatched this aircraft for the emergency task.[60]

It also became necessary for seaplane tender *Pine Island* (AV-12) to enter Danang in order to recover a P5M Marlin seaplane, from Patrol Squadron (VP) 40, which lost an engine and came down during a routine patrol flight. On 20 and 21 December, following diplomatic clearance from the South Vietnamese government, the ship accomplished her politically sensitive mission. The Peking press used the incident to support their contention that the United States had aggressive intentions in South Vietnam.[61]

While standing by to support a military response, naval forces provided other assistance to the U.S.-backed effort in Laos. Following JCS directives, the Chief of Naval Operations authorized the transfer of four Marine H-34 Seahorse helicopters to the CIA-operated Air America, which was aiding General Phoumi with airlift support in Laos. The H-34s would replace H-19As, which were unsuitable for operations in the high terrain and hot temperatures of northern Laos. On 20 December the helicopters were flown from *Bennington* to Bangkok. By the end of the year, maintenance personnel and a mobile training team composed of Marine officers and men were preparing to provide Air America personnel in Laos with assistance in operating and repairing the aircraft.[62]

By 22 December, the crisis atmosphere of the previous week was dissipated. The invasion of Laos, which U.S. leaders feared because of the Russian airlift of arms, ammunition, and supplies, did not occur. On that date, Admiral Felt authorized Pacific Fleet forces in readiness for Laos to resume normal operations, but to remain in the South China Sea "in position to again close the Vietnam coast on short notice."[63] This relaxation enabled the men of the Amphibious Ready Group and the

---

[60]Msgs, *Maury* 160458Z Dec 1960; CPFLT 161745Z; 161910Z.

[61]Msgs, COM7FLT 160354Z Dec 1960; 161030Z; AMEMB Saigon 8:32AM 17 Dec; COM7FLT 220518Z.

[62]Msgs, COM7FLT 171442Z Dec 1960; CNO 172045Z; CHJUSMAG Bangkok 180800Z; CNO 192113Z; CHJUSMAG Bangkok 211035Z; COM7FLT 211046Z; CHPEO Laos 250355Z; CP 290002Z; CTG79.3 291601Z; CG1STMAW 300125Z; MAG16 300240Z.

[63]Msg, CP 230351Z Dec 1960. See also msg, CP 220530Z Dec 1960.

Hunter-Killer Group to spend Christmas in Subic, although all units were kept on a four-hour sailing notice. The *Lexington*, *Parsons* (DDG-33), and *Halsey Powell* (DD-686) task group was directed to proceed to Hong Kong for the holiday and six-day port call. This diminished readiness was extended further on 29 December, when Admiral Griffin allowed the other group commanders to undertake essential maintenance. Believing the Seventh Fleet had experienced one more false alarm, naval commanders prepared to "get back to 'business as usual.'"[64]

The Communist New Year Offensive

At a higher level, military leaders expressed less confidence in late 1960 that the situation in Laos was stabilized. Phoumi's control of the government and the rightist faction was tenuous; and his forces, following the heavy fighting for Vientiane and the pursuit of Kong Le, were overextended and somewhat disorganized. To concentrate on the storming of the capital city, he denuded his garrisons elsewhere in Laos. At the same time, Kong Le remained a serious threat to both Vientiane and Luang Prabang. The Pathet Lao forces, which had husbanded their strength while the other factions engaged in mutual bloodletting, posed an even greater danger. Indeed, intelligence indicated that recent Pathet Lao directives urged increased attacks on Phoumi's forces. In addition to the continuing Soviet airlift, there were reports of stepped-up North Vietnamese troop movements and logistic activities in the border areas of North Vietnam and Laos. The belligerence of the Communist bloc press, and North Vietnamese official assertions of their right to intervene in Laos to counter the U.S. influence, also boded ill.[65]

Admirals Burke and Felt recognized the dangers of an escalating conflict. At one point, the latter officer stated that he was "not unaware of the outside possibility that the level of military activity in Laos could be raised progressively to a point where U.S. and Sino-Sov Bloc forces might become directly involved against each other with all the serious conse-

---

[64] Msg, COM7FLT 050910Z Jan 1961. See also msgs, COM7FLT 220518Z Dec 1960; 230726Z; 232326Z; 290720Z; 290746Z; CTF76 291022Z; ltr, COM7FLT to CNO, ser 002-0027 of 10 Feb 1961.

[65] Msgs, CNO 170021Z Dec 1960; CP 170407Z; 172041Z; 182103Z; OP-60, memo, of 9 Aug 1960; CNO, memo for record, ser 000737-60 of 10 Dec 1960; *U.S.-V.N. Relations*, bk. 2, pt. IV.A.5, tab 3, pp. 61-62.

quences this would entail." The commander of U.S. forces in the Pacific believed that if the Communists intended a military "showdown," then the challenge should be met. However, not knowing what the enemy's plans were, the admiral suggested that "we should find out by knocking off the present airlift," with the Laotians claiming defense of their sovereign air space, to gauge the Communist reaction. Admiral Felt stated his "personal opinion ... that the Reds are bluffing as they were in the Taiwan Strait affair and will back down if we are firm .... U.S. must draw the line in Laos .... We did this in the Taiwan Strait successfully despite substantial international and domestic criticism."[66]

While the JCS and State and Defense Department policymakers considered such options, the Communists struck. On 29 December, strong enemy forces, believed to be North Vietnamese, Pathet Lao, and Kong Le's, attacked government-held outposts in the Plain of Jars. By the 31st, government forces were ejected from strategic points in the plain. CINCPAC, on the day before the new year began, again placed the forces designated to implement or support Operation Plan 32(L)-59 in a high state of readiness.[67]

Once more, Seventh Fleet ships steamed toward operating areas in the South China Sea in preparation to support U.S. actions in Laos. The *Lexington* and *Bennington* task groups were fully deployed to their previous stations 50 to 100 miles off the central coast of South Vietnam by 2 January, while Captain Oliver D. Compton's Amphibious Ready Group, with the 1st Battalion, 7th Marines embarked in *Paul Revere* and *Monticello*, proceeded to a position further south off Phan Thiet. In addition, Admiral Griffin ordered *Coral Sea* (CVA-43) and her task group to sea from Buckner Bay. Loading of Task Force 76 transports also resumed. Aerial photographic aircraft already were embarked in *Lexington* or on standby at Cubi Point. With the officers and men of Joint Task Force 116 and supporting Pacific commands thoroughly familiar with their anticipated task, U.S. forces were at their highest state of readiness yet for a Laos intervention. Commanders awaited the order to act.[68]

---

[66]Msg, CP 282347Z Dec 1960. See also msgs, CP 232339Z Dec 1960; JCS 280226Z; CP 300131Z; memo, OP-61 to CNO, ser 000168P61 of 30 Dec; OP-61, briefing memo, No. 92-60 of Dec 1960.
[67]CINCPAC, Command History, 1961, pt. II, pp. 61-63; Stevenson, *End of Nowhere*, pp. 125-26.
[68]Msgs, CNO 182103Z Dec 1960; CP 311436Z; CPFLT 010501Z Jan 1961; COM7FLT 011230Z; 020834Z; JCS 042210Z; COM7FLT 050910Z; CP 062230Z; memo, OP-40 to CNO, ser 005244P40 of 31 Dec 1960; Robert L. Kerby, "American Military Airlift During the Laotian Civil

Admiral Felt now was fully convinced that the time for unilateral U.S. intervention had arrived. The scale, coordination, and strength of the Communist attack persuaded him that the ultimate goal of the drive, after capture of the Plain of Jars, was the conquest of all northern Laos, including Vientiane and the royal capital, Luang Prabang. CINCPAC stated to the Joint Chiefs of Staff that his Pacific Command forces were ready: "With full realization of the seriousness of a decision to intervene, I believe strongly that we must intervene now or give up northern Laos."[69] The admiral feared that southern Laos would fall soon afterward. That area long was viewed by U.S. strategists as the site of last resort in case pro-Western forces needed to establish a separate government, as in Korea, Germany, and Vietnam. This region also guarded the entrance to the lower Mekong River Valley, an important strategic route into the heart of mainland Southeast Asia.[70]

In Washington, Admiral Burke shared CINCPAC's estimate of the situation. On 31 December, the Chief of Naval Operations presented his sobering conclusions to the JCS. He observed that North Vietnamese forces "appear to have intervened" and were "capable, with Kong Le and Pathet Lao, of defeating Phoumi" even if the latter was provided U.S. material assistance. In addition, he warned that the Chinese Communists were "capable of invading Laos on short notice in great strength." And if this occurred, "they can only be stopped by strong United States forces. Stopping them may well require atomic weapons." The admiral enumerated other dangers resulting from a military response to the hostilities:

> If DRV is in, it will probably be necessary to reinforce Phoumi.... If this happens, the war will probably escalate: more DRV,...then Chicoms, then United States and SEATO. It will be like Korea, except it will be faster, and it is a worse area for us to fight in.[71]

But he also forecast the results of a U.S. failure to act: "If we lose Laos, we will probably lose Thailand and the rest of SE Asia. We will have demonstrated to the world that we cannot or will not stand when challenged. The effect will quickly show up in Asia, Africa, and Latin America."[72]

War, 1958-1963," *Aerospace Historian*, Vol. 24 (Spring 1977), pp. 5-6; ltr, COM7FLT to CNO, ser 002-0027 of 10 Feb 1961.
[69]Msg, CP 312235Z Dec 1960.
[70]*Ibid.*; msg, CPFLT 020255Z Jan 1961.
[71]Msg, CNO 311849Z Dec 1960.
[72]*Ibid.*

Bearing all of these factors in mind, Admiral Burke recommended that a decision be made to "hold Laos" and to "take all actions required, including if necessary open military support." It was essential to "make known United States determination to keep Laos free" through "actions as well as by words."[73] The admiral implied that it was equally important to deter, through a show of strength, further escalation on the part of the Communist powers. He recommended a "graduated response" to the enemy's initiatives with SEATO intervention, then U.S. air operations, and finally U.S. intervention. He cautioned: "Do not escalate the war faster than necessary, leave the enemy all possible opportunity to disengage. The goal is holding Laos, not conquering DRV or Red China."[74]

Also on 31 December, representatives from the State and Defense Departments met with the President to determine the U.S. course of action in Laos. The participants found that there was "insufficient information to form definite opinions as to the existence of overt or covert intervention by foreign troops in the Lao situation and the character, nature, and extent of such intervention, if it existed."[75] Lacking clear proof on this critical point, American leaders deferred a decision on military intervention by U.S. or SEATO forces. Although President Eisenhower stated that "we had to take all the actions necessary to prevent Communist domination of Laos," he approved only limited measures.[76] The President also directed the preparation of a firm diplomatic statement to apprise the Soviet Union of U.S. intent to preserve the Laotian government.[77]

The employment of South Vietnamese resources also was given consideration. The Navy's AD-6 Skyraider aircraft, twelve of which already were transferred to South Vietnam in the aid program, were offered by the commander of the South Vietnamese Air Force for the

---

[73] *Ibid.* See also memo, CNO to JCS, ser 000374P60 of 31 Dec 1960; Burke, "Estimate of Situation," of 31 Dec 1960.

[74] Msg, CNO 311849Z Dec 1960. See also memo, CNO to JCS, ser 000374P60 of 31 Dec 1960; Burke, "Estimate of Situation," of 31 Dec 1960; OP-06, memo, ser BM-5-61 of 5 Jan 1961; OP-60S2, "Adm. Burke's Remarks to Plans and Policies Group," of 9 Jan 1961, pp. 33-34; memo, OP-61 to CNO, ser 000318P61 of 29 Jan 1961.

[75] ASD (ISA), memo for the record, of 31 Dec 1960 in OP-60, briefing memo, No. 4-61 of 5 Jan 1961.

[76] *Ibid.*

[77] *Ibid.* See also msgs, JCS 312255Z Dec 1960; CP 060133Z Jan 1961; memo, OP-61 to CNO, ser 000602P61 of 6 Jan 1961; msg, COM7FLT 100604Z Jan 1961; Stevenson, *End of Nowhere*, pp. 120-26.

conflict in Laos. The conduct of counterguerrilla operations in southern Laos by South Vietnamese troops was discussed by U.S., Laotian, and South Vietnamese leaders as well. Neither of these proposals, however, was implemented.[78]

As happened before, the immediate Communist military threat receded almost as quickly as it appeared. After capturing the towns of Nong Het and Ban Ban and most of the Plain of Jars by 1 January 1961, Pathet Lao-Kong Le pressure on government forces eased considerably. General Heintges believed that external powers were supporting the Laotian Communists in their fight, but he also felt that the evidence available to him did "not support massive intervention claim."[79] Admiral Felt came to the same conclusion. On 6 January, he observed that current rumors in the press of a Chinese invasion of Laos probably were generated by Phoumi:

> Phoumi is under the political pressure gun and is probably following his oft times repeated tactic of manufacturing a [crisis] to gain his ends. It is my opinion this is similar to the exaggerated crises concerning Vietnam invasion of Laos in Jul and Aug of 1959, the many crises reports Phoumi put out during the revolutionary period in Savannakhet and similar crises since that time which he has been wont to bring to our attention whenever he feels the need for additional support or approval of certain actions that he feels we are not in favor of.[80]

Although the extent of North Vietnamese participation in combat during the New Year Offensive is unclear, "volunteer Vietnamese troops," advisors, and other personnel assisted the combined Pathet Lao-Kong Le forces.[81] The Pathet Lao-Kong Le forces were bolstered by the Soviet airlift of arms, ammunition, and equipment. This support was enough to ensure the continued success of the Pathet Lao, while enabling the North Vietnamese to concentrate their efforts and forces southward — along the soon-to-be famous Ho Chi Minh Trail toward South Vietnam. In southern Laos during 1959 and 1960, the North Vietnamese and Pathet Lao secured corridors through the jungle, and, under the control of Group 559, established a sophisticated trail system with way-stations, food

---

[78]Msg, CP 142055Z Jan 1961; memo, OP-61 to CNO, ser 000610P61 of 16 Jan; memo, OP-61 to CNO, ser 00615P61 of 23 Jan; msg, CP 290340Z; CNO, memo for record, ser 0154-61 of 6 Mar; JCS Paper 1992/906.
[79]Msg, CHPEO Laos 040955Z Jan 1961. See also Stevenson, *End of Nowhere*, pp. 126-28.
[80]Msg, CP 060340Z Jan 1961.
[81]Socialist Republic of Vietnam, *Vietnam: The Anti-U.S. Resistance War*, p. 47.

caches, rest areas, and guides. Further, preinfiltration centers and the transportation organizational structure were developed in North Vietnam. During the two-year period, over 4,500 personnel, most of whom were "regrouped" to the north after the Geneva Agreement, infiltrated back into South Vietnam by way of Laos. Once in the South, they waged political warfare, as part of the renewed unification campaign, and laid the groundwork for later arrivals from North Vietnam.[82]

On 6 January 1961, with the battlefield situation once again static, CINCPAC relaxed the readiness of the Laos contingency forces. Admiral Griffin expressed his satisfaction with the performance of his Seventh Fleet when he stated that "as proven twice recently, this ready fleet can shift anytime into high gear without a clutch" to counter Communist moves.[83]

The extended confrontation over Laos did much to alert U.S. naval leaders to the special nature of the conflict in Southeast Asia. The fleet was used increasingly to counter perceived Communist advances into the area. The Navy participated in the Eisenhower administration's program to bolster Phoumi's rightist faction with military assistance and task force deployments into the South China Sea. Nevertheless, as the military fortunes of Phoumi's non-Communist forces waned in the first days of the new year, the fleet anticipated continuing employment in support of U.S. policy in Southeast Asia.

---

[82] M. G. Weiner, J. R. Brom, and R. E. Koon, *Infiltration of Personnel from North Vietnam: 1959-1967* (Santa Monica, CA: Rand Corp., 1968), pp. vi, 7, 39, 41, 53; *U.S.-V.N. Relations*, bk. 2, pt. IV.A.5, tab 3, pp. 55-60; "Aggression from the North: The Record of North Vietnam's Campaign to Conquer South Vietnam," *The Department of State Bulletin* (22 Mar 1965), p. 407; Langer and Zasloff, *North Vietnam and the Pathet Lao*, pp. 71-72, 80, 116, 167-68, 173, 226, 237.

[83] Msg, COM7FLT 120804Z Jan 1961.

CHAPTER III

Confrontation Over Laos, 1961-1962

The continuing crisis in Laos during early 1961 appeared no nearer to solution than it was in the previous year. Increasingly disenchanted with General Phoumi's leadership, U.S. diplomatic officials began to seek suitable substitutes from the center of the Laotian political spectrum. This reassessment of U.S. policy coincided with the advent of the Kennedy administration, which was critical of unsuccessful U.S. actions to establish a viable pro-Western government in Laos or to retard the spread of Communist influence. The new administration eventually adopted a policy toward Laos that was in many ways dissimilar to that of its predecessor. Basic to the new concept was an emphasis on bilateral U.S.-Soviet efforts to establish Laos as a truly neutral buffer state. But convincing the Soviets of the strength of the U.S. position in Laos first required the reestablishment by the Royal Laotian Government of firm military and political control over much of the population. It was recognized that this objective could not be attained without a substantial increase in military assistance and political support by the United States. But, in contrast with the previous emphasis on unilateral actions, the Kennedy administration also stressed the importance of cooperation with the SEATO and pro-Western Southeast Asian nations.[1]

---

[1] CNO, memos for record, ser 030-61 of 10 Jan 1961; ser 0050-61 of 24 Jan; ser 00052- 61 of 25 Jan; msgs, CP 070320Z Jan 1961; 092055Z; Stevenson, *End of Nowhere*, pp. 128-42; Fall, *Anatomy of a Crisis*, pp. 159-61; David K. Hall, "The Laos Crisis, 1960-61" in Alexander L. George, David K. Hall, and William E. Simons, *The Limits of Coercive Diplomacy; Laos, Cuba, Vietnam* (Boston: Little, Brown and Co., 1971), pp. 42-51; Goldstein, *American Policy Toward Laos*, pp. 236-44; Toye, *Laos*, pp. 166-67; Roger Hilsman, *To Move a Nation: The Politics of Foreign Policy in the Administration of John F. Kennedy* (Garden City, NY: Doubleday, 1967), pp. 127-33.

U.S. Military Assistance to the Laotian Armed Forces and the March Alert

Although the military situation in Laos was static during January and February 1961, the respite for government forces was only temporary. CINCPAC reported at the beginning of March that the Communist forces defending the Plain of Jars were at the receiving end of a constant flow of supplies by way of Soviet airlift and road transportation from North Vietnam. He added that the "volume of this Commie supply effort obviously greater than needed to sustain [Pathet Lao] in defensive posture." This conclusion led the commander of U.S. Pacific forces to state: "It needs to be repeated again and again that the only way to save Laos now is by successful military action."[2]

To consider ways to strengthen the FAR, a meeting was called on 9 March at the White House, with the President, State and Defense Department, CIA, and other administration officials in attendance. Admiral Felt also flew in from Hawaii to present his observations in person. As if to reinforce the critical nature of the group's task, the Pathet Lao opened an attack on 6 March. By the time of the meeting, they had thrown Phoumi's forces back from the Plain of Jars in total disarray. At the Washington meeting, President Kennedy approved seventeen measures of support to improve Phoumi's military position.[3]

Of most concern to the Navy was the President's authorization for the transfer to the CIA in Laos of sixteen (later reduced to fourteen) Marine H-34 helicopters crewed with U.S. military volunteers, half of whom were Marines and the other half from the Army and the Navy. This contingent would be supported by 300 Marine maintenance personnel to be deployed to Thailand. The new Secretary of Defense, Robert S. McNamara, assigned this task the highest priority and the Navy made urgent efforts to comply with the directive. In March 1961, the first increment in the helicopter transfer was airlifted from Hawaii to Thailand. On the 18th, CINCPAC ordered a further airlift of the 300 maintenance men of Marine Air Base Squadron 16 from Futema, Okinawa, to Udorn, Thailand. On 22 March, the first elements of the Marine unit arrived at their destination and established facilities to support subsequent helicopter

---
[2] Msg, CP 012300Z Mar 1961. See also CNO, memo for record, ser 000122-61 of 24 Feb 1961; msg, CP 290340Z Jan 1961.
[3] Hall, "The Laos Crisis," pp. 51-58.

operations in Laos. Naval Supply Depot, Yokosuka, Japan, and later the naval facility at Oakland, California, were designated as the supply sources for spare parts and other necessary aircraft material. Simultaneously, Admiral Byng's carrier task group, with *Bennington* and her two escorts, *Braine* (DD-630) and *Cogswell* (DD-651), proceeded to the Gulf of Siam for the helicopter transfer. The helicopters were flown off *Bennington* on the 28th.

Before this additional assistance arrived, however, Phoumi's war effort showed further disintegration in the face of renewed Communist attacks.[4] Late on 19 March, Admiral Felt once again placed Joint Task Force 116 and its supporting forces in a heightened state of readiness. The following day, Major General Donald M. Weller, USMC, received orders to assemble his staff in Okinawa and activate the command. As in previous alerts, much of the Seventh Fleet was concentrated in the South China Sea. These preliminary measures paid off when, late on the 21st, CINCPAC ordered a readiness state just short of the condition where intervention was deemed imminent. In the next several days, additional ships and men of Admiral Griffin's Seventh Fleet converged on this troubled area. Rear Admiral Frank B. Miller's *Lexington* task group headed for a rendezvous with *Midway* and her escorts 200 miles off Danang. Working together, the carrier groups formed Task Force 77, under Rear Admiral Miller's command, to provide necessary air support for the Laos operation. Other air support was provided by shore-based aircraft from Sangley Point in the Philippines, which conducted air early warning patrols for the carrier task force. VMA 212, which deployed earlier to Cubi Point, went to maximum alert in preparation for employment from either a carrier or an airfield on the Southeast Asian mainland. Commander Seventh Fleet also ordered the immediate transfer from Naval Air Station, Atsugi, Japan, to Cubi Point of Marine Fighter Squadron (VMF) 312 and VMF 154 with their thirty-four F8U-1E Crusader aircraft.

Additional naval strength was gathered from other reaches of the Pacific. One element was the 1st Marine Brigade, which was embarking on board Amphibious Squadron 7 ships in Hawaii for scheduled participation in Exercise Green Light off the California coast. Admiral

---

[4]Memos, OP-06, of 10 Mar 1961; Bundy to Brown, of 20 Mar; Laos Task Force to CNO, ser 00039P33 of 21 Mar; ser 00046P33 of 28 Mar; msgs, CNO 162139Z Mar 1961; CP 171935Z; COM7FLT 191430Z; ADMINO CP 242120Z; CNO 040045Z Apr; CPFLT 180316Z; CP 190003Z; CHJCS 210920Z; Kerby, "American Military Airlift," p. 6.

Sides directed Commander First Fleet, Vice Admiral Charles L. Melson, to reorient the amphibious squadron toward Okinawa, once the force put to sea. The formation departed Hawaii on 22 March. It included elements of the 4th Marines and Marine Aircraft Group 13 embarked in 3 APAs, 3 LSDs, and 1 AKA. This movement of naval forces to Southeast Asia reflected the Navy's increased readiness to project forces ashore. It was a harbinger of deployments that occurred later in the Vietnam War.

By 2400 on 24 March, the striking power of the Seventh Fleet was concentrated in the South China Sea in readiness for likely contingencies. *Lexington* and her destroyers arrived on station 200 miles east of Danang. There they joined *Midway* and her escorts. Both *Lexington* and *Midway* carried photographic reconnaissance aircraft. *Bennington*, doubling as a helicopter carrier and an antisubmarine carrier, was enroute to the Gulf of Siam. And the Amphibious Ready Group stood by 100 miles south of Bangkok, ready to dash in and disembark her Marine BLT. In Buckner Bay, the transports and LSTs of Task Force 76 also assembled. Dropping anchor on 24 March, *Calvert* (APA-32) and *Vernon County* (LST-1161) were joined the following day by 2 AKAs, 1 APA, and 1 LSD. *Thetis Bay* also arrived on the 24th to embark combat Marines. In Japan, 5 LSTs, 2 LSDs, and 1 APA loaded the 2nd Battalion, 3rd Marines, ammunition, and other essential cargo. To supply and refuel this vast assemblage of combatant ships, Admiral Griffin dispatched the widely dispersed logistic support units of Task Force 73 to the South China Sea and Okinawa. By the 24th, 5 oilers, 2 repair ships, 3 stores ships, and 1 ammunition ship already serviced the fleet or were enroute to the operational area. The fleet and its embarked forces again stood ready to implement national policy in Southeast Asia.[5]

While U.S. naval, air, and ground forces were stronger and more numerous than they were in any previous Laos crisis, the addition of SEATO resources also became possible. Following the SEATO Military Advisors Fourteenth Conference at Bangkok in March, a great degree of cooperation and coordination was achieved. Admiral Felt reported, following his attendance at the conference, that "SEATO has stood trial

---

[5]Msgs, CPFLT 170322Z Mar 1961; 210839Z; 212316Z; CNO 220021Z; 220035Z; CPFLT 220131Z; COM1FLT 222324Z; COM7FLT LAOS SITREPS 1(221412Z)—5(260806Z); CINC-PACFLT SITREPS 10(222247Z)—13(252151Z); memos, OP-33 (Laos Task Force) to CNO, "Laos—What We Are Doing," ser 00043P33 of 25 Mar; Kerby, "American Military Airlift," p. 6.

this week and came through with a meeting of minds."[6] To better control the large military contingents preparing to take action in Southeast Asia, on 7 April Lieutenant General Paul D. Harkins, USA, the Deputy Commander in Chief, U.S. Army Pacific, established an overall headquarters on Okinawa. Simultaneously, Joint Task Force 116 was deactivated and most of its headquarters staff transferred to General Harkins's new command.[7]

The Fleet Maintains Readiness in the South China Sea

Although the Kennedy administration was somewhat encouraged by the knowledge that allied military unity over Laos was greater than had been the case in previous crises, the primary need for a political settlement was reaffirmed at a White House meeting on 21 March, at which State and Defense Department and CIA representatives were present. U.S. officials sought to bring about a conference at Geneva for this purpose, but obtaining a ceasefire in Laos was seen as an absolute prerequisite to negotiations. To achieve a ceasefire, the Communists would have to be convinced of allied determination to defend the existing government. In the military sphere, this entailed two efforts: the constant readiness of U.S. forces to deploy quickly and in strength to Southeast Asia to back up negotiations and the continuation of military aid to Phoumi's forces.[8]

In this latter regard, the United States continued to strengthen the Laotian armed forces and the transportation system on which they depended. For example, at the end of 1960 the Officer in Charge of Construction, Southeast Asia, in Bangkok, established a resident officer in

---

[6]Msg, CP 020330Z Apr 1961. See also Dommen, *Conflict in Laos*, p. 195; Stevenson, *End of Nowhere*, p. 148; Fall, *Anatomy of a Crisis*, pp. 216-18; Theodore C. Sorensen, *Kennedy* (New York: Harper and Row, 1965), pp. 640-43; Arthur M. Schlesinger, Jr., *A Thousand Days: John F. Kennedy in the White House* (Boston: Houghton Mifflin, 1965), pp. 329-34. The Chinese were apprised of this determination through the U.S. Embassy in Warsaw. See Lee, *Communist China's Policy Toward Laos*, p. 78.

[7]Msgs, CP 020330Z Apr 1961; 050206Z; 050910Z; memo, OP-60 to CNO, ser BM000403-61 of 8 Apr 1961; CINCPAC, Command History, 1961, pp. 135-37; OP-60, briefing memo, No. 155-61 of Apr 1961.

[8]CNO, memos for record, ser 000182-61 and 000183-61 of 21 Mar 1961; Hall, "The Laos Crisis," pp. 59-68; Stevenson, *End of Nowhere*, pp. 143-48; Dommen, *Conflict in Laos*, pp. 187-92.

Vientiane to oversee contract work in Laos, which until then was troubled by inefficiency and some misuse of funds by contractors. Lieutenant John P. Sylva (CEC), designated Resident Officer in Charge of Construction, Vientiane, spent the first months of 1961 standardizing contract procedures and monitoring construction of airfields, roads, and barrack complexes in the capital and other river valley localities.[9]

The second part of the dual politico-military program to deal with the Laotian problem concerned the maintenance of U.S. forces in the Western Pacific in a high state of readiness. In fact, great emphasis was placed on deploying the first increment of the intervention force into Laos within forty-eight hours of an order to execute the contingency plan. To accomplish this, the command elements, the BLT slated for airlift from Okinawa, the air transport units, the afloat BLT in *Bennington*, and other selected Seventh Fleet units were kept in constant alert during late March and April.[10]

At the same time, the fleet also conducted other operations. One of these was the combined SEATO Exercise Pony Express, which was meant to demonstrate to friend and foe alike SEATO's unity and military power at a crucial time. This amphibious exercise was conducted on the coast of North Borneo at the end of April and early May 1961. The exercise included convoy escort, underway replenishment, communications, antisubmarine, and antiaircraft warfare training. The participation of over 60 ships and 26,000 personnel from the combined SEATO nations made it the largest alliance maneuver ever held. The U.S. contingent, most of which sortied from Manila and Subic Bay on 21 April, consisted of the Seventh Fleet flagship *Saint Paul, Coral Sea, Estes* (AGC-12), with Commander Task Force 76 embarked, 1 destroyer division, 1 mine division, and 2 submarines. In addition, *Thetis Bay, Calvert, Catamount* (LSD-71), *Skagit* (AKA-105), *Magoffin*, and *Fort Marion* carried 2 Marine BLTs and HMR 162. Both Admiral Sides, the Pacific Fleet commander, and the JCS feared that U.S. participation in Pony Express might divert ships and men from the primary Laos readiness mission and suggested its postponement. Admiral Felt, however, concluded that the exercise was

---

[9]Sylva, interview.
[10]Msg, CP 052048Z Apr 1961; memo, OP-60 to CNO, ser BM000403-61 of 8 Apr 1961.

Collection of Captain John P. Sylva
The Navy's Resident Officer in Charge of Construction, Vientiane, Laos, Lieutenant John P. Sylva (CEC), meets with Laotian leader Phoumi Nosavan at Savannakhet airfield early in 1961.

too important from many standpoints to defer. Nevertheless, he directed CINCPACFLT to load and position his ships during the exercise so they could readily support Laos contingencies.[11]

---

[11] CINCPAC, Command History, 1961, p. 145; CINCPACFLT, Annual Report, FY1961, p. 24; COM7FLT, Command History, 1961, encl. 1; ltr, Sides to Burke, of 21 Apr 1961; memo, Laos Task Force (OP-33) to CNO, ser 00071P33 of 22 Apr 1961; msgs, CPFLT 012158Z Apr 1961; 032334Z; 060944Z; 070231Z; COM7FLT 130614Z; 200646Z; 270408Z; JCS 272253Z; CNO 020015Z May.

The Laos Crisis Reaches a Climax
April-May 1961

As these military activities continued, the possibility of achieving a negotiated settlement became increasingly bright in the spring of 1961. In April, the United States government acceded to a proposal, put forth by Great Britain and the USSR, co-chairmen of the conference on Laos, for a fourteen-nation gathering, which again would be held at Geneva.[12] The hope was that a neutral Laos would result from these negotiations. However, before this process could be set in motion, the ever evasive ceasefire had to be obtained and adhered to by the contending forces. During March and early April, Communist forces continued to move toward the Laotian population centers in the Mekong River Valley, and the disintegration of FAR increased with each lost engagement. Once again, the Pathet Lao, with the military support and assistance of Communist states, appeared to have the ability to utterly rout government forces and seize the remainder of Laos.

Although a ceasefire was scheduled for 24 April, the Communists, whose forces were in a militarily favorable position, procrastinated. Faced with the rapid deterioration of the FAR's fighting ability and the probability that the fall of Luang Prabang, Vientiane, and most of Laos was imminent, on the 26th Ambassador Winthrop Brown called for drastic action. Specifically, the chief U.S. representative in Laos suggested that the SEATO powers prepare to act on a Laotian government request for intervention. That same day, an urgent meeting was called at the White House to coordinate U.S. moves. Having participated in the meeting and come away with the impression that a decision to intervene shortly would be given, Admiral Burke advised CINCPACFLT to obtain authorization to preposition his fleet and its embarked Marines.[13]

---

[12]Captain William M. Carpenter from the Office of the Chief of Naval Operations, Politico-Military Policy Division, was designated to represent the Navy on an informal working group, under International Security Affair's Rear Admiral Luther C. Heinz, which was to draft position papers relating to the forthcoming conference. The captain subsequently served with the Defense Department delegation to the Geneva Conference. Memo, SECNAV to SECDEF, ser 75P61 of 14 Apr 1961, encl. in memo, Deputy ASD (ISA), ser I-3129/61 of 12 Apr 1961; ACNO (Plans and Policy), memo, ser 90P61 of 3 May.

[13]CNO, memo for record, ser 000221-61 of 21 Apr 1961; OP-61, memo for record, ser 00083P61 of 24 Apr; CNO, memo for record, ser 00085P33 of 24 Apr; msgs, CNO 262027Z Apr; JCS 270256Z.

Kearsarge *(CVS-33)* and her escorts enter Subic Bay in the Philippines in the spring of 1961 as the Seventh Fleet concentrates to deter Communist advances in Laos.

Meanwhile, CINCPAC took immediate steps to alert U.S. forces designated to execute the operation and to bring them close to the Southeast Asian trouble spot. Admiral Felt ordered Lieutenant General Harkins to ready essential commands and directed a Marine aircraft group and the 2nd Battalion, 3rd Marines to deploy forward to Cubi Point. In addition, Admiral Sides ordered *Coral Sea* and her escorts, which in mid-April became the southern CVA group, to a position off Danang. The antisubmarine Hunter-Killer Group, formed around *Kearsarge*, also headed for the South China Sea from Sasebo, Japan. *Thetis Bay*, *Magoffin*, and *Fort Marion* and the embarked 3rd Battalion, 9th Marines, which were engaged in the Pony Express exercise off Borneo, steamed to a position off South Vietnam's Cape Camau. The Amphibious Ready Group, which put in at Subic only the day before, after thirty-seven consecutive days on station in the Gulf of Siam, was ordered to weigh anchor and proceed again to the gulf. *Midway*, on station off Okinawa, headed south in company with four destroyers to back up *Coral Sea*'s operations. Finally, *Lexington*, which recently entered drydock at Yokosuka, Japan, for needed repairs to one of her screws, was alerted to make ready for departure on short notice. In contrast to previous Laos crises, however, the transports and cargo ships of the Amphibious Group, Western Pacific were already in Southeast Asian waters prepared to execute their sealift mission. Commander Task Force 76, Rear Admiral Bernard F. Roeder, in *Estes*, had 1 APA, 1 AKA, 1 LSD, 4 LSTs, and the 1st Battalion, 3rd Marines, close at hand off Borneo with another 2 LSDs, 1 APA, and 2 LSTs off Okinawa and the Philippines.

The fleet swiftly deployed to the South China Sea in what by now was a well practiced maneuver. The *Coral Sea* group arrived at the assigned station east of Danang on the 28th, and the following day *Midway* reached her position east of Hainan Island. Because the threat of Soviet or Chinese Communist intervention was perceived as much greater in this latest confrontation over Laos, additional measures were taken to protect U.S. forces. *Kearsarge*, due to arrive on the 30th, was directed to provide antisubmarine defense on an alternating basis for each attack carrier group. Commander Seventh Fleet also ordered air patrol squadrons from the Philippines, Okinawa, and Japan to give antisubmarine cover over the CVAs operating in the South China Sea, the Taiwan Strait area, and the *Lexington* group, respectively. Air Early Warning Squadron 1 provided early warning support for the carriers. Admiral Griffin also dispatched three destroyers or destroyer escorts to each antisubmarine carrier group, and deployed two attack submarines off Subic Bay. After the great urgency felt on the 26th lessened somewhat, *Thetis Bay*, *Magoffin*, and *Fort Marion* returned to Borneo to continue participation in Pony Express, but prepared to respond on short notice. *Paul Revere* and *Monticello*, however, departed Subic enroute to their old operating area off Bangkok. By 28 April, additional steps were taken to augment the strength of the Laos contingency force. CINCPACFLT ordered *Bon Homme Richard* (CVA-31) to sail for the Western Pacific after departing Pearl Harbor on 2 May.

Renville (APA-227), transporting the 1st Battalion, 5th Marines, had orders to make for Okinawa.

By the end of April, the major part of the Seventh Fleet was deployed to Southeast Asian waters prepared to support the projection of U.S. power onto the Indochinese peninsula. Sailing with the fleet were three Marine BLTs. Another two battalions were available on Okinawa for airlift, and a sixth waited in readiness at Cubi Point. These units were reinforced by the battalion arriving at Okinawa in *Renville*. At the same time, the helicopter and fixed-wing aircraft of the 1st Marine Aircraft Wing were available to support the ground troops.[14]

Decision Against Intervention

Despite the initial inclination of U.S. decisionmakers on 26 April to intervene in Laos, this course of action soon was rejected. Throughout the following day, the President met with officials of the National Security Council, members of Congress, and the Joint Chiefs of Staff. Many of these leaders felt it probable that the Chinese Communists would intervene to counter a similar U.S. or SEATO move and they did not rule out Soviet involvement. The Army Chief of Staff, General George H. Decker, USA, and the Commandant of the Marine Corps, General David M. Shoup, USMC, were especially opposed to American ground operations in the heart of the Southeast Asian mainland. These military officers recognized that U.S. strength might be inadequate to sustain a campaign in Laos. In the crucial first three days of any operation to secure Vientiane, U.S. airlift resources and Laotian airfield capacity would limit the number of troops transported to 1,000 each day. This figure was believed too low to assure a successful defense of the capital. In addition, it already was determined that of the 3,279 short tons of cargo required during the first five days of a Laotian operation, only 1,766 short tons could be transported. During the next five days, the requirement would be 1,053 short tons, but there would only be the capability to airlift 778 short tons. Secretary of Defense McNamara, as reported by the CNO, also was persuaded that "it may be too late to intervene in Laos...that if we put

---

[14]Msgs, COM7FLT 270142Z Apr 1961; CPFLT 271141Z; COM7FLT 271330Z; 280214Z; 280700Z; 280926Z; 280928Z; CPFLT 290426Z; COM7FLT 290850Z; 291418Z; OP-33, memo for record, ser 00094P33 of 29 Apr 1961; Kerby, "American Military Airlift," pp. 6-7.

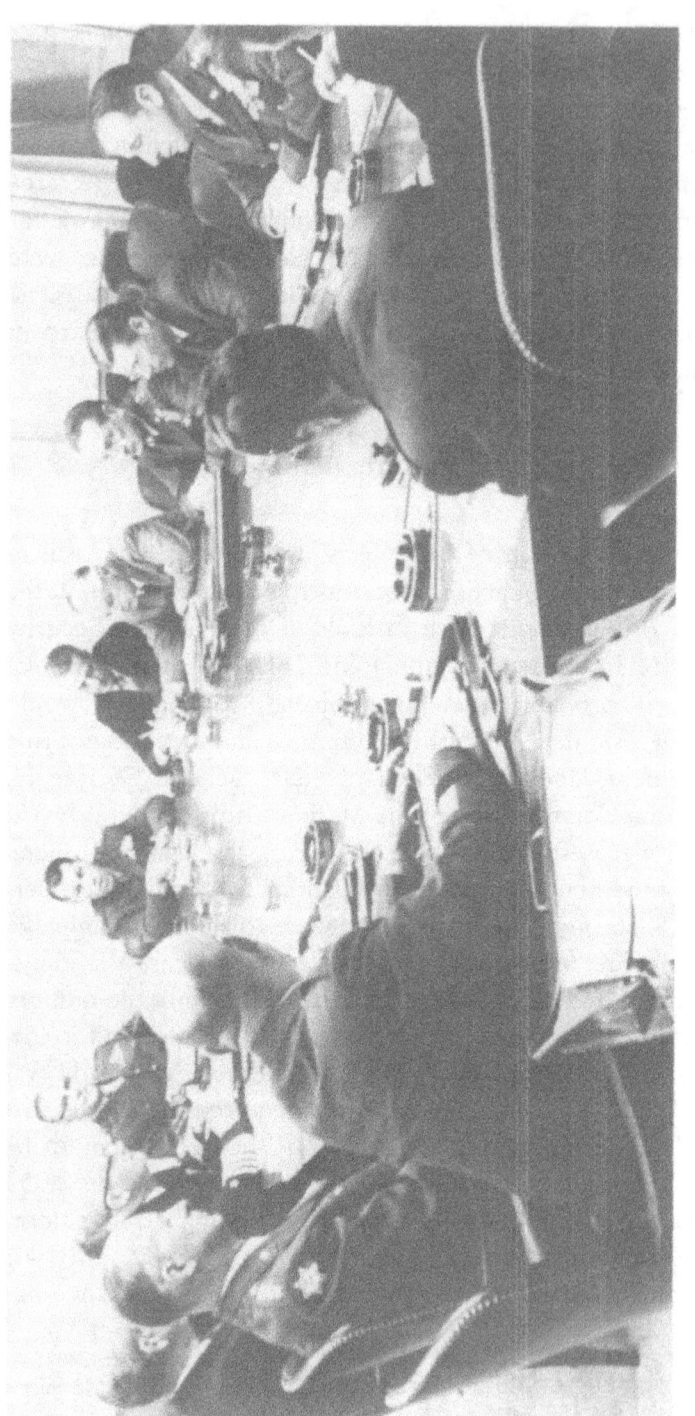

NH-93679
Collection of Admiral Arleigh Burke

Leaders of the national defense establishment confer in April 1961. Those present include, left to right: General George H. Decker, Army Chief of Staff; Admiral Arleigh A. Burke, Chief of Naval Operations; General David M. Shoup, Commandant, U.S. Marine Corps; Paul Nitze, Assistant Secretary of Defense for International Security Affairs (light suit); General Thomas D. White, Air Force Chief of Staff; Secretary of Defense Robert S. McNamara; and General Lyman Lemnitzer, Chairman of the Joint Chiefs of Staff.

troops in Vientiane, they could be driven out."[15] The members of Congress briefed on the situation in Laos, including Senators Mike J. Mansfield, Hubert H. Humphrey, Richard B. Russell, Everett M. Dirksen, Carl Vinson, and Styles Bridges and Representative Sam Rayburn were unanimously opposed to intervention in Laos. The overriding conclusion drawn by the assembled leaders was that Laos was "a terrible place to fight a war."[16]

Of the national leaders present, only Admiral Burke spoke forcefully in favor of a U.S. military stand in Laos.[17] The CNO stated that a failure to act in Laos would result in the eventual, if not immediate, loss of Southeast Asia:

> If the Thais and Vietnamese who were fighting against Communism would come to believe that the United States would not really support them when it came to a showdown, they would then try to accommodate themselves eventually...to Communism because they would not have confidence in the United States coming to their aid if they needed it.[18]

Further, the physical control by a friendly regime of southern Laos would enable the North Vietnamese to markedly increase their support of the war in South Vietnam. The admiral observed that "if Laos were Communist, South Vietnam would...have a long border against a Communist nation. This border is a junction border which could not be patrolled and which could not be guarded even to the extent of preventing a minor degree of infiltration of people across borders to South Vietnam." The Chief of Naval Operations strongly recommended that "regardless of the difficulties of fighting in Laos, regardless of the possibility of escalation of the war, regardless of the possible need to use nuclear weapons eventually, and regardless of all of these things we should try to hold the

---

[15]CNO, memo for record, ser 000231-61 of 27 Apr 1961.

[16]*Ibid.*

[17]Admiral Burke has stated that Vice President Lyndon B. Johnson expressed some agreement with the CNO's views. See Arleigh Burke, transcript of interview with Joseph E. O'Connor, John F. Kennedy Library, in Cambridge, MA.

[18]CNO, memo for record, ser 000231-61 of 27 Apr 1961. See also OP-33, memo for record, ser 00090P33 of 27 Apr 1961; Burke/Ward, transcript of conversation, of 5 May 1961; CINCPAC, Command History, 1961, p. 70; Burke, transcript of conversation with Bob Donovan, *New York Herald Tribune*, of 7 Jul 1961; Burke, transcript of conversation with Hanson Baldwin, *New York Times*, of 27 Jun 1961; ltr, Burke to Griffin, of 27 Jul 1961; memo, OP-40 to OP-60, ser BM00094-61 of 25 Apr 1961; ltr, CINCPACFLT to CINCPAC, ser 41/000146 of 30 May 1961; Hall, "The Laos Crisis," pp. 68-70.

significant part of Laos, including Vientiane." The admiral concluded by asking, "if we do not fight in Laos, will we fight in Thailand where the situation will be the same sometime in the future as it is now in Laos? Will we fight in Vietnam? Where will we fight? Where do we hold? Where do we draw the line?"[19]

Although Admiral Burke's views did not prevail, there appeared to be general agreement that the introduction of U.S. forces into South Vietnam or Thailand, if their fall loomed, should be accomplished. Admiral Burke drew two conclusions from the deliberations on 27 April: first, that airlift and airborne operations could not be conducted or supported in enough strength to ensure success in the crucial first stages of a landing; and second, that Laos, unlike South Vietnam and Thailand, "could not be defended and would go down the drain because it didn't have a sea coast."[20]

While President Kennedy deferred for twenty-four hours a plan of action regarding Laos, the decision not to intervene had, in effect, been made. The CNO informed Admiral Felt that "after a series of meetings today, I am fearful that we may not execute." Planning now was focused on aiding other Southeast Asian nations which had direct access to the sea. Admiral Burke advised CINCPAC that "we may land about 5,000 Marines in Vietnam and an equal number of Army and Air Force troops in Thailand."[21]

Despite the general perception that the odds now were against saving Laos from a Communist takeover, the National Security Council continued to explore various solutions to the problem in that country, if only to forestall the direct threat to South Vietnam and Thailand. By early May, hopes were pinned on the success of United Nations and SEATO diplomatic initiatives. But, military options continued to be considered by President Kennedy, including the possible landing of a U.S. force in Thailand in an effort to hasten Communist acceptance of a ceasefire. On 1 May the chief executive, through Secretary of Defense McNamara, specifically queried Admiral Burke as to the readiness of the BLT afloat off Bangkok. The admiral responded that the battalion and the ships in which it was embarked were ready and waiting twelve-hours steaming time from the Thai capital. Due to the fear that an overt demonstration by

---

[19]CNO, memo for record, ser 000231-61 of 27 Apr 1961.
[20]Ibid.
[21]Msg, CNO 280133Z Apr 1961. See also msg, CNO 271905Z Apr 1961.

the United States would upset the ceasefire negotiations, however, this military measure was not undertaken.[22]

Ceasefire in Laos

Although the Pathet Lao continued to engage in sporadic attacks in the first days of May, and seized the strategically important town of Tchepone near the South Vietnamese border, the military pressure on Vientiane, Luang Prabang, and the other major population centers eased. The reasons for this development were many. While the Kennedy administration decided against intervention in Laos and deferred possible landings in South Vietnam and Thailand, the Communists had reason to fear these initiatives. The resolve of SEATO member nations was demonstrated by the well-publicized Pony Express exercise, which was the largest combined SEATO maneuver to date; and the U.S. contingent of the SEATO Field Forces command was activated in the Philippines. The United States additionally took visible unilateral steps indicating its determination. These included the transfer of helicopters to friendly forces in Laos and the establishment of the Marine helicopter support base at Udorn, close by the Laotian border. On 19 April, the Military Assistance Advisory Group, Laos, was formally established. In the meantime, material and advisory assistance to the FAR increased significantly, and the Seventh Fleet was poised and ready in the South China Sea, within striking distance of the mainland, with its carrier aircraft and amphibious forces.

Conversely, it seemed likely that a ceasefire would leave the Pathet Lao and their supporters in a position of strength. The North Vietnamese then would possess a supply route to South Vietnam, the Ho Chi Minh Trail, and the Pathet Lao would retain the capability to complete the destruction of government forces and seizure of the government. These factors

---

[22]At the same time, Vice President Lyndon Johnson received a briefing by Commander Harry C. Allendorfer, Jr. and Lieutenant (j.g.) S.E. Wood of the Flag Plot Branch in the Office of the Chief of Naval Operations. The briefers revealed that the Vice President's "mind is not made up as to what is the best course of action but he seemed to lean towards taking a stand against Communism in some place other than Laos." Memo, Britten to Burke, of 1 May 1961. See also OP-33, memos for record, ser 00092P33 of 28 Apr; 00093P33 of 29 Apr; 00084P33 of 29 Apr; 00095P33 of 1 May; 00098P33 of 1 May; memo, SECSTATE to PRES, of 1 May; CNO, memo for record, ser 000240-61 of 2 May; Hall, "The Crisis in Laos," pp. 70-72; U.S.-V.N. Relations, bk. 11, pp. 62-66; Stevenson, End of Nowhere, pp. 149-53; Sorensen, Kennedy, pp. 643-47; Schlesinger, A Thousand Days, pp. 334-40.

apparently led the Pathet Lao to agree, on 3 May, to meet with Laotian government officials to arrange a ceasefire.[23]

As these negotiations began, U.S. Pacific forces adjusted to the changing situation. In order to obtain some indication of the amount of military support flowing to the Pathet Lao, CINCPAC requested permission to conduct aerial photographic reconnaissance over key areas in Laos. Following State and Defense Department concurrence, on 3 May the Joint Chiefs authorized the use of Seventh Fleet aircraft. The sorties, conducted between 4 and 8 May, provided valuable information on the Communist military presence in Laos.[24]

On 8 May, five days after the interested parties announced that a ceasefire was agreed to, Pacific naval commanders gradually relaxed once again their high state of operational readiness. Admiral Griffin ordered *Coral Sea* to depart her station in the South China Sea and put in at Subic for replenishment and relief on 13 May by *Bon Homme Richard*. The following day, 9 May, Commander Seventh Fleet directed the Amphibious Ready Group to leave the Gulf of Siam and sail for Subic for a much needed rest, while remaining on twelve-hours steaming notice. Once there, the 2nd Battalion, 9th Marines, would be relieved by the 3rd Battalion of the regiment. The latter unit became the new BLT afloat in *Thetis Bay*, *Paul Revere*, and *Monticello*. And, on the 12th, Admiral Griffin ordered the Task Force 76 elements which assembled in Subic after completion of Pony Express, to sail for Okinawa. Two days later, CINCPAC officially relaxed the alert condition of the forces slated for the Laos operation. Nevertheless, the Seventh Fleet commander was confident that his forces could be quickly concentrated again. He observed:

> With good luck and sufficient time before the [next] "flap," we can pick up the pieces, reassemble MGEN Weller's [Commanding General, 3rd Marine Division] scattered BLT's offload and unscramble the [various] contingency and exercise cargoes in TF 76 ships and fall in, ready to jump again in an orderly fashion if directed.[25]

---

[23]Lee, *Communist China's Policy Toward Laos*, pp. 7-8, 86-87, 91; Hall, "The Crisis in Laos," pp. 172-79.

[24]Wheeler to Burke, transcript of telecon, of 4 May 1961; msgs, CTG77.6 070553Z May 1961; 101415Z; 111334Z; CP, Command History, 1961, pp. 63-64.

[25]Msg, COM7FLT 180808Z May 1961. See also msgs, 050726Z May 1961; CPFLT 050927Z; 060239Z; 062144Z; COM7FLT 070452Z; 070506Z; 071506Z; 080250Z; 080358Z; 090746Z; 090916Z; COM7FLT 111342Z; 121018Z; 121144Z; CP, Command History, 1961, pp. 96-97; Kerby, "American Military Airlift," pp. 7-8.

By mid-June, most U.S. headquarters, ships, aircraft, and ground units of General Harkins's allied command were returned to normal operational deployments. The Pacific Command had weathered another Southeast Asian storm.

Efforts to Form a Laotian Coalition Government

From the time of the May ceasefire, the various factions loosely grouped around the three major Laotian personalities — Souvanna Phouma, Souphanouvong, and Phoumi Nosavan — engaged in complex political and military maneuvers in an effort to form a new coalition government. During this period, the United States continued to seek a Laos that would be truly neutral in its foreign relations, and in August joined with Great Britain and France in calling for the self-proclaimed neutralist Souvanna to head a new coalition government. Admirals Burke and Felt, however, were distrustful of any government which would include Communist elements, and doubted Souvanna's ability to control them. Their views were echoed by leaders of the Thai and South Vietnamese governments, who feared that the establishment of a coalition headed by Souvanna was merely the prelude to their own forced accommodation, if not subjugation, to communism. Reportedly, President Diem was "convinced that Souvanna is nothing but a creature of the Pathet Lao."[26] Diem was particularly alarmed by the dramatic upsurge in Viet Cong activity in South Vietnam during the fall of 1961, which he attributed to the infusion of arms and supplies into his country via the Ho Chi Minh Trail, now completely secured by Communist forces.

U.S. military leaders also recognized the implications if the Pathet Lao retained their hold on the Plain of Jars and on the areas bordering South Vietnam and Cambodia. In their opinion, the ultimate objective of the North Vietnamese was unification with South Vietnam and that the "continued Communist logistic buildup in southern Laos is designed primarily to support Viet Cong activities in South Vietnam."[27] Under these circumstances, U.S. strategists gradually shifted their emphasis to the defense of South Vietnam and Thailand. This was especially the case

---

[26]Memo, OP-61 to OP-06, ser 001962P61 of 13 Sep 1961. See also memos, CNO to JCS, ser 00694P61 of 24 Jun 1961; OP-61 to OP-06, ser 001934P61 of 23 Aug.
[27]Msg, CP 080408Z Nov 1961.

following the Taylor visit to South Vietnam in October 1961, when U.S. measures to strengthen that country increased significantly.[28]

Another Crisis Develops in Laos

Although Laos receded from international focus during late 1961 and early 1962, the internal conflict again burst into the open when the rightist faction led by General Phoumi resisted integration into a national coalition. Having adopted a policy of supporting the Souvanna government, the Kennedy administration now attempted to pressure Phoumi into compliance through various economic and political sanctions. These U.S. efforts, however, were to no avail, as Rear Admiral Arnold F. Schade, head of the CNO's Politico-Military Policy Division, succinctly indicated when he informed the Secretary of the Navy that the "U.S. is piping a lively tune" for General Phoumi, but he is "not dancing to our music." He added, "the rub is that we haven't any effective pressure devices."[29] Policymakers were constrained from implementing more drastic measures by the fear that FAR strength would be weakened and because of the adverse reaction to be expected from Diem.[30]

While the Kennedy administration was reluctant to coerce Phoumi into the Souvanna-led government, the Communists did not hesitate to take forceful action to achieve their goals. During the first week in May 1962, the Pathet Lao attacked and routed Phoumi's forces holding the exposed town of Nam Tha in northwest Laos. U.S. leaders recognized that the Nam Tha battle was an escalation in the level of violence and that the Communists were attempting to resolve the political impasse with a psychological blow to Phoumi's power base, the army. Following the

---

[28]Memo, Director of Intelligence, Joint Staff to Vice Director, Joint Staff, JCS, ser J2DM-333-61 of 18 Sep 1961; msgs, AMEMB Saigon 5PM 7 Oct; CP 080408Z Nov; ltr, CNO to Flag and General Officers, of 4 Jan 1962; Dommen, *Conflict in Laos*, pp. 200-13; Stevenson, *End of Nowhere*, pp. 153-69; Fall, *Anatomy of a Crisis*, pp. 219-31; Toye, *Laos*, pp. 171-79; Sorensen, *Kennedy*, pp. 646-47; Hilsman, *To Move a Nation*, pp. 135-40; Schlesinger, *A Thousand Days*, pp. 363-68.

[29]Memo, OP-61 to SECNAV, ser 001543P61 of 24 Jan 1962.

[30]Memos, OP-61 to CNO, ser 00601P61 of 2 Jan 1962; OP-61 to SECNAV, ser 00608P61 of 18 Jan; ser 00618P61 of 19 Feb; ser 001686 of 3 Apr; ser 00634P61 of 25 Apr; ltr, CNO to Flag and General Officers, of 7 Mar; Donald E. Nuechterlein, *Thailand and the Struggle for Southeast Asia* (Ithaca, NY: Cornell Univ. Press, 1965), pp. 221-38; Stevenson, *End of Nowhere*, pp. 171-73; Marek Thee, *Notes of a Witness: Laos and the Second Indochinese War* (New York: Random House, 1973), pp. 213-25; Dommen, *Conflict in Laos*, p. 216; Schlesinger, *A Thousand Days*, pp. 512-16.

attack, Brigadier General Andrew J. Boyle, USA, the Chief, MAAG Laos, reported that the combat effectiveness of government forces in northern Laos was "nil." The following week, Ambassador Brown added that "Laos [is] now in posit where it can be overrun at [any] time and to the extent of other side's choosing."[31] The danger was that in the absence of a credible internal or external counterweight, the Pathet Lao and their North Vietnamese allies, emboldened and propelled by this singular victory, would complete the destruction of the Royal Laotian Government. On 12 May, Ambassador Brown warned that "it is unlikely we can achieve our objective of a truly neutral government if we do not act in some unmistakable fashion."[32]

Anticipating that this action might be a military response, U.S. leaders took preparatory steps. On the 10th, four days after the fall of Nam Tha, CINCPAC received orders to deploy to the Gulf of Siam those elements of the Seventh Fleet he deemed essential. Admiral Felt immediately alerted relevant commands and activated the Headquarters, Joint Task Force 116 on Okinawa. Rear Admiral Paul P. Blackburn's *Hancock* attack carrier group was directed to proceed to an operating area off Danang, and the Amphibious Ready Group to steam into the Gulf of Siam from Subic Bay. This ready force, under the command of Captain Henry S. Jackson, comprised amphibious assault ship *Valley Forge* (LPH-8), *Navarro* (APA-215), *Point Defiance* (LSD-31) and the embarked Marine Special Landing Force, composed of the 3rd Battalion, 9th Marines and Medium Helicopter Squadron (HMM) 261. Admiral Sides quickly implemented these actions, and took the additional step of advising Commander Seventh Fleet that amphibious units soon might be needed. The fleet's amphibious task force commander, Rear Admiral Edwin B. Hooper, alerted his subordinate task groups and dispatched amphibious ships to the Fuji training area in Japan to embark Marine units. He also ordered the assembly of available shipping in Buckner Bay, Okinawa.

On 12 May, the tempo of events quickened. The antisubmarine warfare aircraft of VP 40, operating from the Philippines, provided aerial

---

[31]Msg, CPFLT 120033Z May 1962. See also msgs, CPFLT 092147Z May 1962; CP 150132Z.
[32]Msg, CPFLT 120033Z May 1962. See also Stevenson, *End of Nowhere*, pp. 174-75; Dommen, *Conflict in Laos*, pp. 217-19; Goldstein, *American Policy Toward Laos*, pp. 257-62; Lee, *Communist China's Policy Toward Laos*, p. 88; Hilsman, *To Move a Nation*, pp. 140-41.

protection for the concentrating forces. Marine helicopter squadron HMM 363 stood ready with twenty-four H-34s at its station in Soc Trang, South Vietnam, to provide emergency support. To increase *Hancock*'s air strength, Commander Seventh Fleet, now Vice Admiral William A. Schoech, called for the movement of VMF 451 from Atsugi to Cubi Point. Once there, eight of the squadron's F8U aircraft flew on board the carrier for temporary attachment. To provide additional antisubmarine support, Rear Admiral Joseph B. Tibbets, who only the day before relieved Rear Admiral Henry L. Miller as commander of the Hunter-Killer Group in *Bennington*, was ordered on 13 May to join *Hancock*.

While U.S. military forces in the Western Pacific made ready, the Kennedy administration contemplated the possible ramifications of the first large-scale deployment of U.S. ground combat forces on the Asian mainland since the Korean War. With the fall of Nam Tha, U.S. policymakers faced the need to reassure friendly nations in Southeast Asia, and were prepared to go beyond the use of fleet movements and other "shows of force." With the FAR now seriously demoralized, U.S. leaders reasoned that only external forces were capable of achieving a return to the ceasefire stability and encouraging international support for a neutralist government headed by Souvanna Phouma. As Admiral George W. Anderson, Jr., the new Chief of Naval Operations, informed his immediate staff on 14 May:

> In its recent decisions and actions the United States was out to demonstrate that it meant business.... We are out to bolster our friends in South Vietnam and Thailand, if unfortunately it was difficult to determine just who were our friends in Laos.... The United States' position involved trying to induce the Communists through pressure to have the Pathet Lao/Viet Minh forces withdraw to the positions they occupied before the attack.[33]

---

[33]CNO, Minutes of Meeting, 14 May 1962. See also msgs, JCS 072159Z May 1962; 110128Z; CP 110625Z; CPFLT 110826Z; COM7FLT 111618Z; CPFLT 112359Z; CTG76.5 121540Z; CPFLT 122201Z; JCS 130231Z; COM7FLT 151936Z; "Summary of Operational Events due to Laos Situation," of 11 May; CNO Flag Plot, "Westpac as of 14 May 1962;" Stevenson, *End of Nowhere*, pp. 176-77; David K. Hall, "The Laotian War of 1962 and the Indo-Pakistani War of 1971" in Barry M. Blechman and Stephen S. Kaplan, eds., *The Use of the Armed Forces as a Political Instrument* (Washington: Brookings Institution, 1976), pp. 4-11; Sorensen, *Kennedy*, pp. 647-48.

U.S. Combat Forces Deploy to Thailand, May 1962

All of these factors were involved in President Kennedy's decision, on 15 May, to deploy large U.S. combat forces to Thailand.[34] The units involved were intended to symbolize the American commitment to defend that country, and by association, South Vietnam. In addition, it was hoped that the deployment would moderate Communist actions in Laos. To command this operation, the Joint Chiefs ordered the establishment of the United States Military Assistance Command, Thailand. Lieutenant General Harkins, who already led a similar command in Vietnam, was designated to direct the actions of both organizations through CINCPAC. At the same time, Lieutenant General James L. Richardson, Jr., USA, was appointed Commander Joint Task Force 116, formerly a Marine general officer's billet.

Already set in motion several days earlier, the air, naval, and ground forces designated to comprise or support the task force continued their forward deployment. During the next week the armed U.S. contingent in Thailand was bolstered significantly. Lieutenant General Richardson and 107 officers and men of his task force staff were airlifted to Bangkok on 15 May, and the following day he assumed operational control of all U.S. combat forces in Thailand, under the command of the Military Assistance Command, Thailand. Subordinate to General Richardson was Brigadier General Ormand Simpson, USMC, the Assistant Division Commander, 3rd Marine Division, who was designated Naval Component Commander, Joint Task Force 116. The naval component was the 3rd Marine Expeditionary Brigade (later changed to 3rd Marine Expeditionary Unit) from the 3rd Marine Division on Okinawa. Reinforcements and support units for Army formations and Air Force tactical and cargo aircraft made the transit to Thailand from bases and installations all over the Pacific theater.

Naval forces assisted these deploying units. Steaming off Danang and providing air support to the operation, *Hancock* was joined on 15 May by the Hunter-Killer Group of Rear Admiral Tibbets in *Bennington*. At the same time, Rear Admiral Hooper collected amphibious shipping from

---

[34]Actually, a U.S. Army regiment already was in Thailand participating in a combined exercise. See Robert A. Whitlow, *U.S. Marines in Vietnam: The Advisory and Combat Assistance Era, 1954-1964* (Washington: History and Museums Division, Headquarters, USMC, 1977), p.88.

throughout the Western Pacific at Buckner Bay and alerted elements of the 3rd, 9th, and 12th Marines for possible embarkation.

The Marine Special Landing Force, embarked in Amphibious Ready Group ships, already was close to the debarkation point when the JCS ordered execution of the landing. At 0424 on 17 May, *Navarro* and *Point Defiance* crossed the bar at the entrance to the Bangkok ship channel as *Valley Forge*, standing offshore because of her deep draft, began the fly-off of the eighteen HMM 261 helicopters. After berthing at Bangkok early that morning, *Navarro* and *Point Defiance* placed ashore 1,500 Marines of the Special Landing Force's battalion landing team, which was composed of the 3rd Battalion, 9th Marines, and attached tank, artillery, and engineer units. The force was quickly transported to Udorn. The unit was prepared for combat, with Marine helicopter and close air support near at hand. The only major problem encountered during this swiftly executed administrative landing was the offloading of ammunition and other cargo from *Valley Forge*. Ship-to-shore lighters, which the Thais agreed to furnish, missed the rendezvous with Captain Jackson's ships on the 16th. As a result, this essential task did not commence until the late morning of 18 May. However, by the end of that day, the work was completed. Soon after, the task group got underway for Subic Bay, where *Talladega* (APA-208) and *Belle Grove* (LSD-2) previously transported the 1st Battalion, 9th Marines, and six remaining helicopters of HMM 261 in order to restore the strength of the Amphibious Ready Group.

The air elements of the Marine force also swiftly converged on Thailand. On 16 May, VMA 332, which deployed from Iwakuni to Cubi Point only days before, departed for Udorn. The squadron's twenty A4D-2N Skyhawks, after in-flight refueling over the South China Sea, reached their destination by 1200. Subsequent airlift brought in some elements of a provisional Marine aircraft group headquarters, Marine Air Base Squadron 12, and Marine Air Control Squadron 4 while *Vernon County* and *Windham County* (LST-1170) delivered the remainder to Bangkok in early June.

At the end of May, the Marine force at Udorn was augmented by a seventy-one man detachment from NMCB 10. The SEABEEs immediately began work on camp facilities and constructed a sawmill to provide tent platforms and frames. To provide the 3rd Marine Expeditionary Unit with more extensive support, a logistic support group was sealifted to Bangkok between 2 and 10 June by *Washtenaw County* (LST-1166), *Whitfield County*

(LST-1169), and *Mathews* (AKA-96). From that port, the unit moved forward to Udorn by air and rail.[35]

Although the deployment of U.S. forces for the Thailand operation was similar in many respects to the actions taken during the crises of 1959 through early 1961, the differences were significant. Unlike the previous military moves at the height of periods of tension, this operation was deliberately kept "low-key." Pacific forces not directly involved with Joint Task Force 116 continued their routine activities and no Pacific-wide increased level of defense readiness was ordered. The relatively small size of the force prepared for possible intervention in Laos was intentionally unthreatening to all but the lightly armed guerrilla forces. Also, in contrast to former confrontations over Southeast Asia, U.S. objectives were fully and publicly explained to avoid any misconceptions on the part of the Communist powers as to U.S. intentions. Through diplomatic channels and various informational media, the Kennedy administration revealed that the goals sought were limited in scope. Secretary of State Rusk stated, for example:

> We have an interest in Laos, where our policy continues to be the reestablishment of a ceasefire and negotiations on a government of national union. We also have obligations to Thailand and to South Vietnam. In the light of all these obligations, the President has ordered certain precautionary moves of the U.S. armed forces, which will improve our flexibility for any contingency that the Communists may force upon us.[36]

Three days later, in announcing the proposed landing, President Kennedy also refrained from threatening rhetoric and made no mention of a movement into Laos, although that action could now be readily accomplished. The President stated that

---

[35]"U.S. Force Disposition Thailand," of 16 May 1962; "Status of U.S. deployments to Thailand," of 18 May; Edwin B. Hooper, interview with Robert H. Whitlow, Marine Corps Historical Center, in Washington, DC, 15 Apr 1974; msgs, JCS 150223Z May 1962; CP 151305Z; JCS 151600Z; CP 151834Z; CPFLT 160420Z; CHJUSMAG THAI 160935Z; ADMIN CPFLT 180119Z; CPFLT 190116Z; COM7FLT 220728Z; COM7FLT SITREPS 7 (171600Z May) — 10 (201600Z); CTG76.5 SITREPS 160006Z — 180650Z May; Kerby, "American Military Airlift," p. 8; Whitlow, *U.S. Marines in Vietnam*, pp. 86-95; Edwin B. Hooper, transcript of interview with John T. Mason, Jr., U.S. Naval Institute, in Annapolis, MD, 1978, p. 344.

[36]Msg, SECSTATE 9:56PM 12 May 1962.

in response to a request of the Government of Thailand, I have today ordered that elements of U.S. military forces, both ground and air, are to proceed to Thailand and to remain there until further ordered. These forces are to help insure the territorial integrity of this peaceful country which now faces a threat of Communist aggression [and to put the United States] in a position to fulfill speedily our obligations under the Manila Pact of 1954, a defense arrangement . . . . I emphasize that this is a defensive act on the part of the U.S.[37]

In subsequent weeks, however, a further movement by U.S. forces into Laos was under consideration. Admiral Felt believed that possible military operations in Laos should not be ignored. He observed to the Joint Chiefs that

actions being taken on both unilateral and international scene to reinforce Thailand are accompanied by statements that no commitment is implied to do anything in Laos should there be another ceasefire violation by the Communist forces. Although I concur with opinions being expressed that Communists are now willing to have a talk and defer fighting for a time to be determined by them, it is essential for us to decide what we shall do when they start another fight . . . . Airborne battle group in Okinawa is readily available as are all forces earmarked for Plan 32-59.[38]

Support for the introduction of U.S. forces into Laos, in the event a ceasefire could not be achieved, was not strong within the administration. Nevertheless, additional planning for this eventuality was undertaken. These measures included a conventional defense of Southeast Asia along a northern South Vietnam-southern Laos line, which was seriously considered by the JCS. Another alternative was offered by Admiral Anderson, who proposed in a memorandum to Secretary of Defense McNamara that in the event a neutralist government was unobtainable and the Communists again violated a ceasefire,

air strikes by U.S. forces against Vietminh and Pathet Lao supply facilities and logistic lines in Laos [which] might suffice [to stabilize the situation]. However, it may be necessary to inflict a series of defeats upon the Communist forces in Laos. A quick strike...making full use of

---

[37]Msg, OSD 151820Z May 1962. See also Hall, "The Laotian War of 1962," pp. 5-11.
[38]Msg, CP 182109Z May 1962. See also msg, CP 230144Z.

air...would be a further step to deter Vietminh and Pathet Lao activities without permanent commitment of U.S. troops in Laos.[39]

The CNO reiterated his belief that large-scale ground combat with Communist forces was inadvisable, but that selective air strikes in Laos should be

> coupled with strongest political warnings to North Vietnam that their continued use of military or subversive actions in Laos and South Vietnam will inevitably result in expanded military action against North Vietnam. It is essential that we convince the North Vietnamese government that we will not tolerate further incursions by them into other Southeast Asian countries. It is possible that military measures may eventually be required in North Vietnam or even in Communist China.[40]

Admiral Anderson concluded by stating:

> A strong warning to North Vietnam accompanied by quick strikes at Communist forces in Laos, following our firm measures in South Vietnam and commitment of U.S. forces in Thailand, may convince the Communists that further aggression could provoke larger scale U.S. intervention, which would pose an unacceptable risk for them.[41]

The Geneva Conference on Laos

All of these possible military measures soon were overtaken by political developments. On 11 June, Ambassador Brown reported that the three factions at last had reached agreement on the composition of a coalition

---

[39] Memo, CNO to SECDEF, of 12 Jun 1962 in memo, OP-06 to CNO, of 12 Jun 1962.

[40] *Ibid.* Several weeks earlier, Admiral Claude V. Ricketts, the Vice Chief of Naval Operations, informed Pacific naval commanders that there was "some sentiment in Executive Department" for a one-time carrier strike against logistic or industrial targets of "great value to Viet Minh" in North Vietnam. The purpose of the attack would be to "demonstrate determination of U.S." This attack would be linked with a presidential statement that "worse will happen if Communist moves not stopped." Msg, CNO 261813Z May 1962.

[41] Memo, CNO to SECDEF, of 12 Jun 1962 in memo, OP-06 to CNO, of 12 Jun 1962. See also memo, Leverton to Persons and Needham, ser 000676P60 of 26 May; NSC Action Memo No. 157 of 29 May in memo, NSC, of 29 May; memos, OP-60 to CNO, ser 000684-62 of 4 Jun; ser 000687-62 of 6 Jun; OP-60 to OP-06, ser BM000691-62 of 6 Jun; OP-60 to CNO, ser 000723-62 of 11 Jun; msg, CNO 042315Z Jun 1962; Hilsman, *To Move a Nation*, pp. 142-51; Stephen E. Pelz, "'When Do I have time to Think?'" John F. Kennedy, Roger Hilsman, and the Laotian Crisis of 1962," *Diplomatic History*, Vol. 3, No. 2 (Spring 1979), pp. 215-29; Roger Hilsman and Stephen E. Pelz, "When is a Document not a Document—And Other Thoughts," *Diplomatic History*, Vol. 3, No. 3 (Summer 1979), pp. 345-48.

government. Reflecting the new balance in the relative strength of the opposing sides, a compromise was reached. Phoumi agreed to join the coalition. The Communist side appeared to be dissuaded from further attacks on the general's troops by the presence of U.S. forces in Southeast Asia. Thus, the U.S. objective of establishing a ceasefire and a government in Laos that was at least nominally neutral, was achieved. Rear Admiral Schade, the Director, Politico-Military Policy Division, observed: "It would appear that we have, in fact, what we bargained for, i.e., a coalition government with the neutrals in the cabinet holding the balance of power." But he also expressed the rather generally held fear that "the exact composition of these neutrals and how long this government will be able to resist Communist subversion remains to be seen."[42]

On 2 July, Great Britain and the Soviet Union, co-chairmen of the fourteen-nation gathering, reconvened the Geneva Conference on Laos to ratify this agreement. Although Thailand and South Vietnam still were hesitant to endorse an accord that held obvious dangers for their own existence, U.S. officials urged the South Vietnamese and Thais to accept the proposed pact. The assembled world powers signed the "Geneva Declaration and Protocol on Neutrality of Laos" on 23 July 1962.[43]

The main provisions of the treaty stipulated that non-Laotian military elements, including North Vietnamese but excepting French military instructors, be withdrawn from the country within seventy-five days. CINCPAC, anticipating the requirement to evacuate U.S. personnel and equipment from Laos, already had directed General Boyle to draw up a plan to this effect. Soon after the signing of the Geneva Agreement, Admiral Felt ordered implementation of this plan. For the next several months, the U.S. military presence in Laos diminished as MAAG components were transferred to Thailand. Finally, on 6 October, the last elements of General Boyle's MAAG departed Laos.

While this process took place, Joint Task Force 116 remained in Thailand as a visible deterrent to any Communist exploitation of the withdrawal and as a symbol to the Thais and South Vietnamese of

---

[42]Memo, OP-61 to SECNAV, ser 001852P61 of 26 Jun 1962.

[43]Memo, OP-61 to SECNAV, ser 001794P61 of 7 Jun 1962; msg, AMEMBVT 111353Z; memos, OP-61 to SECNAV, ser 001814P61 of 14 Jun; ser 001852P61 of 26 Jun; ser 001867P61 of 5 Jul; ser 001891P61 of 12 Jul; ser 001912P61 of 19 Jul; Hall, "The Laotian War of 1962," pp. 23-28; Stevenson, *End of Nowhere*, pp. 177-81; Dommen, *Conflict in Laos*, pp. 219-26; Thee, *Notes of a Witness*, pp. 289-300; Schlesinger, *A Thousand Days*, pp. 517-18.

continued U.S. support. However, the size and composition of the force gradually was altered. As authorized by the President, Marine units began redeploying from Udorn on 2 July. That same day, *Valley Forge* arrived off Bangkok to embark the helicopters of HMM 162 (which had replaced HMM 261) and the A4Ds of VMA 332 flew from Udorn to Cubi Point. With Admiral Schoech in Thailand to observe the redeployment, *Carter Hall* (LSD-3) and *Belle Grove* embarked heavy equipment and personnel of 3rd Marine Expeditionary Unit elements and sailed from Bangkok on 7 July. Rear Admiral Hooper also directed *Seminole*, *Westchester County* (LST-1167), and *Terrell County* (LST-1157) to provide sealift for Marine supplies and equipment. The 3rd Battalion, 9th Marines, "after two and a half months on the muddy frontier of freedom," where they served as a visible deterrent and trained in a new environment, began their airlift to Okinawa on 28 July, as did Brigadier General Simpson's headquarters.[44] As of 11 August, all Marine forces had departed Thailand, leaving behind Army units to oversee the withdrawal of MAAG Laos and to observe developments. By early December, all U.S. combat forces were redeployed and Joint Task Force 116 was disestablished.[45]

Although the Geneva Agreement ended legal justification for U.S. or North Vietnamese military presence in Laos, both sides continued to prosecute the struggle covertly. U.S. officials never placed great faith in North Vietnamese pledges to vacate the country. Their suspicions were not misplaced, as evidence of the departure of North Vietnamese fighting units was scant. Further, by the end of 1962, infiltration operations along the Ho Chi Minh Trail functioned with growing efficiency and sophistication. Protected by most of the 6,000 to 10,000 North Vietnamese troops in Laos, Group 559 oversaw the movement south by vehicle and on foot of the now thoroughly trained "regroupees." Since 1959, some 10,000 to 20,000 personnel had infiltrated into South Vietnam, where they strengthened Viet Cong units, proselytized the populace, and in general abetted the insurgency. In fact, between 1959 and late 1962, the number and size of infiltrating units increased yearly. The war for the South continued in earnest.[46]

---

[44] Msg, COM7FLT 311750Z Jul 1962.

[45] Memo, OP-60 to OP-06, ser BM000820 of 30 Jun 1962; msgs, COM7FLT ADMIN 030856Z Jul; COM7FLT 100820Z; CP 270350Z; memos, OP-60 to OP-06, ser BM00824-62 of 3 Jul; OP-60 to CNO, ser BM000902-62 of 31 Jul.

[46] Stevenson, *End of Nowhere*, pp. 180-88; Dommen, *Conflict in Laos*, pp. 238-40; Arthur J. Dommen, "The Future of North Vietnam," *Current History* (Apr 1970), p. 230; Weiner, Brom, and Koon, *Infiltration of Personnel From North Vietnam*, pp. vi, 7, 39, 41, 53; Langer and Zasloff, *North Vietnam and*

Unconvinced that the North Vietnamese intended to cease funneling troops and supplies through eastern Laos and into Vietnam via the trail, U.S. leaders, after a pause, resumed use of the resources of the CIA to support and train Meo and other hill tribesmen, as well as certain of Phoumi's troops. As Admiral Felt observed in July, the "signing of Geneva Agreement will not end struggle. Laos will continue to have pivotal role in future of SE Asia."[47]

The confrontation over Laos did much to shape current and future developments in South Vietnam. From 1959 through 1962, events in Laos reflected a growing military activism on the part of the Asian Communists, most notably the North Vietnamese. It was matched by growing U.S. determination to resist these advances. But, in the last analysis, the compromise achieved in Laos was less than satisfactory to many American leaders, including top-ranking naval officers. Not only was the Geneva settlement seen as detrimental to South Vietnamese internal security, it was viewed as a psychological blow to Diem's faith in the American commitment. The perceived political failure in Laos greatly stimulated the U.S. effort to aid in the defense of South Vietnam, lest it become another victim of Communist expansion.

In each of the Laos crises, naval forces played a major role in the U.S. response through their presence. This show of strength included the deployment of task forces into the South China Sea, multi-ship fleet exercises, symbolic ship visits to Southeast Asian capitals, aerial reconnaissance, military aid, advisory assistance, and the landing of Marine combat forces, as in Thailand during 1962. The confrontation over Laos reaffirmed the conclusion drawn by naval leaders after the Lebanon and Taiwan Strait crises of the late 1950s that a determined stand by U.S. military forces could forestall Communist actions. Specifically, the presence of the Seventh Fleet in the Southeast Asian

---

the *Pathet Lao*, p. 79; Department of State, *A Threat to the Peace: North Vietnam's Effort to Conquer South Vietnam* (Washington: GPO, 1961), pt. I, pp. 40-42; Department of State, "Aggression From the North," p. 407; Hilsman, *To Move a Nation*, pp. 151-55; Socialist Republic of Vietnam, *Vietnam: The Anti-U.S. Resistance War*, pp. 30-32.

[47]Msg, CP 180651Z Jul 1962. See also ltr, CNO to Flag and General Officers, of 20 Aug; memos, OP-61 (Acting) to SECNAV, ser 00663P61 of 20 Aug; OP-61 to CNO, ser 00673P61 of 19 Sep; OP-61 to OP-06, ser 00682P61 of 1 Oct; Dommen, *Conflict in Laos*, pp. 227-30; Stevenson, *End of Nowhere*, pp. 178-92; Toye, *Laos*, pp. 187-90; Goldstein, *American Policy Toward Laos*, pp. 263-68, 281-89; Thee, *Notes of a Witness*, pp. 300-34; Douglas S. Blaufarb, *The Counterinsurgency Era: U.S. Doctrine and Performance, 1950 to the Present* (New York: The Free Press, 1977), pp. 148-58.

area and its potential for further action were believed by many to have been a primary factor in deterring the Communists from a complete takeover in Laos. The reluctance of political and military leaders alike to commit ground forces — aside from the limited deployment of troops to Thailand — was contrasted with the utility of air and naval forces in influencing enemy behavior. But, the repeated shows of force over Laos also revealed to naval leaders that greater efforts were required to provide a fleet capable of sustained combat. As measures were instituted in this regard, steps also were taken to assist the peoples of Southeast Asia in their fight against insurgencies that posed immediate threats to their continued existence. The testing ground for this latter effort was South Vietnam.

CHAPTER IV

The Navy, Counterinsurgency, and the Growing Threat in South Vietnam, 1959-1961

Throughout the Laos crises, the United States became increasingly concerned that Southeast Asia was most endangered by Communist-inspired insurgency. A number of U.S. leaders were convinced that traditional military actions for dealing with aggression were ill-suited to this threat and they reasoned that the politico-military phenomenon could be successfully countered only through special counter-measures. This approach evolved into the doctrine of "counterinsurgency," which was defined as embodying the "entire scope of military, paramilitary, political, economic, psychological, and civic actions taken by or in conjunction with the government of a nation to defeat insurgency."[1]

Admiral Felt, the Pacific commander, was an early advocate of preparing U.S. and friendly forces to cope with insurgency. He believed that the key "ingredient" to the economic and political prosperity of a Western-oriented Southeast Asia was "internal security against subversion and its accompanying manifestations of banditry, hunger, devastation and chaos."[2] These ideas were reflected in Operation Plan 32-59, issued by Admiral Felt on 16 December 1959, which was the first comprehensive plan concerned with the defense of Southeast Asia. Although the document considered all forms of Communist aggression, it emphasized that the enemy would "seek to gain their objectives by means other than war, general or limited" by employing "political, economic, diplomatic, and psychological means.... Subversion and the fostering of indigenous

---

[1] CNO, "Terminology for Counterinsurgency Matters," ser 361P60 of 29 Mar 1962.
[2] Ltr, Felt to Draper, of 28 Dec 1958. Admiral Felt, when he served on the staff at the Naval War College in the early 1950s, introduced guerrilla and anti-guerrilla warfare to the curriculum.

dissident forces [would] be exploited to the fullest."³

In contrast to Laos, South Vietnam was not believed in imminent danger. U.S. leaders repeatedly affirmed during 1959 that the insurgency in South Vietnam, spearheaded by an estimated 1,000 to 2,000 guerrillas, was being successfully combatted. In November, Lieutenant General Samuel T. Williams, USA, the Chief, Military Assistance Advisory Group (MAAG), Vietnam, went so far as to state that "MAP arms and training [had] enabled the regular forces of [*sic.*] Vietnam to reduce the internal communist threat to the point where the economic growth of the country" could proceed.⁴

This appraisal of Viet Cong strength soon was overtaken by the events of late 1959 and early 1960. Beginning in September 1959, sizeable enemy units attacked government troops and installations, exhibiting aggressiveness and skill in their operations. New intelligence estimates increased the number of armed insurgents to between 3,000 and 5,000. Many of these men infiltrated from North Vietnam, some reportedly by sea. At the same time, assassination of government officials and supporters became epidemic. Conversely, South Vietnamese forces, in general trained in conventional tactics, were increasingly unable to deal with either the guerrilla units or more covert insurgents.⁵

These developments prompted a reanalysis of Communist intentions and capabilities and of measures needed to counter the heightened threat to internal security. On 7 March 1960 the U.S. country team, in a lengthy report, detailed the seriousness of the situation. Admiral Felt also was concerned with the deterioration of South Vietnam's stability and the apparent inability of the Republic of Vietnam Armed Forces (RVNAF) to combat successfully Communist guerrilla tactics and subversion of the population. On 14 March, he proposed the development of an anti-guerrilla capability within the Vietnamese armed forces by a redirection in training of selected units. The following month, CINCPAC, in response

---

³CINCPAC, Operation Plan 32-59, ser 000253 of 16 Dec 1959. See also CINCPAC, Command History, 1959, pp. 37-38; ltr, Hopwood to Burke, of 12 Sep 1959; memos, Kalen to Ricketts, ser 0035P004 of 14 Mar 1959; OP60 to CNO, ser BM96-59 of 19 Mar; OP-60 to CNO, ser BM224-59 of 4 Jun; ser BM420-59 of 12 Sep; Felt, Interview, Vol. II, pp. 577-79.

⁴Msg, CHMAAGVN 300429Z Nov 1959. See also CINCPAC, Operation Plan 32-59; memos, OP-61 to CNO, ser BM39-56 of 13 Dec 1956; OP-004, ser 000600P004 of 11 Dec; OP-60 to CNO, ser BM224-59 of 4 Jun 1959; OP-612 to OP-06, ser BM35-59 of 25 Jun; OP-61 to OP-06, ser BM49-59 of 8 Sep; OP-92B1 to OP-06, ser 000624-59 of 8 Sep.

⁵Msg, AMEMB Saigon of 7 Mar 1960 in *U.S.-V.N. Relations*, bk. 10, pp. 1254-75; bk. 2, pt. IVA.5, pp. 43-48.

to JCS suggestions, also requested that U.S. Army Special Forces teams be assigned to Vietnam to train Vietnamese ranger cadres. This effort began functioning under the MAAG in June 1960.[6]

Naval Leaders Consider Vessels for Counterinsurgency

In addition to Admiral Felt, other naval officers were sensitive to the threat posed by guerrilla warfare and insurgency, especially in Southeast Asia. During 1958 and 1959, CINCPACFLT, Admiral Herbert G. Hopwood, and Commander Seventh Fleet, Vice Admiral Frederick N. Kivette, agreed that there was a need for small gunboats to enable indigenous navies to conduct several types of missions, including counterinsurgency. Long-range projections also indicated the need for craft capable of operating in inland and coastal waters to deal with the guerrilla threat. In February 1959, the CNO's Long Range Objectives Group observed that

> while clearly the most appropriate place for such craft is in navies indigenous to the area, the U.S. Navy's lack of interest or capability now leaves it in no position to demonstrate the potential of such craft, to assist in their development, or to encourage by precept and example the procurement and training of adequate forces.[7]

The group recommended that "as a minimum, prototypes of small, modern combat craft should be procured...and a permanent unit formed to develop and test techniques, and to assist foreign navies through demonstration, development assistance and training activities." While Congress authorized construction of a number of gunboats (approximately 175 feet in length) in shipbuilding programs from 1958 to 1961, the U.S. legislature did not provide actual appropriations for this work.

A similar result attended the efforts to augment indigenous naval forces, and secondarily the U.S. Navy, with craft variously described as small patrol boats, motor torpedo boats, motor gunboats, and finally, fast

---

[6]Msg, AMEMB Saigon of 7 Mar 1960 in *U.S.-V.N. Relations*, bk. 10, pp. 1254-75; bk. 2, pt. IVA.5, pp. 43-48; msg, CP 142351Z Mar 1960; CINCPAC, Command History, 1960, pp. 162-63; OP-60, memo of information, ser 064P60 of 23 Mar 1960; Spector, *Advice and Support*, pp. 329-48.

[7]Long Range Objectives Group (CNO), "Statement of U.S. Navy Long Range Objectives 1969-74" (LRO-59), ser 004P93 of 24 Feb 1959, p. 34.

patrol boats. Beginning in 1958, naval leaders in the Pacific theater recommended that aging and inadequate patrol craft in the inventories of America's Asian allies be replaced with small, fast, shallow-draft boats armed with light weapons, displacing no more than eighty tons — a limit imposed by the capacity of Southeast Asian off-loading cranes — and capable of a top speed of 25 knots. CINCPACFLT concluded that "in view of the instability of these [Southeast Asian] countries, the availability of suitable craft for ready use in restricted waters could be a deciding factor in preventing overt or covert Communist infiltration or even actual aggression."[8] These craft would conduct reconnaissance and raids against enemy vessels and shore defenses. Admiral Kivette proposed, and Admiral Hopwood concurred, that twenty to twenty-five boats be developed and procured. During 1959 and 1960, naval planners in Washington and commanders in the Pacific continued to state the requirement for small patrol craft in order "to establish an operating and training nucleus of this type in the Fleet which could be rapidly expanded when needed in larger numbers."[9]

In July 1959, Admiral Burke stimulated activity within the Office of the Chief of Naval Operations concerning the possibility of developing a new motor torpedo boat. He suggested that "if PT's could be built cheaply and still be efficient, the addition of this type to our operating forces would be extremely useful to us."[10] Two months later, the Material Division in the Office of the Chief of Naval Operations reported favorably on the feasibility of providing small navies with these craft:

> The characteristics of [fast patrol boats] are such that [MAP] nations can professionally operate, maintain, and financially afford to support them in reasonable numbers. To provide FPBs to these countries would be a comparative financial saving to the U.S. and ensure [*sic*] that these boats are located in strategically significant parts of the world, and in friendly hands.[11]

---

[8]Ltr, CINCPACFLT TO CINCPAC, ser 61/00963 of 4 Nov 1958. See also ltrs, COM7FLT to CINCPACFLT, ser 0154 of 7 Jul; CINCPACFLT to CNO, ser 61/00646 of 2 Aug.
[9]OP-415, memo, of 8 Sep 1959. See also ltrs, COM7FLT to CINCPACFLT, ser 0154 of 7 Jul 1958; CINCPACFLT to CNO, ser 61/000140 of 31 May 1959, p. 12; LeRoy Taylor, "Naval Operations in Confined Waters and Narrow Seas," USNIP, Vol. 86, No. 6 (Jun 1960), pp. 55-60.
[10]CNO, memo, ser 00380-59 of 25 Jul 1959.
[11]OP-415, memo, of 8 Sep 1959.

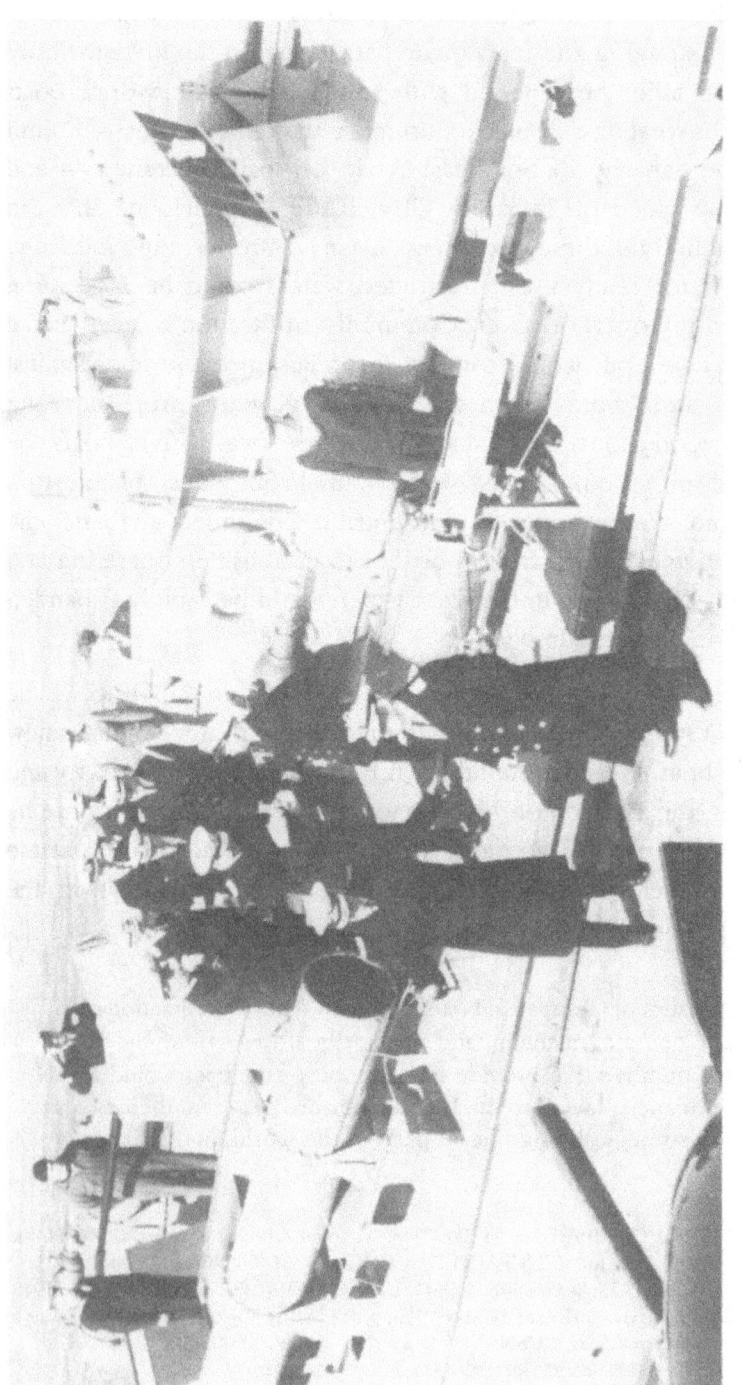

The Commander in Chief, Norwegian Navy, Admiral Erling Hostvedt, and the U.S. Chief of Naval Operations, Admiral Arleigh Burke, after inspection of "Nasty" class PT boat at Haakonsvern, Norway, in May 1960.

Counterinsurgency, and the Growing Threat in South Vietnam

During the latter months of 1959, Admiral Felt initiated study of a Norwegian-produced motor torpedo boat that possessed many desirable design characteristics. These "Nasty" class motor torpedo boats particularly impressed Rear Admiral Paul H. Ramsey, CINCPACFLT Chief of Staff, due to their eighty-foot length; 41-knot speed; ability to carry many light weapons; 3-foot, 7-inch draft that was "well within the maximum recommended for Southeast Asian use;" plastic hulls; and relatively simple operation and maintenance of their diesel engines.[12] It was evident, however, following a comparative analysis of the Norwegian Nasty, a U.S. design motor gunboat, and a Japanese-built motor torpedo boat, that none was entirely suitable. At the end of 1960, consideration still was being given to the characteristics desired.[13]

During 1958-1960, the development of light craft was a relatively low priority for naval leaders in the Pacific in relation to the need to obtain new or modernized aircraft carriers, cruisers, destroyers, and amphibious vessels. Due to budgetary limits, the qualitative improvement and increase in the number of large surface combatants and weapon systems had first priority in the enhancement of the Pacific Fleet's conventional war capability. At the same time, many naval leaders considered the insurgency threat a manageable one, and one that could be handled by existing indigenous forces. These factors contributed to the slow development of new, small craft.

The "Counterinsurgency Plan"

In April 1960, by which time the nature and scope of the Communist threat to Southeast Asia was recognized by an increasing number of U.S. leaders, Admiral Felt forwarded for JCS approval a comprehensive plan to combat insurgency. The document, entitled "Counter-Insurgency Operations in South Vietnam and Laos," was endorsed by the Chief, MAAG, Vietnam, and the Chief, Programs Evaluation Office, Laos. It was a detailed exposition of general solutions to this type of warfare and of particular measures to be taken in these countries. Drawing on the lessons

---

[12]Ltr, CINCPACFLT to CINCPAC, ser 63/00934 of 18 Nov 1959.
[13]*Ibid.*; ltrs, CINCPACFLT to CNO, ser 63/00319 of Apr 1960; CHBUSHIPS (Chairman Ship Characteristics Board) to CNO, ser 420-0172 of 25 Oct 1960; NA London, report, 675-59-A/NA2 of 19 Nov 1959.

learned during successful campaigns against the Communists in the Philippines and Malaya and reflecting Admiral Felt's own views, it stressed that the primary objective in the struggle was assuring the security of the local populace "on a continuing basis;"[14] and securing and holding the hamlets, villages, and towns. But to maintain this control it also was essential for the government to win the allegiance of the affected people by improving their economic, political, and social welfare. Indeed, Admiral Felt stressed that "maintenance of internal security is not a purely military job."[15]

The plan also called for a centrally controlled, well coordinated, and thoroughly planned campaign, involving both regular and paramilitary forces, police, and civil agencies to defeat the insurgency. It suggested intensification of coastal and river patrols by the Vietnamese Navy, augmented by a civilian-manned "coast-watcher" system, to impede infiltration from North Vietnam. Other specific proposals called for the reorganization of the national command structure and strengthening of paramilitary forces.

Finally, the study's summary called attention to the necessity for a much greater expenditure on the part of the United States for the material and financial support of South Vietnamese and Laotian forces. Admiral Felt addressed the problem of the era's frugal defense budgets with the statement that the recommendation "may seem unrealistic in the face of Communist pressures to force greater expenditures by Free World powers," but that "onerous costs in effort, material and money have been found to be essentials in all successful anti-guerrilla campaigns. If Communist expansion is to be prevented without resorting to overt warfare, there is no alternative to making the expenditures required."[16]

Nonetheless, adoption of the plan was delayed for the remainder of President Eisenhower's term in office. In part, this resulted from the need for bureaucratic coordination. Philosophic differences among U.S. officials over the relative priorities of internal political reform as opposed to

---

[14]CINCPAC, "Counter-Insurgency Operations in South Vietnam and Laos," of 26 Apr 1960, pp. 3-4. See also CINCPAC, Command History, 1960, pp. 23, 85-89, 143-44, 217, 232-36; *U.S.-V.N. Relations*, bk. 2, pt. IVA.5, tab 4, pp. 80-83; Felt, Interview, Vol. II, pp. 422, 476, 578, 579, 588, 597, 628, 637.

[15]Msg, CP 272243Z Apr 1960. For the earlier French reaction to revolutionary war in Southeast Asia, see Marc E. Geneste, "Danger from Below," USNIP, Vol. 86, No. 11 (Nov 1960), p. 33.

[16]CINCPAC, "Counter-Insurgency Operations," pp. 14-15. See also memo, OP-61 to SECNAV, ser 00208P61 of 9 Jun 1960.

internal security also slowed the process. In this regard, Washington decided by the end of 1960 to ensure military stability in the countryside before pressing Diem into democratic reforms.

In contrast to its predecessor, the Kennedy administration acted quickly to adopt the plan for use in South Vietnam. Within weeks of his inauguration, President Kennedy "approved the general concept of implementing the CINCPAC outline plan" and authorized funding for a 20,000-man increase in the South Vietnamese armed forces and improvement of the paramilitary forces.[17] That the new administration considered this action important was indicated by Secretary of State Rusk's observation to Admiral Felt that the "White House ranks defense Viet-nam among highest priorities U.S. foreign policy."[18]

On 13 February 1961, the comprehensive plan, based on the April 1960 document, was submitted by U.S. authorities to President Diem for execution. Many provisions contained in the document had been or subsequently would be adopted by the South Vietnamese, but President Diem never completely endorsed or fully implemented all of its facets. The leader of South Vietnam also ignored many suggestions for reform of his government in the political and social spheres. Nonetheless, U.S. and Vietnamese leaders during 1960 had come to recognize the critical nature of the Communist threat to internal security in South Vietnam, and they opted for unconventional measures to deal with the situation.[19]

Early Emphasis on Unconventional Warfare

As a result of renewed interest in guerrillas and insurgency, the Navy gave increasing attention to unconventional warfare as a countermeasure. The Navy long possessed the capability, with its underwater demolition

---

[17]Memo, OP-60 to CNO, No. 55-61 of 3 Feb 1961.
[18]Msg, SECSTATE 020721Z Mar 1961.
[19]*U.S.-V.N. Relations*, bk. 2, pt. IVA.5, tab 4, pp. 80-95; pt. IVB.1, pp. 3, 9-11; bk. 10, pp. 1325-26; bk. 11, pp. 13-16; ltrs, ASD (ISA), of 27 Sep 1960; CHMAAGVN to CINCPAC, of 3 Feb 1961; CINCPAC, Command History, 1960, pp. 217, 230; memos, CINCPAC to JCS, ser 00331 of 30 Jun 1960; OP-605 to OP-06B, ser BM751-60 of 9 Sep; OP-61 to SECNAV, ser 00373P61 of 22 Sep; OP-61 to CNO, ser 00497P61 of 23 Nov; ser 000808P61 of 16 Jan 1961; OP-61 to SECNAV, ser 00626P61 of 1 Feb; JCS, *History of the Joint Chiefs of Staff: The Joint Chiefs of Staff and the War in Vietnam, 1960-1968* (Washington: Historical Division, Joint Secretariat, JCS, 1970) (hereafter JCS, *History*), pt. 1, pp. I-2, 2; Alfred G. Ward, transcript of interview with John T. Mason, Jr., U.S. Naval Institute, in Severna Park, MD, 1970-71, pp. 133-35; Spector, *Advice and Support*, pp. 361-73.

teams, beach jumper units, and other forces, to prosecute unconventional operations, as already demonstrated during World War II and the Korean conflict. With the widespread perception that the Communist powers were intent on guerrilla warfare, subversion, and other forms of indirect aggression short of declared war, however, naval leaders considered using these resources in the Cold War.

As early as 1958, Admiral Burke expressed support for the initiation of covert measures to keep the Communist powers off balance. Writing to Lord Mountbatten, British First Sea Lord, he stated:

> I think it is time that we are willing and have the capability to take other action. Our methods of countering Soviet moves, I personally think, have not been profitable.... It is time, I believe, that we give the communists an opportunity to counter a few moves [of ours].... I am in favor of causing them a little anxiety in some of their peripheral areas, and I think it wouldn't be too difficult to accomplish.[20]

Two years later, the CNO observed that while "most people figure that [covert action] is under the cognizance of CIA and a good deal of it is...we are going to have to contribute and give it more emphasis in both our thinking and planning."[21] In September 1960, Admiral Burke added that he believed it "necessary that the Navy take the lead if our nation is to develop the new concepts and techniques which will be necessary to exploit our maritime advantage in the cold war."[22]

During the same month, Admiral Burke directed the Deputy Chief of Naval Operations (Fleet Operations and Readiness), Admiral Wallace M. Beakley, to study possible contributions by the Navy to unconventional warfare and to summarize what already was being done. Admiral Beakley's response indicated that the Navy then provided planning, transportation, and technical support of operations to the Assistant Secretary of Defense (Office of Special Operations). That organization had certain responsibilities for foreign covert operations in peacetime. He suggested that because of extensive training in small unit actions of this type, the Navy's underwater demolition teams and Marine reconnaissance units were the logical organizations for an expanded naval capability in unconventional warfare. To coordinate planning with the Office of Special

---

[20]Ltr, Burke to Mountbatten, of 15 May 1958.
[21]CNO, memo for record, ser 00389-60 of 11 Jul 1960.
[22]Memo, CNO to OP-03, of 12 Sep 1960.

Operations and to explore ways in which the Navy might further assist or participate in the conduct of covert operations, the admiral recommended the formation of a working group within the Office of the Chief of Naval Operations.[23] Accordingly, an Unconventional Activities Working Group was formally established on 13 September 1960, under the direction of the Deputy Chief of Naval Operations (Plans and Policy). The group was directed to consider "naval unconventional activity methods, techniques and concepts which may be employed effectively against Sino-Soviet interests under conditions of cold war."[24]

During this time, at the fleet command level, unconventional warfare training was not accorded a high priority, since commanders resisted a diversion of scant resources to tasks that were seen as peripheral. For instance, in October 1960, the CNO informed CINCPACFLT, Admiral John H. Sides, that the Army's 1st Special Forces Group required carrier aircraft assistance for unconventional warfare exercises. The proposed training was to be conducted in three two-day periods each during Fiscal Years 1962, 1963, and 1964. Admiral Sides strongly objected to the Army request, and in recommending CNO's concurrence stated that Air Force units were available for such exercises, whereas "under present austere conditions, PACFLT can [not] afford these operations which do not directly support our primary mission."[25] Admiral Burke, however, responded that unconventional warfare did constitute a proper mission for the Navy. Accordingly, he urged his Pacific Fleet commander to comply with the Army request for carrier participation in training, at least a few days each year.

Nevertheless, the Navy's efforts in this lower spectrum of warfare during President Eisenhower's term in office were relatively modest. Further development of concepts and techniques to cope with the perceived worldwide threat from Communist-supported guerrilla wars and insurgencies required the stimulus provided by the Kennedy administration.[26]

---

[23]Memos, CNO, ser 00389-60 of 11 Jul 1960; OP-03 to CNO, ser 109-60 of 12 Aug; OP-09 to OP-06, of 17 Aug.

[24]OP-06, memo, ser 00271P60 of 13 Sep 1960. See also memos, OP-605F to OP-09, ser 00283P60 of 13 Sep; ser BM703-60 of 13 Sep; CNO to SECNAV, ser 00286P60 of 15 Sep; OP-06 to CNO, ser BM00225-60 of 4 Oct.

[25]Msg, CPFLT 232209Z Jan 1961. See also msg, CNO 182223Z Jan; memos, OP-03 to CNO, ser 001515-61 of 27 Jan 1961; OP-03 to CNO, ser 001533-61 of 17 Feb.

[26]Memo, OP-03 to CNO, ser 001533-61 of 17 Feb 1961; ltrs, CNO to Flag and General Officers, of 19 Jan, p. 19; CNO to Chief of Staff, U.S. Army, ser 001503P33 of 19 Feb.

Adoption of the Counterinsurgency Doctrine

President Kennedy for some time held that the Communist bloc would be likely to pursue a limited-risk global strategy of fomenting and supporting guerrilla war and subversion in areas of instability. During the 1960 presidential campaign, he forecast that the Soviet Union's

> missile power will be the shield from behind which they will slowly, but surely advance — through Sputnik diplomacy, limited brushfire wars, indirect non-overt aggression, intimidation and subversion, internal revolution, increased prestige or influence, and the vicious blackmail of our allies. The periphery of the Free World will be slowly nibbled away. The balance of power will gradually shift against us. The key areas vital to our security will gradually undergo Soviet infiltration and domination.[27]

This view of Soviet intentions was reinforced after Premier Khrushchev's speech on 6 January 1961, delivered just fourteen days prior to Kennedy's inauguration. In this address, the Soviet premier proposed to foster "wars of liberation or popular uprisings...wholeheartedly and without reservation," and he specifically mentioned Vietnam as an area for such operations.[28]

The continuing and increasingly threatening encroachment of the Pathet Lao guerrillas in Laos was detailed for Kennedy by outgoing President Eisenhower on 19 January. This briefing was followed by a pessimistic assessment of the situation in Vietnam, made by Brigadier General Edward G. Lansdale, USAF, Assistant Secretary of Defense for Special Operations and long an authority on Asia and guerrilla warfare, in a report read by the new president on 2 February. Lansdale had visited Vietnam from 2 to 14 January. He reached the conclusion that unless the Vietnamese mobilized all their resources and infused a new spirit into their counterinsurgency efforts, and unless the United States revitalized and reoriented its political, military, moral, and material support, "the

---

[27]John F. Kennedy, *Strategy of Peace* (New York: Harper and Brothers, 1960), pp. 37-38, 184.
[28]Quoted in Richard P. Stebbins, *The United States in World Affairs, 1961* (New York: Harper and Brothers, 1962), p. 64. See also Sorensen, *Kennedy*, p. 640; Schlesinger, *A Thousand Days*, p. 320; Thee, *Notes of a Witness*, pp. 16-26; Blaufarb, *Counterinsurgency Era*, pp. 52-55.

free Vietnamese and their government probably will be able to do no more than postpone eventual defeat."[29] Echoing Admiral Felt's recommendation of the previous April, General Lansdale called for recognition of Vietnam as being "in a critical condition" and "requiring emergency treatment" and advised that the United States "treat it as a combat area of the cold war."[30]

The nature of the crises in Vietnam and Laos reaffirmed President Kennedy's conviction that the Communist bloc was embarked on a new course of action, in the worldwide Cold War, which took the form of unconventional warfare and political subversion and that demanded counteraction. President Kennedy's determination led Admiral Burke to suggest once again that the Navy "do as much as we can in guerrilla warfare...even if it is not our primary business." He proposed emphasizing UDT groups, escape and survival training, and the creation of a nucleus of young naval officers trained by the Army in guerrilla warfare.[31] Other activities foreseen at this time by naval leaders included the sealift or airlift of troops and supplies, the conduct of sabotage and anti-shipping measures in foreign ports, river channels, and at sea, and the training of naval personnel in these skills. A number of naval leaders endorsed an improvement in the Navy's capability to conduct unconventional warfare at sea. Similarly, some believed that the fleet should support the Army's prosecution of counterguerrilla operations on land, a conclusion shared by the JCS. But direct naval participation in combat against land-based guerrilla forces was not considered an appropriate role for the Navy. That the Kennedy administration contemplated just such a mission, however, soon became apparent.[32]

On 23 February, in a meeting with the Joint Chiefs of Staff, President Kennedy again stressed the importance of guerrilla and counterguerrilla warfare as responses to Communist actions. This subject was first on a long list of problems to be dealt with by a planning group informally

---

[29]Memo, Assistant SECDEF for Special Operations to SECDEF, of 17 Jan 1961.
[30]*Ibid.* In Oct 1960, Admiral Felt wanted Lansdale assigned to Saigon as a special advisor to Diem.
[31]CNO, memo for record, ser 00086-61 of 6 Feb 1961, pp. 2, 3, 5. See also memo, Special Assistant to President for National Security Affairs to SECDEF, of 3 Feb in *U.S.-V.N. Relations*, bk. 11, p. 17.
[32]Memos, OP-06, ser BM61 of 5 Jan 1961; CNO, memo for record, ser 000111-61 of 17 Feb; OP-60 to CNO, ser BM000210-61 of 21 Feb; OP-60 to CNO, ser BM101-61 of 3 Mar; ltr, CNO to Flag and General Officers, of 14 Mar.

established to review and update basic national security policy. The President urged the military services to expand and hasten their efforts to develop a strong, worldwide capability and to train friendly foreign personnel in the requisite skills. He was not satisfied with the performance of many government agencies and U.S. foreign missions in this respect. The President also suggested that the United States influence the SEATO Council to adopt the new counterguerrilla warfare concepts. Informally briefing Admiral Felt on the meeting, Admiral Burke closed his message to CINCPAC with the comment that "there is going to be an awful lot of guerrilla warfare training by U.S. forces all over [the] world, I'll betcha."[33]

Southeast Asian Crisis and the Bay of Pigs

Events in April 1961 imparted a further sense of urgency to the effort to create stronger counterguerrilla forces in the armed forces. The crisis in Laos, which had become increasingly critical by the middle of April, was perceived by the national leadership to be the result of previous failure to adequately oppose Communist insurgency. By the end of April, the only feasible immediate response to the Communist encroachment would have entailed the use of U.S. regular forces.

The disastrous outcome of the Bay of Pigs operation, which occurred between 17 and 19 April, had an even more dramatic effect on the Kennedy administration. On 20 April, the day after the fighting on the Cuban invasion beaches ceased, President Kennedy, in a speech to the American Society of Newspaper Editors, stated:

> Too long we have fixed our eyes on traditional military needs, on armies prepared to cross borders, on missiles poised for flight. Now it should be clear that this is no longer enough — that our security may be lost piece by piece, country by country, without the firing of a single missile or the crossing of a single border. We intend to profit from this

---

[33]Msg, CNO 240133Z Feb 1961. See also CNO, memo for record, ser 000122-61 of 24 Feb 1961; Burke, memo, of 24 Feb; memos, OP-61 to SECNAV, ser 001602P61 of 1 Mar; OP-60 to CNO, BM104-61 of 1 Mar; BM121-61 of 10 Mar.

lesson. We intend to reexamine and reorient our forces of all kinds — our tactics and our institutions here in this community.[34]

Walt W. Rostow, Deputy Special Assistant to the President for National Security Affairs, reiterated the concept that the United States "must learn to deal overtly with major forms of covert Communist aggression" and added that "we must teach the Free World how to do it." He suggested diminishing the impact of the Bay of Pigs failure by directing attention toward Vietnam: "It is not simple or automatic that we can divert anxieties, frustrations, and anger [focused] on a place 90 miles off our shores to a place 7,000 miles away." But, "a maximum effort — military, economic, political, and diplomatic — is required there...urgently...and a clear-cut success in Vietnam would do much to hold the line in Asia while permitting us — and the world — to learn how to deal with indirect aggression."[35]

Several days later, the President directed General Taylor to head a study group composed of Admiral Burke, Attorney General Robert F. Kennedy, and Allen W. Dulles, the Director of Central Intelligence, to deduce the lessons of the Bay of Pigs. The group was specifically asked to explore ways of strengthening the U.S. capability in military, paramilitary, guerrilla, and anti-guerrilla activities short of overt warfare. During these deliberations, Admiral Burke proposed assigning the Department of Defense greater responsibility for paramilitary and guerrilla actions and suggested adopting the enemy's own techniques by pursuing guerrilla warfare in enemy-held territory. The CNO also called for the assistance of friendly governments fighting insurgency with U.S. forces and civic action groups. He gave as an example the deployment of "Naval construction units to assist in development of under-developed countries. Units such as these would serve as a nucleus for future para-military training."[36]

After a thorough analysis of the Cuban affair, the four members of the study group presented their final report to President Kennedy on 13 June.

---

[34]John F. Kennedy, "Address Before the American Society of Newspaper Editors, April 20, 1961," in *Public Papers of the Presidents of the United States: John F. Kennedy, 1961* (Washington: GPO, 1962), p. 306. See also CNO, memo for record, ser 000221-61 of 21 Apr 1961; *U.S.-V.N. Relations*, bk. 2, pp. ii, 2, 6, 31-32.

[35]Memo, Deputy Special Assistant to the President for National Security Affairs to SECSTATE, SECDEF, Director CIA, of 24 Apr 1961.

[36]CNO, memo for record, ser 000269-61 of 16 May 1961. See also memo, Burke to Taylor, ser 000275-61 of 20 May in memo, CNO to OP-06, of 20 May.

They concluded that the United States was "in a life and death struggle which we may be losing, and will lose unless we change our ways and [marshal] our resources with an intensity associated in the past only with times of war."[37] The report's recommendations included a call for coordination and central direction of all U.S. military, paramilitary, political, economic, ideological, and intelligence resources to counter the Communist threat. On 28 June, the President approved the major recommendations of the group.[38]

Secretary of Defense McNamara echoed the deep concern of the White House with the worldwide course of events in a meeting on 21 April with the civilian heads of the military services and the Joint Chiefs of Staff called to discuss the implications of the Cuban situation. Admiral Burke reported that McNamara wanted to "find out what lessons were to be learned from this exercise. We would have to re-examine the whole business." The Secretary of Defense also stressed the need to "develop a national approach to indirect aggression. . . . We must have a plan for Laos and Vietnam." He doubted that an increase in conventional forces and weapons was the best solution to the problem but suggested instead that "we have to get some new ideas. What is required is a new idea on counter-aggression of the type that we are seeing around the world. . . . We need a major review of the whole problem."[39]

Naval Guerrilla Warfare

Although the Navy, to meet this newly perceived menace, already had taken limited steps to develop underwater swimmer propulsion devices, special parachutes, and survival kits and to enhance related training at naval schools, a number of officers in the Office of the Chief of Naval Operations felt the overall effort inadequate. One of these men, Vice Admiral Ulysses S. G. Sharp, Jr., the Deputy Chief of Naval Operations (Plans and Policy), observed that the Office of the "CNO has done little, if anything, to increase the emphasis on counter-guerrilla warfare" and added that "since this type of operation is held in such high regard in high

---

[37]Cuban Study Group, "Final Report to the President," of 13 Jun 1961, memo No. 4, p. 7.
[38]*Ibid.*, memo No. 3, p. 3; memo No. 4, pp. 4-5.
[39]Quoted in CNO, memo for record, ser 000221-61 of 21 Apr 1961. See also William W. Kaufman, *The McNamara Strategy* (New York: Harper and Row, 1964), p. 65.

places, we had better get going."⁴⁰

A number of promising ideas, however, had been under consideration by one group since early March. On the 10th of that month, Rear Admiral William E. Gentner, Jr., the Director, Strategic Plans Division, approved preliminary recommendations by the Unconventional Activities Committee (successor to the Unconventional Activities Working Group) that would involve the Navy more directly in this lower level of conflict. The group acted to "provide additional unconventional warfare capabilities within, or as an extension of, our amphibious forces" and "specifically adapted to particular country insurgency situations" in "restricted waters."⁴¹ The committee recommended more emphasis on the conduct in these waters of assault landings, reconnaissance, patrolling, transport of troops and supplies, fire support, air support, and the infiltration and exfiltration of personnel. Specific proposals comprised a study of mine warfare techniques and devices, development of armament for small ships and craft, and review of measures to convert ships and craft for guerrilla warfare functions.

Finally, an innovative approach to the naval aspects of guerrilla warfare was indicated in a recommendation for the establishment, under the Pacific and Atlantic amphibious commanders, of one unit each which would become "a center or focal point through which all elements of this specialized Navy capability [in guerrilla warfare] would be channeled." These proposed units, to be designated by the acronym SEAL, "a contraction of SEA, AIR, LAND...indicating an all-around, universal capability," initially would consist of from 20 to 25 officers and 50 to 75 enlisted men. Each detachment would have a three-faceted mission:

> (1) develop a specialized Navy capability in guerrilla/counterguerrilla operations to include training of selected personnel in a wide variety of skills, (2) development of doctrinal tactics, and (3) development of special support equipment.⁴²

---

[40] Memo, OP-06 to OP-60, ser BM0098-61 of 29 Apr 1961. See also memo, OP-06 to JCS, ser 00355P60 of 2 May.

[41] The geographical designation "restricted waters" was defined as including three components: (1) shallow coastal waters, (2) rivers and deltas, and (3) inland seas. Memo, OP-60 to CNO, ser BM00286-61 of 10 Mar 1961.

[42] *Ibid.*

Thus, by the end of April 1961, the Office of the Chief of Naval Operations began to seriously consider the direct participation of the Navy in guerrilla and counterguerrilla warfare and the creation of units specially suited to that type of conflict.

The April-May Crisis in Vietnam

Between 27 and 29 April 1961, the deteriorating military position of the government forces in Laos compelled the U.S. leadership to make critical decisions regarding possible intervention into Southeast Asia with combat forces. With the chance that Laos might fall completely into the Communist sphere, thereby exposing South Vietnam's long border to overt aggression and infiltration from North Vietnam, U.S. leaders began to seriously consider the introduction of American forces into Vietnam. In fact, Admiral Burke felt that South Vietnam "would like to see U.S. come in, [and] in this connection put in special forces [and] part of a division."[43]

On 1 May, an interdepartmental task force report contained proposals to support a two-division increase in the Vietnamese armed forces with two 1,600-man U.S. training teams, in addition to augmenting the current counterinsurgency training program with 400 Special Forces personnel. Of particular importance for the Navy, this report further recommended that U.S. naval forces be directed to mount a coastal patrol with a newly established Vietnamese paramilitary junk force from the Cambodian border to the mouth of the Mekong River. The object of the operation was to prevent seaborne infiltration into the Mekong Delta. To accomplish this mission, Admiral Beakley suggested the use of 180-foot escorts (PCE) and coastal minesweepers (MSC) from the Atlantic and Pacific Fleets. He admitted that the ships were "not ideally suited because of speed and draft limitations but are the best available to handle the shallow waters around Vietnam."[44] The new course of events also required a review of contingency plans for deployment to South Vietnam of a Marine brigade and other conventional forces.

---

[43]CNO, memo for record, ser 00086P33 of 29 Apr 1961. See also msg, CNO 292115Z Mar; CINCPAC, Command History, 1961, pp. 184-85.
[44]OP-33, memo for record, ser 00084P33 of 29 Apr 1961.

Provinces of South Vietnam

During the first week in May 1961, it became increasingly likely that a ceasefire would take effect in Laos and be followed by international peace negotiations at Geneva. These circumstances led Admiral Burke then to view the introduction of U.S. forces into South Vietnam as a way to deter Communist moves at a later date and to reassure U.S. allies and neutral countries throughout the world of American constancy. Many policymakers in the administration and among the military services were greatly concerned that the decision not to meet the Communist advance in Laos with a military response would be perceived by friend and foe alike as a lack of resolve. Admiral Burke was especially troubled that the "Communists were taking our measure" and that the setbacks in Cuba and Laos would induce the Soviets to foment a crisis over Berlin and increase subversive activities throughout Africa, Latin America, and Asia.[45]

After Laos, the country believed to be in the most acute and immediate danger was Vietnam. Without greater support, the CNO feared that President Diem would lose confidence in the United States, which then would hinder the effort to defeat the insurgency. Even in February 1961, Admiral Burke feared that the United States "had lost valuable time with Diem and [we] have damaged his trust in us." Commenting on General Lansdale's report of his January visit to Vietnam, the CNO indicated his attitude toward the anti-Communist leader: "You know how I feel about our friend Diem — as I feel about any leader who strives for the cause of the Free World. Either we back him with our best (people, money, support) or we don't; there is no in-between."[46]

Support for the involvement of U.S. forces also was strong within the Defense Department. A number of officials in the State Department and on the White House staff concurred in the need for such a step. But disadvantages inherent in this course of action were evident. The contemplated measures could be regarded as a breach of the Geneva accords of 1954, which prohibited the entry into Vietnam of military

---

[45] CNO, memo for record, ser 000243-61 of 4 May 1961. See also CNO, memo for record, ser 000221-61 of 21 Apr; Burke/Ward, transcripts of taped conversations, of 3 May; 5 May; OP-33, memo for record, ser 00083P33 of 2 May; memos, Burke to Fontana, ser 000241-61 of 2 May; SECSTATE/SECDEF to President, of 3 May; ltrs, Burke to Bird, of 8 May, encl.. 5; CINCPACFLT to CINCPAC, ser 32/01359 of 11 Aug; telecons, Wheeler to Burke, 0931 of 2 May; McNamara to Burke, 1907 of 2 May; Burke to Fontana, 1935 of 2 May; msgs, CNO 020015Z May; 021347Z; JCS/OSD 022335Z; CNO 042107Z; 042233Z; CP 052130Z.

[46] Ltr, Burke to Lansdale, of 14 Feb 1961. See also Paramilitary Study Group, memo for record, of 26 Apr.

forces, and also would unfavorably affect the Geneva negotiations on Laos, scheduled to begin on 12 May. Further, it was unclear whether President Diem, whose fervent nationalism was well known, would agree to the commitment of foreign troops. Perhaps the most important consideration was the belief that U.S. determination to back the South Vietnamese could be demonstrated in ways that would not commit the United States irrevocably. Accordingly, Secretary of State Rusk, at a meeting with Deputy Secretary of Defense Roswell Gilpatric on 5 May, concluded that "we should not place combat forces in South Vietnam at this time."[47]

The issue, however, did not rest. The following Monday, 8 May, Gilpatric directed the JCS to reconsider the advisability of intervention and the size and composition of forces needed to execute it. The purposes for U.S. intervention continued to be the provision of "maximum psychological impact in deterrence of further Communist aggression from North Vietnam, China, or the Soviet Union, while rallying the morale of the Vietnamese and encouraging the support of SEATO and neutral nations for Vietnam's defense."[48]

Admiral Felt, whose views were solicited, strongly opposed intervention in the war with U.S. forces. He had a number of reasons, including the absence of overt Communist aggression against South Vietnam and the undesirability of U.S. forces usurping Vietnamese responsibilities for conducting aerial surveillance, air-ground support, and coastal patrol. He further observed that the deployment of Pacific Command combat forces would destroy CINCPAC's operational flexibility. Felt also objected to the considered use of Army combat troops on a long-term basis rather than a "USMC Expeditionary Brigade," as called for in operational plans. In addition, Admiral Felt advised that if it was necessary to commit U.S. forces, "it should be with [the] intention of fighting.... Their deployment under the guise of training would be a transparent subterfuge." He warned that the contemplated action "could commit the U.S. to another Korea-type support and assistance situation" and that "if we go in, we

---

[47]JCS, memo for record, of 5 May 1961. See also OP-33, memo for record, ser 00083P33 of 2 May; Burke, memo, of 3 May; CNO, memo for record, ser 000245-61 of 5 May; ltr, Burke to Bird, of 8 May.
[48]JCS Paper 1992/978, p. 6.

can't pull out at will without damaging repercussions."[49] Rear Admiral Henry L. Miller, who became the CINCPAC Assistant Chief of Staff for Operations the following year, later observed that "Admiral Felt's policy was to help the Vietnamese get organized, get trained, given the military equipment to fight their own war, but to keep U.S. troops out of that country."[50]

Nonetheless, on 10 May, the JCS again recommended to Secretary of Defense McNamara that if the "political decision is to hold Southeast Asia outside the Communist sphere, the Joint Chiefs of Staff are of the opinion that U.S. forces should be deployed immediately to South Vietnam...primarily to prevent the Vietnamese from being subjected to the same situation as presently exists in Laos."[51] Admiral Burke, in explaining to Admiral Felt the basis for the JCS decision, confirmed the latter's judgement that the action would in all likelihood commit the United States to the continued existence of South Vietnam. The CNO revealed his own views in a message to CINCPAC on 10 May:

> Where there are no U.S. troops in place, there is no will to send them when the going gets tough. We don't need a lot of troops in there but I feel strongly we do need [a] few organized units.... Decision to reinforce is more easily taken than essential decision to commit. We have missed the boat in Laos by not having foot in door.[52]

Admiral Burke stated further: "Sorry I had to go against your [Admiral Felt's] recommendation South Vietnam but believe this only way to have U.S. take action other than similar to Laos."[53] Several days later, the CNO reiterated one of the primary reasons for the proposed steps with the suggestion that "what we really need is enough troops in Viet Nam to prove to Diem that we intend to stick by him and to keep his confidence in the United States up."[54]

Admiral Felt supported the decision of the JCS, even though he still thought that "there is not sufficient justification to tie up forces which are

---

[49]Memo, OP-60 to CNO, ser BM000511-61 of 9 May 1961. See also memos, SECNAV to SECDEF, ser 000423P60 of 9 May; OP-60 to CNO, ser BM000268-61 of 10 May.

[50]Henry L. Miller, transcript of interview with John T. Mason, Jr., U.S. Naval Institute, in Patuxent and Annapolis, MD, 1971, Vol. II, p. 327.

[51]JCS Paper 1992/983, p. ii.

[52]Msg, CNO 102319Z May 1961.

[53]Ibid. See also msg, JCS 111802Z May 1961; msg, CNO 121413Z May.

[54]Msg, CNO 121413Z May 1961.

now assigned to me." This concern was eased with the knowledge that the proposed ground troops would not be taken from the Pacific Command, but rather deployed from the United States. CINCPAC felt it "quite a different proposition when I can contemplate [being assigned] additional forces to me from" the United States.[55] However, he believed that U.S. naval forces already were assisting the South Vietnamese Navy by deterring a large-scale Communist invasion by sea, and that this protection should not be extended to coastal patrol, which should remain a Vietnamese responsibility. He did suggest that a minimum number of the U.S. Navy's patrol craft be deployed to aid in training and developing an effective South Vietnamese coastal patrol, a proposal that was not implemented.[56]

The issue surrounding the introduction of U.S. forces into Vietnam became less crucial as the month of May wore on. In fact, it was academic when President Diem informed Vice President Lyndon B. Johnson, during the latter's visit to Vietnam from 11 to 15 May, and the new U.S. Ambassador, Frederick Nolting, on 27 May, that no foreign combat units were required short of overt Communist aggression.[57]

The need to deter North Vietnam, China, and the Soviet Union from overt aggression also became less pressing as the ceasefire in Laos held and early negotiations in Geneva indicated that the country would not be lost entirely to the Pathet Lao. The determination to reassure President Diem of American support was satisfied by the dispatch of a new U.S. ambassador to Vietnam and the reported success of Vice President Johnson's highly publicized visit to the country, during which the Vietnamese leader was informed that the United States was "ready to join with you in an intensified endeavor to win the struggle against Communism and to further the social and political advancement of Vietnam."[58]

---

[55]Msg, CPFLT 112238Z May 1961.

[56]Msgs, JCS 111802Z May 1961; CPFLT 112238Z; CP 120544Z; CNO 121413Z; CPFLT 130223Z.

[57]Even earlier, in March, President Diem intimated his feelings in this regard, as related by Admiral Felt. He advised CINCPAC: "If open war breaks out and the U.S. has some idea of landing U.S. troops in N. Vietnam, we should reconsider.... We would have to buck a terrific psychological block — whites invading colored Asia. He recommends the use of S. Vietnam troops or even [Chinese Nationalist] Marines." Ltr, Burke to Bird, of 8 May 1961. See also memo, OP-61 to CNO, ser 00682P61 of 26 May.

[58]Ltr, Kennedy to Diem, of 8 May 1961 in *U.S.-V.N. Relations*, bk. 11, p. 132. See also memo, Lansdale to Gilpatric, of 18 May in *Ibid.*, p. 157; bk. 2, pt. IVB.1, p. 66; memo, OP-61 to CNO, ser 00682P61 of 26 May; CNO, memo for record, ser 000295-61 of 1 Jun.

Admiral Harry D. Felt, Commander in Chief, Pacific Command, bids farewell to Vice President Lyndon B. Johnson at Hickam Air Force Base, Hawaii, on 9 May 1961. The Vice President is enroute to South Vietnam.

Although the Laos crisis temporarily focused attention on the possible direct use of U.S. forces, the Kennedy administration's interest in counterinsurgency as a response to "wars of national liberation" remained paramount. To develop a program for South Vietnam, the President appointed another interdepartmental task force, this one charged with studying measures to strengthen the political, military, and economic capacity of the South Vietnamese to prevent Communist inroads. The final report of the task force, labeled the "Presidential Program," was promulgated on 11 May 1961. It reaffirmed U.S. support for the survival of the South Vietnamese government. The provision that the United States would "seek to increase the confidence of President Diem and his government in the United States" was the underlying assumption of the program.[59] While an increase in the South Vietnamese armed forces to 170,000 and then 200,000 personnel, as well as the size and composition of U.S. forces for possible intervention were to be studied, counterinsurgency warfare again was the primary theme. To prevent the Communist domination of South Vietnam, the United States would initiate "a series of mutually supporting actions of a military, political, economic, psychological and covert character...."[60] In the naval sphere, the program authorized "MAP support for the Vietnamese Junk Force as a means of preventing Viet Cong clandestine supply and infiltration into South Vietnam by water," to include training of junk crews at Vietnamese or U.S. bases.[61]

Acceleration of the Navy's Effort to Prepare for Guerrilla Warfare

As these developments occurred at the national level, Admiral Burke, early in May, took a significant step in broadening the Navy's probable future counterguerrilla role. On 3 May, in a seminal directive, he stated: "I know this is going to be difficult, but we are going to have to take over such operations as river patrol in the Saigon Delta, in the Mekong River, and other areas." Rivers and deltas, soon afterward, were separated from the term "restricted waters" and treated as unique operational environments, reflecting the new emphasis on warfare on inland waterways.[62] To prepare for this eventuality, the CNO called for an increase in the training of naval personnel in guerrilla warfare and an appraisal of the Navy's equipment suited to the conduct of operations in the rivers and swamps of South Vietnam.

---

[59]Memo, McGeorge Bundy to SECSTATE, NSAM 52 of 11 May 1961 in *U.S.-V.N. Relations*, bk. 11, p. 136. See also CINCPAC, Command History, 1961, pp. 172-74.
[60]JCS Paper 1992/978.
[61]*Ibid*.
[62]Memo, CNO to OP-01, ser 00242-61 of 3 May 1961. See also memos, OP-60 to OP-90, ser BM00509-61 of 16 May; CNO to CINCLANTFLT, CINCPACFLT, CINCNAVEUR, ser 0048P34 of 5 Jun.

Soon thereafter, the CNO concurred with the specific proposals of his Deputy Chief of Naval Operations (Fleet Operations and Readiness), Admiral Beakley, redirecting policy toward the actual participation of the Navy in counterguerrilla operations. In this regard, the Deputy Chief of Naval Operations advised that naval forces should be responsible for two general tasks. The first entailed the conduct of armed patrols on inland waters "to suppress either guerrilla activity or the resupply of enemy guerrilla forces" and "minor amphibious operations [in] waters within supporting range of the sea." The second mission consisted of supporting land warfare, "which is the primary responsibility of the Army" through the use of "water-borne forces on inland waterways for various purposes — patrol, protection of flanks, transportation of forces and logistic support."[63]

To implement many of the tasks envisaged in his memorandum, Admiral Beakley, reiterating the earlier 10 March Strategic Plans Division proposal, recommended that special operations teams (SEALs) be established as separate components of the Atlantic and Pacific Fleets underwater demolition commands. These units were to provide a unique naval contribution to the fight against the armed Communist insurgent. The proposed SEAL mission statement remained basically the same as that drawn up in March, but more emphasis was placed on the actual conduct rather than support of combat operations. In the correspondence issued by the Deputy Chief of Naval Operations (Fleet Operations and Readiness) on 13 May, the new primary mission of the special operations teams was to "develop a specialized capability for the conduct of special operations in rivers, bays, harbors, canals, estuaries, and land areas adjacent to coasts."[64] Of ten specific tasks to be assigned the proposed units, eight concerned the overt or covert conduct of operations, including attacks on enemy shipping, demolition raids on targets in close proximity to bodies of water, and the landing of men and material on hostile shores.[65]

Included in the numerous measures submitted in May to improve the Navy's capacity for counterinsurgency was a proposal to reorient the

---

[63] Memo, OP-03 to CNO, ser 0043P34 of 13 May 1961.

[64] *Ibid.* See also Phillip H. Bucklew, transcript of interview with Oscar P. Fitzgerald, Naval Historical Center, in Washington, DC, 10 Jul 1978, pp. 49-55.

[65] Memo, OP-03 to CNO, ser 0043P34 of 13 May 1961. See also memo, OP-60 to CNO, ser BM00286-61 of 10 Mar; OP-60 to CNO, ser BM428-61 of 20 Jul; OP-06B to JCS, ser 00719P60 of 28 Jul.

military construction mission of selected naval construction forces. Inspired by President Kennedy's call for measures to oppose "wars of national liberation," Lieutenant Commander Richard E. Anderson (CEC) and other officers in the Bureau of Yards and Docks and in the Office of the Chief of Naval Operations early in the year developed a concept based on the use of proposed SEABEE technical assistance teams (STATs). These specialized units could provide the people of threatened developing countries with technical training, engineering support, and construction assistance in their nation-building efforts. Rear Admiral Charles O. Triebel, the Director, Logistic Plans Division, adopted the idea. The admiral found that the Navy's STATs could represent an ideal counter to Communist-supported insurgency and infiltration of guerrillas, in that they could be deployed to threatened countries prior to the development of an internal crisis. This preemption would enable the United States to organize the indigenous population to resist Communist political and military incursions before the situation deteriorated.

While the Army's Special Forces were generally recognized as combat troops who performed various paramilitary functions, the SEABEEs were seen as essentially construction and engineering personnel whose primary mission entailed non-combat duties. For this reason, naval construction forces could more readily be introduced to an endangered country to provide technical assistance, but indirectly to provide a military presence. Indeed, SEABEE units already had performed engineering and construction tasks in the developing nations of Southeast Asia. Rear Admiral Triebel stated that naval construction forces personnel were "carefully selected, and given the proper training could become proficient in the field of guerrilla warfare." He recommended that "the utilization of Naval Construction Forces as Technical Assistance Units could then be coupled with a military mission to covertly and overtly oppose Communist aggression in assisting indigenous forces to resist by guerrilla warfare methods if necessary."[66] This proposed concept was approved by the Director, Strategic Plans Division soon afterward.

In line with the reorientation of naval unconventional warfare missions, Admiral Burke recognized the need to adjust the functional organization

---

[66]Memo, OP-40 to OP-60, ser 003107P40 of 16 May 1961. See also Tregaskis, *Southeast Asia*, pp. 13-16, 20-25, 51; COMCBPAC, "Helping Others Help Themselves," of 13 Jan 1969, pp. 2-3; memo, OP-60 to CNO, ser BM428-61 of 20 Jul 1961.

of the Office of the Chief of Naval Operations. In May 1961, the CNO directed that the Office of the Deputy Chief of Naval Operations (Fleet Operations and Readiness) be given additional responsibility for guerrilla warfare readiness. Because the subordinate Amphibious Warfare Readiness Branch already was charged with unconventional and psychological warfare matters, this further task was delegated to that office. Its broad responsibilities included the monitoring of personnel training at service schools, in the fleet, and in military assistance advisory groups overseas, as well as the training of foreign personnel in friendly or allied nations. Also included was the development of tactical plans, concepts, and techniques for the prosecution of special operations. Navy Plans Branch personnel continued to exercise the strategic planning function and, in conjunction with representatives of the Amphibious Warfare Readiness Branch and the Flag Plot Branch, comprised a committee to coordinate guerrilla warfare planning and support within the Navy.[67]

Later in May, a response from Vice Admiral William R. Smedberg, III, the Deputy Chief of Naval Operations (Manpower and Naval Reserve), to Admiral Burke's request for information on the Navy's training programs in unconventional warfare indicated some reluctance to increasing naval activities in this sphere. Admiral Smedberg reported that because responsibility for guerrilla warfare rested with the Army, the Navy did not and should not have its own separate training programs and facilities.[68] Admiral Burke could not concur with these conclusions. Only three days previously, on 16 May, during a luncheon conversation with Admiral Burke and others, President Kennedy stressed the necessity for increasing the guerrilla warfare training of foreign as well as U.S. forces. Accordingly, the CNO directed his deputy for personnel to prepare an "order to double training in [guerrilla warfare]."[69]

Specific suggestions already had been proffered regarding increased guerrilla warfare training for naval personnel. Rear Admiral Gentner, the Director, Strategic Plans Division, proposed that at least one naval officer assigned to a military assistance advisory group or mission in each country "with an existing or potential insurgency threat" be fully indoctrinated in

---

[67]Memos, OP-06B to OP-03B, ser BM393-61 of 5 May 1961; OP-03 to CNO, ser 0040P34 of 13 May.
[68]Memo, OP-01 to CNO, ser c23/00800-1 of 19 May 1961.
[69]Memo, CNO to OP-01, ser 00242-61 of 3 May 1961 . See also CNO, memo for record, ser 000269-61 of 16 May.

the ideological, political, economic, and sociological characteristics of insurgency. This would enable them to develop "an appreciation of the naval aspects and potential of [guerrilla activities in order] to assist in militarily eliminating the threat." Admiral Gentner suggested that these personnel attend pertinent Army courses of instruction, but "in the event U.S. Navy Special Operations units are established, specifically tailored training could be made available to selected personnel within Navy facilities."[70] In line with the new responsibility for the "waterborne conduct of operations and support of guerrilla and other forces" in rivers and restricted waters, Admiral James S. Russell, the Vice Chief of Naval Operations, restated the need for SEAL cadres "to conduct training for selected U.S. and indigenous personnel in a wide variety of skills for use in clandestine operations and the support of same."[71] On 15 June, Admiral Russell directed the future formation of such groups within the underwater demolition units of the Atlantic Fleet and Pacific Fleet Amphibious Forces. It was anticipated that training by SEAL detachments would constitute an important part of the Navy's program to provide instruction on the naval applications to guerrilla warfare.[72]

By the end of July, the program to prepare more naval personnel in guerrilla warfare and related fields at naval and Army schools was ready for implementation. Personnel destined to man proposed special operations teams and SEABEE technical assistance teams, MAAG and Mission instructors, and officers designated to fill relevant fleet staff planning billets were to receive varied training. Instruction would include such subjects as training administration, underwater operations, ranger, airborne, and jungle tactics, communications, psychological warfare, intelligence, languages, and counterguerrilla warfare in general.[73]

Another problem addressed by Admiral Burke in his memorandum of 3 May, which suggested greater efforts on the part of the Navy to prepare for river and restricted water operations, concerned the selection of boats and craft, weapons, and equipment for the prosecution of guerrilla warfare. Impressed with the need for shallow-water craft, in addition to

---

[70]Memo, OP-60 to OP-10/OP-62, ser BM00505-61 of 11 May 1961. See also memos, OP-01 to CNO, ser A232 of 2 Jun; OP-09 to OP-01, encl. in memo, OP-01 to CNO, of 13 Jun.
[71]Memo, OP-09 to OP-01 of 15 Jun 1961, encl. in memo, OP-01 to CNO, of 13 Jun. See also memo, CNO to CINCLANTFLT, CINCPACFLT, CINCNAVEUR, ser 0048P34 of 5 Jun.
[72]Memo, OP-09 to OP-01, of 15 Jun 1961, encl. in memo, OP-01 to CNO, of 13 Jun.
[73]Ltr, OP-06B to JCS, ser 00719P60 of 28 Jul 1961.

coastal patrol craft and special warfare equipment, Admiral Burke called for the accelerated development of suitable material. On 18 May, Admiral Burke directed the Bureau of Ships and the Deputy Chief of Naval Operations (Logistics) to study the problem of providing acceptable craft and "he emphasized the need for boats of many kinds and sizes for real fighting."[74]

To bring some organizational unity to the design selection and developmental process involving small craft and their armament, the Bureau of Ships, on 1 June 1961, established an Unconventional Warfare Equipment Coordinator. And, "because of the urgency of the situation in Viet Nam, great emphasis was placed on fulfilling Vietnamese requirements."[75] Later in June, a counterpart to this position was created within the Office of the Chief of Naval Operations. It was the Special Operations Section of the Amphibious Warfare Readiness Branch, which was designated the contact point for all unconventional warfare equipment, including small water craft. Captain Harry S. Warren headed this section.[76]

In a further effort to improve coordination of the small craft procurement program, on 5 July the Chief of Naval Operations established a panel headed by the Chairman, Ship Characteristics Board, and composed of permanent representatives from the Office of the Chief of Naval Operations, the Bureau of Weapons, the Bureau of Ships, and the Headquarters, Commandant, United States Marine Corps. The Bureau of Naval Personnel, the Bureau of Yards and Docks, and fleet type commanders provided associate members on request and the Army also was invited to participate in the panel's deliberations. The body was charged with determining "the most suitable types of water craft for [guerrilla and counterguerrilla] operations...to meet the needs of the forces of both the U.S. and of military aid countries."[77]

---

[74]OP-09, memo for record, of 18 May 1961. Of interest is Admiral Burke's recommendation that planners read Bernard Fall's *Street Without Joy*, which describes earlier French naval actions in Indochina.

[75]Memo, OP-06 to JCS, ser 001051P60 of 1 Nov 1961. See also memos, OP-414 to OP-09, ser BM00149 of 27 Apr; OP-09 to Chief, Bureau of Ships, ser 24P09 of 24 Jun; msg, CNO 182107Z May.

[76]Memo, OP-09 to Chief, Bureau of Ships, ser 24P09 of 24 Jun 1961; William H. Hamilton/Richard Marcinko, transcript of interview with Edward J. Marolda, Naval Historical Center, in Washington, DC, 28 Feb 1984.

[77]Ltr, CNO to Chairman, Ship Characteristics Board, ser 0432P42 of 5 Jul 1961. See also memo, OP-09 to Chief, Bureau of Ships, ser 24P09 of 24 Jun.

One of the panel's first actions was to receive a report from a naval team which had just returned from South Vietnam. The group, composed of two naval officers and one civilian from the Bureau of Ships and an officer from the Bureau of Weapons, conducted a three-week informational tour of the country. During short stopovers in Hawaii, the team received additional data on Pacific area equipment requirements from CINCPAC and CINCPACFLT. The information acquired during this visit was added to the growing store of knowledge of the Navy's guerrilla warfare needs in Southeast Asia.[78]

In this regard, the CNO already had requested a list of equipment suited to the naval aspects of guerrilla warfare, then available or under development, and also a list of what was required to improve the Navy's material readiness in this area. In response to the CNO's directive, the various offices within the Office of the Chief of Naval Operations and the bureaus with cognizance over related matters, as well as the Office of Naval Research, submitted a consolidated listing. The items then in supply or under development included: aircraft antipersonnel weapons; low-drag, general purpose, and fragmentation bombs; missiles; emergency landing material for air support of guerrilla operations; SCUBA gear; detonators and explosive devices; underwater communication equipment; antipersonnel swimmer weapons; swimmer propulsion units for UDT operations; portable radios, radio and radar identification beacons; direction-finding equipment; jamming devices; and radio intercept units; moored mines for use against wooden or steel-hulled vessels; protective nets; river mine clearance devices; and survival kits, protective clothing, vaccines, insecticides, and repellants for operations in tropical climates. However, the list of new equipment needed to upgrade the Navy's ability to prosecute guerrilla warfare was almost as long. The items in demand included lightweight armor for protection against small-arms fire, air-to-surface weapons, mine detection and destruction devices, and aerial, land-mine laying equipment.[79]

---

[78]Memos, OP-06B to JCS, ser 0071960 of 28 July 1961; OP-06 to JCS, ser 001051P60 of 1 Nov., p. 5; COM7FLT, "Seventh Fleet Briefing for DOD RDT&E Limited War Study Group," ser 00029 of 12 Jul.

[79]OP-07B to CNO, ser 0036P07M of 21 Aug; CNO, memo for record, ser 000230-61 of 28 Apr 1961; memos, CNO to OP-01, ser 00242-61 of 3 May; OP-07B to CNO, ser 0020P07M of 19 May; CNO, ser 0024P07M of 26 May; memo, OP-60 to OP-07, ser BM00659-61 of 21 Jun 1961; ltr, CNO to CINCLANTFLT, CINCPACFLT, CINCNAVEUR, ser 0048P34 of 5 Jun; Hamilton/Marcinko, Interview.

A Temporary Respite in Vietnam

As the Navy prepared for guerrilla warfare during the late summer and early fall of 1961, the administration began to focus on Berlin, where U.S. and Soviet interests clashed sharply and an armed confrontation was a distinct possibility. Hence, the strength of U.S. conventional forces became a prime concern. While the situation in Europe grew more serious, the previous crisis atmosphere surrounding events in Southeast Asia subsided. Negotiations over Laos continued in Geneva, while the military situation remained relatively static.

In South Vietnam, the insurgency still was critical but no climactic turning point loomed in the near future. Conversely, the armed strength of South Vietnam grew due to the increase of U.S. military assistance and Vietnamese manpower levels authorized in the Presidential Program. By mid-August, the South Vietnamese armed forces reached a strength of 157,000 men, including 4,500 in the navy. President Kennedy then authorized U.S. support for a further increase to 200,000 men. Related to these developments was President Kennedy's decision to give first priority to the military effort to achieve internal security. Many U.S. leaders felt that these and other measures would enable the South Vietnamese to effectively deal with the Communist insurgency.[80]

In this non-crisis atmosphere, unilateral activities by the United States Navy in South Vietnamese waters consisted primarily of port calls and other routine functions. For example, on 27 August Mine Division 93's *Leader* (MSO-490) and *Excel* (MSO-439), under the command of Commander George A. Aubert, became the first ships of the United States Navy to make an official visit to Phnom Penh, Cambodia. The Seventh Fleet ships reached their destination without incident, after navigating 180 miles of the Mekong River.[81]

At the same time, the U.S. national leadership explored new ways to complement the efforts of the South Vietnamese in their counterinsurgency struggle. Of particular interest to the Navy were considerations by the Defense Department during July and August of instituting a naval

---

[80]JCS, *History*, pt. 1, pp. 2-16—2-24; *U.S.-V.N. Relations*, bk. 2, pp. 12, 58-71; bk. 11, pp. 239, 241, 245-46; CINCPAC, Command History, 1961, pp. 176-81; COM7FLT, ltr, ser N12 of 9 Aug 1961; msg, JCS 151541Z Aug; memo, OP-60 to CNO, ser BM346-61 of 15 Jun.

[81]Msgs, ADMIN CPFLT 230334Z Aug 1961; ALUSNA Saigon 250245Z; COM7FLT 290952Z; CNO 111914Z Sep; Office of Public Affairs, DOD, "Press Release," of 24 Aug.

USN-1056871

Commander George A. Aubert, Commander Mine Division 93 (left), and Commander Everett A. Parke, U.S. Naval Attache, Saigon, make an official call on Cambodian Defense Minister Lon Nol during the visit of the U.S. minesweeping unit to Phnom Penh in August 1961.

blockade of North Vietnam. This action was contemplated primarily as a punitive measure for that nation's support of the war in the South. Proposals also were advanced for the establishment of air and sea patrols by U.S. naval forces to interdict North Vietnamese sea infiltration. Envisioned were patrols from the 17th parallel southward along the Vietnamese coast and from the coast eastward to the Paracel Islands.

CINCPAC was asked to submit his views on the proposals. Admiral Felt, as he had during the troop involvement issue of April and May, again recommended against the introduction of U.S. forces into Southeast Asia. He specifically cautioned against U.S. military retaliatory actions in the form of a naval blockade because he felt that it was "one thing for the South Vietnamese to take reprisal measures but quite another for the United States to do so." A naval blockade would indicate that the United States was "performing [a] belligerent act." The admiral advised against the augmentation of South Vietnamese coastal patrols with U.S. naval forces because he believed that Americans would not be as effective as the South Vietnamese in identifying infiltrating North Vietnamese boats. Further, Felt knew that President Diem remained adamantly opposed to the use of U.S. forces. The admiral also concluded that

> the best course at this time is to encourage and to assist the Vietnamese forces to develop further their own capabilities and to improve operational coordination.... Our objective is to develop South Vietnamese teamwork and an all-Vietnamese operation.... One of the keys to success in dealing with our Asian friends is to encourage and assist their own initiative.[82]

The JCS, in large part because of Admiral Felt's objections, deferred a decision on a U.S. naval blockade or patrols until further studies were made.

The Navy's Guerrilla Warfare Program in the Fall of 1961

With the administration increasingly distracted by the Berlin crisis and somewhat less concerned about developments in Southeast Asia, the program to expand the naval guerrilla warfare capability lost some momentum later in 1961. The new Chief of Naval Operations, Admiral George W. Anderson, Jr., also reviewed previous actions taken in this area. On 29 August, he specifically questioned the broadened role of the SEABEE technical assistance teams that suggested greater involvement in paramilitary activities by asking the Deputy Chief of Naval Operations

---

[82]Msg, CP 022210Z Aug 1961. See also msgs, CP 270112Z Apr; 250430Z Sep; JCS, *History*, pt. 1, pp. 2-18—2-19; memos, OP-605 to CNO, ser BM454-61 of 1 Aug; BM485-61 of 9 Aug; BM514-61 of 19 Aug.

(Logistics), "How far do we go in this business?"[83] In response, Admiral Triebel stated:

> It is not intended that the Naval Construction Forces become actively engaged in aggressive paramilitary operations, but more that these groups — Technical Assistance Teams, when deployed, possess the capabilities required to extract a maximum of military value from their presence should the international situation and national aims so dictate.[84]

Admiral Anderson then gave tentative approval to this wider use of the Navy's construction forces, although the concept was still subject to further study.

A similar examination of the plan to establish SEAL teams as the Navy's primary counterguerrilla units led to the curtailment of this program. Admiral Anderson advised his fleet commanders in chief: "While it is desirable that naval capabilities in unconventional warfare and paramilitary operations be developed and exploited to full potential, particularly for employment during conditions short of the overt commitment of U.S. forces, current force requirements are of such magnitude that personnel resources are not available for immediate implementation."[85] Billets for 20 officers and 100 men continued to be a requirement, but pending the provision of additional personnel, naval commanders were encouraged to "enhance and augment present naval support capabilities in the area of paramilitary operations by developing the existing capabilities within the Underwater Demolition Teams for demolition, sabotage and other clandestine activities in order to complement the inherent unconventional warfare capabilities of Marine Pathfinder and Reconnaissance Units."[86]

At the same time, specialized training for naval personnel in other than the traditional naval aspects of unconventional warfare lagged. By the end of October 1961, only four officers, including the Navy Liaison Officer at Fort Bragg, the Assistant for Naval Aspects of Special Operations in the Amphibious Warfare Readiness Branch, and two officers from Underwa-

---

[83]OP-403E, memo, ser 003209P40 of 22 Aug 1961.

[84]Memo, OP-04B to CNO, ser 003233P40 of 1 Sep 1961. See also COMCBPAC, "Helping Others Help Themselves," of 13 Jan 1969, p. 3.

[85]Ltr, CNO to CINCLANTFLT and CINCPACFLT, ser 0087P43 of 27 Oct 1961. See also memo, OP-06 to JCS, ser 001051P60 of 1 Nov.

[86]Ltr, CNO to CINCLANTFLT and CINCPACFLT, ser 0087P43 of 27 Oct 1961. See also ltr, Chairman Amphibious Warfare Advisory Board to CNO, ser 0097P34 of 3 Nov.

ter Demolition Team 21, had attended or were attending unconventional warfare courses at the Army's Special Warfare Center. However, another crisis in South Vietnam would put renewed vigor into the Navy's guerrilla warfare effort.

Autumn Crisis in Vietnam

In late September Vietnam again began to draw attention. By that time, progress toward the creation of a strong, stable South Vietnamese government and society had virtually come to a halt. The military picture was even more discouraging. Alarming reports from Saigon indicated that the Viet Cong were on the offensive, initiating three times the number of attacks reported in earlier months. The State Department estimated that Viet Cong "regular" units increased from a strength of 7,000 men at the start of 1961 to 17,000 at the end of September. Increasingly large-scale and large-unit attacks appeared to be fueled by troops and supplies infiltrated through Laos from North Vietnam.

At the end of September, President Diem revealed to the Kennedy administration that, as things stood, the South Vietnamese were unable to cope with the Communist insurgency. On 29 September, in a meeting at which Ambassador Nolting, Admiral Felt, members of the CINCPAC staff, and Lieutenant General Lionel C. McGarr, the new Chief, MAAG, Vietnam, were present, the South Vietnamese president requested a bilateral defense treaty with the United States to ensure the survival of his Asian country. And, contrary to his earlier views, he indicated that American forces now were needed in the struggle. The admission that Diem required direct U.S. military action was a telling indication of the critical nature of the situation.

In recognition of the growing seriousness of the crisis in South Vietnam, the Vietnamese Independence Day celebrations, scheduled for 26 October, were cancelled. A major feature of U.S. participation in the ceremonies was a planned port call to Saigon from 24 to 28 October by Seventh Fleet ships *Coontz* (DLG-9) and *Bugara* (SS-331). But, by this time, it was apparent to many U.S. officials that more dramatic actions were required to demonstrate U.S. support for South Vietnamese national independence.[87]

The JCS viewed the recent developments in South Vietnam with alarm and called for strong action. On 5 October, the military chiefs advised the Secretary of Defense that interim measures would no longer suffice to prevent eventual Communist domination of the area. They further observed:

> Over a period of time, the Joint Chiefs of Staff have examined various alternatives to the solution of the problems of Laos and Southeast Asia. They have recommended certain military actions short of U.S. intervention which might have had the desired effect and could have altered the situation to our advantage. However, the time is now past when actions short of intervention by outside forces could reverse the rapidly worsening situation.... It is the view of the Joint Chiefs of Staff that, lacking an acceptable political settlement prior to the resumption of overt hostilities, there is no feasible military alternative of lesser magnitude which will prevent the loss of Laos, South Vietnam and ultimately Southeast Asia.[88]

Thus, as was true in April and May, the introduction into Southeast Asia of U.S. combat forces again became a primary concern. The rationale for the proposed action continued to be protection of the South Vietnamese border from overt Communist attack; the denial of troop and material support for the insurgency by land, air, and sea; and the consequent freeing of South Vietnamese forces for counterinsurgency operations.

The question of U.S. naval assistance in patrolling South Vietnamese coastal waters also was raised once again when the Assistant Secretary of Defense for International Security Affairs requested information on the legality, probable effectiveness, and influence on other missions of a combined Seventh Fleet-Vietnamese patrol. Admiral Anderson responded by stating that no legal restrictions barred the proposed action and that "naval patrols could effectively help to control infiltration by sea," especially with the use of the search radar on U.S. ships. But, the CNO added that "the assignment of destroyers or patrol aircraft from the

---

[87]Msgs, CPFLT 150048Z Sep 1961; 162352Z; COMDESDIV162 082351Z Oct; memo, OP-61 to SECNAV, ser 00746P61 of 4 Oct.
[88]Memo, JCS to SECDEF, JCSM-704-61 of 5 Oct 1961 in *U.S.-V.N. Relations*, bk. 11, p. 295. See also *Ibid.*, bk. 2, pt. IVB.1, pp. 63-76; JCS, *History*, pt. 1, pp. 2-22—2-24, 3-1; OP-60, memo for record, of 13 Sep; memo, OP-61 to CNO, ser 00752P60 of 19 Oct; msgs, CHMAAGVN 010905Z Sep; 030715Z; 100909Z; JCS 272221Z; CP 020711Z Oct.

Seventh Fleet for patrol action of this type would divert them from the principal threat which they are designed to counter, namely, that of the Soviet submarines," although "they are available for any purpose." The need for such an operation was in doubt, however, as indicated by the estimation of General McGarr that "Viet Cong infiltration is mainly overland through Laos" and that "the sea route is not used to any great extent to infiltrate military personnel or supplies." In any case, the CNO left the "details of carrying out an air-sea barrier...to the unified commander," Admiral Felt, who "would probably wish to augment the South Vietnamese junk force with suitable U.S. forces."[89]

The growing sentiment within the administration for direct U.S. military action against the insurgents was expressed on 10 October by Deputy Under Secretary of State U. Alexis Johnson, who stated that while a reduction of infiltration through Laos as the result of a political settlement "would materially assist the GVN in meeting the Viet Cong threat, there is no assurance that, even under these circumstances, the GVN will in the foreseeable future be able to defeat the Viet Cong." Because of this South Vietnamese inability to eliminate the insurgency, Johnson reasoned that the "real and ultimate objective [of U.S. forces was] the defeat of the Viet Cong...making Vietnam secure in the hands of the anti-Communist government" rather than the previously advanced concept of border and coastal surveillance. "Thus, supplemental military action must be envisaged at the earliest stage that is politically feasible. The ultimate force requirements cannot be estimated with any precision .... Three divisions would be a guess."[90]

The Taylor Mission to South Vietnam

The crucial issue of intervention into Southeast Asia with U.S. ground, air, and naval forces was fully addressed the next day, 11 October, at a meeting of the National Security Council, with President Kennedy in attendance. Support within the administration, especially in the Defense Department, for such a measure was strong. Those in favor of the action included the CNO, Admiral Anderson.[91] Before reaching a decision,

---

[89]Memo, CNO to SECDEF, ser 00981P60 of 9 Oct 1961.
[90]*U.S.-V.N. Relations*, bk. 2, pt. IVB.1, p. 78. See also *Ibid.*, bk. 11, p. 312.
[91]Memo, OP-601 to CNO, ser BM000673-61 of 26 Oct 1961.

however, President Kennedy ordered his personal military representative, General Maxwell Taylor, to proceed to South Vietnam at the head of an interdepartmental group to evaluate the political and military feasibility of the proposed action. Alternative military solutions also were to be investigated, including the "stepping up [of] U.S. assistance and training of Vietnam units, furnishing of more U.S. equipment, particularly helicopters and other light aircraft, trucks and other ground transport, etc."[92] Prior to departure of the Taylor mission, staff officers with the Office of the Secretary of Defense, the Joint Staff, and the military services provided the group with a compilation of twenty possible courses of action. In the naval sphere, suggestions ranged from speeding completion of the junk force construction program to accelerating funding for motor gunboat construction. Also to be considered was the provision of more and better river craft and the possible augmentation of the Vietnamese coastal patrol with Seventh Fleet ships.[93]

During the latter half of October, General Taylor and his group conferred with high U.S. and Vietnamese officials and military officers on the status of the war. General Taylor reported that the situation was extremely critical and he observed a "deep and pervasive crisis of confidence and a serious loss of national morale" among the South Vietnamese resulting from successful Viet Cong attacks, a devastating flood in the Mekong Delta, and other demoralizing factors.[94] Nonetheless, while President Diem appeared greatly concerned over the deterioration of internal security and stability of his country, he now vacillated on the issue of introducing U.S. military forces into South Vietnam. The Vietnamese president requested that the United States assist his armed forces only with support elements, such as tactical aviation, helicopter companies, ground transportation units, and coastal patrol forces.[95]

General Taylor's initial intention, buttressed by JCS recommendations, was to bring about the introduction into South Vietnam of U.S. combat

---

[92]Deputy Secretary of Defense, memo for record, of 11 Oct 1961 in *U.S.-V.N. Relations*, bk. 11, p. 323.
[93]*Ibid., U.S.-V.N. Relations*, bk. 11, pp. 322-23; bk. 2, pt. IVB.1, p. 121; memo, OP-601 to CNO, ser BM000673-61 of 26 Oct 1961.
[94]*U.S.-V.N. Relations*, bk. 2, pt. IVB.1, pp. 90-92. See also msgs, CP 180250Z; 200713Z Oct 1961; 210441Z; CHMAAGVN 260347Z.
[95]*U.S.-V.N. Relations*, bk. 2, pt. IVB.1, pp. 15, 90-92; memo, OP-61 to SECNAV, ser 002049P61 of 25 Oct 1961; msgs, AMEMB Saigon 132000Z Oct; CHMAAGVN 200713Z; AMEMB Saigon 201900.

formations. In order to deploy these forces, the significance of which would be obvious, General Taylor advanced a unique proposal of General McGarr's. Instead of deploying units in a border security role, the president's military representative suggested dispatching a flood relief task force (eventually 6,000 to 8,000 men) to the inundated Mekong Delta area "for humanitarian purposes with subsequent retention if desirable."[96] At first, the force was to be composed primarily of engineer and construction, medical, quartermaster, ordnance, transportation, military police, and other support units. Infantry units would come later to protect the force. Also included would be a naval construction battalion and an H-34 light helicopter squadron from the Seventh Fleet, the latter to conduct aerial reconnaissance of the flooded area. In addition, the Seventh Fleet was to provide an attack cargo ship (AKA) with twenty-seven small boats and a landing craft repair ship (ARL).[97]

While the Secretary of Defense, his deputy, Roswell Gilpatric, and the JCS favored the introduction into South Vietnam of sizeable U.S. forces, they opposed the flood relief task force idea as a half-measure. Others, such as Secretary of State Rusk, were concerned that any intervention would be disadvantageous to the United States. Admiral Felt, the commander of U.S. forces in the Pacific theater, also counselled against the proposed action. Reiterating his earlier opposition to the use of American forces, the admiral warned that it would renew charges of "white colonialism throughout the world, prompt Communist countermeasures on a like scale, result in a long-term deployment, and ultimately engage U.S. personnel in combat." He concluded that the disadvantages of the action "added up in favor of our not introducing U.S. combat forces until we have exhausted other means for helping Diem."[98] Subsequently, Admiral Felt elaborated on this view. Although opposed to the introduction of combat forces before attempting lesser measures, he stated that the action should not be ruled out "if their presence becomes necessary to keep [South Vietnam] from being overwhelmed." But, he added that "we have a wide range of U.S. military actions at our disposal which will not

---

[96]*U.S.-V.N. Relations*, bk. 2, pt. IVB.1, pp. 15-18. Taylor, in Michael Charlton and Anthony Moncrieff, *Many Reasons Why: The American Involvement in Vietnam* (New York: Hill and Wang, 1978), pp. 74-75, downplays the significance of the task force proposal.

[97]Msg, CP 200401Z Oct 1961. See also *U.S.-V.N. Relations*, bk. 2, pt. IVB.1, pp. 88-90, 122-23; msg, CP 040220Z Nov; CHMAAGVN 080021Z.

[98]Msg, CP 152015Z Nov 1961.

kick off war with Communist China" and that the United States should "use forces flexibly in a way of our own choosing when their use is required."[99]

As a result of these many reservations, the final report of the Taylor mission, issued on 3 November, did not recommend the deployment to South Vietnam of U.S. combat troops. However, the team called for other means of increasing the U.S. military commitment. In order to demonstrate the resolve of the United States to stand by the South Vietnamese, one step proposed was the deployment of "some U.S. military forces" other than training and advisory personnel. In addition, a shift would occur

> in the American relation to the Vietnamese effort from advice to *limited partnership* [italics added]. The present character and scale of the war in South Vietnam decrees that only the Vietnamese can defeat the Viet Cong; but at all levels Americans must, as friends and partners — not as arms-length advisors — show them how the job might be done — not tell them or do it for them.[100]

Specific courses of action in the naval sphere also were suggested by the Taylor group. These included assistance by the United States to "the GVN in effecting surveillance and control over the coastal waters and inland waterways, furnishing such advisors, operating personnel and small craft as may be necessary for quick and effective operation."[101]

The issue concerning the composition and role of U.S. forces to be introduced into South Vietnam was resolved on 11 November, when Secretary of Defense McNamara and Secretary of State Rusk concurred with the recommendations of the Taylor mission. Although a decision to act on the report was not formalized until its promulgation as National Security Action Memorandum (NSAM) 111 on 22 November, the concurrence of his principal advisors led President Kennedy to take preparatory action. On 14 November, he directed Ambassador Nolting to inform President Diem that the United States was "prepared to join the

---

[99] *U.S.-V.N. Relations*, bk. 2, pt. IVB.1, p. 102. See also *Ibid.*, pp. 100-01, 110; memos, OP-06 to OP-60, ser BM0001161-61 of 8 Nov 1961; OP-60 to CNO, ser BM001168-61 of 9 Nov.

[100] *U.S.-V.N. Relations*, bk. 2, pt. IVB.1, pp. 96-97. See also CINCPAC, Command History, 1961, pp. 188-89; msgs, CHMAAGVN 130825Z Oct 1961; AMEMB Saigon 260330Z.

[101] *U.S.-V.N. Relations*, bk. 11, p. 400. See also *Ibid.*, pp. 359-66, 400-05, 419-21; msg, Naval Communications Station, Washington 160745Z Nov 1961; JCS, *History*, pt. 1, pp. 3-5—3-9.

Government of Viet-Nam in a sharply increased joint effort to avoid a further deterioration in the situation in South Vietnam and eventually to contain and eliminate the threat to its independence."[102]

Many factors contributed to President Kennedy's decision to limit the United States to an expanded supporting role. One was the danger that the Berlin crisis would lead to an armed confrontation in Europe which would command priority attention. The JCS repeatedly informed the President that a simultaneous commitment of U.S. ground, air, and naval forces to both Southeast Asia and Europe would require mobilization of additional U.S. reserves, with all of the political and military ramifications of such a move. On the other hand, the deployment of U.S. support forces would signal American resolve, while at the same time allowing the South Vietnamese to fight their own war. This step also was less likely to damage the precarious Laos negotiations or to provoke overt Communist attack.

In other respects, a limited U.S. response was in keeping with the flexible response concept of the Kennedy administration, in view of the relatively modest force of Viet Cong guerrillas. The measure also was consistent with the President's evolving counterinsurgency theories that placed great emphasis on preparing and motivating indigenous populations to deal with the Communist insurgencies. The war was meant to remain essentially a Vietnamese affair, despite U.S. initiation of a program of "limited partnership."[103]

Thus, the involvement of the Navy and the other U.S. Armed Forces in South Vietnam's anti-Communist struggle increased dramatically during this period. Initially, in 1959, the most serious threat to the existence of Southeast Asia's non-Communist nations, especially South Vietnam, was seen as internal subversion and insurgency. Before 1961, neither the development of counterinsurgency concepts nor the particular nature of the situation in South Vietnam had a major impact on the United States Navy. But the response to Communist insurgency by the Kennedy administration motivated the Navy to give increased attention to its capability to engage in low-level conflict. The Laos and Bay of Pigs crises

---

[102] *U.S.-V.N. Relations*, bk. 11, p. 400. See also *Ibid.* bk. 2, pt. IVB.1, pp. 83, 98, 106; bk. 11, pp. 295, 337, 344; memo, OP-60 to CNO, ser BM0001155-61 of 6 Nov 1961; CINCPAC, Command History, 1961, pp. 24-26.

[103] *U.S.-V.N. Relations*, bk. 2, pt. IVB.1, pp. 133-37; bk. 11, pp. 400-18; JCS, *History*, pt. 1, pp. 3-2—3-12.

accelerated this effort. Thereafter, the Navy took steps to develop specialized SEAL and STAT units and related administrative organizations. South Vietnam would become the testing ground for these forces and the counterinsurgency warfare doctrine in general.

CHAPTER V

U.S. Military Assistance and the Vietnamese Navy

From the end of the French Indochina War in 1954, the Republic of Vietnam received direct U.S. military aid through the U.S. Military Assistance Advisory Group, Vietnam. The MAAG's mission was to support the Vietnamese armed forces so that they could ensure internal security and offer initial resistance to a foreign invasion until the United States or the other SEATO nations came to their assistance.

The Navy Section of the MAAG had the specific task of building up the Vietnamese Navy to conduct antisubmarine warfare (ASW), coastal patrol, and harbor defense against infiltration and minor naval threats. The naval force also was to be prepared to carry out river patrols in support of counterinsurgency operations and to undertake minelaying and minesweeping measures in the country's territorial waters.[1] Admiral Herbert G. Hopwood, the Commander in Chief, U.S. Pacific Fleet, summarized the intended role of Southeast Asian navies, including Vietnam's, in a letter to Admiral Burke in March 1959:

> My basic concept is that the small indigenous navies are not and cannot be expected to become capable of offensive type naval operations other than having a limited capability for their own amphibious lift, local escort and patrol, limited local ASW, local mine warfare, and harbor defense. In short, they should be capable of taking over those local defensive missions which will allow us to keep the Pacific Fleet free, flexible and available to conduct the offensive missions whenever and

---

[1] Memo, OP-60 to CNO, ser 253-63 of 30 Apr 1963. For information on the early years of the Navy Section, see Edwin B. Hooper, Dean C. Allard, and Oscar P. Fitzgerald, *The Setting of the Stage to 1959*, Vol. I in series *The United States Navy and the Vietnam Conflict* (Washington: Naval History Division, 1976).

wherever they are required; thus maintaining the punch to counter local contingency actions while still retaining a ready...posture.²

One of more than fifty U.S. military assistance activities throughout the world, the MAAG in Vietnam formulated the aid program for the Vietnamese, administered deliveries, and advised the recipients on the use of the equipment. The first military aid programs for Greece and Turkey after World War II were planned and implemented by the individual services under the Mutual Security Act of 1947. Subsequent changes in the program soon concentrated more and more responsibility in the hands of the Secretary of Defense. With the establishment of the Office of the Deputy Secretary of Defense for International Security Affairs (ISA) in 1953, that office became the locus for military assistance decisionmaking. By 1959 the services merely provided the hardware and technical advice for programs which were shaped in ISA. The Joint Chiefs of Staff set the overall dollar amounts of military aid for each country and established general policy and force objectives. The MAAG drew up aid proposals and ISA gave final approval to the military part of the aid budget which then was submitted to Congress. The State Department handled economic aid, and although vested with overall responsibility for the entire aid program, generally delegated the details of military aid to the Defense Department.³

In 1958, President Eisenhower appointed a committee headed by William H. Draper, an investment banker, to study the foreign aid program, which had become increasingly controversial. Draper's committee, which included among its members Admiral Arthur W. Radford, former Chairman of the Joint Chiefs of Staff, detailed a number of recommendations for making the system more responsive. Their report was submitted to the President in August 1959. President Eisenhower endorsed the Draper Committee recommendations and by the end of 1960 most of them were implemented.⁴

---

²Ltr, Hopwood to Burke, of 13 Mar 1959. See also CINCPAC, "Material for Discussion with the President's Committee on Military Assistance Programs (Draper Committee)," of 28 Jan 1959; msg, CP 172354Z Apr 1959. For an overview of the U.S. naval advisory effort, see Oscar P. Fitzgerald, "U.S. Naval Forces in the Vietnam War: the Advisory Mission, 1961-1965" in Robert W. Love, Jr., ed., *Changing Interpretations and New Sources in Naval History* (New York: Garland Publishing, 1980).

³Harold A. Hovey, *United States Military Assistance: A Study of Policies and Practices* (New York: Frederick A. Praeger, 1965), pp. 139-41.

⁴Amos A. Jordan, Jr., *Foreign Aid and the Defense of Southeast Asia* (New York: Frederick A. Praeger, 1962), p. 60.

Some of the Draper Committee's ideas were incorporated in the Foreign Military Assistance Act of 1961. The military aid budget, which previously was appropriated separately, became a part of the overall defense budget. This measure was in recognition of the fact that military aid contributed to U.S. security in the same manner as did the armed forces. Long-range planning also was required. Beginning with the Fiscal Year 1962 program, military assistance requirements were projected five years into the future. Planning for the long term was particularly important, because the services had exhausted much of the surplus World War II equipment suitable for aid programs, and longer lead times were necessary to develop new hardware.[5]

The new act also mandated important changes in the administration of the military aid program. Responsibility for overall direction of foreign aid, both military and economic, continued to rest with the State Department. On the military side, however, the 1961 act created a Director of Military Assistance, in the Office of the Assistant Secretary of Defense for International Security Affairs, who could devote full time to the administration of the program. This subordinate office reviewed the program proposals for the Secretary of Defense.

In an attempt to make foreign aid more responsive to the needs of recipients, the task of drawing up the initial military assistance program was transferred from ISA to the unified commanders. CINCPAC, the unified commander for the Pacific theater, directed the MAAGs in his area to put together preliminary lists of these requirements. Working within Defense Department ceilings and JCS guidelines for force levels and objectives, the three service representatives attached to MAAGs in each country balanced priorities to reach agreement on a preliminary program. After approval by the ambassador, the aid requirements then were sent to CINCPAC headquarters in Hawaii where they were put into final form. At that time, Admiral Felt routinely solicited comments from each of the service representatives on his staff before reviewing the proposals himself. He then sent the program on to ISA in Washington, which obtained cost data, information on specific hardware, and delivery schedules from each of the military departments. After final approval by

---

[5]The U.S. President's Committee to Study the United States Military Assistance Program, *Composite Report* (Washington: the Committee, 1959) (Draper Report).

U.S. Organizational Structure for Military Assistance

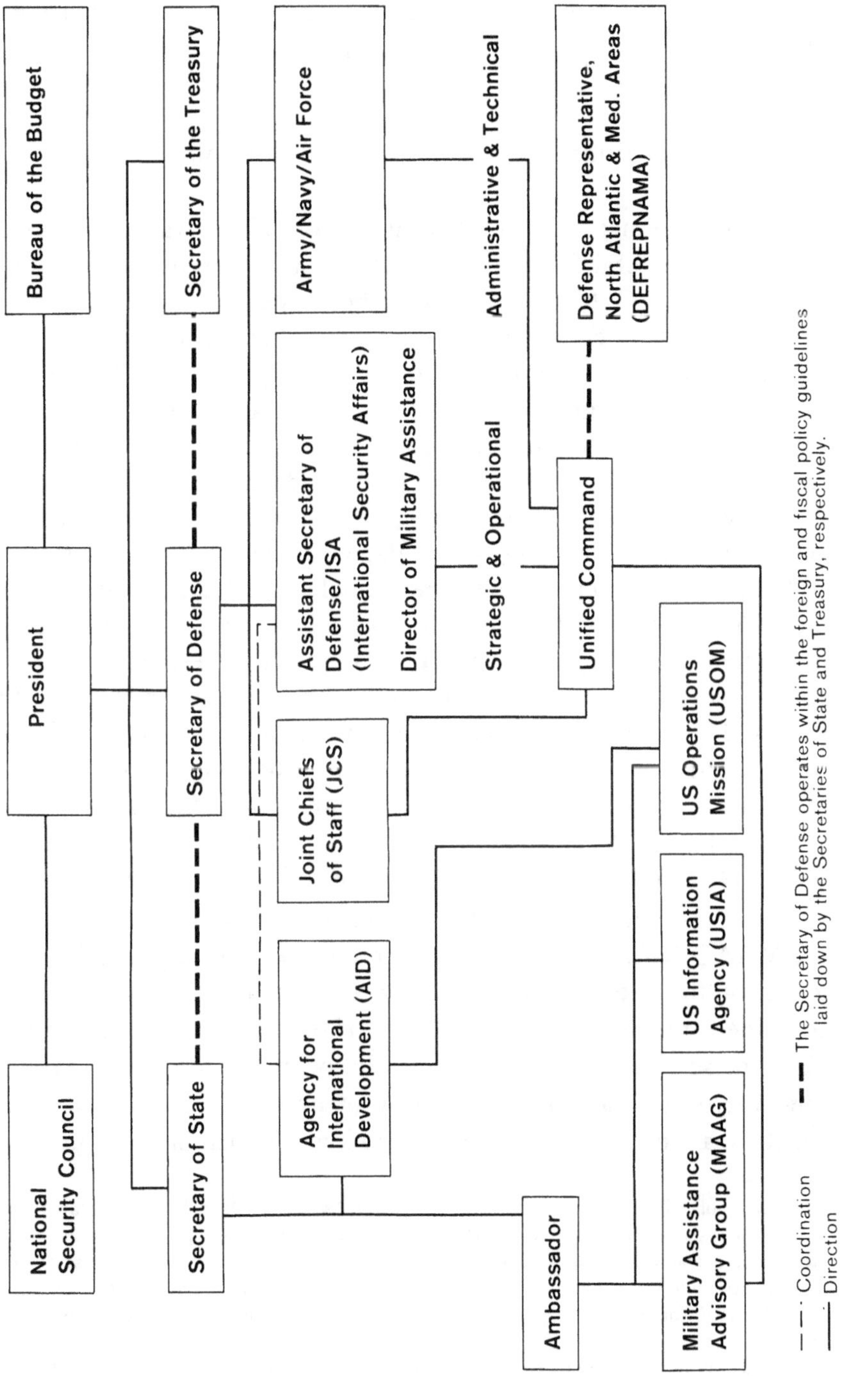

ISA and the Joint Chiefs, and concurrence by the State Department, the Military Assistance Program was submitted to Congress.[6]

The Military Assistance Advisory Group, Vietnam

MAAG Vietnam at the beginning of 1959 was commanded by Lieutenant General Samuel T. Williams. He was relieved by Lieutenant General Lionel C. McGarr in September 1960. Captain John J. Flachsenhar commanded the twenty-six-man Navy Section of the MAAG until Captain Henry M. Easterling relieved him in July 1960. The small naval staff, including a senior Marine advisor, could do little more than process aid requests from the Vietnamese and draw up their navy's portion of the aid program. What actual advising they did accomplish was primarily at the Naval School at Nha Trang, where instruction concentrated on electronics, gunnery, navigation, damage control, and engineering. In addition to these men, 14 naval personnel and 2 Marines were assigned to the MAAG headquarters. Another 22 men served with the Temporary Equipment Recovery Mission (TERM), which was established in 1956 to salvage surplus American equipment left in Vietnam by the French. Finally, 15 individuals worked in an administrative section. In all, 79 naval officers and men, representing 9 percent of the roughly 700 U.S. military in Vietnam, were in-country at the beginning of 1959. Their number was commensurate with the Navy's 12 to 14 percent share of the overall MAP budget and was typical of most MAAGs around the world.[7]

Both President Diem and U.S. officials in Saigon wanted an increase in the MAAG staff, maintaining that the legal strength of the MAAG under terms of the Geneva Agreement could be as high as 888 men, the combined number of French and U.S. advisors working with the Vietnamese at the end of the French Indochina War in 1954. U.S. policy, however, was to adhere to a ceiling of under 350 men in the MAAG, which was the number of U.S. advisors in Vietnam at the signing of the

---

[6]Director of Military Assistance, DOD, "Military Assistance Manual," of 15 May 1960; DOD, "Military Assistance Facts," of 1 May 1966; Joseph B. Drachnik, transcript of interview with Oscar P. Fitzgerald, Naval Historical Center, in Sacramento, CA, 25 Jan 1978; Malcolm C. Friedman, transcript of interview with Oscar P. Fitzgerald, Naval Historical Center, in Sunnyvale, CA, 24 Jan 1978; USAF, "The Journal of Military Assistance," Sep 1961, Office of Air Force History, pp. 200-09.

[7]NA Saigon, reports, 5-59 of 12 Jan 1959; 5-60 of 12 Jan 1960; memo, OP-63 to CNO, ser 0222-63 of 25 Oct 1963; CNO, Joint Table of Distribution MAAG Vietnam, of 1 Jul 1959.

Geneva Agreement. In November 1959, the South Vietnamese government notified the International Control Commission (ICC), set up to oversee implementation of the Geneva Agreement of 1954, that TERM would complete its mission by 31 December 1960. On 19 April 1960, the ICC agreed to an increase in the MAAG to 685 men, which was about the size of the MAAG and TERM combined. Ambassador Eldridge Durbrow in Saigon called the ICC action the "most stunning diplomatic defeat suffered by DRV under Geneva Agreements for Viet-Nam."[8]

The phaseout of the TERM began immediately and its personnel were absorbed by the MAAG. The disestablishment of TERM ended the fiction that the group was only recovering obsolete equipment. In fact, advising the Vietnamese on logistic problems had been its primary role since formal activation in 1956. After the reorganization, which was completed by the beginning of 1961, naval members of the MAAG totaled twenty-nine officers and thirty-four enlisted men, approximately the same number as in the combined MAAG and TERM before the merger.

Despite the expansion of the group, General Williams believed that the MAAG "should and can work itself 'out of [a] job' with possible reduction [by] approximately 15% in June 1961 and approximately 20% reduction yearly thereafter."[9] These reductions, however, were not possible. Instead, in May 1961, as part of the Presidential Program, Washington authorized an expansion in the MAAG by 100 men, including 12 for the Navy. The additional naval personnel were to advise the newly established Coastal Force. This decision, the first to increase the number of U.S. advisors beyond the total authorized at Geneva, initiated a long series of increases in U.S. military force levels in Vietnam.[10]

The Vietnamese Navy

At the beginning of 1959, the Vietnamese Navy was a modest force in comparison with the other services in the RVNAF. 5,100 men (1,500 of

---

[8]NA Saigon, Joint Weekly Analysis, 17 of 23 Apr 1960. Canada and India voted in favor of the expansion and Poland against. See Anita Lauve, *The Origins and Operations of the International Control Commission in Laos and Vietnam*, Rand study RM-2967 (Santa Monica, CA: Rand Corp., 1962), pp. 85-88.

[9]Quoted in *U.S.-V.N. Relations*, bk. 2, pt. IVA.5, tab 4, p. 81.

[10]Msg, CHMAAG Saigon 200711Z May 1960; memos, ISA to SECARM, of 12 Mar 1960; Chief of Staff, MAAGVN to All Division Chiefs and Chief TERM, of 4 Apr 1960; MAAGVN, General Order No. 24 of 1 Jun 1960; CINCPAC, Command History, 1961, pp. 174-75; *U.S.-V.N. Relations*, bk. 2, pt. IVB.1, p. 29.

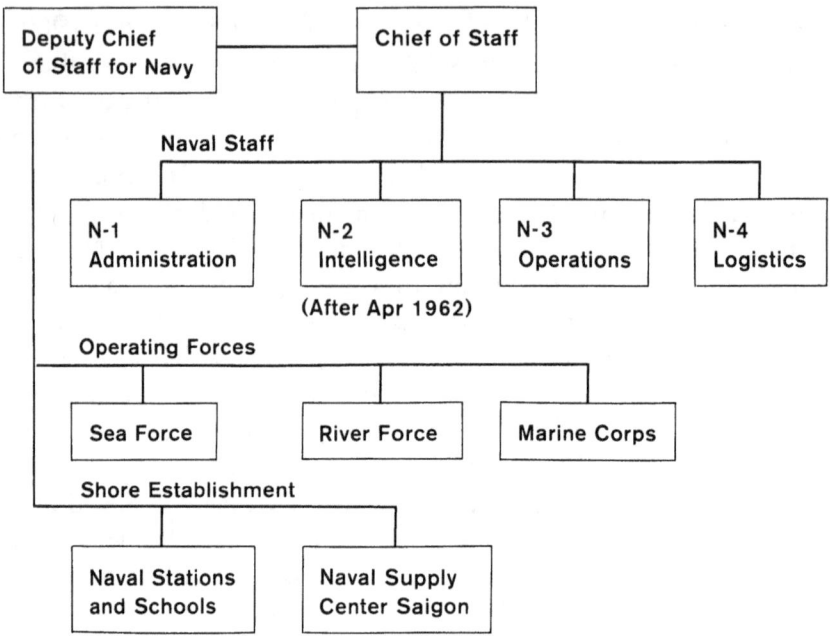

whom were marines) were assigned to the service. The navy's two major combat components were the Sea Force and the River Force, which operated a total of 119 ships, boats, and landing craft of various types. The largest vessels were 5 173-foot submarine chasers (PC).

The Vietnamese Navy was led by the Deputy Chief of Staff for the Navy, who in early 1959 was Commander Tran Van Chon. He served under the Chief of the General Staff of the Vietnamese armed forces. The chain of command then extended to the Secretary of State for National Defense and finally to President Diem. The naval head was not a member of the Joint General Staff, which was composed entirely of army officers. Thus, the navy had little influence in the high-level military decisionmaking process. The small role played by the navy partly reflected the fact that the maritime service then comprised only 3.4 percent of the armed forces' authorized personnel strength of 150,000 men.

To assist the Naval Deputy in his command function, a Chief of Staff coordinated the work of the Naval Staff, which consisted of Administration (N-1), Operations (N-3), and Logistics (N-4) Departments. The Naval Deputy exercised direct control of the operating forces and shore establishments, which comprised the Sea Force, River Force, Marine Corps, Naval Supply Center, Saigon, and Naval Stations and Schools. The Commander Naval Stations and Schools, headquartered in Saigon, in addition to overseeing all training, exercised command of the facilities at Danang, Nha Trang, Vung Tau, and An Thoi. Each of these stations was the headquarters of a coastal district command, from the 1st Coastal District in the north to the 4th Coastal District in the Gulf of Siam. The coastal district commander controlled all naval forces operating within his section of coastline, both afloat and ashore.[11]

During the period from 1959 to 1961, the navy experienced modest growth. As part of the Presidential Program of May 1961, the United States agreed to support an additional 20,000 men in the Vietnamese armed forces, 200 of whom would be sailors. Shortly afterwards, however, President Diem requested that support for an overall figure of 270,000 men be provided. Stepped-up Communist activity in Laos and South Vietnam that year gravely concerned Diem. The Kennedy administration shared his apprehension, but felt a total force of 200,000 men would be adequate. In August this latter force level was approved. By the end of 1961, the Vietnamese Navy's personnel numbered 4,497, of an authorized strength of 5,712.[12]

During this time, a number of newer ships were provided. The United States turned over to the South Vietnamese 1 PC, 1 PCE, 1 LSM (landing ship, medium), and 3 MSCs. Only the latter three ships were of recent construction. The others were built in World War II. However, these vessels replaced less capable units that had been retired from the active list. While the Vietnamese fleet did not increase in number, the newer ships were a qualitative improvement.

The one-for-one replacement process was stipulated in the Geneva Agreement and U.S. naval advisors were not displeased with this restriction. A survey of long-range military assistance requirements,

---

[11]CIA, National Intelligence Survey, "South Vietnam, Armed Forces," 1959, pp. 2, 31-32.
[12]NA Saigon, reports, 20-S-60 of 21 Sep 1960; 32-S-60 of 23 Dec 1960; *U.S.-V.N. Relations*, bk. 2, pt. IVB.1, pp. 29-30, 59-60.

completed in October 1960, concluded that the South Vietnamese did not have the ability to absorb great increases in strength. The U.S. Naval Attache noted at the end of 1961 that the problem did not appear to be the need for additional equipment and material but more efficient organization and use of available resources.[13]

Admiral Felt expressed a similar assessment during the visit of Nguyen Dinh Thuan to his headquarters in Hawaii on 1 April 1960. Thuan, the Secretary of State for National Defense, requested a step-up in the delivery of ships scheduled over the next five years. Admiral Felt did not agree, however, because he reasoned that the existing rate of delivery was based on the limited Vietnamese ability to man and operate the ships. He also believed that the Vietnamese could make better use of the equipment they already possessed. For example, the admiral suggested that with some additional effort the number of ships on coastal patrol could be increased from an average of seven to eleven or twelve.[14]

Small Boats for the Delta

At the same time, the Vietnamese also requested special craft to operate on the flooded plains of the Mekong Delta. General Duong Van Minh, commander of the Army Field Command, sent a list of these requirements to Washington, prior to his visit in April 1960, which included the request for a swamp boat with a large propeller. It would be used by the army to lift troops into flooded Mekong Delta areas, particularly in the Plain of Reeds west of Saigon and in the U Minh Forest area on the southwest coast. In addition to shallow water, boats also had to contend with weeds and grass which choked the flood plains. The need for such a boat became apparent in 1960 when the Viet Cong, using small motorized sampans, outmaneuvered a larger army force and defeated it soundly. The government troops could not pole their own sampans fast enough to evade the enemy nor effectively fire from their boats. The requirement for a shallow-draft boat was passed to the Bureau of Ships, and in the spring of 1960 the Landing Craft, Amphibious Boats Section recom-

---

[13] NA Saigon, report, 87-59 of 16 Apr 1959; Naval Ship Systems Command, Military Assistance Program Ship and Craft Summary, Vol. I of 15 Oct 1966; NA Saigon, report, 23-S-60 of 9 Nov 1960.
[14] Msg, CP 020430Z Apr 1960.

mended a nineteen-foot rescue boat, with aircraft engines and propellers similar to those used on boats in the Florida Everglades.

At a meeting between Admiral Burke and Secretary Thuan, during the latter's visit to Washington in April 1960, the two discussed both the rescue boat and a turbo-powered boat to fill Vietnamese requirements. Subsequently, two of each of these craft were added to the Military Assistance Program and sent to Vietnam. The MAAG tested the boats, but in April 1961 reported that they were unsatisfactory. The turbo craft, although possessing good speed and shallow-draft characteristics, was deemed unsuitable because it was not sufficiently maneuverable and its water jets clogged easily. The air boats also were ill-suited for use in Vietnam and William H. Godel of the Advanced Research Projects Agency in the Department of Defense stated why:

> The continued insertion of standard American weaponry and standard American logistics over-complicates the maintenance and support problem and consumes an inordinate amount of time of the American personnel.... There is, for example, no reason to introduce U.S. made air-boats into the Viet Nam fighting. These items are expensive, noisy, hard to maintain, and identify the rider to all Viet Cong who hear or see him for 100 miles around as an enemy to be shot on sight.[15]

The subject of boats for the delta was raised again in a second visit to Washington by Mr. Thuan in April 1961. In a conference with Admiral Burke, Thuan observed that the craft which the U.S. had sent to Vietnam were indeed unsatisfactory. After the meeting, Admiral Burke asked the Bureau of Ships to expedite the analysis of more suitable shallow-draft boats for Vietnam. "If we take too long on this study and evaluation," he said, "their country may fall. An effective picket boat might mean the difference between success and failure of Viet-Nam."[16]

During the spring and summer, several other types of boats were considered. Captain Easterling suggested reevaluation of the Wizard, a twenty-foot, fiberglass runabout powered by a twenty-five-horsepower outboard engine. The United States provided the Vietnamese 300 of these craft at the end of the French Indochina War. Since then they had remained in storage at the Saigon Naval Shipyard. The Vietnamese Army

---

[15]Memo, Director, Policy and Planning Div. to ISA, of 15 Sep 1960.
[16]Memo, CNO to OP-04, ser 0224-61 of 23 Apr 1961.

declined Easterling's proposal because it sought a boat capable of speeds greater than the Wizard's maximum of 6 to 8 knots.

On the other hand, the Zodiac boat, a French-made inflatable craft with an outboard engine, was deemed eminently suitable. At the end of 1961, 125 of these boats were ordered for delivery. Another shallow-water craft finally adopted was the swimmer support boat. The thirteen-foot, fiberglass craft was powered by a forty-horsepower engine. By August 1962, 222 of the boats, constructed both in the United States and Saigon, operated in the delta.[17]

The Leadership Problem

Of the many problems that beset the fledgling Vietnamese Navy during the period from 1959 to 1961, perhaps the most debilitating was the lack of sound leadership. It was a prime concern to U.S. naval observers. The U.S. Naval Attache in Saigon explained: "As in the past, the main shortcoming seems to be weak leadership down the line, caused by inexperience and a lack of 'espirit de corps.'"[18] His diagnosis was not surprising, in view of the fact that the French did not relinquish their control over the Vietnamese Navy until 1955, and most of its officers, even the senior men, were only in their early thirties.

Compounding the lack of experience was the instability at the top of the naval command caused in large part by political intrigue. On 6 August 1959, Commander Ho Tan Quyen, then thirty-one years old, replaced Commander Chon as Acting Naval Deputy, when the latter departed for the U.S. Naval War College at Newport, Rhode Island. Many U.S. officers hoped that Lieutenant Commander Lam Nguon Tanh, who impressed them with his leadership ability, would get the job upon his return from the General Line School at Monterey, California. But political

---

[17]MAAG Indochina, Monthly Activity Reports, Jun, Jul, Aug 1954; CINCPAC, Command History, 1961, pp. 183, 194; ISA, "Briefing Book for Visit to U.S. by Sec State for the Presidency, Nguyen Dinh Thuan, on 5-6 Apr 1960;" *U.S.-V.N. Relations*, bk. 2, p. 388; memos, OP-63 to CNO, ser 00142-60 of 5 Apr 1960; OP-04 to CNO, ser 00237-414 of 21 Jun 1961; Burke/Townley/Gatacre Conversation, of 18 May 1961; memo, OP-06 to JCS, ser 001051P60 of 1 Nov 1961; msgs, CHMAAGVN 150725Z Sep; 240801Z Oct; 240935Z; 010341Z Nov; 280257Z Aug 1962; BUSHIPS 262232Z Oct 1961; 062140Z Nov; 022201Z Jan 1962.

[18]NA Saigon, report, 23-S-60 of 9 Nov 1960. See also ltr, CINCPAC to CINCPACFLT, ser 00171 of 16 Feb 1963.

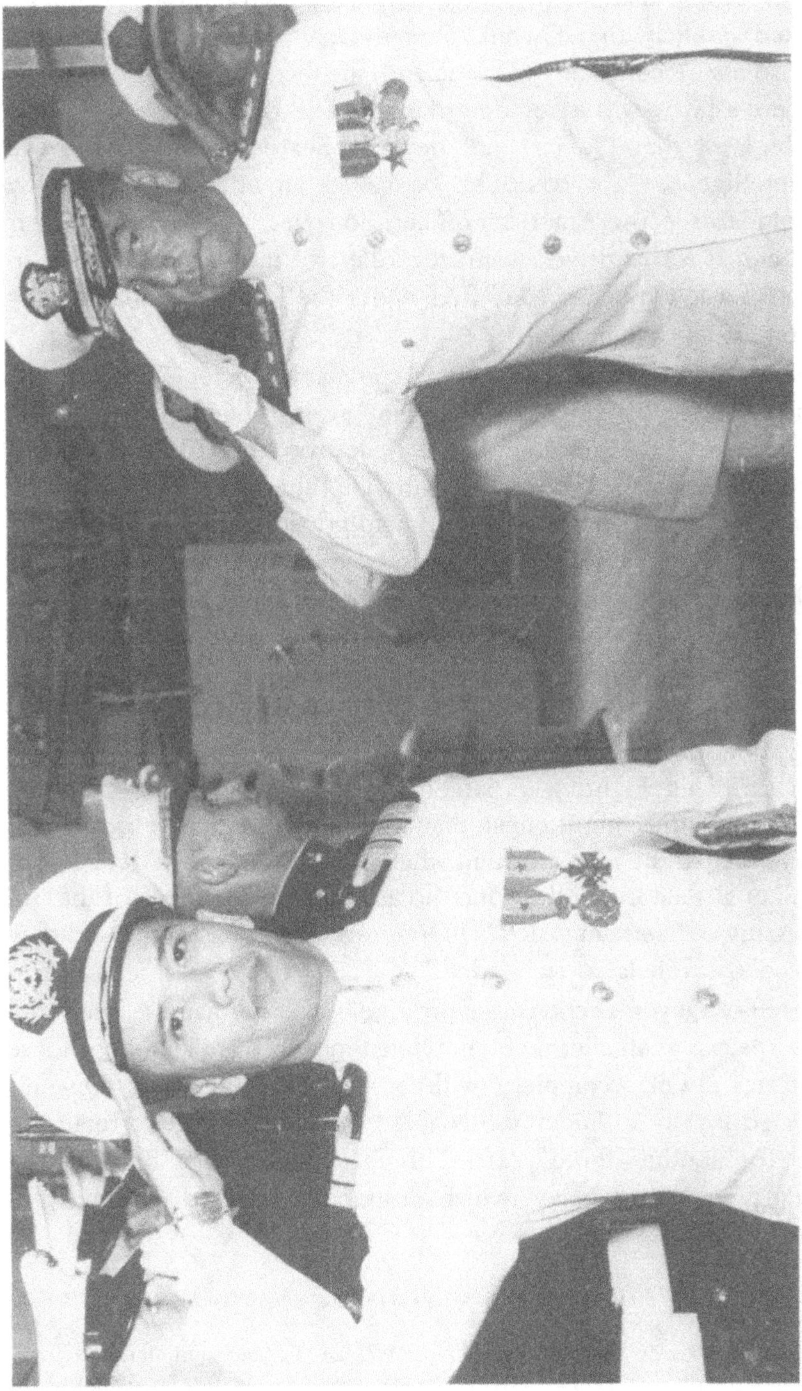

NH-94339

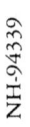

Commander Ho Tan Quyen, Acting Naval Deputy of the Vietnamese Navy, and Rear Admiral Alfred G. Ward, Commander Cruiser Division 1, on board heavy cruiser Toledo *(CA-133) during the ship's visit to Saigon on 26 October 1959.*

connections rather than ability often influenced promotion. Although Diem stated publicly that Quyen, then the navy's Chief of Staff, was appointed to assure continuity of command, the fact that the officer was in the president's favor was a key determinant. The U.S. Naval Attache in Saigon observed that Quyen "has never appeared to be [of] above average intelligence, nor could he be called an educated person by western standards." The American officer, however, was hopeful: "He is a worker, and it is this drive which, regardless of the purpose behind it, will touch off a few much-needed fires under the local navy and thereby effect various improvements."[19]

Little more than a year after assuming command, Quyen's position was solidified as the result of a coup attempt against Diem. In the early morning hours of 11 November 1960, a paratroop brigade commanded by Lieutenant Colonel Nguyen Chanh Thi attempted to storm the Presidential Palace and overthrow the Diem government. As soon as the attack began, Commander Quyen ordered two marine companies to defend the palace and hurried there himself. His actions probably saved the government by giving the president time to rally his forces.

In the meantime, elements of the Seventh Fleet, which had been assembled in readiness to respond to developments in Laos, speedily concentrated off the South Vietnamese coast prepared to evacuate American nationals. Fighting in Saigon was temporarily halted at noon. Negotiations with the rebels began that afternoon. A tentative agreement was hardly reached the next morning when the fighting broke out again at the Presidential Palace. By this time, however, loyal elements of the 5th and 21st Army of Vietnam (ARVN) Divisions arrived in Saigon and they soon forced the rebels to surrender.[20]

As a result of Quyen's actions, the prestige of the Vietnamese Navy and Marine Corps was at an all-time high. Quyen moved from a modest house in Saigon to a villa, complete with a sentry at the gate. Quyen's demonstrated loyalty to Diem also enabled the naval officer to retain his command for another three years. This fact alone was a boon to the developing Vietnamese Navy, which desperately needed continuity of command.

---

[19]NA Saigon, report, 204-59 of 19 Aug 1959. See also NA Saigon, Joint Weekly Analysis, 29 of 18 Jul.
[20]NA Saigon, Joint Weekly Analysis, 47 of 10 Nov 1960; USAF, "Journal of Mutual Security," Dec 1960, Office of Air Force History, p. 149; Spector, *Advice and Support*, pp. 369-71.

Material and Maintenance Shortcomings

The effect of leadership on material readiness was clearly revealed in the Vietnamese Navy. An evaluation in the spring of 1959 of ships in the Sea Force indicated that only four were even in fair material condition. In the River Force, fully half the vessels were down for repairs. Routine inspection reports by U.S. advisors at the end of 1959 on ships turned over to the Vietnamese highlighted the maintenance problem. The evaluations ranged from an overall very satisfactory to unsatisfactory. The inspecting officer of *Long Dao* (HQ-327), an LSIL built in 1944, noted that "the officers and men have pride in their ship and are showing an effort to make it one of the best in the fleet."[21] *Ham Tu II* (HQ-114), commanded by Lieutenant Commander Chung Tan Cang, a future head of the Vietnamese Navy, also received a superior rating. The newly built MSC was transferred to the Vietnamese in July 1959. The crew took pride in the ship and worked to keep it in the same condition as when it was received. At the other extreme was *Ninh Giang* (HQ-403), an LSM built in 1944 which saw heavy service during the French Indochina War and was turned over to the Vietnamese in 1956. "The overall condition of the ship is deplorable," read the report. "There is evidence of neglect throughout the ship's interior as well as exterior." Rust and dirt were everywhere, and some topside fixtures were corroded completely because of years of neglect. In one case, the cord to a fan was missing a plug and the bare wires were inserted directly into a socket.[22]

Lack of knowledge, initiative, and supervision on the part of many Vietnamese naval officers certainly contributed to the problem, but the poor material condition of the ships, most of which already were suffering from old age when the Vietnamese received them, discouraged all but the most diligent officers. Thus, the aid program often created excessive maintenance problems for the recipient nation. A report on *Tuy Dong* (HQ-04), a submarine chaser built in 1944, illustrated the point:

> The hull appears to have lost a lot of strength through years of corrosion. The holes that have [eroded] through have been patched, and at present there are no leaks. The thin sheet iron deck plates in the

---

[21] NA Saigon, report, 14-59 of 19 Jan 1959.
[22] NA Saigon, report, 15-59 of 19 Jan 1959. See also NA Saigon, reports, 113-59 of 9 May 1959; 14-60 of 27 Jan 1960.

144 *United States Navy and Vietnam Conflict*

Vietnamese Navy LSIL Long Dao (HQ-327) patrolling a river in South Vietnam.

various compartments have reached a state where they are dangerous. The securing screws have [eroded] away, plates are warped and buckled, presenting a hazard for men to walk around the compartment in the local type of foot wear.

The PC's commanding officer was Lieutenant Ho Van Ky Thoai, a competent and rising officer in the Vietnamese Navy. The report concluded that despite the deplorable condition of the ship, Lieutenant Thoai was making progress in preventing further deterioration.[23]

In December 1961 a CINCPACFLT survey team, headed by Captain Nathan Sonnenshein, completed its inspection of twenty-two ships and sixty-six boats of the Vietnamese Navy deadlined for repair in Saigon. Of the twenty-two ships, about two-thirds were rated in excellent to satisfactory condition, while the rest were rated unsatisfactory. The team found definite improvement, compared to similar inspections eight months earlier, in the material readiness of the ships. The group also was impressed with their cleanliness. The survey found that newer ships received more maintenance attention than the older vessels. Much of the improvement was credited to the efforts of the American naval advisors.[24]

Despite some progress in accomplishing routine shipboard maintenance, most Vietnamese commanders continued to rely almost exclusively on the shipyard. Until 1959 all major overhauls were performed by the U.S. Navy at Subic Bay. Thereafter, the Saigon Naval Shipyard began to do most of the major repair work for the Vietnamese Navy.

The Saigon Naval Shipyard was the largest of its type in Southeast Asia, with the exception of the facilities in Singapore. The yard had existed at its location on the Saigon waterfront since the mid-19th century, when France established its Arsenal there for support of the Far Eastern Fleet. By the early 1960s, it was the largest industrial plant in South Vietnam, with eighty-seven concrete buildings, consisting of a foundry, boat repair, structural, carpenter, instrument, diesel engine, ordnance, electronics, electrical, and machine shops, warehouses, and administrative offices. In addition, the fifty-three-acre site contained a 520-foot graving dock, a 119-foot graving dock, a 1,000-ton-capacity floating drydock, and four

---

[23]NA Saigon, report, 103-60 of 14 May 1960. See also NA Saigon, report, 20-59 of 24 Jan 1959; NAG, Staff Study, "Naval Craft Requirements in a Counterinsurgency Environment," of 1 Feb 1965; Ho Van Ky Thoai, transcript of interview with Oscar P. Fitzgerald, Naval Historical Center, in Washington, DC, 21 Sep 1975.
[24]Msgs, CHMAAGVN 120917Z Dec 1961; CP 130506Z.

marine railways. These facilities and their seven mobile, gantry, and floating cranes enabled the shipyard to service all but the largest ships.[25]

Since command of the Saigon Naval Shipyard was one of the most desirable positions in the Vietnamese Navy, top Vietnamese naval officers were assigned to the billet. Nevertheless, poor planning and supervision by the lower echelons resulted in long delays in scheduled overhauls. For example, the submarine chaser *Chi Lang* (HQ-01) spent twenty-one months in the yard but still had work to be done after she was released at the end of 1959.[26] To alleviate the backlog, some overhauls continued to be scheduled for the U.S. Naval Ship Repair Facility, Subic Bay. This was the case with six LCMs transported from Saigon on board USNS *Core* (T-AKV-41) in mid-December 1961. A proposal to station one of three Seventh Fleet repair ships at Saigon, however, was rejected. A survey team of the U.S. Navy found that such a ship would use only 20 percent of its capacity due to the type of work required on the relatively small Vietnamese ships. On the other hand, U.S. naval officers were confident that an increase in the number of advisors from five to seventeen at the shipyard would enable the Vietnamese to rectify the situation.[27]

Training

One long-term solution to the leadership and maintenance problems in the Vietnamese Navy was better training. The principal training center of the naval service was based at Nha Trang. Here Lieutenant Commander Bang Cao Thang, at the beginning of 1959, commanded a staff of 14 officers and 204 enlisted men. Advising him was a detachment of three American naval officers and six men. The Nha Trang facility included a recruit school, Class A schools offering specialized classes, and the Vietnamese Naval Academy. As one example, a recruit class of 103 students completed their four weeks of basic training in March 1959 and the graduates were assigned to Class A schools in such specialties as engineering, communications, clerical work, electronics, seamanship, damage control, and logistics. These schools lasted from one to six weeks.

---

[25]CINCPACFLT, report, ser 73/0023 of 9 Jan 1962.
[26]NA Saigon, report, 12-60 of 27 Jan 1960; LeRoy R. Hagey, Jr., End of Tour Report, of 30 Mar 1965.
[27]Msgs, CP 030625Z Dec 1961; CPFLT 040508Z.

When the Naval Academy's eighth class of forty-five midshipmen graduated on 2 April 1960, the Vietnamese pointed with pride to the fact that this class was the first to be completely trained by Vietnamese instructors.[28]

Training was not exclusive to the classroom. Off Vung Tau between 22 and 24 July 1959, for example, two submarine chasers conducted underway training, which included gunnery, shipboard drills, and battle problems. The embarked U.S. naval advisors observed the operation and offered suggestions on improving procedures, particularly damage control and gunfire techniques.[29]

Formal training at Nha Trang and operational exercises by the River and Sea Forces was augmented by training of Vietnamese naval personnel in the United States. During Fiscal Year 1960, forty Vietnamese officers and sixty enlisted men received such instruction. Officers were sent to both the Naval War College in Newport, Rhode Island, and to the Naval Postgraduate School in Monterey, California. The Fiscal Year 1961 Military Assistance Program called for the training of 406 men of the Vietnamese Navy at facilities in the United States. In addition, the MAAG requested training of Vietnamese on board Seventh Fleet ships for short periods of time. The proposal was approved and implemented in the Fiscal Year 1961 aid program. Some of the best instruction was received by Vietnamese crews who picked up new ships in the United States and sailed them to South Vietnam.

In early May 1961, Commander Quyen proposed that Vietnamese naval officers be sent to five European countries, Japan, Canada, and Australia, in addition to the United States. He criticized instruction given to his officers in American schools as too basic and limited to data on equipment currently in the Vietnamese Navy. Instead, the commander suggested that his naval officers receive training in shipbuilding, engine manufacturing, metalwork, hydrography, atomic propulsion, and weapons manufacturing in order to make the Vietnamese Navy self-sufficient and free of U.S. control. The U.S. Naval Attache in Saigon concluded, however, that such a goal was beyond the technical and industrial capability of the Vietnamese at that time. Furthermore, the attache

---

[28]NA Saigon, report, 52-59 of 27 Feb 1959; Le Ba Thang, transcript of interview with Oscar P. Fitzgerald, Naval Historical Center, in Arlington, VA, 19 Sep 1975, pp. 1-4.
[29]NA Saigon, report, 192-59 of 31 Jul 1959.

believed that Quyen was using the plan to attract the favorable attention of his superiors. In the end, the unrealistic nature of the program doomed it to rejection by the Vietnamese Department of State for National Defense. Consequently, only one officer received training in a country other than the United States through 1961.[30]

Another Quyen proposal was for the establishment of a UDT capability within the Vietnamese Navy to improve protection for ships, piers, and bridges. U.S. naval advisors initially recommended against the idea because they believed the Vietnamese Marine Corps was charged with that responsibility. Later in 1960, however, the Vietnamese turned to Taiwan for UDT training. The Vietnamese naval officer and seven men who completed this course subsequently formed the nucleus of the *Lien Doc Nguoi Nhia* (LDNN), or literally, "soldiers who fight under the sea." This Vietnamese underwater demolition unit was formally established in July 1961. The naval force was authorized forty-eight officers and men and given the mission of removing underwater obstacles, protecting military ports, and mounting special operations in waterways.[31]

The River Force

As with this training, the operations of the Vietnamese Navy were oriented toward accomplishment of its dual mission of defending the country against overt external aggression and maintaining internal security. Because the first responsibility had top priority before 1959, the River Force, primarily operating on inland waterways, was not the favored branch of the service. As the U.S. Naval Attache explained in 1959, "they play a definite second fiddle to the sea forces," which steamed along the coast and out to sea.[32] With the increase of Viet Cong activity in 1959 and 1960, however, U.S. and Vietnamese naval officers devoted greater attention to the River Force.

---

[30]Ltrs, Williams to Burke, of 11 May 1960; Hopwood to Burke, of 24 May; Griffin to Hopwood, of 31 May; Hopwood to Burke, of 9 Jun; Burke to Hopwood, of 18 Jun; CINCPACFLT to CINCPAC, ser 61-00740 of 26 Aug; Bang Cao Thang, transcript of interview with Oscar P. Fitzgerald, Naval Historical Center, in Arlington, VA, 21 Aug 1975, pp. 4-7; Ho Van Ky Thoai, Interview.

[31]Peter W. Willits, End of Tour Report, of 29 Feb 1964; Nguyen Van Duc, transcript of interview with Oscar P. Fitzgerald, Naval Historical Center, in Hayfield, VA, 4 Dec 1976, pp. 2-3.

[32]NA Saigon, report, 113-59 of 9 May 1959. See also ONI, "Report from Vietnam," *ONI Review* (Oct 1962), pp. 437-39.

This Communist guerrilla activity was concentrated in the Mekong Delta region of South Vietnam, the most populous part of the country. In mid-1959, President Diem described the southern provinces as "in a state of siege."[33] The MAAG agreed with the South Vietnamese conclusion that the situation in the delta was worse than it had been in 1954 or 1955. It also was evident that the Vietnamese Navy's River Force, which patrolled the waterways, and transported troops and supplies, had a critical role to play in restoring security to the area. Because few roads traversed the area, the 1,500 miles of waterway was the most important network for travel and commerce.

From his headquarters, recently moved from Saigon to the delta city of Can Tho, the River Force commander in 1959 controlled ninety-six boats and craft, organized into five river assault groups (RAGs). Each RAG could support a battalion in the field for up to fourteen days. The river assault groups, each containing approximately 2 officers and 100 men, were located at My Tho, Vinh Long, Saigon, Can Tho, and Long Xuyen. The RAGs rotated between one month of operations and one month of training. During the training period, an Underway Training Group of six officers and fourteen enlisted men from Saigon offered lectures and specialized instruction. The remainder of the training period was spent in overhauling boats.[34]

Individual RAGs operated nineteen boats, mostly modified World War II U.S. landing craft. In each RAG one commandament, an LCM-6 with the bow ramp replaced by a pointed steel prow, served as a command ship and provided communications and gunfire support during operations. The RAGs also contained one monitor, which was similar to the commandament but possessed more firepower. Its armament included one 40-millimeter cannon, two 20-millimeter cannons, one 50-caliber machine gun, and an 81-millimeter mortar. The troops and supplies were carried by five LCMs and twelve LCVPs and STCANs. Only the highly maneuverable STCAN, left over from the French era, was especially designed for river operations.[35]

---

[33] NA Saigon, report, 18-S-59 of 7 Aug 1959.

[34] NA Saigon, report, 113-59 of 9 May 1959.

[35] The STCAN also was called a vedette, the French equivalent of a patrol boat. The boat also was known as a FOM, which is the French acronym for the French shipbuilding company which designed and built the craft. Richard T. Gray et al., "Revolutionary Warfare on Inland Waterways: An Exploratory Analysis," Naval Ordnance Test Station, China Lake, California, Jan 1965, pp. 228-40.

The main operational area of the River Force was the Mekong Delta where the RAGs and the four battalions of the Vietnamese Marine Corps sought out the enemy. At one time during 1959, for example, 6 LCMs, 4 LCVPs, 2 vedettes and several marine ground units conducted assaults in An Xuyen Province. Another 2 LCMs and 2 LCVPs patrolled the Cambodian border region near Chau Doc, while 1 LCM and 2 LCVPs operated on the Tranh Dong River in the Rung Sat swamp below Saigon. At the same time, 2 LCVPs operated near a Vietnamese Army fuel depot upriver from Saigon. Although by 1960 the Marine Corps was assigned to South Vietnam's strategic reserve with the army's airborne formations, individual battalions continued to work with the navy. In addition, the River Force mounted numerous operations with the army. In 1961, for instance, joint army-navy actions numbered twenty-seven.[36]

In October 1960, the River Force assumed the added responsibility for escorting convoys laden with charcoal from Nam Can and rice from Camau, Rach Gia, Chau Doc, and Bac Lieu in the Mekong Delta to Saigon. On occasion, the Viet Cong virtually cut off Saigon from these vital staples. The River Force commander allocated 18 STCANs, 4 LCMs, and 8 LCVPs to a command which became the River Transport Escort Group. The unit escorted an average of six to eight round-trip convoys per month. During 1961, the navy assisted in transporting over one million tons of cargo from the delta. The Communists harassed the convoys a number of times, and in five instances set off mines, but none of the transports suffered appreciable damage that year.

Even before receiving the additional burden of the new convoy support assignment, the River Force suffered from a shortage of personnel to fully man its vessels. In December 1960, the manning level of boats was more than 50 percent below the requirement. For that reason, the combat effectiveness of the River Force was reduced. Commander Quyen recommended a future increase in the navy's total personnel, but in the interim he transferred men from other parts of the navy to the River Force. In 1960, the five river groups were authorized 602 men, but had only 340 on board. By March 1961, primarily through Quyen's efforts, the total rose to 422, which represented some improvement. Admiral Felt discussed the problem with President Diem during CINCPAC's 29 September 1961 visit to Vietnam. Still, in October U.S. advisors reported

---

[36]NA Saigon, reports, 113-59 of 9 May 1959; 23-S-60 of 9 Nov 1960.

that the River Force remained 30 percent under strength.[37]

The River Force was not used to its maximum potential. Naval advisors felt that a shortage of personnel was one explanation for this problem, but there were other reasons as well. Because the army seldom included naval officers in planning for operations, the River Force contingent often was concentrated at the last minute, which limited the number of boats available. The small group employed for the mission was thus more vulnerable to attack by even modest Viet Cong forces. And because only the landing craft, utility (LCU), LSILs, and the LCM monitors and commandaments were equipped with adequate communication equipment, calling for reinforcements sometimes was difficult.

Similarly, the army feared the devastating effect on their units of a successful Viet Cong mining attack. Mining assaults usually followed the tactics used by the enemy during the French Indochina War. A command-detonated mine would stop the lead boat dead in the channel and then the enemy would rake the stalled convoy from the banks of the waterway. The River Force attempted to counter these tactics with crude but effective minesweeping devices, which consisted of grapnels dragged behind LCVPs, or cables strung between two LCVPs, to cut the detonation wires.

No minesweeping precautions were taken on 25 November 1960, however, when an LCM was mined near the village of Hau My in Dinh Tuong Province. This operation began when the army regional commander, without soliciting naval advice, ordered the River Force to transport an army battalion from Tay Ninh to a position on the edge of the Plain of Reeds. About 1800, as the three LCMs, loaded with 150 men each, approached Hau My on the Hai Muoi Tam Canal, an explosion rent the air. Its force lifted the lead LCM out of the water, stove in the bulkheads near the bow ramp, and caved in the roof over the tank deck. The men seated in the tank deck were thrown against the overhead, their gun muzzles punching holes through the wooden planking. Gunfire from both sides of the canal struck the force. The LCMs replied with their 20-millimeter guns. The boats then beached on the left bank and disembarked their troops. More firing came from a strong enemy force 100 meters from the canal. After a ten-minute firefight, the enemy withdrew

---

[37]NA Saigon, report, 20-S-60 of 21 Sep 1960; msg, CHMAAGVN 260347Z Oct 1961; ltr, NAVSEC to CHMAAGVN, ser 001 of 6 Jan 1961; memo, Taylor to Craig, of 24 Oct; Chung Tan Cang, transcript of interview with Oscar P. Fitzgerald, Naval Historical Center, in Arlington, VA, 31 Jul 1975, pp. 42, 46.

and the South Vietnamese counted their casualties. Eight men were killed and twenty-three seriously wounded, mostly by gunfire.[38]

In July 1961 the River Force played a more successful role in the largest and most productive operation against the Communists since 1954. The operation, named Dong Tien, took place in Kien Phong Province in a marshy area of My An District. It was bordered on the north by the Dong Tien Canal, on the south by the Thap Muoi Canal, on the east by the Tu Moi Canal, and on the west by the Mekong River. The area long had been a Viet Cong stronghold. On the morning of 14 July, river craft and army artillery units took up positions along the Thap Muoi and Tu Moi Canals and began blasting enemy camps. During that night other River Force units landed a paratroop battalion along the Dong Tien Canal, and at dawn the troops began to advance south to the village of My Qui. When the surrounded Communists tried to escape north, they ran into the paratroopers. The enemy force finally was crushed in a six-hour battle on the morning of the 16th. The 502nd Viet Cong Battalion and a company from the 504th Battalion sustained 167 men killed, 11 captured, and 85 weapons lost. After the operation, the forces involved returned to Saigon for a hero's welcome. General McGarr, the MAAG chief, later commented:

> The operations in the delta area which were successful were preplanned set-piece operations. Plenty of time was given to their planning and moving into position and tactical surprise together with superiority of force was gained. Even though the planning, movement to contact and actual operations were surprisingly well done, errors were committed which could have caused failure. In these operations, the Viet Cong in some instances were either cooperative enough or forced by encirclement to stand and fight in larger groups against stiff opposition — which is not their tactic. The reorganization of the Armed Forces with the single chain of command and the progress we have made in our training over the past ten months in developing joint operations gave these divisions the capability to fight the set-piece battle.[39]

---

[38] Ltrs, NAVSEC to CHMAAGVN, ser 001 of 6 Jan 1961; CINCPACFLT to CINCPAC, ser 32/00693 of 9 Aug 1963.

[39] *The Times of Viet Nam Magazine*, Vol. III, No. 28 (22 Jul 1961), encl. in NA Saigon, report, 168-61 of 3 Aug 1961. See also NAVSEC Joint Weekly Analysis, 29 of 16 Jul 1960; ltr, McGarr to Lemnitzer, of 12 Oct 1961.

Mekong Delta

The Sea Force

At the beginning of 1959, the Sea Force, headquartered in Saigon, consisted of 5 PCs, 4 LSMs, 7 LSILs or landing support ships, large (LSSL), 3 auxiliary motor minesweepers (YMS), and 1 light cargo ship (AKL). These ships were divided into three groups plus a reserve group, with theoretically one group in upkeep, another in training, and the third in operations. In practice, however, because of delays in overhaul completions and routine upkeep, plus lack of initiative on the part of Sea Force commanders, some two-thirds of the ships were out of commission.

The other ships could barely meet operational commitments, which included six-week patrols by a PC or LSSL/LSIL in the Danang area and an LSSL/LSIL off Phu Quoc. Another ship served six weeks of duty as a training vessel at the Naval School in Nha Trang. The same Underway Training Group which served the River Force also provided training for the crews of two other ships.[40]

The PCs and LSSL/LSILs were the backbone of the patrol force. The 173-foot submarine chaser, with a crew of fifty-four, had a range of over 5,000 miles at a speed of 10 knots. Its armament of one 3-inch/50-caliber gun; one 40-millimeter gun; four 20-millimeter guns; and one 60-millimeter mortar was more than a match for any seaborne infiltrator, and also was effective against shore targets. The shallow draft of both the PC and LSSL/LSIL allowed them to operate close inshore, particularly in the shallow waters of the Gulf of Siam. The 160-foot LSSL/LSIL was capable of carrying sixty to seventy combat-equipped troops and could operate on the rivers of the Mekong Delta, as well as the open sea.

Although the Sea Force concentrated on coastal patrol, it also provided logistic support to garrisons on Phu Quoc Island, transported prisoners and supplies to the military prison on Son Island, and carried marines to garrison the Paracel Islands. In all, during 1961 the Sea Force transported 10,000 men and 5,000 tons of cargo. The navy also assisted the Certeza Surveying Company of the Philippines in a survey of all islands in the Gulf of Siam claimed by the Vietnamese.[41]

Usually the resupply missions were routine, but on 8 August 1961 an operation by *Long Dau* almost ended in disaster. While beached and unloading cargo 300 yards from the Duong Dong Light on Phu Quoc Island, the ship broached in the surf and was driven hard aground. The LSIL listed badly and was completely out of the water at low tide. Following several unsuccessful attempts to pull the ship free with a submarine chaser, a small tug, and other landing craft, the South Vietnamese, on 15 August, requested U.S. help. *Lipan* (ATF-85) and *Reclaimer* (ARS-42) were dispatched to the Gulf of Siam to salvage the LSIL. On 24 August, after thirteen attempts, *Lipan* pulled the vessel off the beach and refloated her.[42]

---

[40]NA Saigon, report, 20-59 of 24 Jan 1959; msg, CPFLT 302026Z Nov 1961.
[41]NA Saigon, report, 23-S-60 of 9 Nov 1960.
[42]SERVPAC, Command History, 1961; msgs, NA Saigon 151150Z Aug 1961; CHMAAGVN 191508Z; CTF73 200056Z; NA Saigon 200500Z.

Most Vietnamese Sea Force operations were uneventful throughout 1959, 1960, and 1961, but operations in the Paracel Islands proved to be an exception. Since 1954 the Vietnamese had maintained a small garrison and weather station on Pattle Island in the Paracel group about 230 miles east of Danang. In 1956 the Chinese Communists, who also claimed the Paracels, established a colony on Woody Island, fifty miles from Pattle. In February 1959, when reports reached Vietnam that the Chinese had sent fishermen to occupy Duncan Island as well, LSSL *No Than* (HQ-225) sallied from Danang to verify the reports. The Vietnamese feared that the Chinese were attempting to assert sovereignty over the islands by colonizing them. Five additional ships plus a company of marines joined *No Than*. The marines landed on Duncan Island and captured thirty-one prisoners, who were transported to Danang for interrogation, and then returned to the Paracels. The Chinese protested sharply, but South Vietnam was determined to press its claim to the islands.[43]

Aside from the psychological and strategic importance of the Paracels, which lay adjacent to the shipping lanes between Southeast Asia and the Far East and Japan, the islands also contained rich deposits of guano fertilizer. Early in 1959 a Vietnamese commercial group made plans to exploit the deposits. In April the navy transported the businessmen to the Paracels to study the feasibility of the venture. The first shipments of guano arrived in South Vietnam by November 1959 in Vietnamese merchant ships.[44]

The main tasks of the Sea Force were interdiction of Communist infiltration from North Vietnam, intracoastal enemy traffic, and smuggling along the 1,200-mile coastline. Communist seaborne movement from the North was the chief worry, and the most difficult to verify. But, periodically, hard evidence of enemy activity was uncovered. In one such instance, in the spring of 1961, a Vietnamese naval vessel on patrol near Danang stopped a suspicious junk. One of the South Vietnamese recognized a man on the junk who had been missing from the local area for some time. Upon questioning, the suspected individual confessed that he and his four fellow sailors were involved in a maritime infiltration effort. Several of the men admitted that they were officers in the North

---

[43] NA Saigon, report, 7-S-59 of 3 Mar 1959; memos, OP-61 to CNO, ser 029P61 of 19 Jan 1959; ser 039P61 of 27 Feb; USAF, "Journal of Mutual Security," May 1959, Office of Air Force History, p. 154.
[44] NA Saigon, reports, 85-59 of 13 Apr 1959; 253-59 of 30 Nov.

Vietnamese People's Army, while the others identified themselves as Viet Cong. Nguyen Chuc, leader of the group, revealed that he had participated in seventeen seaborne missions since June 1959.

Through the testimony of this group and other information, the organization of the Communist maritime infiltration effort became better known. Since 1959, it appeared that the North Vietnamese used two organizations for maritime infiltration into South Vietnam. One was political, being attached to the Lao Dong Party (the Communist Party of North Vietnam), and was in contact with party cadre and intelligence agents in the South. This organization operated about eight three to four-ton sail boats, with five-man crews, which blended in with local fishing junks. Each boat made about one trip a month, except during the bad weather between August and December, when they could not operate because of their small size.

The other organization was the 603rd Battalion of the North Vietnamese People's Army, headquartered at Quang Khe, fifty-five miles north of the Demilitarized Zone. The unit transported military supplies and personnel to the South. This battalion was manned by about 258 men, most of whom were southerners with some experience as seamen. One of the battalion's three companies stockpiled supplies to be infiltrated, a second built and maintained the boats, and the third manned the boats on missions to the South. By 1961, the Communists had available for infiltration of men and supplies by sea about ten small fishing boats with crews of six each and equipped with radios and machine guns.[45]

In light of the information available, U.S. intelligence agencies concluded at the end of 1961 that "only a small percentage of Viet Cong support comes by junk traffic, and that this mode is used more to infiltrate agents, couriers and instructions."[46] General McGarr estimated that 25 percent of the Viet Cong force was infiltrated from the North, and that only about 1 percent of these men came by sea. Ambassador Nolting also concluded that "infiltration of arms as well as personnel by sea continues to be relatively small as available information indicates."[47]

---

[45] A Communist history of the war relates that from 1959 to 1961 maritime infiltration was controlled by Group 759, directly under the North Vietnamese General Staff, and that no major effort was mounted. See Socialist Republic of Vietnam, *Vietnam: The Anti-U.S. Resistance War*, p. 32. See also State Department, *Threat to the Peace*, p. 34.

[46] Memo, Craig to Taylor, of 24 Oct 1961.

[47] Msgs, AMEMB Saigon 3:11PM 10 Oct 1961. See also msg, 3:12PM 10 Oct; Director Far East Region ISA, memo for record, of 20 Dec 1961.

The Sea Force did not have adequate resources to control even low levels of sea infiltration from outside of Vietnam, or Viet Cong movement along the coast within South Vietnam. It was almost an impossible task to detect the handful of infiltrators mingling with the 10,000 junks which plied the South Vietnamese coastal waters each day. The Sea Force could deploy one or two ships at the 17th parallel and in the Gulf of Siam, which were the most vulnerable areas, but they could not patrol off all the countless landing spots along the 1,200-mile coastline. It was not surprising that the U.S. Naval Attache in Saigon could not rate the Sea Force as even "moderately effective" in controlling sea infiltration. In his analysis, "there is too much coastline, too many junks, too few patrol craft, and inadequate authority to prevent the junks from doing almost as they please." On the last point, the Sea Force commander complained that his ships were prohibited from even firing on suspected infiltrators because the government feared inflicting friendly casualties.[48]

At the end of 1961, Admiral Felt observed that the Vietnamese needed to concentrate on deploying more ships on the line. Of the twenty-one ships in the Sea Force at the end of the year, only eight or nine were operational and only one actually was on patrol. He explained that the low utilization rates were caused by a "lack of preventive maintenance, by slow shipyard work and by poor operational planning and complete lack of command drive."[49]

Establishment of the Coastal Force

Vietnamese officers and their U.S. advisors also thought of new ways to control coastal traffic. Even though the evidence indicated that the level of Communist seaborne infiltration was slight during this period, the potential for expansion was there. As early as 1956, Commander Quyen, then commander of the Danang Coastal District, had purchased ten junks to patrol the 17th parallel. Soon thereafter, Quyen was transferred to Saigon and the force dissolved. But, in 1958 he persuaded President Diem to create a nationwide junk force. Diem placed the unit under the navy. Little became of the force, however, according to Quyen, because

---
[48]NA Saigon, report, 45-60 of 8 Mar 1960. See also NA Saigon, report, 20-59 of 24 Jan 1959.
[49]Msg, CP 252239Z Nov 1961. See also msg, CP 010340Z Dec.

the navy did not have adequate resources to support it, did not understand the fishermen who manned the junks, and had no clear idea of the mission. Another debilitating factor was the construction of unseaworthy junks.

As Communist activity in the South intensified in the next two years, Quyen again pressed for establishment of a junk force. Then, in January 1960, a junk with six men on board was captured off the coast of Quang Ngai Province. These men, who went north at the end of the French Indochina War, were caught transporting supplies to Communists in the South. The following month, the Vietnamese asked General Williams to comment on ways to deter large-scale infiltration by Communist boats. General Williams responded that sea and air patrols alone could not cope with the threat. Local fishermen and civilians living on the coast would have to help with surveillance to make an interdiction effort effective. After considering the American suggestions, President Diem established the Coastal Force in April 1960. The junk force was placed under the Department of State for National Defense, but the Naval Deputy exercised operational control through his coastal district commanders.[50] The creation of the Coastal Force was in line with the growing U.S. interest in counterinsurgency concepts being developed at the time. Admiral Felt's budding Counterinsurgency Plan called for intensified coastal surveillance and reflected the new American emphasis on South Vietnamese internal security.

Quyen's project followed closely a program which the French drew up during the Indochina War but never implemented. His plan called for a force of 420 sailing junks and 63 motorized junks, manned by 2,200 fishermen, with an annual budget of $1,500,000, to patrol the inshore coastal waters within five miles of shore. The proposed twenty-one junk divisions, each comprising twenty-three junks, would patrol about thirty miles of shoreline. In addition to the mission of interdicting maritime infiltration and smuggling, the force also was responsible for collecting intelligence on fishermen, pursuing a psychological warfare program among them, and maintaining government authority in the populous coastal areas. When fully deployed, the force also was to curtail Viet Cong

---

[50]CINCPAC, Command History, 1960, p. 168; NA Saigon, report, 86-60 of 18 Apr 1960; G. A. Carter et al., *User's Guide to Southeast Asia Combat Data* (Santa Monica, CA: Rand Corp., 1976), p. 380; "History of the Coastal Force," (Unpublished Manuscript).

intracoastal traffic, a task beyond the capability of the navy.⁵¹

Several unexpected but surmountable problems plagued the establishment of the force. Quyen had conceived of the force as a clandestine group that would blend with the local fishing traffic. It soon became apparent, however, that the junks unavoidably revealed their identity by boarding and searching other junks rather than fishing. Quyen hoped to recruit fishermen who needed only a minimum of training and were familiar with local junk traffic. But, this group proved difficult to recruit because of their traditional independence. Therefore, in the first 400-man class, which began training at Danang in July 1960 under Lieutenant Nguyen Van Thong, only 25 percent were former fishermen. The rest were refugees from North Vietnam living in camps near Danang. As a result, it was necessary to extend the training program past the 15 October completion date.⁵² By November, however, training was completed. On 4 December 1960, four divisions of twenty junks each deployed along the northern coast of Vietnam, between Quang Nam Province and the Demilitarized Zone, at Cua Viet, Hue, Danang, and Hoi An. The junkmen spent most of January and February 1961 establishing their bases, and by March were conducting limited patrols.

Setting up a communication network for the force proved difficult. The initial plan called for Civil Guard or army units to man small coastal outposts, to which junks would send messages for relay back to the main base or to Sea Force ships offshore. These outposts were never established and radios for the junks were diverted to army units. U.S. carbines and other weapons destined for the junk force also went to army units, leaving the junkmen with old French submachine guns and repeating rifles.⁵³

The activity of Coastal Division 11, based at the mouth of the Cua Viet River about ten miles south of the Demilitarized Zone, was typical during this period. The army commander in the area, Major General Tran Van Don, was sympathetic to the program and agreed to help ease the unit's officer shortage by providing an army lieutenant to command the twenty sailing junks and 104 men. A naval petty officer and two seamen assisted the lieutenant. All administrative and logistic support came from the naval

---

⁵¹NA Saigon, reports, 86-60 of 18 Apr 1960; 87-60 of 19 Apr; CINCPAC, Command History, 1960, p. 293; *U.S.-V.N. Relations*, bk. 2, pt. IVA.5, tab 4, p. 93.

⁵²NA Saigon, reports, 109-60 of 25 May 1960; 16-S-60 of 3 Aug; 230-60 of 17 Nov; "History of the Coastal Force."

⁵³Heinz, memo for record, of 19 Apr 1961.

base at Danang. The army officers in this and sister units turned out to be more of a liability than an asset, however. They seemed to be the worst officers in General Don's command and had little interest in learning naval procedures.

By the end of March 1961, the division patrolled about twenty miles of coastline and five miles out to sea. Quyen hoped that local fishermen would report suspicious junks to the Coastal Force, but since the majority of the Coastal Force sailors were alien to the area, little such information was received. On three occasions, however, junks gave chase to suspected North Vietnamese sailing junks. In these instances, the security office under the Quang Tri Province chief had alerted the junk force to the infiltrators. The Communist boats, however, eluded the sailing junks because the former craft possessed greater speed and the deputy province chief prohibited firing anything but warning shots.[54]

By mid-1961, U.S. policymakers were convinced that the threat of internal subversion was more serious than that of conventional cross-border attack and were looking for ways to increase counterinsurgency capabilities. The relatively inexpensive support required by the Coastal Force impressed American observers and convinced them that this was an ideal counterinsurgency technique. The Presidential Program for Vietnam, which John F. Kennedy approved in May 1961, contained a pledge of support for the Vietnamese junk force, to include training of junk crews "as a means of preventing Viet Cong clandestine supply and infiltration into South Vietnam." This support, in addition to twelve training advisors, included U.S. funding for radios and weapons. Until then, the junk force had been equipped, manned, and funded solely by the Vietnamese.[55]

That the newly formed Coastal Force was a threat to Communist activity was indicated by their action on 9 July 1961. On that date, the Communists sent fishing boats south across the 17th parallel from a base on Gio Island, just north of the Demilitarized Zone, to lure South Vietnamese patrols. When six junk force boats pursued, they were suddenly surrounded by twenty motorized and armed boats and taken under fire. However, the South Vietnamese return fire compelled the North Vietnamese to withdraw, leaving behind one of their fishing boats.

---

[54]CINCPAC, Command History, 1960, p. 169.

[55]*U.S.-V.N. Relations*, bk. 2, pt. IVB.1, p. 30. See also CINCPAC, Command History, 1961, p. 180; ONI, "Briefing by former Naval Attache, Saigon," in Saigon, report, 11-S-62 of 3 Oct 1962.

Such actions as these gave promise to the developing coastal surveillance effort.

The Persons Visit

In mid-November 1961, Admiral Felt sent his Deputy Chief of Staff for Military Assistance Affairs, Rear Admiral Henry S. Persons, to Saigon to consult with MAAG personnel on ways to improve the Vietnamese Navy's contribution to the overall military effort. His report summarized the major problems facing the Vietnamese Navy at the end of 1961, and served as a focus of advisory attention in 1962.

Admiral Persons found the most serious problem to be the low utilization of the Vietnamese Navy's ships and craft. U.S. naval advisors told him that two-thirds of the patrol ships and half of the river boats were unavailable for operations because of repair, maintenance, or scheduling difficulties. He identified poor supervision at the Saigon Naval Shipyard as the root cause of delays in repairing ships and craft. In this regard, General McGarr pointed out that the expected arrival of additional U.S. advisors for the shipyard promised to improve performance. In addition, the recent decision of the Vietnamese Navy to make force commanders responsible for maintenance as well as operations promised to improve preventive maintenance performance.

Admiral Persons also recommended that the navy be represented on the Joint General Staff if naval resources were to be used effectively. General McGarr agreed wholeheartedly, but his attempts to convince the Vietnamese Army of this necessity met with little success. Admiral Persons also urged the MAAG's Navy Section to press harder for the establishment of separate naval organizations, such as an intelligence office, that would provide better support for the maritime service.

At the same time, Admiral Persons called for increased U.S. support for the Coastal Force. The complete coastal surveillance plan, under consideration at the end of 1960, was not implemented due to difficulties coordinating it with the army and the air force. General McGarr also explained that high contractor bids, which totalled more than the budget approved by the Department of State for National Defense, delayed construction of junks. Furthermore, the deployment of a command junk was set back when the prototype to be constructed at the Saigon Naval Shipyard proved to be unsuitable.

Admiral Persons identified several other major deficiencies in the Vietnamese Navy. Training was unsatisfactory because of a lack of qualified Vietnamese instructors in the naval schools at Nha Trang. The arrival of a U.S. mobile training team, however, promised to alleviate this situation. The same remedy was prescribed for the supply center at Saigon, where records were in such bad shape that the Vietnamese did not know all the items they had on hand.

Finally, some consideration was given to expediting the delivery of patrol ships to the Vietnamese in order to bolster their coastal patrol resources. Admiral Persons recommended against this action because the Vietnamese would not be able to accept the patrol vessels without a corresponding slowdown in the delivery of an LST due in April and an LSM due in June 1962. These latter ships were critical because of the need to provide logistic support to Danang, Nha Trang, and other coastal ports. The Communist threat to cut railroad lines to these cities made supply especially important. Admiral Felt concurred, and added that in general "materials and people are not lacking; organization, training and maintenance, all interrelated, must be jacked up."[56] He added that "our problem is one of inculcating into the VN Navy a desire to utilize better the tools which are at hand."[57]

During the period from 1959 to 1961, the number of U.S. naval advisors and new ships and craft provided the fledgling Vietnamese maritime service was small. This modest level of U.S. military assistance partly reflected the relatively minor importance of the Vietnamese Navy in the worldwide aid program. But, U.S. officials also believed the navy incapable of absorbing a great number of ships, boats, weapons, and U.S. advisors due to the many problems faced by that service. Many leaders of the navy lacked experience, were too involved in South Vietnamese domestic politics, and often lacked motivation. The training received by officers and men was marginal. The obsolescence of ships, river craft, and weapons, as well as the inadequacies at repair and logistic facilities,

---

[56]Msg, CP 242055Z Nov 1961. See also msgs, CHMAAGVN 140315Z; 270745Z.
[57]Ltr, Felt to Anderson, of 30 Nov 1961.

hampered operations, as did the absence of adequate shipboard maintenance.

The Vietnamese Navy registered some selective improvement in administration, organization, training, logistic support, and operational performance during this period, partly as a result of the work of U.S. naval advisors. Still, much remained to be done before the naval arm could be considered ready to accomplish its mission in the rivers and coastal waters of South Vietnam.

CHAPTER VI

The Seventh Fleet's Contribution to the Limited Partnership, 1961-1963

In late 1961, the United States increased the scope and magnitude of the effort to preserve the struggling South Vietnamese government. Largely as a result of General Taylor's fact-finding mission to Vietnam, President Kennedy directed his policymakers to implement a program of additional naval, military, economic, and financial assistance. Reflecting the high priority accorded this program, Secretary of Defense McNamara took personal and close interest in its execution. From December 1961 to March 1962, he attended monthly conferences at CINCPAC headquarters in Hawaii to monitor and maintain the momentum of the project. Thereafter, he visited Hawaii or South Vietnam periodically to assess the course of events.

In December, McNamara was apprised by Admiral Felt, Ambassador Nolting, and General Harkins that the Viet Cong were making considerable inroads in South Vietnam and that Diem's government was not meeting the threat adequately. Admiral Felt concluded pessimistically that the "situation in Southeast Asia has never been more favorable for advancement of Communist aims.... In South Vietnam, VC making good progress in field.... Although various US/SVN actions may slow down VC somewhat, Communists still hold edge in the countryside."[1]

U.S. military and civilian leaders regarded one of the greatest obstacles to a reversal of South Vietnamese fortunes as President Diem himself. Throughout the year Diem resisted implementing various provisions of the U.S.-conceived Counterinsurgency Plan and the Presidential Program of May, and greater popular support for his regime was not in evidence.

---

[1] Msg, CP 232035Z Dec 1961. See also *U.S.-V.N. Relations*, bk. 3, p. 3.

Admiral Anderson, the CNO, informed his flag officers that "unfortunately, it is clear that Diem is strongly opposed to taking any action which might tend to undermine his one-man rule, and he resents American advice as to the necessity for military and political reforms."[2] Indeed, Rear Admiral William E. Gentner, Jr., director of the Strategic Plans Division, proposed advising Diem that unless changes were made, he would have to "accept the real possibility that the United States will stand aside while Vietnamese select a new Chief of State."[3] At the first conference in Hawaii, on 16 December 1961, however, the Secretary of Defense stated that U.S. officials would have to assume that "Diem is going to continue to be Diem" and "since he is all that we have, we must work with him."[4]

McNamara went on to stress that the survival of South Vietnam was the first priority of the administration and that money would be no object in the provision of military assistance. Everything short of combat troops would be offered. Nevertheless, the use of U.S. ground units in Vietnam was not ruled out. As the Director, Politico-Military Policy Division, Rear Admiral Arnold F. Schade, noted in a briefing to Vice Admiral Schoech, Commander Seventh Fleet, "if we get by short of introducing U.S. or SEATO troops, it will be a long hard pull." He added that "we can't see any light at the other end of the tunnel yet."[5]

The Combined U.S.-South Vietnamese Coastal Patrol

While this was short of full-scale intervention, units of the U.S. Armed Forces, for the first time in the Asian conflict, were ordered to provide the Vietnamese with direct support. Army light helicopter units were quickly dispatched to South Vietnam, as were other U.S.-manned transport aircraft. On 11 December 1961, *Core*, an aircraft ferry operated by the MSTS, arrived in Saigon and offloaded the Army's 8th and 57th

---

[2] Ltr, CNO to Flag and General Officers, of 4 Dec 1961. See also memo, OP-60 to CNO, ser BM1330-61 of 29 Dec; *U.S.-V.N. Relations*, bk. 3, pp. 6, 19; bk. 12, pp. 439-41.

[3] Memo, OP-60 to OP-06, ser BM00011-62 of 3 Jan 1962.

[4] CINCPAC, "Record of the Secretary of Defense Conference held 16 December 1961 at Headquarters, Commander-in-Chief Pacific," ser 000300 of 18 Dec 1961, pp. 4-6. See also CINCPAC, Command History, 1962, pp. 149-53.

[5] Ltr, OP-61 to COM7FLT, ser 00225P61 of 22 Dec 1961. See also CINCPAC, SECDEF Conference, of 16 Dec 1961, pp. 1-2; ltr, CNO to Flag and General Officers, of 4 Jan 1962; msg, JCS 171615Z Jan.

Transportation Companies (Light Helicopter).⁶ In addition, as its role in the new strategy of "limited partnership," the Navy was called upon to help establish a coastal patrol. On 27 November, Secretary of Defense McNamara implemented one provision of a presidential directive that the South Vietnamese be provided with "small craft, including such United States uniformed advisors and operating personnel as may be necessary for operations in effecting surveillance and control over coastal waters and inland waterways."⁷ Several days later, this instruction was amplified to state that the proposed U.S. patrol would be conducted until the South Vietnamese Navy had the capability to unilaterally carry out the coastal control mission. This addition obviously reflected the perception that the South Vietnamese Navy's Sea Force was then unable to provide an adequate patrol force.

Under these circumstances, Admiral Felt did not oppose the use of U.S. ships or aircraft in a coastal patrol, as he did earlier in 1961. He hoped that the presence of U.S. ships on patrol would infuse the Vietnamese with the "can do" spirit, provide needed training in conducting a multi-ship operation, and demonstrate the value of coordination between air, sea, and coastal forces. Admiral Felt stated that the employment of the U.S. units was to "augment [Vietnamese Navy] capability temporarily and for the purpose of working with and assisting in training SVN Sea Force."⁸ Captain Joseph B. Drachnik, newly assigned Chief of the MAAG's Navy Section, stated that the object was to get the Vietnamese Navy's "ships in such condition that they could operate for extended periods of time, convince the sailors that they could go to sea for more than three days without everybody getting seasick or running out of water or food, and developing incentives and showing them procedures whereby they could do this."⁹ Additionally, there was a need to determine the extent and nature of seaborne infiltration from North Vietnam. CINCPAC specifically wanted to know if the upsurge of Communist activity in South Vietnam during the latter part of the year "had been preceded or accompanied by increased junk traffic."¹⁰

---

⁶*U.S.-V.N. Relations*, bk. 3, p. 7; pt. IVB.3, pp. ii-iii.
⁷Memo, SECDEF to SECARM/SECNAV/SECAF/Chairman JCS/ASD (ISA) of 27 Nov 1961.
⁸Msg, CP 010340Z Dec 1961.
⁹Joseph B. Drachnik, transcript of interview with William W. Moss, John F. Kennedy Library, in Norfolk, VA, 27 Jul 1970, p. 3.
¹⁰Msg, CP 292316Z Nov 1961.

The Seventh Fleet's Contribution to the Limited Partnership 167

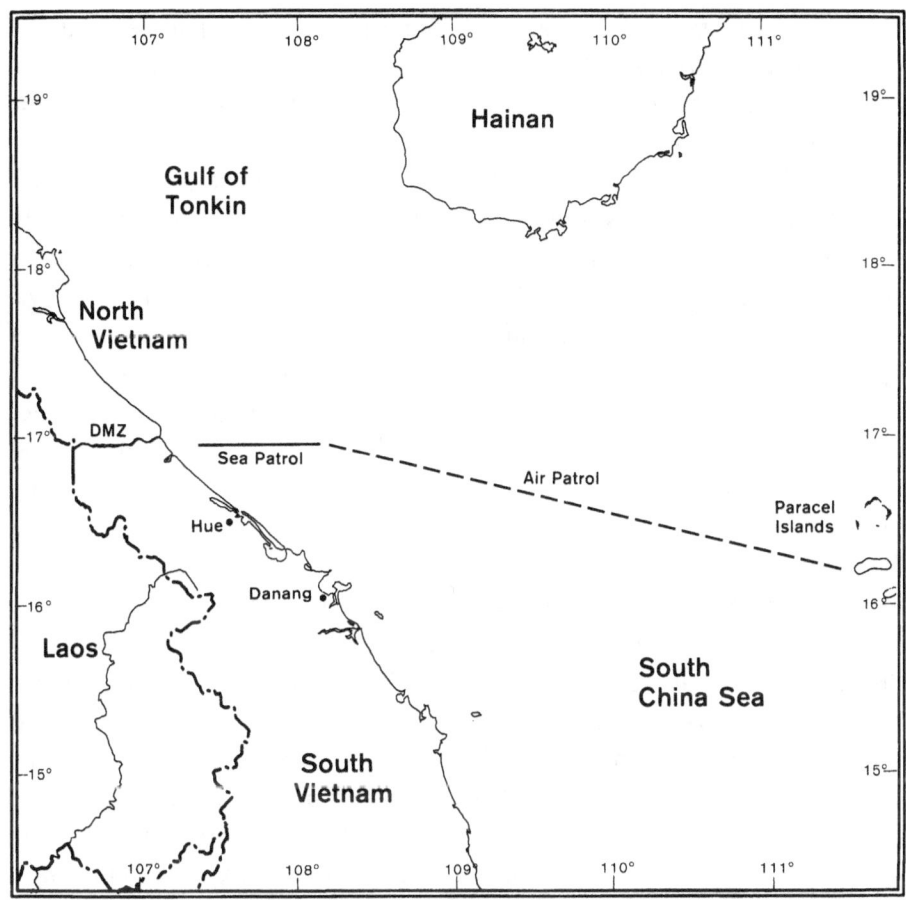

17th Parallel Patrol

Because the coastal patrol mission was requested on an urgent basis, the naval command met the requirement for U.S. vessels with the most suitable ships then in the Southeast Asian area. These were the five 165-foot ocean minesweepers (MSO) of Minesweeping Division 73, that had just recently completed an exercise in the Gulf of Siam and were due to call at Saigon on 8 December 1961. Admiral Sides, the Pacific Fleet commander, directed Vice Admiral Schoech to organize a meeting in the South Vietnamese capital to work out the details of the proposed patrol. Prior to the conference, it was thought that the areas of responsibility would include the sea around Phu Quoc Island and Cape Camau, although the major effort was to take place between the 17th parallel and the Paracel Islands. It soon became evident, however, that only the 17th parallel sector could be adequately covered by the five ships of Minesweeping Division 73.[11]

Guided by instructions from Admirals Felt and Sides, CINCPACFLT and Seventh Fleet representatives, General McGarr, Commander Ralph E. Graham, the Minesweeping Division 73 commander, and Captain Drachnik met with Commander Quyen and other South Vietnamese naval officers in Saigon on 10 December. The conferees drew up a concept of operations that provided for the establishment of a "fixed barrier patrol" ten miles south of the 17th parallel and extending eight to thirty miles from the South Vietnamese coast. This area was believed to hold the most promise for intercepting North Vietnamese coastal traffic to the South, but provision was made to shift the patrol to other locations to the east if warranted. The combined patrol force was to consist of two Vietnamese PCs operating in conjunction with two to three MSOs. The U.S. ships would guide their Vietnamese counterparts to suspect craft and stand by during boarding and search operations. U.S. personnel were not allowed to board suspicious boats. Commander Minesweeping Division 73 was assigned the tactical command. Commander Quyen stated that his ship captains would be directed to "carry out the orders of the U.S. patrol commander."[12] But, in keeping with the U.S. advisory role in South Vietnam, Admiral Sides changed "orders" to read "recommendations."[13]

Although both Admirals Felt and Sides preferred to operate the U.S. contingent of the patrol force from Subic Bay, the conferees decided that Danang was suitable as a staging base and was closer to the patrol area. Most logistic support would be provided by the Seventh Fleet Mobile Logistic Support Force (Task Force 73), although a Vietnamese fuel-oil barge was available at Danang to refuel U.S. ships. The Saigon planning group also requested that air surveillance of the sea from the South Vietnamese coast to the Paracels be instituted to complement the surface patrol and a limited U.S. Air Force reconnaissance effort already

---

[11]Msgs, CPFLT 302026Z Nov 1961; CP 030626Z Dec; memo, Military Assistant, SECDEF to SECARM/SECNAV/SECAF/Chairman JCS, of 6 Dec.

[12]Msg, CHMAAGVN 110757Z Dec 1961.

[13]Msg, CPFLT 120131Z Dec 1961. See also SECSTATE 8PM 4 Dec; CPFLT 052359Z; CP 060343Z.

underway. With this general concept agreed upon, it was affirmed that the combined operation would commence on 22 December.[14]

On 14 December, CINCPACFLT issued his Operation Plan 75-61 governing U.S. conduct of the combined 17th parallel patrol. While the plan stated that only "small scale infiltration by sea" into South Vietnam then existed, Minesweeping Division 73 was assigned the mission of conducting "patrol, surveillance and training operations in the coastal waters off SVN in order to assist CHMAAG Vietnam and SVN naval forces in preventing infiltration."[15] CINCPAC approved the patrol plan the following day, and CINCPACFLT immediately ordered its execution. On 16 December, Secretary of Defense McNamara, meeting with Pacific Command representatives at CINCPAC's Hawaiian headquarters on the situation in South Vietnam, endorsed the proposed measures "as a beginning, subsequent action dependent on experience."[16]

At the same conference Admiral Felt directed that Seventh Fleet reconnaissance aircraft, in the course of their routine flights, assist U.S. Air Force units operating from South Vietnam in making a count of the junks plying the waters between the 17th parallel and the Paracels. Soon afterward, however, Admiral Schoech ordered Commander Patrol Force, Seventh Fleet to establish a formal air patrol by SP-5B Marlin aircraft of VP 40, with random flights conducted at least every other day. The patrol force commander was to provide Commander Graham and the MAAG with intelligence on maritime traffic patterns and density. Admiral Sides cautioned that the reconnaissance planes not fly any closer than thirty miles to the coast. This gap would be filled by the ships of the combined surface group. CINCPAC subsequently approved this revised plan.[17]

On 22 December 1961, six days after the Vietnamese deployed, the U.S. ships of the combined patrol force assumed their stations five miles south of the 17th parallel, marking the first time major units of the Seventh Fleet participated directly in the Vietnam conflict. The force consisted of *Conquest* (MSO-488), *Esteem* (MSO-438), *Pledge* (MSO-492),

---

[14]Msgs, COMINDIV73 101233Z Dec 1961; CHMAAGVN 110757Z.
[15]Msg, CPFLT 142351Z Dec 1961. See also CHMAAGVN 131733Z.
[16]CINCPAC, SECDEF Conference, of 16 Dec 1961, pp. 8-D-1— 8-D-2, 8-D-5. See also memo, OP-60 to CNO, ser 0001296-61 of 18 Dec 1961; msgs, CP 111920Z Dec; 151915Z; CPFLT 152329Z; ADMIN CPFLT 181114Z; CP 202326Z.
[17]Msgs, CHMAAGVN 190245Z Dec 1961; ADMIN COM7FLT 190448Z; CPFLT 200203Z; CP 222112Z; CINCPAC, SECDEF Conference, of 16 Dec 1961, p. 8-D-2.

Ocean minesweeper Pledge *(MSO-492) searches for Communist infiltrators off the South Vietnamese coast.*

and *Gallant* (MSO-489), in company with two South Vietnamese PCs. A fifth U.S. ship, *Illusive* (MSO-448), remained in readiness in Danang. For the next two months, the American and Vietnamese ships of the patrol force ranged the area east of Danang. Normally, U.S. ships steamed at staggered intervals on an east-west track in proximity to the parallel. Early in the period numerous junks and other small craft, as well as several steel-hulled trawlers, evaded search by beating to the north across the parallel. Of the craft actually stopped and searched, few produced suspects requiring further identification. In one instance, a man under investigation was found to be the brother of a political commissar in the North Vietnamese People's Army. However, Captain Drachnik reported in mid-

February that all persons detained in Danang for interrogation subsequently were released.[18]

While the air and surface patrol might have been effective as a deterrent to North Vietnamese sea infiltration, the lack of firm evidence of enemy activity did not indicate the need for continued U.S. participation. Admiral Felt, along with other naval officers close to the scene, previously believed that only small-scale, cross-border movement was taking place; and he continued to believe, as he intimated to Admiral Anderson during the latter's trip to the Pacific in late December, that the U.S. air and sea effort was not "particularly useful."[19] However, several factors combined to require extension of the 17th parallel patrol, not the least of which was Secretary of Defense McNamara's undiminished interest in the coastal effort. During his second monthly meeting with Pacific commanders in Hawaii, on 15 January 1962, he was briefed on the number of junks stopped and suspects taken. Admiral Sides reported that McNamara felt the Navy had "done a truly marvelous job during the past couple of months.... The apparent efficiency with which the fleet ships have established their patrols is extremely impressive."[20] In addition, the Secretary of Defense added that he wanted "intelligence reports on what we have gotten from captured junks" at the next monthly meeting.[21]

Another factor was the coming availability of five destroyer escorts (DE) from the Reserve Fleet which were activated during the Berlin crisis of late 1961. These 306-foot ships were much better suited to the coastal patrol mission than the MSOs. Since they were faster and had better seakeeping abilities, each destroyer escort could perform the work of two minesweepers. In addition, the patrol was seen as a temporary operation and the Naval Reserve ships were scheduled for deactivation at the end of June.[22]

---

[18]CINCPAC, "Record of the Secretary of Defense Conference held 19 February 1962 at Headquarters, Commander-in-Chief Pacific," ser 00062 of 20 Feb 1962, p. 3-12; msgs, CTU70.5.7 190913Z Dec 1961; 250433Z; 290545Z; CTF72 250539Z Jan 1962; memo, OP-60 to J-3/Joint Staff, JCS, ser 0020P60 of 8 Jan 1962.
[19]CNO, Daily Diary, of 29 Dec 1961.
[20]Ltr, Sides to Anderson, of 16 Jan 1962.
[21]CINCPAC, "Record of the Secretary of Defense Conference held 15 January 1962 at Headquarters, Commander-in-Chief Pacific," ser 00021 of 16 Jan 1962, pp. 3-9, 3-7. See also memo, OP-601C4 to OP-60, ser BM00069-62 of 18 Jan.
[22]Ltr, Sides to Anderson, of 16 Jan 1962; CINCPAC, SECDEF Conference, of 15 Jan 1962, pp. 3-8—3-9; msg, CPFLT 170301Z Jan; memo, OP-60 to CNO, ser BM0076-62 of 22 Jan 1962.

The change in ship types also afforded naval commanders the opportunity to reorganize the patrol operation to increase its flexibility and effectiveness. To ease logistic support requirements, CINCPACFLT again proposed basing the U.S. patrol force at Subic Bay, especially since he felt that the use of Danang was "not necessary for accomplishing mission of training VN Navy."[23] Admiral Sides also requested authority for U.S. ships to conduct surveillance or pursue craft north of the 17th parallel. The admiral was distressed that "to date 52 contact[s] have turned north upon sighting patrol and have escaped interception." He added that "limitation of 17th parallel if left in effect too long can become a real fence in politico-military thinking."[24] Finally, CINCPACFLT proposed centralizing command of both the U.S. air and sea patrol under Commander Patrol Force, Seventh Fleet, Rear Admiral Bernard M. Strean. This step was especially desirable since that officer was better able to control operations through his staff and mobile flagship, seaplane tender *Pine Island*.

CINCPAC approved these measures and they soon were embodied in Commander Seventh Fleet Operation Plan 75-62, which took effect on 17 February 1962. On that date, a patrol force component, under the temporary command of Commander John B. Lewis, USNR, and composed of *Edmonds* (DE-406) and *Walton* (DE-361), relieved Minesweeping Division 73.[25]

As the destroyer escorts took their stations near the border between North and South Vietnam, the U.S. Navy also became involved in countering infiltration from Cambodia. In early January the South Vietnamese government, through Captain Drachnik of the MAAG, requested U.S. assistance in patrolling the waters off the Mekong Delta, where Vietnamese authorities reported significant infiltration from Cambodia by way of the many islands in the Gulf of Siam. The major points of entry were believed to be along the east and west coasts of the Camau Peninsula, long a Viet Cong stronghold. The South Vietnamese stressed that their navy possessed insufficient patrol ships to interdict this Communist traffic; but Captain Drachnik and other Americans, including

---

[23]Msg, CPFLT 170301Z Jan 1962.
[24]*Ibid.*
[25]Msgs, CP 192347Z Jan 1962; ADMIN COM7FLT 211326Z; CTF72 250534Z; CP 090308Z Feb; CTF72 100312Z.

Admiral Anderson and his chief Pacific naval commanders, were skeptical that major infiltration actually was underway. Nevertheless, the captain felt that the enemy certainly had the ability to infiltrate arms and supplies from Cambodia and was probably doing so on a minor scale. Captain Drachnik noted the need for the South Vietnamese Navy to gain experience and proficiency in the conduct of open-sea patrol, training he then believed Sea Force crews on the northern patrol were receiving. For these reasons, he recommended U.S. participation and assistance in the establishment of combined U.S.-Vietnamese patrols from the Cambodian border to Cape Camau and from that point to Son Island. Eventually, however, the latter segment was dropped for lack of a suitable number of South Vietnamese patrol ships.

Admiral Felt shared the skepticism of American naval commanders regarding the amount of infiltration in the Gulf of Siam. But, to resolve the issue, CINCPAC ordered the establishment of a U.S.-Vietnamese patrol from Cape Camau to Phu Quoc for a period of two weeks in order to "determine degree of, and to counter, sea infiltration in progress from Cambodia via Gulf of Siam," and additionally to "train [the Vietnamese Navy's] ships in patrol and surveillance procedures."[26] Remaining under the operational control of Commander Seventh Fleet and patrolling in conjunction with 2 or 3 South Vietnamese PCs, 1 gasoline barge, self-propelled (YOG), and 1 AKL, 1 or 2 U.S. destroyer escorts would direct their counterparts to suspicious craft in the manner of the 17th parallel patrol. South Vietnamese ships would be vectored to infiltrating boats in order to board and search them and to investigate further suspicious seafarers.[27]

On 19 February 1962, at the third consecutive monthly meeting dealing with the situation in South Vietnam, Secretary of Defense McNamara was briefed on the proposed southern patrol. In addition, the effectiveness of the surface and air patrols along the 17th parallel was discussed. Captain Drachnik expressed his belief that U.S. participation was most useful in providing the Vietnamese Navy with on-the-job training in extended patrolling. Admiral Felt also explained the function

---

[26]Msg, CP 172350Z Feb 1962.
[27]Memos, OP-60 to CNO, ser BM00199-62 of 12 Feb 1962; OP-60 to OP-06, ser BM00213-62 of 15 Feb; OP-60 to CNO, ser BM00233-62 of 20 Feb; msgs, CHMAAGVN 071107Z Feb; 110549Z; CP 172353Z; CNO 021445Z Mar; CPFLT 160429Z.

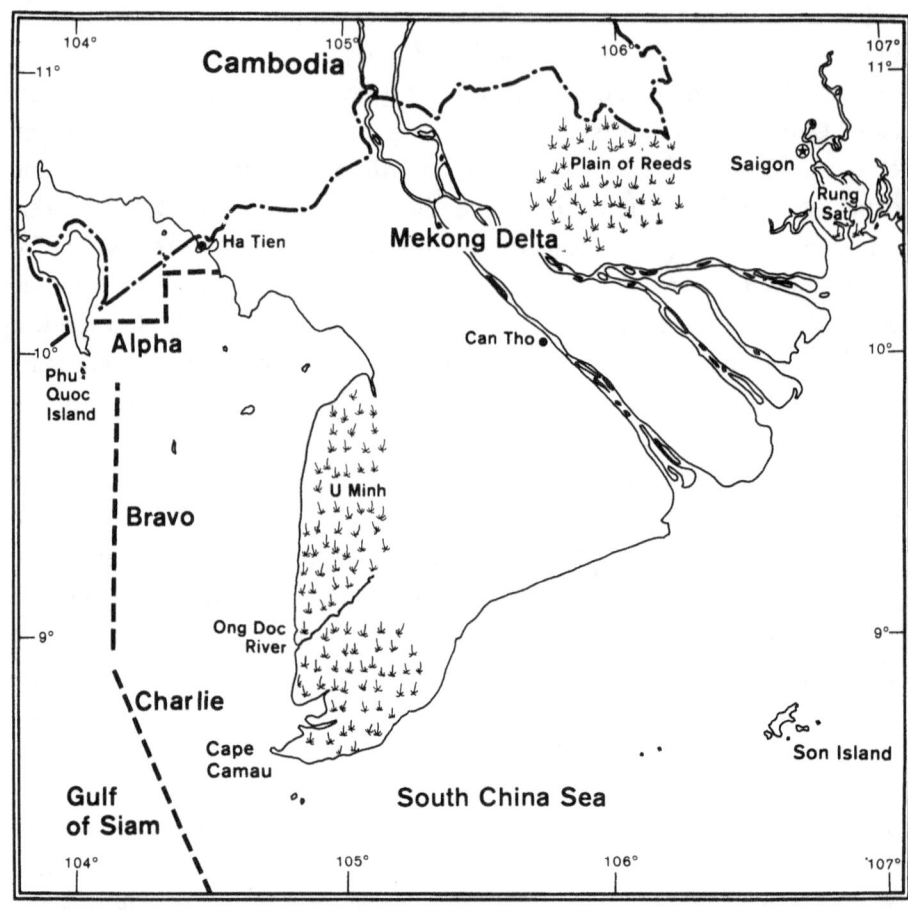

Coastal Patrol in the Gulf of Siam

of the air surveillance effort in determining junk traffic density and patterns. As he did at the previous meeting, McNamara endorsed these measures and commended the Navy for doing a "wonderful job."[28]

Wiseman (DE-667) and *Walton* were the initial U.S. ships assigned to the Gulf of Siam patrol that began on 27 February 1962. In conjunction with South Vietnamese units, the destroyer escorts established three patrol lines to screen the western coast of the delta. Patrol line Alpha extended from three miles south of Ha Tien to the east coast of Phu Quoc Island.

---

[28]CINCPAC, SECDEF Conference, of 19 Feb 1962, pp. 3-17, 3-13— 3-15.

Because the State Department feared that a U.S. presence in this area, which contained islands claimed by both Cambodia and Vietnam, would damage relations with Norodom Sihanouk's government, only Vietnamese vessels operated here. Line Bravo began at the lower tip of Phu Quoc and continued south to a point thirty-five miles west of the mouth of the Ong Doc River. From here, patrol line Charlie extended to a point thirty-five miles south of Cape Camau. One U.S. and one South Vietnamese ship cruised at random intervals along the Bravo and Charlie patrol lines.[29]

Throughout the spring of 1962, naval leaders evaluated the effectiveness of the two combined patrols in detecting Communist infiltration and improving the South Vietnamese Navy's open-sea performance. At the end of March, Commander Seventh Fleet reported that after thousands of junk sightings, searches, and seizures by both the northern and southern patrols, infiltration from Cambodia or North Vietnam was not substantiated. He stated:

> To date there has been no concrete evidence of massive or even significant infiltration.... From results attained to date it must be concluded that the patrols have not been effective in capturing infiltrators if significant infiltration is taking place, although the patrol's presence may have discouraged attempts.[30]

Admiral Schoech also addressed the question of the ability of the South Vietnamese to unilaterally carry out the patrols. He concluded that because of "poor state of training and material readiness, lack of forceful leadership in some ships, and need for additional experience at sea by all SVN ships...the SVN Navy is not capable of assuming full responsibility for conducting effective patrols at present without U.S. assistance."[31] At the same time, naval commanders believed that the American training effort eventually would enable the South Vietnamese Sea Force to operate independently. Initial reports were encouraging. The Sea Force had been motivated by the U.S. example to keep more of their ships on longer

---

[29]The exact coordinates were: Alpha — 3 miles south of Ha Tien, along 10°20'N, to 104°20'E, then to 10°16'N/104°6'E; Bravo — 10°0'N/104°13'E to 9°0'N; Charlie — 9°0'N to 8°0'N/104°45'E; msgs, ADMIN CPFLT 200112Z; CP 230420Z; AMEMB Saigon 2:25AM 24 Feb 1962; 250019Z; AMEMB Saigon 8:02PM 26 Feb; 4:10PM 27 Feb; CPFLT 271923Z; memo, OP-60 to CNO, ser BM00263-62 of 5 Mar.
[30]Msg, COM7FLT 291038Z Mar 1962.
[31]*Ibid.*

patrols and to enhance their communications, seamanship, gunnery, and tactical skills.

In the meantime, U.S. ships carried out their mission. *Whitehurst* (DE-634), *McGinty*(DE-365), *Alvin C. Cockrell*(DE-366), *Marsh* (DE-699), *Vammen*(DE-644), and *Charles E. Brannon* (DE-446) of Escort Squadron 7 increased the strength of the surface patrol group in March and early April. By mid-April, however, the Reserve destroyer escorts began relinquishing their northern patrol stations to make ready for rotation back to the United States and inactivation. Minesweeping Division 91, consisting of *Conflict* (MSO-426), *Dynamic* (MSO-432), *Endurance* (MSO-435), *Implicit* (MSO-455), and *Persistent* (MSO-491), assumed responsibility for the northern patrol on 19 April as the Special MSO Patrol Group. The Seventh Fleet received two additional MSO divisions on 1 May to support the patrol effort.

Again, in May, U.S. naval officers analyzed the results of the combined operation. Conclusive evidence of enemy infiltration still was lacking. By this time, it was clear that American training assistance on the southern patrol had not been productive. Because of their deeper draft, U.S. ships were unable to operate efficiently with their Vietnamese counterparts in the shallow waters of the Gulf of Siam. The commander of the American patrol group felt that "training is impractical and radar assistance in surveillance [is] of negligible value."[32] The converse was true of the 17th parallel patrol. There, the American presence was beneficial to the Vietnamese open-sea effort. For instance, the Sea Force increased its steaming miles per month from 10,000 in May 1961 to 37,000 in May 1962.[33]

As a result of these findings, CINCPACFLT concluded that further U.S. participation in the northern patrol was warranted. However, he recommended to CINCPAC that the American role in the Gulf of Siam patrol, already extended one month at the request of Commander Quyen, be ended. Admiral Felt concurred with these proposals. Following the detachment of *Charles E. Brannon* and *Vammen* for support of the landing in Thailand, *Wiseman* and the other three ships of Escort Division 72, on

---

[32]Msg, CTG72.7 120615Z May 1962.

[33]On the other hand, some South Vietnamese naval officers privately observed that the U.S. support was not constructive since it "so saps the initiative of the [Vietnamese] officers on the patrol as to cancel any training or motivational advantages achieved." CTG72.7, report, ser 002 of 18 May 1962, p. 2.

21 May, departed South Vietnamese waters for their scheduled return to the United States. The destroyer escorts might have been deployed to the 17th parallel but Admiral Sides decided that "these ships could be more profitably utilized in other employment."[34]

On 14 June, Admiral Sides, after consultation with Admiral Schoech, forwarded a study that recommended termination of the northern U.S.-Vietnamese coastal patrol as of 1 July 1962. The Pacific Fleet commander felt that the U.S. Navy's effort had served its purpose in preparing the Sea Force to conduct unilateral open-sea patrols, although technical deficiencies, such as the lack of suitable radar, would reduce their effectiveness somewhat. He also was convinced that there was no "appreciable infiltration" by sea.[35] Admiral Felt basically agreed with these views, but concluded that the U.S. operation would be continued for an additional month. This reflected the fears of the South Vietnamese who were not yet confident the Sea Force could assume full responsibility for the patrol. Admiral Felt also was concerned that the close of the northern patrol so soon after the U.S. withdrawal from the southern sector could have a negative impact on South Vietnamese morale.

Through the month of July, Minesweeping Division 71, under Commander Robert L. Morgan, with *Engage* (MSO-433), *Fortify* (MSO-446), and *Impervious* (MSO-449), manned patrol stations along the 17th parallel. Finally, on 1 August 1962, after seven months, the Seventh Fleet brought to a close its first major operation in direct support of the South Vietnamese armed forces.[36]

The Seventh Fleet Provides Additional Support

The Navy's Pacific Fleet also undertook other operations in South Vietnamese waters. Among these were intelligence gathering missions

---

[34] Msg, CPFLT 150038Z May 1962.
[35] Msg, CPFLT 142201Z Jun 1962.
[36] Msgs, COM7FLT 201146Z Feb 1962; COMUSMACV 070747Z Mar; CP 130506Z; CPFLT 160429Z; 302358Z; COM7FLT 102246Z Apr; 150325Z; CTG72.7 270005Z; 120615Z May; ADMIN CPFLT 150038Z; CP 170007Z; COMUSMACV 191004Z; CPFLT 042059Z Jun; CP 060457Z; CPFLT 130219Z; 142201Z; COM7FLT 311750Z Jul; CP 112025Z Aug; memos, OP-60 to CNO, ser 00533-62 of 23 Apr 1962; OP-601C6 of [2 May]; OP-60 to CNO, BM00649-62 of 26 May; CINCPACFLT, Annual Report, FY1962; NA Saigon, report 33-S-62 of 29 Mar 1962; COMPHIBPAC, reports, 8-62 of 19 Jul; 7-S-62 of 10 Aug; 9-S-62 of 10 Oct; ONI, report, 11-S-62 of 3 Oct; CTG72.7, report, ser 002 of 18 May; Drachnik, Interview with Fitzgerald.

motivated in part by CINCPACFLT's appreciation that "the present conflict in South Vietnam could expand in scope with little warning and require extensive commitment of U.S. naval forces. Amphibious, mine warfare, and more intensive barrier/surveillance operations are all distinct possibilities; all require the greatest possible knowledge of South Vietnam's coastal waters."[37]

This requirement already was recognized at the end of 1961 when CINCPAC authorized his naval component commander to deploy *Cook* (APD-130) for a beach survey on the South Vietnamese coast. At that time, CINCPACFLT noted that the information available on landing beaches was "not sufficiently [detailed] for tactical use for either administrative or opposed landings."[38] Admiral Sides was particularly interested in beaches in the vicinity of Quang Tri, Danang, Nha Trang, Cam Ranh Bay, Vung Tau, and Qui Nhon. After *Cook*'s executive officer conducted a liaison and coordination visit to Saigon on 22 December, the ship proceeded to the South Vietnamese coast and on 4 January 1962 began her mission. UDT detachments carried out most of the required surveys of beach configurations, gradients, underwater obstacles, and tides in the assigned areas. The work was completed without incident on 27 January.[39]

Another naval support mission took place at the end of January 1962, when the Army's 93rd Transportation Company was lifted by sea to Southeast Asia. USNS *Card* (T-AKV-40), an aircraft ferry operated by the MSTS, brought this unit — the third of its type to deploy to South Vietnam — to Subic Bay, where its personnel and H-21 helicopters were reembarked in *Princeton* (LPH-5), LST-629, and LST-630. The three ships departed the U.S. naval base on the night of 23 January, initially feinting in the direction of Hong Kong but changing course for Danang. Arriving off that South Vietnamese port late on the 25th, *Princeton* launched the Army helicopters for the short flight to shore, while the landing ships discharged their cargo in the harbor.[40]

---

[37]Ltr, CINCPACFLT to CNO, ser 32/00351 of 23 Apr 1962.
[38]CINCPACFLT's views were reported in msg, CP 010517Z Dec 1961.
[39]COMPHIBPAC, report, 6-61 of 9 Nov 1961; memo, OP-61 to OSD (ISA), ser 002157P61 of 8 Dec; msgs, CP 010517Z Dec 1961; CNO 061727Z; ALUSNA Saigon 120710Z; 150200Z; SECSTATE 220035Z; CTF76 230140Z Jan 1962; memo, OP-60 to CNO, ser BM00164-62 of 5 Feb 1962.
[40]Msgs, CTG76.5 170735Z Jan 1962; 220516Z; 260330Z; CHMAAGVN 270107Z.

At the second Secretary of Defense conference in Hawaii, on 15 January, McNamara pledged an additional U.S. light helicopter company if CINCPAC and the Chief, MAAG, Vietnam, decided a fourth unit was required. Admiral Felt and General McGarr determined that another helicopter company was needed to increase South Vietnamese mobility in the difficult Mekong Delta environment. Since the Army was unable to provide the unit immediately, plans were made to deploy a Marine medium helicopter squadron from Okinawa. On 21 March, CINCPAC ordered CINCPACFLT to lift HMM 362 to South Vietnam by approximately 15 April. Admiral Sides concurred with Admiral Schoech's decision to use *Princeton* for the task, especially since this would facilitate a fly-off of the squadron directly to its destination, and avoid a conspicuous offloading at Saigon, which was considered undesirable by the State Department. By the end of March, Soc Trang, a former Japanese fighter strip located south of Can Tho in Ba Xuyen Province, was selected as the operating site of the Marine helicopter unit. On 10 April *Princeton*, having just participated in Exercise Tulungan, sailed from Buckner Bay, Okinawa, with the 259 officers and men and twenty-four H-34D helicopters of HMM 362 on board. The ship rendezvoused in the South China Sea with *Hancock* and two destroyers of Task Force 77. The carrier's aircraft were directed to provide air cover for the fly-off but to approach no closer than twenty miles from the shore. At first light on 15 April 1962, from a position thirty miles southeast of Soc Trang, the Marine squadron flew off *Princeton* to join advance elements already airlifted to the base. In short order, HMM 362 was prepared to begin troop-lift operations as the first Marine combat support unit deployed to South Vietnam. The effort was named Operation Shufly.[41]

As part of the continuing effort to bolster South Vietnamese morale and assure the populace of U.S. support, periodic ship visits were conducted in 1962. One of these resulted from information that the Viet Cong were spreading rumors among the people of being supplied by sea from Communist submarines. When Commander Quyen requested an appro-

---

[41]CINCPAC, Command History, 1962, pp. 191-92; Hooper, Interview with Whitlow, pp. 4-6; Archie J. Clapp, "Shu-Fly Diary," USNIP (Oct 1963), pp. 14, 16; msgs, JCS 192142Z Mar 1962; ADMINO CP 210412Z; JCS 291549Z; CPFLT 300316Z; CGFIRSTMAW 300700Z; COM7FLT 030918Z Apr; CTG79.3 041046Z; 041244Z; CP 072036Z; CTG76.5 090300Z; COMFLT 091134Z; CTU79.3.5 150450Z; CGFIRSTMAW 160850Z; memos, OP-331 to Admin Aide to SECNAV, of 10 Apr 1962; OP-601C6, of 14 Apr; Fails, *Marines and Helicopters, 1962-1973*, pp. 28-32; Whitlow, *U.S. Marines in Vietnam*, pp. 57-65.

priate U.S. action to counter this propaganda, Commander Seventh Fleet dispatched *Bluegill* (SS-242) to South Vietnam. During the first three days of April, the ship became the first U.S. submarine to visit Saigon, where an estimated 2,500 people, including President Diem and other U.S. and South Vietnamese dignitaries, boarded for a tour. Admiral Felt was pleased by the reaction of the capital's populace to the visit and to a diving demonstration in the Saigon River which he described as an "especially effective eye-popper."[42] Leaving Saigon, *Bluegill* proceeded northward along the coast, participating with the South Vietnamese Navy in antisubmarine practice and making her presence known to Vietnamese fishermen and observers on shore. The ship's crew also bartered for fish and passed out Polaroid pictures. After skirting within 1,200 yards of the beaches near Nha Trang, Danang, and Hue, *Bluegill* headed for the open sea on 7 April.[43]

In the fall, another Seventh Fleet ship called on the South Vietnamese capital to demonstrate U.S. support. In August, Captain Quyen requested the visit to Saigon of a guided missile cruiser or destroyer type during the annual Independence Day celebration. Commander Everett A. Parke, the Naval Attache, considered a cruiser preferable from a public relations standpoint, but impractical because of limited port space and facilities at Saigon. He recommended a destroyer for the occasion, believing its presence "would strengthen respect and prestige of Vietnamese people toward the U.S. Navy" and bolster their morale.[44] Soon afterward, CINCPACFLT nominated *Mahan* (DLG-11) for the task. This ship was one of the most modern guided missile frigates in the fleet. During her visit, from 25 to 28 October, many Saigon inhabitants boarded *Mahan* to view at close hand her missiles and other weapons. The guests included President Diem and other high-ranking officials of the South Vietnamese and U.S. governments.[45]

At the end of November 1962, the Pacific Fleet began planning for an additional intelligence-gathering mission, this time by *Weiss* (APD-135), which would survey possible landing sites near Cape Vung Tau, Qui

---

[42]Msg, CP 280106Z Apr 1962.
[43]Msgs, ALUSNA Saigon 250640Z Jan 1962; CPFLT 070236Z Feb; ALUSNA Saigon 130030Z Mar; *Bluegill* 171053Z; ALUSNA Saigon 221009Z; CPFLT 242129Z; ALUSNA Saigon 260936Z; 041020Z Apr; CPFLT 182159Z; CP 280106Z.
[44]Msg, ALUSNA Saigon 290700Z Aug 1962.
[45]Msgs, CPFLT 312346Z Aug 1962; COM7FLT 300726Z Oct.

President Ngo Dinh Diem visits modern guided missile frigate Mahan (DLG-11) during the ship's call at Saigon for the annual South Vietnamese Independence Day celebrations on 26 October 1962. He is flanked by U.S. Ambassador Frederick E. Nolting, Jr., and Commander Ivar A. Johnson, the ship's commanding officer.

Nhon, Danang, and Bac Lieu. On 27 January 1963 Commander Amphibious Force, Seventh Fleet (Task Force 76), COMUSMACV, and Naval Attache, Saigon, representatives met to coordinate their actions. Intelligence reports indicated that the coastal areas were relatively quiet, although landing parties might encounter small arms or sniper fire. The conferees recommended that armed landing craft be positioned off the beaches and that only the UDTs carry weapons for defense ashore. The "frogmen" were to survey to the high-water line, but to proceed no further inland. However, Commander Seventh Fleet subsequently amended these instructions to allow a Marine reconnaissance team "in areas of safe operation, [to] conduct hinterland reconnaissance...on beaches for which it would appear profitable."[46]

On 21 February 1963, *Weiss*, with UDT 12's Detachment Bravo and a team from the 3rd Marine Reconnaissance Battalion on board, began survey operations near Danang. Three days later, while surveying a beach south of the port city, the Marine reconnaissance party received sniper fire. No casualties were sustained, and the entire shore party safely reembarked. The survey operation continued routinely as *Weiss* moved south along the coast. The one exception was the broaching in heavy surf of one of *Weiss*'s LCVPs, which suffered severe damage.

About noon on 12 March, the inland Marine detachment once again came under small arms fire, this time in an area five miles east of Vinh Chau on the Mekong Delta coast. The estimated twelve to fifteen Viet Cong attackers made withdrawal from the beach difficult, but all U.S. personnel safely returned to *Weiss* by 1500. Because of the shallow water, the ship's boats were unable to aid the shore party, but fortunately the enemy troops did not press their attack. Naval leaders, however, were not so sure that luck would remain with *Weiss* for a third time. Admiral Griffin, now the Deputy Chief of Naval Operations (Fleet Operations and Readiness), communicated his concerns to Admiral Sides from Washington:

> The many potentially inflammable incidents involving WEISS activities lead me to wonder if the programmed activities are worth the effort. Furthermore, we have a large mass of info concerning Vietnam coastline gathered over the years. Just a thought as seen from this end where little incidents sometimes assume big proportions.[47]

---

[46]Msg, COM7FLT 060252Z Feb 1963. See also ADMIN CPFLT 300226Z Nov 1962; 120241Z Dec; CTF76 290919Z Jan 1963; 300709Z; 010620Z Feb; 011534Z; 020525Z.

[47]Msg, CNO 121439Z Mar 1962.

In light of Admiral Griffin's observation, and satisfied that *Weiss* had collected sufficient intelligence, Admiral Sides ended the mission. On 14 March 1963, after refueling at Saigon, the ship got underway for Subic.[48]

Naval Air Operations over South Vietnam

A different type of naval mission grew out of reports in March 1962 of unidentified, low-flying, low-speed aircraft entering South Vietnamese air space at night near Pleiku in the Central Highlands. U.S. leaders feared that the Viet Cong might be receiving supplies from North Vietnam by this clandestine method. To deal with Communist air intrusions, the Joint Chiefs, in late March, directed the Navy and Air Force to determine the best U.S. aircraft to counter that threat and then to plan for the alternate basing of detachments of these units in Vietnam. The Navy soon determined that the AD-5Q Skyraider, equipped with a technologically advanced combination of APS-31 and APS-19 radars, had the best means to detect, track, and close with air targets over both mountainous and flat terrain. But, the only aircraft of this type then available in the Western Pacific were embarked in *Hancock*, *Lexington*, and *Coral Sea* as detachments of Air Early Warning Squadron (VAW) 13. If these were removed, the Seventh Fleet's carriers would be denuded of the only airborne electronic countermeasures (ECM) systems available. For this reason, Commander Seventh Fleet objected "strongly to the use of these aircraft for any other mission until this ECM capability is in other aircraft."[49] Admiral Sides concurred with this view, but because of high-level interest in the fate of South Vietnam, the project, named Waterglass, went forward.

On 7 May 1962, Admiral Schoech ordered the establishment at Cubi Point, effective 15 May, of VAW 13 Detachment 1, consisting of six AD-5Qs from *Coral Sea* and *Hancock* and support personnel, in order to train with Air Force ground-control radar. By early June, CINCPACFLT reported the VAW 13 detachment ready for deployment to South

---

[48] Ltr, CINCPACFLT to CNO, ser 62/00033 of 30 Jan 1963; msgs, CTF76 110950Z Feb; 240137Z; *Weiss* 240225Z; 240300Z; 240535Z; CTF76 240753Z; ALUSNA Saigon 250700Z; *Weiss* 260600Z; 260900Z; 261416Z; 040630Z Mar; 041200Z; 060600Z; CTF76 060245Z; *Weiss* 090215Z; 120325Z; 120500Z; 120635Z; 120700Z; COMUSMACV 120802Z; CTF76 121148Z; *Weiss*140400Z; OP-331C2, memo for record, of 24 Feb 1963; memo, OP-33 to OP-03, of 28 Feb.

[49] As reported in msg, CPFLT 212042Z Apr 1962. See also CPFLT 310249Z Mar 1962; JCS 291629Z; CP 012100Z Apr; COMNAVAIRPAC 030253Z; 141932Z.

Vietnam. He proposed basing three aircraft for three weeks at an airfield near the area where air intruders were detected. Admiral Sides suggested Pleiku, if that airfield possessed night lighting, crew accommodations, and other ground support facilities. COMUSMACV, however, designated Tan Son Nhut Airfield outside Saigon as the operations base because he felt it better suited to the VAW 13 detachment's requirements.

In mid-July, CINCPAC authorized his naval component commander to deploy this special AD-5Q interceptor team to South Vietnam for orientation, once a similar Air Force unit equipped with F-102 aircraft completed its own shakedown there. In the early morning hours of 10 August 1962, the three AD-5Q aircraft of VAW 13 Detachment 1, under Lieutenant Wallace A. Shelton, the flight leader, landed at Tan Son Nhut, initiating the Navy's first direct effort to protect South Vietnamese air space. The naval air unit was placed under the operational control of COMUSMACV for the duration of the deployment. The vanguard soon was followed by the remainder of the unit of eleven officers and thirty-four enlisted men. The naval air unit normally had three teams on standby alert, one on routine duty, and one off duty. The AD-5Qs were "scrambled" and vectored to suspicious contacts by ground-control radar and by their on board systems.

For the remainder of August and much of September, five naval pilot-radar operator teams refined their skills in intercepting unidentified aircraft. Since March 1962, U.S. aircraft had been authorized by the JCS to shoot down hostile aircraft discovered in South Vietnamese air space, in which case the victory could have been attributed to the RVNAF.[50] Although no hostile Communist aircraft were identified by the time VAW 13 Detachment 1 redeployed to Cubi Point on 21 September, after relief by an Air Force contingent, fleet commanders deemed the operation a success in preparing for such foes. Of 399 practice intercept attempts using American aircraft during the period of operations, 366, or 91 percent, were judged successful; and U.S. military leaders were satisfied that the Navy's aircraft possessed unique attributes for the air intercept role. Admiral Felt stated:

> The EA-1F [AD-5Q] has proven to be highly suitable to the air defense mission in RVN. It has demonstrated a high intercept probability

---
[50]CINCPAC, Command History, 1962, p. 189.

(consistently above 90 percent); it has flight performance characteristics compatible with pursuit and identification of slow targets; and is equipped with 4-20 mm cannon which can be fired accurately using [onboard] radar or visual sight. It can be effectively used on [combat air patrol] missions and can be deployed to airfields with minimum support facilities and short runways.[51]

Due to the apparent success of this operation in providing the South Vietnamese with a potential defense against or deterrent to Communist air intrusions, CINCPAC decided to continue the program. On 23 October he directed both services to deploy their respective detachments from the Philippines to South Vietnam on an alternating basis for six-week periods. Following the Air Force F-102 unit's deployment at the end of 1962, the Navy's AD-5Qs (now designated EA-1F) resumed their air alert position at Tan Son Nhut from 3 January to 17 February 1963.

Although the Navy's Waterglass teams were scheduled to relieve the F-102 element on 1 May for another operational period in South Vietnam, Commander Seventh Fleet, now Vice Admiral Thomas H. Moorer, objected. The admiral felt that the "continued employment VAW-13 Det 1 aircraft in Water Glass ops [was] detrimental [to] Seventh Fleet training and readiness."[52] The admiral also was concerned about the diversion of the fleet's attention and funds to train and deploy the EA-1F teams. Additionally, fleet training in ECM had of necessity been limited to the Philippines area, thereby depriving operational ships and aircraft in other parts of the Western Pacific of capabilities in this field. The admiral equally stressed the need for carrier-based ECM aircraft in view of the Soviet Union's increasing long-range air searches and noted that "no contact in RVN has ever proven hostile."[53]

At the end of February, Admiral Sides endorsed his fleet commander's proposal for termination of the Navy's participation in Waterglass. On 23 March CINCPAC approved cancellation of the May-June naval deployment, extending instead the Air Force unit's tour. But readiness for air

---

[51]Msg, CP 262132Z Jun 1963. See also msgs, JCS 270251Z Mar 1962; CPFLT 282223Z Apr; COM7FLT 072328Z May; ADMIN CPFLT 220242Z; 022151Z Jun; 110431Z Jul; CP 130145Z; ADMIN CPFLT 172158Z; COM7FLT 310908Z; PACAF 040213Z Aug; VAW 13 Det 1 071019Z; 090637Z; 092209Z; COMUSMACV 100739Z; COM7FLT 140612Z; VAW 13 Det 1 240830Z; 060837Z Sep; VAW 13 Det 1 210405Z; CP 260500Z; CPFLT 272133Z; CINCPAC, Command History, 1962, pp. 188-89.
[52]Msg, COM7FLT 150202Z Feb 1963.
[53]*Ibid.*

USN-1077833

An EA-1F Skyraider of Air Early Warning Squadron 13 at the Naval Air Station, Cubi Point, Philippines, in early 1963.

intercept missions continued to be a requirement, since Admiral Felt considered it possible that the Communists might resort to night air operations if the conflict escalated further. To ease the concerns of Commander Seventh Fleet, VAW 13 Detachment 1's EA-1F complement was increased to seven aircraft in September. Two of these planes were configured for night intercept missions.[54]

---

[54]Msgs, ADMIN COM7FLT 290728Z Sep 1962; PACAF 022043Z Oct; CPFLT 121923Z; ADMIN COMNAVAIRPAC 131711Z; CP 230115Z; 280002Z; PACAF 070026Z Feb 1963; CP 120400Z; CPFLT 122034Z; COM7FLT 150202Z; CPFLT 202219Z; CP 242312Z; COM7FLT 260750Z; CPFLT 270146Z; CPFLT 260301Z Mar; COMUSMACV 261006Z; CPFLT 050004Z

On 30 September 1963 CINCPAC informed COMUSMACV of his desire to reinstitute the alternating Navy-Air Force air intercept training program in South Vietnam on a random basis. With General Harkins's concurrence, Waterglass was restarted. Following the commitment of the Air Force F-102 teams for a two-week period in October, two EA-1Fs of VAW 13 Detachment 1 deployed to Tan Son Nhut in late November for the last Waterglass mission. For one week, the naval aircraft resumed the operational training and readiness mission last conducted in February. Thus, the Navy instituted one more measure to prevent external Communist support for the Viet Cong movement.[55]

Other measures of naval air support were begun in the spring of 1962. In March CINCPACFLT was informed that photographic reconnaissance by naval aircraft was required to supplement ongoing Army and Air Force mapping programs. CINCPAC and the Naval Attache in Saigon urged quick action before the approaching seasonal monsoon cut short the effort. On 28 April Admiral Felt authorized the Navy's participation in the aerial photographic operation. Commander Seventh Fleet directed Heavy Photographic Squadron (VAP) 61, under Commander Donald B. Brady, to undertake the mission. During May the unit's RA-3B Skywarriors, flying from Cubi Point, photographed much of the area from Danang to the Demilitarized Zone. After a five-month respite, VAP 61 again conducted aerial mapping operations over South Vietnam from November 1962 to February 1963. By then, about 90 percent of the project was completed. Soon thereafter, the entire squadron deployed to Guam for other assignments.[56]

In summary, this era of limited partnership was characterized by the employment of American armed forces to support and complement the actions of their South Vietnamese counterparts. The Seventh Fleet surface and air patrols at the 17th parallel and in the Gulf of Siam, the air intercept readiness maintained by VAW 13 Detachment 1, and the

---

Apr; ADMINO CP 130025Z; CNO 091929Z May; CP 262132Z Jun; COMNAVAIRPAC 222242Z Aug; CPFLT 010508Z Sep; CNO, "Allowances and Location of Navy Aircraft," of 30 Sep 1963.
[55]Msgs, CP 302345Z Sep 1963; ADMINO CP 262023Z Oct; CP 291935Z Nov.
[56]Msgs, ALUSNA Saigon 230937Z Mar 1962; CPFLT 240331Z; 180142Z Apr; ALUSNA Saigon 230636Z; CPFLT 250221Z; 290739Z; CINCUSARPAC 182006Z Aug; CTU70.3.1 051413Z Sep; VAP 61 020401Z Oct; CTU70.3.1 170803Z Nov; CINCPACFLT, Annual Report, FY1962, p. 37; VAP 61, Aviation Historical Summary, of 15 Oct 1962; 12 Apr 1963; 19 Oct; ltr, CINCPACFLT to CINCPAC, ser 23/00330 of 18 Apr 1962.

delivery of U.S. helicopter units to Danang and Soc Trang by *Princeton* were in this vein. The Navy also took steps to prepare for future contingencies, whether these included a continuation of low-level warfare or the introduction of U.S. combat forces in strength. In that event, surveys by *Cook* and *Weiss* would provide the fleet with current intelligence on the physical environment.

For the Kennedy administration and for the Navy, the period 1962 to 1963 represented a significant transition in the Vietnam conflict. In the preceding era, from 1950 to 1961, U.S. involvement had consisted of advisory support and material assistance. Beginning in 1964 the activities of American combat forces — naval, air, and ground — overshadowed all other aspects of the war. The interim period from 1962 to 1963 witnessed an effort by the administration to provide the South Vietnamese with more than advice and aid, but to avoid the introduction of U.S. combat forces.

CHAPTER VII

The Navy Enters the Fight Against Communist Insurgency

As Seventh Fleet units assisted the South Vietnamese in traditional naval operations, other naval commands developed less conventional measures for combating the Communist insurgency. As a result of renewed high-level interest in counterinsurgency from late 1961 on, the Navy further developed its ability to participate in this type of conflict by creating and deploying to Southeast Asia SEAL, STAT, and PT boat units. In the same period, it reordered pertinent naval administrative responsibilities.

Development of SEAL Teams

Following final authorization by the CNO, Admiral Anderson, sixty-man SEAL units were established in the Atlantic and Pacific Fleets on 1 January 1962. After its activation at Coronado, California, and assignment to Commander Amphibious Force, U.S. Pacific Fleet, SEAL Team 1 quickly prepared for Southeast Asian commitments. Under the guidance of Commander David Del Giudice, SEAL Team 1 began assimilating officer and enlisted volunteers, most of whom initially came from Underwater Demolition Teams 11 and 12. To establish liaison with the MAAG and to determine the specific requirements of the South Vietnamese environment, two officers from the unit spent part of January and February in-country. One of the team's first missions was to provide guerrilla warfare training to personnel of Mobile Training Team 7, who were scheduled for advisory duty with the South Vietnamese River Force. At the same time, the training of SEAL personnel was given a high priority, since it was necessary to prepare detachments for deployment to Southeast Asia within eight to ten weeks. These men received instruction through the Pacific Fleet amphibious command in special forces techniques, evasion and escape, jungle warfare, unconventional warfare equipment use, and river and restricted waters operations.[1]

By the end of February, with half of its officers and all the enlisted men on board, SEAL Team 1 finalized plans to deploy detachments to South Vietnam. On 10 March two instructors arrived in Saigon to begin a six-month tour training South Vietnamese personnel in clandestine, maritime operations. Soon after the end of this tour, another was instituted. From January to December 1963, a SEAL detachment of two officers and ten men based in Danang continued training South Vietnamese personnel in small boat operations, sabotage, landing techniques, and other related skills.

In April 1962, Mobile Training Team 10-62, composed of one officer, Lieutenant (j.g.) Philip P. Holts, and nine men from both SEAL Team 1 and SEAL Team 2, reported to General Lionel C. McGarr, the Chief MAAG Vietnam, to commence a half-year training cycle. The SEAL Team's purpose was to train selected Vietnamese Coastal Force personnel in reconnaissance, sabotage, and guerrilla warfare; and to prepare them to instruct succeeding classes of "Biet Hai" commandos. By October, sixty-two men had graduated from the grueling course. With completion of the follow-on six-month cycle by Mobile Training Team 4-63, commanded by Lieutenant (j.g.) Alan C. Routh, the Vietnamese were able to assume most of the training mission performed by the SEALs.[2]

As experience was gained on the likely activities of the SEALs, steps were taken to codify the tactics and techniques of these naval special warfare forces. At the end of December 1962, the Assistant Chief of Naval Operations (Fleet Operations and Readiness), Rear Admiral Allan L. Reed, issued "SEAL Teams in Naval Special Warfare," Naval Warfare

---

[1] Msgs, CP 090409Z Jan 1962; CNO 091955Z; CPFLT 171857Z; CNO 241707Z; CP 242341Z Feb; ltrs, CINCPACFLT to CINCPAC, ser 62/0035 of 12 Jan; CINCPACFLT to CINCLANTFLT, ser 31/00220 of 9 Mar; SEAL Team 1, Command History, 1966; Phillip H. Bucklew, transcript of interview with John T. Mason, Jr., U.S. Naval Institute, in Fairfax, Virginia, 1980, pp. 360-65; Hamilton/Marcinko, Interview.

[2] OIC MTT 10-62, report, of 22 Sep 1962; CINCPAC, Command History, 1962, p. 197; Lionel Krisel, "Special Maritime Operations in Vietnam, 1961-1972," unpublished history in Naval Historical Center, 1973, pp. 73-75; memo, OP-60 to CNO, ser BM00199-62 of 12 Feb 1962; ltr, OP-61 to SECNAV, ser 1640P61 of 9 Mar; msg, CPFLT 210012Z; ltr, CINCPACFLT to CINCPAC, ser 62/00299 of 10 Apr; SECDEF, "Record of Third Secretary of Defense Conference, 19 Feb 1962," p. 3-18; Charles Donald Griffin, transcript of interview with John T. Mason, Jr., U.S. Naval Institute, in Washington, D.C., Dec 1975, Vol. II, pp. 522-24; SEAL Team 2, Command History, 1962-1966, ser 019 of 31 May 1967.

USN-1120449

One of the Navy's highly trained SEAL commandos searches for the Viet Cong in South Vietnam's dense Rung Sat swamp.

Information Publication 29-1, which embodied the experience gained in South Vietnam and elsewhere during the preceding year. It remained the basic directive for SEAL operations for much of the Vietnam War. As was true when the concept was first developed in mid-1961, the primary mission of the SEAL team was to "develop a specialized capability for sabotage, demolition, and other clandestine activities conducted in and from restricted waters, rivers, and canals and to conduct training of selected U.S., Allied, and indigenous personnel in a wide variety of skills for use in naval clandestine operations."³

The publication further defined SEAL tasks as conducting attacks on enemy maritime installations, bridges, railway lines, and shipping; protecting similar friendly supply lines and installations; landing and recovering friendly guerrillas, agents, special forces, and downed aviators; carrying out reconnaissance; and developing boats, equipment, and tactics for special warfare. In addition to being used as waterborne units, SEAL detachments also would be prepared to land from submarines or surface craft, parachute from aircraft, and move overland by traditional methods. They would be lightly armed and as "small and highly mobile units [would] confine most logistic support items to those which are portable and are carried by the individual, craft, or vehicle."⁴ Also detailed were operating procedures for the planning, preparation, and employment of SEALs in all phases of warfare. However, the emphasis clearly was on the type of counterinsurgency situation existing in South Vietnam.

SEABEE Technical Assistance Teams Enter Southeast Asia

In addition to SEALs, naval leaders had considered creation of SEABEE technical assistance teams (STATs) since mid-1961. As a consequence of the administration's renewed focus on counterinsurgency forces, on 19 February 1962, Admiral Anderson authorized establishment of these units. They would "provide technical assistance in both socio-economic and military construction areas...gather field and engineering intelligence," and "provide military and engineering support for other U.S. or friendly forces" in selected countries.⁵

By May 1962, CINCPACFLT had plans to staff, organize, and train four teams by 1 October for deployment to Southeast Asia. Initially, two of these units were slated for South Vietnam. Admiral Sides, the Pacific Fleet commander, planned to prepare an additional six teams by 1 February 1963. These units were manned by members of the Pacific Fleet's five mobile construction battalions and each would consist of 13 individuals, including 1 Civil Engineer Corps junior grade officer (officer

---

³OP-03, "SEAL Teams in Naval Special Warfare," NWIP-29-1, of 27 Dec 1962, pp. 1-1— 1-2. See also CINCPACFLT, ltr, ser 00482 of 11 Jun 1962; Hamilton/Marcinko, Interview.
⁴OP-03, NWIP-29-1, pp. 1-4, 1-2—1-3.
⁵Ltr, CINCPACFLT to CNO, ser 45/00415 of 18 May 1962 cites this directive.

in charge), 2 builders, 1 engineering aide, 1 steelworker, 2 construction mechanics, 1 construction electrician, 3 equipment operators, 1 utilities man, and 1 hospital corpsman. Admiral Sides sought highly motivated and skilled men who were prepared to volunteer for STAT service for a minimum period of sixteen months. Intensive training, which was to commence in June 1962 at the Construction Battalion Base Unit, Port Hueneme, California, consisted of language indoctrination and instruction in the customs, technological state, and general characteristics of the countries where the men would serve.

Admiral Sides also recognized that the new program would require officers from outside the Pacific Fleet to conduct the training at Port Hueneme and fill vacated billets in the mobile construction battalions. In addition, extra funds were needed to equip the teams. It would cost $1.2 million to provide each of the STATs with a basic allowance of personal gear, weapons and ammunition, radios, camp components, tools, vehicles, and trailers. Heavier construction equipment, fuel, rations, vehicles, and spare parts suited to specific tasks, entailed an additional outlay of $800,000. Even though Admiral Sides recognized that "complete equipage and material requirements must be deferred until funds become available,"[6] the Pacific Fleet's Service Force was directed to implement the STAT program.

A number of factors caused delay in the deployment of the first units to South Vietnam. Funding problems remained serious, as did the shortage of qualified personnel. Another difficulty arose over possible areas of deployment. Captain Drachnik, the head of the Navy Section of the MAAG in Saigon, initially requested STAT construction assistance for the South Vietnamese Navy. But Rear Admiral Ray C. Needham, CINCPACFLT Chief of Staff, felt that Drachnik's proposals offered "little opportunity to accomplish the objectives of the STAT programs" and were "of such scope as to exceed the direct construction capability of a STAT."[7]

At the same time, Captain Jesse B. Gay, Jr., the CINCPACFLT Deputy Chief of Staff, directed Commander Construction Battalions, U.S. Pacific Fleet, to effect liaison with the military assistance command in South Vietnam, as well as in other countries, to determine the exact nature of

---

[6]Ltr, CINCPACFLT to CNO, ser 45/00415 of 18 May 1962.
[7]Ltr, CINCPACFLT to CINCPAC, ser 45/00802 of 27 Sep 1962.

STAT employment. Captain Gay advised subordinate commands that the "development of appropriate projects will require initiative on the part of the U.S. Navy to make the unique capabilities and mission of the STATs known to in-country U.S. personnel who are in a position to recommend suitable areas of employment."[8] He also cautioned that

> great care must be exercised to insure that projects undertaken reflect credit on the United States. They must make a meaningful contribution to the counterinsurgency efforts or civic actions in the country concerned so that the time, effort, and money expended on the training and equipping of the STAT will not be wasted on projects that might better be accomplished by some other means.[9]

Still acting on the assumption that the units would be deployed after 1 October, the CINCPACFLT Deputy Chief of Staff also directed Commander Construction Battalions, U.S. Pacific Fleet, to be prepared by that date to begin the six-month rotation of teams to their operational areas. However, continued funding problems and the effort to determine STAT missions delayed movement to Southeast Asia of the now fully trained and ready teams.

The fiscal hurdle was surmounted when arrangements were made by MACV for another U.S. government agency to provide the STATs with interim funding support. And by the end of the year, Navy and MACV representatives concluded that the STATs were singularly qualified to take part in the Civilian Irregular Defense Group (CIDG) program. This effort was an attempt to group Vietnamese and Montagnards inhabiting remote regions of the country into more easily defended villages. U.S. Army Special Forces detachments were responsible for overseeing the defense of these outposts, but they needed assistance to construct fortifications, develop water supplies and irrigation systems, improve roads, and erect schools, hospitals, and dwellings. This was seen as an ideal use of STAT capabilities. In November CINCPAC ordered STATs 0501 and 0502 to

---

[8] Ltr, CINCPACFLT to COMCBPAC, ser 45/00786 of 20 Sep 1962.
[9] Ltr, CINCPACFLT to COMCBPAC, ser 45/00786 of 20 Sep 1962. See also memo, OP-405 to OP-04, ser 00022P405 of 27 Apr; ltrs, CINCPACFLT to CNO, ser 45/00582 of 13 Jul; CINCPACFLT to CINPAC, ser 45/00583 of 13 Jul; OSD, "Minutes of the 16 July 1962 Staff Meeting," of 26 Jul; msg, CPFLT 242352Z Aug; ltr, CINCPACFLT to CNO, ser 45/00750 of 8 Sep; msg, CP 110435Z Sep.

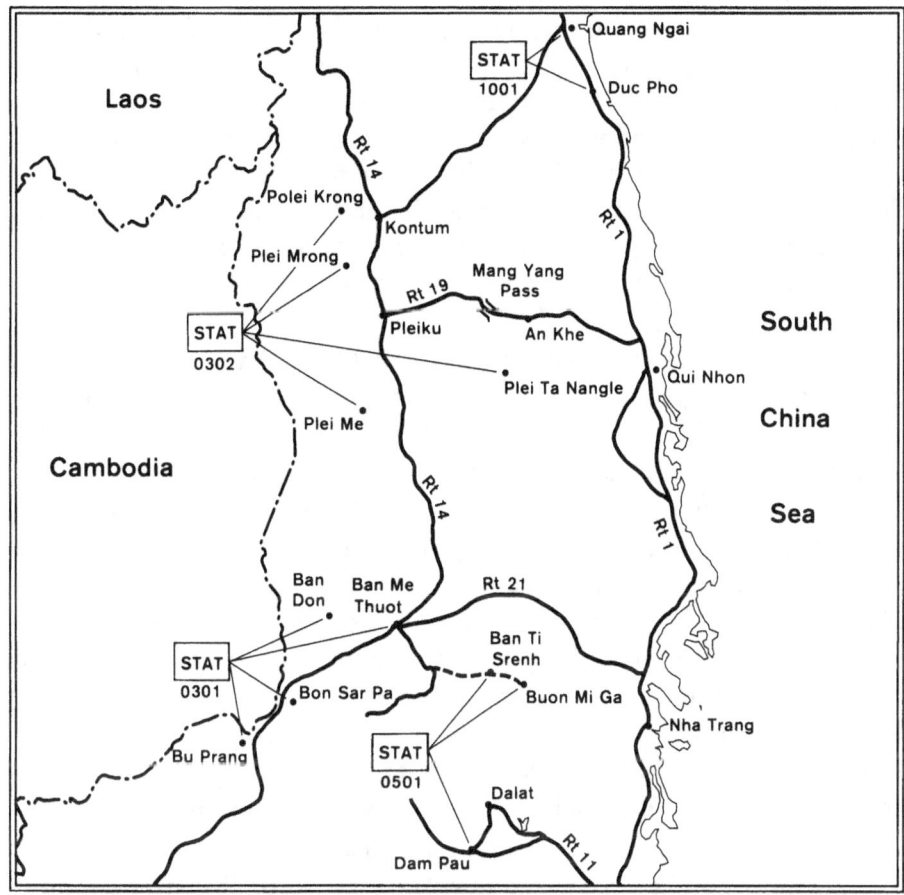

SEABEE Team Deployments in Central South Vietnam, 1963-1964

deploy to South Vietnam for this purpose.[10]

On 25 January 1963, the first of the Navy's technical assistance teams organized and trained for the Kennedy administration's "nation building" tasks arrived in South Vietnam. This was STAT 0501 from Naval Mobile Construction Battalion 5, under the command of Lieutenant (j.g.) Robert L. Ferriter, which initially was assigned to the Special Forces camp at Dam Pau in Tuyen Duc Province. For the next several months, the team

---

[10]Ltrs, CINCPACFLT to COMCBPAC, ser 45/00786 of 20 Sep 1962; CINCPACFLT to CNO, ser 45/00853 of 12 Oct; memo, OP-04 to OP-06, ser 001215P401 of 5 Nov; ltrs, CINCPACFLT to CNO, ser 45/00977 of 21 Nov; CINCPACFLT to CNO, ser 45/0022 of 10 Jan 1963; msgs, CP 120155Z Jan; CINCUSARPAC 232122Z Feb.

labored at such tasks as improving and nearly doubling the length of the 800-foot airstrip, clearing forty-five acres of jungle for farm land, upgrading twenty miles of roadway, and teaching villagers how to produce simple concrete blocks. In mid-March STAT 0501 redeployed to even more remote Darlac Province in order to reopen fourteen miles of abandoned road from Ban Ti Srenh, their temporary site, to the Special Forces camp at Buon Mi Ga. By mid-July the road project was completed and the team capped the effort by constructing at the terminus a Special Forces "A team" camp for the better protection of the local Rhadé tribesmen.

Lieutenant Clyde V. Popowich's STAT 0502 was based in a completely different operating environment far to the south in Tri Ton, Chau Doc Province, near the "Seven Mountains" area on the Cambodian border. This Mekong Delta location was heavily populated with the enemy, and the team underwent periodic attacks and harassment. Soon after the thirteen-man detachment's arrival in January, the Viet Cong revealed their recognition of the STAT's potential by killing and mutilating a village elder who had provided the team with laborers. Nevertheless, STAT 0502 succeeded in upgrading or constructing over forty miles of road, which included work on four bridges and twenty-two culverts, and in building a helicopter pad and an 1,800-foot airstrip for the "Green Berets." The team also aided the populace by drilling water wells, constructing a dam, and grading the site of a proposed refugee settlement.

The delicacy of the STAT program was clearly revealed in one instance. To ease the lot of the people in one village, the SEABEEs began drilling a well. Formerly, water could be obtained only at the local Buddhist pagoda, a situation which had enabled the monks to oversee the spiritual development of the villagers. The religious leaders evidently were disturbed over the new course of events. Recognizing the monks' importance in countering Communist influence, Lieutenant Popowich quickly suspended work on the village well, and, with the monks' relieved assent, sank a new one within the temple grounds. As a final effort, STAT 0502 built a Special Forces camp at Don Chau on the coast in Vinh Binh Province. As evidence that the deployment had been fraught with peril, Lieutenant Popowich was awarded the Bronze Star with Combat "V."

On 1 July 1963, a final solution to the funding problem was reached when the STATs were put under the operational control of Commander U.S. Military Assistance Command, Vietnam (COMUSMACV). At the same time, STATs 0301 and 0302 from Naval Mobile Construction Battalion 3 relieved the first teams deployed to Southeast Asia. Lieutenant (j.g.) Richard Wisenbaker's STAT 0301 was assigned to construct a Special Forces camp at Bon Sar Pa, two miles from the Cambodian border in a mountainous, densely wooded, and exposed corner of Darlac Province. The team was subjected to a light probing attack by the Viet Cong, on the morning of 16 September, but fortunately no casualties were sustained. In addition to the fortified encampment, STAT 0301 built a 2,000-foot airstrip, drilled a well, improved local roads, and erected a two-room schoolhouse. The team's hospital corpsman, T. L. Veatch, provided the Montagnards with medical attention and sanitation instruction. A detachment from Lieutenant Wisenbaker's unit also constructed an 1,800-foot airstrip and sank a 110-foot well at Bu Prang. After road work in the vicinity of Ban Don at the end of the year, STAT 0301 moved to Ban Me Thuot, the provincial capital. Completing a 1,500-foot taxiway at the airfield, the SEABEE team departed the country on 18 January 1964.

As part of the same deployment, STAT 0302, under the command of Lieutenant (j.g.) James H. Abing, arrived in Saigon on 7 July 1963 and relieved STAT 0502. After the equipment turnover was completed, separate detachments of the team moved to Plei Mrong and Polei Krong. Both were north of Pleiku city in the Central Highlands. At the former location, team members built structures for South Vietnamese paramilitary forces and for a leper colony, and conducted road and bridge repairs. At Polei Krong even greater demands were placed on the naval constructionmen. While STAT 0302 constructed a 1,500-foot airstrip and a 114-foot bridge, Vietnamese personnel were given on-the-job training and local laborers were provided employment. The Viet Cong were not idle either. On 1 October the enemy destroyed a 38-meter bridge that was half-finished. A South Vietnamese river ferry also twice fell victim to the stealthy foe. However, the SEABEEs were able each time to refloat it.

After completing their tasks at Plei Mrong and Polei Krong, Lieutenant Abing's team reassembled in the provincial capital, and on 21 October 1963 moved to a third site, Plei Me. Action around this village in 1965 was to ignite one of the fiercest battles of the war — that of the Ia Drang Valley. In order to reach this site with the necessary earth movers and construction equipment, Lieutenant Abing and the twelve men of his team had to repair the road as they moved forward. Escorted by Special Forces soldiers and 300 South Vietnamese irregulars, STAT 0302 completed the two-day convoy south into the jungled region. By early December another characteristically shaped triangular CIDG camp had been constructed.

Once again, the SEABEE detachment was called upon to build a camp for the Special Forces, this time at Plei Ta Nangle, south of An Khe. During the move to Pleiku, one of the SEABEE trucks detonated a Viet Cong mine and was heavily damaged, but no casualties were suffered. On 6 December STAT 0302 convoyed from Pleiku through the famed Mang Yang Pass and southeast on Route 19 to An Khe. Then, the combined force pushed south toward their destination on a long unused, and now barricaded and booby-trapped road. While engaged in clearing hazards, Chief Utilityman James W. Cigainero, assistant officer in charge of the team, became the first SEABEE casualty in the Vietnam conflict when he stepped into one of the simple but effective Viet Cong punji traps and received leg wounds. After constructing the fortified encampment and clearing land for an airstrip, the much traveled unit returned to Pleiku and departed South Vietnam in January 1964.[11]

Even as STATs 0301 and 0302 relieved the original teams, 0501 and 0502, in July 1963, proposals were made to deploy an additional two units to South Vietnam. Largely through the efforts of Mr. Ogden Williams, Assistant Director for Rural Affairs in the United States Operations Mission (USOM), plans were made to use these SEABEE technical assistance teams in support of the foreign aid program, instead of the Special Forces. With less emphasis on military construction, the STATs could then be available for civic action and village socio-economic projects. Accordingly, COMUSMACV recommended deployment of two additional teams, for a total of four in-country at any one time, and the assignment of the new units to USOM's Rural Rehabilitation Program, better known as the Strategic Hamlet Program, which received funding from the Agency for International Development (AID). CINCPAC, who

---

[11]COMCBPAC, Detachment RVN, "Completion Report, 1963-1972," of 30 May 1972, pp. 1-3, 3-3; COMCBPAC, "Helping Others Help Themselves," of 13 Jan 1969, pp. 4, 29-35; Francis J. Kelley, *U.S. Army Special Forces, 1961-1971*, in series *Vietnam Studies* (Washington: Department of the Army/GPO, 1973), pp. 35-44; msgs, CP 082158Z Jun 1963; COMUSMACV 051044Z Mar; ltrs, CINCPACFLT, ser 45/00350 of 16 Apr; CINCPACFLT to CINPAC, ser 32/00693 of 9 Aug; CBTEAM 0501, Completion Report, ser 30 of 15 Jul; CBTEAM 0302, Completion Report, ser 8 of 2 Nov; CBTEAM 0501, Completion Report, ser 103 of 17 Jan 1964; Charles J. Merdinger, "Civil Engineers, Seabees, and Bases in Vietnam," *U.S. Naval Institute Naval Review* (May 1970), pp. 258-59; Cigainero, UTC James W., Casualty Report of 27 Dec 1963; Tregaskis, *Southeast Asia*, pp. 60-61.

was aware of the successes of the STATs in Southeast Asia, authorized the increased use of the SEABEE teams on the condition that the necessary billets be filled from MACV and not CINCPACFLT resources. He added that stipulation because at that time U.S. military and political leaders were considering the return to the United States in October 1963 of 1,000 U.S. military personnel. General Harkins complied with the reallocation of personnel within his command and, as a result, on 1 September Admiral Felt authorized the provision of two more STATs to operate in more populated areas.[12]

In mid-October, STATs 1001 and 1002 of Naval Mobile Construction Battalion 10 arrived in South Vietnam and quickly deployed to their assigned operating areas. The former team, under the command of Lieutenant (j.g.) Vincent L. Kontny, set up headquarters in Quang Ngai city on the Annam coast. In keeping with the reemphasized civic action role, STAT 1001 provided Vietnamese hospitals, orphanages, and schools with badly needed maintenance and repair work. Still operating from Quang Ngai, the team then participated in a hamlet construction project south of the city in Duc Pho. There Lieutenant Kontny's men drilled wells, built bridges, and graded local roads and footpaths for the inhabitants. Steps were also taken to help the government reassert its control of the population through pacification measures. Once areas of the Duc Pho District were swept by South Vietnamese forces, STAT 1001 moved in to repair roads and bridges destroyed by the enemy. By 13 February 1964, thirteen bridges with a combined span of 325 feet were reconstructed. At the same time, Hospital Corpsman 1st Class T. G. Gardner, the team corpsman, provided the Vietnamese with badly needed medical attention, especially during one of the country's periodic cholera epidemics.

STAT 1002, which deployed to Hue, engaged in similar activities in and around the old imperial capital. In addition to road and bridge repair and well-sinking work, the team, led by Lieutenant (j.g.) Warren M. Garbe, cleared land and constructed airstrips. The socio-economic aspect of the STAT's mission was maintained especially by the provision of medical assistance and the erection of a school and a dispensary. When

---

[12]COMCBPAC, "Helping Others Help Themselves," p. 35; msgs, CP 102329Z Jul 1963; COMUSMACV 300824Z; CP 060258Z Aug; 170147Z; COMUSMACV 291209Z; CP 010506Z Sep; CPFLT 011944Z; CINCPAC, Command History, 1963, pp. 236, 247.

STATs 1001 and 1002 ended their South Vietnamese tour in April 1964, government influence over the daily lives of the people in the respective operating areas was enhanced, to some extent, as a result of the units' work.[13]

With the SEABEE effort in South Vietnam expanding in the fall of 1963, steps were taken to bring more centralized naval direction to the program. On 30 September CINCPACFLT established the billet of Commander Naval Construction Battalions, U.S. Pacific Fleet Detachment, Republic of Vietnam. Thereafter, operational control of the STATs was exercised by COMUSMACV and command by Commander Service Force, U. S. Pacific Fleet, through Commander Construction Battalions, U.S. Pacific Fleet. To facilitate liaison, the SEABEE Vietnam detachment headquarters was co-located in Saigon with the Deputy Officer in Charge of Construction. Lieutenant Commander John A. Wright (CEC), an early proponent of the STAT concept, became the first officer in charge of the South Vietnam detachment.[14]

After one year in the field, the SEABEE technical assistance teams impressed U.S. political and military leaders with their contribution to the counterinsurgency effort. General Harkins summarized the views of many observers in commenting that "the magnitude and quality of the work of the STATs...has shown conclusively that small military engineering units properly equipped, manned, and trained are extremely valuable in every phase of unconventional warfare."[15]

The Initiation of Maritime Operations Against North Vietnam

As the Navy worked to counteract the Communist insurgency in South Vietnam, U.S. leaders gave greater attention to covert, clandestine operations against North Vietnam. As early as November 1960, Admiral Felt gave consideration to striking the enemy in his rear bases in order to

---

[13]COMCBPAC, "Helping Others Help Themselves," pp. 30, 35-36; CBTEAM 1001, Completion Report, ser 133 of 15 Apr 1964; CBTEAM 1002, Completion Report, ser 62 of 22 Apr; Tregaskis, *Southeast Asia*, pp. 60-61.
[14]COMCBPAC, "Helping Others Help Themselves," p. 28; COMCBPAC, Detachment RVN, Completion Report, pp. 1-4, 2-3, 3-3.
[15]Quoted in Naval History Division, "History of Naval Operations in Vietnam, 1946-1963," unpublished history in Naval Historical Center, 1964, pp. 205-06.

upset "some Communist apple carts."[16] Following the benchmark Bay of Pigs and Laos crises in April 1961, U.S.-trained South Vietnamese personnel carried out increasingly energetic covert actions against North Vietnam. In keeping with the "flexible response" concept of the Kennedy administration, North Vietnamese guerrilla warfare and subversive activity demanded and justified like countermeasures. The number of U.S. personnel engaged in training and supervising the Vietnamese in these operations was increased and now included military advisors from the MAAG. By the end of 1961, South Vietnamese motorized junks, carrying agents and supplies, were delivering their cargo to points in North Vietnam at least once each month.[17]

As a result of the dramatic decisions made following the Taylor visit to South Vietnam and the institution of the "limited partnership," the nature and degree of U.S. participation in covert operations changed in early 1962. The operation received high-level support when the Special Group (Counterinsurgency), composed of senior White House, State Department, Defense Department, JCS, CIA, and other representatives, was established on 18 January. The group was charged with ensuring the unity of U.S. and allied efforts to combat insurgency and indirect aggression.

Considering new approaches to the Southeast Asian problem, CINCPAC observed that the North Vietnamese were particularly susceptible to covert action:

> When Ho Chi Minh acquired full title to former French assets in North Vietnam he also logically acquired the vulnerability which such assets represent. Power plants, railroads, bridges, VIP residences, and the like — all represent relatively vulnerable holdings totally unknown to Viet Minh before 1954. We should exploit this vulnerability. So far, DRV has been enjoying the best of two worlds —conventionality in the North and uninhibited terrorism in the South.[18]

---

[16]Msg, CP of 2 Nov 1960.
[17]CNO, memo for record, ser 00020-61 of 28 Aug 1961; memo, OP-60 to Joint Staff (J-3), JCS, ser 0020P60 of 8 Jan 1962; msgs, CP 111920Z Dec 1961; CTU70.5.7 270611Z; 090530Z Jan 1962; OSD 102358Z; CPFLT 172042Z; CP 192142Z; ADMIN COM7FLT 211356Z; CP 050548Z Feb; Krisel, "Special Maritime Operations in Vietnam," pp. 55, 58-62, 66-67; William Colby, *Honorable Men: My Life in the CIA* (New York: Simon and Schuster, 1978), pp. 172-75, 219; William E. Colby, transcript of interview with Edward J. Marolda, Naval Historical Center, in Washington, D.C., 9 Jun 1980, pp. 1-10.
[18]Msg, CP 250501Z Apr 1962.

Admiral Felt added that in any proposed actions against North Vietnam,

> we should strive for a direct cause-and-effect relationship. A mining of Dong Ha-Saigon railroad ideally would be followed within a week by slightly larger destruction of the DRV Lao Kay-Hanoi line.... In a case such as a VC ambush of a GVN convoy, where retaliation in kind is impossible, a submarine transported commando raid on some DRV coastal facility would serve the purpose.... By utilizing our superiority in means of transporting clandestine operators via [aircraft] and submarines against which DRV has little or no defensive capability and by use of special techniques such as UDT forces.[19]

Admiral Felt believed that the North Vietnamese would become so concerned about the loss of material resources and the possibility of an insurrection developing that they would ease pressure on the South.

Many of these recommendations were echoed in Admiral Anderson's proposals of July 1962 for a policy on Communist activities in Southeast Asia. The CNO recommended a "campaign of harassment" against North Vietnam if the Communists persisted in their support of insurgency. The program would be implemented in relation to the Communist reaction: "Step up the harassment campaign as Viet Cong activities increase and slow it down as the Viet Cong slow down.... Select harassment measures which most nearly represent retaliation in kind, on a higher scale."[20]

Specific actions already had been taken to implement CINCPAC's proposals. Psychological warfare broadcasts over clandestine radios and leaflet drops into North Vietnam were conducted, as was infiltration of South Vietnamese reconnaissance teams. U.S. planners then chose a target for sabotage that utilized the great advantage afforded by the U.S. Navy's control of the sea. Preparations were made to land in North Vietnam, from a motorized junk, specially trained South Vietnamese "frogmen" in order to sink a Swatow class gunboat. Prior to this action, a U.S. submarine would remain submerged at the entrance to likely Swatow bases and report the vessels' arrivals and departures. On 16 May CINCPAC ordered his fleet commander to provide a submarine for the intended operation, named Wise Tiger. *Catfish* (SS-339) was directed to proceed to the mouth of the Giang River in order to observe maritime activity around the Swatow base at Quang Khe. Equipped with a special

---

[19]Msg, CP 250501Z Apr 1962. See also CINCPAC, Command History, 1962, p. 48.
[20]Memo, CNO to JCS, ser 000762P60 of 13 Jul 1962.

communications circuit, the submarine was to remain in international waters no closer than three miles from shore and signal information on the Swatows and other vessels. At the beginning of the last week in May, *Catfish* set out from Manila on her sensitive mission. However, there is no evidence that a Swatow was sunk in succeeding months as a result of this surveillance.

Although the existing CIA-directed program against North Vietnam had CINCPAC's strong support, various problems arose to limit its effectiveness. The motorized junks and other craft used in the maritime operation were proving inadequate for the rigorous forays into northern waters, since they were neither fast enough nor sufficiently armed. CINCPAC soon became dissatisfied with the conduct of the operation as well. Admiral Felt believed that the CIA's planners in Saigon were not suitably trained to mount a naval mission of this type or make use of the Navy's resources, in particular submarines and SEALs. In September, the admiral observed to COMUSMACV that the "program should have been under full head of steam a long time ago."[21]

But, steps already had been taken to inject U.S. naval support and equipment into maritime operations. In late August, COMUSMACV proposed the use of U.S. motor torpedo boats, supported by a naval logistic unit based in Danang, for the runs to the North. Non-Americans would form crews for the boats. This concept was forwarded to Washington for high-level consideration.[22] On 27 September 1962, the administration's Special Group (5412) formally suggested the use of PTs, as well as SEALs, in covert operations against North Vietnam.

The following week, on 6 October, Deputy Secretary of Defense Gilpatric directed the Navy to reactivate by January 1963 two aluminum-hulled motor torpedo boats, both of which were built in 1950. In response, the CNO ordered the Chief, Bureau of Ships to prepare for sea PT-810 and PT-811, then mothballed at the Philadelphia Naval Shipyard. The boats would each be armed with two 40-millimeter guns and two 20-millimeter guns, and would be rigged for quiet operations.

---

[21]Msg, CP 040745Z Sep 1962. See also Democratic Republic of Vietnam, *Facts and Figures Concerning U.S. and U.S. Agents' Sabotage Activities in North Vietnam* (Hanoi: Ministry of Foreign Affairs, 1963).

[22]Msgs, JCS 281850Z Apr 1962; CP 140912Z May; 160032Z; ADMIN CPFLT 162209Z; COMSUBFLOT 7 210415Z; 220543Z; CP 040745Z Sep; 060013Z; 082355Z; Krisel, "Special Maritime Operations in Vietnam," pp. 72-79; CINCPAC, Command History, 1962, pp. 177-78; Colby, *Honorable Men*, pp. 219-20; Colby, Interview, pp. 10-12.

While the Secretary of Defense believed this measure to be "a step in the right direction," he also felt there was a need to "get us moving ahead more rapidly in developing this operational support capability."[23] Accordingly, he expressed his

> desire that priority attention also be given to the procurement of foreign-made craft of the PT boat category. Specifically, unless you have objections or considerations of preference with which I am not familiar, I desire that you take immediate action to procure two boats of the Norwegian Navy's NASTY class.... General Lansdale, my Assistant for Special Operations, has been directed to monitor this undertaking and to provide such additional information as may be required.[24]

During the winter of 1962-1963, the small boat force resulting from these directives assembled on the East Coast and prepared for fleet service. PT-810 and PT-811, redesignated PTF-1 and PTF-2, respectively, were reactivated and refitted with more serviceable equipment and with the prescribed weapons. Sea trials, however, soon revealed that further work was needed on the boats. PTF-1 developed an engine malfunction and a fuel leak into the engine compartment. PTF-2 also was found to have a faulty exhaust system. Necessary repairs at the Philadelphia Naval Shipyard and the presence of ice in the Delaware River delayed the boats' departure for service with Commander Amphibious Force, U.S. Atlantic Fleet at Little Creek, Virginia, until spring.

Two Nastys, purchased by the Navy from Norway, arrived in the United States early in 1963 and almost immediately began crew familiarization, sea trials, and refitting with American equipment. By 3 May, both boats, designated PTF-3 and PTF-4, were placed in service at Little Creek.[25]

---

[23]Memo, SECDEF to SECNAV, of 12 Oct 1962. See also memos, VCNO to SECNAV, ser 054134 of 22 Mar 1962; OP-03 to CNO, ser 00023-63 of 25 Jan 1963; DOD, News Release, No. 1879-62 of 19 Nov 1962.

[24]Memo, SECDEF to SECNAV, of 12 Oct 1962.

[25]Ltrs, CNO to CHBUSHIPS, ser 0326P46 of 16 Oct 1962; ser 0100P03B1 of 18 Oct; Director, Navy Department Program Evaluation Center, ser 00215PEC of 23 Nov; memo, CHBUSHIPS to CNO, of 19 Dec 1962; msgs, NAVSHIPYD PHILA, COMPHIBLANT, CINCLANTFLT, CNO, BUSHIPS 3 Jan 1963 — 6 May 1963; memo, OP-03 to OP-09, ser 00023-63 of 25 Jan; *Jane's Fighting Ships, 1968-1969*, Raymond V. B. Blackman, ed. (London: McGraw-Hill, 1970), pp. 430-31; Krisel, "Special Maritime Operations in Vietnam," pp. 80-81; Michael L. Mulford, transcript of interview with Edward J. Marolda, Naval Historical Center in Washington, DC, 21 Apr 1983.

The Navy Enters the Fight Against Communist Insurgency 205

To publicize the capabilities of the newly assembled PTF force, on 30 April the CNO directed his Atlantic Fleet commander to dispatch one of the Norwegian boats to Washington for a three-day visit. On 13 May PTF-3, under the command of Lieutenant (j.g.) John R. Graham, arrived at the Washington Navy Yard. The press was informed that the boats were "designed to perform amphibious support and coastal operations" and also for use "by the Navy's Sea-Air-Land (SEAL) Teams in unconventional and paramilitary operations."[26] On the 15th the Secretary and Under Secretary of the Navy and high-ranking naval officers embarked in the craft for a thirty-minute demonstration on the Potomac River.[27]

Soon afterward, preparations were made to deploy PTF-3 and PTF-4 to Southeast Asia in order to conduct the long-contemplated special operations. On 28 June, Admiral Anderson assigned the two Nastys to CINCPACFLT's Amphibious Group 1. However, before the transit from the East Coast was made, Admiral Sides, the Pacific Fleet commander, after a thorough study of the proposed operating environment, directed modifications to the PTFs' armament. Specifically, in addition to the two single-mount, 40-millimeter, and two single-mount, 20-millimeter guns, the admiral stipulated that the boats be equipped with two 3.5-inch rocket launchers and two or more flamethrowers.

At the end of August, after the completion of much of this work, the PTFs were loaded on board *Vancouver* (LPD-2) and transported via the Panama Canal to San Diego. Once there, Commander Amphibious Force, U.S. Pacific Fleet was given the first opportunity, albeit a short one, to prepare the boats and train the crews for service in the Western Pacific and to evaluate their future needs.

Two days of exercises with SEALs and UDT personnel, including delivery and recovery operations, night interdiction, sneak attack, beach marking and buoy laying, and day and night rendezvous followed. The SEALs found the PTF a suitable craft for their type of activity, but the crews were considered not yet fully familiar with their unconventional warfare role. Weapons firing practice by boat personnel was somewhat more satisfactory, considering the fact that the men had conducted live-fire only twice before. Habitability of the PTFs, with crews and ten-man

---

[26]DOD, News Release, No. 671-63 of 13 May 1963.
[27]Msgs, CINCLANTFLT 012056Z May 1963; 031756Z; CHINFO 062148Z; COMNAVAIRLANT 072053Z; COMUDUTWO 111533Z; Schedule, "Secretary of the Navy Visit to the PTF-3 at Quantico," of 15 May; *Washington Post*, 16 May 1963.

SEAL detachments on board, was determined adequate, but only for operations lasting forty-eight hours or less. The critical factor was the lack of stowage space for fresh water and provisions. The Pacific Fleet amphibious commander also advised CINCPACFLT that the boats needed specialized logistic support to remain operational in Southeast Asia. Special high-grade diesel fuel, lubricating oil, and coolants were essential. With most of the spare parts of European manufacture, an efficient supply system also was required. In addition, the need for frequent screw replacement, engine overhauls, and a one-month drydocking period every six months demanded sophisticated base support, such as then could be provided only at Subic Bay in the Philippines.

The amphibious commander further observed that the boat crews should be provided with instruction in self-defense, evasion and escape, and specialized training in covert operations support. Extended training in San Diego could not be conducted because *Point Defiance* (LSD-31) was scheduled to lift the boats to Pearl Harbor on 17 September. But the admiral suggested that training personnel be embarked, and a mobile training team continue the process in Hawaii and in Subic. Vice Admiral Ephraim P. Holmes, the commander of the Pacific Fleet amphibious force, finally concluded that without a sophisticated forward support and training base in South Vietnam, "this operation will soon come apart and probability of highly detrimental effects is apparent."[28]

With training officers embarked, *Point Defiance* transported PTF-3 and PTF-4 to Hawaii, where preparations for the Southeast Asian commitment proceeded in late September and early October 1963. At the same time, naval leaders began to grow concerned about the heavy publicity given the new additions to the fleet. As a result, emphasis was placed on the boats' capability to counter Soviet motor torpedo boats rather than on their special operations role. The CNO allowed the Office of Information to provide press and film coverage while the PTFs were in Hawaii, but felt that "in view of the ultimate operations planned for PTF-3 and PTF-4, they should be given a minimum of publicity" thereafter.[29]

---

[28]Msg, COMPHIBPAC 121747Z Sep 1963. See also msgs, CNO 262043Z Jun 1963; 282313Z; CPFLT 031953Z Jul; CLFLT 101434Z; CPFLT 160229Z; CLFLT 252016Z; COMPHIBPAC 210115Z Aug.

[29]Msg, CNO 251847Z Sep 1963. See also COMPHIBPAC 221711Z Aug; CPFLT 140614Z Sep; COMPHIBPAC 141629Z; CPFLT 151943Z; Mulford, Interview.

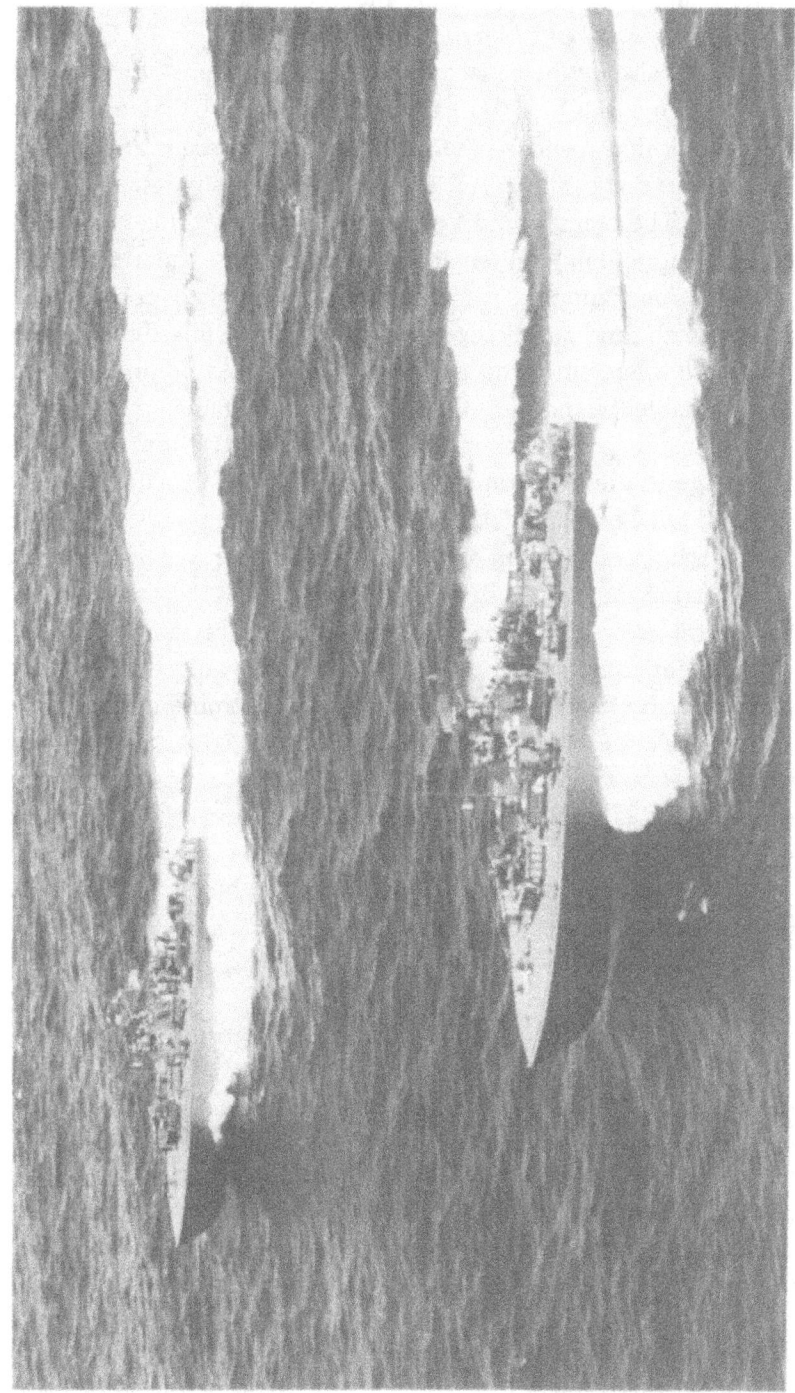

The Navy's first contingent of Nasty fast patrol boats, consisting of PTF-3 and PTF-4, proceed at high speed off Pearl Harbor, Hawaii. The boats soon were transported to Southeast Asia.

As the boats and their crews made the month-long transit to the Western Pacific on board *Point Defiance*, arriving in Subic on 22 October, the naval command also refined plans for the establishment of a forward base in South Vietnam. On 10 October CINCPACFLT detailed his proposal for establishing a shore-based mobile support team at Danang, rather than a light cargo ship (AKL) as previously suggested at the Washington level. The team would be composed of two officers and ten men, including personnel in engineman, electrician's mate, quartermaster, electronics technician, gunner's mate, shipfitter, damage controlman, machinery repairman, and storekeeper ratings, taken primarily from the PTF crews. Berthing, messing, and repair facilities would be provided by the MAAG. To enable the mobile support team to maintain and repair the boats in Vietnam, it was planned to transport a 100-ton tool and machinery package to the site from Subic. Fuel could be procured locally through the Shell Oil Company. CINCPACFLT also attempted to secure a small floating drydock and a ten-ton crane for heavier repair tasks. In addition to preferring the mobile support team to the AKL, because it was a more economical use of naval resources, Admiral Ulysses S. G. Sharp, the new Pacific Fleet commander, felt the small team would be less likely to compromise security. In that regard, he strongly recommended that the "boats be stricken (under MAP or other appropriate cover) at least for record purposes from U.S. Navy records...to preclude possible future embarrassment to the U.S. Navy and the U.S. Government."[30] Action on this proposal, however, was not taken until late 1964. Although South Vietnamese personnel operated the boats when in North Vietnamese waters, they remained under U.S. register.

Administrative Preparations for Counterinsurgency Warfare

To better control and coordinate the Navy's counterinsurgency effort, the CNO instituted several organizational changes. In early January 1962 Admiral Anderson established a Navy-Marine Corps Cold War Advisory Panel to disseminate relevant information among the planning offices in Washington and to "conceive, develop and process ideas by which the

---

[30] Msg, CPFLT 102342Z Oct 1963. See also CP 030350Z May 1963; CNO 051937Z Jun; CPFLT 302031Z; CNO 271759Z Aug; CP 112011Z Oct.

Navy and Marine Corps can better serve the United States in gaining advantage in the cold war."[31] Placed under the supervision of the Deputy Chief of Naval Operations (Plans and Policy), the panel was chaired on an alternating basis by the Assistant Chief of Naval Operations (Plans and Policy) and the Director, Politico-Military Policy Division. Its members were drawn from those offices, from the Bureau of Naval Personnel, and from the Headquarters, U.S. Marine Corps.

Soon afterward, the CNO fixed responsibilities within the Office of the Chief of Naval Operations for counterinsurgency matters. The Deputy Chief of Naval Operations (Fleet Operations and Readiness) was designated the central point of contact. Within that office, the Strike Warfare Division ensured the Navy's operational readiness for the conduct of counterinsurgency actions through training, development of tactical doctrine, and determination of operational requirements. Similarly, the Deputy Chief of Naval Operations (Plans and Policy) was assigned responsibility for planning as regards counterinsurgency. That office's Politico-Military Policy Division provided advice on the political ramifications of an intended operation, while the Strategic Plans Division coordinated planning so as to attain the "maximum counter-insurgency effectiveness...as may be achieved in balance with limited war and general war readiness."[32]

In addition, due to the increasing number of SEAL and other units involved in unconventional warfare in Southeast Asia and elsewhere, it became apparent by the fall of 1963 that greater centralization of administrative support and control of naval special operations forces was required. Accordingly, on 10 October 1963, Naval Operations Support Groups were established in the Pacific and Atlantic Fleets. The groups assumed administrative control of fleet SEAL, beach jumper unit, underwater demolition team, and PT boat units.[33]

In addition to organizing commands to provide more responsive administrative support, the Navy took steps to prepare personnel for counterinsurgency warfare in the hostile Southeast Asian environment. This was especially the case after Admiral Anderson learned early in 1962 that the "President was quite emphatic...that he wanted people from all

---
[31]CNO, OPNAV Instruction 3410.5A, ser 9P06B1 of 2 Jan 1962.
[32]CNO, OPNAV Instruction 5430.22, ser 129P60 of 27 Feb 1962.
[33]Ltr, McDonald to Kennedy, of 21 Nov 1963; CINCPACFLT, Annual Report, FY1964, p. 34.

Services trained in antiguerrilla warfare, including the Attaches."[34] As a result, on 6 January the CNO informed his fleet commanders in chief that "all U.S. Navy personnel now in Vietnam or sent to Vietnam or such places in the future should receive sufficient training in the use of small arms and other appropriate weapons for individual protection should they become involved in combat with guerrilla-type adversaries."[35]

To implement this directive, the Bureau of Naval Personnel established at fleet training activities indoctrination courses in small arms use and self-defense to qualify individuals for Southeast Asian duty. For the next six months, naval training programs and courses of instruction in subjects related to counterinsurgency were increased significantly. Both the U.S. Naval Academy and the Naval War College intensified their teaching efforts. At the same time naval personnel, in growing numbers, received relevant instruction at non-Navy schools, such as the Armed Forces Staff College, the National War College, and the Army's Special Warfare Center. In addition, the Office of the Chief of Naval Operations and the technical bureaus concerned with unconventional and Cold War military activities dispatched key personnel to selected areas of the world. Admiral Anderson explained to his flag officers that the "broad objective of the overall [counterinsurgency training] program is to prepare officers for command, staff, country team and departmental positions involved in planning and conducting counterinsurgency operations, with emphasis on improving U.S. capability for countering subversive insurgency in emerging nations."[36]

On 19 July 1962, the Chief of Naval Operations issued a formal instruction establishing the Navy's "Counterinsurgency Education and Training Program." This comprehensive effort was designed to "familiarize officers of all grades with the history of insurgency movements, in order that they will understand the problems, characteristics, tactics and

---

[34]CNO, Minutes of Meeting of 5 Jan 1962. President Kennedy also expressed his desire that training in and knowledge of counterinsurgency operations be a prerequisite for selection to flag and general officer rank. See OP-09A, memo for record, ser 0037P09 of 9 Mar 1962. See also memo, OP-601C to OP-06, ser BM0269-62 of 10 Mar; *U.S.-V.N. Relations*, bk. 12, pp. 457-59.
[35]Msg, CNO 061353Z Jan 1962. See also BUPERS 021323Z Feb.
[36]Ltr, CNO to Flag and General Officers, of 15 May 1962. See also memos, OP-60 to Joint Staff, ser 001193P60 of 8 Dec 1961; OSD to CNO, of 19 Mar 1962; OP-60 to OP-01P, ser 0513-62 of 20 Apr 1962.

techniques of these movements."³⁷ Under the guidance of the Bureau of Naval Personnel, the General Line and Naval Science School, Officer Candidate School, Navy Supply Corps School, Civil Engineer Corps Officer School, U.S. Naval School, Pre-Flight, and various Navy Medical Corps schools were directed to provide ten-hour academic orientation courses in such subjects as "Communist Exploits in Revolutionary Change," "Functions of Guerrilla Warfare," "Civil-Military Relationships," and "Problems of Cross-Cultural Communications." There were plans for the U.S. Naval Academy and the General Line and Naval Science School to conduct a minimum of eight hours of "study of the social, economic, political and psychological aspects of the revolutionary process including insurgency movements and counterinsurgency operations, guerrilla warfare, psychological warfare and legal aspects of insurgency."³⁸

For the middle and senior level officers at the Naval War College, an understanding of the role of U.S. government organizations and country team counterinsurgency efforts was deemed essential. This would be coupled with teaching in the capabilities of U.S. naval forces to carry out counterinsurgency operations and in the related weapons, training, supply, transportation, medical, engineering, psychological, intelligence, civil affairs, communications, political, and planning areas.

Responsibility for functional training rested with the fleet commanders in chief. In addition to specialized training for SEALs and STATs, CINCPACFLT and CINCLANTFLT were to instruct MAAG naval mission officers, selected fleet staff officers, and personnel assigned to certain mobile training teams and overseas duty stations. The military assistance advisors would receive comprehensive instruction at the Special Warfare Center in countering guerrillas and the spread of insurgency. This training was augmented by a two-week course conducted by area fleet amphibious commands in small arms use, self-defense, evasion and escape, and orientation in the functions of SEAL, STAT, boat, and mobile training teams. The mobile training team personnel also received this indoctrination. Staff officer training consisted of preparation for planning the organization, employment, and logistic support of friendly counter-

---

³⁷CNO, OPNAV Instruction 01500.17, ser 01666P10 of 19 Jul 1962; OPNAV Instruction 01500.17A ser 0187P34 of 12 Mar 1965, which superseded 01500.17, was modified to include enlisted personnel in the general training program.
³⁸CNO, OPNAV Instruction 01500.17.

guerrilla forces.[39]

A third element in the naval instruction of July 1962 was the suggestion that personnel conduct self-orientation programs in counterinsurgency matters. Because of the forward positioning of naval forces near troubled areas of the world, it was altogether likely that the Navy would be called upon to undertake activities in these regions. The Chief of Naval Operations apprised the service that "at this point in conflict, the role may shift from a show of force (i.e., port visits, goodwill, civic action, and MAP assistance) to one of participation in counterinsurgency operations."[40] Hence, naval personnel were instructed to enhance their awareness and understanding of insurgency movements, including their causes, characteristics, and solutions. In addition to academic preparation, individuals were advised to acquire knowledge of endangered countries through simple observation. Officers and men stationed in foreign lands, passing through, or attached to ships on port calls, were requested to analyze what they saw and to pass on that knowledge to other personnel.[41]

Thus, the Navy prepared its personnel to cope with and to counter the perceived threat of Communist insurgencies worldwide, and particularly in Southeast Asia. By mid-1962, the naval training program in counterinsurgency warfare was fully underway. Within a year, most of the personnel in the Pacific Fleet received basic instruction in counterinsurgency at the ship or unit level. Over 400 personnel assigned to commands in the Western Pacific experienced more intensive training by Commander Amphibious Force, U.S. Pacific Fleet. And 1,200 officers completed programs of self-orientation. Similarly, most amphibious exercises included special warfare training.[42]

The Navy's Adaptation to the Counterinsurgency Doctrine

Although the Navy accommodated the administration's stress on counterinsurgency, principally with the establishment of the SEALs and STATs, there was a continuing effort by Defense Department officials to encourage additional measures. At one point, Admiral Anderson privately

---

[39] CNO, OPNAV Instruction 01500.17.
[40] CNO, OPNAV Instruction 01500.17.
[41] CNO, OPNAV Instruction 01500.17.
[42] CINCPACFLT, Annual Report, FY1963, pp. 19, 29, 35.

The Navy Enters the Fight Against Communist Insurgency 213

complained to his Pacific Fleet commander that "we are constantly besieged with inquiries as to what the Navy is doing in this realm."[43] This focus continued throughout the period, as President Kennedy, Secretary of Defense McNamara, and subordinate officials worked to reorient U.S. conventional forces for the conflict in Southeast Asia.

At the same time, a number of naval staff officers and commanders in the field also called for the restructuring of forces to fight the Communist guerrilla. In one example, the Office of the Chief of Naval Operations, Amphibious Warfare Readiness Branch, with the assistance of the Navy Plans Branch, prepared a study based on the assumption that "U.S. national policy will permit the use of effective military means short of open warfare to combat Communist expansion" and that the "U.S. Navy will be called upon to conduct sublimited warfare in restricted waters, rivers, maritime areas, and on the high seas."[44] This document, whose principal author was Captain Harry S. Warren of the Amphibious Warfare Readiness Branch, concluded that "expansion beyond the SEAL team concept is considered necessary to provide a truly effective capability."[45] Captain Raymond S. Osterhoudt, the Navy Plans Branch representative on the project, also called for a "new look" regarding naval participation in special warfare and added that

> some degradation of readiness for limited war and/or general war is a factor which must be recognized and accepted prior to employment for sub-limited war purposes.... It is reasonable to assume that some specialized sub-limited war forces would be necessary to augment existing forces. Such forces would provide capabilities complementary to limited war and general war forces, rather than adding one more mission to existing forces.[46]

Both captains recommended the creation of a special operations group, as first suggested in a CINCLANTFLT study, to exercise operational control of SEAL teams, "Restricted Waters Units," and "River Operations Units," and to train personnel in the requisite skills. The group also would

---

[43]Ltr, Anderson to Sides, of 30 Jan 1962. See also memo, OP-60 to OP-06, ser BM0033-62 of 11 Jan 1962.
[44]Memo, OP-03 to OP-09, ser 00111P34 of 5 Dec 1961. See also CNO, memo for record, ser 00020-61 of 28 Aug 1961; memos, BUWEPS to CNO, ser 06430 of 21 Nov; OP-09 to OP-03, ser 053P09 of 25 Nov; OP-60 to Joint Staff, JCS, ser 001193P60 of 8 Dec.
[45]Memo, OP-03 to OP-09, ser 00111P34 of 5 Dec 1961.
[46]Memo, OP-06 to OP-03, ser BM001238-61 of 9 Dec 1961.

contain a support element possessing aircraft, transport submarines, helicopter carriers, amphibious ships, and other boats and craft. The force would be manned by 200 officers and 1,300 men.

In another instance, in August 1962, Captain Drachnik, head of the MAAG Vietnam Navy Section, forwarded to Washington a concept for a U.S. "River Warfare Force." The unit would consist of several river groups, each composed of a Marine rifle company, fifteen river craft (LCVP type), thirty swimmer support boats, a UH-1B helicopter, a mother ship (LSM), and a major support ship (an LSM, LSD, LPD, or APA). Air support would be furnished by carrier and shore-based aircraft. Captain Drachnik envisioned positioning the major support ship at a river mouth or nearby port and the mother ship thirty to thirty-five miles from the area of operations. From the latter floating base the naval group would sortie into the rivers to "locate, harass, and destroy guerrilla-type insurgency units in order to assist a friendly government to resist covert aggression."[47]

However, a number of naval leaders resisted the creation of additional special purpose units. In the words of Rear Admiral Waldemar F.A. Wendt, Director of the Strategic Plans Division, it was "uneconomical in manpower, equipment, and money to develop specialized units and forces solely for counterinsurgency operations"[48] when traditional naval forces possessed the requisite characteristics. Admiral Wendt further observed that "within current resources, improvement of naval cold war/counterinsurgency activities world-wide is desirable and should continue to be stimulated." But, he concluded that "such activities should be secondary to considerations of readiness for limited and general war."[49] Noting that the Navy's prompt and forceful response to the Cuban Missile Crisis demonstrated the need for optimum strength at sea, the admiral also pointed out that while the service could "contribute significantly to meeting cold war/counterinsurgency requirements, these activities are primarily land oriented and properly a primary responsibility of the Army."[50]

---

[47]"U.S. River Warfare Force," encl. in ltr, Drachnik to Anderson, of 17 Aug 1962. See also Charles N. Crandall, Jr., "Naval Warfare On Inland Waterways," unpublished thesis for U.S. Army War College, 1962.

[48]Memo, OP-60 to OP-93, ser 0338-63 of 19 Apr 1963. See also Bucklew, Interview with Mason, pp. 338-39, 358.

[49]Memo, OP-60 to OP-34, ser 00337-63 of 16 Apr 1963.

[50]Memo, OP-60 to OP-34, ser 00337-63 of 16 Apr 1963.

Several months later, before a congressional committee, Captain Donald N. Clay, the Head, Special Operations Section, gave another statement indicating the Navy's overall position. He noted:

> Since counterinsurgency is but one part of the cold war...one part of the spectrum of conflict...the Navy does not consider it necessary or desirable to have its general purpose forces separately organized for counterinsurgency operations.... Because of their flexibility and multipurpose functions...Navy general purpose forces...have inherent capabilities. Deployed fleet forces are ready to respond quickly and effectively to requirements throughout the spectrum of [conflict] including insurgency.[51]

For these reasons, neither the proposal to establish a special operations group nor the River Warfare Force then were adopted. In the latter case, Admiral Anderson concluded that the "development of a separate U.S. River Force does not appear to be justified to my mind at the present time in view of our already considerable capabilities in the form of amphibious naval craft and the complementary amphibious capabilities of our Marines."[52]

The Chief of Naval Operations also pointed out to Captain Drachnik that "we are required to remain in an advisory role [which prevents] our development of a 'U.S.' force for use in your area."[53] Under these circumstances, Admiral Anderson felt that the further development of tactics, techniques, and equipment for this type of warfare could be achieved by "improving the River Force capabilities of our friends, the Vietnamese and others by providing appropriate material and competent advisory support."[54]

---

[51] Memo, OP-343 to OP-03, ser 00526-63 of 9 Sep 1963.

[52] Ltr, Anderson to Sides, of 11 Sep 1962. Commander Howard A. I. Sugg, executive officer of the Navy Section, MAAG, Vietnam, on the other hand, subsequently observed that the "U.S. Navy is sadly deficient in its knowledge of and capability for any type of operations in restricted waters, other than conventional amphibious tactics, which, although having some application, are entirely inadequate to the wide range of problems of a nation like Vietnam." Memo, OP-941P to OP-941, of 16 Jan 1963. See also ltrs, Anderson to Dennison, of 11 Sep 1962; CINCPAC to JCS, ser 00635 of 24 Jun 1963; memos, OP-09 to OP-03, ser 0055P09 of 18 Dec 1961; OP-60 to OP-06, ser BM001238-61 of 1 Dec; ltr, CNO to Comptroller of the Navy, ser 00114P34 of 22 Dec.

[53] Ltr, Anderson to Drachnik, of 10 Sep 1962.

[54] Ltr, Anderson to Sides, of 11 Sep 1962. See also ltr, Anderson to Dennison, of 11 Sep; memo, OP-60 to CNO, BM550-62 of 4 Sep.

Although top naval leaders were reluctant to establish further special purpose forces, there were continuing efforts to adapt existing resources to the growing requirements of counterinsurgency. Indeed, Admiral Robert B. Pirie, the Deputy Chief Naval Operations (Air), observed that

> while the other services...are busily developing a multitude of new requirements, and programs...the Navy is quietly contributing both a large share of the aircraft currently involved, and of those planned for use in the immediate future in South Vietnam, with very little credit redounding to us but with no little effort on training and readiness.[55]

Similarly, late in April 1962, Admiral Sharp, then the Deputy Chief of Naval Operations (Plans and Policy), noted the potential value of naval helicopters and fixed-wing aircraft (including the A3D, P2V, and P5M) in supporting counterinsurgency troops with attack, communications, surveillance, reconnaissance, and transport operations. The admiral recommended further evaluation of these aircraft and their specialized armament in an operational environment.[56]

Another system adaptable to the requirements of Southeast Asia was the amphibious assault ship, whose helicopters could carry South Vietnamese troops on strikes against Viet Cong coastal concentrations from one end of the elongated country to the other. CINCPACFLT, who favored their use, believed that ship-based helicopter lift was inherently superior to the shore-based mode because of the advantages of surprise, greater flexibility, and freedom from enemy fire over water.[57]

Greater attention was given to other existing ships that were suited to special transportation duties, such as submarines. These vessels could land and supply friendly guerrillas, collect intelligence, or perform rescue

---

[55] Memo, OP-05 to OP-06, ser 0003P50 of 14 Apr 1962.

[56] Memos, OP-605 to Joint Staff (JCS), ser 001193P60 of 8 Dec 1961; OP-60 to OP-06, ser BM0033-62 of 11 Jan 1962; OP-60 to OP-34, ser BM00249-62 of 2 Mar; OP-60 to OP-35, ser 00358-62 of 19 Mar; OP-06 to OP-05, ser 000504P60 of 28 Apr; ltr, OP-60 to Leake, of 6 Jun; memos, OP-60 to OP-06, ser BM000691-62 of 6 Jun; OP-60 to OP-06, ser 00716-62 of 15 Jun; OP-60 to OP-34, ser 00965-62 of 14 Aug.

[57] Ltr, CINCPACFLT to CINCPAC, ser 62/00072 of 21 Mar 1962. In the fall of 1962, COMUSMACV briefly broached a proposal for placing an LPH under his operational control, but the CNO, CINCPAC, and CINCPACFLT consistently opposed the concept as a usurpation of roles assigned the Navy and Marine Corps. See msgs, COMUSMACV 220445Z Sep 1962; CPFLT 272134Z; CINCPACFLT, "Type Commanders' Conference, 19-20 February 1962," ser 00/00192-62 of 2 Mar 1962, p. 9; ltr, CINCPACFLT to CINCPAC, ser 62/00048 of 6 Mar; OP-605F, memo, ser 0001514P60 of 29 Nov. See also W. M. Miller, "The BLT/LPH in South Vietnam: A Proposal," unpublished thesis for Naval War College, 1963.

operations in enemy waters. To provide the fleet with this capability, transport submarines *Perch* (APSS-313) and *Sealion* (APSS-315) were recommissioned in the fall of 1961. *Perch*, commanded by Lieutenant Commander Charles H. Hedgepeth, thereafter engaged in training exercises off the West Coast, Hawaii, and the Philippines with Marine reconnaissance, SEAL, and UDT units. Homeported in Subic Bay after March 1963, the submarine prepared for special operations in Southeast Asia.[58] In a like vein, Captain Daniel V. James, the Director of Communications, Plans and Policy Division, stressed the relevance to counterinsurgency of the Navy's beach jumper units in conducting "electronic warfare, particularly in the fields of electronic jamming and electronic deception" against such countries as North Vietnam and Communist China.[59]

Regardless of these efforts to adapt its forces to counterinsurgency situations, senior officials outside the Navy continued to urge the development of special formations. President Kennedy himself, shortly before his death, wrote the Chief of Naval Operations and Secretary of the Navy that

> when I was in Norfolk in 1962 I noted particularly the members of the SEAL Teams. I was impressed by them as individuals and with the capability they possess as a group. As missiles assume more and more of the nuclear deterrent role and as your limited war mission grows, the need for special forces in the Navy and Marine Corps will increase.[60]

The President ended his correspondence with the pointed question, "what is the status of your Special Forces?"[61]

On 21 November 1963, Admiral David L. McDonald, the new CNO, in what was to be his last report to President Kennedy, summarized the Navy's accomplishments in the counterinsurgency effort of the past two years. The admiral detailed the establishment and deployment to South

---

[58] OP-93, "Statement of U.S. Navy Long Range Objectives, 1969-1974 (LRO-59)," ser 0018P93 of 19 Mar 1959, p. 34; ltr, Griffin to Burke, ser 00029 of 12 Jul 1961, enclosing "Seventh Fleet Briefing of DOD RDT&E Limited War Study Group," pt. 3, p. 3; ltr, McDonald to Kennedy, of 21 Nov 1963; Naval History Division, *Dictionary of American Naval Fighting Ships*, Vol. V (Washington: GPO, 1970), p. 262; Naval History Division, *Dictionary of American Naval Fighting Ships*, Vol. VI (Washington: GPO, 1976), p. 418; OSD, memo, of 26 Jul 1962.
[59] Memo, OP-94 to OP-94G, ser 00079P94 of 14 Jun 1962.
[60] Memo, Kennedy to Nitze/McDonald, of 7 Nov 1963.
[61] Memo, Kennedy to Nitze/McDonald, of 7 Nov 1963.

Vietnam of the SEAL and STAT units which he believed were "definitely proving their worth." He added that the "remainder of our Cold War (and potential limited war) requirements of this type are met from our general purpose forces."[62]

In the period from 1962 to 1963, the Navy established the basic structure for its contribution to counterinsurgency warfare. The SEAL and STAT teams, the PTF detachments, and the Naval Operations Support Groups formed the core of this program for much of the Vietnam War. At the same time, the role and composition of naval forces in this particular type of conflict were refined, partly as a result of experience in the operational theater. As a result of these developments, naval personnel were better prepared to assist the South Vietnamese in their fight against the Communist insurgents.

---

[62]Ltr, McDonald to Kennedy, of 21 Nov 1963.

CHAPTER VIII

The Naval Advisory and Logistic Support Effort in Vietnam, 1961-1963

As a result of the presidential decisions of November 1961, the U.S. military assistance and advisory effort took a new turn. At that time, the United States took the position that continued aggression by North Vietnam in blatant contravention of the Geneva Agreement of 1954 justified and necessitated the setting aside of the restrictions of the agreement regarding the introduction of military personnel and material into South Vietnam. On 11 December 1961, *Core* arrived in Saigon with the first military equipment not authorized by the 1954 accord.

Similarly, the administration allowed an expansion of the MAAG to 1,905 men and, as a result of the stepped up Communist activity in the fall, Diem authorized American advisors to accompany and advise Vietnamese units during combat operations. Thereafter, U.S. naval advisors were assigned to individual ships and craft, rather than to headquarters alone. Captain Drachnik believed this to be an effective way to strengthen the Vietnamese Navy to defeat the Communists.[1]

To better control and coordinate the numerous, varied, and growing U.S. military activities in South Vietnam, early in November 1961 Secretary of Defense McNamara directed the JCS to draw up plans for the creation of an overall American command. He envisioned a unified command, separate from CINCPAC, reporting directly to the JCS and through the Joint Chiefs to the Secretary of Defense.

Opposition to this proposal quickly developed within the JCS and from CINCPAC. Admiral Anderson, the Chief of Naval Operations, was concerned that the new command arrangement would erode Admiral

---

[1]Drachnik, Interview with Fitzgerald; memo, OP-61 to CNO, ser 00770P61 of 11 Dec 1961.

Felt's authority in the Pacific. The Navy's head pointed out that South Vietnam should not be militarily segregated from the rest of the Far East, for which CINCPAC was responsible, especially since the size of U.S. forces in the country or the nature of the conflict did not seem to warrant an independent theater type command. The JCS concurred with the Navy's position and recommended establishment of a unified command subordinate to CINCPAC. McNamara accepted the JCS conclusion. Accordingly, the U.S. Military Assistance Command, Vietnam (MACV), was established on 8 February 1962 under General Paul D. Harkins, USA. The new headquarters was authorized a staff of 216 individuals, 35 of them from the Navy. Naval captains filled the assistant chief of staff for personnel and comptroller billets. President Kennedy assigned General Harkins, commanding under the policy direction of the U.S. ambassador, a difficult task: "He was to save the country without escalating the situation there."[2]

Expanded Naval Advisory Effort

During 1962 and 1963 there was a dramatic growth in the number of U.S. military advisors in South Vietnam. By November 1963, the number of personnel in the MAAG had increased to 3,500. More than doubling in strength, the Navy Section grew to 154 U.S. Navy and Marine Corps advisors. Naval officers and men were assigned to every major command and component of the Vietnamese Navy, including Sea Force ships, River Force RAGs, and junk force coastal divisions. As a result, the ability to exert influence on the development of the Vietnamese Navy was enhanced considerably.[3]

While the number of U.S. naval advisors sent to Vietnam increased, Captain Drachnik encountered problems obtaining exceptional American

---

[2] As reported by Admiral Anderson in CNO, minutes of meeting, Thursday, 4 Jan 1962. See also CNO, minutes of meeting, Thursday, 16 Nov 1961; CNO, minutes of meeting, Friday, 24 Nov 1961; msgs, CP 141212Z Nov 1961; JCS 282248Z; CP 290301Z; 081600Z Feb 1962; CINCPAC, Command History, 1962, p. 154; memos, Shoup to Anderson, of 18 Nov 1961; OP-60 to CNO, ser BM727-61 of 22 Nov; Military Assistant to SECDEF to SECARM/SECNAV/SECAF/CHJCS, of 29 Nov; OSD, of 29 Nov.

[3] CINCPAC, Command History, 1961, fig. 13; *U.S.-V.N. Relations*, bk. 3, pt. IVB.4, p. i; Fitzgerald, "U.S. Naval Forces in the Vietnam War;" JCS, "Report of Visit by JCS Staff Team to South Vietnam," Jan 1963; NAG, Progress Report, of 30 Aug 1962.

officers for the advisory program. The naval advisor's job was extremely difficult. He had to deal with a type of inshore and coastal warfare with which the U.S. Navy had little modern experience. He was expected to advise the Vietnamese in operating old ship types that, in many cases, he had never seen in the U.S. Fleet. Furthermore, the advisors lacked command authority and could only influence their counterparts through persuasion and example. Overeager officers who pushed too hard or tried to command the Vietnamese found their effectiveness sharply reduced.

Not surprisingly, most American officers did not consider the job of advisor as career enhancing. Captain Drachnik stated frankly that "careerwise it was...horrible duty." He explained: "I was out there the only Navy captain that side of Hawaii practically...surrounded by...Army officers writing [my fitness] reports."[4] When informed that he would relieve Drachnik, Captain William H. Hardcastle felt that, "it certainly sounded like a dead-end job. I would go as a loyal naval officer, but I certainly didn't see any future in that."[5] Captain Drachnik also reported that the caliber of personnel assigned to his command indicated "a distinct lack of interest in the naval effort in Vietnam."[6] Since the Navy's share of the military assistance budget worldwide was only about 10 to 15 percent of the total, the Navy understandably gave the program relatively low priority compared to the more pressing needs of the fleet.[7]

In December 1961 Secretary McNamara expressed dissatisfaction with the experience and quality of advisory personnel in Vietnam. As a result, he directed the services to send highly qualified personnel to the MAAG. Two years later, McNamara voiced similar complaints. At that time a survey of senior naval billets assigned to the MAAG found that many were filled by junior officers or by officers who had failed their first selection to the next higher grade. There was noticeable improvement in the caliber of officers subsequently sent to Vietnam, but the selection of advisors continued to be a concern.[8]

---

[4] Drachnik, Interview with Fitzgerald, p. 2.
[5] William H. Hardcastle, transcript of interview with Oscar P. Fitzgerald, Naval Historical Center, in Norfolk, VA, 22 Apr 1975, p. 15.
[6] Ltr, Drachnik to Ricketts, of 13 Mar 1964, p. 12.
[7] *Ibid.* p. 6; Hardcastle, Interview; memo, Special Assistant, Counterinsurgency, ISA to Assistant for Counterinsurgency, ISA, of 2 Dec 1964.
[8] Msgs, CNO 301739Z Dec 1961; COMUSMACV 310330Z Dec 1963.

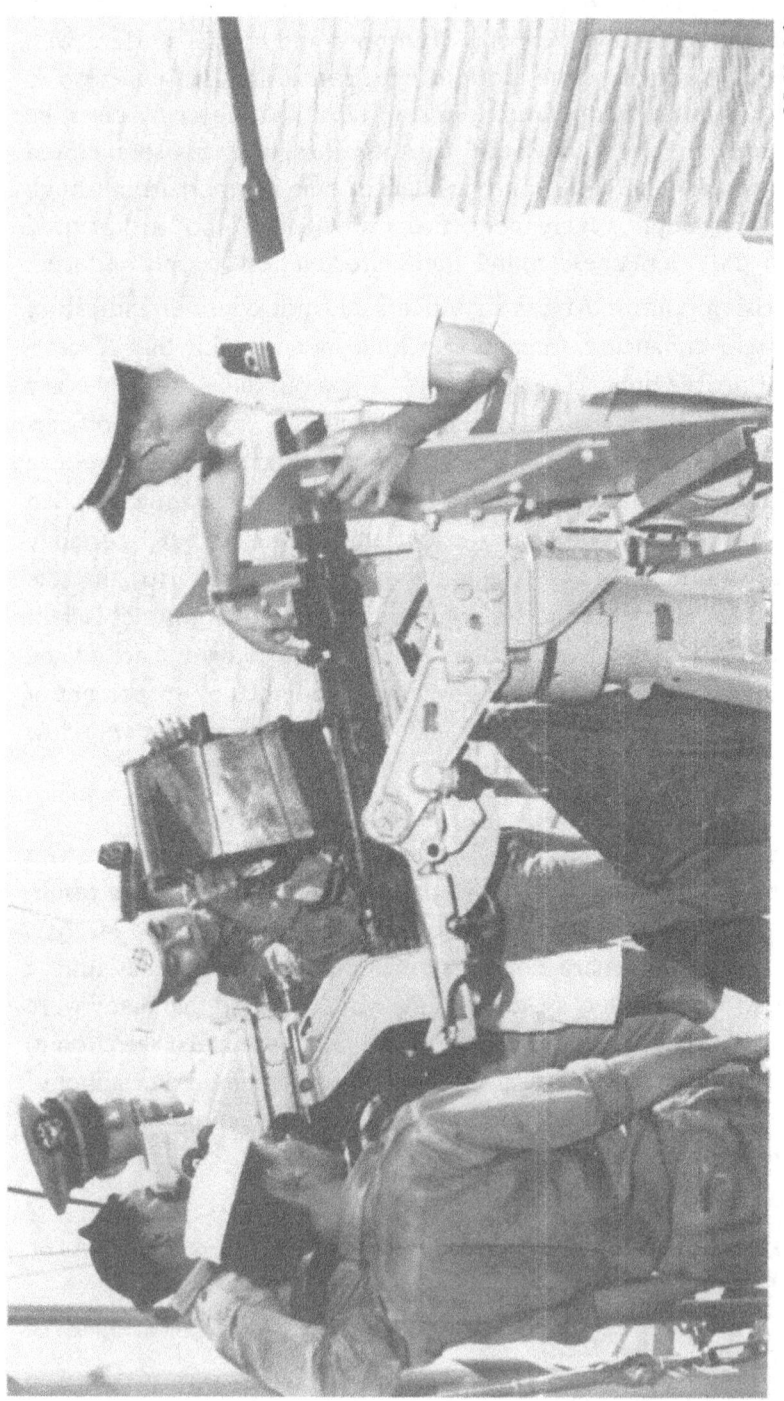

A U.S. naval advisor, Lieutenant Thomas Howley, observes an officer of the Vietnamese Navy train his men to operate a 20-millimeter deck gun.

A continuing problem for the advisors assigned before 1964 was the absence of even brief instruction in the culture and customs of the country, much less the language. The need for their expertise was so critical, however, that there was no time for comprehensive predeployment training. Advisors could develop a rapport with the Vietnamese, but lack of language training complicated an already difficult task. At the end of 1961, only three officers in the U.S. Navy had received training in Vietnamese. Interpreters were scarce and Vietnamese documents often had to be sent to Saigon for translation at MAAG headquarters.[9]

Although the number of Americans conversant in Vietnamese remained low, many more Vietnamese learned English, especially those officers in the higher commands. Further, English competency was a prerequisite for the growing number of Vietnamese naval officers sent to the United States for training. Captain Drachnik observed that almost everyone he worked with in Vietnam spoke English.[10]

At best, it took an average of six to eight months for an advisor to learn his role and understand the Vietnamese system. But in March 1962, the Secretary of Defense approved a reduction in tour lengths to twenty-four months for naval personnel accompanied by their families, fifteen months for unaccompanied men, and twelve months for naval advisors serving alone in the field outside of Saigon. Initially, Admiral Felt favored longer tours in order to preserve advisor continuity. He supported the new shorter tour lengths, however, believing that more personnel should be exposed to the learning experience. Also, as more and more advisors were assigned to the Vietnamese units in the field, Admiral Felt concluded that a year was long enough exposure to the isolation, tropical climate, and health problems associated with duty in remote areas of Vietnam. Most advisors, however, agreed with Captain Drachnik that the effectiveness of the advisory effort would have been substantially improved by lengthened tours.[11]

---

[9]G.C. Hickey and W.P. Davison, *The American Military Advisor and His Foreign Counterpart: The Case of Vietnam* (Santa Monica, CA: Rand Corp., 1965), pp. 19-20, 30-33; MTT 3-62, report, of 11 Jan 1963; ltr 1st Coastal District Advisor to Senior Junk Force Advisor, of 31 May 1963; 1st Coastal District Advisor to CHNAVSEC of 5 Jul.

[10]Drachnik, Interview with Fitzgerald; msg, CNO 301739Z Dec 1961; NAG, Fact Sheet, "Training," of 1963.

[11]Ltr, Drachnik to Ricketts, of 13 Mar 1964, p. 14; Hickey and Davison, *American Military Advisor*, p. 43; msg, CP 062320Z Feb 1962; memo, OP-01 to CNO, ser BM37-62 of 6 Mar.

Expansion of the Vietnamese Navy

The increase in the number of U.S. advisors in Vietnam reflected the growth of the Vietnamese Navy. From 3,200 men in June 1961 the navy, exclusive of its subordinate marine corps, grew to 6,000 men in February 1963. This burgeoning of the navy placed severe demands on the Vietnamese training establishment. To meet the growing need for officers, in August 1962 classes at the Vietnamese Naval Academy were increased from 50 to 100 men and the training time reduced from two years to eighteen months. The Vietnamese also set up a special petty officer training program. To assist this effort, Mobile Training Team 3-62, headed by Chief Radarman Elden Baldwin, arrived at Nha Trang in January 1962 for an eleven-month tour. These steps helped the Vietnamese Navy to fulfill the training needs of its expanding forces.[12]

As the Vietnamese Navy grew, better command-control procedures were necessary, particularly at the naval headquarters in Saigon. There efficient communications were needed to replace the patchwork system left over from the French era. Briefed on the problem during his visit to Saigon in December 1961, Secretary McNamara directed that communications in the navy be modernized. Lieutenant John R. King was assigned temporarily to Vietnam on 28 December 1961 to develop plans for improving the Vietnamese system. During June and July 1962, the headquarters network, by then operated by a communications section, was completely rehabilitated, based on King's plans. Work was conducted on systems for four coastal surveillance centers and four River Force bases as well.[13]

Another essential requirement for an effective Vietnamese military command was intelligence. Before 1962, Vietnamese naval intelligence responsibilities were handled by the operations department of the naval staff; by a twenty-man section, which kept current information on the North Vietnamese naval order of battle, on the Joint General Staff; and by

---

[12]Navy Section, MAAG, "Agenda Items for Conference with President Diem, Aug 63;" Navy Section, MAAG, Fact Sheet, "Training in the VNN," of Sep 1963; Navy Section, MAAG, Progress Report, "Navy Schools," Aug 1962; Thomas M. Browne, transcript of interview with Dean Allard, Naval Historical Center, in Washington, DC, 31 Jan 1964; CHNAG, memo, ser 0070 of 10 Jul 1964; ltr, Drachnik to Ricketts, of 13 Mar, p. 2; MTT 3-62, report, of 11 Jan 1963; Education and Training Advisory Team, report, of 18 Jul 1962; Drachnik, Interview with Moss.

[13]MTT 5-62, report, of 28 May 1962; NAG, Progress Report, "VNN Communications Improvement," of 23 Aug 1962; CINCPAC, Command History, 1962, pp. 164, 196.

another twenty-man group, which carried out counterintelligence and counterespionage duties, serving with the Military Security Service. On 1 April 1962, the Joint General Staff created a separate twenty-one-man Intelligence Department (N-2) of the naval staff. Staff officers with the Sea Force, River Force, and coastal district commands were also given intelligence responsibilities as a collateral duty. In August 1962, Captain Drachnik requested that a mobile training team be dispatched to Vietnam to provide elements of the Vietnamese Navy with instruction in operational intelligence. U.S. fleet commanders objected to even the temporary loss of these key personnel. Admiral Anderson was sympathetic with their views, but he approved Captain Drachnik's request on 25 September. Consequently, Lieutenant Commander Philip B. Shepard arrived in Vietnam in October and, working with Lieutenant (j.g.) Ray B. Huttig, intelligence advisor to the Vietnamese Navy, developed a two-week course of instruction. By mid-1963, over 200 Vietnamese officers and petty officers had received this intelligence training.[14]

In addition, an important command reorganization improved relations between army and naval commands in the field. The reorganization was part of the National Campaign Plan, devised by MACV in mid-1962 to streamline the Vietnamese command structure and make it more responsive. On 1 January 1963, the Vietnamese Army increased from three to four the number of areas controlled by a corps headquarters. Captain Quyen immediately submitted a proposal to the Joint General Staff calling for a reorganization to facilitate coordination between the army and the navy. As adopted on 16 October 1963, the new structure established four naval zone commands to work in conjunction with the army's four corps tactical zone commands. The naval zone commanders exercised operational control over Coastal Force, River Force, and Sea Force units in their area. With a few exceptions, the Coastal Force and River Force controlled only administrative and logistic functions. The Sea Force retained operational control of its ships only when they were not operating in territorial waters.[15]

---

[14]*U.S.-V.N. Relations*, bk. 11, pp. 419-20; CINCPAC, Command History, 1961, p. 196; memo, DCNO (Logistics) to DCNO (Plans and Policy), ser 001215P401 of 5 Nov 1962; MTT 5-63, report, of 3 Dec 1962; Navy Section, MAAG, Fact Sheet, "Naval Intelligence Organization," of 16 Aug 1962; msg, CHMAAG 190039Z Sep 1962.

[15]Navy Section, MAAG, "Agenda Items for Conference with President Diem, Aug 63;" *U.S.-V.N. Relations*, bk. 3, pt. IVB.4, pp. 5-6.

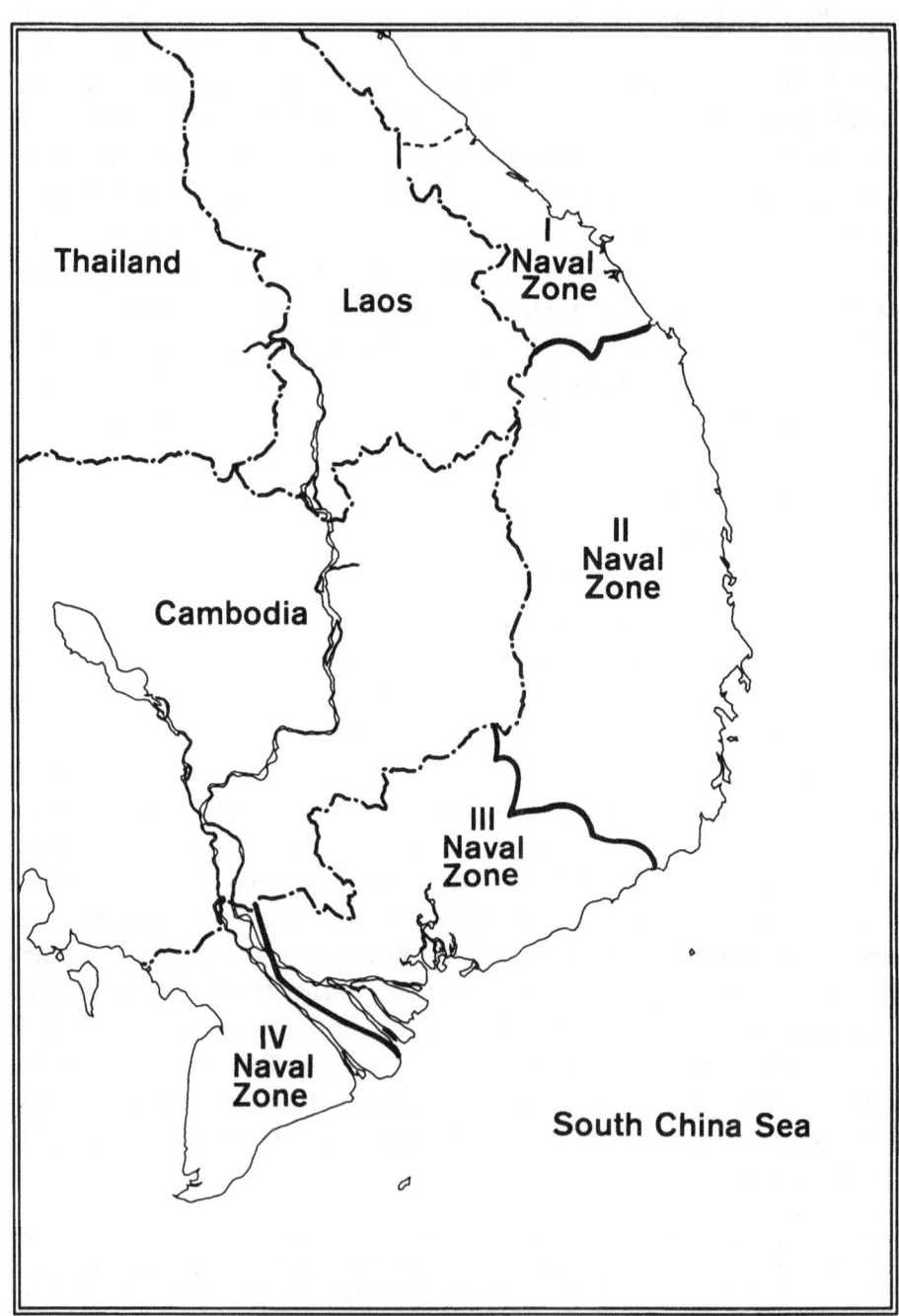

Vietnamese Naval Zone Commands

As the size of the navy grew, the demands on the supply system increased correspondingly. During the first six months of 1962, the advisory team at the Naval Supply Center in Saigon expanded from six to sixteen men and their efforts to streamline supply management helped the center process twice the amount of supplies handled in all of 1961. Another important accomplishment of these naval advisors was the publication of a supply manual designed to speed up the system, although the Vietnamese were slow to accept it.[16]

Steps also were taken to upgrade the Vietnamese Navy's ship and boat repair facilities. In order to ease the workload at the Saigon Naval Shipyard, Mobile Training Team 7A, consisting of eleven U.S. naval officers, arrived in Saigon in February 1962. During the next three months, the team reactivated an abandoned French repair yard at Cuu Long, adjacent to the shipyard, and placed its two marine railways back in operation. The new yard, named the Eastern Repair Facility, serviced the boats of three River Force groups stationed in the Saigon area. No longer would these units be forced to use the distant Western Repair Facility at Can Tho for repair work.[17]

At the shipyard itself, naval advisors concentrated on improving repair support through better long-range planning, work scheduling, and waterfront operations and strengthening the technical proficiency of the 1,500-man civilian work force through training. Partly as a result of this assistance, the number of boat overhauls undertaken increased from an average of fourteen per month in 1961 to fifty-six per month in 1962, and most of them were completed on time. The shipyard additionally was able to take on the construction of fiberglass swimmer support boats, for use by army troops in the delta, and to do conversion work on newly arrived LCMs and LCVPs.[18]

---

[16] Browne, Interview; Navy Section, MAAG, Progress Report, "Naval Material Center," of 30 Aug 1962.
[17] Navy Section, MAAG, Fact Sheet, "Development of the Eastern Repair Facility," of 16 Dec 1963; COMPHIBPAC, report, 2-S-62 of 22 Jun 1962; Navy Section, MAAG, "Agenda Items for Conference with President Diem."
[18] Evenson M. Burtis, End of Tour Report, of Jun 1964; H.H. Reichert, End of Tour Report, of 6 Apr 1964; Navy Section, MAAG, Progress Report.

The Coastal Force Comes of Age

Diem had established the Coastal Force as an autonomous unit directly under the Department of State for National Defense, while the navy was assigned operational control of the force. In November 1961, however, Quyen recommended that the force be placed totally under the naval headquarters in order to avoid duplication and delays in support. U.S. advisors supported the recommendation. Accordingly, in July 1962 Secretary of State for National Defense Thuan directed that the junk force thereafter rely upon the naval staff for all support. Lieutenant Commander Bruce A. Bryer, the Coastal Force advisor, commented several weeks later:

> The Junk Force is a new and vital addition to the VNN. It will soon be the largest force afloat — both in personnel and number of craft. It has already demonstrated its potential in unconventional warfare. Due to recent publicity, the eyes of the free world are upon it. It will be spread over the entire 1500 [sic.] mile coastline making support problems acute. We must not allow this great new force to sink before it swims due to lack of support from its Mother Navy.[19]

The navy was slow in assuming this responsibility, but by the end of the year was providing full staff support to the Coastal Force.

During this same period, the Kennedy administration agreed to support a sizeable increase in Coastal Force strength. At his meeting with Admiral Felt in Hawaii on 19 February 1962, Secretary of Defense McNamara approved the expenditure of MAP funds to expand the junk force from the initial 80 to 644 junks, formed in twenty-eight divisions. The United States would fund the building of 501 junks (including 61 command junks) in South Vietnamese yards. The Vietnamese Navy contracted for the construction of 40 motorized junks at a private yard in Rach Gia. The Saigon Naval Shipyard was to build the remaining 23 command junks. MAP support would also provide arms, engines, POL, and communications equipment.

---

[19]Junk Force Advisor, Fact Sheet, "Support of the Junk Force by the VN Navy," of 21 Aug 1962. See also ltr, Junk Force Advisor to CHNAVSEC, of 24 May 1962; Chung Tan Cang, Interview, pp. 42-45; ltrs, CHMAAGVN to SECDEF, of 18 Dec 1961; CHMAAGVN to CINCPAC, of 18 Dec 1961.

There were three types of standard vessels: sailing junks; junks with a motor-sail combination, sometimes referred to as the northern type; and motorized or southern type junks. The command junks were similar to fishing junks used at the mouth of the Mekong River, but the design was modified for naval requirements by Lieutenant Commander William E. Hanks of the MAAG's Navy Section. The craft were powered by 225-horsepower Gray diesel engines.[20]

The ordnance initially carried on the junks consisted only of small arms, including M-1 rifles, a Thompson submachine gun, and a 45-caliber pistol. A Browning automatic rifle was carried on the command junks. Later, the shipyard installed a 50-caliber machine gun forward and a 30-caliber machine gun aft on the command junks. But in March 1963 Quyen ordered all 50-caliber machine guns removed to avoid the possibility of their loss to the Viet Cong and subsequent use against friendly aircraft, a fear which had been expressed at CINCPAC headquarters. Although U.S. naval advisors and the Vietnamese Coastal Force commander felt that the decision would hamper operations, particularly in the 3rd and 4th Coastal Districts, the decision to remove the weapons stood. To offset the loss, and in view of increasing operations in the delta region, 168 30-caliber machine guns were procured by mid-October 1963 and installed forward where the 50-caliber weapons had been.[21]

By the end of June 1962, the U.S. Navy had let two contracts to boat yards at Phan Thiet and three to the naval shipyard at Saigon to construct 501 junks, at a cost of $850,000, for delivery beginning in August 1962. Although poor performance by several of the Vietnamese building firms and financial difficulties delayed the program, the first contractor completed his junks by January 1963 and the last finished his work by May of that year.[22]

At the suggestion of President Diem, General Harkins expressed a concern about the quality of junks which the United States was buying. Captain Drachnik ordered an investigation in October 1962, after which he was convinced that the U.S. contract junks under construction were of

---

[20]CHNAVSEC, Instruction 9000.1, of 26 Sep 1962; CINCPAC, Third Secretary of Defense Conference, of 19 Feb 1962; ARPA, R & D Field Unit, "Junk Blue Book," of 6 Aug 1962.

[21]Msg, CP 160115Z Nov 1962.

[22]This included all but twelve junks, which were never built. Junk Force Advisor, memos for record, of 25 May 1962; 28 Jun; ltr, Drachnik to BUSHIPS, ser 0207 of 2 Jun 1962; CHNAVSEC to Garner, of 25 Oct 1962.

high quality and were superior to those being constructed under Vietnamese contract.[23]

By July 1962, one coastal division from the 1st Coastal District was deployed to the 2nd Coastal District and four divisions were activated in the 4th Coastal District. At the end of 1962, 179 sailing junks were operational in ten junk divisions in the 1st, 2nd, and 3rd Coastal Districts. Several command junks and forty-four motorized junks were deployed in the 4th Coastal District off the Mekong Delta and the Camau Peninsula. By the end of March 1963, the last five of the twenty-eight divisions were activated and the construction program was accelerated to fill the complement of each division. The Vietnamese Navy also established coastal surveillance centers in each of the four coastal districts to coordinate the inshore patrol of the junks with Sea Force ships farther out to sea. The first facility opened at Danang in early September 1962, followed by those at Vung Tau, Cam Ranh, and An Thoi in 1963.

The junkmen received three months of training at small centers established at Danang, Nha Trang, Phu Quoc, and Vung Tau. Initially, the curriculum concentrated on small arms and land warfare techniques, subjects which naval advisors deemed peripheral. The advisors soon revised the training programs to emphasize naval topics, and the Vietnamese readily adopted the new curriculum. A permanent junk training facility was planned for Phu Quoc Island but, due to its inaccessibility, the location was shifted to Cam Ranh Bay in February 1963. At that time, 92 officers and men occupied an old dilapidated French base which had been garrisoned by a Vietnamese Marine security force. In addition to training at Cam Ranh Bay, over 700 junkmen received specialized instruction at Saigon and Vung Tau in the operation and maintenance of engines, communications, first aid, intelligence, and psychological warfare.[24]

In the spring of 1962 the junk force numbered about 800 men, in addition to a small cadre of Vietnamese naval officers and men. With the decision to expand the Coastal Force to twenty-eight divisions came authorization to increase manning levels to 459 military and 3,640 paramilitary billets. By December 1962 the Vietnamese reported 3,243

---

[23]Ltr, Drachnik to Harkins, ser 0495 of 15 Oct 1962. By the end of 1963, this conclusion was called into question, as almost all junks suffered from severe wood shrinkage. In some cases the hull planks had spread three inches apart.

[24]Donald C. Schroder, End of Tour Report, of 14 Jan 1965.

personnel on board. In late February 1963, however, the U.S. Joint Chiefs of Staff authorized support for an even larger junk force of 4,425 paramilitary men.[25] Throughout this period, recruiting proved difficult because the relatively prosperous Vietnamese fishermen, a group targeted for enlistment, were not interested in joining the low-paying junk force. In addition, many prospective enlistees were North Vietnamese recruited from refugee camps. They required a certification of loyalty from the province chief, which often was hard to get. Desertion also was a serious problem in the Coastal Force. As more and more junks were built, the personnel shortages began to affect operations. Junks were operated with reduced crews and others lay idle. Commander Charles K. Presgrove, the Senior Junk Force Advisor, persuaded Captain Quyen to organize special recruiting teams to fill the quotas. The requirement for security checks was eased. Training periods were shortened from three months to five weeks, with on-the-job training substituting for classroom instruction. By 1 November 1963, the Coastal Force included 66 officers, 375 enlisted men, and 3,359 paramilitary junkmen.

Despite their myriad problems, many junkmen exuded confidence, believing that they were building a special organization. One indication of this esprit de corps was the practice adopted by some junkmen of tattooing *Sat Cong*, translated as "let us kill the Communists," on their chests. Captain Quyen revived the custom which had originated in the fourteenth century when sailors, under the naval hero Tran Hung Dao, tattooed "let us kill the Mongols" on their skin.[26]

Besides the personnel problem, the major concern in the Coastal Force was repair and maintenance of the junks. The 1962 Vietnamese budget for the junk force only funded seven divisions, while during the year the force was expanding to the planned twenty-eight division force. In order to fund the increased junk units and personnel, money was diverted from repairs, material, and equipment; but this came at a time when the original boats deployed in 1960 were sorely in need of repair. The absence of regular preventive maintenance and the common Vietnamese attitude of "run it until it quits," aggravated the problem. The condition of twenty junks in Coastal Division 24, as reported by Lieutenant Commander Louie L. Lindenmayer, was typical. He explained that the boats had

---

[25] Memo, OP-60 to CNO, ser BM0047-63 of 18 Feb 1963.
[26] Msg, COMUSMACV 030945Z Jul 1962.

been in service in the First District since November 1960 with little or no maintenance or repairs. Their material condition has deteriorated until none of the junks are sea worthy enough to permit off shore patrol. All 20 of the junks require complete replacement of sails and most running rigging. Some require new masts and standing rigging. 10 of the 20 junks have woven bottoms that have rotted beyond repair. The 10 remaining all wooden hull junks are in need of repairs, extensive in some cases.[27]

Other districts experienced similar difficulties. Lieutenant Wesley A. Hoch reported in August 1963 that in the 4th Coastal District, the problem was a "complete lack of adequate Civilian or Military repair facilities" which "creates endless problems in repairing the junks."[28]

The establishment of repair facilities in each of the districts proceeded slowly, but by the end of 1963 each one had the capability for repairing junks locally. A center at Danang handled all junk work for the 1st Coastal District. A marine railway at Nha Trang, completed in November 1963, facilitated repairs in the 2nd Coastal District. A marine railway at Cat Lo, serving the 3rd Coastal District, began operation in January 1964, and some junks were sent to the Western Repair Facility at Can Tho. In the 4th Coastal District, small civilian yards at Song Ong Doc and Duong Dong did some jobs and were augmented by a Vietnamese Navy mobile repair team at Rach Gia. In addition, as a result of efforts by U.S. advisors, the 1963 Vietnamese defense budget ensured funds for maintenance and repair work in the Coastal Force.[29]

The primary mission of the Coastal Force was to patrol the coast and randomly search craft for Communist agents or contraband. A search consisted of checking the identification card of the fisherman and the registration of his boat. This was possible because the U.S. Operations Mission in the U.S. Embassy had sponsored a program to register the 35,000 junks and 200,000 fishermen of South Vietnam. The project was completed in 1962 by the Vietnamese customs service, with the help of the Coastal and Sea Forces. During a search, the junkmen looked for crewmen with northern accents or those who were unskilled in fishing, which might indicate that they were Communist agents. Similarly, salt, tea,

---

[27] Memo, Lindenmayer to CHNAVSEC, of 18 Dec 1962.
[28] 4th CD Advisor, report, of 22 Aug 1963.
[29] Ltr, Lindenmayer to CHNAVSEC, of 25 Jan 1963.

string, wood, and tobacco could often be identified as originating in North Vietnam.[30]

Another aid in separating the innocent fishermen from the Communist agents was the "Junk Blue Book," first issued in August 1962. This undertaking, sponsored by the Research and Development Field Unit of the Advanced Research Projects Agency of the Department of Defense, was headed by Lieutenant Colonel Marion C. Dalby, USMC, and Commander William L. Thede. Three-man field teams visited each of the twelve major population centers along the Vietnamese coast. Their research was augmented by aerial photography. Published with both English and Vietnamese texts, the book identified thirty-two distinct junk types and the areas where they were most commonly found. The book served as a training aid and identification handbook for U.S. advisors and Vietnamese officers assigned to coastal patrol duties.

Initial planning called for two-thirds of the force to be at sea while one-third was in port to rest the crews, maintain the boats, and defend the base. By the summer of 1963, when the construction program was completed, the proportion of junks on patrol averaged between 40 and 50 percent daily. The night, however, belonged to the Communists until the installation of searchlights on motorized junks resulted in some patrolling after dark. Repair and personnel problems were the main causes of the low operational figures, but poor leadership was a contributing factor. By the end of the year, the operational readiness rate remained between 40 and 45 percent.[31]

The quality of the coastal divisions varied. Commander Jerome L. Ashcroft reported, after a visit to Coastal Division 33 in September 1963, that it was "without qualification, the best trained and most effective division visited by the Senior Junk Force Advisor. [The commander] is a professional and his men model him."[32] On the other hand, Ashcroft's unannounced visit to Coastal Division 37 about the same time found none of its junks on patrol. Somewhere in between were Coastal Divisions 15 and 16. Lieutenant (j.g.) Bruce Ryan, the 1st Coastal District advisor, reported that

---

[30]JCS, report, "Project Beef-Up," of 5 Dec 1961; Navy Section, Progress Report, "Coastal Infiltration," of Aug 1962; "Weekly Progress Report," of 28 Aug-3 Sep 1963; Senior Junk Force Advisor, report, of 4 Dec 1963; JCS, report, "Visit of Team to South Vietnam," of Jan 1963.
[31]Navy Section, MAAG, "Weekly Progress Reports," of Aug-Dec 1963.
[32]Ltrs, Ashcroft to CHNAVSEC, of 5 and 12 Sep 1963.

both 15th and 16th Divisions appear to be keeping their [sailing] junks in good condition and frequently underway; and, although the 16th's primary activities seem to be commercial fishing and woodcutting as opposed to the more routine patrol activities of Division 15, the net results of the two divisions appear the same — no significant contacts.[33]

The work of the junkmen was monotonous, but also dangerous, as one action on 19 August 1963 revealed. At 0300 that day, eight junks set sail from Cam Ranh Bay for Vinh Hy, about twenty miles to the south. The group patrolled the seaward approach to Vinh Hy until daybreak. Then, the eight junks sailed through the inlet in column about sixty yards apart, while *Nam Du* (HQ-607), a motor gunboat (PGM), stood by just outside the bay. At 0745 the junks fired on a deserted village which was suspected of harboring Viet Cong agents. When there was no return fire, the junks beached and prepared to land a shore party. At that point an estimated ten to twenty Viet Cong opened up on the beach party with small arms fire. As the junks pulled away from the beach, Lieutenant Dallas W. Shawkey, the 2nd Coastal District advisor, was hit. The junks returned the fire while Vietnamese corpsmen attended Shawkey. The wounded advisor was transferred to the PGM which steamed for Nha Trang, about two hours away. There he was taken to a U.S. Army field hospital to recover from his wounds.[34]

During 1962 the Vietnamese Navy caught 320 enemy junks and captured 111 confirmed Viet Cong. All of the prisoners were engaged in intracoastal transport within South Vietnam. However, six Communists were captured in March 1962 carrying explosives in sampans across the Cambodian border on the Mekong and Bassac Rivers. By April 1963, when all twenty-eight coastal divisions were deployed, U.S. advisors evaluated control of the coast as 90 percent effective. In the first six months of the year, only one incident involved a North Vietnamese junk, which was captured near Hue. In 1963 only a small number of sampans was infiltrating across the Cambodian border on the Mekong River. By year's end, the Coastal Force and Sea Force had checked 127,000 junks and 353,000 fishermen. Of the 3,000 suspects detained, the Sea Force took 500 and the Coastal Force 2,500. The coastal surveillance efforts

---

[33]Ltr, 1STCDADV to CHNAVSEC, of 15 Apr 1963. See also Navy Section, Fact Sheet, of Aug 1962; ARPA, "Junk Blue Book."

[34]Msg, COMUSMACV 190450Z Aug 1963; ltr, B.D. Graham to Senior Naval Advisor, of 19 Aug 1963.

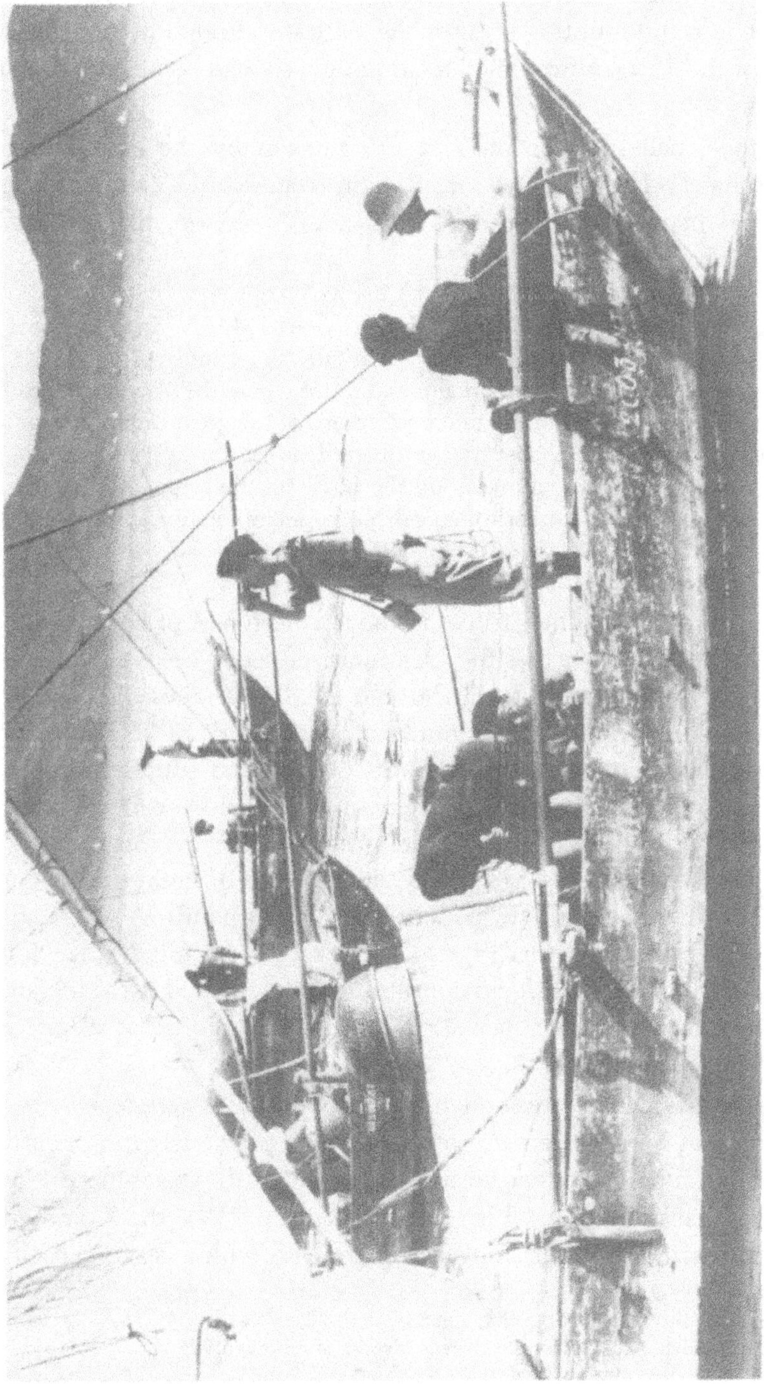

USN-1111101

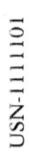

Officers and men of the South Vietnamese Coastal Force scan the coast to locate junks or other small craft carrying arms and munitions to Viet Cong forces ashore.

continued to discover mostly internal Viet Cong traffic, rather than infiltration into the country. This conclusion was indicated by the fact that, in 1963, of the 150 confirmed Viet Cong only six had come from outside the country.[35]

From the small number of Viet Cong taken by the junk force, it appeared that no large-scale sea infiltration from North Vietnam of men and supplies had occurred. Lieutenant Mark V. Nelson, the 1st Coastal District advisor, reported:

> [The Vietnamese commander] and I, as does [MACV Intelligence] think that there is a very small chance that the VC are infiltrating by sea. Most of the VC are in the mountains and this is where the operations are going on. Resupply is highly unlikely because of the great distances that goods must be carried through government held land. It is true that Psy War personnel are operating along the coast but these people do not carry weapons and it is next to impossible to catch them except through the use of agents.[36]

Communist support for their forces in the northern part of South Vietnam probably came directly across the Demilitarized Zone or over the border from Laos. Most Communist traffic along the 1,200 miles of coastline in South Vietnam consisted of infiltration of small bands of key cadre or of intracoastal movement of small amounts of men and supplies. The junk force certainly hampered such movement but by no means completely stopped it. The appearance of Communist-made heavy weapons in the Mekong Delta suggested that some equipment was brought into that area by sea, but there was no evidence in 1963 to confirm this. Captain Drachnik later observed that "I was convinced in my mind...that during those years there was no effective infiltration by sea...and Mr. McNamara told me later when I was on his staff in the Pentagon that he too was convinced."[37]

However, evidence subsequently obtained adds credence to the contention that North Vietnam stepped up the previously minor infiltration effort in 1963. Under the aegis of the North Vietnamese Navy's 125th Sea Transportation Unit (formerly Group 759), the Communists began construction in their shipyards of trawlers with a cargo capacity of

---

[35]Navy Section, Fact Sheet, "Coastal Infiltration," of 1963.
[36]Ltr, 1st CO Advisor to Senior Junk Force Advisor, of 16 Aug 1963.
[37]Drachnik, Interview with Moss, p. 8.

50 to 100 tons. During 1963, the first full year of operation, the unit conducted eight trips to the South. The small trawlers carried arms and ammunition primarily to the Camau Peninsula area, to the mouth of the Mekong River, and to the central coast of Vietnam. This latter area included delivery sites in northern Khanh Hoa, Phu Yen, and Binh Dinh Provinces. Often flying the Chinese Communist flag to conceal their identity, these ships sailed on moonless nights to a point about sixty miles offshore. This placed them beyond the effective surveillance zone of the Vietnamese Navy. At the optimum time, the ships made a run to the beach or unloaded into junks offshore. None of these trawlers was detected in 1963, much less stopped or sunk.[38]

In view of the unexciting patrol routine and meager results, it was not surprising that the junk commanders favored independent raiding operations. The commander of Coastal Division 33 mounted a typical operation in July 1963. He had received reports from local villagers that the 206th Viet Cong Company was headquartered at the village of Dong near the mouth of the Soirap River. The reports indicated that the Viet Cong unit planned to attack a nearby village on the 20th, leaving behind in Dong only a small garrison. Deciding to assault the lightly manned base, the division commander sortied with a command junk and a River Force vedette from his base at Vam Lang, six miles to the north. He entered the channel to Dong about noon on 20 July. With machine guns blazing, the command junk landed the thirty-man raiding party, which started inland to Dong. Almost immediately the machine guns on both the vedette and the command junk jammed and the troops were called back to the boats, which withdrew to repair the weapons. A second landing was attempted, but then the Communists drove off the boats. Four men were wounded. In the meantime, requests for air support were turned down by the sector headquarters. The sailors faced the entire Viet Cong company, which had returned earlier than expected. Undaunted, the force mounted a second attack the next day, this time with a PGM in support. Beginning about noon on the 21st, the PGM began a two and one-half hour bombardment

---

[38]MACV, "SECDEF Conf Agenda Book, General Harkins," of 19 Dec 1963; CICV, report, "VC/NVA Gunrunners," No. SR67-002 of 9 Aug 1966; NAVFORV, "Maritime Infiltration into the Republic of Vietnam," of 4 Mar 1967; CINCPAC, "CINCPAC/COMPONENTS Assessment of Sea Infiltration, Committee B," of Jul 1967; CINCPAC, "Infiltration Study," of 1 May 1968; DIA, "Viet Cong Use of Cambodia," No. 6028 3647 68 of 10 May 1968; CIA, report, No. FIR-311/01873-74 of 27 Jun 1974; Judith Erdheim, *Market Time*, study CRC 280 (Washington: Center for Naval Analyses, 1975); Socialist Republic of Vietnam, *Vietnam: The Anti-U.S. Resistance War*, p. 32.

of Dong, which drove off the defenders. The raiding party landed at 1430 and met no resistance. After searching the area and finding numerous booby traps and mud fortifications, the junkmen departed.[39]

The Vietnamese wanted to increase their small force of paramilitary commandos, named Biet Hai, and assign thirty-eight-man units to each of the twenty-eight divisions. But Captain Drachnik discouraged the plan because of the logistical problems of supporting such a large force and the danger that the original Coastal Force mission of patrolling would be diluted by commando operations. As a result, the Vietnamese Department of State for National Defense did not approve further funding for the commandos, and the program died early in 1963. Forty-two of the Biet Hai were transferred to Saigon to fill the ranks of the regular navy's LDNN "frogman" force. The remainder of the men were dispersed among the coastal divisions, where they filled critical billets in the rapidly expanding command.[40]

The Coastal Force also participated in joint operations with army and local paramilitary forces. A typical action occurred in January 1963 in Phuoc Tuy Province. While Civil Guard and army ranger companies swept toward the coast, the Coastal Force patrolled off the beach to stop the enemy's evasion by water. Four motorized sailing junks, with two sailing junks in tow, arrived on station at 0800 on the 17th about twenty-five miles up the coast from Vung Tau. The junks sailed up and down the coast forming a three and one-half mile barrier before moving six miles farther up the coast to Tuan Bien to land a thirty-man commando force. A small group of three Viet Cong stumbled on the landing party. One man was seized as his two companions fled, after which the junkmen destroyed those captured Viet Cong stocks of rice, lumber, and potatoes that they could not carry back to Vung Tau. During the landing one sailing junk was grounded and then pounded by the surf. The force commander ordered the craft dragged onto the beach for repairs. By 2000 a platoon of Civil Guards arrived to reinforce the junkmen and a short time later the defenders drove off an attacking Communist platoon, killing two of the enemy. The operation ended on the 22nd when the junk was abandoned as unsalvageable. Then a seventy-man force of sailors marched inland and destroyed a Viet Cong village one mile from the coast. Reaching the main

---

[39] 3rd CD Advisor, report, of 25 Jul 1963.
[40] Peter W. Willits, End of Tour Report, of 29 Feb 1964.

road to Vung Tau, the force boarded trucks which returned them to their base.

Often the Coastal Force was called upon to transport men and materials along the coast. For example, in December 1962, when the province chief of Phuoc Tuy Province asked for Coastal Force assistance in relocating villagers in his province, the junkmen agreed, even though operating on inland waterways was not one of their functions. On the 6th junks picked up a platoon of Vietnamese Army rangers and a platoon of Self Defense Corps troops and landed them at positions along the waterways between the old village near the coast and the new hamlet at Phuoc Hoa, about six miles inland on Route 15. Then, the five motorized and twenty sailing junks transported the villagers and their belongings to the new homes. When the operation was over on the afternoon of the 8th, the junks and several civilian craft had relocated 1,400 villagers.

The Sea Force Improves its Blue Water Capability

The inauguration of the combined U.S.-South Vietnamese coastal patrol in December 1961 touched off a concerted effort to provide the Sea Force with more and better ships. The original Fiscal Year 1962 Military Assistance Program called for the delivery of 212 fifty-six-foot minesweeping launches (MLMS). In view of the Coastal Patrol Plan, approved by the Joint Chiefs of Staff in January 1962, the Chief of the MAAG decided that implementation of the plan should take precedence over developing the minesweeping capability of the Vietnamese Navy. Therefore, he recommended that twelve PGMs be substituted for the MLMS craft.

The 100-foot PGM, built especially for foreign navies, was an ideal ship for the Vietnamese considering its small crew, simple design, and low maintenance demands. The Vietnamese Naval Deputy, Quyen, promoted to captain in June 1962, planned to deploy the PGM inshore so its speed, maneuverability, fire power, radar, and excellent communication equipment could be put to best use. Because labor shortages at the U.S. shipyard delayed initial delivery, however, the first ships did not arrive in Vietnam until 1963.[41]

---

[41] Msgs, CHMAAGVN 230409Z Jan 1962; 021029Z Feb; CP 062321Z Jul; memo, CHNAVSEC to CNO VNN, ser 00214 of 15 Oct 1962.

The PGM was a welcome addition to the Vietnamese Navy's coastal patrol capability, but spare parts for the foreign-made Mercedes Benz engines proved hard to obtain. As early as November 1961, Captain Easterling questioned the use of these engines in the PGM based on his staff's study of the Philippine Navy's less than positive experience with them. Captain Drachnik, Easterling's successor, expressed similar reservations. The Bureau of Ships assured the MAAG that spare parts would not be a problem, observing that the navies of Burma, Thailand, the Philippines, India, and Indonesia all used the same engines and stocked parts for them. In addition, no U.S.-made engine could meet the size, horsepower, and delivery requirements. The PGMs were in operation less than a year, with the engines generally performing well, when a spare parts problem began to appear. By the end of 1963 less than half the spare parts requested had been received from the Mercedes Benz supplier in New York.[42]

In addition to 10 of the PGMs, the U.S. Navy transferred to the Sea Force 2 LSMs, 3 LSTs, 1 YOG, 12 MLMSs, and 2 fleet minesweepers (MSF) in 1962 and 1963. The Vietnamese accepted MSTS LSTs rather than combat-configured ships, which would have required costly reactivations from the Reserve Fleet. The two MSFs (formerly *Gayety* (MSF-239) and *Sentry* (MSF-299)) were not used as minesweepers by the Vietnamese but converted to escorts (PCE). The MLMSs were reconfigured to counter the major mining threat — command detonated mines on inland waters. Even though they operated primarily in the Rung Sat swamp below Saigon, the MLMSs remained a part of the Sea Force.

The 3 LSTs, the 2 new LSMs, and the 5 LSMs already in the Vietnamese Navy gave the fleet a capability to transport over 10,000 tons of cargo a month. Because of poor planning, however, the ships hauled only 5,000 to 8,000 tons of cargo a month during 1962 and 1963. Although naval advisors wanted the Vietnamese to develop an amphibious capability, the primary use of the landing ships was for logistic support of the army along the coast of South Vietnam, particularly in the northern part of the country where the rail line was usually cut by Viet Cong sabotage. In a

---

[42]Ltrs, CHBUSHIPS to CHNAVSEC, ser 009083 n.d.; CHNAVSEC to CHBUSHIPS, ser 0081 of 27 Nov 1961; ser 0011 of 18 Jan 1962; B.H. Palmer to CHNAVSEC, of 15 Nov; msg, CHMAAGVN 160255Z Nov 1963; Hardcastle, Interview.

typical operation, in the summer of 1963, five LSMs carried ammunition from Saigon to army forces in Danang and returned with excess equipment and prisoners. The LSMs were often directed to pick up or deliver cargo to Nha Trang or Qui Nhon on these cruises, which lasted from seven to ten days.[43]

Vietnamese crews accepted transfer of most of the larger ships in the United States and, after receiving several weeks of training and familiarization, sailed them to Vietnam. Mobile training teams were dispatched to Southeast Asia to give instruction in the operation of smaller craft, such as the MLMSs. Mobile Training Team 3-63, commanded by Lieutenant (j.g.) Dennis McInerby, trained ninety-one Vietnamese crewmen in the operation of the MLMSs at Vung Tau between August and December 1963.[44]

Because high-level U.S. planners looked at Vietnam and other MAP recipients as part of the overall collective security system in Asia, these navies were intended not only to defend their own countries, but to contribute to the allied effort. Although the North Vietnamese did not have submarines, the Soviets and Chinese Communists did. Thus, Admiral Felt expressed his concern about the low priority given to antisubmarine warfare by countries in the Pacific Command. While Captain Drachnik observed that "there is insufficient evidence to support a theory of a submarine threat from the VC or the DRV,"[45] broader defense needs required South Vietnamese readiness to deal with the undersea danger. Accordingly, the Force Objective Plan of April 1963, as had others before it, called for the continued development of an ASW capability in the Vietnamese Navy.

Until the policy was reviewed in 1965, PCs were required to keep their antisubmarine warfare equipment operational and from time to time to participate in exercises. Submarine chaser *Van Don* (HQ-06) engaged in one exercise with *Bluegill* (SS-242) on 6 April 1962, two days after the American submarine visited Saigon. Similarly, between 29 August and 6 September 1962, four of the Vietnamese Navy's PCs and one PCE operated with *Queenfish* (SS-393) about forty miles off Nha Trang. The final combined antisubmarine warfare exercise in this period occurred

---

[43] COMPHIBPAC, report, 6-S-62 of 25 Jul 1962; ONI, report, 11-S-62 of 3 Oct.
[44] Ltrs, OICMTT 3-63 to CHNAVSEC, of 26 Nov 1963; OICMTT 3-63 to CNO, ser 4950 of 13 Dec; Le Ba Thang, Interview, pp. 5-7.
[45] Ltr, CHNAVSEC to CO VNN, ser 0378 of 23 Aug 1962.

between 7 and 14 April 1963, when *Capitaine* (AGSS-336) trained with six Vietnamese Navy PCs and PCEs under the command of Lieutenant Commander Dinh Manh Hung. No exercises were scheduled in the latter half of 1963 and thereafter, because Captain Drachnik felt that the Sea Force ships could not be spared from the more crucial coastal patrol mission.[46]

A similar theater defense planning requirement motivated the Vietnamese Navy's preparation to sweep coastal waters for sophisticated magnetic and acoustic mines. Hence, in March 1962 three MSCs sailed to the Philippines to conduct degaussing (demagnetizing) operations with *Surfbird* (ADG-383). On board the Vietnamese ships were forty-five midshipmen from the Vietnamese Naval Academy taking their first training cruise. Then, from 20 to 22 August two of the MSCs participated with a British flotilla in a minesweeping exercise off Vietnam. In August 1963, to save time, *Surfbird* visited Cam Ranh Bay to provide the same services she had at Sangley. Late that year, a portable degaussing range was installed at Cam Ranh Bay, so that the Vietnamese were no longer dependent upon the United States for these services.[47]

More relevant to the current military situation in South Vietnam were amphibious operations, in which the Sea Force figured prominently. Throughout the period, U.S. advisors encouraged the Vietnamese to carry out landings with amphibious ships rather than use them on logistic operations. Showing initiative in this regard, the Vietnamese Navy undertook a large-scale amphibious operation on the Camau Peninsula in January 1963. The start of the operation was delayed, partly because of controversy over control of the forces. The IV Corps commander, an army general, disagreed with plans to give overall command to the navy. Nonetheless, the operation was finally placed under the direct control of Captain Quyen for both the landing and ground phases of the action. Although the command setup caused no serious problems, U.S. naval

---

[46]Msg, ALUSNA Saigon 181001Z Apr 1962; memo, SECNAV to SECDEF, of 8 Aug 1962; ltrs, CO *Capitaine* to CHNAVSEC, ser 028 of 18 Apr 1963; Senior Junk Force Advisor to CHNAVSEC, of 19 Apr; J.O. Richter, Jr., End of Tour Report, ser 5213 of 23 Apr 1964; ltr, CHNAVSEC to CO VNN, ser N0438-63 of 3 May 1963; CINCPACFLT, Annual Report, FY1963; Dinh Manh Hung, transcript of interview with Oscar P. Fitzgerald, Naval Historical Center, in Alexandria, VA, 19 and 21 Aug 1975, pp. 4-7.

[47]Ltr, CHNAVSEC to CO VNN, ser 875 of 18 Oct 1960; memos, SECNAV to SECDEF, of 16 Nov 1962; CO *Surfbird* to CHMAAGVN, ser 091 of 17 Sep 1963; msg, CHNAVSEC 110053Z Apr 1963; Browne, Interview.

advisors recommended that in future operations the command arrangements follow more closely the American practice, which passed control of the operation to a Marine or Army officer once the landing force was established ashore.

A naval task force of 1 LST and 4 LSMs, carrying two marine battalions and their American Marine advisors, later joined by 2 LSILs, and 1 LSSL, sailed on 1 January 1963 to begin the largest naval and amphibious operation ever mounted by the Vietnamese. A second LSSL, plus units of the 22nd RAG and two junk divisions, also participated. Because of the shallow depth of the water off the Camau Peninsula, the marines landed in small assault boats. They met no resistance and in fact found the intended objective stripped of military material. Apparently, the Viet Cong had expected the attack and fled. On the 8th both marine battalions were picked up and transported to Tan An by an LST and an LSM in order to begin Phase II of the operation. Meanwhile, RAG units patrolled inland waterways to cut off food shipments to Communist troops and provide troop lift and gunfire support if the need arose.[48]

By the end of the month the Vietnamese encountered only light resistance, but they accomplished their mission of expanding government control in an area which long had been a Communist stronghold. Casualties stood at 5 killed and 28 wounded, while Communist losses were estimated as 40 killed and many more wounded. During the rest of January Vietnamese engineers also constructed several strategic hamlets and resettled 3,000 people in the vicinity of Nam Can. In February Communist opposition to government inroads into their territory intensified. The land phase of the operation was terminated on 4 March 1963. Not until the mid-1960s would regular government troops return here in strength.[49]

Even though the marines departed in March, the Sea Force continued to patrol the area in support of the Civil Guard-manned outposts at Nam Can, Ong Trang, and Tan An. The seven-day patrol of LSSL *Linh Kiem* (HQ-226) on the Bo De and Cua Lon Rivers in mid-1963 was typical. Beginning on 27 August, the ship escorted an LSM to Tan An,

---

[48]Navy Section, "Weekly Progress Reports," of 28 Dec 1962-3 Jan 1963; 4-10 Jan; 11-17 Jan; ltrs, CHNAVSEC, ser 1100-63 of 23 Apr 1963; CINCPAC, ser 00394 of 29 Apr.
[49]Naval History Division, "History of Naval Operations in Vietnam, 1946-1963," pp. 224-27.

Linh Kiem *(HQ-226)*, an LSSL of the Vietnamese Navy's Sea Force, patrols one of South Vietnam's innumerable inland waterways.

transported Viet Cong prisoners to Ong Trang, and fired shore bombardment exercises along the river banks. After observing the operation of the LSSL, an American advisor, Lieutenant Jon A. Askland, stated that "of the seven day patrol, few tangible results can be reported. [But] the LSSL is on patrol primarily as a deterrent, and as a deterrent, the ship was effective." The Viet Cong chose not to risk exposure to the LSSL's one 3-inch, four 40-millimeter, and four 20-millimeter guns.[50]

---

[50] Ltr, J.A. Askland to CHNAVSEC, of 4 Sep 1963.

The River Force

As with the other components of the Vietnamese Navy, the River Force expanded as a result of the U.S. government's decision of November 1961 to give added support to the Vietnamese. During 1962 a sixth RAG, with nineteen boats and about 250 men, was activated. One LCM arrived from the United States in February and seven LCVPs in April to fill the unit's complement. The other eleven boats were former derelicts reconditioned at the Saigon Naval Shipyard. The new RAG was conceived as a mobile group which would operate from a mother ship, an LCU, in the Saigon River and the Rung Sat in support of Vietnamese Army forces.[51] The new RAG, designated the 22nd River Assault Group, became operational on 1 September 1962. Less than two weeks later, the unit sailed for the Rung Sat, with one company of marines embarked, to test the new mobile concept during the thirty-day deployment. The unit landed small parties of marines dressed in civilian clothes to gather intelligence and then transported larger units to the area to take advantage of the information collected. The operation was concluded on 8 October with the following results: 26 enemy soldiers killed and 1 arms factory, 1 hospital, 1 training camp, and 1 sector headquarters destroyed, at a cost of 1 sailor killed and 3 wounded. A captured Communist document bemoaned the success of the operation: "Disruption of traffic lines and shortage of food stuffs is critical. All units and elements send inventory of anti-boat weapons for coordination of counter-action."[52]

In addition to the boats for the new RAG, the River Force received twenty-four monitors, LCVPs, and other craft. The River Force controlled a total of 208 boats at the end of 1963, almost twice the number in the force in 1959. However, only 157 of the 208 boats were armed and armored. The remaining craft, consisting of LCUs and LCVPs, provided local transportation at Danang, Nha Trang, Cam Ranh, Vung Tau, Phu Quoc, Can Tho, and Saigon.

As the River Force grew in size, its primary mission remained the same: to support army operations in the Mekong Delta. Other than occasional efforts during army operations, the River Force did not attempt significant

---

[51] Navy Section, Progress Report, "22nd River Assault Group," of 18 Jul 1962.
[52] Navy Section, Progress Report, "Status of VNN River Force," of 6 Sep 1962. See also Undated Brief, "Activation of 22nd River Assault Group;" msg, ALUSNA Saigon 172210Z Oct 1962.

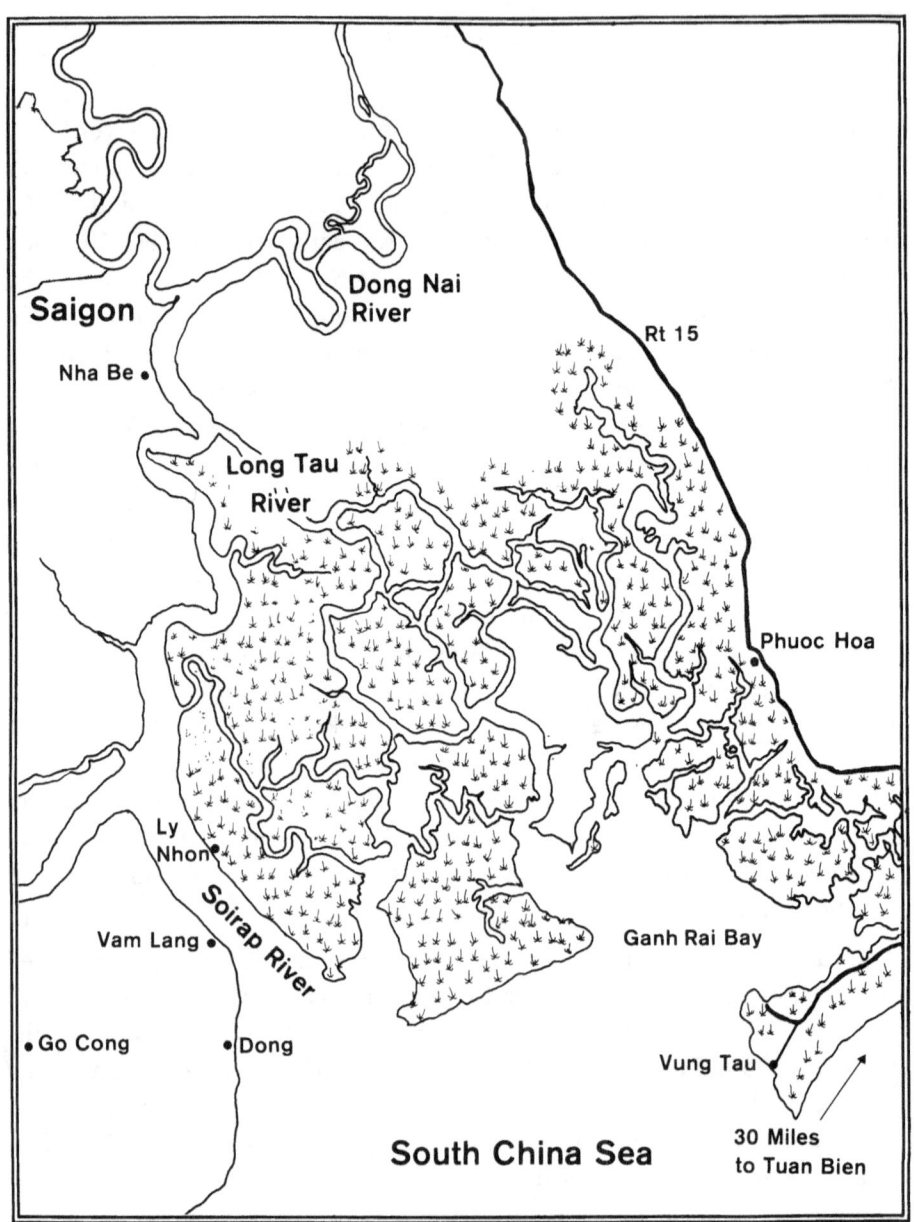

Rung Sat Swamp

interdiction of Communist waterway traffic in the delta. During 1963, for example, a typical daily deployment consisted of 12 boats on combat operations, 9 in static guard duty, 12 operating with province chiefs, 15 in training, upkeep, or repair, and 66 idle. Considering that a small percentage of the RAG boats were being used, naval advisors deleted the proposal for yet another RAG, which the Vietnamese had requested, from the Fiscal Year 1963 MAP budget.[53]

Only an expansion of the mission of the River Force to include river interdiction, it was reasoned, could justify additional boats. Secretary McNamara raised the possibility of adding new functions during his visit of September 1963, but Captain Drachnik resisted attempts to broaden the mission of the River Force. He saw its main role as one of transport. In addition, he believed that there was little Viet Cong use of the rivers and felt that extensive interdiction efforts would yield only meager results.[54]

Despite Captain Drachnik's views, on 1 June 1963 the Vietnamese Navy established a patrol area along the Cambodian border, where Vietnamese customs agents and units of the River Force and Self Defense Corps had reported seven attempts at cross-border smuggling of explosives during the previous three months. The patrols were conducted by one Sea Force ship, usually an LSSL or LSIL with a shallow enough draft to navigate the rivers, and two River Force LCVPs or STCANs. The patrols, which continued through the end of the year, normally found only contraband goods of a non-military nature. U.S. advisors speculated that the Viet Cong could hear or see the vessels far enough away for the Communists to hide or jettison their cargo. Still, night patrols and stationary, noiseless ambushes were no more successful. On the other hand, the presence of well-armed ships and craft in their area was comforting to pro-government Vietnamese in the border towns threatened with Communist attack.[55]

In October 1963, General Harkins appointed a study group of four MACV intelligence officers and six MAAG officers from the Navy Section to study the extent of inland waterway and coastal infiltration. The group learned that sixteen tons of explosive components had been found on junks searched during the March to September period. Also, the group found that much intracoastal movement of Communist personnel occurred

---

[53]MACV, "Agenda Items for Conference with President Diem, Aug 1963."
[54]Ltrs, Drachnik to Ricketts, of 13 Mar 1964, p. 2; A.A. Levine to CHNAVSEC, of 18 Nov 1963.
[55]Drachnik, Interview with Fitzgerald; ltrs, J.O. Richter, Jr., to CHNAVSEC, of 10 Jun 1963; J.A. Askland to CHNAVSEC, of 17 Dec; Navy Section, Fact Sheet, "VNN Boats," of 30 Oct 1963; Navy Section, "Study of Requirements for Additional River Craft in Delta," of 18 Oct 1963 Tab I to report of Delta Infiltration Study Group (Bucklew Board), of Feb 1964.

in the delta. The members concluded that "Cambodia's broad Mekong River system, flowing generally from north to south, represents the most convenient channels for Communist supplies destined for the VC in southern Vietnam." They also decided that "coastal seaborne infiltration would appear to be limited to specialized items of equipment and high level VC cadre and agents." However, these evaluators added that although the Vietnamese Navy's control of inland waterways was "woefully inadequate," there was not enough verified intelligence available to judge the extent of Viet Cong use of these avenues.[56]

The major mission of the River Force continued to be support of army troops in the Mekong Delta. Often, however, the army did not permit naval officers to participate in the planning of operations, which sometimes had detrimental effects. Such was the case in three operations mounted between 27 March and 5 April 1962, the purposes of which were to lift troops to an objective and then patrol the adjacent waterways to prevent Communist escape by water. In the first operation, three LCMs carrying troops reached a bridge north of Saigon, where they had to wait ten hours for the next low tide before further passage was possible. In the second operation, a convoy of 4 LCMs, 4 LCVPs, and 4 STCANs were delayed for nine hours at a Viet Cong barricade, on the Thap Muoi Canal, which military engineers had failed to clear to a depth that would allow passage at low tide. In a third operation, two LCVPs landed troops at low tide, which forced the soldiers to wade 500 meters through mud and water before they reached the river bank.

During the next month, the Vietnamese tested a new system of coordination where they established a naval operations command center at army headquarters. After studying copies of the operation plan, detailed charts of the area, and tide and current tables, the center advised the army commander on the employment of the navy's units. At least during that month, the delays of earlier operations were avoided. As a further solution, in the fall of 1963, operational control of most of the RAGs was transferred from the army corps commanders to the newly created naval zone commanders. Under the new arrangement, the mobile RAG and the River Transport Escort Group remained under the direct operational control of the River Force commander.[57]

---

[56]Navy Section, "Study Requirements for Additional River Craft."

[57]NA Saigon, report, 59-62 of 13 Jun 1962; Navy Section, Progress Report, "Status of VNN River Force," of Sep 1963.

Another organizational hindrance was the common practice of province chiefs drawing on the navy's river fleet to perform static defense missions. Captain Quyen had long opposed this practice, which limited the number of boats available for mobile operations and hindered an orderly maintenance program for the River Force. Addressing this problem in 1962, the United States provided 145 LCVPs to form twenty boat companies for use by Vietnamese province chiefs. These paramilitary Civil Guard boat units were created in June 1962. The Vietnamese Navy trained the first boat crews. Then, in July 1963, a formal Civil Guard Boat Operation Training Center was established on the Saigon River. The boat companies were deployed to most of the provinces in the III and IV Corps areas, where they relieved Vietnamese River Force units of many support duties. Each company usually contained eight boats and two platoons of troops, with a strength of 4 officers and 134 men. The boat units supported counterinsurgency operations, provided vessels for static guard duty, and occasionally went out on patrol. Although the boat companies suffered from the usual problems with poor preventive maintenance, repair, supply support, and operational readiness, they did improve the mobility of local forces and eased the burden on River Force resources.[58]

While bettering the command structure and acquiring additional resources for the riverine war, the River Force took steps to help counter Viet Cong ambush and mining attacks, which totalled seventy-three incidents in the first ten months of 1963. U.S. and Vietnamese naval officers mounted flamethrowers on selected LCMs, as was done during the French Indochina War, and developed anti-mining equipment. One such device consisted of a chain with cutters welded on, which proved effective against the wires controlling the electrically detonated mines used by the enemy.[59]

The personnel situation in the River Force also improved from 1961 to 1963. While a number of craft were laid up for lack of crews early in the period, an increase in personnel allocations soon solved that problem. The River Force school, which opened in Saigon on 15 December 1961,

---

[58]U.S. Army Advisory Detachment, "LCVP Density River Patrol (Boat) Companies, Regional Force," of 13 Jan 1965; "Regional Force River Patrol Group," of Nov 1965; msg, CHMAAG 220841Z Jan 1962.
[59]CHMAAGVN, report, 2 Sep 1961-8 Feb 1962; Ray C. Nieman, End of Tour Report, of 10 May 1962; Navy Section, "Requirements for Additional River Craft;" ltr, River Force Advisor to CHNAG, of 6 Mar 1964.

began graduating 200 men every month. By late 1963, the RAGs were fully manned.[60]

U.S. Naval Augmentation of the Vietnamese Air Force

As might be expected, the primary focus of naval interest in Vietnam was on improving the Vietnamese Navy, but the U.S. Navy also played a part in the development of the Vietnamese Air Force. The principal tactical aircraft in the Vietnamese Air Force inventory was the aging Grumman F8F Bearcat, built for the United States during World War II. The durable Bearcat was deemed the most appropriate aircraft for the fledgling Vietnamese Air Force in the mid-1950s. By 1960, however, they had seen hard service and were at the end of their useful life. The decision was made to replace them with the U.S. Navy's AD-6 attack aircraft, the single-engine Skyraider built by the Douglas Aircraft Corporation during the 1950s. SS *Breton* sailed for Vietnam on 1 September 1960 with the initial consignment of six aircraft, along with supporting equipment. Another nineteen aircraft reached Vietnam in increments, until all twenty-five planes of the proposed first squadron had arrived by the end of May 1961.

A total of eighteen qualified pilots also were trained to fly the plane at the Navy's schools in the United States, and another six pilots received instruction in the T-28 trainer, before progressing to the AD. Additionally, eleven mechanics and five radio specialists received instruction in the United States, while a six-man American mobile training team prepared maintenance technicians in Vietnam from September to December 1960.[61]

During 1961 the U.S. Air Force programmed forty T-28B Nomad aircraft, a modified, high-performance version of the T-28, to replace the older trainers in the Vietnamese air arm. However, when the U.S. Air Force could not make the Nomad immediately available, the U.S. Navy agreed to loan the Vietnamese fifteen T-28Bs. All of the aircraft had

---

[60]MACV, "February 1962 Secretary of Defense Conference, Agenda Book;" Drachnik, Interview with Fitzgerald; T. T. Beattie, Jr., End of Tour Report, of 16 Dec 1964.Navy Section, Progress Report, 1963; Chung Tan Cang, Interview, pp. 42-46.

[61]CINCPAC, Command History, 1960, pp. 141-42, 156; 1961, p. 186; USAF, "Journal of Mutual Security," of Jun 1961, Office of Air Force History, p. 159.

arrived by 29 December 1961. On 4 December 1961, a joint Navy-Air Force training group arrived at the Nha Trang airfield to instruct Vietnamese pilots and maintenance personnel. In addition, sixty-five T-28 pilots were trained under the Fiscal Year 1962 Military Assistance Program, thirty-five by the Navy and thirty by the Air Force. A total of twenty of these pilots trained by the Navy also received instruction flying the AD-6. By June 1962, the fifteen T-28s on loan were transferred permanently to the Vietnamese Air Force.[62]

During 1962 and 1963, the U.S. Navy continued to provide some support to the Vietnamese Air Force. In addition to the original twenty-five AD-6 aircraft (redesignated A-1Hs in 1962), the Navy furnished eleven replacement aircraft in the Fiscal Year 1962 and Fiscal Year 1963 Military Assistance Programs. In March 1963 a second squadron of twenty-five A-1Hs was approved for the Vietnamese Air Force. The Navy also provided pilot and maintenance training. Mobile Training Team 8-63, composed of three instructors headed by Lieutenant Commander Thomas J. Conway, arrived in South Vietnam on 1 May 1963 for a five-month assignment. The training included day and night flying and the teaching of Vietnamese instructors. By the time the team departed Vietnam on 26 September 1963, it had prepared thirty pilots for A-1H operations. While the earlier aircraft and training that the U.S. Navy provided for the Vietnamese Air Force was included in the Air Force portion of the Military Assistance Program, the twenty-five aircraft provided in Fiscal Year 1964 were funded by the Navy.[63]

Mobile Training Team 1-64, composed of ten aircraft technicians and commanded by Lieutenant Commander Philip S. Arp, arrived in Vietnam in October 1963 to provide training in maintenance of the A-1H. Over the next five months the team trained 181 Vietnamese Air Force enlisted personnel. Not one of the students dropped out of the course. Lieutenant Commander Arp commented that the success of the team "was due primarily to the excellent facilities, remarkable receptiveness and eagerness of the students and to the complete and wholehearted support of the

---

[62]USAF, "Journal of Military Assistance," of Sep 1961, Office of Air Force History, pp. 6-7; Jun 1962, p. 179; msg, CP 201947Z Mar 1962.

[63]USAF, "Journal of Military Assistance," of Sep 1964, Office of Air Force History, p. 178; Dec 1964, pp. 180-81; MTT 8-63, report, of 9 Aug 1963; USAF, report, "Study Group on Vietnam," of May 1964.

U.S. Air Force."[64] However, the Navy, in particular the mobile training teams, was in large part responsible for the success of this program to strengthen the Vietnamese Air Force during the years from 1961 to 1963.

The Support Establishment in Saigon

With the U.S. military community in South Vietnam rapidly expanding after the presidential decisions of late 1961, steps were taken to establish a logistic command. The proposed command would provide support to the newly created MACV and to MAAG and other American personnel in the Saigon area. Logically the Army, with the greatest number of personnel in Vietnam, might have been expected to assume this new function. But, under a directive of the Secretary of Defense that divided worldwide responsibilities, issued in 1958, the Navy was charged with assuring administrative and logistic support for unified commands in the Pacific area. This requirement included the provision of food, pay, billeting, medical care, and other support common to all the services.[65]

Previously, Army elements of the MAAG had taken care of in-country needs, but the smaller naval contingent assisted in the effort. Naval doctors and dentists staffed a dispensary established in 1959 to serve Americans in Saigon. The Navy also furnished commissary services. In August 1959, the facility in Saigon was separated from the parent Naval Exchange at Subic Bay and established as an independent function soon afterward.[66]

The proposal to increase the service's role in the logistic support of U.S. forces in South Vietnam was not endorsed enthusiastically by all naval leaders. Admiral John H. Sides, the Commander in Chief, U.S. Pacific Fleet, argued that "Navy support is not logical in this case nor required by existing" directives. He cited Japan, Korea, and Okinawa as places where naval administrative support of U.S. forces had not been considered necessary: "The HQ will be predominately Army and it simply does not make sense that we be the janitors." Admiral Sides reached this conclusion after considering a study prepared by Captain Malcolm C. Friedman, who

---

[64]MTT 1-64, report, of 21 Mar 1964.
[65]DOD Directive 5100.3, of 12 Sep 1958; memo, OP-40 to Callahan, ser 0063P401 of 12 Jan 1962.
[66]Memo, OP-40 to CNO, ser BM14-62 of 12 Feb 1962; HSAS, "Notes for History."

The Naval Advisory and Logistic Support Effort in Vietnam 253

handled military assistance matters on the CINCPACFLT staff.[67]

Admiral Sides's objections reached Washington during the controversy over the command relationships of the soon-to-be established U.S. Military Assistance Command, Vietnam. The Navy's case would have been weakened considerably in that issue if it was not prepared to assume responsibilities to support subordinate commands. Accordingly, Admiral Anderson, the CNO, replied to Admiral Sides: "Appreciate your views, but as you know there are command implications in this proposed new organization which Navy cannot overlook. Consensus in OPNAV is that we should provide required logistic support."[68] Admiral Anderson elaborated on his thinking in a letter to Admiral Felt on 9 February 1962. He agreed with Admiral Felt's concern "over the Army's efforts to make inroads on our control of the Pacific Command. With the increased attention being given to limited war matters, they can generate many plausible reasons why CINCPAC should be an Army officer. We cannot afford to add weight to their arguments by needlessly increasing the size of their role in the Military Assistance Program." He added that he thought support of the MAAG was a proper role for the Navy. Hence, when MACV was activated, the Navy should be ready to support it, "despite the price we must pay in personnel and Navy dollars."[69]

Anticipating a JCS decision to proceed with the establishment of a support activity, Admiral Anderson directed Admiral Sides to submit a proposal for the headquarters organization and staffing. Ironically, Captain Friedman, who had earlier recommended against the establishment of a naval support activity, was selected as the prospective commanding officer. He was ordered to head a survey team which was dispatched to Saigon to carry out the study directed by the CNO. Friedman's study was completed by the end of February 1962. The team used as a model the Naval Support Activity, Taipei, which supported the unified Taiwan Defense Command and the Military Assistance Advisory Group, Republic of China. The commands supported by the Navy in Taiwan were similar to the MAAG and MACV in South Vietnam. In line

---

[67] Msg, CPFLT 120223Z Dec 1961; see also Friedman, Interview.

[68] Msg, CNO 131633Z Dec 1961.

[69] Ltr, Anderson to Felt, of 9 Feb 1962. See also Friedman, Interview; memo, OP-40 to Callahan, ser 0063P401 of 12 Jan 1962; ACNO, memo for record, ser 0011-62 of 27 Jan; memo, OP-40 to CNO, ser BM14-62 of 12 Feb; CINCPAC, Command History, 1964, p. 330; MACV, Command History, 1964, p. 135.

with general CNO policy statements, the team recommended that the proposed activity be limited to supporting units in the immediate Saigon area. Admiral Anderson and other leaders were greatly concerned that support for the rapidly expanding forces in Vietnam might be interrupted. So, to ensure a smooth transition, the team recommended that the personnel in the MAAG, performing functions which would be taken over by the support activity, should be transferred to the activity. The Navy's presence would increase when naval personnel replaced many of the Army people at the end of their tours with the MAAG. Within several years, the support activity would be staffed primarily by naval personnel. With regard to command relationships, the team suggested that the activity be placed under Commander Naval Forces, Philippines. That command had a similar relationship with the Naval Support Activity, Taipei, and was in relative proximity to South Vietnam. Operational control of the naval support facility would be delegated to Commander U.S. Military Assistance Command, Vietnam.

After accepting the team's recommendations, Admiral Sides set 1 July 1962 as the commissioning date for the support activity. To minimize the disruption of a transfer of functions from the MAAG to the new command, CINCPACFLT dispatched Captain Friedman and a small advanced staff to Saigon in April.[70] Captain Friedman worked out agreements to establish each military service's responsibilities within the activity. The Navy agreed to provide common administrative and logistic support, including supply and fiscal, public works, medical and dental, commissary and exchange, special services, and housekeeping functions to MAAG and MACV, and also to Army and Air Force components in the Saigon area. The Army provided a small contingent of military police units for the Saigon area and a small group of supply specialists. Aircraft would be attached to the support function when needed, until several transports were permanently assigned in subsequent months. The Air Force assigned personnel to handle postal service, supply problems, and airlift traffic coordination.[71]

---

[70]Friedman, Interview; memo, OP-40 to CNO, ser BM14-62 of 12 Feb 1962; HSAS, Draft History.

[71]Msgs, CNO 221613Z May 1962; CPFLT 131951Z Dec; memo, OP-405C to CNO, ser BM80-64 of 1 Dec 1964.

Headquarters Support Activity, Saigon

As planned, the Headquarters Support Activity, Saigon (HSAS) was established on 1 July 1962. The MAAG provided the nucleus of personnel for HSAS, but because MACV was a larger organization, HSAS required more than twice as many men as had been involved in the MAAG's support effort. By the end of December, HSAS was staffed by 445 men, 251 from the Navy, 188 from the Army, and 6 from the Air Force.[72]

The activity began operations with an $11 million budget from a small building adjacent to the MAAG headquarters on Tran Hung Dao Street. Early in 1963 the HSAS headquarters was moved to the Cofat factory building, the site of an old French cigarette firm. As more and more of the naval personnel programmed for the support activity arrived, they moved into former MAAG facilities, which were scattered throughout the city.[73] This decentralization was, for the most part, beneficial. HSAS offices and compounds melted into the metropolis, so that the Vietnamese, sensitive about their sovereignty, were not confronted with a monolithic headquarters. Furthermore, the decentralized offices offered less attractive targets for Viet Cong terrorists and, because HSAS was not restricted to a single location, expansion was much easier. Any available building could be obtained rather than having to construct a new one at a centralized compound. The most pressing problem facing Captain Friedman after the commissioning was to find warehouse space in Saigon to store common supplies for U.S. forces. But within a short time, the Real Estate Division located a compound, which soon was renovated and expanded to receive the stocks.[74]

Other HSAS responsibilities, such as messing and billeting, were handled on a more routine basis. The activity assumed control from the MAAG of nine bachelor officers quarters (BOQs) and seven bachelor enlisted men's quarters (BEQs), with the capacity to house about 2,000 men. In 1962 and succeeding years, eight additional BOQs and five BEQs

---

[72] Msg, MACV 290543Z Dec 1962.
[73] CINCPAC, Command History, 1962, pp. 159-60; MACV, Summary of Highlights, of 20 Mar 1963, pp. 74-75; ltr, CNO to SECNAV, ser 00155P10 of 20 Apr 1962. Edward J. Marolda, "Saigon" in *United States Navy and Marine Corps Bases, Overseas*, Paolo E. Coletta, ed. (Westport, CT: Greenwood Press, 1985), pp. 287-91.
[74] Ltr, Friedman to Kuntze, of 23 Dec 1965; HSAS, Draft History.

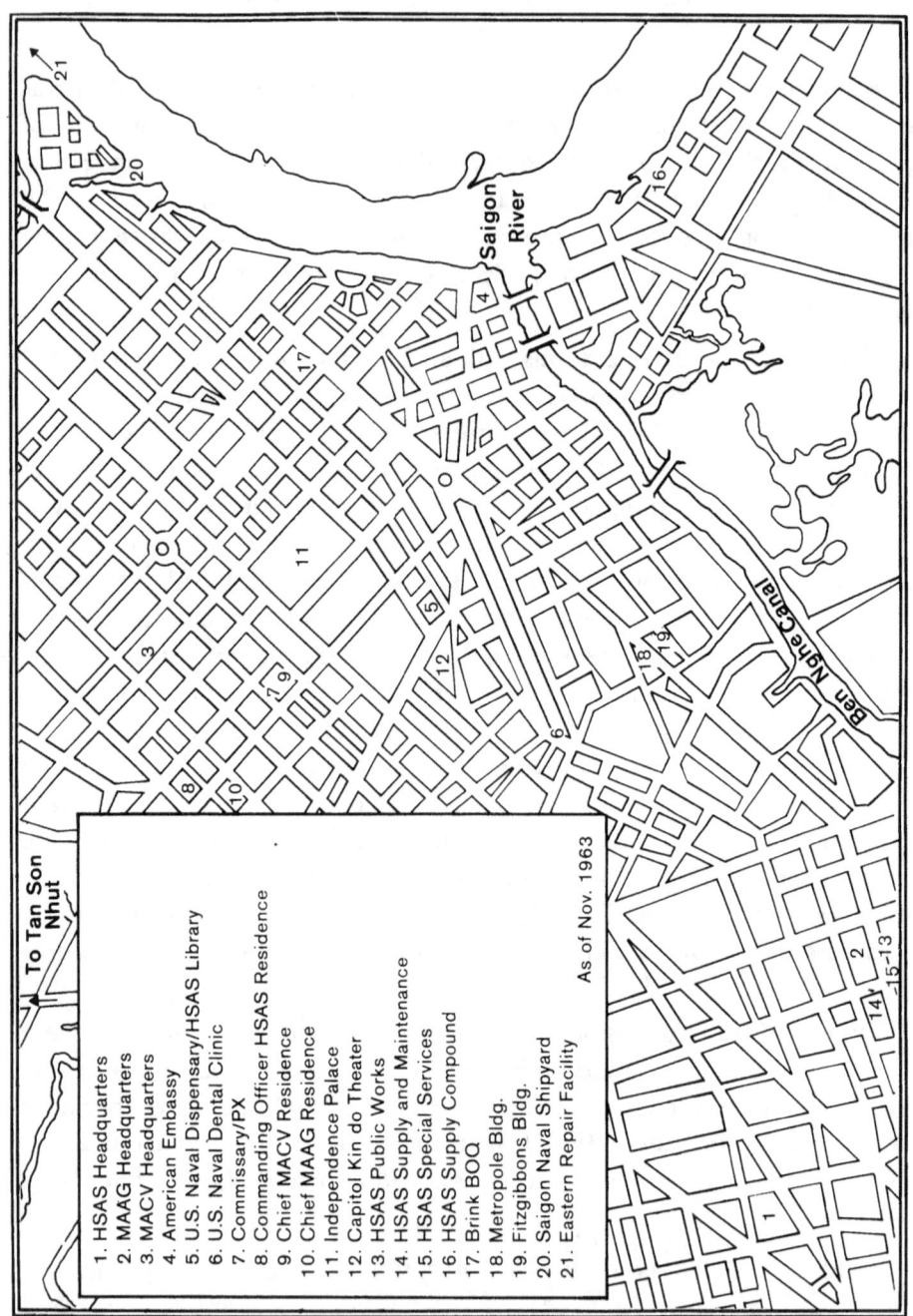

Saigon

were acquired to house 1,700 more men. The Billeting Division administered three other quarters, with a capacity of about 500, for personnel passing through Saigon for duty elsewhere. The division also managed a number of individual villas for senior officers and their families and for visiting dignitaries. American servicemen in Saigon generally received quarters with air conditioning, maid service, and potable hot and cold running water. Most of the hotels and apartment buildings leased as billets also had messing facilities. Under the Army, these messes were independent. HSAS placed them under centralized control for more efficient management and accounting and converted them to the Navy's standard mess system.

A large Public Works Department, similar to those at any naval shore establishment, was responsible for maintenance, cleaning, fire protection, and security of U.S. quarters. In addition, the department furnished utilities to HSAS buildings and operated a bus and taxi service for the scattered elements of the command.

Along with billets and messes, the activity took over the limited recreation facilities of the MAAG and immediately began an expansion of the program to entertain Americans. Most of the effort was in the Saigon area but HSAS also organized USO shows for U.S. units throughout Vietnam. With profits from the naval exchange, a bowling alley, craft shop, swimming pool, and a complete athletic complex were created for American servicemen to use during their free time. HSAS also distributed moving picture films. But the most popular services offered by HSAS were the rest and recuperation (R and R) flights inaugurated in February 1963. About 1,000 men each month were flown by Air Force planes to Bangkok and Hong Kong. This program continued throughout the war. In addition, HSAS ran a library in Saigon and branches in outlying areas that were heavily used. To provide the U.S. community in Saigon with news and music, HSAS established the Armed Forces Radio Service. The station first broadcast on 15 August 1962.

In support of U.S. forces, the activity employed Vietnamese civilians, who numbered 1,700 by February 1963. HSAS established a miniature civil service system based on local wage rates and customary fringe benefits. One of the most difficult initial problems was the inordinately long security clearance procedures required to hire Vietnamese for sensitive positions. The delays, which ran as long as nine months, soon were reduced to a few days or a few weeks by the use of the HSAS military police to conduct the investigations. The majority of the Vietnamese worked in the extensive U.S. mess system in Saigon, which became the largest single employer in the city.[75]

HSAS also provided medical and dental care to all American servicemen and their dependents in Saigon. To accomplish this task, HSAS controlled only a seventeen-bed dispensary, taken over from the MAAG. The Air Force operated a thirty-six-bed tactical hospital at Tan Son Nhut airport. In the fall of 1962, Captain Friedman, working through General Harkins and Admiral Felt, sought to acquire a suitable facility in Saigon to accommodate a 100 to 200-bed hospital. However, the Navy's cumbersome leasing procedures delayed the hospital effort and others as well, as Admiral Sides related to Admiral Anderson:

> The Navy has accepted the job to be done in Saigon, yet is hampering itself in many instances by inflexible administrative decisions and the absence of an adequately funded financial plan and related implementing procedures. HSAS cannot carry out its mission in the unique environment now existing in SVN without prompt and adequate support.[76]

While this issue was being resolved, Captain Friedman recommended that the Fitzgibbons BEQ, with a seventy-two-bed capacity, be converted into a hospital, on an interim basis. He proposed construction of a new hospital for the long term. Admiral Felt approved the use of the Fitzgibbons facility and the establishment of an outpatient clinic in the Metropole Hotel. But CINCPAC deferred a decision on the erection of a new hospital because at that time planning for a phaseout of U.S. forces was underway. Instead, he approved measures to make the Fitzgibbons a semipermanent medical facility. On 1 October 1963, the building on Tran Hung Dao Street was commissioned as the Saigon Station Hospital. It then was the only naval facility equipped to receive battle casualties directly from the field.[77]

In addition to caring for U.S. casualties, HSAS medical and dental facilities contributed to the high priority civic action effort. Whenever

---

[75]HSAS, Draft History.
[76]Msg, CPFLT 131951Z Dec 1962.
[77]Msgs, CNO 112040Z Jul 1962; CP 032356Z Aug; MACV 160019Z Sep; HSAS 061425Z Oct; CP 150231Z; CNO 212149Z Dec; CP 290316Z; CINCPAC, Command History, 1962, pp. 87-88; 1963, pp. 220-21; memo, Head Medical Department to CO HSAS, of 17 Nov 1965; CINCPACFLT, Annual Report, FY1962, p. 84; 1 Jul-30 Sep 1963, p. 10; Friedman, Interview.

possible, hospital personnel tendered services to the Vietnamese people. Naval doctors and dentists volunteered countless hours of their own time to care for the sick and injured. One naval dentist commuted all the way to Phu Quoc Island in the Gulf of Siam on weekends to treat people in that isolated area. In another program, Vietnamese nurses, doctors, and corpsmen from the *Cho Ray* Hospital received training at the Saigon Station Hospital.[78]

The chaplains were equally active in civic action projects. A Protestant Chapel Fund was begun in October 1962 soon after the arrival of Lieutenant Commander Harry R. Miller (CHC), the first chaplain of HSAS. The fund supported a number of worthy projects in Vietnam, including the Pleiku Leprosarium, the Hue Vietnamese Church, and a summer institute for the Wycliffe Bible Translators. Portable organs, tape recorders, and film projectors were purchased for Vietnamese churches. Chaplain Calvin J. Croston (CHC), who relieved Chaplain Miller in August 1964, took a personal interest in Project Handclasp which brought to Vietnam in the Navy's ships donated food, clothing, toys, medical supplies, and other items collected in the United States. Chaplain Croston distributed Handclasp materials to orphanages and refugee villages in every part of Vietnam.[79]

Up-Country Support

By the end of 1962, HSAS was effectively supporting U.S. forces stationed in the Saigon area with a myriad of services ranging from graves registration and dependent schooling to legal counseling and chaplain services. The Navy, however, hoped to avoid providing full support for the outposts of American troops scattered throughout Vietnam. During planning for HSAS in 1962, Admiral Sides added the adjective, "headquarters," to the name of the activity to reinforce that idea. He recommended that the MAAG continue the practice of assigning support personnel from other services to the field detachments. However, even

---

[78] Ltrs, Head Medical Department to CO HSAS, of 17 Nov 1965; COMPHIBTRACOM, PACFLT to CNO, ser 0031-66 of 11 Jul 1966; CNO, OPNAV Instruction 5450.100A, of 5 Nov 1962.

[79] Withers M. Moore, *Navy Chaplains in Vietnam, 1954-1964* (Washington: Office of the Chief of Chaplains, Bureau of Naval Personnel, 1968), pp. 109, 112, 116; Withers M. Moore, Herbert L. Bergsma, and Timothy J. Demy, *Chaplains with U.S. Naval Units in Vietnam, 1954-1975: Selected Experiences at Sea and Ashore* (Washington: Office of Chief of Chaplains, 1985), pp. 17-34.

the initial Office of the Chief of Naval Operations instruction detailing the mission of the HSAS implied some responsibility for U.S. forces outside of Saigon. For example, HSAS was charged with delivering mail to all personnel in South Vietnam. And HSAS was directed to "coordinate or arrange support of MAAG Vietnam field detachments."[80] In November 1962, an updated instruction was issued which assigned responsibility for the purchase and shipment of commissary and exchange supplies and food intended for units in the field. Other areas of support for up-country units included maintenance of vehicles, water purification, real estate acquisition, and engineering support.[81]

The task of transporting supplies, mostly the commissary and exchange items, to the up-country outposts fell to the Operations Department. Commander Robert E. Begley, who headed the department during 1963, observed:

> Supplying the up country messes was always a problem due to poor coordination and lack of transportation and the always present pilfering of items especially of the PX type. Trying to convince the Army that people in the field did not need ice cream...was quite a chore.[82]

At the port of Saigon the Operations Department served as the local MSTS representative and arranged for the unloading there of all U.S. supplies. Since Viet Cong ambushes threatened road and rail transportation, air and sea transport generally was relied on to move the cargo to field units.

The U.S. Air Force 2nd Air Division in Saigon operated a centralized airlift system to move cargo to American units all over Vietnam. But air transportation was expensive and subject to weather and operational delays, so the bulk of the cargo for up-country bases moved by water. HSAS depended on MSTS ships to transport the material along the coast to Danang, Nha Trang, and Qui Nhon, where major concentrations of American troops were located. Additionally, a commercial shipper was employed to transport refrigerated supplies.[83]

In January 1963, General Harkins recommended that HSAS take over responsibility for port services throughout Vietnam, which then was being

---

[80]CNO, OPNAV Instruction 5450.100, of 22 Jun 1962. See also Friedman, Interview.
[81]CNO, OPNAV Instruction 5450.100A, of 5 Nov 1962; Friedman, Interview.
[82]Ltr, Begley to Kuntze, of 27 Dec 1965.
[83]HSAS, Draft History; Friedman, Interview; ltr, CINCPAC to JCS, ser 001931 of 23 Dec 1964.

handled separately by each service. Admiral Sides strongly opposed General Harkins's recommendation, observing that HSAS did not have the resources to take on the expanded task. CINCPACFLT saw this as the first step in a move to make HSAS a country-wide logistic organization. He pointed out that HSAS had assumed additional support responsibilities outside of Saigon, not because it had the resources to do so, but "more from energetic attitude of personnel assigned." He proposed that the Army deploy its own logistic organization to take over country-wide logistic support responsibilities. Admiral Felt, however, overruled him and directed MACV to work out interservice support agreements to centralize the task in HSAS.[84]

None of the armed services wanted to divert manpower for the new responsibility. An initial agreement failed when all the services temporarily had to reduce personnel in South Vietnam at the end of 1963. As an interim measure, HSAS hired civilians in some of the ports. Finally, in June 1964, after nineteen months of tedious negotiation, an interservice agreement was signed that stationed HSAS advisory personnel in the ports of Danang, Nha Trang, and Qui Nhon. Their function was to receive and forward cargo and ensure that it was not lost before transshipment. The service was extended to U.S. Embassy cargo and MAP material, as well as to military supplies.[85]

By the end of 1962, HSAS was supplying thirty exchange stores scattered throughout Vietnam. Another store was supported in Cambodia. These facilities, contrary to the Navy's practice, were run by the unit they supported. HSAS acted only as the supplier. In the fall of 1963, discussions were held to determine the merits of continuing this system or setting up country-wide exchanges. Consideration also was given to allowing the Army and Air Force exchange service to operate the entire system, since those services provided most of the customers. The decision was made to continue with the current arrangement. Similarly, HSAS provided for the special needs of the American diplomatic communities in Phnom Penh and Bangkok. Despite problems, HSAS accomplished its mission of "Service to the Services" by shouldering the major logistic burden for Americans in Vietnam. Captain Friedman aptly summed up the early years of HSAS when he observed that the command

---

[84]Msgs, MACV 300922Z Jan 1963; CP 270430Z Feb; 290036Z Mar; CPFLT 200327Z Nov.
[85]MACV, Command History, 1964, p. 113; CINCPAC, Command History, 1963, pp. 219-20; memo, OP-40 to CNO, ser BM82-64 of 8 Dec 1964.

was established to meet rather unique responsibilities for a Navy activity. Its early development was, therefore, unorthodox in many respects. Its major problem was to discharge its responsibilities within the umbrella of peace time regulations but in a war time environment and with a war time sense of urgency.[86]

The period from 1961 to 1963 witnessed a dramatic increase in the size of the Vietnamese Navy and the U.S. naval establishment that helped train and support it. American naval advisors and their Vietnamese counterparts improved the command structure with the creation of naval zone commands, coastal surveillance centers, and the naval staff departments for communications and intelligence. Setting up the Civil Guard boat companies freed the River Force from duties that were a drain on its resources and flexibility. The U.S.-Vietnamese team also strengthened the fighting potential of the Sea Force, River Force, and Coastal Force with the integration into the naval arm of a large number of new ships, river-combat craft, and junks. New repair facilities were built and the performance of existing yards was improved; the supply system was reorganized; and new training schools were established for the Coastal Force and the River Force.

Although defying permanent resolution, many long-standing problems in the Vietnamese Navy were alleviated by Vietnamese naval leaders and their American advisors. The combat forces enlisted an adequate number of personnel to accomplish their missions, despite continued difficulty with recruitment and desertion. Poor leadership adversely affected the motivation of naval personnel at all levels and this, in turn, diminished the operational performance and readiness of individual units. Nonetheless, corrective measures showed promise of improving the Vietnamese Navy's ability to combat the Communist enemy.

During this same time, the U.S. Navy's Headquarters Support Activity, Saigon, provided logistic support to a major portion of the American military contingent in South Vietnam. Although hard-pressed to keep pace with the rapid increase in numbers, the naval activity furnished U.S. personnel in the Saigon area, and to a lesser extent up-country, with

---

[86]Ltr, Friedman to Kuntze, of 23 Dec 1965.

adequate housing, messing, medical, chaplain, fiscal, transportation, port service, and morale support. These logistic requirements would continue to demand the Navy's attention as the struggle in Vietnam grew in intensity.

CHAPTER IX

Perceptions of the Conflict in South Vietnam and the Diem Coup

As the U.S. advisory and military support program built up the material, personnel, and organizational strength of the Vietnamese armed forces from 1961 to 1963, many American leaders expressed guarded confidence in the allied ability to counter the Communist insurgency. Although developments in the military sphere initially gave reason for hope, the increasing weakness of the South Vietnamese political structure undermined this optimism and led to a climactic turning point in the war.

At the third Secretary of Defense conference, on 19 February 1962, both General Harkins and Ambassador Nolting agreed that there was improvement in South Vietnamese internal security. The number of Viet Cong initiated incidents had declined steadily since the end of 1961, and government forces were expanding their operations against the enemy. The U.S. civilian officials, and Admiral Felt, summarized their estimation of the situation thus: "South Vietnam had earlier been described as a country going down a steep slope to disaster. We can't say that the direction has been reversed — but for the moment the slope has leveled out a bit."[1] CINCPAC soon afterward, however, cautioned that while Viet Cong activity had diminished, the enemy still possessed the ability to strike at will and in force in his long-term battle of attrition. The CNO reiterated the perception that the campaign to root out and destroy the insurgency would be a slow, extended process, requiring years of effort.[2]

---

[1] SECDEF, "Record of Third Secretary of Defense Conference, 19 Feb 1962," pp. 1-10, 1-5.
[2] Msg, CP 230815Z Feb 1962; memo, OP-60 to CNO, ser BM00250-62 of 26 Feb; ltr, CNO to Flag and General Officers, of 7 Mar.

By mid-March 1962, U.S. civilian officials and military leaders concerned with South Vietnam began to exude a "cautious optimism." U.S. military support forces were in-country and many provisions of the plan of action to buttress the South Vietnamese counterinsurgency program were being implemented. At the fourth Secretary of Defense meeting at CINCPAC headquarters, on 21 March, General Harkins expressed gratification over the industry of U.S. military personnel and the growing enthusiasm and amenability to advice of the South Vietnamese armed forces. Citing the general's reports to him of encouraging Viet Cong-to-ARVN loss ratios, during the preceding weeks, Admiral Felt stated that the "pendulum seems to be swinging our way."[3] Secretary of Defense McNamara also was encouraged by the apparent change in the situation. By the end of the conference he was questioning Ambassador Nolting "whether the fact that we are beginning to win the war was realized by the people."[4] As a result of the confident reports given at this meeting, the Secretary of Defense cancelled the monthly gatherings and, soon after, the semi-weekly "Beef-up" reports on the status of the U.S. aid program.[5] McNamara's perception of gradual improvement in the counterinsurgency struggle was reaffirmed during his whirlwind tour of Southeast Asia from 9 to 11 May. After inspecting various U.S. military installations and Vietnamese fortified hamlets, and talking with officials of both governments, he praised General Harkins for his leadership of the burgeoning American command.[6]

Naval officers also revealed increasing satisfaction with the course of events. In late July Admiral Anderson conducted a three-day visit to the Southeast Asian trouble spot, primarily in response to Secretary of Defense McNamara's request that members of the Joint Chiefs of Staff personally evaluate the situation there. The CNO also was aware of Captain Drachnik's complaint that since the preceding December only one senior naval officer had visited South Vietnam. The captain was concerned that "there have been almost no Navy people who have [shown] an interest in what we are doing. It does get a little lonely here."[7]

---

[3]SECDEF, "Record, Fourth Secretary of Defense Conference, 21 March 1962," pp. 1-5, 1-1.
[4]*Ibid.*, pp. N-2, 1-5.
[5]*Ibid.*; memo, OP-60 to CNO, ser BM00425-62 of 2 Apr 1962; ltr, CNO to Flag and General Officers, of 13 Apr; CINCPAC, Command History, 1962, pp. 49-50.
[6]*U.S.-V.N. Relations*, bk. 12, pp. 479-80.
[7]Ltr, Drachnik to Anderson, of 22 May 1962 encl. in ltr, Anderson to Drachnik, of 11 Jun. Admiral Hooper, COMPHIBFOR, Seventh Fleet, at the time, has observed that the Navy generally regarded

From 27 to 29 July, Admiral Anderson toured U.S. and South Vietnamese military installations in Saigon, Soc Trang, Tuy Hoa, and Nha Trang and held discussions with military and civilian leaders. The CNO was impressed that President Diem "appeared knowledgeable and seemed to be coming around to ideas of decentralizing."[8] The admiral also observed that General Harkins, Captain Drachnik, and the other U.S. military personnel in South Vietnam were doing an outstanding job. Admiral Anderson recorded that "what we saw is a sound basis for cautious optimism," while pointing out that "of course, we have not yet received the full impact of the communist reaction."[9] At the same time in Washington, Captain Donald N. Clay, who headed the Special Operations Section in the Office of the Chief of Naval Operations, informed high-level conferees at a Defense Department staff meeting that the Communists had been stopped in South Vietnam, "for here our efforts to train and equip the small Vietnamese navy have paid off."[10] Similarly, Commander Everett A. Parke, who served as Naval Attache, Saigon, from August 1960 to August 1962, observed on his return to Washington that he felt "somewhat cautiously optimistic at this point."[11] However, he tempered his evaluation:

> I think there is some hope, but we must not expect to see a sudden dramatic improvement. We are up against people who are capable of outsitting us and outwaiting us, and unless we make our minds up to try and get this thing put into long-term perspective, I think we will be deluding ourselves.[12]

Nonetheless, key indicators continued to reflect a favorable trend. A MACV analysis of the military situation in March 1963 showed that Viet Cong incidents were below the 1962 average, and the rate of company and battalion-size Viet Cong attacks also had fallen. Further, the rate of

---

the conflict there as a land effort. See Hooper, Interview, p. 353. See also memos, OP-60 to Persons/Needham, ser 0608P60 of 14 May 1962; OSD, of 26 Jul.

[8] Anderson Diary of 6 Aug 1962. See also CNO, Itinerary of Pacific Tour, Anderson Diary.
[9] OP-09, memo, ser 00133P09 of 10 Aug 1962. See also Anderson Diary, of 6 Aug.
[10] OSD, memo, of 26 Jul 1962, p. 4-1.
[11] Everett A. Parke, "Report From Vietnam," *ONI Review* (Oct 1962), p. 441.
[12] *Ibid.* p. 441. See also ltr, Anderson to Nolting, of 28 Dec 1962; CINCPAC, Command History, 1962, pp. 147-49; *U.S.-V.N. Relations*, bk. 12, pp. 487-89, 504-05.

weekly losses of government weapons to the Communists dropped markedly from 1961 and 1962 levels.[13]

As a result of the general optimism over Vietnam, Secretary McNamara began to think about scaling down U.S. forces once the Viet Cong threat was further contained. Responding to a Secretary of Defense query, General Harkins estimated that this might be accomplished by the end of 1965. His estimates were accepted for planning purposes, even though the Joint Chiefs commented that it was impossible to make such a forecast with any accuracy.

Serious planning for an initial 1,000-man reduction began in the spring of 1963 and was scheduled for completion by the end of the year. Most of the personnel to be withdrawn were in support units. Only about 200 were attached to MAAG and MACV and a handful of these were naval advisors. However, Captain Drachnik was unhappy about these reductions, which he considered unjustified by the situation in Vietnam and motivated solely to show the American people that progress was being made in the conflict. Even though the proposed reduction would amount to only about 10 percent of the naval advisors, in a small unit such as the Navy Section there were few billets which could be spared. Since the Bureau of Naval Personnel had not yet filled some billets in the Navy Section, Drachnik recommended that those be the positions cut. He was told that the cuts had to come from occupied billets. A total of 1,000 men did leave Vietnam by the end of 1963, but this withdrawal process was stillborn and a general buildup immediately followed.[14]

Internal Turmoil

Events in South Vietnam soon began to erode the confidence of some U.S. officials in Diem's government and armed forces. In the battle of Ap Bac, on 2 January 1963, South Vietnamese regular and paramilitary forces

---

[13] MACV, Summary of Highlights, of 20 Mar 1963; JCS Paper 2315/223; msgs, CP 260440Z May 1963; COMUSMACV 060556Z Jul; CP 212210Z; *U.S.-V.N. Relations*, bk. 3, pt. IVB.4, pp. 4, 15, 17.

[14] *U.S.-V.N. Relations*, bk. 3, pt. IVB.4, pp. 15, 17; Drachnik, Interview with Fitzgerald; CINCPAC, Command History, 1963, pp. 204, 216-19; msgs, CP 212210Z Jul 1963; COMUSMACV 070655Z Nov.

performed unevenly and suffered heavy casualties. CINCPAC, however, described the action as atypical of most South Vietnamese operations. Admiral Felt also criticized the U.S. press for exaggerating the negative aspects of the fight. Admiral Anderson reiterated that evaluation and added that the "Ap Bach [sic.] operation is considered a success for the South Vietnamese forces." The CNO also observed that the "overall U.S. effort in Vietnam vis-a-vis the Communist[s] continues to show substantial and gratifying progress and the Vietnamese armed forces, after a year of reorganizing and training by the U.S., are only now beginning to move into high gear."[15] In June Admiral Anderson expressed an even greater confidence. He assured Captain Quyen that "all available evidence indicates that the high tide of the Viet Cong insurgency may have been reached and is now ebbing." The CNO added that "the dark days of 1961 and 1962 have given way to a more hopeful present and the bright promise of ultimate victory now looms on the horizon."[16]

On the other hand, Commander Seventh Fleet's liaison officer with the MACV headquarters in Saigon reported a difference of opinion among in-country personnel over the success of the war effort. He found staff officers optimistic, but "informal and unofficial comments from personnel working with the RVN forces point more toward 'escalating stalemate.'"[17]

Deficiencies in the South Vietnamese armed forces, made evident during the battle of Ap Bac, were mirrored in the country's political fabric. Beginning in May, South Vietnamese Buddhists, including many monks, began active street demonstrations to protest perceived and real government abuses. The regime's reaction was swift and harsh. The crisis became increasingly widespread and violent in the summer. The self-immolation of Buddhist monks in the streets of Saigon revealed the fervency of the religious opposition to Diem's government. Other anti-Diem factions used the turmoil to advance their causes. Rumor of planned attempts to overthrow the South Vietnamese leader began to circulate freely.[18]

---

[15] Ltr, CNO to Flag and General Officers, of 24 Jan 1963. See also *U.S.-V.N. Relations*, bk. 3, pt. IVB.5, pp. 1-2; CINCPAC, Command History, 1963, p. 203; msg, CP 100910Z Jan 1963.

[16] Ltr, Anderson to Quyen, of 28 Jun 1963.

[17] Msg, COM7FLT 070938Z May 1963.

[18] Memo, OP-61 to SECNAV, ser 00680P61 of 26 Jul 1963; *U.S.-V.N. Relations*, bk. 3, pt. IVB.5, pp. 4-12.

Nonetheless, some U.S. officials considered the situation manageable. At the end of July Rear Admiral Henry L. Miller, Assistant Chief of Staff for Plans on the CINCPAC staff, reported:

> In regard to the COMUSMACV business, it is all going exceptionally well. As a matter of fact, we have a comprehensive plan for South Vietnam which wraps up the whole counterinsurgency effort by 13 December 1965. However, if we can settle the Buddhist problem and get the "coup" scares settled down, and continue the Phase II Campaign Plan wherein the ARVN troops in all four areas push as hard as they have since 1 July of this year, Harkins believes that it can be over by 1 January 1964.[19]

Other U.S. leaders were less optimistic at this point, as it was becoming increasingly clear that Diem's hold on the government, and consequently the war effort, was loosening.

The Kennedy administration, not wanting to instigate action against Diem by moving away from him, but uncertain of his longevity as head of the government, adopted a "wait and see" policy. Public demonstration of close association between the U.S. and South Vietnamese governments was avoided. In this regard, routine ship visits took on added significance. *Providence* (CLG-6), flagship of the Seventh Fleet, was scheduled to visit Saigon for the traditional South Vietnamese Independence Day celebration on 26 October. Admiral Felt, citing the gravity of the situation in Saigon, postponed the annual port call.

The possibility of having to protect or even evacuate Americans from South Vietnam, in the event of a coup, was now deemed real. Planning for such an eventuality was undertaken. By late August the internal situation had grown so serious that U.S. leaders took steps to ensure the safety of non-combatant Americans. Late on 25 August CINCPAC directed the Pacific Fleet commander to station naval forces off the South Vietnamese coast prepared to evacuate 4,600 U.S. nationals. Captain John Boyum's Amphibious Ready Group sortied from Subic Bay the next day and proceeded to a point within one day's sailing time from the mouth of the Saigon River. *Princeton*, *Noble* (APA-218), and *Thomaston* carried the Marine Special Landing Force. The group was escorted by *DeHaven* (DD-

---

[19]Ltr, Miller to Stroh, of 30 Jul 1963. The view that the military struggle was still favorable to the South Vietnamese was shared by other U.S. military leaders. See msgs, JCS 112003Z Sep 1963; CP 122055Z.

727) and *Lyman K. Swenson* (DD-729). Also on the 26th, Rear Admiral Daniel F. Smith was ordered to sail his Attack Carrier Task Group 77.5 to within 200 miles of Boyum's force in order to provide air cover for the possible evacuation. *Hancock*, in company with three destroyers, quickly made for the designated operating area.

These preparatory steps shortened transit time when, on 28 August, the JCS directed the evacuation force to concentrate off Vung Tau. At the same time, CINCPACFLT readied two Marine battalion landing teams on Okinawa and Marine transport aircraft in Japan for movement to Saigon. By 30 August, with a naval task force close off shore and transport aircraft ready on Okinawa, Admiral Felt possessed the resources to land three Marine BLTs almost simultaneously, covered by naval aviation. And that same day a fourth Marine battalion was embarked in attack transport *Lenawee*, which promptly put to sea bound for the Southeast Asian coast.

To avoid precipitating a panic in the South Vietnamese capital, the movement of U.S. naval forces in the South China Sea was publicly described as a routine training exercise. This discretion paid off when the internal crisis temporarily eased. Accordingly, on 3 September, Admiral Felt returned the transport aircraft to normal activities. The rest of the alerted evacuation and protection force remained in readiness for another week as the situation in Saigon was assessed by U.S. leaders. Then, on 11 September CINCPAC returned all naval forces to normal operations, although a carrier task group and the Amphibious Ready Group were retained in the South China Sea on twenty-four hours notice.[20]

This deployment proved to be the first of several in the worsening South Vietnamese internal crisis. Buddhist protest demonstrations subsided during September and October 1963, but the government appeared leaderless and disoriented to the Kennedy administration. U.S. leaders increasingly feared that the Diem regime was incapable of uniting the fractious South Vietnamese body politic and that the Communists would

---

[20]CNO Flag Plot, WESTPAC Situation Charts, 26 Aug-13 Sep 1963; CINCPAC, Command History, 1963, pp. 230-32; COM7FLT, "RVN SITREPS 1 (011018Z Sep)-12 (121210Z Sep); ltrs, Miller to Moorer, encl. in memo, CINCPAC to COM7FLT, ser 00684-63 of 8 Jul 1963; Moorer to Anderson, of 26 Jul 1963; memo, OP-61 to SECNAV, ser 00680P61 of 26 Jul; msgs, ALUSNA Saigon, COMUSMACV, AMEMB Saigon, CP, AMCONSUL Hue, COM7FLT, CTF76, CPFLT 5 Aug-11 Sep 1963; COM7FLT, Command History, 1963, p. 7; CPFLT, Preparatory Actions RVN SITREPS 1 (300032Z Aug)-7 (130244Z Sep); CINCPACFLT, Annual Report, FY1963 Supplement, ser 15/00838 of 30 Sep; *U.S.-V.N. Relations*, bk. 3, pt. IVB.5, pp. 12-36; bk. 12, pp. 526-35, 546-47. 554-73.

Aircraft carrier Hancock (CVA-19) steams in the South China Sea off Vietnam during the turbulent late summer and fall of 1963.

exploit internal differences. The Republic of Vietnam and the American investment in it of lives, material resources, and prestige were seen in jeopardy.

Then, late in October 1963, American officials learned of a concerted plan to overthrow the Diem government by high-ranking South Vietnamese military officers. This activity was not discouraged. Precautionary steps were again taken to protect Americans caught in the political maelstrom that was Saigon in late 1963. On 29 October the JCS directed the Pacific Command to repeat the movement to South Vietnam's coastal waters of U.S. naval forces. At first light on 31 October, the *Oriskany* (CVA-34) attack carrier task group got underway from Iwakuni, Japan, bound for the South China Sea. Although *Hancock*'s task group was closer to Southeast Asia in Hong Kong, the departure of this force would have been more conspicuous. The Amphibious Ready Group, now composed of *Iwo Jima* (LPH-2), *Point Defiance*, and *Noble* also headed for its former station off Vung Tau. As before, the movement was carried out under the guise of a routine training exercise. Ironically, the exercise, Yellow Bird, was intended to test Seventh Fleet readiness for Southeast Asian contingencies. Two Marine battalion landing teams and 1st Marine Aircraft Wing KC-130 transports were placed on alert on Okinawa. As naval forces steamed for operating areas off Vung Tau, Saigon exploded in yet another coup attempt.

The Coup

The military coup foreseen by U.S. government leaders began shortly after noon on the first day of November 1963. Although Diem had weathered attempts to overthrow his regime in the past, this time he lacked a key element to his survival — Vietnamese Navy support. Since the first days of Vietnamese independence, when President Diem used the navy to defeat several religious sects in the Mekong Delta, that service had enjoyed a special relationship with the president. The quick reaction of Commander Quyen, the Vietnamese Naval Deputy, had saved Diem during the coup attempt of November 1960. A little over a year later, on 26 February 1962, two disgruntled Vietnamese Air Force pilots flying AD-6s bombed the Presidential Palace and made strafing runs on the shipyard and police headquarters. The navy's ships anchored in the Saigon

River went to General Quarters immediately and *Huong Giang* (HQ-404), a recently received LSM, shot down one of the rebel planes. Quyen threw a security cordon around the shipyard and the naval headquarters and ordered the marines to establish a command post in the shipyard. Diem considered moving his offices to the yard, but the limited nature of the attack made it unnecessary. Largely as a result of their actions, Quyen, in June 1962, was promoted to Captain and Le Nguyen Khang, the Commandant of the Marine Corps, became a lieutenant colonel.[21]

The overthrow of Diem on 1 November 1963 came as a surprise to most leaders of the Vietnamese Navy. However, several officers were known to have been involved in planning the coup. One officer visited the Naval Deputy on the morning of 1 November, which ironically was Quyen's birthday, and offered to drive him to a party in his honor. In reality, he was trying to determine Quyen's reaction to the planned revolt. When Quyen rejected his inducements to join the conspirators, a struggle ensued, and he killed Quyen with three pistol shots to the head. The assassination occurred on the highway from Saigon to Thu Duc. The officer then went to the Vietnamese naval headquarters and arrested Quyen's staff.[22]

Meanwhile, Lieutenant Commander Dinh Manh Hung, the Sea Force commander, got underway on the Saigon River in LST *Cam Ranh* (HQ-500), accompanied by five other ships. He tried to gain the support of other naval commands but without success. At this point the Joint General Staff, which backed the coup, called in an air strike on the naval headquarters and the shipyard. At least four of the ships fired at the A-1H aircraft, but when Hung saw the strikes, and by 1800 had received no support from other commands, he returned to the dock.[23]

To American military leaders, 1 November was a day of confusion and uncertainty. Reports on the success or failure of the attempt, the opposing sides, and the condition of President Diem were sketchy and contradictory. In this uncertain situation, additional U.S. evacuation forces were marshaled. With news of the coup now public, Commander Seventh Fleet

---

[21]Msgs, ALUSNA Saigon 270510Z Feb 1962; 281031Z.
[22]Bang Cao Thang, Interview, pp. 8-9; Dinh Manh Hung, Interview, pp. 7-8; Ho Van Ky Thoai, Interview, pp. 15-22; Nguyen Van Duc, Interview, pp. 2-3; Hoang Co Minh, transcript of interview with Oscar P. Fitzgerald, Naval Historical Center, in Reston, VA, 8 and 18 Sep 1975; Nguyen Huu Chi, transcript of interview with Oscar P. Fitzgerald, Naval Historical Center, in Falls Church, VA, 21 Aug 1975, pp. 9-12; Drachnik, Interview with Fitzgerald.
[23]Msg, ALUSNA Saigon 040958Z Nov 1963; Drachnik, Interview with Moss, pp. 13-15.

USN-1099485

Admiral Ulysses S.G. Sharp, Commander in Chief, U.S. Pacific Fleet, and Vice Admiral Thomas H. Moorer, Commander Seventh Fleet, confer at Subic Bay in the Philippines three days after the overthrow of South Vietnam's Diem regime.

ordered *Hancock* and her escorts to depart Hong Kong at first light on 2 November and to proceed at 25-knot speed for a station southeast of the Saigon River mouth.

In the early morning hours of that day, the Amphibious Ready Group arrived at its position off the South Vietnamese coast. The force was prepared to begin at dawn launching Marines by air into Tan Son Nhut Airfield or to land and secure the Vung Tau Peninsula as a base for further

Perceptions of the Conflict in So. Vietnam and the Diem Coup   275

operations. The naval command, however, adhered to JCS instructions to keep sea forces out of sight of land and to take no actions "which would represent visible support either for or against the coup in RVN."[24]

By 2400 on 2 November *Hancock*, accompanied by her escorts, *Buchanan* (DDG-14), *Southerland* (DDR-743), and *Lyman K. Swenson*, was in range to provide air support for an evacuation. *Oriskany* was prepared to do the same two hours later while steaming southwest with *King* (DLG-10), *Hanson* (DDR-832), *Marshall* (DD-676), and *Mahan*.

At the same time, the course of events in the South Vietnamese capital became clearer. President Diem, his brother Nhu, and the Naval Deputy had been assassinated by the conspirators. Further, the new regime, led by Generals Minh and Don, had ended significant opposition, reestablished order, and begun the task of forming a government. Since these new leaders immediately proclaimed a continuation of the anti-Communist struggle and a desire to maintain close relations with the United States government, concern for the safety of Americans in-country abated rapidly.

On 4 November CINCPAC released airlift resources and the Marine BLTs on Okinawa to routine tasks. However, the naval forces afloat off South Vietnam remained on station to await developments and to conduct evacuation rehearsals, especially since the political situation remained confused in Hue. On 5 November Admiral Felt ordered his naval component commander to shift one of the carrier task groups to the north. That same day *Oriskany* sailed for a position 150 miles east of Hue. Soon after arriving on station, however, conditions in the old imperial capital stabilized. On 7 November, *Oriskany* and her escorts were released for normal operations by Commander Seventh Fleet, acting on JCS instruction. The following day, the Joint Chiefs authorized the return to routine pursuits of the two task groups still positioned off Vung Tau.[25]

The measured progress in the development of the Vietnamese armed services, growing strength of the American combat support forces in-

---

[24]Msg, JCS 011617Z Nov 1963.
[25]CINCPAC, Command History, 1963, pp. 232-36; COM7FLT, Command History, 1963, p. 9; CNO Flag Plot, "7th Fleet Response to 1 Nov 1963 Coup D'Etat and Overthrow of Diem Government;" msgs, JCS, CPFLT, ALUSNA Saigon, CTF76, COM7FLT, CTG77.5, CTG77.7, CP 29 Oct-9 Nov 1963; *U.S.-V.N. Relations*, bk. 3, pp. 37-68; bk. 12, pp. 574, 578-605; ltr, CO *Iwo Jima* to CNO, ser 015 of 27 Jan 1964; Tran Van Don, *Our Endless War: Inside Vietnam* (San Rafael, CA: Presidio Press, 1978), pp. 87-115.

country, and favorable statistical analyses of the war in the years from 1961 to 1963 led Secretary of Defense McNamara, General Harkins, Admirals Anderson and Felt, and other leaders to suggest that success in the struggle was within reach. In fact, limited steps were taken to withdraw U.S. personnel from Vietnam. This optimism, however, was premature. The battle at Ap Bac highlighted continued weakness in the South Vietnamese military. Of greater import, the Diem government increasingly was unable to cope with either the militant Buddhist and other opposition groups or the coup plotters in the armed forces. By the fall of 1963, American leaders had come to accept this reality, as demonstrated by the deployment of Seventh Fleet units to South Vietnamese waters in readiness to evacuate non-combatants from the country. Ngo Dinh Diem's assassination on 1 November 1963 marked the close of an era in which it was believed possible for the South Vietnamese, with only limited U.S. assistance, to overcome the Communist threat. Thereafter, the use of major units of the fleet and the other U.S. Armed Forces to reverse the pattern of events became a prime consideration.

CHAPTER X

Readiness of the Fleet for Limited War, 1961-1964

Even while fighting the Communist insurgency in South Vietnam, the Kennedy administration and the Navy accelerated efforts begun in the late 1950s to rebuild the conventional warfare strength of the U.S. Fleet, especially its capability to project power ashore. Although high-priority items in the defense budgets of 1961-1964 limited funding for a number of important programs of naval readiness, the Navy's ability to conduct a limited, non-nuclear war improved significantly. This was particularly true of the Pacific Fleet, which prepared to counter aggressive Communist military actions in Southeast Asia.

The Navy's long-standing concern with limited war challenges was endorsed, and indeed championed, by the Kennedy administration for the entire U.S. military establishment. During the 1960 presidential campaign, John Kennedy and his national security advisors subscribed to many of the concepts advanced by the flexible response advocates and supported the revitalization of the U.S. conventional warfare capability. His campaign program emphasized the need for a marked improvement and augmentation of conventional forces and weapons, especially U.S. airlift and sealift resources. Kennedy stated that no aspect of defense policy was "cause for greater concern" than the weakness in this area and that completion of the task was essential in order to "prevent any quick Communist takeovers on the ground — enough to let them know that they will be in for a long, costly struggle, if they pursue this means of attaining their objectives."[1]

On assuming office, President Kennedy initiated actions to upgrade this part of the defense structure. The new Secretary of Defense, Robert S. McNamara, who oversaw this redirection of defense policy, stated that he

---

[1] Kennedy, *Strategy of Peace*, pp. 183, 186.

was assigning "our conventional forces early and high priority in 1961" in order to improve their "organization, manning, equipment, training, mobility and, most especially, the balance among all elements of the forces."[2] The new Secretary of State, Dean Rusk, elaborated on the military support needed to further U.S. policy in the Far East. He observed that the "free world's military posture along the Asian rim of the [Communist] bloc should be capable of rapid response to a wide spectrum of threats" because "Chinese Communist policy is likely to pose such threats." He added that to free indigenous forces for the fight against insurgency, it was "important not only to have mobile, flexible and substantial U.S. forces...but also to have them deployed in forward areas of the Western Pacific, in order to present our allies and the Communists with tangible evidence of our capacity to respond to aggression."[3]

Soon after taking office, the new administration requested additional funds, which totalled more than $6 billion by July 1961, for the Fiscal Year 1962 Defense Department budget then under review. The Navy's share of this increase was more than $2.7 billion. The impact of these steps on conventional warfare readiness was reflected in manning levels. The Navy's personnel ceiling was raised by 32,000 persons, of whom 90 percent would man general purpose units. This ceiling was subsequently raised again. By mid-1964 the Navy had reached a strength of 667,600 personnel, 40,500 more than the June 1961 total. Following a request by the President, the Congress authorized an increase in Marine Corps personnel from 175,000 to 190,000 and proportionately more men were assigned to the operating forces than before. In addition, over $100 million in additional funds were allocated to research and development in the limited warfare field. The naval capacity for sealift of troops and equipment was also strengthened by the reactivation of a number of transports, the deferred inactivation of others, and the authorization for construction of additional amphibious ships. Aircraft carriers, while still charged with readiness for general war, were increasingly considered as the Navy's chief resource for limited war and projection of power ashore, especially since the Polaris ballistic missile-firing submarines entering the

---

[2]Robert S. McNamara, *The Essence of Security: Reflections in Office* (New York: Harper and Row, 1968), p. 78.
[3]Memo, Rusk to McNamara, "Foreign Policy Considerations Bearing on the U.S. Defense Posture," of 4 Feb 1961.

fleet freed the carrier force from most strategic retaliation responsibilities.[4]

In 1961, no less than three new attack carriers entered the U.S. Fleet, including *Kitty Hawk* (CVA-63), *Constellation* (CVA-64), and *Enterprise* (CVAN-65). The latter vessel was the world's first nuclear-powered carrier and the largest warship then afloat. Major advances also were made adapting naval aircraft to non-nuclear attack roles. The F-4 Phantom II fighter, which soon symbolized to many the air war in Southeast Asia, became a valuable attack plane with the addition of new multiple bomb racks. During the years from 1961 to 1964, work was begun on a close air support aircraft capable of carrier-based, all-weather operation and able to deliver rockets, bombs, and guided missiles, as well as small nuclear weapons. This aircraft was designated the A-6 Intruder. The newly designed A-7 Corsair II was intended for a similar role. Another effort was the development of the P-3 Orion patrol plane, a planned successor to the P-2 Neptune. The growing importance of helicopters was reflected in development of the CH-46 and CH-53 helicopters for the Marine Corps and the UH-2A and SH-3A for the Navy.[5]

During the period from 1961 to 1964, the Navy initiated programs to develop more effective aviation ordnance for conventional warfare, as well. Several improved variants of the successful Sidewinder and Sparrow air-to-air missiles were accepted and pushed through production for delivery to the fleet in 1965. At the same time, the accurate Bullpup air-to-ground missile was reconfigured to carry a larger 1,000-pound warhead. The Shrike missile, designed to home in on ground radar, and the TV-guided Walleye glide-bomb, were both the result of the greater attention devoted to non-nuclear ordnance in the early 1960s.[6]

---

[4]DOD, *Annual Report of the Secretary of Defense*, FY1961 (Washington: GPO, 1962), pp. 4, 14, 16-18, 28, 201, 218, 371; DOD, *Annual Report of the Secretary of Defense*, FY1964 (Washington: GPO, 1965), pp. 15, 252; President, "Special Message to the Congress on the Defense Budget," of 28 Mar 1961 in *Public Papers of the Presidents of the United States: John F. Kennedy, 1961*, pp. 229-32, 236-37; McNamara, *The Essence of Security*, p. 78; Adam Yarmolinsky, *The Military Establishment: Its Impacts on American Society* (New York: Harper and Row, 1971), p. 9; Gregory Palmer, *The McNamara Strategy and the Vietnam War: Program Budgeting in the Pentagon, 1960-1968* (Westport, CT: Greenwood Press, 1978), pp. 49-52; Futrell, *Ideas, Concepts, and Doctrine*, pp. 317, 322, 329-39; Jerome H. Kahan, *Security in the Nuclear Age: Developing U.S. Strategic Weapons Policy* (Washington: Brookings Institution, 1975), p. 75.

[5]OP-902, "Ship Operating Forces of the U.S. Navy-Historical Force Levels by Category Types," of 6 Feb 1980; Burke, memos for record, ser 0099-61 of 13 Feb 1961; ser 000112-61 of 17 Feb; CNO, "Position on Matters of Current Interest," 1964; Futrell, *Ideas, Concepts and Doctrine*, pp. 339-44, 349-50.

[6]CNO, "Naval Aviation Summary," of 1 Oct 1964.

Perhaps the most innovative measure taken to improve the Navy's projection forces was Admiral Burke's endorsement of amphibious assault ship (LPH) construction. *Iwo Jima*, the first in her class, entered fleet service in 1961, followed in succeeding years by *Okinawa* (LPH-3), *Guadalcanal* (LPH-7), *Guam* (LPH-9), and *Tripoli* (LPH-10). These 23-knot vessels could embark a Marine BLT of 1,900 men, much of the unit's basic equipment and supplies, and a full-strength Marine helicopter squadron. The combination of fast amphibious ship and airborne Marine landing force proved to be a versatile resource for Cold War and limited war employment. In another move to provide amphibious forces capable of strong and quick reaction to crises, the Navy built a class of modern amphibious transport docks (LPD). The ships possessed the 20-knot speed deemed the goal for the future amphibious fleet. Designed as an improved LSD, the LPD transported forces ashore through the use of its organic LCMs and LCUs. Cargo and troop loading was greatly accelerated through the use of the ship's enclosed well deck. *Raleigh* (LPD-1) was commissioned in 1961, followed by *Vancouver* (LPD-2) and *LaSalle* (LPD-3) in the years thereafter. The authorization, in September 1961, to build the new *Austin* (LPD-4) class ships heralded the subsequent award of nine more such ships during the period. With these commissionings and the activation of older vessels, the amphibious fleet rose from 113 ships in 1961 to 133 ships in 1964.[7] The increase in Marine personnel strength allowed the full manning of the three active Marine division-air wing teams and the provision of a nucleus for the fourth reserve division-air wing team. Three additional assault helicopter squadrons were established to accommodate the new, more capable CH-46 assault helicopters being procured.[8]

The Navy introduced other ships which promised to ease the underway logistic support of deployed forces in forward areas. When *Sacramento* (AOE-1), which combined the functions of an oiler, an ammunition ship,

---

[7]OP-902, "Listing of Ships by Delivery Dates by Fiscal Year FY1958-FY1988," of 31 Mar 1980; OP-902 "Ship Operating Forces;" CNO, Naval Aviation Summary, ser 001002P50 of 1 Apr 1963; ser 001009P50 of 1 Oct 1964; SECNAV, "Annual Report," in DOD, *Annual Report*, FY1961, pp. 197-98; Burke, memo for record, ser 000112-61 of 17 Feb 1961; ltrs, CINCPACFLT to CNO, ser 61/000112 of 15 Apr 1961; Burke to Taylor, of 22 Apr; CINCPAC to JCS, ser 000103 of 3 Apr 1962; William Case, "USS Sacramento (AOE-1)," USNIP (Dec 1967), pp. 88-102; Fails, *Marines and Helicopters*, pp. 23-26; John S. Rowe and Samuel L. Morison, *The Ships and Aircraft of the U.S. Fleet* (Annapolis: Naval Institute Press, 1972), pp. 68, 114, 124, 171-77; Marolda, "The Influence of Burke's Boys on Limited War," pp. 36-41.

[8]OP-508, "Naval Forces Summary," of May 1980; Fails, *Marines and Helicopters*, pp. 52-55.

and a cargo ship, entered the fleet in 1964, she was capable of supplying the entire carrier task force with 165,000 barrels of aviation and ship fuel, ammunition, and materials, a task made easier by her 26-knot speed. The combat stores ship (AFS) combined the functions of the older stores ship (AF), stores issue ship (AKS), and aviation supply ship (AVS). The construction contract for *Mars* (AFS-1), the first of a seven-ship class, was awarded in May of 1961. The 581-foot floating depot could carry and dispense 118,000 cubic feet of refrigerated stores and 308,000 cubic feet of non-refrigerated provisions. *Mars* possessed the first shipboard computer designed to speed the processing of supplies. And, as with *Sacramento*, the AFS boasted several UH-46A helicopters to augment traditional ship-to-ship supply transfer procedures with the innovative "vertical replenishment" method that later would figure so prominently in the logistic support of a fleet in combat.[9]

Strengthening the Pacific Fleet

During the Kennedy years, major improvements were made in the Pacific Fleet. Many were a continuation of efforts begun late in the Eisenhower administration, while others reflected the Kennedy administration's stress on conventional warfare. Specifically, the fleet was strengthened by the activation, in December 1961, of 1 attack cargo ship, 1 transport submarine, 2 high-speed transports (APD), 2 oilers, and 2 stores ships. CINCPAC also took steps to retain MSTS troopships and civilian-manned LSTs in the Pacific in order to support limited war contingencies. To improve the readiness of amphibious forces to react to Southeast Asian developments, important organizational changes also were initiated. In January 1962, Commander Amphibious Group 1, Rear Admiral Edwin B. Hooper, assumed the responsibilities of Commander Amphibious Force, Seventh Fleet and established a permanent home port for the command at Subic Bay, close to the troubled Indochinese peninsula. Previously, amphibious group commanders and their staffs rotated between the Eastern and Western Pacific.[10] Nearby, at Cubi Point,

[9] Op-902, "Listing of Ships;" *Mars*, Ship History.
[10] CINCPACFLT, Annual Report, FY1962, pp. 9, 10; CINCPAC, Command History, 1962, pp. 32-79; COMPHIBGRUONE, Command History, 1964; COM7FLT, "Weekly Summaries," May 1961-May 1962; "Seventh Fleet Briefing of Limited War Study Group" in ltr, Griffin to Burke, ser

a Marine battalion landing team and its supporting aircraft were kept in readiness to respond quickly to developments across the South China Sea. On Okinawa an alert SEABEE battalion was established, ready to react on six-days notice with most of its basic allowance of materials and supplies. Naval Mobile Construction Battalion 3 was prepared for rapid deployment anywhere in the Western Pacific. Another battalion, on Guam, was prepared to deploy on ten-days notice.[11]

To further prepare the fleet for the type of operations anticipated in Southeast Asia, in 1961-1964 stocks of "Lazy Dog" antipersonnel munitions and related ordnance were provided Seventh Fleet naval forces on a priority basis. Training in their employment was also undertaken. Extended operations in the South China Sea and contiguous tropical waters also highlighted the deleterious effects of high temperatures and humidity on ships and men, especially in the amphibious forces. As an expedient, commercial air conditioners available at Subic Bay were installed in ships of the Amphibious Ready Group. For the long term, Admiral Sides pressed for a program to air condition the older ships in the fleet.[12]

At the same time, intelligence efforts were expanded and intensified. By mid-summer 1962, Seventh Fleet aerial photographic squadrons had almost completed the mapping of South Vietnam as well as other critical areas in Southeast Asia. To improve photographic intelligence by carrier-based units, instruction in collection requirements and proper equipment use was pressed. And, in anticipation of future emergencies, two photo interpretation teams were kept in readiness at Cubi Point with Detachment Alpha of VAP 61 in order to augment Seventh Fleet sections. In addition, the photographic interpretation facility at Cubi Point was upgraded to a "Special Fleet Lab" and provided with extra equipment and personnel.[13]

Reflecting the growing concern with the possible need for a landing on the Southeast Asian mainland, Rear Admiral Ray C. Needham, CINC-

---

00029 of 12 Jul 1961, p. 4; Norman Polmar, *Aircraft Carriers: A Graphic History of Carrier Aviation and Its Influence on World Events* (Garden City, NY: Doubleday and Co., 1969), pp. 612-13.

[11]CINCPACFLT, Annual Report, FY1962, pp. 48-49; ltr, CINCPACFLT to CNO, ser 45/00527 of 23 Jun 1962; Tregaskis, *Southeast Asia: Building the Bases*, pp. 52-57.

[12]CINCPACFLT, Annual Report, FY1961, p. 62; FY1962, pp. 24, 31; CINCPAC, Command History, 1961, p. 72; msgs, CNO 111741Z Feb 1961; COMNAVAIRPAC 251856Z Mar; CHBUWEPS 260609Z Mar; CPFLT 120540Z Apr.

[13]CINCPACFLT, Annual Report, FY1962, pp. 2, 37-38; msg, CTU70.3.1 131709Z Oct 1961.

PACFLT Chief of Staff, in October 1961 requested that the Amphibious Objective Studies Program again concentrate on this area. He recommended that the updating of existing studies on the Nha Trang-Cape Ke Ga, Danang, Cape Vung Tau-Phan Thiet-Qui Nhon, and Vinh (the latter site in North Vietnam) landing areas be given top priority and that new coverage be obtained on the Quang Tri-Hue area, as well as the Dong Hoi and Thanh Hoa regions of North Vietnam. In contrast to previous submissions, it was requested that the coverage be extended out to the 100-fathom curve and 100 miles inland.[14]

With most indicators pointing to a continuation of low-level armed conflict in the countries of Southeast Asia, and possibly the involvement of external powers, the importance to the fleet of U.S. naval support facilities on Okinawa, Guam, and especially the Philippines became paramount. Early in 1961, CINCPACFLT expressed his strong opposition to Pacific base reductions recently under consideration by the Eisenhower administration. Admiral Sides stated that "in view of potentially explosive situation SE Asia any reduction or phase out West Pacific Navy Bases can only be accomplished with acceptance of fact that ability to support contingency Ops will be jeopardized."[15] This view was echoed several months later by the Naval Inspector General, who conducted a survey of naval shore activities with representatives from other offices and commands from 21 February to 22 March 1961. In the group's final report, it was emphasized that the Subic Bay-Sangley Point complex was a "convenient gateway and an excellent staging base for possible local war situations arising in the politically unstable South East Asian and Indonesian Archipelago countries."[16] With the need for a greatly improved logistic complex in the Western Pacific soon graphically demonstrated during the Laos crisis of April-May 1961, and the alarm in South Vietnam in the fall, Pacific naval leaders pressed anew for a revitalization of support bases.

On the other hand, the progress of the effort to strengthen the support facilities closest to Southeast Asia was limited. Early in 1962 Commander Service Force, U.S. Pacific Fleet, Rear Admiral Redfield Mason, recommended that serious consideration be given to shifting shore-based logistic

---

[14]Ltr, CINCPACFLT to CNO, ser 62/000244 of 11 Oct 1961.
[15]Msg, CPFLT ADMINO 090008Z Feb 1961.
[16]Ltr, Naval Inspector General to SECNAV, ser 015P008 of 24 Apr 1961. See also ltr, CINCPACFLT to CNO, ser 42/00492 of 7 Jun 1963.

resources from Japan to the Philippines. Admiral Charles D. Griffin, the Deputy Chief of Naval Operations (Fleet Operations and Readiness), did not concur. He observed that the United States had definite commitments to Japan and that there "are many people more fearful of the threat from North Korea than that existing in Southeast Asia."[17]

Nevertheless, in the Philippines themselves, a number of steps were taken in 1961-1964 to prepare for future contingencies. Stocks of ship parts, electronic equipment, medical and dental, and other emergency fleet support items were increased at the Naval Supply Depot, Subic Bay. Throughout the Philippines, construction of fuel storage facilities at U.S. installations was expanded and expedited. At the Cubi-Sangley Point complex, which had witnessed a dramatic increase in air operations during the previous year, approval was granted to construct a pipeline extension to the carrier fueling wharf and to rebuild the airfield runway. The shore bases in the Western Pacific were being prepared to deal with an increased tempo of operations that recent events presaged.[18]

Exercise Tulungan

While the Navy improved units, facilities, aircraft, weapons, and material for non-nuclear operations, it also trained Pacific Fleet forces for this type of combat, with a focus on Southeast Asia. Specifically, during 1962-1963, greater attention was devoted to the conduct of small-scale amphibious exercises using the recently instituted Amphibious Ready Group and its Special Landing Force. In addition to numerous helicopter, over-the-beach, and reconnaissance exercises carried out unilaterally, the units of the U.S. Navy and Marine Corps also participated in combined training with the other nations in the area. This included jungle warfare and over-the-beach training with Thai marine and naval units in Exercise Jungle Drum and mining familiarization with Thai and British forces as part of Exercise Experience IV. Under SEATO auspices, U.S. naval forces took part in Sea Devil, which involved the control of shipping in the South

---

[17]CINCPACFLT, "Type Commanders' Conference, 19-20 February 1962," ser 00/00192-62 of 2 Mar 1962. See also CINCPACFLT, "Type Commanders' Conference, 19-20 February 1962," Agenda Items, ser 001/00131 of 10 Feb 1962, item 34.
[18]CINCPACFLT, Annual Report, FY1962, pp. 48, 55-57.

China Sea. Another SEATO exercise, Air Cobra, simulated an air-ground defense of Thailand against an aggressor.

The most noteworthy exercise during this period was Tulungan, meaning "mutual assistance," which involved over 70 ships, 400 aircraft, and 37,000 men in the largest amphibious training operation in the Pacific since World War II. It was conducted from 2 March to 12 April 1962. Tulungan had been in various stages of planning since 1960, but these efforts only came to fruition with the announcement in August 1961 by the SEATO Military Advisors Council that the multinational event would take place early the following year. The intent and relevance of this undertaking was clear from the beginning — to deter the Communist powers from pursuing a campaign of indirect aggression in Southeast Asia by demonstrating the military strength and collective resolve of the SEATO alliance to counter any such threat. U.S. leaders felt that aggression might consist of guerrilla warfare and subversion, as well as cross-border invasion. The initial scenario depicted a situation where an

> aggressor guerrilla force had infiltrated into [hypothetical country later called "Tahimik"] a Southeast Asian country which had appealed to SEATO for assistance. By February 1962, these guerrilla elements had become so strong that by direct assaults on military posts and subversion and terrorism of local population, aggressors were able to seize control of central area of country *without overt commitment of military units* [italics added for emphasis]. However, reports had been received that some aggressor regular military forces had moved into this area.[19]

Because the British objected to the implicit acceptance of SEATO action before proof of overt attack had been obtained, however, the final scenario simulated allied military assistance to a country being invaded by large forces. Secretary of State Rusk accommodated the British view, but he emphasized that he did "not accept principle that there must be proven case overt aggression before we can contemplate use of SEATO military force."[20]

Although the nature of the exercise made it applicable to operations in Thailand or other Asian nations on the Communist periphery, the secret Tulungan operation order specifically identified South Vietnam

---

[19] Msg, AMEMB Bangkok 10:55AM 12 Feb 1962.
[20] Msg, SECSTATE 8:20PM 13 Feb 1962. See also msgs, COM7FLT 261008Z Jan 1962; CTF72 151001Z Feb; 011203Z Mar; 011205Z.

as the model for the fictitious country of "Tahimik." Indeed, Rear Admiral Edwin B. Hooper, Commander Amphibious Force, Seventh Fleet, who was appointed exercise director, fashioned the planned landing area on Mindoro in the Philippines to reflect the "mirror-image" of the Southeast Asian mainland. The landing itself was to take place in that portion of the land mass corresponding to the northern provinces of South Vietnam — the I Corps Military Region.[21]

While a primary objective of Tulungan was the accomplishment of combined SEATO training on a large scale and the development of close working relationships among participating members, only the United States and the Philippines, the cosponsors, contributed sizeable forces. Continuing disagreement over the nature of the exercise prompted Britain and New Zealand to drop out, and Australia reduced its contingent to one squadron of tactical aircraft. In overall command of Tulungan as exercise director, Admiral Hooper also served as commander of the amphibious task force. Major General John P. Condon, USMC, Commander Fleet Marine Force, Seventh Fleet, was in charge of the combined landing force. This contingent was composed of the 1st Philippines Battalion Combat Team, the 9th Marine Expeditionary Force of the 3rd Marine Division, 1st Marine Aircraft Wing elements, an Air and Naval Gunfire Liaison Company team, a SEABEE battalion, and other miscellaneous units.

Beginning with the loading of equipment and embarkation of personnel at Yokosuka, Iwakuni, Buckner Bay, and Manila on 2 March, the exercise proceeded through various stages. By 14 March, *Eldorado* (AGC-11) with Rear Admiral Hooper on board, *Princeton*, and the ships of Amphibious Squadron 1, Amphibious Squadron 7, and Landing Ship Squadron 9 were assembled off Okinawa. Provided antisubmarine escort by *Bennington* and ten destroyers, the group sailed for Subic Bay. The U.S. naval force intentionally made known its presence to the Chinese Communists when it steamed through the Taiwan Strait enroute to the Philippines.

The main amphibious assault on Mindoro by 15,000 Marines and the Filipino battalion got underway on the morning of 26 March with Rear Admiral Hooper's traditional order, from his flagship *Eldorado*, to "land the landing force." On the southern, or Blue Beach, the Filipino battalion combat team stormed ashore while the 2nd Battalion, 9th Marines were

---

[21]Hooper, Interview with Mason, p. 333.

flown off *Princeton* to a landing zone inland. Major General Robert E. Cushman, USMC, the 3rd Marine Division commander, was in charge of the Blue Beach forces. To the north, at Red Beach, Brigadier General Ormand Simpson, USMC, commanded the assault of the 3rd Marine Regimental Landing Team. Once ground troops secured the airstrip at San Jose, where a SEABEE unit and MABS 12 elements had readied a Short Expeditionary Landing Field (SELF) before the exercise, C-130 transports airlifted the 3rd Battalion, 9th Marines from Okinawa. Air support was provided by the *Hancock* aircraft of Commander Carrier Division 3, Rear Admiral Paul P. Blackburn, Marine aircraft of VMA 332 from Cubi Point, and Filipino and Australian land-based aircraft. By 2400 the following day, 27 March, the off-loading of personnel, equipment, and cargo was completed, as was the airlift operation.

For the rest of the month, the expeditionary force sought their elusive foe. Perhaps as a foretaste of the later cost and frustration in bringing the Viet Cong to battle, early reports in the exercise indicated that for 6 captured "aggressors," the Marines lost 8 "killed" and 55 "wounded." Asked by a public relations representative whether this was "an indication that a handful of skilled and well-led guerrillas would win this war," General Condon replied, "no, SEATO will gain the advantage and win the war."[22] Several days later the landing force still had not made solid contact with the guerrillas, as the latter withdrew "further into the back country of Tahimik." The press release stated that "undoubtedly, a strong action will be encountered as the aggressors are pushed against the wall."[23] However, this had not occurred when the land operation was terminated on 31 March and the 9th Marine Expeditionary Force began reembarking in Seventh Fleet ships for return to normal stations.

One of the stated objectives of Tulungan, the development of improved coordination and cooperation among SEATO forces for contingency operations on the Southeast Asian mainland, was only partially successful, due to the limited international composition of the forces involved. But the training received by U.S. naval, land, and air forces in an undertaking of such size and complexity served the fleet well in succeeding years.[24]

---

[22]Msg, CTF72 271445Z Mar 1962.
[23]Msg, CTF72 291033Z Mar 1962.
[24]Several of the higher commanders who participated in Tulungan were in positions of importance in the later period of the Vietnam conflict. Both Generals Cushman and Simpson led Marine forces in South Vietnam, Rear Admiral Blackburn became Commander Seventh Fleet, and Rear Admiral

Shortfalls in Conventional Warfare Readiness

Although the administration and the Navy gave greater emphasis to preparation for conventional warfare and projection of power ashore during this period, progress in strengthening the fleet was not uniform. Significant deficiencies remained that threatened to hamper the successful conduct of operations. This situation resulted from a number of factors. The Kennedy administration increasingly focused on the rapid development of unique forces — the special units slated for counterinsurgency warfare — sometimes to the detriment of the more traditional forces. And the conventional forces that were favored with budgetary support were primarily those of the other services. Between 1961 and mid-1964 the number of Army divisions grew from eleven to sixteen, the number of Air Force tactical air squadrons increased by half, and the Army's aircraft inventory, comprising helicopters, observation planes, and transports, rose from 5,564 to over 6,000. Marine ground forces received priority attention as well.[25]

Within the Navy's budget, the Polaris program continued to receive primary funding support. By the end of Fiscal Year 1964, twenty-one submarines had entered fleet service for the strategic retaliatory function, compared with only five by June 1961. The importance of the sea control mission, especially with regard to the threat from the powerful Soviet submarine fleet, also demanded concentration on resources for antisubmarine and antiaircraft warfare. Funds for the construction or reconfiguration of attack submarines and surface escort ships were a prime requirement. Arming surface ships with modern missile systems was another high

---

Hooper commanded the Service Force, U.S. Pacific Fleet. Exercise Director (CTF-260) and COMPHIBGRUONE, OPORD 301-62 of 13 Jan 1962; CINCPAC, Command History, 1961, p. 146; 1962, p. 131; CINCPACFLT, Annual Report, 1962, p. 34; COM7FLT "Weekly Summaries," 28 Feb-24 Apr 1962; COMPHIBGRUONE/COMPHIBFOR7FLT, Command History, 1962; Hooper, Interview with Whitlow; Hooper, Interview with Mason, pp. 324-29, 332-39; memo, CINCPACFLT to CNO, of 20 Mar 1962; msgs, CTF260 SITREPS 1 (220359Z Mar)-7(280530Z Mar); CTF72, Press Releases 1(191051Z Feb)-46(291033Z Mar); CTU261.8 111450Z Mar; ltr, CINCPACFLT to CINCPAC, ser 21/001031 of 4 Dec 1962.

[25]Memos, SECNAV to Chairman, JCS, of 25 Apr 1961; OP-601C7 to CNO, BM000251-61 of May; SECNAV, "Annual Report" in DOD, *Annual Report*, FY1964, pp. 3-4, 21-22; Kaufman, *McNamara Strategy*, pp. 98, 100; Alain C. Enthoven and K. Wayne Smith, *How Much Is Enough?* (New York: Evanston, 1971), pp. 223, 268-69; McNamara, *Essence of Security*, pp. 80-84; Edward A. Kolodziej, *The Uncommon Defense and Congress, 1945-1963* (Athens: Ohio Univ. Press, 1966), pp. 406-08; Futrell, *Ideas, Concepts, and Doctrine*, pp. 361-63, 378-82; Kahan, *Security in the Nuclear Age*, p. 78; Yarmolinsky, *The Military Establishment*, pp. 7-9, 15, 20-21.

priority item. But, with the exception of the favorable treatment accorded the LPH, LPD, AOE, and AFS building programs, the fleet's projection forces and the logistic units needed to support them generally received lean support. At the end of 1962, CINCPACFLT complained that "lack of sufficient personnel and money are the causes of all our worries and the continued shortage of both are causing a gradual but sure degradation of our overseas readiness."[26]

The competition for funding support also adversely affected the Navy's budding motor gunboat (PGM) project. U.S. participation during 1962 in the coastal patrol off South Vietnam clearly revealed that the Navy required craft more suitable to this mission than ocean minesweepers and destroyer escorts. This deficiency had long been recognized by naval leaders, but plans — and funds — for the development of prototype coastal patrol craft were consistently deferred for higher priority construction. This pattern was repeated in late 1961 when Secretary of Defense McNamara changed from sixteen to two the number of motor gunboats scheduled for construction in the Fiscal Year 1963 building program. Only two more ships subsequently were approved for the Fiscal Year 1964 plan.

Despite their limited number, the Navy felt the PGM a promising vessel for coastal warfare. As a result, on 5 March 1962, the Chief of Naval Operations directed that the PGM prototypes be designed with "good seakeeping abilities and an adequate endurance suitable for patrol, blockade or surveillance missions in waters other than the open seas and rivers."[27] The characteristics of the PGM included a 165-foot length, 23.5-foot beam, and a 230-ton displacement fully loaded. Powered by both diesel engines and gas turbines, the motor gunboat would be capable of attaining a speed of 30 knots and a range of 1,700 miles. Armament included one 3-inch/50-caliber gun mounted forward, one 40-millimeter gun mounted aft, two 50-caliber machine guns, two 81-millimeter mortars, and twelve Redeye antiaircraft missiles. For close-in coastal work,

---

[26]Ltr, Sides to Ricketts, of 21 Dec 1962.
[27]CNO, OPNAV Instruction 09010.175, ser 0184P42 of 5 Mar 1962. See also memos, OP-34, ser 8-62 of 12 Jan 1962; OP-93 to OP-42, ser 09P93 of 12 Jan; msg, CLFLT, 232344Z Jan; ltrs, CINCPAC to CNO, ser 057 of 29 Jan; CINCPACFLT to CNO, ser 61/00116 of 6 Feb; memos, OP-93 to OP-03, ser 031P93 of 1 Mar; OP-34 to OP-03, ser 0541-62 of 9 Aug; ltr, Griffin to Burke, of 12 Jul 1961 encl. in ltr, Burke to Griffin, of 27 Jul 1961.

Asheville (PGM-84), lead ship of a new class of motor gunboats, carries out training exercises prior to deployment to Southeast Asia.

the PGM was thought to be a good amalgam of weapons, hull design, and power plant.[28]

Naval aviation experienced a similar constraint on its full development. In the first half of 1961, the CNO observed that the procurement of aircraft was not keeping pace with losses through wear, obsolescence, accidents, and other causes. He added that the fleet required 7,200 operating aircraft. More capable planes, such as the Phantom II which joined the fleet in 1961, were not compensation enough for the overall shortage. Admiral Burke advised Secretary of the Navy John B. Connally, Jr., that "the Navy has the best tactical aircraft and the best close air support aircraft in existence in the world but we don't have very many of them."[29] As late as July 1962 CINCPACFLT identified another problem: "The continued evolution of the attack aircraft toward a special purpose, supersonic, nuclear weapon delivery aircraft has seriously impaired its effectiveness in the Close Air and Helicopter Support roles."[30] Significant progress was made, however, by June 1964, in adapting strike aircraft, such as the A-5 Vigilante and the A-3 Skywarrior, to conventional roles, primarily in the photographic reconnaissance configuration.

The lack of required numbers in the Navy's inventory was not reversed. During the period from 1961 to mid-1964 the total number of operating aircraft rose by 167, but because of a low production rate, the overall inventory decreased by 1,168 to 10,274 aircraft. And while several categories of aircraft registered gains, the critical fighter, attack, and transport type planes were 197 fewer in number in June 1964 than three years earlier. As a result, one naval and two Marine attack-fighter squadrons were deactivated during this period.[31]

The dearth of adequate amphibious shipping and sealift resources for the provision of troops, reinforcements, and their logistic support continued to plague naval planners. The new LPHs and LPDs were not able to fully compensate for the advancing age of the World War II amphibious fleet. Rather than institute a large-scale shipbuilding program,

---

[28]CNO, OPNAV Instruction 09010.175, ser 0184P42 of 5 Mar 1962; Rowe and Morison, *Ships and Aircraft*, p. 62.

[29]Memo, CNO to SECNAV, ser 00359-61 of 18 Jul 1961. See also CNO, Statement before House Armed Services Committee, of 8 Mar 1961.

[30]Ltr, CINCPACFLT to CNO, ser 32/00606 of 19 Jul 1962.

[31]OP-508, "Naval Forces Summary," of May 1980; ltrs, SECNAV to SECDEF, ser 00121 of 31 Aug 1962; CINCPACFLT to COMNAVAIRPAC, ser 32/00894 of 24 Oct; CNO, "Naval Aviation Summary," of 1 Oct 1964.

as the Navy advocated, the Kennedy administration suggested that the optimum service life of these and other ships be extended from twenty to thirty years through ship conversion and rehabilitation measures. However, the Fleet Rehabilitation and Modernization (FRAM) program concentrated on the highest priority surface combatants. In August 1963 Admiral Sides stated that "the funding level in recent years has proven barely adequate, and in some instances, less than adequate" to support the material readiness of the operating forces.[32] Shipboard material and spare parts deficiencies and limitations on combat training resulted from this situation. The material condition of the fleet remained marginal as funds for ship overhauls and maintenance were often cut back.[33]

The average 12-14 knot speed of the amphibious fleet and growing obsolescence remained as detriments to readiness. The reactivation in 1961 of additional amphibious ships from the Reserve Fleet helped the numbers situation somewhat, but by June 1964 there were twenty fewer amphibious ships in the Pacific Fleet than CINCPACFLT thought essential. In mid-1962, the Pacific Fleet was able to lift simultaneously only half of the Marine forces required for the defense of Southeast Asia in CINCPAC Operation Plan 32. The Seventh Fleet's Task Force 76 was required to transport 24,800 Marine personnel and 10,000,000 cubic feet of cargo but had the capacity to lift simultaneously only 11,500 personnel and 2,000,000 cubic feet of cargo. The First Fleet, responsible for carrying Marine forces on the U.S. West Coast and the 1st Marine Brigade in Hawaii to the Western Pacific, was similarly ill prepared to do so. These deficiencies were exacerbated in late 1962 when much of the Pacific Fleet's amphibious resources passed through the Panama Canal to support the military buildup generated by the Cuban Missile Crisis. The Pacific Fleet commander, Admiral Sides, privately informed the CNO that "their absence has really put a crimp into my readiness to back up Tom Moorer in case anything should pop in WESTPAC."[34] The shortage of these forces continued through 1963 and early 1964. Although CINCPAC had access to MSTS and merchant shipping in a crisis, it was obvious that more

---

[32] Ltr, CINCPACFLT to CINCPAC, ser 41/00694 of 9 Aug 1963.

[33] CINCPACFLT, "Type Commanders' Conference," 1962, pp. 48-49, 56-58, 60-64; Agenda, items 29, 30, 92, 93; "Conference, 6-7 Feb 1963," ser 001/0089 of 29 Jan 1963, Agenda, tabs B, I; "Conference, 6-7 February 1963," ser 001/00195 of 25 Feb 1963, pp. 1-25, 56-66; Roswell Gilpatrick, transcript of speech to National Association of Manufacturers, of 25 Jan 1963; msg, CNO 212349Z Jan 1964.

[34] Ltr, Sides to Anderson, of 5 Nov 1962.

vessels would be needed to transport ground troops and provide a dependable logistic pipeline to Southeast Asia in the event of war.[35]

Early in the Kennedy administration, Secretary of Defense McNamara concluded that U.S. airlift resources, because of their ability to respond quickly to distant crises, should be used primarily to carry troops, light weapons, and material while the slower sealift should be designated to transport heavy equipment and bulk supplies. Admiral Burke and other naval leaders, however, believed that too heavy reliance should not be placed on aircraft transportation because of its much lower personnel and cargo capacity in comparison to that of sealift. The Laos crisis of April and May 1961 highlighted the constraints on air operations in Southeast Asia. Conversely, the deployment and support of major Marine, Army, and Air Force contingents in Thailand the following year demonstrated the important contribution of sealift to strategic readiness.

Still, the Secretary of Defense became concerned with the response time required by Pacific shipping in certain limited war contingencies. To rectify this situation, McNamara favored the prepositioning in critical forward areas of ships loaded to equip troop units airlifted in during a crisis. In 1963 this "Floating Forward Depot" concept was tested with the deployment at Subic Bay of converted Victory ships USNS *Provo* (T-AG-173), USNS *Cheyenne* (T-AG-174), and USNS *Phoenix* (T-AG-172) under MSTS control. But top naval leaders were unenthusiastic about immobilizing scarce ships that would require secure ports in which to disembark their cargo. Rear Admiral George H. Miller, the Director, Long Range Objectives Group, expressed the Navy's inclination to rely instead on naval task forces "'prepositioned' by the U.S. government before potentially dangerous situations reach the crisis stage."[36] Admiral McDonald, the CNO, endorsed the view of the Commandant of the Marine Corps that "prepositioning should not be considered as a substitute for ready forces in the forward area which are required for initial reaction in

---

[35]Memo, Burke to Moorer, ser 0083-61 of 5 Feb 1961; CNO, Statement before House Armed Services Committee, of 8 Mar; ltrs, CINCPACFLT to CNO, of 15 Apr; Griffin to Burke, of 12 Jul encl. in ltr, Burke to Griffin, of 27 Jul; CINCPAC to JCS, ser 000103 of 3 Apr 1962; CINCPACFLT to CHBUMED, ser 75/00523 of 22 Jun 1962; CINCPACFLT to CGFMFPAC/COMPHIBPAC, ser 61/00465 of 27 May 1963; CINCPACFLT to CNO, ser 32/00718 of 19 Aug; CINCPACFLT to CINCPAC, ser 41/00146 of 30 May 1964; CINCPACFLT, "Type Commanders' Conference," 1962, Agenda, items 79, 80; CINCPACFLT, "Conference, 6-7 February 1963," pp. 35-39, tab E; CINCPACFLT, Annual Report, FY1964.

[36]Memo, OP-93 to OP-09, ser 0053P93 of 18 Aug 1964.

crisis situations."[37] The Navy's reluctance to adopt the Floating Forward Depot concept resulted in a continual search for solutions to the shortage of amphibious shipping, but the immediate problem was not solved.

While new, improved conventional ordnance entered fleet service, problems with air and surface weapon systems and munitions continued to trouble naval commanders. The stress on deploying guided missiles in the fleet resulted in a decrease in the number of large-caliber guns capable of effective shore bombardment in support of ground operations. In 1963 Admiral Sides observed that the active fleet possessed no 16-inch guns, only eighteen 8-inch guns, and only eighteen 6-inch guns. Since 1959, the number of 5-inch guns had decreased from 596 to 463. Compounding the problem, at the beginning of the decade, twenty-four landing ships, medium, rocket (LSMR), important vessels for close inshore fire, were inactivated. And by mid-1964 only one all-gun cruiser, *Saint Paul*, sailed with the Pacific Fleet.[38] As a related problem, naval commanders noted a lack of proficiency in gunnery resulting from the emphasis on missile warfare. Commander Training Force, U.S. Pacific Fleet, reported in early 1962 that "even upon completion of refresher training some ships cannot demonstrate a satisfactory gunnery capability, and the majority are barely satisfactory."[39]

Difficulties were also experienced with conventional ammunition and other ordnance. In mid-1961 the Secretary of the Navy reported that the World War II and Korean War stocks of gun ammunition were dwindling because the low level of procurement authorized by the Defense Department did not equal expenditures. At the same time, the Long Range Objectives Group found air ordnance stockpiles inadequate. The Bureau of Weapons, after a "critical inspection," concluded that because of attention to nuclear warfare there were "serious deficiencies in the Attack Carrier Striking Forces non-nuclear attack capabilities."[40]

---

[37]Ltr, CMC to SECNAV, ser 003A21364 of 31 Jul 1964. See also memos, CNO to OP-03/OP-06, ser 0234-61 of 30 Apr 1961; OP-60 to OP-09, ser BM00853-61 of 23 Aug; SECNAV to SECARM/SECAF/CHJCS of 26 Sep; OP-93, of 30 Oct; SECNAV to SECDEF, ser 0004310P40 of 7 Nov; SECNAV to CNO, of 16 Feb 1962; CNO to SECNAV, ser 0029P401 of 30 Jun; ltr, CINCPACFLT to COMNAVPHIL, ser 41/00777 of 17 Sep; Executive Asst, CNO, ser 00191-64 of 16 Jul 1964.

[38]Ltr, CINCPACFLT to CNO, ser 32/00606 of 19 Jul 1962; ser 31/00109 of 27 Dec; CINCPACFLT, "CINCPACFLT Conference, 6-7 Feb 1963," p. 36, tab E; Rowe and Morison, *Ships and Aircraft*, p. 65; CINCPACFLT, Annual Report, FY1964; ltr, CINCPACFLT to CNO, ser 32/00359m of 19 Apr 1963.

[39]CINCPACFLT, "Type Commanders' Conference," 1962, Agenda, item 55.

[40]OP-07, memo, ser 47-61 of Feb 1961.

After 1962, increased procurement was authorized for these munitions, but critical items continued to be in demand. In August 1963, the Pacific Fleet itemized those resources that were in short supply or would quickly be consumed in combat. These items included 3-inch and 5-inch shells, Tartar, Terrier, and Talos surface-to-air and Bullpup air-to-surface missiles, and torpedoes. The fleet was especially short of conventional aerial munitions, such as low-drag 250, 500, and 2,000-pound bombs and napalm bombs.[41] At the end of May 1964, CINCPACFLT reported that a period of extended air action in Southeast Asia would "result in aircraft out of commission for parts and conventional ammunition stock expenditures that will severely reduce available parts and stocks."[42]

Pacific Naval Forces on the Eve of War

While a number of deficiencies detracted from its capability to fight a non-nuclear war, and especially to project conventional power ashore, the Pacific Fleet in mid-1964 was a good deal stronger than it had been four years earlier. The general purpose forces of the fleet consisted of 434 active ships. The 13 attack and antisubmarine aircraft carriers deployed throughout the Pacific constituted the backbone of the fleet's striking force. They were supported by 7 cruisers, 117 destroyer types, and 43 submarines. The amphibious force comprised 72 ships, including 3 LPH, 1 LPD, 15 LSD, 23 LST, 3 amphibious force flagships (AGC), and 27 cargo and troop transport ships. To defend against any mine threat, the Pacific Fleet could deploy 43 coastal and ocean minesweepers. With the need for readiness to conduct coastal patrol, especially in Southeast Asia, the Navy had augmented the Pacific command's 19 DEs and radar picket escort ships (DER) with 9 escorts from the Naval Reserve Training Fleet. Enabling this powerful naval force to maintain a continuous presence throughout the vast Pacific were 111 auxiliary ships, including ammunition, stores, cargo, surveying, and repair ships and oilers, tankers, tenders, and fleet tugs.

---

[41]Ltr, CINCPACFLT to CINCPAC, ser 41/00694 of 9 Aug 1963; msg, CNO 212349Z Jan 1964; CINCPACFLT, "CINCPACFLT Conference, 6-7 Feb 1963," pp. 83-86, tab M.

[42]Ltr, CINCPACFLT to CINCPAC, ser 41/000146 of 30 May 1964. See also memos, OP-93 to CNO, ser 00209-61 of 30 Oct 1961; SECNAV to SECDEF, ser 00121 of 31 Aug 1962; SECNAV to SECDEF, of 12 May 1964; CINCPACFLT, "Type Commanders' Conference," 1962, Agenda, item 56.

An F-4 Phantom II test fires a Sparrow III air-to-air missile off Point Mugu, California.

The Pacific Fleet's Naval Air Force, consisting of both carrier and land-based aircraft, added considerably to U.S. strength in that ocean. The force was organized into 10 attack carrier air wings, 5 ASW carrier air groups, and 31 separate squadrons. The latter units performed special functions, such as airborne early warning, photographic reconnaissance, electronic intelligence collection, patrol, and training. The Marine Corps contributed another 2 air wings to the total. First-line aircraft included the F-4 Phantom II, F-8 Crusader, A-4 Skyhawk, A-3 Skywarrior, propeller-driven A-1 Skyraider, and all-weather A-6 Intruder in the fighter and attack roles. The S-2 Tracker was responsible for ASW tasks, while the EC-121 Warning Star provided the fleet with early warning, weather, and electronic support. Patrol duties were carried out by the P-2 Neptune, the newer, all-weather P-3 Orion, and the P-5 Marlin seaplane. Mainstays of the naval helicopter force were the UH-34 Seahorse, the SH-3A Sea King, and the UH-2 Seasprite.[43]

During this era, the Navy made a concerted effort to improve its ability to fight non-nuclear limited wars. The naval service built ships that promised to enhance the fleet's mobility, versatility, and endurance, qualities deemed essential to deterring or conducting a limited conflict. New types, such as the LPH, LPD, AFS, and AOE, soon entered fleet service. The Navy built three new carriers and also developed fixed-wing aircraft and helicopters especially suited to a conventional role. Greater research and development and manufacturing effort was devoted to non-nuclear ordnance.

Despite the overall improvement in the Navy's conventional readiness, a number of problems persisted throughout the period, including the shortage of adequate numbers of key aircraft, amphibious vessels, and ships for sealift of troops and cargo. The material condition of the Pacific Fleet remained marginal. Similarly, naval forces were deficient in the number of large-caliber guns available for shore bombardment and in training for their use. Stocks of some conventional ordnance and spare parts remained low in the Pacific area.

Even with these shortfalls, the Pacific Fleet was the strongest single naval force in the world. By mid-1964, the fleet possessed the resources to conduct and support a limited war 7,000 miles from the continental United States in Southeast Asia.

---

[43]CINCPACFLT, Annual Report, FY1964; CNO, "Naval Aviation Summary," of 1 Oct 1964.

CHAPTER XI

The Advisory Program and the Vietnamese Navy in a Year of Turmoil, 1964

The overthrow of the Diem government brought about a profound change in the nature of the war in Southeast Asia and each side's perception of the conflict. Although briefly hopeful that new political leadership would galvanize South Vietnam's counterinsurgency struggle, U.S. leaders soon expressed growing doubt that the country could survive its troubles. The problems were many and varied, but the lack of strong, durable leadership from the South Vietnamese government and the armed forces was the most fundamental defect.

The Don-Minh-Kim regime which seized power from Diem succumbed after only several months of ineffectual and disharmonious government. On 31 January 1964 army General Nguyen Khanh ousted these leaders in a bloodless coup and established himself as the head of state. Although U.S. officials initially thought highly of Khanh, who was recognized as staunchly pro-American, his hold on power and direction of the country was tenuous. Khanh remained as the head of government until the fall, but that feat required an inordinate devotion to political intrigue, inaction on controversial but necessary policies, and greater reliance on U.S. resources.

The Diem coup also did serious injury to the Vietnamese Navy's officer corps. The close association of many top officers with the old regime resulted in their replacement by more junior and often less qualified men or by those who were politically acceptable to the new government. Captain Chung Tan Cang, formerly head of the River Force and sometime antagonist of the assassinated Quyen, was appointed Naval Deputy. Cang and General Nguyen Van Thieu, one of the chief officers involved in

Diem's overthrow, served together in the merchant marine in the early 1950s before the latter man joined the army. Although Cang was well thought of by some U.S. naval advisors, Captain Drachnik, a close friend of Quyen, found him "a very poor officer" who had revealed "traitorous" tendencies some time before the Diem coup. The American believed that Cang "certainly was not the kind of person you would want for a senior job in the Vietnamese Navy."[1] Other American advisors viewed Vietnam's naval leadership with concern. For example, the new head of intelligence in the naval headquarters, a Cang loyalist, reportedly concerned himself more with politics than the war effort. Similarly, Lieutenant Frank T. Lazarchick, a Sea Force advisor, observed that "approximately one-half of the commanding officers lack the experience necessary to command" their seagoing units.[2] This condition was reflected in the high number of groundings by Sea Force ships that year, especially the PGMs. In general, the development of a professional, dedicated, and cohesive officer corps was dealt a sharp blow by the Diem assassination of November 1963. As Captain Drachnik observed, the coup and the following political turmoil in South Vietnam "just eroded the two years of effort that we put in" the advisory program.[3]

The enemy clearly recognized and took advantage of the dissension in the South Vietnamese armed forces and a weakening in the war effort. Thus, the North Vietnamese leadership resolved at a meeting of the Central Committee of the Vietnam Workers' Party in December 1963 to significantly increase its support of the southern insurgency. As detailed in the top secret record of the meeting, later captured by American forces, Communist leaders determined that "the North must bring into fuller play its role as the revolutionary base for the whole nation."[4] The directive specified that while being progressively strengthened, Communist forces would simultaneously destroy the Strategic Hamlets and concentrate on the regular units of the South Vietnamese armed forces.

---

[1] Drachnik, Interview with Moss, pp. 14-15. See also Drachnik, Interview with Fitzgerald, pp. 23-24.

[2] F. T. Lazarchick, End of Tour Report, of 1 Jun 1964.

[3] Drachnik, Interview with Fitzgerald, p. 52. See also Sea Force SITREP, of 9 Nov 1963; R. N. Channell, End of Tour Report, of 16 Jan 1964.

[4] "The Viet-Nam Workers' Party's 1963 Decision to Escalate the War in the South," in U.S. Mission, South Vietnam, "Viet-Nam Documents and Research Notes," Document No. 96 of Jul 1971, p.i. See also, msg, CP 102155Z Dec 1963; Don, *Our Endless War*, pp. 116-24; Felt, Interview, pp. 621-23.

U.S. naval advisors, including, from left to right: Captain Joseph B. Drachnik, Chief of the Naval Advisory Group, Vietnam; Lieutenant Wesley A. Hoch, 4th Coastal District advisor; an unidentified U.S. naval officer; and Captain William H. Hardcastle, Drachnik's successor, inspect crews quarters of the Coastal Force base at An Thoi in 1964.

If the U.S. strategy of counterinsurgency failed, the North Vietnamese expected their adversary to escalate the conflict to the limited war level with the introduction into South Vietnam of U.S. and allied combat troops. The North Vietnamese also recognized the necessity to prepare "to cope with the eventuality of the expansion of the war into North Viet-Nam." Hoping to avoid this occurrence, however, the Central Committee report stressed the "necessity to contain the enemy in the 'special war' [counterinsurgency] and confine this war within South Viet-Nam."[5]

Soon afterward, the movement south of men, weapons, and supplies increased dramatically. In contrast to 1963 when the flow of infiltrators actually declined, 1964 witnessed the introduction into South Vietnam of over 12,000 men, mostly indigenous North Vietnamese. The type of weapons being provided also signaled a change in the nature of the conflict. Rather than having the Viet Cong rely on their own sundry small arms of different calibers and captured U.S. weaponry, the North Vietnamese began providing the southern forces with weapons suited to heavy combat with regular Vietnamese Army units. Chinese-made recoilless rifles, heavy machine guns, rocket-propelled grenade launchers, large mortars, and anti-tank mines began appearing in 1964 in quantity.[6]

Most of the enemy men and material reaching South Vietnam in 1964 arrived via the Ho Chi Minh Trail complex in Laos. This logistical pipeline, however, soon was overloaded. To alleviate this bottleneck and to provide immediate assistance to Viet Cong forces in close proximity to the South Vietnamese coastal population, the Communists turned to the sea route. As revealed by Communist prisoners later in the war, infiltration of steel-hulled trawlers, with a capacity of 50 to 100 tons, increased six-fold from 1963 to 1964. The ten ships built in North Vietnamese yards were augmented in 1964 by another fifteen trawlers provided by Communist China. Each of the vessels reportedly conducted two voyages a month to the South laden with arms and ammunition. By the end of 1964 this operation constituted a consequential part of the overall North Vietnamese effort. Clearly, the enemy saw the year

---

[5]"The Viet-Nam Workers' Party's 1963 Decision," pp. 40, v, vii, viii, x, 6, 8, 15, 17, 21-23. See also msg, CPFLT 222148Z May 1964.

[6]Weiner, Brom, and Koon, *Infiltration*, pp. 5, 7, 43-45; State Department, *Aggression From the North*, p. 15; William C. Westmoreland, *A Soldier Reports* (New York: Doubleday and Co., 1976), pp. 101, 104; DIA, Special Intelligence Supplement, "Military Fact Book on the Republic of Vietnam," of Jul 1965.

following Diem's ouster as a time of decision and used every means to bring about the total collapse of South Vietnam.[7]

Of particular concern to the U.S. Navy was increasing evidence that infiltration of arms and supplies into the Mekong Delta region of South Vietnam was coming by sea. In the early months of 1964, small "freighters" were reported to be carrying contraband from Singapore to the Camau Peninsula and submarines purportedly were sighted off the southern coast. However, the Navy was unable to confirm that the Viet Cong were procuring munitions in Singapore and Captain Drachnik dismissed the submarine reports with the observation that the shallow water off the southern coast would preclude even surface running by these vessels. He believed the "freighters" were actually 100 to 150-foot fishing vessels that purchased inexpensive fish off South Vietnam for resale in Singapore.

Nonetheless, the possibility of seaborne infiltration worried other U.S. leaders. Following his trip to Southeast Asia at the end of 1963, Admiral Claude V. Ricketts, the Vice Chief of Naval Operations, recorded his impressions: "I heard that there is much infiltration coming in by sea, particularly in the south. Material is coming over from Cambodia, transferred into shallow draft craft and then going into the waterways and becoming lost."[8] Secretary of Defense McNamara, in the Pacific theater during December 1963, also was concerned that the waterways of the delta were being used by the Communists to transport war material. Upon his return to Washington he suggested to Admiral Felt that a team be sent to Vietnam to study the delta infiltration and to recommend ways of controlling it.[9]

Further, the Secretary was troubled that the Vietnamese Navy units in the delta were not prepared to counter the enemy threat. Admiral Sharp, the Pacific Fleet commander, reported that McNamara "did not believe the Vietnamese Navy was being used to best advantage." In addition, "he thought their material condition was steadily improving and that Captain Drachnik was doing a good job, but that what they needed was more

---

[7]Erdheim, *Market Time*; CINCPAC, "Infiltration Study," of 1 May 1968; DIA, "Viet Cong Use of Cambodia," No. 6 028 3647 68 of 10 May 1968; MACV, report, "Likely Locations for Sea Infiltration," ser 0636 of 5 May 1965; Socialist Republic of Vietnam, *Vietnam: The Anti-U.S. Resistance War*, pp. 32-33.

[8]Ricketts, memo for record, of 20 Jan 1964.

[9]Msg, DOD 211932Z Dec 1963.

attention to naval concepts."[10] For these reasons, the state of South Vietnamese naval forces in the delta became an important consideration at the beginning of 1964.[11]

The Bucklew Report

To evaluate the extent of the Communist movement of men and munitions into the Mekong Delta and the effectiveness of South Vietnamese countermeasures, in January 1964 Admiral Felt directed the creation of a survey team headed by Rear Admiral Paul Savidge, Jr., Commander Amphibious Training Command, U.S. Pacific Fleet. When bad health incapacitated Admiral Savidge, Captain Phillip H. Bucklew, commander of the Naval Operations Support Group, U.S. Pacific Fleet, took charge. Captain Bucklew, who served with Rear Admiral Milton Miles's Naval Group China during World War II, had considerable experience in intelligence matters and guerrilla warfare.

The nine-man team, officially known as the Vietnam Delta Infiltration Study Group, including representatives from the Pacific Fleet, the First Fleet, MACV, the Navy Section of the MAAG, and SEAL Team 1, arrived in Vietnam in January. Based on interviews with naval advisors and their own observations throughout the country, the group formulated it views. The final Bucklew Report agreed with earlier assessments that the primary Communist supply route extended "from North Vietnam, via Laos and Cambodia, with delivery accomplished via the Ho Chi Minh trail, via major rivers, and by combination of man carried and inland water-borne transfers." It concluded, however, that the rivers in the delta probably were used by the Communists more for the transportation of troops than as avenues of infiltration of munitions. The team recognized the potential for sea infiltration into the area but believed that this approach was used mostly "for deliveries of high priority items and key cadre personnel," a conclusion most naval officers in Vietnam had shared for several years.[12]

---

[10]Ltr, Sharp to Ricketts, of 26 Dec 1963.

[11]*Ibid.*; Ricketts, memo for record, of 20 Jan 1964; OP-922H, Newsletter, ser H-002-64 of Jan 1964; msgs, CTF35 270907Z Jan 1964; CP 082044Z Feb.

[12]Senior Member, Vietnam Delta Infiltration Study Group, "Report of Recommendations Pertaining to Infiltration into South Vietnam of Viet Cong Personnel, Supporting Materials, Weapons and Ammunition," ser 0076 of 15 Feb 1964 (hereafter Bucklew Report), p. 2.

As one means of meeting the Communist threat in the Mekong Delta, Captain Bucklew and the members of his group recommended that a landing force component be assigned to the River Force for "raiding and pursuit" purposes. The logical forces for such a mission were the Vietnamese Marines. But there was resistance to this proposal by both Vietnamese and U.S. Army officers, who worried about interference with Vietnamese Army efforts in the same area. For that reason, the American observers considered it unlikely that a marine force would be assigned. They emphasized, however, that "Navy patrols are limited in effectiveness and vulnerable to destruction without neutralization of the shorelines."[13] Their suggestion that the navy be given increased authority in the Vietnamese defense structure was designed, in part, to assure the more effective participation of naval forces in riverine campaigns.

With regard to coastal patrol, the report concluded that augmentation with resources was necessary for the Coastal Force and Sea Force to cover the South Vietnamese littoral completely. At the same time, it found that the Vietnamese surveillance effort functioned with "reasonable effectiveness," considering the shortage of adequate numbers of operational ships, craft, and junks.

Many of Captain Bucklew's recommendations centered on improving coordination between various agencies of the Vietnamese government. For example, he observed that the activities of the Vietnamese customs agents and river pilots were not coordinated with any agency responsible for stopping infiltration. Yet, these officials had a unique opportunity to observe and report on possible smuggling and infiltration if requested to do so.

Both Admiral Felt and General Harkins had a chance to comment on the Bucklew Report's recommendations and generally concurred with the conclusions. The report was then submitted to the Joint Chiefs, who used it in a comprehensive review of the U.S. Navy's role in the Vietnam conflict in the spring of 1964. The Bucklew Report also served as a basis for much of the work conducted in the naval advisory program that year and some of the team's recommendations were incorporated into the *Chien Thang*, or Victory Plan, which replaced Diem's discredited Strategic Hamlet Program on 22 February 1964. The new plan assigned first

---

[13] *Ibid.*

priority to operations against the Communists in the Mekong Delta and called for more integration of civil and military operations.

One of the Bucklew recommendations was acted upon immediately. Responding to the conclusion that the Vietnamese Navy lacked a strong voice in strategy-making councils, on 8 April the Joint General Staff established the billet of Chief of Naval Operations, to replace the former Naval Deputy to the Chief of Staff of the Armed Forces. This position was filled by Captain Cang, Quyen's successor, who was promoted to the rank of commodore. In October 1964 Cang received a further promotion to rear admiral. Still, the CNO only took part in Joint General Staff deliberations when naval matters were discussed.[14]

Consolidation and Buildup of the Advisory Program

One of the issues raised by McNamara upon his return to Washington from the Pacific in early 1964 was the possibility of streamlining the U.S. command organization by integrating the Military Assistance Advisory Group into the Military Assistance Command, which already was charged with coordinating the total American effort in Vietnam and advising senior South Vietnamese military and political authorities.[15]

Admiral Felt opposed this reorganization. He believed that the MACV commander could not effectively control the large organization which would result from the merger of the two commands. Further, the existing setup allowed MACV to concentrate on the counterinsurgency effort without getting bogged down in the details of the Military Assistance Program and the direction of the growing number of field advisors. The admiral reported to the Joint Chiefs that "we will be unduly rocking the boat to no practical purpose since COMUSMACV already clearly exercises operational command over MAAG and advisors."[16] Secretary McNamara, however, was not persuaded. During his trip to Saigon in

---

[14]*Ibid.*; CINCPAC, Command History, 1964, p. 356; MACV, Command History, 1964, p. 65; Fitzgerald, "U.S. Naval Forces in the Vietnam War," pp. 455-56; ltr, Drachnik to Ricketts, of 13 Mar 1964; memo, JCS to SECDEF, of 1 Jul; Hardcastle, Interview; DIA, Biographic Data, "Chung Tan Cang," of Feb 1973; Bucklew, Interview with Fitzgerald; Bucklew, Interview with Mason, pp. 322-55.

[15]CINCPAC, Command History, 1964, Chart I-1; MACV, Command History, 1964, pp. 3-10.

[16]Quoted in MACV, Command History, 1964, p. 10. See also msg, CP 220912Z Mar 1964.

March, he directed General Harkins to prepare a study of the proposed merger for consideration by Admiral Felt and the Joint Chiefs.

Captain Drachnik favored the reorganization, based on his observation of several problems resulting from the divided command. He noted that although operational control of the American effort in Vietnam rested with MACV, the MAAG allocated the Military Assistance Program supplies that supported operations. Since operations obviously depended on supply, he argued that the two functions should not be separate. Captain Drachnik also concluded that since the MACV commander only advised high-level Vietnamese officers, he functioned with little feel for the problems of MAAG's field advisors. The Joint Chiefs submitted a split opinion to the Secretary of Defense, with the Army favoring the consolidation and the Navy opposing it. Admiral Felt continued to doubt the need for the reorganization.

Nevertheless, on 8 April McNamara approved the merger. The MAAG was disestablished on 15 May. At the same time, the Navy Section of the MAAG was redesignated the Naval Advisory Group, MACV, under Captain William H. Hardcastle, who relieved Captain Drachnik in January 1964.[17] As a result of the reorganization, the number of men authorized for MACV increased slightly from 3,369 to 3,677. At the beginning of the year the number of naval advisors in Vietnam numbered 154. But these figures soon increased substantially. When the Kennedy policy of phasing down U.S. involvement in Vietnam was set aside in 1964, the JCS authorized an increase of MACV advisory personnel. By the end of 1964, they numbered 4,889, 235 of whom were from the Navy. Additional supporting units attached to MACV brought the total of U.S. military forces in Vietnam to over 23,000 at that time.

The eighty-one additional naval advisors who reached South Vietnam in 1964 were assigned primarily to field billets, although psychological warfare, personnel, and medical advisors also were added at the headquarters level. The twenty-one new billets for the Sea Force allowed advisors to ride individual ships on a regular basis in order to promote more aggressive patrolling. Advisors with the River Force increased from ten to thirty-two, which enabled the establishment of three-man detachments with each of the six existing RAGs, with a new assault group, and with the

---

[17]Hardcastle, Interview, p. 17; CINCPAC, Command History, 1964, pp. 306-08; Chart I-1, MACV, Command History, 1964, pp. 3-14; Drachnik, report, of 13 Mar 1964, pp. 1, 7, 9; msg, CP 220912Z Mar 1964.

An American naval advisor and his Vietnamese Navy counterpart. Lieutenant Mark V. Nelson, 1st Coastal District advisor, and Commander Phong, 1st Coastal District commander, on board a Coastal Force junk off Vietnam.

River Transport Escort Group. A total of two advisors each were assigned to the Eastern and Western Repair Facilities. The remaining personnel staffed administrative positions. The assignment of additional advisors to the Coastal Force in 1964 enabled the stationing of two men at each of the junk repair facilities at Danang, Nha Trang, Cat Lo, and Rach Gia, and three with each of the eight advisory detachments assigned to the coastal districts. Besides instructing Vietnamese on ways to improve naval operations, the advisors now were able to provide Captain Hardcastle and the Military Assistance Command in Saigon with more information on the true situation in the field.[18]

Personnel and Training in the Vietnamese Navy

The increase in advisors partly reflected the growth of the Vietnamese armed forces, the expanded support of which was authorized after Secretary McNamara's visit to Vietnam in March 1964. The number of Vietnamese Navy personnel rose from 6,467 in January to 8,162 officers and men in November. General Khanh's National Public Service Decree, signed in April 1964, which made all men between the ages of twenty and forty-five subject to the draft, aided the navy's recruiting program, although the service was manned solely by volunteers. The additional personnel manned the ships and craft arriving from the United States, raised the manning level of other units and repair facilities, and filled the training pipeline.[19]

The Vietnamese Navy had little trouble recruiting for the regular forces, but meeting the allowance for the paramilitary Coastal Force remained difficult. As of 1 January 1964, the Coastal Force was authorized 6,640 men. But the force never had more than 3,700 men on board during the year. Desertions, which since April 1963 averaged about 100 men each month, were the chief problem. Between May and August 1964, only 264 men were enlisted to offset this loss. Undermanning was most serious in the 3rd and 4th Coastal Districts. Coastal Division 34, for

---

[18]MACV, Command History, 1964, p. 180; *U.S.-V.N. Relations*, bk. 3, pt. IVB.3, pp. 38-39; CINCPAC, Command History, 1964, pp. 317-18; Hardcastle, Interview; memo, Hardcastle to DEPCOMUSMACV, ser 0046 of 31 May 1964; NAG, "VNN Background Information," of May 1964; NAG, "Historical Review of Naval Advisory Group Activities, CY1964," ser 0024 of 1 Jan 1965 (hereafter NAG, Historical Review, 1964), p. 17; NAG, Briefing for CINCPAC, of Jul 1964.

[19]NAG, Historical Review, 1964, pp. 4-5; *U.S.-V.N. Relations*, bk. 3, pt. IVC.1, p. A-6.

example, had only 40 junkmen of the 145 authorized actually on board. At the same time as recruiting fell behind, almost one-third of the Coastal Force personnel were assigned to duties other than the primary one of coastal patrol. Thus, the number of junks on patrol hovered around 40 percent of the total operational force.

As a long-term solution to the personnel shortage, U.S. advisors called for the formal integration of the junk force into the Vietnamese Navy. This step would make personnel eligible for all the benefits of the regular service, including higher pay and allowances, and thus enhance the desirability of Coastal Force service.[20] Although the Joint General Staff expressed concern that the action would increase personnel costs and set an undesired precedent for the other paramilitary units in the armed forces, it approved the integration plan in December. During the following summer, the Coastal Force formally joined the Vietnamese Navy.[21]

The training programs set up to handle the rapid expansion of the navy in 1962 and 1963 began to function routinely by 1964. With the graduation of the Naval Academy class in October 1964, the previous officer shortage ended. An eight-week tour of duty with Seventh Fleet ships was provided to 25 percent of each class. To give refresher training to Vietnamese technicians in engineering, deck and gunnery procedures, and operational skills, U.S. advisors helped the Vietnamese set up thirty-five courses, varying in length from three days to four weeks, at the Naval Advanced Training Center in Saigon.

The Vietnamese also continued to benefit from specialized training by U.S. mobile training teams. Mobile Training Team 1-65, for example, conducted simulated brigade-level amphibious exercises at the army's General Staff College in Dalat in October. Mobile Training Team 3-65, which deployed to Saigon for six months later in 1964, trained the medical staff of a Vietnamese LSM that was refitted with two medical vans and equipment. The ship then steamed along the coast treating offshore fishermen and naval personnel and their families at isolated bases.

A restructured intelligence school in Saigon also yielded good results. A ten-day basic intelligence course for officers was begun late in 1963. As the graduates of the new program went into the field, the amount of

---

[20]NAG, Fact Sheet, of 27 May 1964; NAG, "Coastal Force Paramilitary Strength Figures," of 16 Sep; NAG, Monthly Evaluation, of Aug 1964.
[21]NAG, Historical Review, 1964, p. 10; NAG, memo, ser 00121 of 16 Nov 1964.

intelligence information submitted by operational units increased commensurately. In May 1964, the first agent net was established in order to collect information on infiltration into the Mekong Delta. The progress made in the field was not matched at the headquarters level, where coordination between naval intelligence officers and their army counterparts was limited.

Since most of the recruits for the Coastal Force had little education, special training programs were established to instruct them in technical subjects, such as engine maintenance and radio procedure. In January 1964, the Engineering School was moved from Saigon to Cam Ranh Bay, and by the end of the year the facility had trained over 500 men in diesel engine maintenance. Other personnel received medical and communications training at army schools. In March 1964, a Junk Skippers School was established in Nha Trang, and a Junk Division Commanders School opened in April at the Naval Advanced Training Center in Saigon.[22]

U.S. naval advisors further developed the Vietnamese capability for special warfare. The LDNN naval commando force numbered one officer and forty-one men at the beginning of 1964. On 20 March, however, the only officer and most of the enlisted men were transferred to Danang for special operations. When Lieutenant Franklin W. Anderson became advisor to the LDNN in July, he found only eleven men, all who remained of the first unit. After an intensive three-month screening process, sixty additional men were selected to augment the unit's strength. Training of this group began on 25 September at Nha Trang. The arduous sixteen-week course included "Hell Week," during which each student paddled a boat 115 miles, ran 75 miles, carried a boat 21 miles, and swam 10 miles. Even before the completion of their training, team members participated in salvaging a sunken LCVP at Nha Trang and a downed Vietnamese Air Force Skyraider in Binh Duong Province. Of this group, thirty-three men completed their LDNN training in January 1965 and were based thereafter at Vung Tau, under the direct control of the Vietnamese Deputy Chief of Naval Operations for Operations.[23]

---

[22]NAG, memo, ser 0181 of 10 Jun 1964; NAG, Historical Review, 1964, pp. 5-6, Annex A; MACV, Command History, 1964, p. 44; R.N. Channell, End of Tour Report, of 16 Jun 1965; NAG, Fact Sheets, of 27 May 1964; 10 Jul; MTT 1-65, report, ser 1500 of 13 Nov 1964; Hardcastle, Interview; ltr, CHBUMED to OP-09B92, ser 38 of 11 Feb 1966.

[23]Franklin W. Anderson, Jr., End of Tour Report, of 23 Jun 1965; A3, report, of 23 Jun 1964; NAG, Fact Sheet, "VNN SEAL/UDT Teams," of 8 Jun 1965.

Further, the U.S. Navy continued the program to equip and train units of the Vietnamese Air Force begun in 1960. During his visit to Saigon in March 1964, Secretary of Defense McNamara decided to replace all of the T-28s in the Vietnamese Air Force with A-1H aircraft. On 29 April a squadron of twenty-five A-1Hs landed at Danang, ferried to Vietnam by pilots of the U.S. Navy. There, on the same day, a U.S. naval training detachment of 23 officers and 150 enlisted men from VA 152 began training 98 Vietnamese pilots and 277 maintenance men.[24] Before this detachment departed on 24 November, the Navy's Mobile Training Team 4-65 reached Vietnam for a six-month tour starting on 21 September. This team concentrated on instructing Vietnamese at the Bien Hoa Airbase in maintenance techniques, in anticipation of the deployment of another A-1H squadron, due to arrive in-country early in 1965. Mobile training teams usually worked well with the Vietnamese, but this team, headed by Lieutenant (j.g.) Douglas E. Story, had a number of difficulties. Thus, after a month in Vietnam, Lieutenant Story reported that maintenance progress was slow, "because of the reluctance of VNAF personnel, both officer and enlisted, to accept advice offered by U.S. advisors. They seek help only when a situation becomes critical. A general lack of initiative and leadership is exhibited by officers and senior enlisted personnel."[25] Nonetheless, the U.S. Navy was instrumental in providing the Vietnamese Air Force with equipment and training assistance that would be invaluable in meeting the enemy's threat.

New Resources for the Vietnamese Navy

In addition to training assistance, the Vietnamese Navy received new ships, junks, small craft, and material through the U.S. Military Assistance Program. The last two of the twelve specially designed MAP motor gunboats, programmed for delivery to Vietnam in Fiscal Year 1965, arrived early in 1964. One of these ships, originally destined for Cambodia, was diverted to Vietnam when Prince Sihanouk severed

---

[24]Msgs, MACV 111132Z Mar 1964; JCS 181712Z; CPFLT 210159Z; CP 220028Z; CHMAAGVN 080809Z May; CINCPAC, Command History, 1964, pp. 318-32; MTT 4-65, report, of 1 Dec 1964.

[25]MTT 4-65, report, of 1 Dec 1964. See also CINCPAC, Command History, 1964, pp. 318-22; msg, CHMAAGVN 080809Z May 1964.

economic and military ties with the United States in November 1963. The only other seagoing ships which the Vietnamese received during 1964 were two fleet minesweepers, *Serene* (MSF-300) and *Shelter* (MSF-301), which were converted to escorts (PCE) before their assignment to the Sea Force. With the arrival of the MSFs and PGMs, the upgrading and expansion program for the Vietnamese Sea Force, begun as a result of U.S. decisions in 1961, was complete. At the end of 1964 the Sea Force comprised forty-four seagoing ships.

Military assistance funds were also used to upgrade the junks in the Coastal Force. Poor quality control on the first U.S.-contracted boats was revealed in the breakdown of many junks in 1964. Captain Hardcastle explained the problem in these words: "These had been built on a crash program by, to say the least, incompetent house carpenters. They were built of green [wood] and after the wood dried out, I have seen junks with seams open that were about three-fourths of an inch. It was just terrible."[26] In addition, the original boats proved highly susceptible to teredo worms, a marine borer which riddled wooden hulls, particularly in the Gulf of Siam.

Captain Hardcastle suspected that many of the junks which the Vietnamese reported operational were in fact beyond economical repair and in May 1964 he directed a survey team from the Navy Section to make an accounting of the junk force's material condition. The team found that of the 644 junks planned in 1962 for construction, 12 were never built, 16 were lost at sea, and 13 were scrapped because they were beyond feasible repair. Of the remaining 603 junks, 378 were operable, 174 were laid up but repairable, and 51 were not worth repairing. With an effective fleet of only 552 junks and an optimum 50 percent utilization rate, the Coastal Force had no hope of deploying junks at the ideal spacing of one for every two miles of coast.

Many of the craft in poor condition were the sailing junks, which were the subject of constant complaint by Coastal Force advisors. This type was particularly unsuited to duty in the Gulf of Siam where most of the civilian junks were motorized and therefore faster. In addition, it was difficult for the cumbersome and slow sailing junks to avoid ambush by the Viet Cong, who controlled much of the coastline in that area. Attempts to install

---

[26]Hardcastle, Interview, p. 32.

engines in the sailing junks proved unsatisfactory because that step required the virtual rebuilding of the junk.

Despite the problems with existing vessels, the Bucklew Report recommended expanding the junk fleet. The new COMUSMACV, General William C. Westmoreland, USA, on the other hand, demurred, concluding that the Vietnamese did not have the ability to man a larger number of units. After reviewing a similar proposal for expansion at the end of the year, Captain Hardcastle reaffirmed the general's conclusion:

> Based upon the past multitude of problems which has faced the Coastal Force and the dismal outlook for any significant improvement, it is not considered appropriate to further compound the problems by increasing the number of junks in the Coastal Force at this time.[27]

The captain determined that new construction should be directed only at replacing the sailing junks and that no new programs should be initiated until operational and support problems were solved. A Naval Advisory Group staff study completed at the end of May concluded that ninety new motorized junks were required to replace lost and surveyed junks and to allow the deployment of patrol units spaced at five-mile intervals north of Vung Tau and at three-mile intervals south of that port.

The prototype junk selected for construction was a 57-foot boat with a fiberglassed wooden hull, one of which had been built in 1961 from the design of a Japanese engineer, Mr. Yabuta, at the Saigon Naval Shipyard. CINCPAC approved funding for ninety of these craft in the Fiscal Year 1965 Military Assistance Program budget and Admiral Cang enthusiastically approved construction of the craft in the Saigon shipyard. The program began in October 1964, with all the boats scheduled for completion within one year.[28] Captain Hardcastle later cited the Yabuta program as one of the outstanding achievements of the advisory effort. He explained: "You get the Vietnamese in on the ground roots of planning. Let them have a part in it, and if they believe in it, they are going to succeed and they are capable." The Vietnamese had never mass-produced anything in the shipyard, but they assimilated the new techniques and fulfilled all of their commitments. An American advisor coordinated the

---

[27]Hardcastle, memo for record, of 17 Dec 1964. See also Richard Knapp, End of Tour Report, of 2 Oct 1964.
[28]Msg, CP 190050Z Mar 1964.

project, but the Vietnamese did the work. Captain Hardcastle concluded: "They did a beautiful job."[29]

To the disappointment of U.S. advisors, however, the total strength of the Coastal Force actually decreased in 1964. At the end of the year, the 1st Coastal District advisor, Lieutenant Robert C. Perkins, reported:

> The trend is more and more junks out of commission (55 this week with 11 at the Navy Base). Even though the repair effort was improved, I expect this figure to increase. The same old story, too much time required for repairs and poor quality hull work in the past, and we still have a long way to go in improving hull work.[30]

By the beginning of 1965, there were 81 command junks, 91 combination motor-sail junks, 120 motorized junks, and 239 sailing junks distributed among twenty-eight bases on South Vietnam's coast.[31]

In addition to the Yabuta, Captain Hardcastle gave consideration to obtaining a steel-hulled craft requiring less maintenance and offering a longer useful life than the wooden-hulled junks. The Chief of the Advanced Research Projects Agency's field unit in Vietnam was sympathetic to Captain Hardcastle's request for an evaluation of such a vessel. He commented:

> The concept of the Junk Force was a stop-gap quick fix at best. At a time when the Army of Vietnam is using M113 Armored Personnel Carriers and the Air Force is using A1H Skyraiders, the Navy of Vietnam is attempting to patrol its coast with craft which might have held their own in the Battle of Salamis.[32]

The most promising type was the landing craft, personnel, large (LCPL), which could be armed with one 50-caliber and two 30-caliber machine guns. Four LCPLs, representing the U.S. Navy's entire active stock, were added to the Fiscal Year 1965 Military Assistance Program. By that time, however, the United States began deploying American-made Swift units

---

[29]Hardcastle, Interview, pp. 35-36. See also Bang Cao Thang, Interview, pp. 9-12; Tanh Nguon Lam, transcript of interview with Oscar P. Fitzgerald, Naval Historical Center, in Fall River, MA, 14 Apr 1976, pp. 4-5.
[30]1st Coastal District Advisor, SITREP, of 10 Dec 1964.
[31]OP-324, Staff Study, of 1 Jan 1965.
[32]Memo, Director, ARPA Field Unit, Vietnam, to Director for Remote Area Conflict, of 14 Nov 1964.

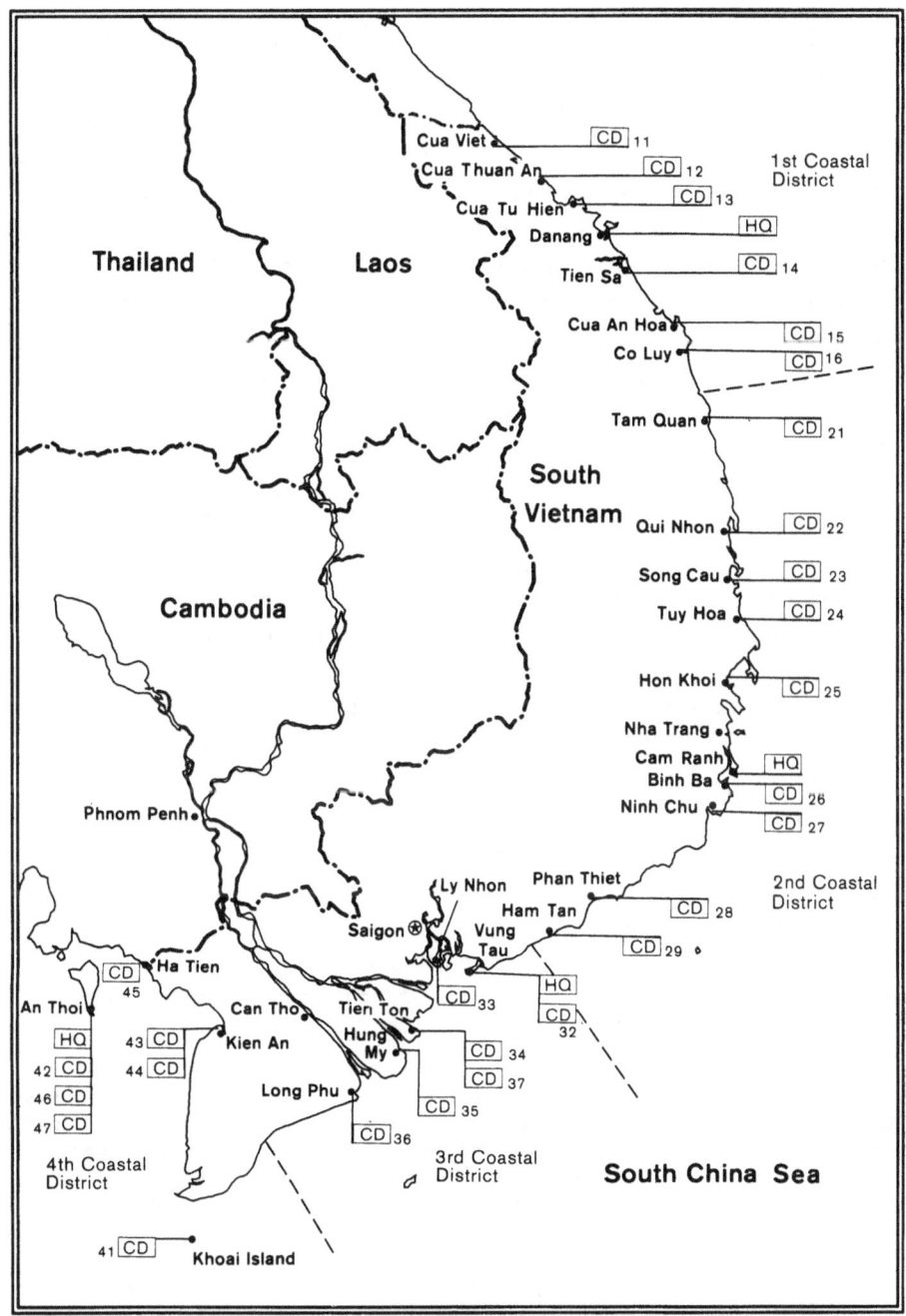

Coastal Force Dispositions, January 1965

along the coast. Their presence obviated the need for LCPLs with the Coastal Force.[33]

To strengthen the River Force in the critical Mekong Delta region, on 17 March 1964, President Johnson approved use of MAP funds to create a seventh river assault group. Secretary of Defense McNamara first raised the possibility of another Vietnamese RAG during his visit to Vietnam in December 1963. Initially, Admiral Felt and Captain Drachnik opposed creation of the unit because of the low operational rates of existing RAGs. General Harkins, however, eventually persuaded the naval officers that the shift of a Vietnamese Army division from the northern provinces to the delta and an expanded river patrol mission demanded a net increase in riverine forces.

When established in early 1965, the unit, designated the 27th River Assault Group, was composed of fourteen U.S.-built river patrol craft (RPC), six LCM-8s, a commandament, and a monitor. The LCM-8 was selected rather than the LCM-6, which was standard in earlier RAGs, because it could carry the new M-113 armored personnel carriers used by some army units in the delta. The RPC, a 36-foot craft, was designed by the Bureau of Ships to replace the French-built STCAN. The RPC's 15-knot speed was nearly twice as fast as the STCAN and its cruising range of 200 miles was four times that of the old French boat.[34]

Additional measures to increase the resources of the River Force included augmentation of two existing RAGs with 2 commandaments, 4 monitors, 12 LCMs, and 6 river patrol craft and the transfer from the condensed River Transport Escort Group to combat units of 12 STCANs. The latter craft were especially suited to assault operations, since their V-shaped hulls lessened mine damage and their pointed bows, when wedged in mudbanks, held well against the current for the debarking of troops.[35]

---

[33]Hardcastle, Interview; CINCPAC, Command History, 1964, pp. 314, 357-58; NAG, Historical Review, 1964, pp. 4-5, 13; Drachnik, Interview with Fitzgerald; Bucklew Report; NAG, Monthly Evaluation, Sep 1964; msgs, CP 190050Z Mar 1964; 220002Z; 242155Z; MAAG, "Revision of RVN Military Assistance Program Review," of 15 Nov 1963; ltrs, CHNAG to J. L. Ashcroft, ser 0055 of 10 Jun 1964; CHNAG to COMUSMACV, of 24 Jun; Hardcastle, memo for record, of 17 Dec 1964; memo, DCNO (Plans and Policy) to CNO, ser 00269-64 of 24 Dec; NAG, "VN Navy Background Information;" ltrs, J. L. Ashcroft to CHNAG, of 30 May 1964; Chung Tan Cang to CICRVNAF, of 1964; OP-324, Staff Study, "Number of Junks Required in the Coastal Force to Provide Effective Surveillance," of 1 Jan 1965.

[34]Gray, et al., "Revolutionary Warfare on Inland Waterways," pp. 264, 279; CHNAG, Briefing, "The Vietnamese Navy and Vietnamese Marine Corps," of 30 Jun 1964.

[35]Msg, CP 220002Z Mar 1964; NAG, Staff Study, "Requirements for Additional VNN River Assault Group," of 9 Apr 1964 in "VN Navy Background Information;" ltr, CHNAG to CO VNN,

MACV's Joint Research and Test Activity, an organization established in Vietnam in April 1964, and composed of American military and civilian personnel, worked to provide the Vietnamese with craft, weapons, and material best suited to combat in the riverine environment. Although the widespread introduction of the helicopter by the end of 1964 lessened the requirement for them, the activity tested several potentially useful air boats in the Rung Sat swamp. Another craft, the 14-foot marsh screw, was evaluated in the United States in late 1964. Propelled by two rotating pontoons with spiralled tracks, the amphibian could cross flooded plains and climb muddy river banks. The Naval Advisory Group was asked to comment on the new boat and decide if it should be tested in Vietnam. Lieutenant Commander Thomas F. Wooten, a River Force advisor, described the reaction to the proposal:

> We didn't like it. We didn't think it had any function. We thought it was just one more thing to put in-country that we really didn't have any great need for .... They didn't need anything else. They had enough trouble running and operating the equipment they had. So the thought was to keep the exotic equipment out.[36]

The development of the marsh screw for Vietnam was not pursued.

Another in-country group, the Advanced Research Projects Agency, studied techniques to counter Viet Cong mining incidents, which averaged about three per month in 1964. To support this effort, the Navy's Mine Defense Laboratory at Panama City, Florida, developed improved sweeping devices. Tests conducted in Vietnam in March 1964 found that one particular chain sweep was effective against bottom mines. The anchor-drag system was less useful because the anchor tended to bounce along the river bottom, skipping over some mines. Twenty-one detection sonars also were programmed for delivery to the RAGs during the year.

Other equipment considered by the testing activities included various radars, infrared sniper scopes, night image intensifiers, and anti-ambush weapons for use with the River Force. Some concepts, such as the rigging of boats with Claymore mines, proved too dangerous or impractical. More effective against ambush was the shoulder-fired M-79 grenade launcher,

---

ser 0374 of 7 Dec 1964; CINCPAC, Command History, 1964, pp. 358-59; *U.S.-V.N. Relations*, bk. 3, pt. IVC.1, pp. 15, 46.

[36] Thomas F. Wooten, transcript of interview with Oscar P. Fitzgerald, Naval Historical Centr, in Little Creek, VA, 23 Apr 1975, pp. 29-30.

100 of which were distributed to the River Force beginning in August 1964. This weapon, with its high trajectory, could lob grenades over the high river banks which lined many delta waterways.[37]

Material Readiness Improvements

A major thrust of the Bucklew Report was to enhance the readiness of the Vietnamese Navy's units by improving maintenance, repair, and supply. The report reaffirmed what advisors already knew — that these were major weaknesses of the Vietnamese Navy. American advisors reported that many Vietnamese line officers believed they should not be concerned with maintenance or repair. As a result, the facilities at the Saigon Naval Shipyard were overloaded with minor preventive maintenance work. Fully half of the shipyard's jobs involved unscheduled work. The remainder constituted regularly scheduled overhauls, 150 of which the yard completed for the Sea Force and River Force in 1964.

While U.S. advisors tried, with mixed results, to change Vietnamese attitudes, they had more success expanding the physical plant of the Saigon shipyard, such as the establishment of a spare-engine shop in 1964 and an apprentice school, in January 1965, which promised to expand the limited pool of semi-skilled labor. Specialized training in hull fabrication, and other specialized shop practices was provided by Mobile Training Team 7-64. Mobile Training Team 2-65 instructed technicians at the gyrocompass repair shop. At the end of the year, U.S. advisors could point to a more skilled work force and better management at the higher levels, although mid-level supervision remained a problem.

The shipyard was the largest customer of the Vietnamese Navy's supply center. That center operated more smoothly once a thorough inventory allowed disposal of excess stocks by October 1964. A program to package engine and electronic parts, in order to preserve them from deterioration

---

[37]Msg, COMUSMACV 100151Z Jun 1964; Advisory Board, report, "Long Tau Soirap River Area Security," encl. 9; Joint Research and Test Activity, Third Semi-Annual Report, 1 Jan-30 Jun 1965; First Semi-Annual Report, 1 Jan-30 Jun 1964; Wooten, Interview; NAG, Historical Review, 1964, p. 9; msg, CP 180140Z Dec 1964; ARPA, "Riverine Minecountermeasures in Vietnam, 1964," of 15 Apr 1964, pp. 30-31, 109; ltrs, Senior River Force Advisor to CHNAG, ser 22-64 of 6 Mar; NAG, ser 0042 of 22 May.

in the tropical climate, continued throughout the year. Still, the work of the center was hindered by a dearth of qualified personnel. For example, at the beginning of 1964 the facility had only 97 of its authorized 164 enlisted storekeepers.

The new PGMs presented a particularly difficult supply problem. The ships used 2 types of main engine, 3 types of generators, and 2 types each of fresh water pumps and air compressors. Spare parts for the Mercedes-Benz main engines were not in the U.S. Navy's supply system. The Bureau of Ships sent a five-man team to Vietnam in September to assess the problem and, as a result, the Navy established a direct supply line for engine parts between Vietnam and the Navy Purchasing Office in London. This direct link and the stocking of spares at Subic reduced to four weeks the previous two-to-four month delay in receiving parts.

Separate repair facilities in the coastal districts served the Coastal Force. In January, after spending three months training junkmen in maintenance and logistic procedures, Mobile Training Team 2-64 helped establish a new repair facility at Rach Gia. Upon completion of the team's work, in March, each coastal district had a junk repair facility. During 1964, each yard received a mobile, thirty-ton crane capable of handling junks needing repair. The Vietnamese completed the renovation of the Eastern Repair Facility at Cuu Long, which had been in limited operation since 1962.

The Coastal Force also opened repair parts depots at Rach Gia and An Thoi in May, similar to facilities already in operation at Danang, Nha Trang, and Vung Tau. But supplying these depots from Saigon was difficult. After the November 1963 coup against Diem, a fleet of trawlers, formerly owned by Diem's sister-in-law, Madame Ngo Dinh Nhu, was taken over by the new government. Two of these 30-meter vessels were turned over to the junk force. By October 1964 they carried repair teams, generators, engines, and fuel to the isolated coastal bases. Hence, Sea Force LSMs, which formerly made the runs, were freed for other duty.[38]

---

[38]NAG, Historical Review, 1964, pp. 6-8, 12; End of Tour Reports, Evenson M. Burtis, of 24 Jun 1964; Donald A. Still, of 8 Aug; J.P. Tyson, of 5 Feb 1965; W. F. Calloway, of 12 Jan; LeRoy R. Hagey, of 30 Mar; Completion Reports, MTT 2-64, n.d.; MTT 7-64, of 15 May 1964; MTT 2-65, ser 2141-100 of 15 Dec; NAG, Fact Sheets, of 6 Jan 1964; 27 May; 7 Oct; NAG, "Country Logistics Improvement Plan," of 13 Jan 1964; NAG, "Summary of Military Assistance Advisory Effort," 27 Dec 1964-2 Jan 1965, ser 08 of 6 Jan 1965; CHNAG, memo, ser 0065 of 6 Jul 1964; ltr, CHNAG to CO VNN, ser 761 of 8 Jul; msgs, COMUSMACV 120110Z Sep; Gray et al., "Revolutionary Warfare on Inland Waterways," pp. 59-60.

The An Xuyen Quarantine

As directed by the South Vietnamese Victory Plan, and in line with recommendations of the Bucklew Report, the navy mounted a major effort during 1964 to inhibit Communist movement in the Gulf of Siam and off the Mekong Delta coast, especially around the southernmost province of An Xuyen. Credible intelligence reports indicated that Viet Cong arms, ammunition, and supplies were moving from the Cambodian border area to offshore islands, primarily Phu Quoc, and then to the coast of An Xuyen and Kien Giang Provinces. In January 1964, the Vietnamese Navy initiated an operation, soon known as the An Xuyen Quarantine, to interdict this Communist traffic. Routinely, the patrol force consisted of 1-3 PCEs, 1 LSIL, and 4 PGMs (except during the heavy weather of the southwest monsoon) and 70 junks from eight coastal divisions. An AKL or YOG periodically replenished the patrol force.

American destroyers *Philip* (DD-498), *Lyman K. Swenson*, and *Berkeley* (DDG-15) steamed with Vietnamese units in the Gulf of Siam on several occasions during the year and SP-2 patrol aircraft from Tan Son Nhut Airfield and from Vung Tau flew a number of coastal surveillance missions in support of the An Xuyen Quarantine. These were only short, one-time operations, however. The coastal patrol effort was the primary responsibility of the Vietnamese Navy and its ships and craft.[39]

The An Xuyen Quarantine area consisted of a small sector around Panjang Island, which was patrolled by one junk division, and three major sectors — the waters off the northwestern coast of An Xuyen Province, Phu Quoc Island, and the Camau Peninsula. The Sea Force ships were usually distributed equally among the latter three areas. Each patrol ship operated with several junks drawn from coastal divisions based in the Gulf of Siam. Junks patrolled inshore in groups of at least two or three, while Sea Force ships patrolled up to ten miles out to sea. The larger units used their communications, radar, and firepower for long-range surveillance and gunfire support and for vectoring Coastal Force junks to suspicious contacts. Although assigned to a specific station, Sea Force ships had

---

[39] NAG, Historical Review, 1964, p. 16; NAG, Briefing, 8-14 Nov 1964; Naval Advisory Board, "An Xuyen Quarantine," encl. 5, p. 5; Naval History Division, "History of U.S. Naval Operations in the Vietnam Conflict, 1965-1967," unpublished history in Naval Historical Center, 1971, pt. 1, p. 230; msgs, CP 082044Z Feb 1964; CPFLT 152159Z; COMDESRON9 020300Z May.

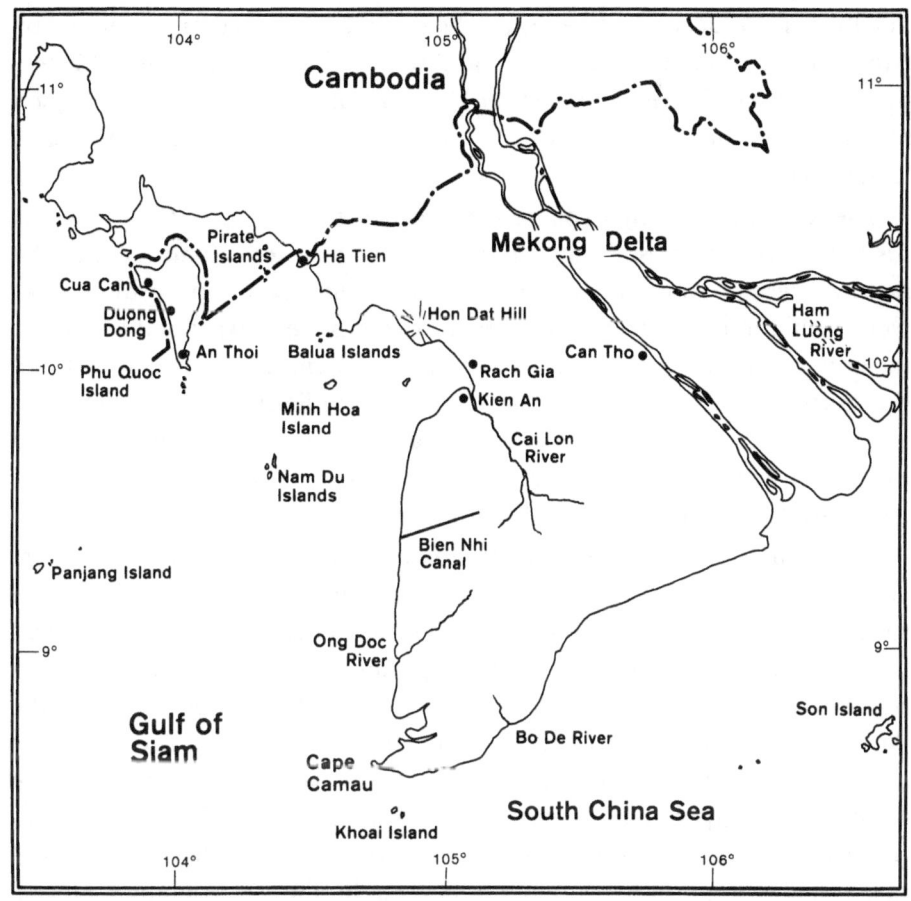

Area of the An Xuyen Quarantine

orders to make random cruises along the coast to establish the government's presence.

The senior Sea Force commander assigned to the operation served as the officer in tactical control. From his ship he commanded the numerous junks and other patrolling vessels. Bypassing the IV Naval Zone commander and the Coastal Force district commanders, he reported directly to the Operations Officer (N-3) on the Vietnamese CNO's staff. However, this arrangement proved faulty because the commander often was isolated from his command while at sea. Further, Sea Force ships and their officers were rotated every month, disrupting command continuity.

Finally, on 16 December 1964, partly as a result of recommendations by American naval advisors, the command structure was reorganized. Hence, the 4th Coastal District commander based ashore at An Thoi was assigned operational control of the An Xuyen Quarantine under the IV Naval Zone commander.[40]

The quarantine employed several tactics to interdict infiltration. A restricted zone was established five kilometers to sea, along most of the northwestern coast of An Xuyen Province, where boats and fishing junks were forbidden to operate. The restricted zones were expanded in June to include most of the western coast of the Camau Peninsula and the northern coast of Phu Quoc Island. From a military point of view, the concept made sense, and American naval advisors favored it. But to exclude fishermen from economically vital areas was politically difficult. As a result, the Vietnamese did not enforce the ban.

A similar fate befell the tactic of creating free-fire zones in Viet Cong-controlled territory. During 1964 the Vietnamese established only one such zone, at the tip of the Camau Peninsula. Hence, ships in that area could conduct harassing fire without permission. The Bucklew Report recommended expansion of the concept; and U.S. advisors studying the An Xuyen Quarantine identified the Viet Cong-controlled coastline between Ha Tien and Rach Gia, the northern coast of Phu Quoc, and the coast of An Xuyen from Kien An to the mouth of the Bo De River as other promising areas for free-fire zones. Admiral Felt, however, recognized that such an indiscriminate policy might alienate friendly civilians. The Vietnamese shared these concerns and declined to so designate these areas.

While there was only one free-fire zone, Sea Force ships often carried out previously approved shore bombardment missions. Since none of the sixteen Sea Force ships with 3-inch/50-caliber guns possessed modern fire-control systems, the fire was often inaccurate, especially during indirect fire missions, when target spotting was difficult. To improve indirect fire techniques, in October U.S. advisors recommended procedures for air-spotted and preplotted missions, which produced excellent results for the Vietnamese in exercises conducted during the month.

---

[40]Memo, Senior Junk Force Advisor to Senior Forces Advisor, of 29 May 1964. See also ltr, A34.6 to A34, of 7 Jul; W. A. Hoch, End of Tour Report, 1 Jul 1964.; Naval Advisory Board, "An Xuyen Quarantine," encl. 3, p. 1; encl. 4, pp. 1-2; 3rd Coastal District Advisor, Action Report, of 22 Apr 1964.

The April cruise of Command Junk 471 was typical of operations in the Gulf of Siam during 1964. It involved the boarding of 150 junks and sampans, during which the crew checked identification papers of Vietnamese seafarers, searched for contraband, and detained suspects, whom they turned over to provincial officials for further investigation. The junk operated at three separate check points, one near Phu Quoc Island, another in the Balua Island chain, and a third at the mouth of the Cai Lon River, without finding enemy contraband. Then, toward the end of the patrol, on 14 April, the junk chased and fired on a 40-foot fishing boat fleeing toward the beach. When the Viet Cong returned fire from entrenched shore positions, the junkmen withdrew and called in air strikes. The next day, the command junk discovered several men transferring food and clothing from a boat to a small sampan in the Ben Nhi Canal. Three men escaped in the sampan, but the junk crew captured the suspicious boat and turned it over to Coastal Division 43 headquarters.[41]

While coastal and open-sea patrol was the primary responsibility of the units in the An Xuyen operation, naval gunfire support of friendly forces afloat and ashore also was important. In one instance, in January 1964, PCE *Chi Lang II* (HQ-08) bombarded enemy shore defenses from which four Coastal Division 43 junks drew fire. In July, another Sea Force ship, this time a PGM, silenced enemy gunners who attacked Coastal Division 44 units from positions on Hon Dat Hill northwest of Rach Gia. The following month, just after midnight on the 27th, an LSIL used its 81-millimeter mortar and machine guns to drive off a Viet Cong company that attacked the Coastal Division 34 base at the mouth of the Ham Luong River.[42]

---

[41]Msg, COMUSMACV 170525Z Jan 1964; R.P.W. Murphy and E.F. Black, "The South Vietnamese Navy," USNIP, Vol. 90 (Jan 1964), p. 60; NAG, "Vietnamese Navy's Role in the Counterinsurgency," of 12 Jun 1964; 3rd Coastal District Advisor, Action Report, of 22 Apr 1964.

[42]W. A. Hoch, End of Tour Report, of 1 Jul 1964; ltr, Coastal Force Advisory Detachment 6 to CHNAG, of Mar 1965; Advisory Board to Study Critical Operations, "An Xuyen Quarantine Operation," of 31 Dec 1964; NAG, Briefing, 8-14 Nov 1964; NAG, Monthly Evaluations, 1964; msg, COMUSMACV 101011Z Aug 1964; Naval History Division, "History of U.S. Naval Operations Vietnam, 1964," of 22 Jan 1970, p. 182; NAG, "Progress 12-18 April 1964;" NAG, "Progress 14-20 June 1964;" memo, CHNAG to COMUSMACV, ser 0069 of 9 Jul 1964; Advisory Board, "An Xuyen Quarantine," encl. 5, p. 13; NAG, Historical Review, 1964, pp. 11, 16; ltr, Hardcastle to Commanding General U.S. Army Support Command, ser 0173 of 4 Jun 1964; NAG, Monthly Evaluations, 1964; Gordon E. Abercrombie, End of Tour Report, of 8 Apr 1965; Bucklew Report; VNN OPORD of 3 Jan 1964; msgs, CP 030513Z Jul 1964; COMUSMACV 131221Z; 071023Z Sep.

Vietnamese naval forces also were charged with civic action duties, as the April patrol of Command Junk 471 off An Xuyen demonstrated. After each junk search was completed, the Vietnamese sailors distributed matches, magazines, soap, calendars, an medicine. Moreover, they called at a number of islands off the west coast of An Xuyen, where no government representative had visited for years. On 3 April, in the Pirate Island group, the boat's corpsman held sick call for 300 people from eight surrounding islands. Three days later, at Minh Hoa Island, the corpsman set up a medical station, one of five established during the patrol, and trained the local village teacher in first aid. During its entire patrol the junk's crew treated 5,000 people, showed movies to another 5,000, and distributed 200 pounds of candy and 100 articles of clothing.

Although these missions were important, the success of the An Xuyen campaign depended on effective ocean patrolling and in this the Vietnamese naval force was deficient. At the beginning of 1964, Lieutenant Hoch, the 4th Coastal District advisor, found most of the Coastal Force junks "in port or hiding behind islands." He added that he "put them at sea but am sure that they returned as soon as I got out of sight." He further concluded that "the Sea Force if anything is worse."[43] Apparently, little had changed by October when Captain Hardcastle reported that "it appears that patrol ships are almost always not in their patrol areas and almost all are anchored."[44] Lieutenant Donald C. Schroder, another Coastal Force advisor, was more optimistic regarding the operational performance of the junk units as well as the effectiveness of the command structure. However, his overall appraisal of the military situation in the Mekong Delta coastal regions at the end of 1964 was less sanguine. He commented that "in speaking of VC controlled areas, I have seen a gradual loss of land and waterways to the VC in the last several months, and the war effort has gradually gone down hill."[45]

Through the end of 1964, the naval task force in the Gulf of Siam searched 211,121 junks, of which 316 were seized as suspected enemy craft. The South Vietnamese sailors conducted identity searches of 889,335 persons during the year. Of this number, 1,938 persons were detained for further interrogation. But this great effort notwithstanding,

---

[43]Msg, Coastal District Phu Quoc 091630H Feb 1964.
[44]Memo, Hardcastle to A-10, of 20 Oct 1964. See also CHNAG, Briefing for MAAG Senior Advisors Conference, of May 1964.
[45]Donald C. Schroder, End of Tour Report, of 14 Jan 1965.

only 11 individuals were confirmed as Viet Cong. U.S. naval officers suspected that some enemy craft evaded the blockade and delivered their cargo ashore, especially at night. But the magnitude of the South Vietnamese coastal patrol effort and the meager results convinced many U.S. advisors that significant infiltration was not occurring. Lieutenant Hoch reported, after eighteen months as an advisor in the Camau Peninsula area, long a Communist stronghold, that he found no evidence of intense enemy waterborne movement. He shared the belief held by many U.S. naval advisors that, with control of much of the delta's land routes and virtual freedom of navigation on the area's innumerable waterways, the Communists had no real need to use the sea route from Cambodia.[46]

Mekong Delta Operations

Coincident with the patrol operation to limit enemy movement along the Mekong Delta coast, the Vietnamese Navy stepped up its efforts to counter the Communist threat to the strategically vital interior. The Vietnamese Navy's operations in this region during 1964 increasingly were focused on the river patrol mission rather than the army-navy assault role. This new emphasis resulted from recognition by Vietnamese naval leaders, as well as Admiral Felt, Captain Hardcastle, and the Bucklew group, that the Vietnamese Navy's resources had not been efficiently employed in the past by the army command. Many army leaders understood little of naval tactics and were reluctant to assign ground troops for riverine missions. But along the narrow, heavily foliated canals and rivers of the delta, they were essential for protecting the naval craft. Despite U.S. and Vietnamese Navy recommendations that marines or paramilitary troop units be assigned permanently to the river assault groups, however, the army-dominated Joint General Staff did not concur. As a result, a vigorous joint riverine campaign was not realized.

To avoid idling units, the navy's River Force increasingly deployed combat craft on the major waterways in search of Communist infiltrators. The pattern of these operations was revealed on a typical day in February 1964, when 32 of the 67 operational River Force ships and craft were on

---

[46]W. A. Hoch, End of Tour Report, of 1 Jul 1964.

patrol while 7 supported ground actions. Convoy escort occupied 11 others; 7 were stationed in the Saigon area; 4 were assigned to province chiefs; and 6 were engaged in training exercises. Each day during the last week in June, an average of 28 vessels conducted patrols while 10 supported the army. By October, only 8 percent of River Force units carried out assault actions with ground troops.[47] Despite the concentration on patrolling, the River Force uncovered little enemy contraband or personnel. During 1964, the naval force searched 993 junks, 40 of which were held for further inspection. 3,620 persons were checked for identification and 190 were detained. Only 12 Viet Cong were identified.[48]

In addition to patrols, the navy mounted operations with units from each of its three combat components and the army in critical sectors of the delta, such as the area around the mouths of the Mekong River. The Bucklew Report suggested strengthening patrols in this area and the establishment of stringent curfews on civilian boat traffic, the latter a politically unpopular measure. During April, after urging by U.S. advisors, the Vietnamese government reluctantly approved plans for a curfew for parts of the major rivers in the delta and the inshore waterways of Ba Xuyen and Vinh Binh Provinces. The plans designated a large curfew zone fifteen kilometers off the coast, where any boat could be attacked without warning. Fishing boats were allowed along the Ba Xuyen coast, from the shoreline to three kilometers seaward, only if they showed running lights. On 8 April, the curfew went into effect on the Co Chien River, at the mouth of the Bassac, and on the Mekong near Cao Lanh at the Cambodian border.[49]

Although the Vietnamese River Force had primary responsibility for enforcing inland curfews, Sea Force ships assisted with gunfire support, river mouth blockade, and the transportation of combat troops and

---

[47]David J. Anthony, End of Tour Report, of 16 Mar 1965; F.J. Barnes, III, End of Tour Report, of 17 Jun 1965; David N. Orrik, End of Tour Report, of 26 Mar 1965; ltrs, Cang to CICRVNAF; NAG, ser 1166 of 9 Oct 1964; Bucklew Report; memo, OP-60 to CNO, ser BM000954-64 of 29 Jun. James W. Johnson, *River and Canal Ambush Problems, Republic of Vietnam, 1962*, Washington: (Research Analysis Corporation Study, 1963), pp. 47-48; NAG, "Waterway Barricades;" NAG, Monthly Evaluation Report, Oct 1964; msgs, COMUSMACV 290955Z Jun 1964. Wootten, Interview, p. 11; T. T. Beattie, Jr., End of Tour Report, of 16 Dec 1964.
[48]MACV, Weekly Reports, 1964; NAG, "Vietnamese Navy's Role in the Counterinsurgency," of 12 Jun 1964.
[49]Msg, COMUSMACV 140127Z Apr 1964; Charles J. Timmes, Debriefing Report, of 10 Jun 1964.

supplies. In November, the success of these operations led the Naval Advisory Group chief, Captain Hardcastle, to urge the South Vietnamese to expand the Sea Force role there. As a result, three ships were permanently assigned to the river mouth patrol[50]

Units of the Vietnamese Navy occasionally raided Viet Cong bases in the same area. Representative of this action was Operation Sea Dog, a joint army-navy effort which was commanded personally by the Chief of Staff of the Vietnamese Navy. It began on 4 January 1964, when LST *Cam Ranh*, PGM *Phu Du* (HQ-600), and LSIL *Than Tien* (HQ-328) sailed from Saigon for My Tho, where the LST embarked an army battalion. At 0600 on 6 January, the LST reached Ilo Ilo Island at the mouth of the My Tho River and bombarded landing beaches while the troops boarded six landing craft for an assault. The soldiers secured their objective, despite antipersonnel mines and enemy fire, and during the next two days destroyed a Viet Cong medical training center and two munitions factories. Naval commandos, the LDNN, destroyed six Viet Cong junks. Amphibious ships and Coastal Force junks supporting the Ilo Ilo assault blockaded the island. The LSIL fired 81-millimeter mortars, while an LCM picked up captured equipment or ferried water to the beach for the thirsty troops. The six junks of Coastal Division 33 searched twelve boats and sank nineteen others. Vectored by the LSIL to suspicious craft, four River Force STCANs searched ten of the boats. Of the estimated thirty Viet Cong on the island, one was killed and one was wounded. The rest evaded the sweep.

The secondary mission of the operation was to relocate the population of Ilo Ilo to the mainland. On 7 January a psychological warfare team explained the relocation plan to the people. The group of fifty-one men, women, and children was then transported in the LST to the mainland where they received food and money to help them reestablish their new homes. The navy's ships blockaded the island for three more days, broadcasting propaganda and distributing leaflets to convince the remaining Viet Cong to surrender. Finally, on the 11th, the ships withdrew.[51]

In addition to the Mekong River mouth area, South Vietnamese naval forces were also concerned with securing the approaches to Saigon, as part

---

[50]NAG, "Briefing Given General Westmoreland," ser 00121 of 16 Nov 1964.
[51]Operating Forces Advisor, Action Report, "Operation Sea Dog I Phase I, 6-8 Jan 1964," of 12 Jan 1964.

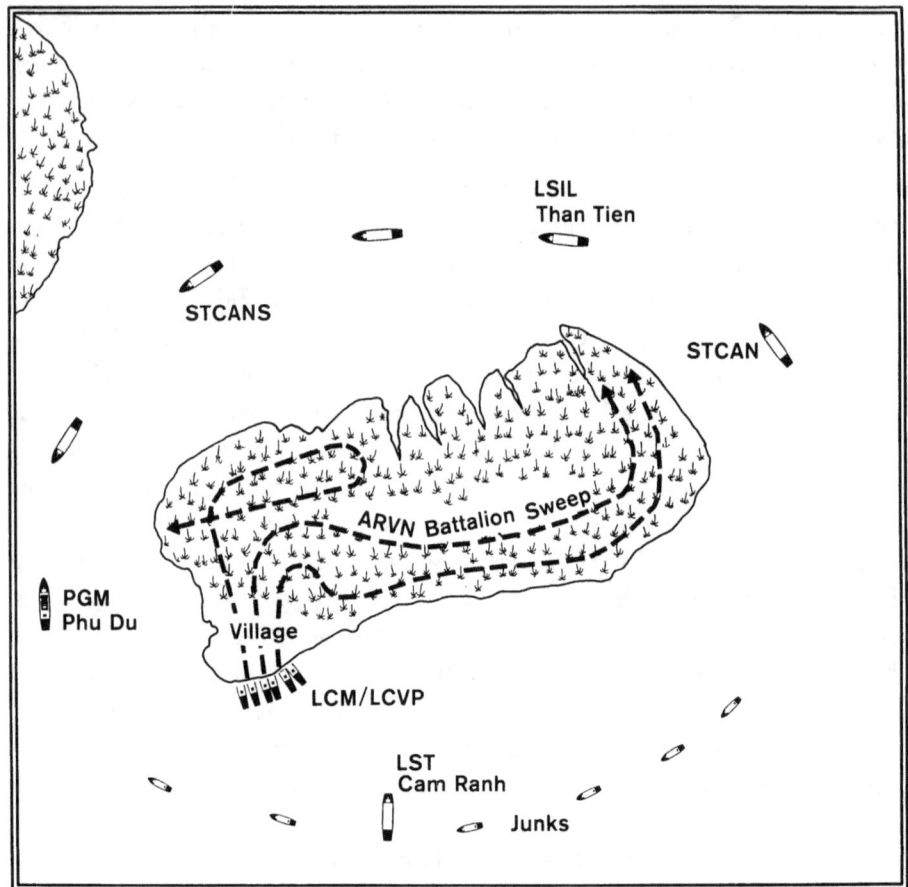

Joint Operation at Ilo Ilo Island

of a general strategy to secure the provinces around the capital. Ships bound for the capital passed Vung Tau, on a peninsula at the mouth of the ship channel, and followed forty-six miles of winding river to the city. The Long Tau River was one of many rivers which traversed the Rung Sat, a thirty by thirty-five kilometer mangrove swamp at the northeastern edge of the Mekong Delta. The Rung Sat was both a haven for an estimated 200 local Viet Cong and a rest area for neighboring Communist units.

On 15 April 1964, the responsibility for securing this strategic area was transferred from the army to the navy. General Khanh felt that the army had not devoted enough attention to this region. Under the new arrangement, the commander of the Rung Sat Special Zone reported to the local River Force commander who came directly under the Vietnamese Navy's headquarters in Saigon. Major Edward J. Bronars, USMC, and two assistants worked in the Rung Sat as advisors. At the end of the year, several other U.S. advisors, including a psychological warfare expert of the U.S. Navy, were assigned to the Rung Sat command.

The Vietnamese commander had at his disposal two paramilitary companies of about 200 men each, plus eight to ten river craft. Sea Force ships were attached for specific operations. Also, the Vietnamese converted eight of the twelve MLMSs received in 1963 to armored motor launches with one 50 and two 30-caliber machine guns and shields for gunners and the coxswain. The reconfigured craft began operating on the rivers in the Rung Sat in April. The other four MLMSs were used for training at Vung Tau.

Mining of these constricted waterways, however, was still a threat. To diminish the risk, LCVPs from the 22nd RAG, the rapid reaction unit based at Nha Be, swept the Long Tau, the main shipping channel, four times a week and the Soirap, an alternate channel, twice a week. At the end of 1964, Captain Hardcastle appointed a board to survey anti-mining operations in the critical Rung Sat. That group reported that much progress had been made during the year to improve security, but recommended an even greater effort in the coming months. Even though no minings occurred during 1964, the board cautioned that the Viet Cong could be waiting for the best moment tactically or psychologically to close the channel.[52]

In addition to minesweeping, the River Force periodically mounted operations against Viet Cong strongholds in the Rung Sat. In one instance, on 16 April, 2 LCMs, supported by 1 LSIL command ship, 1 monitor, 4 STCANs, and 3 junks from Coastal Division 33, embarked two companies of South Vietnamese troops. Their objective was to destroy two Viet Cong companies which threatened the junk base at Ly Nhon. The Vietnamese also hoped to catch troops resting there while moving between Long An and Go Cong Provinces. The 2 LCMs disembarked their troops at 0600 as the LSIL fired her 3-inch guns at suspected Viet Cong concentrations.

---

[52] E. J. Bronars, transcript of interview with Oscar P. Fitzgerald, Naval Historical Center, in Little Creek, VA, 22 Apr 1975; NAG, Monthly Evaluation, Apr 1964; Bucklew Report; NAG, Fact Sheets, N-5, N-13, of 7 Oct 1964; NAG, Historical Review, 1964, p. 10; Advisory Board, "Long Tau-Soirap River Area Security," of 30 Nov 1964.

Meanwhile, the monitor, the junks, and the STCANs patrolled the banks to block escape across the Soirap River. Firing ceased at 0830, shortly after the troops had landed. The 1,100 South Vietnamese soldiers encountered a thirty-man Viet Cong platoon and, in a twenty-minute firefight, killed three of the enemy and captured three. Making no further contact, the troops reembarked at 1400.

Later in 1964, RAG units participated in the first joint army-navy-air force assault operation in the Rung Sat. The action began at dawn on 24 December with a Vietnamese Sea Force diversionary bombardment north of the target, a Viet Cong supply base near the mouth of the Soirap River. The bombardment was followed by Vietnamese Air Force strikes. Then, helicopters and River Force craft landed paramilitary forces to secure the objective. The operation resulted in the seizure of 600 kilograms of rice, 10 sampans, 1 motorized junk, and 50 rounds of Russian-made ammunition.

As in An Xuyen Province, free-fire zones were established in the Rung Sat in 1964. Sea Force ships transiting the Saigon shipping channel, ships engaged in training exercises, and ships directed to support besieged Rung Sat hamlets fired shore bombardment missions into these areas. An L-19 Cessna aircraft, assigned to the Rung Sat commander, usually spotted for the bombarding ships. The 3-inch guns on board Sea Force ships, with a range of 9,000 yards, could cover the entire zone during a five-hour cruise, while three ships stationed at predetermined locations could blanket the zone simultaneously. A typical mission took place on 24 October, when LSMs *Huong Giang* and *Hau Giang* (HQ-406) shelled Viet Cong training and staging areas. During the operation, Lieutenant Keith L. Christensen, a U.S. advisor, flew overhead in the L-19 to direct Vietnamese fire. He termed the fire of *Hau Giang* the most accurate he had observed from the Vietnamese Navy.[53]

Although the Vietnamese Army and Navy were successful in a number of operations, especially in the river mouth and Rung Sat regions, their control over much of the Mekong Delta during 1964 was lost to the enemy. The Viet Cong extended their influence throughout the area, mauling government forces and dispersing paramilitary units. In April, for

---

[53]Advisory Board, "Long Tau-Soirap River Area Security," encl. 11, p. 1-2; NAG, Historical Review, 1964, p. 14; Naval History Division, "History of U.S. Naval Operations, Vietnam, 1964," unpublished history in Naval Historical Center, 1970, p. 203.

A converted LCM monitor and three STCAN patrol craft of the Vietnamese Navy's 25th River Assault Group prepare to depart their base at Can Tho for an operation on the Bassac River.

instance, the Communists overran a district capital in Chuong Thien Province and killed over 300 South Vietnamese soldiers. Concerned by growing Viet Cong power, units of the army and navy often avoided offensive actions, indirectly surrendering control of key land areas and waterways to the enemy. With the South Vietnamese armed forces unable to reverse the course of events, by December 1964 the region around the capital of the Republic of Vietnam itself was host to regimental-size Viet Cong forces.[54]

The year 1964 was a time of turmoil. The political upheaval following in the wake of the coup against Diem in November 1963 brought nation-building and the military effort to a standstill. The Communists seized the opportunity to attempt to deal South Vietnam a death blow. To help counter this threat, U.S. leaders strengthened the advisory effort by substantially increasing the number of advisors and the level of military aid. In addition, the Navy dispatched the Bucklew team to South Vietnam to evaluate naval operations and recommend improvements in the Vietnamese Navy. The group highlighted the primary importance of interdicting Communist coastal infiltration and securing the inland waterways of the Mekong Delta region.

The Vietnamese Navy registered some progress during 1964. Establishment of the Chief of Naval Operations billet, with its more direct access to the Joint General Staff, and actions to integrate the Coastal Force into the regular navy improved the command structure. The naval service grew in size as the United States provided more ships, craft, weapons, and equipment and supported higher personnel levels. This enabled creation of a seventh river assault group, the development of promising anti-mining and anti-ambush resources, and construction of the more capable Yabuta junks. Training was accelerated with the establishment of new schools for the combat and support forces and deployment to Vietnam of additional U.S. mobile training teams. The supply system was better organized and new repair facilities and parts depots were opened.

Nonetheless, by the end of the year, the Vietnamese Navy was less able than it had been to fight the war. The officer corps, disorganized by the Diem coup, was hindered further by the political intrigue, inexperience,

---

[54]Sharp and Westmoreland, *Report on the War in Vietnam*, pp. 83-95; *U.S.-V.N. Relations*, bk. 3, pt. IVC.1, pp. 30-46, 58-76; Westmoreland, *A Soldier Reports*, pp. 62-85.

and lack of motivation of many of its leaders. The combat forces were unable to deploy consistently a sizeable proportion of their units for primary missions because of diversions for secondary duties, poor preventive maintenance of vessels, and overloaded repair facilities. In addition, low recruiting and desertion caused serious personnel shortages in the Coastal Force. The Sea Force, the River Force, and the especially troubled Coastal Force, discovered little Communist infiltration into the Mekong Delta or movement on its waterways, even though the evidence now available suggests a significant enemy effort that year. Despite a number of successful actions along the An Xuyen coast, at the mouths of the Mekong River, and in the Rung Sat, the Vietnamese Army and Navy were losing control of the vital delta region. It became increasingly clear that the South Vietnamese Navy required more than U.S. advisors and material assistance to stem the rising enemy tide.

CHAPTER XII

Naval Support to the Counterinsurgency Struggle

Increasingly frustrated in attempts to revitalize the foundering politico-military effort in South Vietnam, the administration of President Lyndon B. Johnson focused greater attention in late 1963 and early 1964 on the insurgency's base of aid and command control — North Vietnam. Johnson's strategists concluded that bringing war to the North Vietnamese in increasing measure would sap their will to continue the struggle. At the same time, U.S. civilian and military leaders continued the in-country programs to win the support of the South Vietnamese people for their government and to diminish the Communist threat to internal security.[1]

Plans for intensified covert action against Hanoi were under review for most of 1963. In May of that year, the JCS directed CINCPAC to develop a program of U.S. military support for South Vietnamese covert, hit and run actions against North Vietnam. In keeping with the guidance drawn up after the Bay of Pigs, large covert operations were controlled by the Defense Department. Hence, Admiral Felt, who also pressed for such a program, had his staff prepare Operation Plan 34, which he dispatched to Washington on 17 June. But, various difficulties, including delays in the operational employment in the Western Pacific of two fast patrol boats (PTF), to be used in the maritime phase of the plan, prevented quick approval and implementation of the proposed program. Further, the Diem government, preoccupied with internal political troubles, evinced little enthusiasm for these extraterritorial actions.

The pace quickened in the last two months of 1963. General Harkins found Diem's successors more amenable to expanded operations and on 18 November the general informed Admiral Felt that the "climate is

---

[1] Memo, OP-09A to OP-002, of 21 May 1963; JCS, *History*, pt. 1, pp. 7-37—7-39.

right" for the contemplated program.² On 20 November, at the Secretary of Defense conference in Honolulu, COMUSMACV and the CIA's Chief of Far Eastern Operations, William Colby, were ordered to prepare a twelve-month, three-phase plan for actions against North Vietnam in a campaign of graduated intensity. The final program was to draw heavily upon CINCPAC's work, and indeed would be labeled Operation Plan 34A. The new president allowed planning for covert operations against the North to proceed as before. Johnson, however, cautioned that the credibility of a U.S. denial of involvement, the degree of destruction to be expected in the North, possible North Vietnamese retaliation, and the worldwide reaction should be taken into account.³

Throughout the month of December 1963, Vietnamese, MACV, CIA, Seventh Fleet, and CINCPACFLT representatives made urgent preparations to refine the maritime aspect of the plan, to outline command relationships, and to ready the boats, men, and equipment for the prospective actions. On 18-19 December, a conference proposed by General Harkins to discuss modifications to the PTFs and their future support at Danang was convened at the Subic Bay Naval Base. The conferees agreed that the boats would be stripped of the 40-millimeter gun forward and non-essential equipment, and fuel tanks added to enable fast, long-range forays into North Vietnamese waters. A naval Mobile Support Team, initially consisting of eleven men; the 100-ton tool-machinery package for on-site repair and maintenance support; and necessary spare parts were scheduled to arrive in Danang on 15 February 1964. It was anticipated that the boats and their crews would be ready to deploy from Subic by 20 March.⁴

The speed of preparation was accelerated on 20 December, following a Secretary of Defense conference in Saigon. At that time, Secretary of Defense McNamara reviewed and approved the concept of operations of the completed plan 34A and "showed great interest in developing full

---

²Msg, CP 182345Z Nov 1963. See also U.S.G. Sharp, *Strategy For Defeat: Vietnam in Retrospect* (San Rafael, CA: Presidio Press, 1978), pp. 28-29; JCS, *History*, pt. 1, pp. 7-37—7-39.
³*U.S.-V.N. Relations*, bk. 3, pt. IVC.1, pp. 1-7; pt. IVC.2a, pp. 1-2; msg, CP 301841Z Nov 1963; Chester L. Cooper, *The Lost Crusade, America in Vietnam* (New York: Dodd, Mead and Co., 1970), p. 224; Lyndon B. Johnson, *The Vantage Point: Perspectives of the Presidency, 1963-1969* (New York: Holt, Rinehart and Winston, 1971), pp. 42-46; JCS, *History*, pt. 1, pp. 7-39, 8-1.
⁴Msgs, CPFLT 062104Z Nov 1963; CNO 182315Z; CP 301933Z; CNO 061959Z Dec; 062029Z; BUSHIPS 062351Z; COMUSMACV 070407Z; CPFLT 100649Z; 110357Z; 130321Z; CNO 132115Z; COM7FLT 160630Z; Commander Naval Base, Subic 190615Z.

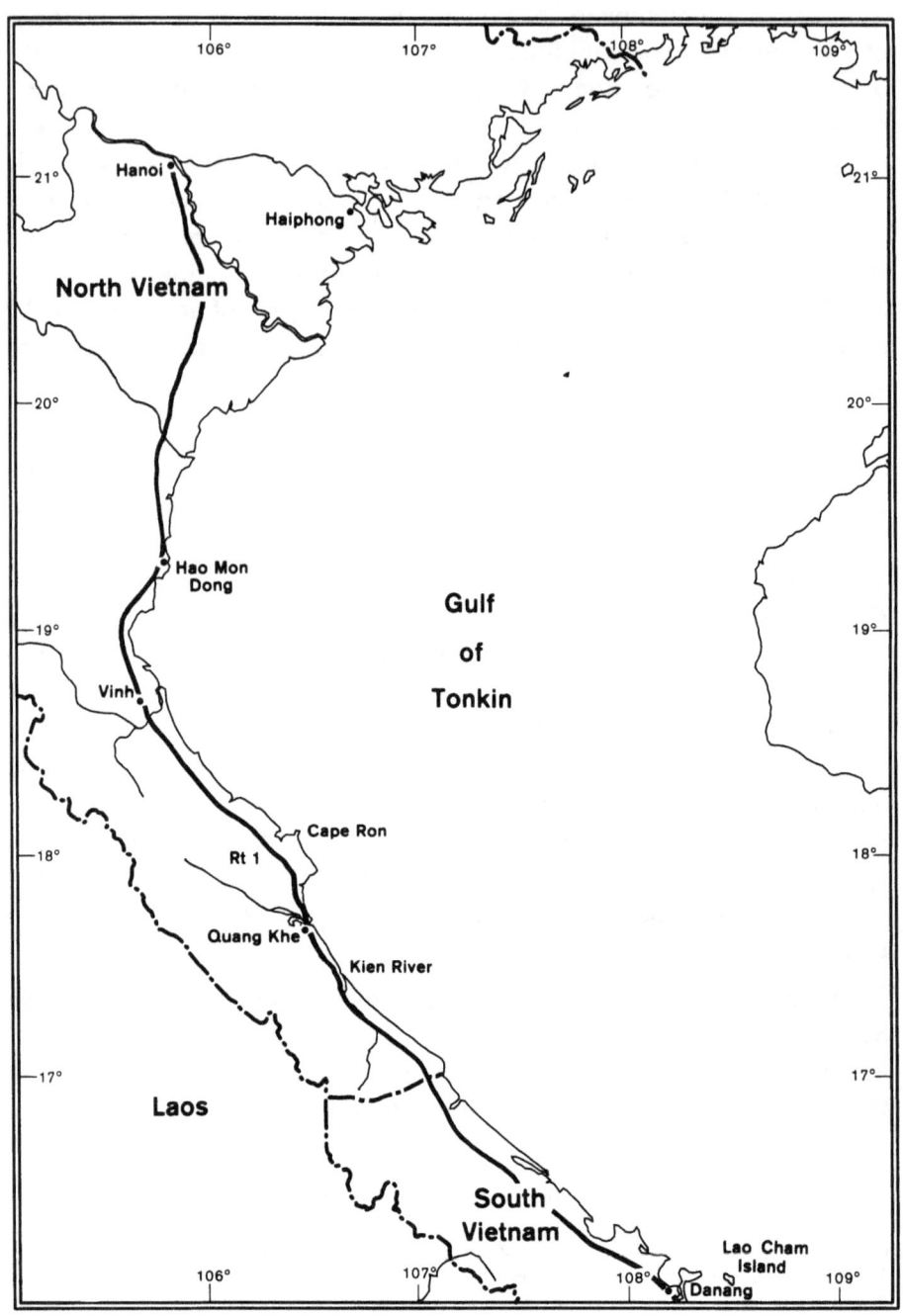

Coast of North Vietnam

capability for early implementation of several actions" contemplated.[5] When Admiral Felt expressed his view that the few Nastys and Swift boats available would only be capable of small-scale actions, the Secretary of Defense directed the Navy to purchase four more Nastys from the Norwegian government, to "be made available in Vietnam for maximum readiness [as soon as possible]."[6] The Secretary of Defense also called for the deployment to the Western Pacific of PTF-1 and PTF-2, the two American-made boats then serving with the Atlantic Fleet.

CINCPAC, appraising the dangers inherent in the proposed operations, observed that "the U.S. must be prepared to back up RVN [Republic of Vietnam] and be willing to commit U.S. forces in the event reaction from DRV and CHICOMS escalates to a threshold beyond RVN capabilities or [possibly] if actions in this plan are not sufficiently persuasive."[7] For these reasons, provisions for expanded U.S. support or the commitment of forces to counter Communist escalation were incorporated into the final plan, which then was carried by hand to Washington. McNamara informed President Johnson the following day, 21 December, that the 34A plan was "an excellent job...[presenting] a wide variety of...operations against North Vietnam from which I believe we should aim to select those that provide maximum pressure with minimum risk."[8]

As Operation Plan 34A underwent review at the highest levels of the administration, the naval command quickened the pace of preparations for the maritime phase by advancing deadlines for completing the boat modifications and providing personnel and logistic support. The Bureau of Ships was directed to obtain the additional Nastys and, on the last day of 1963, the CNO, Admiral McDonald, authorized Commander in Chief, U.S. Atlantic Fleet, to initiate action to transfer the U.S.-made PTFs, their crews, and necessary spare parts to Subic Bay.[9]

By mid-January 1964, the continued instability of the South Vietnamese military government convinced U.S. leaders that additional steps were

---

[5]Msg, CP 201807Z Dec 1963.
[6]*Ibid.* See also msgs, CP 180549Z Dec 1963; JCS 211951Z.
[7]Msg, CP 180549Z Dec 1963.
[8]Memo, McNamara to President, of 21 Dec 1963 in Gareth Porter, ed., *Vietnam: The Definitive Documentation of Human Decisions*, Vol. II (Standfordville, NY: Earl M. Coleman Enterprises, Inc., 1979), p. 232.
[9]Msgs, JCS 211951Z Dec 1963; CNO 231723Z; CPFLT 232311Z; COMUSMACV 240325Z; COMSERVPAC 240542Z; Naval Ship Repair Facility Subic 260849Z; CNO 281927Z; CPFLT 282311Z; CNO 312145Z; memos, DEPSECDEF to SECNAV, of 26 and 27 Dec; ltr, CINCPACFLT to CINCPAC, ser 02/001 of 2 Jan 1964.

necessary to reverse the tide. The Johnson administration now felt it essential to demonstrate to the North Vietnamese that their support of the southern insurgency would become increasingly costly. At the same time, some U.S. leaders, in particular General William C. Westmoreland, then Deputy COMUSMACV, felt covert operations "represented probably the only action we could take against the North without provoking a level of reaction which the South Vietnamese would be unable to absorb."[10] On 16 January, President Johnson approved implementation, to begin on 1 February, of Operation Plan 34A. But in keeping with the concept of graduated response, he allowed the execution of only the four-month Phase I segment, which consisted of the least-risk intelligence collection, psychological, and sabotage operations.[11]

At the end of 1963, the CIA relinquished support and control of most covert operations in the North to MACV. Established on 24 January 1964 under General Harkins's command, the Special Operations Group (later Studies and Observation Group), or MACSOG, exercised operational control from Saigon of 34A activities, including maritime operations. However, Washington kept a tight rein on these operations through the Defense Department's Office of the Special Assistant for Counterinsurgency and Special Activities (SACSA), which superseded General Lansdale's Office of Special Operations in the fall of 1963.

Direct oversight of the naval program was exercised by the U.S. Naval Advisory Detachment (NAD) in Danang, the base used by boats operating on missions to the North. Subordinate to NAD was the Mobile Support Team, which consisted of a Repair and Maintenance Team and a Boat Training Team. The former detachment, eventually numbering five officers and forty men, provided unit-level repair and maintenance service for the boats from a floating drydock, placed in operation by Amphibious Construction Battalion 1 in April. The unit also operated a crane barge, and electrical, electronic, carpentry, welding, and machinery repair shops. Major repairs and overhauls were available only in Subic. The Boat Training Team, with two American officers and ten men for each

---

[10] Westmoreland, *A Soldier Reports*, p. 106.

[11] Palmer, in *The McNamara Strategy*, p. 109, avers that the 34A program was the first test of McNamara's use of the Planning Programming Budgeting System (PPBS) to monitor and direct U.S. military actions in support of foreign policy. See also *U.S.-V.N. Relations*, bk. 3, pt. IVC.2(a), pp. 1-4; msg, CP 210314Z Jan 1964; memo, OP-60 to CNO, ser BM000397-64 of 27 Feb 1964; JCS, *History*, pt. 1, pp. 8-3, 8-20—8-23.

Vietnamese boat crew, instructed their counterparts in small craft handling, basic maintenance, and tactics. The NAD also supervised the SEAL Training Team (two officers and ten men) preparing LDNN commandos for their dangerous work, as well as the Marine Reconnaissance Team (one officer and three men), and three fast patrol craft (PCF), or Swift boats.

Except during operations, the naval forces in Danang were commanded by the Naval Operations Support Group, of the Pacific Fleet Amphibious Force, based in Coronado, California. Under this headquarters was SEAL Team 1, which directed the SEAL detachment in Danang. Also subordinate to the Naval Operations Support Group was Boat Support Unit 1. The mission of this unit, established on 1 February 1964 under Lieutenant Burton L. Knight, was to (1) develop, test and evaluate procedures, techniques and equipment and to improve and document tactics in river and restricted water warfare, and (2) to man, maintain and operate assigned craft in support of naval special operations and to provide trained personnel to support the PTF/PGM programs.[12] The Mobile Support Team in Danang, with naval personnel assigned on six-month tours of duty, was the forward area component of Boat Support Unit 1. Because the distance between California and South Vietnam hindered the effective administration and support of the Mobile Support Team, however, in March 1964 Lieutenant Knight took direct charge of the detachment. While HSAS supplied the naval forces with general stores and certain other special supplies, most administrative and logistic support for Danang was channeled through the Subic Bay Naval Base of Commander Naval Forces, Philippines.[13]

In initiating maritime operations, Washington policymakers sought to send a clear signal to Hanoi of U.S. potential for retribution. Initially, however, this communication was muffled. The first phase of the program started slowly. The delays usually associated with establishing base and logistic facilities; deploying boats from the assembly line in Norway

---

[12]Ltr, OICBSU1 to CNO, ser 012 of 15 Sep 1964. See also msg, NOSGPAC 160325Z Mar 1965; Colby, *Honorable Men*, p. 219; Colby, Interview; Merdinger, "Civil Engineers, Seabees, and Bases in Vietnam," p. 264; Bucklew, Interview with Mason, pp. 317-22, 358-60; Mulford, Interview.

[13]Msgs, CP 292126Z Jan 1964; CPFLT 280342Z Feb; COMNAVPHIL 021003Z Mar; JCS 271625Z; ltr, CINCPACFLT to CNO/CINCPAC, ser 61/00527 of 16 Jul; memo, OP-01 to CNO, ser BM61-64 of 15 Jun; MACV, Command History, 1964, Ann. A, pp. I-1—I-2, IV-13—IV-16; Westmoreland, *A Soldier Reports*, pp. 106-07; BSU1, Command History, 1967; NOSGPAC, Command History, 1963-1966.

directly to the operating area in Southeast Asia; creating a necessary spare parts pipeline for the Nastys, Swifts, and the American-made PTs; and assembling trained U.S. and Vietnamese personnel were aggravated by seasonal heavy weather. In addition, a period of adjustment was required to test boats, men, equipment, and operational techniques.

PTF-3 and PTF-4, the Norwegian-built Nastys that had been in Subic since the preceding fall, were soon ready for deployment to the forward operating base at Danang early in 1964. After removal of their forward 40-millimeter gun to allow installation of fuel tanks, the boats were loaded on board *Carter Hall* for the transit. On 22 February, the first two PTFs arrived at their destination, after the six-month transit from Norfolk. Unfortunately, during off-loading PTF-3 was smashed into the ship by a freak swell, causing severe damage to the hull and necessitating return to Subic for repairs. The boat rejoined PTF-4 in Danang at the end of the month.

In the meantime, the other six boats were expeditiously delivered to Subic. SS *Pioneer Myth* departed Norfolk on 19 January 1964 with PTF-1 and PTF-2 on board and entered Subic Bay during the first week of February. Purchased from the Norwegian government, four Nastys, designated PTF-5, PTF-6, PTF-7, and PTF-8, were shipped from Bergen, Norway, on 1 February in *Point Barrow* (AKD-1). The ship arrived in the Philippines on 3 March. From March until the end of May 1964, these boats underwent time-consuming but essential modifications at the Ship Repair Facility and conducted sea trials to test the work done. Leaking fuel tanks necessitated their replacement on all the boats, including the two at Danang which returned to Subic for the fifteen-day alteration. Problems with armament caused the greatest delays. Captain Phillip S. Bucklew, Commander Naval Operations Support Group, U.S. Pacific Fleet, felt that the "NASTY Class PTF's are examples of excellent hull and propulsion systems with inadequate armament."[14] Following prolonged study, 81-millimeter mortars were installed on two of the boats as compensation for loss of their 40-millimeter guns.

Problems also arose with PTF-1 and PTF-2, the American-built boats. Although Secretary of Defense McNamara mandated their deployment to Southeast Asia, naval commanders were dubious of their compatibility with the rest of the force. At one point, for example, Admiral Ricketts, the Vice Chief of Naval Operations, noted that the boats were too limited in

---

[14]Ltr, COMNOSGPAC to COMPHIBFORPACFLT, ser 062 of 1 Jun 1964.

range. Further, after an inspection trip to South Vietnam, Admiral Sharp reported to CINCPAC that naval officers in Danang and with MACSOG in Saigon had "misgivings" about the craft and were "somewhat reluctant" to have them in Danang.[15] Nonetheless, the decision was made to keep the two American gasoline-powered boats — or "gassers" — with the force in Danang. In contrast to the Nasty boats, PTF-1 and PTF-2 retained their forward 40-millimeter guns. Two 50-caliber machine guns also were installed amidship on each boat.[16]

These efforts to prepare the boats for the maritime campaign delayed the initial phase of 34A operations and explained some of the problems encountered after 16 February 1964, when the first missions into North Vietnamese waters were launched. On that date, South Vietnamese "frogmen," the LDNN, attempted unsuccessfully to sabotage a ferry on Cape Ron and the Swatow patrol craft at the Quang Khe base. Subsequently, swimmers were again sent against the boats at Quang Khe, with the same result. Attempts to destroy Route 1 bridges below the 18th parallel were twice aborted.

Dissatisfaction among U.S. leaders over the slow progress and limited results of the overall 34A program was enunciated during the spring. For instance, in April the U.S. Ambassador to Saigon, Henry Cabot Lodge, emphatically stated that 34A activities "might be good training but were certainly having no effect on Hanoi."[17] Disenchantment with the 34A program, especially the maritime operation, also was expressed by some naval commanders. Admiral Sharp observed:

> We have spent a lot of time, effort and money on the PTF program. I have been watching this program closely and see...some of our early reservations on the PTF concept becoming reality.... The NVN defensive posture in potential areas may be more extensive and effective than originally assessed.[18]

---

[15]Memo, Sharp to Felt, of 14 Feb 1964. Colby also felt that the American-built boats would create problems. See memo, Colby to Krulak, encl. in memo, Riley to Ricketts, of 4 Jan 1964. See also msg, CNO 102333Z Jan 1964.

[16]Msgs, COMUSMACV, CNO, COMSERVPAC, CPFLT, Naval Ship Repair Facility, Subic, BUSHIPS, Commander Naval Base, Subic, *Carter Hall*, 2 Jan-16 Apr 1964; OP-434, memo for record, No. 0021 of 8 Jan; memos, OP-03 to Director, Joint Staff (JCS), ser 002P43 of 9 Jan; Sharp to Felt, of 14 Feb; OP-343E, of 22 Jun; ltrs, CINCPACFLT to CNO, ser 71/0071 of 5 Feb; CNO to SECNAV, ser 213P43 of 11 Feb; CNO, ser 360P43 of 16 Mar; MACV, Command History, 1964, Ann. A, pp. IV-11—IV-16; Krisel, "Special Maritime Operations in Vietnam," pp. 104-06; Cooper, *Lost Crusade*, p. 228.

[17]Quoted in William P. Bundy, memo for record, of 27 Apr 1964.

[18]Msg, CPFLT 190259Z May 1964.

CINCPACFLT also was concerned that South Vietnamese personnel were not yet prepared for the missions. He stated, "we know that generally for the Vietnamese, under their own leadership, the unexpected circumstance can defeat an entire operation.... The competency of the Vietnamese UDT/SEAL Team has not been fully developed and is a questionable capability."[19] Nevertheless, other key American leaders, including Secretary of Defense McNamara, General Maxwell Taylor, Chairman of the JCS, and General Earl Wheeler, Army Chief of Staff, concluded that some advantage was gained from harassing North Vietnam and causing that country to divert limited resources to its defense. Hence, despite the negligible results achieved before late May 1964, the 34A maritime operation was continued.[20]

The Tempo of the 34A Operation Quickens

By this time, however, the maritime force was better prepared to carry out its mission in the North. Administrative and logistical procedures were better developed, knowledge of the enemy's defenses was greater, and most of the operation's resources were deployed to the forward area. The pier and support building at the port were erected and a fuel tank farm neared completion. Both the Repair and Maintenance Team and the first increment of the Boat Training Team of the Navy's Mobile Support Team were in place. Commodore Cang, the South Vietnamese Chief of Naval Operations, also detailed the cream of his service's volunteers for this dangerous duty. After sixteen weeks of training and limited operation, four Vietnamese boat crews were prepared, in various degrees, for action, as was the SEAL-trained LDNN team.[21]

On 27 May the maritime operation scored its first significant success with the capture of a North Vietnamese junk and subsequent interrogation of its six passengers. The detainees were taken to a special facility on Lao Cham Island off Danang, questioned for intelligence, and released in

---

[19]*Ibid.*
[20]Msgs, JCS 262339Z Mar 1964; COMUSMACV 311037Z; memo, OP-601 to CNO, ser BM000569-64 of 29 Apr; JCS, *History*, pt. 1, pp. 8-22—8-23, 9-11.
[21]Msgs, CP 272258Z May 1964; memo, Sharp to Felt, of 14 Feb 1964; OP-343, memo, of 22 Jun; ltr, Drachnik to Ricketts, of 13 Mar, p. 13.

the North with their junk soon afterward. Thus began a phase of the program that would become a valuable means of gathering intelligence on North Vietnam and a vehicle for conducting psychological warfare activity against the enemy.[22]

In June and July sabotage operations also were attended with success. On June 12 a storage facility was destroyed and two weeks later a Route 1 bridge near Hao Mon Dong was dropped. A sabotage mission carried out on the night of 30 June–1 July clearly demonstrated the hazards but also the opportunity for threatening and harassing the North Vietnamese in their own territory. This action began soon after midnight when PTF-5 and PTF-6 closed the North Vietnamese coast near the mouth of the Kien River and launched rubber boats carrying South Vietnamese attack teams. Unfortunately, the raiding force soon was sighted by a fishing sampan which promptly raised the alarm. Undeterred, the sabotage party scouted the beach with two swimmers, set up a five-man security force on shore, and moved inland to attack the target, a reservoir pump house. After illuminating the building with a 60-millimeter mortar, the team destroyed it with eighteen rounds of 57-millimeter recoilless rifle fire at 0215. Meanwhile, the North Vietnamese surrounded the security force on the beach and took it under heavy fire. But, the PTFs, which were standing by, moved close inshore and shelled the enemy with their 40 and 20-millimeter guns, causing the North Vietnamese attack to subside. At the same time, the landing party fought their way to the beach in hand-to-hand combat and launched their rubber boats. By 0240 PTF-5 had reembarked all but two of the team members, who were believed killed, and set course for Danang. Despite the loss of two men and three abandoned 57-millimeter guns, twenty-two of the enemy were reported killed and the target destroyed. The mission was a success.[23] During July the maritime force conducted several more successful junk captures and psychological warfare actions directed against the Swatow bases at Ben Thuy and Quang Khe. The only failure since May occurred on the night of 15 July, when two men were lost during an aborted attack on a security post near Cape Ron.[24]

---

[22]Msgs, COMUSMACV 031115Z Jun 1964; MACSOG 041100Z; MACV, Command History, 1964, Ann. A, p. IV-2; Westmoreland, *A Soldier Reports*, pp. 108-09.
[23]Msg, MACSOG 022331Z Jul 1964.
[24]MACV, Command History, 1964, Ann. A, p. IV-2; msg, MACSOG 081215Z Jul 1964; Krisel, "Special Maritime Operations in Vietnam," pp. 116-18.

Naval Civic Action in the Pacification Campaign

Although the execution of covert operations against the North commanded increasing attention in early 1964, the effort to foster a closer association of the South Vietnamese people with their government retained a high priority. An occasion to demonstrate the U.S. commitment to the welfare of the South Vietnamese people arose in January 1964 when a cholera epidemic swept the Saigon area, striking over 20,000 inhabitants. Following a request from the South Vietnamese government, CINCPACFLT alerted his Naval Medical Research Unit 2 on Taiwan and soon afterward airlifted the men, supplies, and equipment to Saigon. Throughout late January and February the fifteen-man medical unit, under the command of Captain Robert A. Phillips, treated 1,877 cholera victims, only 2 of whom died. The unit operated from Saigon's *Cho Quan* Infectious Disease Hospital, where it established a three-ward, 160-bed treatment facility. At the same time, members of the naval medical unit instructed 425 Vietnamese physicians, nurses, technicians, and students in the most effective methods for combatting the dread disease. When the team departed South Vietnam on 26 February, the epidemic was largely under control, an achievement the naval unit helped make possible.[25]

The long-standing practice of "showing the flag" to bolster South Vietnamese morale and demonstrate allied solidarity also continued during the year. In January light guided missile cruiser *Providence*, flagship of the Seventh Fleet, called at Saigon to the enthusiastic acclaim of the city's residents. The ship delivered over thirty-eight tons of humanitarian and educational materials as its part in the Navy's Project Handclasp effort to aid underprivileged peoples. Buoyed by the reception accorded the ship and crew, Admiral Moorer, Commander Seventh Fleet, commented that the visit was "certainly a clear demonstration of the stabilizing and reassuring influence of sea power on the political climate of unsettled areas."[26] In the spring, attack transport *Paul Revere* also visited Saigon. The ship's commanding officer, Captain William S. Bradway, and his crew delivered Project Handclasp supplies to a local church serving refugees from North Vietnam.[27] Later in the year, Admiral Moorer's successor,

---

[25]Ltr, CHBUMED to OP-09B92, ser 38 of 11 Feb 1966; State Department, "Memorandum on Situation in South Vietnam," of 13 Jul 1964.
[26]Ltr, Moorer to Ricketts, of 24 Jan 1964.
[27]Friedman, Interview; msg, COMPHIBRON5 200856Z May 1964.

KN-9448

Guided missile cruiser Oklahoma City *(CLG-5), the Seventh Fleet flagship, steams through the Rung Sat swamp enroute to an official port call at Saigon in July 1964.*

Vice Admiral Roy L. Johnson, paid a three-day visit to the South Vietnamese capital in his flagship, *Oklahoma City* (CLG-5).[28] In November, *Princeton* carried 1,000 tons of emergency flood relief supplies from Hong Kong to Quang Ngai. At the same time, *Winston* (AKA-94) and *Bexar* (APA-237) used their ship's boats and landing craft for lighterage services in storm-damaged Danang harbor.

Throughout this period, the Headquarters Support Activity, Saigon, undertook civic action work. The men of the command and their wives

---

[28]COM7FLT, Command History, 1964, p. 7.

distributed food, clothing, furniture, and toys to orphanages. In addition, HSAS personnel erected playgrounds, showed films, and arranged for tours in visiting ships for the South Vietnamese. Most U.S. naval personnel acted spontaneously to better the lot of unfortunate Vietnamese. Captain Friedman, who commanded Headquarters Support Activity, Saigon, until relieved by Captain Archie C. Kuntze in June 1964, stated later:

> It was just such an obvious need and the people didn't need any encouragement, and the support that [the Vietnamese] received from their government was so marginal according to our standards that it was one of those obvious things.[29]

As during the previous year, the Navy's most direct contribution to the counterinsurgency struggle was made by the SEABEEs. In 1964, the State Department's Agency for International Development, in conjunction with the Defense Department, proposed a new use of these personnel. AID's recommendation was that SEABEE well digging teams, working with Army engineers, participate in a rural water supply project, especially by providing needy areas in the Mekong Delta with potable water. The drilling rigs and other equipment were available in-country, but at least seventy skilled personnel were needed to operate the equipment and eventually train the South Vietnamese to take over the job. To coordinate the provision of the Navy's SEABEEs and the Army's engineer personnel, CINCPAC convened a conference on 7 January 1964 at his headquarters. It was determined that the first contingent, composed of fifty SEABEEs and twenty Army engineers, would deploy to South Vietnam at the beginning of March. To prepare for the deployment of the teams, the Construction Battalion Center at Port Hueneme conducted a crash course in deep well drilling operations near the California base. Because of funding difficulties, movement of the first contingent was delayed. But on 18 March, sixteen men under Chief Equipment Operator Willie Gipson from Naval Mobile Construction Battalion 9 departed for Saigon.

COMUSMACV had operational control of the well drilling teams and the United States Operations Mission (USOM), in a combined program with the South Vietnamese, provided the equipment, materials, and

---

[29]Friedman, Interview, p. 17. See also HSAS, Draft History; Moore, *et al.*, "Chaplains With Naval Units in Vietnam."

General William C. Westmoreland, Commander U.S. Military Assistance Command, Vietnam, and Captain Paul J. Knapp, Commanding Officer of Princeton *(LPH-5), on board the ship during flood relief operations off northern South Vietnam in late 1964.*

funding support. The units were commanded, however, by the Naval Construction Battalions, U.S. Pacific Fleet Detachment, Republic of Vietnam. Administrative and personnel support was channeled through this headquarters from Commander Construction Battalions, U.S. Pacific Fleet.

The naval constructionmen, eventually numbering twenty-six individuals, although fifty had been authorized, worked at four separate drilling sites in the Mekong Delta and one on the central Vietnamese coast. Teams 1 and 2 sank their wells at Tan Hiep and Ben Luc, southwest of Saigon.

Team 3 operated at Tac Van, deep in the Viet Cong-controlled province of An Xuyen, and Team 4 drilled at Cat Lo near Vung Tau. Team 5 provided the Army Special Forces camp at Dong Ba Thin, just north of Cam Ranh Bay, with a deep well.

As often in modern naval history, the SEABEEs performed their work in close proximity to the enemy. On 16 July, the Viet Cong triggered a road ambush on a SEABEE truck near isolated Tac Van. Steelworker 2nd Class William W. Trottno, Steelworker Thomas M. Charles, Utilitiesman 2nd Class L. W. Hanson, Equipment Operator 3rd Class W. T. Brown, and Equipment Operator Constructionman E. J. Hoskins all received wounds, fortunately of a superficial nature. In September, the team site was attacked again. This time, two South Vietnamese defenders were killed and the drilling rig was damaged extensively.

By mid-October, the South Vietnamese appeared able to perform the well drilling task with only USOM civilian advisors providing limited assistance. Hence, Lieutenant Commander John R. Wear (CEC), the newly assigned Officer in Charge, Naval Construction Battalions, U.S. Pacific Fleet Detachment, Republic of Vietnam, initiated actions to phase out the Navy's personnel. By the end of the year the existing well drilling program was completed and all but one of the SEABEE teams had left South Vietnam. The remaining unit, Team 5, completed its work at Dong Ba Thin on 10 February 1965. As a result of this SEABEE effort, pure water became available to villagers who previously were forced to rely on tainted sources. Further, South Vietnamese drillers were trained to continue this flow of fresh water to their people.[30]

In addition to the well drilling units, the SEABEE Technical Assistance Teams continued their work in civic action and military construction. At any given time, two teams assisted the Army's Special Forces in erecting fortifications and facilities at isolated border camps, constructed airstrips, and improved roads; two other teams participated in rural pacification efforts under USOM. Based on their record in 1963, the STATs were

---

[30]COMCBPAC, "Helping Others Help Themselves," pp. 40-41; COMCBPAC, Detachment Republic of Vietnam/Thailand, Completion Report, of Oct 1964, pp. 2, 3, 5; COMCBPAC, Detachment Republic of Vietnam, Completion Report, 1963-1972, pp. 3-3, 3-4, 4-9, 5-23—5-25; CINCPAC, Command History, 1964, pp. 348-49; MACV, Command History, 1964, pp. 78-80; Naval History Division, "History of U.S. Naval Operations Vietnam, 1964," pp. 133-34; msgs, CP 072152Z Jan 1964; 082252Z; 292124Z; 260246Z Feb; COMCBPAC 100227Z Mar; CINC-PACFLT, Annual Report, FY1964, p. 65; Tregaskis, *Southeast Asia: Building the Bases*, p. 62; Flag Plot Briefer, of 17 Jul 1964; COM7FLT, Command History, 1964, p. 7.

highly prized for their contribution to the nation-building and counterinsurgency campaign. In fact, after his tour of Southeast Asia, Admiral Ricketts, the Vice Chief of Naval Operations, reported that "there is no doubt that our STATs are turning in an outstanding performance, and doing more than any other similar agency in this area."[31]

This appreciation led the South Vietnamese government and USOM to request a marked increase in the number of STATs deployed to the country. The Saigon officials wanted ten teams for civic action projects, in addition to the technical assistance and well drilling units already scheduled for South Vietnam. Early in 1964, however, CINCPACFLT recommended against an expanded STAT program, because he felt that action would weaken Pacific Fleet SEABEE units and necessitate reduction of other vital construction work in his command area. As an alternative, Admiral Sharp proposed use of SEABEE battalion detachments to perform specific construction tasks. When COMUSMACV reiterated the need for the additional teams, CINCPACFLT responded that manning both the STAT and well drilling units had strained his resources to the maximum. Admiral Sharp also observed that the "counter insurgency experience in RVN is, in my opinion, the most valuable and realistic experience available to today's SEABEEs. Their accomplishments have been outstanding in furthering the interest of the United States." With that in mind, he added: "I would welcome the opportunity to incorporate STAT teams from SEABEE sources outside PACFLT into this highly important and excellent training program."[32]

Several months later, in May 1964, Secretary of Defense McNamara directed CINCPAC to detail future counterinsurgency requirements and the number of STATs to meet them. Admiral Felt concluded that in addition to the present 4 STATs, 12 more STATs and 12 port construction or "waterfront" teams could profitably be put to work in South Vietnam and Thailand. But, it soon became evident that this large increment could not be provided from the Navy's resources because of the fiscal and personnel costs involved. Although the proposal would receive further study, STAT force levels remained the same throughout the year of 1964.[33]

---

[31]Memo, OP-09 to OP-04, ser 010P09 of 10 Feb 1964.
[32]Msg, CPFLT 222147Z Feb 1964.
[33]Memo, OP-60 to OP-40, ser BM0905-64 of 2 Jul 1964; msgs, CPFLT 100951Z Dec 1963; SECSTATE 200520Z; CPFLT 270847Z; CP 160117Z Feb 1964; CPFLT 222147Z; CP 112350Z

As part of the Special Forces program of establishing border posts to monitor and impede Viet Cong infiltration, STAT 0503, under Lieutenant (j.g.) Francis M. Oxley, landed in Saigon on 7 January 1964. The team soon began work on a Special Forces camp at Minh Thanh, deep in the Viet Cong-controlled War Zone C northwest of the capital. That job finished, the unit redeployed to Moc Hoa in the Plain of Reeds. There, the terrain dictated the nature and method of building the fortified base. Earthmoving equipment was needed to raise the site above the monsoon water level and to cope with the eroding rains. STAT 0503 then enabled the U.S. and South Vietnamese defenders of the camp to take advantage of the area's waterways. The naval constructionmen created a boat basin, dug a canal 300 yards long, and fashioned several wooden boats. Then, at the end of June, Lieutenant Oxley's team was airlifted by C-123 aircraft to Bu Gia Map, 100 miles northeast of Saigon in forested hill country near the Cambodian border. The thirteen-man STAT improved and lengthened an existing airstrip, repaired camp facilities, and carried out its civic action responsibilities in the local Montagnard community.

When STAT 1003 relieved Lieutenant Oxley's team in mid-August 1964, the new arrivals continued work on the airstrip at Bu Gia Map, extending the runway to over 4,000 feet. In addition to other military construction and civic action activities, STAT 1003 built a 120-foot earthen dam for the mountain tribesmen. Departing the hill country at the end of the year, Lieutenant (j.g.) Warren M. Garbe's naval constructionmen deployed to the Mekong Delta west of Saigon at Binh Thanh Thon, where they began work on a new Special Forces "A Team" camp. At the end of the unit's tour in February 1965, most of the task was completed.

The Navy's SEABEEs also were deployed to another critical sector of the South Vietnamese border area. STAT 0504, under Lieutenant (j.g.) Henry Frauenfelder, arrived in the Central Highlands in January 1964. During the first one and one-half months, the team operated in the Pleiku area, constructing airstrips, erecting facilities, and clearing vegetation for fields of fire. In mid-February the STAT embarked on a hazardous undertaking when they accompanied Special Forces men and 350 South Vietnamese troops on a seventy-five-mile convoy into Viet Cong territory

---

Mar; CP 090500Z Jun; memo, OP-60 to OP-04, ser BM0905-64 of 2 Jul; CINCPAC, Command History, 1964, pp. 160-61.

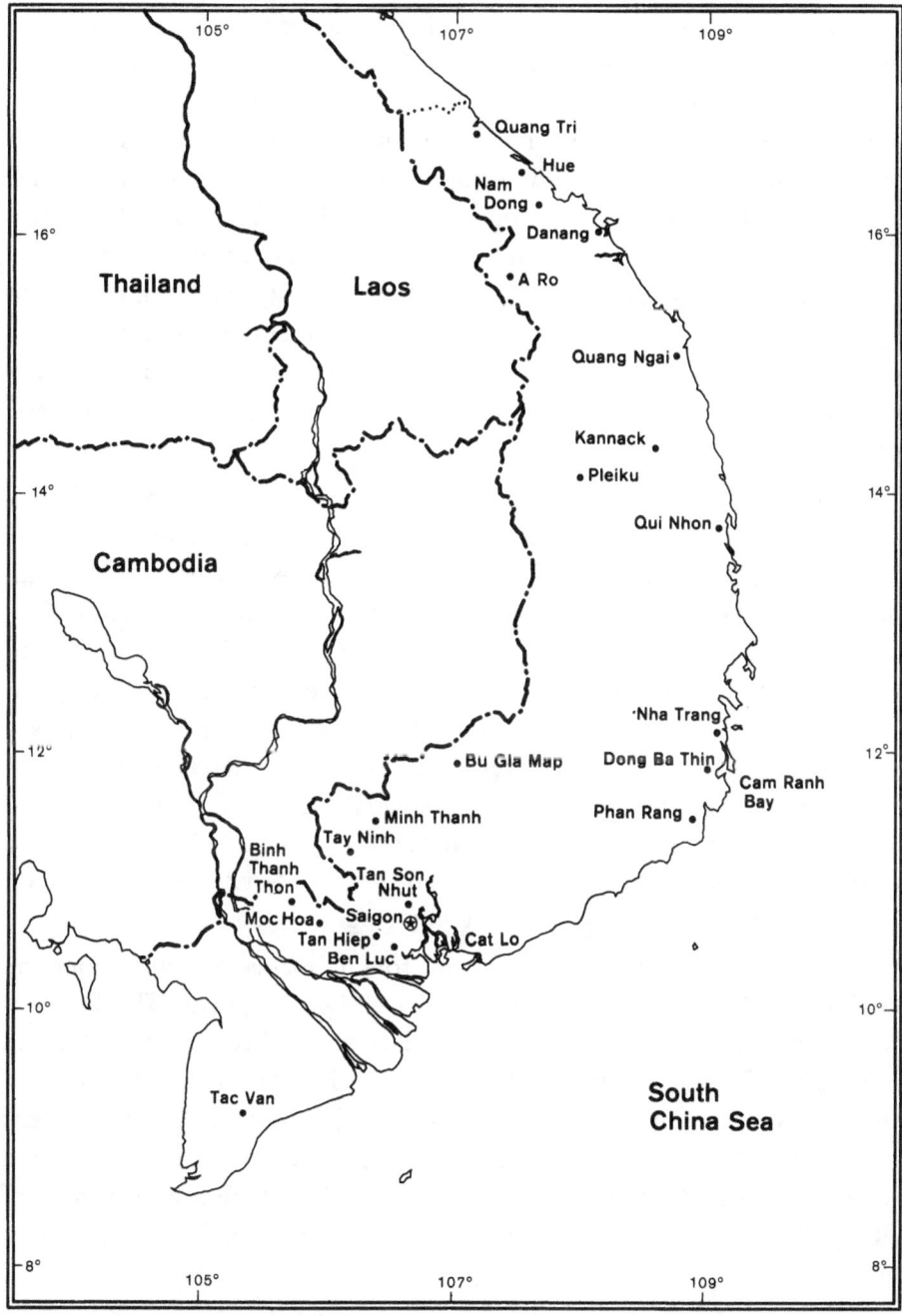

SEABEE Team Deployment Sites in South Vietnam, 1964-1965

to establish a new camp. After a difficult but uneventful journey, the SEABEEs and their protectors arrived at Kannack, the site of an old French fort, and began the construction project. Two months later, Lieutenant Frauenfelder and his twelve men had built a fortification system with underground ammunition and communication bunkers, camp buildings, and an airfield capable of accommodating C-123 transports. STAT 0504 next traveled with their equipment by road to Qui Nhon, from there to Nha Trang by LST, and finally on land again thirty miles southward to Dong Ba Thin. There the team devoted their attention to developing a landing strip for transport aircraft. When the unit departed South Vietnam in August 1964, after a seven and one-half month tour, the airfield was receiving vital logistic aircraft.

Unfinished tasks and new projects were soon handled when STAT 1004 arrived at Dong Ba Thin in August. For the remainder of the year Lieutenant (j.g.) William F. Pitcher's team worked on installations and defensive works at the Special Forces camp and extended the 3,000-foot airstrip. Much of the work was accomplished despite frequent rains and flooding. During September a detachment of the team deployed to a post on the Cambodian border at A Ro, where the men performed military construction. The team was again split when one detachment briefly remained at Dong Ba Thin while two others carried out building tasks at Tay Ninh northwest of Saigon and at Tan Son Nhut Airfield. At the end of the team's deployment period, in February 1965, vital construction on three "Green Beret" camps was completed.

Although civic action was important for the teams working under the aegis of the Army's Special Forces, for the USOM-supported STATs it was the primary goal. To continue the already established program, STATs 0903 and 0904 deployed to South Vietnam in April 1964. The first of these SEABEE teams, led by Lieutenant (j.g.) Roger E. Wiedmer, spent their seven-month tour providing a wide range of assistance to the populace around Quang Ngai city. This aid included medical treatment of fifty patients daily and the construction and repair of roads, bridges, wells, and schools.

Lieutenant (j.g.) Allen N. Olsen's STAT 0904 did similar work in the vicinity of Hue and Quang Tri. During the team's Southeast Asian deployment, Hospital Corpsman 2nd Class Roger C. Necas provided medical help to over 3,700 South Vietnamese. The team's construction efforts also were designed to promote the economic and environmental betterment of the local people. One of STAT 0904's most important projects was the erection near Quang Tri of a sawmill, using equipment that had not been assembled since its shipment from the United States in 1956. Despite its non-military construction, the team's activities concerned the enemy. On 19 June the Viet Cong ambushed three SEABEEs and seriously wounded Petty Officer R. L. Bowers. Fortune was with the SEABEEs on another occasion, however. The team departed the site near Hue — at Nam Dong — one month before the Viet Cong all but overran the Special Forces camp there on 6 July, killing 55 South Vietnamese, 2 Americans, and 1 Australian advisor.

The attempt to win the "hearts and minds" of the South Vietnamese people for their government continued when STATs 0505 and 0506 relieved their predecessors in October 1964. Team 0505, led by Lieutenant Lowell H. Ruff, completed the sawmill begun by STAT 0904 at Quang Tri and began to move to a new site at Phan Rang, in Ninh Thuan Province. At that point, however, the unit was caught by the torrential rains and catastrophic flood which hit the northern part of South Vietnam in November 1964. For the remainder of the year the SEABEEs and their heavy equipment were convoyed by road, with great difficulty, to their destination. Flood relief assistance to the people in the Phan Rang area consumed the team's efforts in the first part of 1965. Distribution of emergency supplies, repair of roads, culverts, and bridges, and removal of debris were major tasks. Before the team departed the country in early May 1965, it was able to prepare the seventeen-acre site for a New Life Hamlet, formerly called a Strategic Hamlet, whose inhabitants had fled from enemy controlled areas.

The SEABEEs of STAT 0506, commanded by Lieutenant (j.g.) William H. Roche, also began their deployment to South Vietnam's northern region in the midst of the monsoon flood. Based at Quang Ngai city, the team coordinated relief efforts with a sideband radio. Food and emergency supplies were called in via airlift from Saigon and delivered through flood waters with the unit's earth-moving equipment and other heavy vehicles. In addition to post-flood recovery activities, STAT 0506 personnel sank ten wells, erected five single-span bridges, and built a road. The paramount mission of civic action was continued with improvements to orphanages, schools, and hospitals and highlighted by the provision of medical assistance to almost 3,000 South Vietnamese. These SEABEEs left the country in May 1965.

Through the end of 1964, the SEABEEs accomplished many projects aimed at improving the economic plight and increasing the security of the population under government control. At fifty-two separate locations throughout the country the naval constructionmen completed work on 11 airstrips, 298 miles of road, and 87 bridges and repaired 18 more bridges, drilled 35 wells, designed and built 36 New Life Hamlets, and trained 1,800 Vietnamese in their trades. In addition, the SEABEEs built numerous fortifications and Special Forces camps. Civic action work on schools, dispensaries, orphanages, and other facilities, as well as flood relief activities, was considerable.

The accomplishments of the STATs and the well drilling detachments were widely recognized. For example, Senator Hubert H. Humphrey apprised Congress on 21 August that the STAT program was "an impressive success." He added:

> The STAT has been called the military peace corps and the reasons for comparison are obvious. Like the Peace Corps, the STAT put something into the country: They develop human resources. Such a contribution is valuable indeed. Dollar for dollar, the STAT program has been called one of our best overseas investments.[34]

A USOM official found their work the "finest form of civic action that could have been done by any military unit in this country so far."[35]

---

[34] Quoted in COMCBPAC, "Helping Others Help Themselves," p. 139.

[35] Quoted in Naval History Division, "History of U.S. Naval Operations Vietnam, 1964," pp. 134-35. See also COMCBPAC, "Helping Others Help Themselves," pp. 30-45; COMCBPAC, Detachment Republic of Vietnam, Completion Report, 1963-1972, pp. 3-3—3-5, 4-9, 5-5—5-7; COMCBPAC, Detachment Republic of Vietnam/Thailand, Completion Report, of Oct 1964, p. 5-6; Naval History Division, "History of U.S. Naval Operations Vietnam, 1964," pp. 128-33; MACV, Command History, 1964, pp. 78, 190; CINCPAC, Command History, 1964, pp. 328-29, 346-47; CBTEAM 0904, Completion Report, ser 41 of 13 Jun 1964; CBTEAM 0503, Completion Report, ser 54 of 14 Aug; CBTEAM 0504, Completion Report, ser 55 of 20 Aug; CBTEAM 0904, Completion Report, ser 141 of 20 Nov; CBTEAM 1004, Completion Report, ser 60 of 3 Mar 1965; CBTEAM 1003, Completion Report, ser 17 of 20 Mar; CBTEAM 0505, Completion Report, ser 4905 of 5 May; CBTEAM 0506, Completion Report, ser 42 of 19 May 1964; Kelley, *U.S. Army Special Forces*, pp. 54-57; Flag Plot Briefer, of 16 Nov; memos, OP-33A to OP-09A of 13 Nov 1964; OP-333E to

Although the STAT and other U.S. programs attained a measure of success, the overall U.S.-South Vietnamese civic action campaign faltered during the tumultuous months of 1964. The ineffective execution of the program by the South Vietnamese bureaucracy, the instability of the political leadership, and the growing presence of North Vietnamese in the South left U.S. policymakers gravely concerned over the course of the struggle.

Protection of U.S. Ships and Installations

Not only were American leaders concerned about the failing counterinsurgency effort in the countryside, but also the increasing threat to U.S. ships in the country's ports and rivers and to installations in the cities. For instance, at 0515 on 2 May 1964, Viet Cong saboteurs mined the MSTS aircraft ferry *Card*, which had just offloaded planes and helicopters at the Saigon waterfront. The explosion tore a 28-foot hole in the starboard side. The civilian crew suffered no casualties, but the ship's engine room flooded and *Card* settled to the bottom in 48 feet of water. Captain Friedman and naval officers from the Military Assistance Command immediately initiated emergency damage control measures, saving *Card* from progressive flooding and possible capsizing in the Saigon shipping channel.[36] The next day, a Vietnamese LDNN team determined that several small, electrically detonated mines, often used by the Viet Cong, apparently caused the explosion. The saboteurs evidently approached their target through a sewer main which emptied into the Saigon River under the pier about 50 feet from the blast area.[37]

Admiral Thomas H. Moorer, Commander Seventh Fleet, placed Rear Admiral Russell Kefauver, Commander Service Squadron 3, under the Service Force, U.S. Pacific Fleet, in charge of *Card*'s salvage. Four divers arrived from the Philippines and the salvage ship *Reclaimer* reached Saigon on 5 May. Assisted by the Vietnamese Navy, the salvage force made temporary repairs and refloated *Card*. On 20 May, only a fortnight after the mining, the ship departed Saigon for the Philippines, towed by fleet

---

OP-002, of 24 Nov; COM7FLT, Command History, 1964, p. 10; msg, CPFLT 022029Z Dec 1964; Blaufarb, *The Counterinsurgency Era*, pp. 205-25; Don, *Our Endless War*, pp. 125-37.

[36]Msgs, HSAS 020500Z May 1964; MACV 030214Z; Friedman, Interview.

[37]Msg, HSAS 070715Z May 1964.

ocean tug *Tawakoni* (ATF-114). Five months later, *Card* was back at sea with the Military Sea Transportation Service. Immediately after the *Card* incident, Admiral Moorer diverted destroyer *Lyman K. Swenson*, then enroute to Yokosuka, to Saigon for a two-day visit to show that the United States would not be intimidated by sabotage.[38]

A second incident occurred on 3 June. Civilian crew members of SS *A and J Mid-America* abandoned the old Liberty ship in Saigon harbor when they were not paid on time and accepted as true rumors that the ship's owner was bankrupt. During the next few days, as local thieves looted the ship, Ambassador Lodge requested police protection. On the 25th, Lodge also asked the Navy to remove the ship, which was moored in such a position that, if sunk, she could slide into the main channel and block military and commercial transportation on the vital waterway.[39] A crew of twenty-five officers and men flew in from *Piedmont* (AD-17) to take over the ship. Under the command of *Piedmont*'s executive officer, Commander Lyle R. Hays, the merchant ship, in company with *Tawasa* (ATF-92), departed Saigon on 4 July. Five days later Commander Hays delivered *A and J Mid-America* to the American Consul General in Hong Kong.[40]

In a third incident, on the evening of 30 October, guards captured a young saboteur near the USNS *Muskingum* (T-AK-198) tied up in Danang harbor. He carried a bomb concealed in his school books and had orders to "get" the ship or a nearby MSTS LST beached forward of *Muskingum*. *Muskingum*'s captain was appalled by the close call. He termed Vietnamese security for his ship "practically nil," and declared that he would anchor out in the harbor on his next visit to Danang rather than risk another attack.[41]

In the aftermath of each of these incidents, both U.S. and Vietnamese authorities took steps to improve port security. In May the Vietnamese increased river patrol vessels in the Saigon channel from one to four vedettes, placed two other patrol boats on twenty-four-hour alert, and ordered divers to make random underwater inspections of ship hulls. Sea Force ships and Vietnamese Air Force planes continued to escort all vessels up the river to Saigon.[42]

---

[38]Msgs, COM7FLT 030038Z May 1964; 030214Z; HSAS 030535Z; COMDESRON9 070835Z; CTF73 191033Z; COMSTS 100501Z Dec.
[39]Msgs, HSAS 101140Z Jun 1964; AMEMB Saigon 250245Z.
[40]Msgs, COM7FLT 300809Z Jun 1964; CTU73.4.2 090145Z Jul.
[41]Msg, COMSTSFE 090555Z Nov 1964. See also CINCPAC, Command History, 1964, p. 335.
[42]Msgs, CP 022233Z May 1964; COMUSMACV 210259Z.

On 29 July Admiral Sharp directed Admiral Moorer to study the vulnerability of the Saigon harbor and river channel to Viet Cong mining. The study concluded that the many sharp turns on the forty-six-mile channel from Vung Tau to Saigon made the route particularly vulnerable to Viet Cong mines. The turning point at the Ben Nghe Canal, on the southern border of the city, posed a special danger, since here a mine could be detonated under a ship while it was virtually dead in the water and broadside to the main channel. Most of the commercial port of Saigon was downstream of this point, but a large ship sunk at the mouth of the Ben Nghe Canal could block the up-river transit of all but the smallest craft and embarrass the governments of the United States and South Vietnam.[43]

In September CINCPACFLT reported that clearance from certain sections of the Saigon shipping channel of a 10,000-ton merchantman, severely damaged and submerged as a result of mining, would be extremely difficult "if it could be cleared at all."[44] He proposed the activation and stationing in Subic Bay of two salvage lifting ships (ARSD) and one salvage craft tender (ARST) and the creation of a nucleus harbor clearance unit of two officers and twenty-five men. Action on this proposal, however, was deferred. At the same time, serious thought was given to dredging an alternate shipping channel to Saigon which would follow the Soirap River all the way from the sea. However, studies concluded that while the straighter and wider river would be easier to secure, the waterway's tendency to silt up would make it difficult to keep open. The most significant result of these studies was to inspire the Vietnamese to heed U.S. advisor recommendations and begin regular mine sweeps of the river approaches.[45]

HSAS was responsible for the security of the cargos once they were unloaded from the ships. Pilferage was always a problem, particularly during the transit of non-containerized goods from the docks to the warehouse. Exchange and commissary goods, such as televisions and radios, were especially prized by thieves. Several local stevedore companies, owned by Vietnamese generals, were suspected of complicity and, in

---

[43]Msg, CPFLT 010218Z Aug 1964.
[44]Ltr, CINCPACFLT to CNO, ser 73/00686 of 3 Sep 1964.
[45]Msg, CP 010218Z Aug 1964; ltr, CINCPACFLT to CNO, ser 73/00686 of 3 Sep; CINCPAC, Command History, 1964, pp. 336-37; Bronars, Interview.

several cases, HSAS flatly refused to employ some of the more suspect firms. Military policemen were assigned to ride trucks from the port to the warehouse and officers at the port carefully checked manifests as the cargo was unloaded. On the other hand, Captain Friedman felt that, in many cases, goods were missing even before the ship reached Saigon and were probably lost in the Philippines.

Terrorist attacks on U.S. facilities ashore also increased in 1964. The first serious incident occurred at Pershing Field, an athletic facility run by HSAS. During a baseball game in February, a Viet Cong device exploded in the bleachers, killing two Americans and wounding twenty-five other persons. Witnesses noted that the Vietnamese children who usually played around the field disappeared before the blast. Because it was impossible to provide future security for such a large open area, HSAS reluctantly closed the facility. Not more than a week after the Pershing Field attack, a Viet Cong suicide squad gunned down a military policeman guarding the door of the Capital Kin Do Theater and placed a bomb in the lobby, while Vietnamese and Americans watched a Sunday afternoon movie. Alerted by the attack, Captain Donald E. Koelper, USMC, leaped to the stage to warn the audience to take cover. He was still there when the bomb blast killed him and wounded thirty-six others.[46]

Logistic Support of a Growing Conflict

The increase of U.S. military activities in South Vietnam, which placed great demands for support on the Headquarters Support Activity, Saigon, emphasized the need for a larger logistic establishment. HSAS, staffed by 600 officers and men at the end of the year, was barely able to cope with the deployment into Vietnam of more and more U.S. units and resources. All departments of HSAS experienced an increased workload. Even at the beginning of the year, the Port Terminal Division handled thirty ships and 30,000 to 40,000 measurement tons of cargo each month. To prevent a backlog of ships in port awaiting offloading, the division took extraordinary measures. Port personnel were placed on a twelve-hour day, seven-

---

[46]Westmoreland, *A Soldier Reports*; Malcolm Browne, *The New Face of War* (New York: Bobbs-Merrill, 1965), pp. 258-59; MACV, Command History, 1964, p. 189; *New York Times*, of 2 Feb 1964; msg, COMUSMACV 161540Z Feb; Friedman, Interview.

day work-week schedule and Cargo Handling Battalion 2, of the Service Force, U.S. Pacific Fleet, was deployed to Saigon to augment the HSAS personnel. Efforts also were made to acquire additional warehouse space near the docks. To ease the problem, the Public Works Department approved acquisition of 57,000 square feet of new warehouse space and seven 6,800 cubic foot, advanced base refrigerators in the port area. By the end of 1964, HSAS open storage capacity totaled 127,000 square feet, warehouse space 186,000 square feet, and cold storage 201,000 cubic feet.

Much of the increase in port operations was attributed to the expansion of the exchange and commissary system operated by HSAS. In May 1964 Navy Exchange sales topped $1 million and this figure reached $1.7 million at the end of the year. Construction of a new exchange building, scheduled for completion by April 1965, was begun. The field exchange system grew from 12 branches to over 100. To supply these field exchanges, the chartered private fleet of vessels was replaced by two Japanese-manned MSTS LSTs early in 1964. By the end of the year, these LSTs numbered seven and hauled 12,000 tons of supplies monthly.

As with the other departments, the workload of the Fiscal and Supply Departments expanded dramatically. By July the fiscal branch was disbursing about $3 million in pay and allowances each month. There were corresponding increases in the supply workload. The main logistic source was located at the Naval Supply Center, Oakland, California, but urgent requests were sent to the Naval Supply Depots at Subic, Yokosuka, or Sangley Point. An inter-service support agreement allowed the Navy to use the Army Support Command for assistance, but according to Commander Lennus B. Urquhart (SC), who headed the Supply Department in 1964, "this proved very frustrating and we finally gave up trying and went Navy all the way." Even the Navy's support was sometimes insufficient, however. Urquhart stated that "of all the activities in the U.S., only Oakland seemed to understand our problems and did their best to meet our requirements."[47]

By mid-year, the adequacy of medical facilities in South Vietnam became an additional concern. The anticipated increase in American personnel pointed to the need for greater resources. In addition, General

---

[47] Ltr, Urquhart to Kuntze, of 29 Dec 1965. See also HSAS, Draft History; CINCPACFLT, Annual Report, 26 Jun 1964 - 30 Mar 1965, pp. 65-66.

A Military Sea Transportation Service tank landing ship, operated by Headquarters Support Activity, Saigon, loads supplies at Saigon for delivery to outlying ports along the coast of South Vietnam.

Westmoreland was dissatisfied with the fire security and physical layout of the Saigon Station Hospital. An alternate building was considered but rejected when Rear Admiral James R. Davis, the Commander Pacific Division, Bureau of Yards and Docks, found it unsatisfactory as well. Thought was given to activation of a hospital ship, but because of the poor security situation in the port of Saigon, and the limited berthing space available, this proposal too was dropped. The issue was closed when Admiral Ulysses S. G. Sharp, shortly after becoming CINCPAC on 30 June 1964, reaffirmed an earlier decision to expand the existing facility. In the meantime, despite the crowded conditions, the Saigon Station Hospital continued to serve the American community. Its staff of 10 medical officers, 2 medical service officers, 16 nurses, and 90 hospital corpsmen, the great majority of whom were naval personnel, performed admirably, especially after each major attack by the Viet Cong against U.S. installations during 1964.[48]

HSAS had been established in 1962 to support a maximum of 9,000 men. By the end of 1964 the activity supported 23,000 U.S. military personnel and 2,700 U.S. government civilians in 240 scattered locations. With the exception of fuel provision and construction assistance, accomplished by large U.S. corporations under contract to U.S. government agencies in Saigon, HSAS provided the major common-item support to all U.S. forces in Vietnam.

In July 1964, CINCPAC sought ways to increase the efficiency of the logistic organizations in Vietnam. Specifically, Admiral Sharp recommended that the Army establish a major logistic command which could take over from HSAS if contingency plans were implemented for a major U.S. and allied buildup in Vietnam, as anticipated. General Westmoreland agreed with Admiral Sharp's assessment and in late October completed his own study of the logistic situation. He concluded that an Army logistic command should be introduced immediately into Vietnam to prepare for the likely transition. The proposed new command would accommodate any increase in U.S. or SEATO troops.

---

[48]CINCPAC, Command History, 1964, pp. 341-44; CINCPACFLT, Annual Report, 26 Jun 1964-30 Mar 1965, pp. 65-98; MACV, Command History, 1964, p. 141; CINCPACFLT, Annual Report, 10 Oct 1963-26 Jun 1964, p. 107; F. O. McClendon, Jr., "Doctors and Dentists, Nurses and Corpsmen in Vietnam," *U.S. Naval Institute Naval Review* (May 1970), pp. 278-79; msgs, CP 150206Z Jul 1964; CPFLT 290421Z Sep; CP 210348Z Nov; COMUSMACV 091022Z Dec; CP 160457Z; 160459Z; Marolda, "Saigon" in *United States Navy and Marine Corps Bases, Overseas*, pp. 287-91.

NH-93962

Nurses serving with the Navy's Saigon Station Hospital receive Purple Heart medals from Captain Archie C. Kuntze, Commander Headquarters Support Activity, Saigon, for wounds they received when the Viet Cong sabotaged the Brink Bachelor Officers Quarters on Christmas Eve, 1964. Left to right are Lieutenant Barbara Wooster (NC), Lieutenant Ruth A. Mason (NC), and Lieutenant (j.g.) Ann P. Reynolds (NC).

In November the JCS directed Admiral Sharp to develop a support system which could expand on short notice to serve a buildup of American or allied forces in Vietnam. Admiral Sharp decided to use the Westmoreland study as the basis for his own work. Agreeing with the MACV study, CINCPAC concluded that "existing logistic arrangements in RVN are not adequate to meet present intensity of operations. Common user support concept currently being followed in RVN does not provide all of the common user supply nor has it established the necessary retail facilities and services."[49] Admiral Sharp also concurred with the recommendation to deploy an Army logistic command to Vietnam. He thought that additional manpower for command and control functions and for maintenance and supply support in up-country locations was needed. Admiral Sharp believed that HSAS should be integrated into the logistic command, but only after the new command was fully established and operating. He felt that the need was so great that the Army command should be deployed immediately, even before resolution of the question of support for the allied nations which might be sending forces to Vietnam.[50]

On 9 December 1964, however, the JCS informed Sharp that the Department of the Army was reluctant to assume the large personnel and budgetary responsibility associated with the Army takeover of all common logistic support in Vietnam. Therefore, the JCS directed Sharp to plan for a smaller Army logistic command to augment the U.S. Army Support Group which had been in Vietnam since 1962. The new unit would have the initial function of supporting only Army units, but its responsibilities subsequently could be expanded. As the command gradually took over all the common support duties of HSAS, the Navy's activity would be phased out.

As also requested by the JCS, Admiral Sharp directed General Westmoreland to prepare a more comprehensive logistic plan. The MACV document identified a number of deficiencies in HSAS support resulting from the rapid growth of the number of U.S. military personnel in Vietnam. The plan identified inadequate supervision of U.S. cargo shipped to isolated ports and airfields as a problem. Even in Saigon, there was insufficient maintenance support of vehicles, radios, small arms, office machinery, and utilities and an absence of certain categories of common supply items, such as medical, automotive, electronic, munitions, and construction material. Many items had to be procured on the local economy. The fifteen logistic support systems operating in Vietnam overlapped, particularly in the supply of goods from Saigon to up-country locations. This developed because HSAS limited its support primarily to the Saigon area, with the major exception of commissary and exchange

---

[49]Msg, CP 272339Z Nov 1964.
[50]Msgs, CP 150116Z Nov 1964; JCS 190047Z; CP 272339Z; HSAS 311315Z Dec; CINCPAC, Command History, 1964, pp. 329-33; 1965, p. 550.

goods. The proposed Army logistic command would be able to centralize military construction, medical services, maintenance, and transportation throughout Vietnam. The final MACV plan, which Admiral Sharp considered a realistic guideline, was submitted to the JCS on 21 December 1964. To support a 40,000-man U.S. and allied buildup, which was one contingency considered, an Army logistic command of 2,100 men was required. HSAS would not be phased out immediately, but planning would begin for a gradual turnover of responsibilities to the Army command.[51]

The JCS approved this plan for Vietnam on 15 January 1965. They sent it on to the Secretary of Defense for approval with the recommendation that an advance party of 230 men be deployed immediately. Cyrus Vance, Deputy Secretary of Defense, replying to the JCS recommendations of 27 January, expressed general agreement with the overall proposal. Due to his concern, however, that the JCS proposals only added another organization to the existing structure, he sent the Deputy Assistant Secretary of Defense for Installations and Logistics, Glen Gibson, to Vietnam for an on-site survey. Gibson departed Washington on 29 January, stopping in Hawaii for a briefing by Admiral Sharp, and returned to Washington on 5 February. His report concurred in general with the JCS recommendations but noted that any major augmentation of U.S. forces was "limited by availability of facilities and will continue to be so limited until additional funds are made available." He echoed Captain Friedman's complaints that "many of the present difficulties result from peacetime funding procedures and crash organization concepts."[52] Gibson was particularly impressed with the use of Vietnamese personnel and American contractors by HSAS, thus holding down the number of U.S. military personnel required. HSAS employed three times as many Vietnamese as Americans and contracted with corporations such as Vinnell, Philco, and Pacific Architects and Engineers for specialized support. He agreed with the new U.S. Ambassador, Maxwell Taylor, that the contractor organizations should be expanded before increasing U.S. military personnel levels. Based on Gibson's report, Vance approved "in principle" the introduction of a U.S. Army logistic command, but authorized an advance deployment of only seventy-five men. He directed

---

[51]CINCPAC, Command History, 1964, pp. 329-33; 1965, pp. 550, 552; msgs, CP 162340Z Dec 1964; 240120Z; 240121Z; COMUSMACV 301205Z.
[52]JCS Paper 2343/486-11, p. 56.

the JCS to draw up a new proposal for staffing the logistic command that avoided a large increase in U.S. personnel. The first increment of the Army logistic command arrived in Vietnam in March 1965. Finally, in 1966, the functions of HSAS were transferred to the Army's organization, as planned.[53]

Beginning in early 1964, the Johnson administration considered covert military actions against North Vietnam necessary to support the counterinsurgency struggle in the South. Hence, the limited 34A program was launched. Nonetheless, President Johnson continued to emphasize the primacy of the campaign within South Vietnam. In this context, the Navy's Headquarters Support Activity, Saigon, SEABEEs, and fleet units worked to enhance South Vietnamese internal security. It became increasingly apparent, however, that despite U.S. and Vietnamese efforts, the anti-Communist campaign was failing. Measures to strengthen the allied logistic base in the South later in the year, which reflected the increased presence of American forces in-country, coincided with a search for new solutions to the expanding conflict.

---

[53]Memo, Deputy SECDEF to Chairman JCS, of 12 Feb 1965; Friedman, Interview; JCS Paper 2343/486-11; Edwin B. Hooper, *Mobility, Support, Endurance: A Story of Naval Operational Logistics in the Vietnam War, 1965-1968* (Washington: Naval History Division/GPO, 1972), pp. 25-28.

CHAPTER XIII

Fleet Air Operations Over Laos

During 1964 U.S. leaders increasingly doubted that the counterinsurgency campaign in South Vietnam and the covert program in the North were sufficient to deter North Vietnamese support of the Viet Cong. Greater consideration now was given to the conduct of military actions by American conventional forces. Within this context, senior naval officers gave particular attention to maritime measures. In mid-January Vice Admiral Alfred G. Ward, Deputy Chief of Naval Operations (Plans and Policy), issued a study proposing steps to be taken to pressure the North Vietnamese. The Navy's chief planner suggested the implementation of various actions in sequence, proceeding from warnings and movement of forces to covert and overt activities by South Vietnamese armed forces. These latter measures included sabotage, coastal raiding, harassment of shipping, small-scale amphibious landings, and air strikes in ascending degrees of intensity. Another sequence involved the introduction of South Vietnamese ground forces into southern Laos to interdict infiltration. In the final sequence, direct and overt actions by U.S. naval forces would escalate from show of force deployments, intensive air and sea reconnaissance over and off North Vietnam, and harassment of shipping, to overt attacks on the North. These latter operations included the isolation of Haiphong, the country's major port, through aerial mining, the sinking of a block ship in the narrow approaches, and the imposition of a naval blockade. Another option proposed was the bombing of airfields, bridges, naval facilities, and critical components of the industrial sector. Admiral Ward believed that the program would have a positive effect on North Vietnamese policymaking. He observed that

> should destruction of North Vietnam's facilities be undertaken, the North Vietnamese means to a better future, as they see it, will be shattered. The government has nothing to offer as a substitute except, possibly, defense of the fatherland — a theme not too impressive to the general Vietnamese population. Accordingly, it can be expected that an

erosion of the authority of the regime and NVN economy would result.[1]

On 22 January 1964 the JCS recommended that necessary steps be taken to convince the Communists of the unequivocal U.S. determination to preserve the existence of South Vietnam. The Joint Chiefs of Staff paper contained many of the actions prescribed in the Ward study and in Admiral Anderson's similar proposals of July 1962 and concluded that the "United States must be prepared to put aside many of the self-imposed restrictions which now limit our efforts, and to undertake bolder actions which may embody greater risks."[2]

While the Secretary of Defense deferred action on the JCS proposals, the concept of direct measures against the North remained under serious consideration. In late February 1964 the military chiefs reiterated their recommendation for a stronger military policy. Admiral Ricketts, representing Admiral McDonald in JCS deliberations, observed that the American position as leader of the non-Communist world was deteriorating and that the passage of time would favor the Communists, a view shared by Admiral Ward. Admiral Ricketts reasoned that military power was the key element in the unrelenting competition for influence among the nations of Southeast Asia between the Communist powers and the United States. Ricketts proposed the use of air and naval forces to interdict enemy lines of communication to the South through Laos and southern North Vietnam and to strike at military and economic targets in all parts of North Vietnam. The admiral observed that "there has not been a time in the past when the communists have not backed down in the face of U.S. force, except possibly at the beginning of the Korean conflict."[3] He cited the Lebanon and Taiwan Strait crises of 1958, and the Cuban Missile Crisis of 1962 as instances where firm action had resulted in Communist retreat from confrontation. The admiral concluded:

> We must balance the long-range effect of our positive actions against the resulting small risk to buy tremendous advantages . . . . It seems strange that in the face of examples where we have used United States' military power and have obtained such tremendous results, we are hesitant to

---

[1] Memo, OP-06 to SECNAV, ser 0001070P60 of 14 Jan 1964, p. 11 encl. in memo, Zumwalt to Nitze, of 15 Jan 1964.
[2] Memo, JCS to SECDEF, JCSM-46-64 of 22 Jan 1964.
[3] Memo, CNO to JCS, CNOM 59-64 of 24 Feb 1964.

use it again in the particular and serious crisis we now face.... We must learn how to use it as an instrument of national policy.[4]

Senior officials in the Johnson administration, including the Secretary of Defense and the Secretary of State, feared that outright actions might cause Chinese Communist or even Soviet retaliation, a concern shared by the President.[5] For this reason, and because of the other possible international political and military ramifications of this action, U.S. decisionmakers were loath to commit large forces to combat in Southeast Asia.

The Joint Chiefs, however, doubted that China would intervene in Southeast Asia unless U.S. actions impinged directly on that nation's security. Accordingly, on 2 March 1964 the JCS recommended to Secretary of Defense McNamara that overt military operations against North Vietnam be executed to dissuade the Communists from further support of the southern insurgency. The chiefs called for a program of growing intensity and increasing U.S. involvement that would include low-level aerial reconnaissance over Laos and North Vietnam and eventually strikes by South Vietnamese or American aircraft on northern targets. The final steps included U.S. air attacks and cross-border operations into Laos and North Vietnam and the mining and blockading of North Vietnamese ports. Admiral Ward, who played an important role in developing this position, recognized the possibility of Chinese involvement when he reflected on their response to similar threats in Korea and on the Indian border in 1962. However, he felt that risks would have to be accepted, noting that "if action beyond the scope of current operations is not initiated now it will have to be initiated later, and at greater cost."[6]

Although Admiral Ricketts doubted that Chinese intervention was probable, he also pointed out that this unlikely contingency could be countered by the United States. Until his untimely death on 6 July 1964, Admiral Ricketts argued that if large, enemy armies needed to be dealt with, U.S. and allied troops could be landed along the coasts fronting the Gulf of Tonkin. When the enemy reacted to this threat to his eastern flank, by concentrating forces there, he could be hit with crippling blows by U.S. air and naval forces.

---

[4]*Ibid.*
[5]Johnson, *Vantage Point*, p. 66.
[6]Memo, OP-06 to SECNAV, ser 0001070P60 of 14 Jan 1964, p. 16 encl. in memo, Zumwalt to Nitze, of 15 Jan 1964.

Secretary of the Navy Paul H. Nitze also felt that a coordinated program of escalating pressures by the United States would bring about a North Vietnamese retrenchment, without the danger of Chinese intervention. He observed that

> in the case of North Vietnam with her exposed position to the combined assault of U.S. air and naval power, there is little that she could do to put the outcome of a military conflict in doubt. In other words, the balance of combat power would favor the United States so greatly that regardless of what North Vietnam did we would prevail in a comparatively short period of time.[7]

At the same time, Admiral Ricketts observed that "there is no question but what we could flatten Laos and North Vietnam were such to be necessary, but the harvest of reaction that the United States would reap is an undesirable prospect to contemplate when lesser heroic actions offer probability of being effective." The naval leader felt that "we can get the signal across to Hanoi without too much difficulty" through the moderate application of force. He reaffirmed the "Navy's recommendation for measured and graduated response enunciated by Admiral McDonald and me in the forum of the JCS."[8]

Admiral Ricketts addressed the fears of others in the defense establishment over becoming mired in a land war on the continent of Asia. In an exchange of correspondence with the noted newspaper columnist Walter Lippman, the admiral stated that the use of large numbers of ground troops was unnecessary in the current situation. He reasoned that because of their elongated shapes and respective positions on the Indochinese peninsula, both North and South Vietnam and southern Laos "are accessible to the sea, and most targets are within reach of our sea based and land based air." Hence, the enemy's lines of communication in these countries were "relatively easy to interdict."[9] The admiral also observed that the limited measures taken to date in South Vietnam failed to prevent Viet Cong depredations. The Vice Chief of Naval Operations stressed that if protection of South Vietnam required "escalation of the war into North Vietnam, then that must be done, because it is from North Vietnam that

---

[7]Memo, SECNAV to SECDEF (transmitted orally on 12 Jun 1964) encl. in memo, OP-60 to SECNAV, ser 000493P60 of 12 Jun.

[8]Draft memo, CNO(OP-09) to SECNAV, of 9 Jun 1964.

[9]Ltrs, Ricketts to Lippmann, of 4 and 24 Jun 1964.

the vast majority of the guerrillas are coming." He concluded that "it would be militarily acceptable to use our overwhelming power in such gradually escalating actions that North Vietnam cessation could come before the destruction of their country."[10]

The Cautious Approach Continues

Other military leaders were not convinced that the risk of Chinese reaction in the face of overt actions against North Vietnam and Laos could be largely dismissed. In fact, this threat had much to do with the cautious and limited application of the measures ultimately adopted. Admiral Felt concluded, for instance, that the imposition of a naval blockade of Haiphong probably would generate Chinese air attack on the American naval force conducting the operation. CINCPAC added that this step "is neither a suitable nor an acceptable action unless taken in conjunction with other actions. [One] of the necessary conjunctive actions would be to gain control of the air in the area of operations."[11] The JCS, as well, made it clear that if strong actions against the North were taken, the United States would have to be prepared for a higher level of warfare and all its possible consequences. The military command in Saigon also was unenthusiastic about initiating overt hostile acts against North Vietnam, due to the possibility that the Viet Cong and North Vietnamese would intensify their assault on the already beleaguered South Vietnamese forces.

The political situation in South Vietnam and in the United States during the spring and summer of 1964 also deterred American escalation. Many key U.S. civilian leaders, with the notable exception of Ambassador Lodge, were reluctant to deepen U.S. involvement by spreading the conflict to North Vietnam when the South Vietnamese government, indeed the society itself, might collapse. Another factor noted by some observers was the approaching presidential election in the United States and lack of strong domestic support for expanding hostilities into North Vietnam. Rear Admiral Henry L. Miller, CINCPAC's Assistant Chief of Staff for Plans, observed shortly after McNamara's visit to Hawaii in

---

[10]*Ibid.*

[11]Msg, CP 280311Z Feb 1964. Subsequently, Admiral Felt expressed his opinion that Chinese intervention probably would not have occurred. See Felt, Interview, Vol. II, pp. 627-28, 638-39; CINCPAC, Command History, 1964, p. 361. See also JCS, *History*, pt. 1, p. 9-11.

March that "from what goes on to date, I do not believe Washington is going to approve any strikes against North Vietnam. This is an election year."[12]

At the same time, Admiral Felt and COMUSMACV believed that the counterinsurgency campaign in South Vietnam should be enthusiastically pursued before initiating stronger actions against the North. These officers believed that the covert air and naval operations embodied in Operation Plan 34A, if fully and properly executed, should do much to moderate North Vietnamese behavior. Admiral Felt stated: "I think that Hanoi can be influenced to quit the Communist overt military action in SVN" if those steps were taken. He added that "if the pressures are applied selectively and subtly militarily, psychologically and diplomatically, I believe that the desired effect can be attained without CHICOM invasion of SEASIA."[13]

All these views were taken into account during Secretary of Defense McNamara's visit to South Vietnam from 8 to 14 March 1964. Enroute to Southeast Asia he conferred with Admiral Felt. After extensive consultation with other U.S. and South Vietnamese officials, McNamara concluded that the policy of fighting the insurgency within South Vietnam, supplemented by the modest covert program against the North, should be continued. The secretary, at the same time, was hopeful that the Khanh administration in Saigon would emphasize its national mobilization and pacification plans. McNamara's conclusions formed the core of National Security Action Memo (NSAM) 288, approved by the President at the National Security Council meeting on 17 March. All but minor measures to widen the war into Cambodia, Laos, and North Vietnam were deferred. Thus, U.S. policy essentially remained as before. This decision was reaffirmed on 1 and 2 June, at a meeting in Honolulu of the chief U.S. civilian and military leaders concerned with Southeast Asia.[14]

During this same period, the Johnson administration initiated diplomatic communications with the North Vietnamese through J. Blair Seaborn, a Canadian ICC representative then in Hanoi. This intermediary was asked

---

[12]Ltr, Miller to Moorer, of 12 Mar 1964. Admiral Sharp also alludes to these political exigencies in *Strategy For Defeat*, p. 34, as does Westmoreland in *A Soldier Reports*, pp. 105-09.

[13]Msg, CP 250022Z Feb 1964.

[14]MACV, Command History, 1964, pp. 360-61; Flag Plot Briefers, of 28 Feb 1964; 3 Mar; ltr, Drachnik to Ricketts, of 13 Mar, pp. 12-13; memo, SECDEF to President, of 16 Mar; Sharp, *Strategy For Defeat*, pp. 4, 31-34; memo, OP-60 to CNO, ser BM000579-64 of 14 May; Johnson, *Vantage Point*, pp. 65-67; JCS, *History*, pt. 1, pp. 8-31—9-21.

to inform the North Vietnamese that while the United States did not wish to escalate the conflict in Southeast Asia, it was determined to defend South Vietnam from Communist encroachment, even if this required forceful actions against the North. The nature and tone of the response by the Hanoi government throughout the summer of 1964 suggested that the North Vietnamese were not especially fearful of American military pressure. Still, Hanoi did not cut off this secret line of communication with the United States.[15]

Although the Johnson administration all but dropped consideration of overt air and naval actions against North Vietnam during the spring and summer of 1964, military planning for this contingency continued. Following the issuance of NSAM 288 in March 1964, the Secretary of Defense called for the preparation of plans treating several possible courses of action in Laos, Cambodia, and North Vietnam. In response, on 30 March, CINCPAC submitted Operation Plan 37-64, entitled "Actions to Stabilize the Situation in the Republic of Vietnam," which after considerable refinement became the basic document for the proposed conduct of military operations against North Vietnam. Admiral Felt's plan embodied three major provisions: border control measures in Laos and Cambodia; "tit-for-tat" retaliatory actions in response to North Vietnamese attacks; and a program of graduated overt military pressures against the Democratic Republic of Vietnam. In each category both U.S. and South Vietnamese forces might be involved, but in the first two the U.S. role would consist of aerial reconnaissance, airlift, and advisory support and the ready positioning in Southeast Asia of major fleet units and other forces. Only in the latter phase would U.S. combat forces — two B-57 bomber squadrons — participate in attacks on North Vietnamese targets, and then as reinforcement for South Vietnamese air forces. The JCS approved Operation Plan 37-64 on 21 April 1964.

The issue of striking the North was kept alive by the South Vietnamese when General Khanh, reversing his previous stand, began strongly advocating open attacks on his external foe. Some U.S. officials saw this development as an effort to deflect attention from the chaotic domestic scene in South Vietnam during the late spring. To mollify the South Vietnamese, the U.S. leadership explored various measures for attacking

---

[15]George C. Herring, ed., *The Secret Diplomacy of the Vietnam War: The Negotiating Volumes of the Pentagon Papers* (Austin: Univ. of Texas Press, 1983), pp. 4-35.

the Communists in Laos both by air and land. In July the JCS also proposed an intensification of the covert 34A operations in the North. But these actions were primarily intended to satisfy the South Vietnamese while the counterinsurgency struggle was pushed anew.[16]

Developments in Laos Precipitate Greater U.S. Military Activity

The policymakers in the Johnson administration who desired to bring pressure on the North Vietnamese through actions outside South Vietnam were aided by political and military events in Laos. Since the signing of the Geneva accords in July 1962, Laos had receded from international focus as the relative positions of the various contending factions remained essentially static. Each of the three major parties — the neutralists, the rightists, and the Pathet Lao — provided representatives to the coalition formed at Geneva but retained their power bases and geographic strongholds. The North Vietnamese continued to support the Pathet Lao with arms and material and made increasing use of southern Laos for the infiltration of their own men and supplies into South Vietnam. At the same time, the United States trained and armed through the CIA an effective guerrilla force of Meo tribesmen under Colonel Vang Pao. Ties with rightists in the government and armed forces also were maintained. But the political, if not military, balance had begun to swing toward the West. In contrast to previous assumptions, Souvanna Phouma and the military forces under Kong Le drew closer to the United States rather than to the Communists.

---

[16]Memo, OP-61 to OP-06, ser 000666P61 of 13 Jun 1963; ltrs, CINCPACFLT to COM7FLT, ser 32/00844 of 1 Oct; CINCPACFLT to CINCUSARPAC, ser 62/000257 of 14 Nov; OP-09, memo for record, ser 0011P09 of 10 Feb 1964; memos, Sharp to Felt, of 14 Feb; OP-09 to OP-06, of 22 Feb; OP-60 to OP-06, ser BM000395-64 of 25 Feb; OP-60 to CNO, ser 000398-64 of 28 Feb; msgs, SECSTATE 3:53PM 17 Feb 1964; CP 242253Z Apr; 1:34AM 2 Jun; VCNO, memo for record, ser 00043P09 of 27 Jun; memo, OP-60 to CNO, ser BM000952-64 of 29 Jun; ltr, Zumwalt to Moorer, of 16 Jul; JCS, *History*, pt. 1, pp. 8-27—8-31, 9-1—9-23, 9-33—10-33; MACV, Command History, 1964, p. 160; *U.S.-V.N. Relations*, bk. 3, pt. IVC.2(a), pp. 5-40; bk. 4, pt. IVC.2(b), pp. ii, iii, 1-4; CINCPAC, Command History, 1964, pp. 49-52, 54-56, 61-64, 82-92, 360; JCS Papers 2343/326, 329, 330, 332, 345, 346, 348, 350, 367, 382, 384, 392, 394, 797; 2319/114; 2054/627-5; Felt, Interview, pp. 623-29; William Momyer, *Airpower in Three Wars* (Washington: USAF, 1978), pp. 14-15.

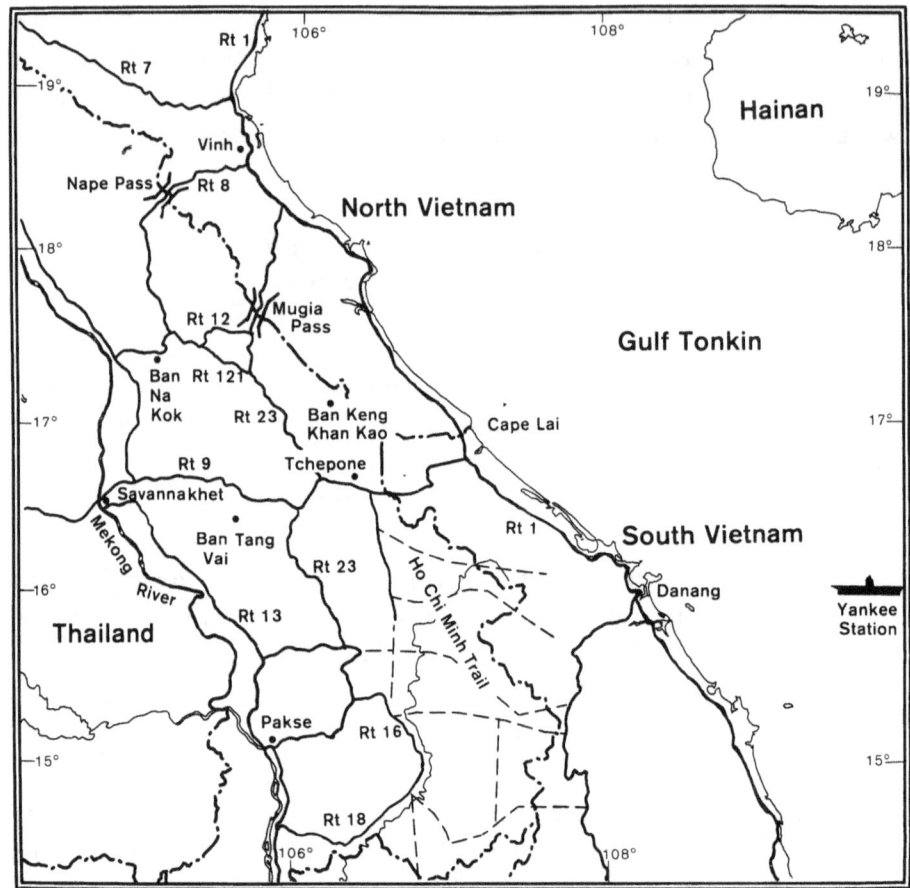

Laotian Panhandle

This development was brought about in 1962 when the Soviets ended their direct airlift of supplies and arms to the neutralists and rerouted them through the North Vietnamese. Attempting to exert political control of the neutralists, the North Vietnamese proved to be far from generous. Hence, the neutralists gradually turned to the United States to replace this interrupted logistic support. When outright hostility between the Communists and the neutralists ensued in March and April of 1963, the shaky coalition government dissolved. Thereafter, Souvanna and his neutralist allies governed Laos.

At the beginning of 1964, several events dramatically altered the situation in Laos. The fall of the Diem government in South Vietnam, which prompted the North Vietnamese to accelerate the war in the South, necessitated increased use of the Ho Chi Minh Trail in southern Laos for the infiltration of men and supplies. To accommodate the surge, North Vietnamese and Pathet Lao forces, in January, began a successful campaign to push government forces further away from the border area. These operations weakened Souvanna's credibility as the leader of the Laotian government.

On 19 April rightists ousted Souvanna in a swift coup. After U.S. insistence, the new leaders were compelled to reinstate Souvanna as head of the government, but they retained actual control of the governmental apparatus. As the non-Communist factions became decidedly more pro-American, the Communists opened attacks on Kong Le's forces in mid-May and soon drove them from the Plain of Jars. At the same time, Souvanna skillfully integrated his neutralist political organization and Kong Le's forces with those of the rightists to form a new government that was closely associated with the United States.

During the April coup in Laos, Secretary of State Rusk, who was visiting Saigon at the time, proposed stationing fleet units at either Danang or Cam Ranh Bay to demonstrate U.S. support to both the Laotian and South Vietnamese governments and possibly deter Communist activity. The JCS did not concur in this proposal. As an alternative, however, the military chiefs recommended periodic and temporary fleet sorties into South Vietnamese waters. Specifically, they endorsed adoption of Admiral Felt's concept of deploying a carrier task group for several days in an area 200 miles in diameter that would bring the force as close as 30 miles from Hainan and 75 miles from North Vietnam's Cape Lai. This force, whose air operations "would be painted on Communist radar screens,"[17] was intended to deter the other side. In accordance with this concept, a task group built around aircraft carrier *Kitty Hawk* proceeded to the South China Sea on 22 April 1964. On the next day, with Souvanna back in power, the formation was ordered to return to normal operations, but to remain within forty-eight hours steaming time of a point off South

---

[17]Msg, CP 222333Z Apr 1964. COMUSMACV also stressed that the force should sail close to North Vietnamese waters. See msgs, COMUSMACV 231020Z Apr 1964; SECSTATE 200208Z.

Vietnam at 16° north 110° east. This position soon became known as Point Yankee or Yankee Station.[18]

Connected with the possibility of an extended naval presence in Southeast Asia was Ambassador Lodge's suggestion on 2 May for an austere naval facility at Cam Ranh Bay, "that the layman would call a 'U.S. Naval Base' [and where] the flag would fly"[19] to signal the fleet's presence. The Cam Ranh base had other potential uses. During a visit to Saigon, on 11 May, General Taylor met with the U.S. Ambassador, who suggested a course of action, in the event Khanh was ousted or assassinated. Lodge

> suggested the possible need of a U.S. presence to take over and run the government. In such a case, he thought a naval base at Cam Ranh Bay might be used as a U.S. headquarters external to Saigon. He apparently feels that in a situation of civil turmoil, the U.S. facilities in Saigon would not be available.[20]

Although Admiral Felt was concerned about immobilizing a large naval force at Cam Ranh Bay, he believed that the idea of stationing some fleet units there had merit. First, however, he recommended that CINC-PACFLT conduct a careful, comprehensive survey of the bay and its environs. By its nature, the survey would be time-consuming and prolonged. In the meantime, the immediate need for a naval presence would be served by the ships and aircraft of the survey team.

Following JCS approval, on 9 May 1964, CINCPAC directed his fleet commander to conduct the required survey. Soon afterward, Nha Trang and Ben Goi were included in the locations to be evaluated. The first phase of the program to determine the area's suitability as a fleet anchorage and amphibious training location began at the end of the month when an RA-3B Skywarrior overflew Cam Ranh Bay on an aerial photographic mission. Other flights by Seventh Fleet aircraft followed. In

---

[18]In 1966 Yankee Station was shifted to 17°30'N 108°30'E. Memos, OP-61 to CNO, ser BM00154-63 of 31 Jan 1963; SECNAV to SECDEF, of 4 May; OP-60 to CNO, ser BM000566-64 of 24 Apr 1964; OP-61 to SECNAV, ser 000624P61 of 29 Apr; msgs, CPFLT 230207Z Apr 1963; CP 012332Z May; JCS 221512Z Apr 1964; CP 222137Z; COMUSMACV 231020Z; CP 231427Z; 242149Z; JCS 282111Z; Flag Plot Briefers of 22 and 23 Apr; CINCPAC, Command History, 1964, pp. 259-69; Stevenson, *End of Nowhere*, pp. 180-205; Roland A. Paul, "Laos: Anatomy of an American Involvement," *Foreign Affairs* (Apr 1971), pp. 533-47.

[19]Msg, AMEMB Saigon 021052Z May 1964.

[20]JCS Paper 2343/379, encl. A, p. 1.

June, *Currituck* (AV-7), a seaplane tender, carried out the first surface survey of all three locations. When, in July, Cam Ranh Bay was determined to be the most valuable for use by fleet seaplanes, Mine Flotilla 1 with *Epping Forest* (MCS-7), Mine Divisions 31, 32, and 33, *Current* (ARS-22), Navy explosive ordnance disposal and UDT units, and Marine beach survey units, swept the area for mines, made hydrographic studies, investigated landing beaches, and updated charts. After meeting with U.S. and South Vietnamese officials in Saigon, Commander Seventh Fleet, on board *Oklahoma City*, called at Cam Ranh Bay on 25 July. Vice Admiral Roy L. Johnson toured the area by helicopter and observed the site's natural advantages. At the end of August, CINCPACFLT reported that Cam Ranh Bay could serve as a fleet anchorage and amphibious exercise area. Nha Trang and Ben Goi were seen as less suitable for these functions.

In the second phase of the survey mission, conducted during the fall, Seventh Fleet Mobile Logistic Support Force (Task Force 73) units under Rear Admiral Joseph W. Williams, Jr., evaluated the feasibility of establishing an austere naval facility at Cam Ranh. After examining the site's ability to physically accommodate building, airfield, and fortification construction, Admiral Williams concluded in his 1 November report to Commander Seventh Fleet that the Cam Ranh area possessed the capability to support a limited fleet shore facility. The potential for later expansion also was present.

Despite these preparations, more direct measures to influence Hanoi's behavior came to the fore in the latter half of 1964. For this reason, on 8 December Admiral Sharp informed the JCS that, while Cam Ranh could serve a future need, there was no current requirement for a shore station at this location. The JCS concurred in this recommendation and the survey report was shelved. Ironically, it would soon be dusted off and prove invaluable to military planners concerned with providing a logistic support complex on the South China Sea for the U.S. armed forces who entered South Vietnam in 1965.[21]

---

[21]Msgs, AMEMB Saigon 021052Z May 1964; CPFLT 042344Z; CP 052336Z; JCS 091445Z; CP 292016Z; CPFLT 142131Z Jun; 260021Z; CP 140322Z Jul; COMUSMACV 221031Z; COM7FLT 281325Z; 182145Z Aug; 230356Z; CTF73 260350Z; CPFLT 262132Z; CP 310737Z; ADMIN CPFLT 050447Z Sep; COM7FLT 110359Z; CPFLT 201055Z; CP 080257Z Dec; COM7FLT, Command History, 1964, p. 7; Flag Plot Briefers, of 5 May and 2 Jun; memos, OP-60 to CNO, ser BM000513-64 of 6 May 1964; BM000584 of 18 May.

Yankee Team Reconnaissance

The search by U.S. policymakers in the spring of 1964 for the means to exhibit American military strength was partially resolved in mid-May when the Communist attacks on the neutralists in Laos compelled Souvanna Phouma to seek direct U.S. assistance. The Laotian leader thereafter allowed American civilians to fly Laotian aircraft. He also authorized U.S. transport aircraft to enter the country's airspace and his air force to accept new delivery of U.S.-made planes. The most important measure, however, was his authorization of low-level reconnaissance flights over Laotian territory by U.S. military aircraft.

U.S. leaders pressed for an aerial reconnaissance effort over Laos as a means of sending Hanoi a message of American resolve. The missions were required for other reasons as well. One was the obvious need for accurate intelligence on both Pathet Lao and North Vietnamese military capabilities and activities. Two geographic areas were seen as critically important: the Plain of Jars in central Laos and the territory to the east of it stretching to the North Vietnamese border; and the eastern reaches of the elongated Laotian panhandle. The first region contained Pathet Lao forces and some North Vietnamese auxiliary troops, both directed against Souvanna's government. North Vietnamese forces controlled the second area, for the most part, even though Pathet Lao units also were present there. Although the Pathet Lao were concerned primarily with their struggle against Souvanna Phouma and the North Vietnamese were intent on securing the Ho Chi Minh Trail that allowed them to prosecute the conflict in South Vietnam, this distinction in aims was blurred. Each of the Communist allies fought in conjunction with the other and in the same operational areas.

Recent high-level flights by U.S. reconnaissance aircraft had revealed intensive logistic activity by the North Vietnamese in the Plain of Jars and the panhandle. U.S. military planners expressed the need for more detailed intelligence, which could only be obtained by aerial reconnaissance at low level. Hence, provision for low-level photographic flights by U.S. aircraft was embodied in NSAM 288 and CINCPAC Operation Plan 37.

When Souvanna acceded to the U.S. request for periodic low-level flights on 17 May, the measures were quickly implemented. The next day the JCS directed CINCPAC to initiate the operation, soon named Yankee

Team, using aircraft from the Air Force's South Vietnam-based 2nd Air Division and from the Navy's aircraft carriers. On 19 May the Air Force carried out the first "reconnaissance/show of force" mission over central Laos.[22] On the same day *Kitty Hawk*, carrying the flag of Rear Admiral William F. Bringle, Commander Carrier Division 7, arrived at Yankee Station. The aircraft carrier was in company with *Berkeley*, *Samuel N. Moore* (DD-747), *Duncan* (DDR-874), and soon-to-be famous *Maddox* (DD-731). *Kitty Hawk*'s aerial reconnaissance assets initially included three RF-8A Crusaders and two RA-3B Skywarriors.

On 21 May 1964, Rear Admiral Bringle received orders to execute the aerial reconnaissance mission over Laos. At 0800 two RF-8A aircraft from Light Photographic Squadron 63 launched from the carrier and made for the target area in the Plain of Jars. While photographing Communist road traffic on Routes 4, 6, and 7, one of the planes was hit by ground fire over Xieng Khouang. Although a fire broke out on the port wing and burned for twenty minutes, the pilot managed to return to *Kitty Hawk* and land safely. The first of many such Yankee Team flights revealed a significant Communist military presence in northern Laos.

Augmented expeditiously by 3 RF-8As from *Bon Homme Richard*, then in Subic, 2 RA-3Bs from Cubi Point, 4 RF-8As from a Marine squadron, and 2 EA-3Bs from Fleet Air Reconnaissance Squadron (VQ) 1 in Japan, the naval aircraft of the carrier task group continued operations over Laos during succeeding days. At the same time, *Kitty Hawk* provided the extended naval presence off Southeast Asia that was sought by Washington. This symbolic measure was enhanced when *Constellation* and her escorts joined the Yankee Team formation off the coast on 6 June.

Between 21 May and 9 June, Air Force and Navy Yankee Team aircraft conducted more than 130 flights over Laos. Most of the photographic reconnaissance focused on the Plain of Jars and surrounding areas, but approximately fifty missions were flown over the infiltration routes into South Vietnam. Naval aircraft normally operated north of 18°31' north, while Air Force RF-101s flew south of that unofficial dividing line. The intelligence these units provided confirmed the extensive use of southern Laos by the North Vietnamese in their increasing support of the insurgency in South Vietnam.

---

[22] CINCPAC, Command History, 1964, p. 269; msg, CNO 171439Z May 1964; memo, OP-60 to CNO, ser BM000584-64 of 18 May.

Two weeks after the start of the reconnaissance flights, Admiral Moorer, Commander Seventh Fleet, concluded that Navy-Air Force cooperation and coordination "has been excellent and communications between them and *Kitty Hawk* have been good."[23] General Westmoreland was assigned by CINCPAC as coordinator, rather than commander, of Yankee Team operations, because while he had operational control of the 2nd Air Division at Tan Son Nhut, the Seventh Fleet units remained under CINCPACFLT. But, to ensure the efficient conduct of the overall mission, Admiral Moorer posted a mobile air control team to Saigon and liaison officers from each service worked with counterpart commands. The successful conduct of the joint operation was exemplified by the use of *Kitty Hawk*'s A-3B aerial tankers to refuel Air Force RF-101s along the route to Laos.

The Seventh Fleet commander was not equally impressed with the tight control over operations exercised from Washington. By this time, the Defense Department had fully established an elaborate command network for the worldwide direction of U.S. military forces known as the National Military Command System. This measure was prompted by the necessity for immediate readiness in the nuclear war environment, but the system also enabled close attention to conventional operations. Through the sophisticated National Military Command Center, located in the Pentagon, the JCS could order instantaneous implementation of directives from the President and the Secretary of Defense. Conversely, field commands were obligated to submit detailed message reports of operations in their theater.[24]

Under the current Yankee Team operational procedures, the Seventh Fleet commander provided the national command center with proposals for upcoming missions thirty-six hours in advance. There, the Secretary of Defense closely monitored the program and made modifications that appeared to be appropriate. The result, as Admiral Moorer noted in a private letter to Admiral McDonald, was that

> our total capability has not been utilized and...we have been restricted as to the number of sorties, have been directed as to the specific type

---

[23] Ltr, Moorer to McDonald, of 2 Jun 1964.
[24] Memo, CNO to SECNAV, ser 0004P35 of 3 Apr 1964; CNO, OPNAV Instruction 003020.7, "Master Plan for the National Military Command System," ser 008P35 of 22 Jul; DOD, *Report to the Secretary of Defense on the National Military Command Structure* (Washington: GPO, 1978).

camera to use and have had late changes in target assignments. The restrictions as to the number of aircraft to use, combined with a directive to cover a certain area is sometimes contradictory since the aircraft simply do not carry sufficient film to properly cover the specified area. An additional aircraft is often needed to complete the job. Also, the present thirty-six hour advance notice is unrealistic when viewed within the context of tactical reconnaissance. The situation on the ground and the weather changes too fast.[25]

Despite these difficulties, Seventh Fleet forces carried out the missions assigned them.

Shortly thereafter, a string of events began that would alter the nature of Yankee Team flights and signal for the Navy the start of a new era in Southeast Asian operations. On 6 June 1964, Lieutenant Charles F. Klusmann, of *Kitty Hawk*'s Light Photographic Squadron 63, Detachment C, became the first naval aviator shot down by Communist fire in Southeast Asia. His RF-8A was photographing Pathet Lao installations in an area of central Laos between Khang Khay and Ban Ban referred to as "lead alley" because of the heavy concentration there of antiaircraft weapons. Making low passes to enhance the quality of the photographs, Lieutenant Klusmann's plane was hit by fire from a 37-millimeter antiaircraft gun. When the plane became uncontrollable, the naval aviator was forced to bail out northeast of Xieng Khouang. He passed through a hail of small arms fire in landing, but only suffered a wrenched knee. Alerted by distress calls from Klusmann's wingman, Lieutenant Jerry Kuechmann, American recovery aircraft quickly converged on the spot and attempted to rescue the pilot. The heavy fire from the ground, however, made the task impossible without air cover and covering aircraft were not within range. Klusmann was soon captured by the Pathet Lao.

For the next eighty-six days the young lieutenant was held in captivity in central Laos, primarily at a location near Khang Khay. He was subjected by his captors to the subtle, but unrelenting psychological pressure long practiced by Communist interrogators. The mental stress was exacerbated

---

[25] Ltr, Moorer to McDonald, of 2 Jun 1964. See also msgs, JCS 301648Z Apr; CP 190032Z May; CPFLT 190244Z; 190459Z; CTG77.4 210152Z; 210436Z; 210504Z; 220941Z; CP 052030Z Jun; JCS, NMCC Summaries, of 19, 21, 22, 30 May; CINCPAC, Command History, 1964, pp. 261-62, 269-72; JCS, *History*, pt. 1, pp. 9-28—9-33; Seventh Fleet, Weekly Summaries, of 26 May, 9 Jun; Flag Plot, "Laos Chronology 17 May-17 June 1964;" memo, OP-60 to CNO, ser BM000584-64 of 18 May.

by his solitary confinement and debilitated physical state. He was finally forced to sign a contrived political statement which attacked U.S. policy in Southeast Asia.

Soon afterward, the Communists confined Klusmann with other prisoners, mostly Laotians and Thais, at a different location. Security at this new compound was not as rigorous. The less than attentive vigil of his guards allowed him to plan an escape. After one unsuccessful, but undiscovered attempt to burrow out of the hut to which they were confined, Lieutenant Klusmann and five other Thai and Laotian prisoners finally succeeded. The group managed to steal away and evade Pathet Lao patrols, but three members became separated and were not seen again. Another man, in search of food, entered a village that turned out to be occupied by the enemy. He was led away at gunpoint to an uncertain fate. Finally, on 21 August 1964, three days after their escape, the naval aviator and his remaining companion reached friendly Meo forces near Bouam Long. Thus, Lieutenant Klusmann became the first, and one of the few, naval personnel to escape from Communist captivity during the long conflict in Southeast Asia.[26]

Klusmann's capture and interrogation by the Pathet Lao and subsequent flight highlighted the importance of preparing naval personnel for possible imprisonment. Since 1962, the Pacific Fleet command had devoted considerable attention to refashioning prisoner of war procedures, especially since CINCPACFLT felt that "no doctrine or policy has been developed by any military service that covers the present antiguerrilla operations in Southeast Asia."[27] Subsequently, the Pacific Fleet commander issued new evasion and escape materials that incorporated the latest intelligence on Communist interrogation methods and the geographical characteristics of enemy-held areas. Reflecting the peculiar nature of the conflict in Southeast Asia, "evasion and escape" then became "Survival, Evasion, Resistance and Escape [SERE] so as to place proper emphasis on survival, and resistance to interrogation if captured."[28]

On 13 August 1964 the CNO promulgated a new instruction on SERE that superseded guidance followed since 1957. Adherence to the Code of

---

[26]Klusmann was awarded the Distinguished Flying Cross at the end of June 1964. "Klusmann Debriefing Report" encl. in ltr, COMNAVAIRPAC, ser 36/0150 of 12 Feb 1965; msgs, CTG77.4 061415Z Jun 1964; USAF 2nd Air Division 100530Z; CHINFO 301548Z; USAF 235th Tactical Group 011949Z Sep.
[27]Ltr, CINCPACFLT to CNO, ser 21/00943 of 10 Nov 1962.
[28]CINCPACFLT, Annual Report, FY1963, p. 41.

Lieutenant Charles F. Klusmann, a naval aviator who escaped from captivity in Laos in August 1964, relates his experiences to Vice Admiral Roy L. Johnson, Commander Seventh Fleet, and an unidentified officer.

Conduct was emphasized as the basic factor determining the actions of naval personnel held captive in enemy territory. The document also stated that the experience gained from World War II, the Korean conflict, and the nation's still limited involvement in Southeast Asian actions demonstrated the need for intensified SERE training to "insure that individuals are provided a thorough understanding of the standards of conduct expected of them, and are provided the means to survive and evade if isolated, resist if captured, and escape from captivity if possible."[29] Fleet commands, type commands, and training commands were instructed to establish programs for all personnel, but to place priority emphasis on those individuals most subject to capture and imprisonment. Soon afterward, Commander Naval Air Force, U.S. Pacific Fleet, began SERE training at the North Island, Whidbey Island, and Barbers Point naval air stations in the United States.

Unfortunately for Lieutenant Klusmann, this guidance was not available prior to his capture. Air intelligence officers on board *Kitty Hawk* provided the naval aviator with a wealth of detail on the political and military situations in South Vietnam, North Vietnam, and Laos, on the capabilities of friendly and enemy forces, and on survival, evasion, and escape procedures. But, with regard to resisting his interrogators, Klusmann was influenced by the Air Force 2nd Air Division manual, "E&E/Survival in South Vietnam," which recommended in essence that prisoners outwit their captors with false information. Following Klusmann's recovery, Admiral Moorer expressed his concern that "some doubt exists as to which line of resistance a pilot should follow if downed in SEASIA." He added that the tactic of outsmarting interrogators was "directly opposed to Navy policy on POW conduct which authorizes disclosure of name, rank, serial number and date of birth only." The admiral ordered that the section of the Air Force document "which suggests going beyond article V of the fighting men's code shall be disregarded by all Navy and Marine Corps personnel detained by forces inimical to U.S. efforts in SEASIA."[30] This advice would soon be followed by many naval aviators faced with the harsh and persistent interrogation of their Communist warders.[31]

---

[29] CNO, OPNAV Instruction 00305.1, ser 0063P34 of 13 Aug 1964.
[30] Msg, CPFLT 180227Z Sep 1964.
[31] Ltrs, CINCPACFLT to CINCPAC, ser 21/00866 of 15 Oct 1962; CINCPACFLT to CNO(DNI), ser 21/00872 of 18 Oct; CINCPACFLT to CNO, ser 21/00943 of 10 Nov; CINCPACFLT to CO Fleet Intelligence Center, Pacific, ser 21/00960 of 16 Nov; ser 21/001022 of

The U.S. reaction to Klusmann's loss brought the level of military involvement in Laos one step higher. The same day Klusmann's plane was shot down it was decided at the highest levels of the government to demonstrate U.S. determination to continue the reconnaissance flights and to provide them with fighter escort. This response was planned and directed from Washington. The Secretary of Defense ordered an aerial photographic mission in Laos, starting on 7 June, by two reconnaissance aircraft and eight escorting fighters. Instructions to the Pacific military command further stated that the accompanying aircraft were to be armed with an "optimum mix of weapons for anti-aircraft suppression [and] authorized to employ appropriate retaliatory fire against any source of anti-aircraft fire against reconnaissance or escort aircraft."[32]

The first of these missions took place on 7 June 1964. In the early morning hours, one RF-8A from *Constellation* and four F-8D Crusaders from *Kitty Hawk* proceeded from their launching point in the South China Sea. Over the Plain of Jars the flight received heavy fire from the ground and one of the escorts sustained minor damage. In accordance with their new instructions, the other escorts returned fire on the antiaircraft site. The group then returned safely to the carrier task force.

A second echelon planned for the same day was less fortunate. Mechanical trouble forced its launching to be delayed and reduced the number of Crusaders escorting the one RF-8A to three. This group also ran into flak over central Laos. At this point, an F-8D, piloted by Commander Doyle W. Lynn from *Kitty Hawk*'s Fighter Squadron (VF) 111 became the second naval aircraft to fall prey to Communist gunners over the Plain of Jars. Commander Lynn bailed out of his plane and landed safely in a wooded area thirty-five miles south of Xieng Khouang. Until their fuel was almost exhausted, his compatriots circled overhead.

An air rescue effort was immediately put into effect. Having learned from the unsuccessful attempt to recover Klusmann, U.S. commanders were better prepared on this day. A group of four A-1H aircraft, kept on standby over Danang, was dispatched to the location, as were F-8Ds from the carrier task group. An A-3B served as a communications relay plane

---

11 Dec 1963; *Kitty Hawk*, Cruise Report, ser 0045 of 18 Jul 1964, pp. iv-19, iv-24, iv-25; CNO, OPNAV Instruction 00305.1, ser 0063P34 of 13 Aug; CINCPACFLT, Annual Report, FY1964, p. 49; FY1965, pp. 5, 25.
[32]Msg, JCS 061632Z Jun 1964.

and used its electronic equipment to pick up the pilot's signals. Guided by the transmissions from Commander Lynn's survival radio and flares, the searching aircraft finally pinpointed his location early the next day, 8 June. An H-34 helicopter, finding its rescue cable six feet too short to lift the pilot from the forest floor, and nearly crashing in the effort, finally took him on board at a small clearing. The uninjured naval aviator was flown to Udorn in Thailand and soon afterward returned to his squadron.[33]

The reaction of Secretary of Defense McNamara to the mission conducted on 7 June revealed Washington's desire to maintain detailed control of operations. Thus, McNamara questioned the decision of naval commanders to split the mission into separate elements and to position the fighter escorts above rather than below the reconnaissance aircraft, actions which he considered as rendering the F-8Ds more vulnerable. Fleet commanders responded through the Secretary of the Navy that the mountainous terrain and low cloud ceiling in central Laos precluded the type of formation that he had in mind. The Secretary of Defense also wondered why some Sidewinder air-to-air missiles were carried, when the targets were antiaircraft guns, and why only a small portion of the other ordnance available was expended on the enemy. The Navy answered that defense against possible North Vietnamese MiG intervention made it essential to arm several of the Crusaders with Sidewinders. The low expenditure of ordnance reflected Commander Seventh Fleet's belief that only limited retaliation against enemy antiaircraft sites was to be undertaken. Washington policymakers had wanted the enemy's weapons to be silenced in order to convince the Communists of U.S. resolve, but their intentions had not been communicated effectively. Secretary of the Navy Paul H. Nitze concluded that in the future operational requirements should be more precisely stated, while commanders should be given "maximum practicable flexibility in manner of execution."[34]

Having lost two aircraft in as many days, the Washington leadership was especially determined to demonstrate to the Communists the consequences of attacking U.S. military forces. Specifically, the JCS was directed

---

[33]Tragically, Commander Lynn was killed the following year during a mission over Vinh, North Vietnam. See CINCPACFLT, "The United States Navy in the Pacific, 1965," pp. 74-75.

[34]Memo, SECNAV to SECDEF, of 10 Jun 1964. See also msgs, SECSTATE 061625Z Jun 1964; JCS 061632Z; 080654Z; CPFLT 081553Z; AMEMBVT 081921Z; JCS, NMCC Summary, of 8 Jun; Flag Plot Briefers, of 8 and 9 Jun; Flag Plot, "F-8 Flap Summary, of 6 June-8 June;" ltr, Ricketts to Moorer, of 20 Jun.

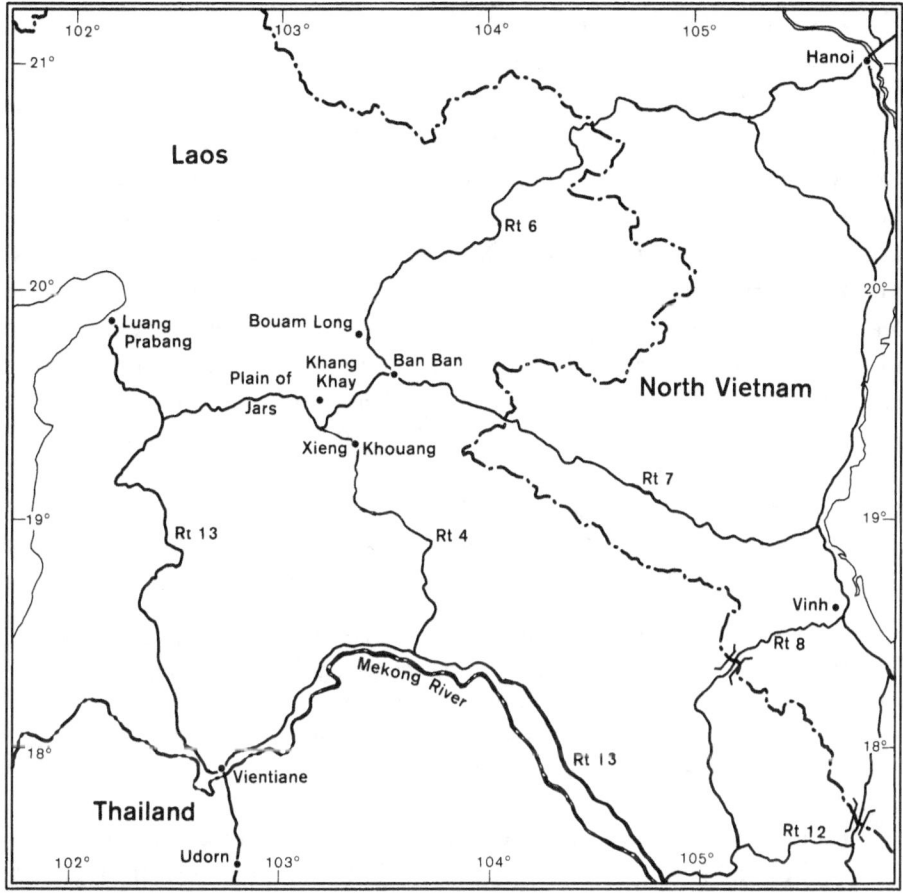

Central Laos

to initiate retaliatory air strikes by Air Force and Navy aircraft on antiaircraft installations at Xieng Khouang and Khang Khay, respectively. On 9 June Air Force F-100s based in South Vietnam hit their targeted sight with 750-pound bombs, rockets, and cannon fire. Actual damage to the antiaircraft facility was not great, but the signal to Hanoi and Peking sought by U.S. policymakers presumably had been sent. However, the naval strikes at Khang Khay, planned for the following day, were cancelled when Souvanna Phouma requested that no further offensive missions be undertaken in his country. He was disturbed both by the air attack and by U.S. disclosure of the fact that American aircraft were conducting escorted reconnaissance flights over Laos. At that point, *Kitty*

Hawk was released for normal flight operations, leaving only one carrier, *Constellation*, at Yankee Station.[35]

There followed a five-day hiatus in operations as U.S. officials negotiated with the Laotian leader. It was only after assurances were made to Souvanna that the escorted reconnaissance flights would no longer be publicly acknowledged that he agreed to their resumption in mid-June. At the same time, Secretary of Defense McNamara called for a new "minimum risk approach" to lessen future American losses.[36] Pacific naval leaders responded that the best way to achieve the secretary's goal was to give operational commanders greater flexibility in fashioning missions according to the strength of enemy defenses, the weather, and other continually changing tactical factors. CINCPAC also suggested

> that low level photo recce of well defended targets must be preceded by an air strike of adequate weight against the target, to be followed up immediately by post-strike recce supported by armed escort.... This is a militarily sound concept and should be adopted as the strategy.... In the north, I would start with anti-aircraft concentrations and raise the level of activity to include military camps and supply dumps if the [Pathet Lao/Viet Minh] do not rpt not concede to political demands made by our side. In the south, I would hit supply facilities and conduct armed recce along routes of supply.[37]

The recommendations were not accepted in Washington. But, on 16 June, when the JCS issued new operational instructions, they directed that reconnaissance missions be conducted at altitudes above 10,000 feet, in order to remain outside the effective range of most Communist guns, unless it was absolutely necessary to obtain low-level photographs. Further, areas of high enemy antiaircraft concentrations, primarily around the Plain of Jars, would be avoided. Only when it was essential to obtain intelligence at low level in lethal areas were aircraft allowed to attack and neutralize antiaircraft defenses in advance of the aerial photographic planes. Authority for this type of operation was granted only on a case-by-case basis. The JCS also reiterated their requirement for prior approval in

---

[35]Msgs, JCS 072022Z Jun 1964; AMEMBVT 081036Z; 082050Z; 082145Z; 082200Z; JCS, NMCC Summaries, of 9 and 10 Jun; memo, OP-60B to Executive Assistant to CNO, ser BM000607P60 of 8 Jun; OP-601C9, Point Paper, of 10 Jun; Flag Plot Briefers, of 8, 9, 10, 11, 12 Jun.
[36]Memo, SECNAV Aide to CNO, of 9 Jun 1964.
[37]Msg, CP 122146Z Jun 1964.

Washington of the purpose, time-span, number and type of planes involved, flying formation, tactics to be employed, altitude, and route to the target of each contemplated mission. For the remainder of the year, these instructions constituted Yankee Team standard operating procedures. Since only two Air Force and no Navy planes were lost over Laos by the end of 1964, this new directive apparently was effective.[38]

When aerial photographic flights over Laos were resumed by Air Force planes on 14 June, *Constellation* was positioned off the South Vietnamese coast, prepared to launch her aircraft. On the 19th, this carrier launched the first Seventh Fleet reconnaissance mission since the halt in operations when an RF-8A and an RA-3B, each escorted by two Crusaders, overflew sites in the Laotian panhandle. In line with the new operating procedures, greater reliance now was placed on the carrier's RA-3B Skywarriors, which were best suited for photography above 10,000 feet. For the more hazardous low-level reconnaissance, the faster and smaller RF-8As were used because of their ability to evade enemy flak. However, the heavy monsoon weather, typical in Laos during the summer months, limited these operations. Before her relief on 12 July, *Constellation* launched only five other aerial intelligence collection missions.

When *Constellation* steamed for Japan, *Ticonderoga* (CVA-14) and her escorts, under the command of Rear Admiral Robert B. Moore, took position at Yankee Station. Because of a relative improvement in weather conditions, Admiral Moore's task group was able to launch reconnaissance flights on six separate days during the remainder of July. Both the Plain of Jars and the panhandle were covered, but to minimize risks most overflights were conducted at medium-level altitudes. These operations succeeded in photographing Communist troop movements, supply traffic, and military installations. Similarly, the Laotian air force received post-bombing damage assessments and other intelligence that improved the government's military position. By the end of July the Navy had conducted 93 of the 189 missions carried out under the Yankee Team program.

As a result of the Gulf of Tonkin attacks in August, Yankee Team operational procedures were altered to counter the growing Communist military threat. Shortly after the incidents in early August, U.S. intelligence confirmed the presence in North Vietnam of MiG-15s and MiG-17s

---

[38]Msgs, JCS 102316Z Jun 1964; 121419Z; CP 122146Z; JCS 122227Z; 161904Z; memo, OP-60B to CNO, ser 000499P60 of 13 Jun; Flag Plot, "Laos Chronology 17 May–17 June."

An RF-8A Crusader aerial reconnaissance aircraft of Light Photographic Squadron 63 flies over aircraft carrier Ticonderoga (CVA-14) in December 1964.

provided by Communist China. Accordingly, escort aircraft now carried air-to-air weapons and were permitted to attack hostile aircraft in Laos and to carry "hot pursuit" into Thailand and South Vietnam. Unless in actual combat with enemy planes, however, Yankee Team escorts were barred from North Vietnamese air space and prohibited from entering China for any reason. Despite these precautions, however, no air-to-air encounters took place over Laos during 1964.

Following the Gulf of Tonkin naval engagements, there was a buildup in the number of Seventh Fleet carrier task groups operating in Southeast Asian waters. During August and most of September two aircraft carriers shared Yankee Team duties, as well as the now primary mission of exhibiting U.S. military strength in the confrontation with North Vietnam. Hampered by bad weather and other operational commitments, Task Force 77, under Admiral Moore, initially launched only a limited number of reconnaissance flights. Between 28 August and 10 September, however, thirty-two such missions were conducted. For the remainder of 1964, only forty more photographic missions over Laos were accomplished by *Ticonderoga*, *Constellation*, and *Hancock* aircraft, but the requirement for aerial photographic missions was lessened, in part, because of the introduction into the fleet late in the year of the more advanced and capable RA-5C Vigilante. The first operation by this aircraft took place on 1 December from the deck of *Ranger* (CVA-61).[39]

By the end of 1964, Seventh Fleet aircraft had carried out more than half of the joint Yankee Team missions, which included 198 photographic, 171 escort, and 81 weather flights. The information collected, especially through the low-level flights, provided U.S. and friendly governments with useful intelligence of enemy intentions and capabilities, including confirmation of the suspected increase in the number and size of enemy units infiltrating into South Vietnam by way of the Ho Chi Minh Trail complex. On the negative side, it is evident that the political purpose of these flights was not achieved, since the enemy showed no sign of halting his support of the insurgency in South Vietnam.

At the same time, the Navy profited from participation in the Yankee Team program. Commanders, recognizing that their military operations would be to a great extent controlled at the Washington level, adapted their actions to this method of command, which would be exercised throughout the Vietnam conflict. Similarly, search and rescue (SAR) procedures were modified and refined in accordance with the special Southeast Asian operating environment. SERE training benefited from the lessons learned the hard way by naval aviators. The officers and men of Task Force 77 gained valuable experience with the extended deployment

---

[39]Previously, CINCPAC prohibited use of the technologically advanced plane over Laos for fear of loss. See OP-03, memo for record, of 22 Sep 1964.

at Yankee Station that would prepare them for the later aerial offensive against North Vietnam.[40]

The Yankee Team reconnaissance operation, in addition to the Seventh Fleet's "show of force" deployments into the South China Sea, and the anchorage and naval base surveys on the South Vietnamese coast, represented the Johnson administration's growing focus during 1964 on overt military measures against North Vietnam in order to preserve the faltering government of South Vietnam. Key American naval leaders were influential advocates of this course of action, convinced as they were that the North Vietnamese lacked the will or physical capacity to prevail against an increasingly strong application of U.S. air and naval force. Further, they minimized the likelihood of a Chinese military response. Continued weakness of the South Vietnamese politico-military effort, concern by other U.S. leaders over Chinese intentions, ongoing diplomatic activities, and other considerations, however, dictated a limited use of American military power in Southeast Asia.

---

[40]JCS, NMCC Summaries, of 19, 26 Jun, 13, 16, 21, 23, 24, 31 Jul 1964; memos, OP-333E to OP-002, of 29 Jun 1964; OP-33B of OP-09B, ser 003131-64 of 27 Aug; ser 003132-64 of 3 Sep; ser 00032P33 of 17 Sep; msgs, COMUSMACV 021345Z Aug; CPFLT 030104Z; CP 120323Z; 200325Z Sep; JCS 281438Z; CTF77, "Standard Operating Procedures (SOP) for Yankee Team (YT)," ser 0031205 of 7 Dec; COM7FLT, Weekly Summaries, Jun-Dec 1964; CINCPAC, Command History, 1964, pp. 271-72; CINCPACFLT, Annual Report, FY1964, pp. 4, 51; FY1965, pp. 5, 54, 55; Flag Plot, "Laos Chronology 17 June-31 July;" JCS Paper 2344/92; MACV, Command History, 1965, pp. 208-10.

CHAPTER XIV

Naval Engagements in the Gulf of Tonkin

The Tonkin Gulf crisis of August 1964, which focused American attention on Southeast Asia in a highly dramatic fashion, traced its origin to March 1962, when Admiral Schoech, Commander Seventh Fleet, proposed a destroyer patrol in international waters along the Chinese Communist coast. The purpose was to "collect intelligence concerning CHICOM electronic and naval activity...establish and maintain Seventh Fleet presence in area [and] serve as a minor cold war irritant to CHICOMs."[1] Soon afterward, the JCS, through CINCPAC, authorized inauguration of the operation, designated the Desoto Patrol, in international waters off the Chinese mainland.

In mid-April 1962, *DeHaven* conducted the first operation. The ship steamed along the northern coastline of the Peoples Republic of China. Once each month for the next five months, U.S. destroyers cruised the same general area without significant incident, although the Chinese broadcast protests. The October patrol of *Hollister* (DD-788) and the November mission of *Shelton* (DD-790) were extended to include, for the first time, surveillance along the North Korean littoral. As before, there was no significant Communist reaction.

---

[1]Msg, COM7FLT 140536Z Mar 1962. The following sources, of varying usefulness and quality, specifically treat the Tonkin Gulf crisis. U.S., Congress, Senate, Committee on Foreign Relations, *Hearings on the Gulf of Tonkin, the 1964 Incidents* (90th Cong., 2nd sess.) (Washington: GPO, 1968); Anthony Austin, *The President's War* (New York: Lippincott, 1972); John Mecklin, *Mission in Torment* (Garden City, NY: Doubleday and Co., 1965); Joseph C. Goulden, *Truth is the First Casualty: The Gulf of Tonkin Affair — Illusion and Reality* (New York: Rand McNally, 1969); Eugene G. Windchy, *Tonkin Gulf* (Garden City, NY: Doubleday, 1971); John Galloway, *The Gulf of Tonkin Resolution* (Rutherford, NJ: Farleigh Dickinson Univ. Press, 1970); U.S., Congress, Senate, Committee on Armed Services, *Nomination of Admiral Thomas H. Moorer, USN, to be Chairman, Joint Chiefs of Staff* (91st Cong., 2nd sess.) (Washington: GPO, 1970); Jim and Sybil Stockdale, *In Love and War: The Story of a Family's Ordeal and Sacrifice During the Vietnam Years* (New York: Harper and Row, 1984); Samuel E. Halpern, *WEST PAC 64* (Boston: Branden Press, 1975).

The first surface surveillance of North Vietnamese coastal waters, as part of the Desoto Patrol program, was carried out in mid-December 1962. Departing Keelung, Taiwan, on 16 December, *Agerholm* (DD-826) sailed around Hainan Island and into the Gulf of Tonkin to 21° north latitude. As with the other ships, *Agerholm* was directed to approach no closer than twenty miles to Communist territory. The mission of the patrol was to "collect general and electronic intelligence [and] increase U.S. knowledge concerning CHICOM and North Vietnamese military forces."[2] The cruise coincided with reconnaissance flights over the same area by EC-121 and EA-3B electronic intelligence planes. Thus, Communist radar emissions were monitored from the air and the sea. In keeping with past practice, the Chinese protested the approach of the U.S. patrol to their territorial waters, but took no further action.

During 1963, there were six additional Desoto Patrols along the Chinese, Soviet, Indonesian, and North Vietnamese coastlines. Once again, the patrolling destroyers were prohibited from approaching closer than twenty nautical miles from the Communist mainland. In mid-April, *Richard S. Edwards* (DD-950) operated off Hainan and North Vietnam. The Seventh Fleet ship was shadowed by five or six North Vietnamese submarine chasers and coastal minesweepers and a number of Chinese aircraft. The Chinese again issued "serious warnings."[3]

On 7 January 1964, Commander Seventh Fleet issued a revised directive governing conduct of the Desoto Patrol. The mission of the operation was broadened to include the collection of "all-source intelligence" in order to "increase both COMSEVENTHFLT and national fund of information concerning both military and civil activity of the Asiatic Communist bloc." In addition, the restriction that U.S. ships approach no closer than twenty miles from Communist territory was eased to allow patrol vessels to sail as near as twelve miles offshore. Aerial intelligence collection aircraft continued to form part of the Desoto team. The following information was sought:

A. Seaward defense posture: disposition of forces and capability. Deployment and operations of naval units, particularly submarines.

---

[2]Msg, ADMINO COM7FLT 080250Z Dec 1962.
[3]H.E. Fitzwater, JRC (JCS), memo for record, of 13 Aug 1964. See also CINCPAC, Command History, 1962, pp. 44-45; 1963, pp. 55-57; 1964, p. 367; CINCPACFLT, Annual Report, FY1962, p. 12; msgs, CP 172231Z Mar 1962; COM7FLT 080250Z Dec; *John R. Craig* 151020Z Dec 1963.

B. Air defense posture: disposition and capability. Response to unexpected surface and air contacts.

C. Merchant shipping activity.

D. [Electronic] intelligence collection in support of objectives above.

E. Photography and visual identification in support of objectives above.

F. Hydrographic and meteorological observations.

G. Such additional recurring or nonrecurring collection as may be directed by higher authority.[4]

The potential value of the operation to U.S. actions in Southeast Asia was recognized by key leaders. In mid-January 1964, COMUSMACV requested that the Desoto Patrol scheduled for February be designed to provide the forthcoming 34A program with critical intelligence. CINCPAC informed the JCS that there was a "continuing requirement for obtaining INTEL on DRV forces capable [of resisting] projected operations in conjunction with OPLAN 34A. Desoto platform offers excellent means for obtaining this INTEL."[5] Accordingly, Admiral Moorer, the Seventh Fleet commander, scheduled a patrol by *Radford* (DD-446) for the first week in February. The destroyer was to steam along a designated track off the North Vietnamese coast, orbiting in certain areas for up to twenty-four hours. For the first time, a Desoto Patrol ship was authorized to close up to four nautical miles to Communist territory. In addition to satisfying existing needs, *Radford* had orders to photograph items of interest on the coast and offshore islands, to locate and identify coastal radar transmitters, to monitor junk activity, and to provide "information on Viet Cong supply routes to fulfill long standing requirement this area."[6] To ensure that General Harkins received intelligence specifically suited to the maritime operation based in Danang, a MACV officer would be embarked in *Radford*. Shortly afterward, however, the patrol was postponed until after mid-February in order not to interfere with 34A missions planned for the first two weeks of the month.[7]

---
[4]Msg, COM7FLT 070524Z Jan 1964. See also msg, COM7FLT 151741Z Aug 1963.
[5]Msg, CP 240124Z Jan 1964.
[6]Msg, COM7FLT 220602Z Jan 1964.
[7]Msgs, COM7FLT 151741Z Aug 1963; CP 290100Z Jan 1964; COM7FLT 300300Z.

As a result of this delay, *John R. Craig* (DD-885) replaced *Radford* as the patrol ship. At the end of January 1964, Admiral Sharp, the Pacific Fleet commander, directed Commander James H. Doyle, the commanding officer of *John R. Craig*, to conduct the postponed mission from 25 February to 12 March. The closest point of approach to Communist China remained twelve nautical miles, while that to North Vietnam was more precisely defined as eight miles to the mainland and four miles to the offshore islands. Because the State Department had no record of a specific North Vietnamese assertion regarding their territorial waters, U.S. officials concluded that international waters extended to three miles offshore, which was the limit established by the French when they controlled Indochina. Only on 1 September, after the August incidents, did the North Vietnamese state a claim to a twelve-mile limit.[8] In addition to standing requirements, General Harkins requested that the Desoto Patrol provide him with radarscope photography of the North Vietnamese littoral. Assessing the threat from the Communists as minimal, Admiral Sharp decided not to provide carrier air support. He observed that "CHICOM air attack on Desoto ship highly unlikely and North Vietnam air capability for attack almost non-existent."[9] *Ingersoll* (DD-652), however, was ordered to the entrance of the Gulf of Tonkin prepared to assist *John R. Craig* with on-call surface support against destroyers and smaller naval vessels and antiaircraft protection.

On 25 February, *John R. Craig* steamed from Keelung, Taiwan, with Captain Edward A. Williams, Commander Destroyer Division 12, and several intelligence collection equipment vans embarked for the first Desoto Patrol of 1964. A MACV representative, Lieutenant Commander Donald P. Darnell, accompanied the ship during part of the patrol. *John R. Craig* conducted the surveillance operations for eleven days in international waters near the Chinese and North Vietnamese coasts without eliciting a significant reaction from either Communist nation. Aside from shadowing *John R. Craig* with a Kronstadt class patrol vessel and an aircraft, both from considerable distances, the Chinese restricted their response to issuing a "serious warning," one of many in a long series. No North Vietnamese reaction was detected. By 9 March, the American destroyer

---

[8]Memo, Office of the Judge Advocate General to SECNAV, of 1 Feb 1968; msg, CPFLT 140203Z Jul 1964; COM7FLT, OPORD 201-64, Ann. D, app. XI.
[9]Msg, CPFLT 311834Z Jan 1964.

completed its mission, made difficult by ubiquitous coastal fog, and sailed for Taiwan.[10]

Another Desoto Patrol was conducted in July. This time, Soviet coastal waters in the Sea of Japan were the prime interest. Between 14 and 24 July, *George K. MacKenzie* (DD-836), with Commander Destroyer Division 32 on board, sailed as close as fifteen nautical miles to Soviet territory in the vicinity of Vladivostok and Sakhalin Island. The ship collected valuable electronic, photographic, visual, hydrographic, and other intelligence. Numerous Soviet ships and aircraft approached *George K. MacKenzie,* but no incidents occurred.[11]

Preparation for the August Patrol

Even while *George K. MacKenzie* cruised through northern waters, planning was underway for another mission in the Gulf of Tonkin. Since March 1964, COMUSMACV's requirements for current intelligence on North Vietnam had increased significantly. During the spring, the 34A maritime force suffered losses and accomplished little, partly owing to the dearth of information on the enemy's defenses. In April Admiral Felt, CINCPAC, reported that the "lack of adequate intelligence is a prime factor in the failure of maritime operations." He added that "as a result of increased state of alert and mobilization of resources by the DRV sabotage targets are more difficult to reach than was visualized at the time [Operation Plan 34A] was written.... The odds against pulling off operations under present conditions are high."[12]

At the beginning of July, General Westmoreland, the new COMUSMACV, detailed his specific needs for an improved 34A program. He required intelligence on the enemy's coastal ground forces and naval craft capable of intercepting the South Vietnamese PTFs and Swifts. Knowledge of radar sites from which the maritime force could be detected and

---

[10]Msgs, CP 010022Z Feb 1964; 010308Z; ADMIN CPFLT 120142Z; 120423Z; COM7FLT 140200Z; 291015Z; 051132Z Mar; Fitzwater, JRC (JCS), memo for record, of 13 Aug 1964; Roy L. Johnson, transcript of interview with John T. Mason, Jr., U.S. Naval Institute, in Virginia Beach, VA, Dec 1980, p. 235.

[11]Msgs, CPFLT 212103Z Jun 1964; COM7FLT 300740Z; CP 150015Z Jul; CTU72.1.2 200420Z; CTG72.1 211447Z.

[12]Msg, CP 012205Z Apr 1964. See also msg, COMUSMACV 311037Z Mar 1964.

tracked also was essential. The general requested coverage of those areas specifically targeted for sabotage missions during July. Vinh Son and the islands of Hon Me, Hon Nieu, and Hon Matt were the sites of prime importance. Concern about the enemy's patrol craft was heightened when, on 3 July, COMUSMACV reported that ten Swatow motor gunboats had swelled the defense forces at Dong Hoi. An additional four boats were discovered at Quang Khe. Westmoreland observed that the "cause of these movements not known but could be attributable as reaction to recent successful 34A MAROPS."[13]

Accordingly, on 10 July, Admiral Sharp, the new CINCPAC, directed Admiral Moorer, now CINCPACFLT, to finalize planning for a Desoto Patrol into the Gulf of Tonkin, to begin not later than 1 August, for the "primary purpose of determining DRV coastal patrol activity."[14] CINCPACFLT was authorized direct liaison with General Westmoreland to determine if additional intelligence was required, to set up any communications that were desired, and to ensure mutual non-interference between proposed 34A and Desoto Patrol operations.

The following day, Vice Admiral Johnson, the newly designated Commander Seventh Fleet, issued his initial instructions. *Picking* (DD-685), with Commander Destroyer Division 192, Captain John J. Herrick, embarked, was slated to carry out the mission under the operational control of Commander Taiwan Patrol Force, Rear Admiral Robert A. MacPherson. The destroyer would depart Keelung on 28 July and proceed southwestward to the patrol area. After underway replenishment in the vicinity of $17°N$ $108°30'E$, the plan called for *Picking* to steam along the following track, arriving near the following points at the times indicated:

A.	$17°5'N$	$107°18'E$	311300H
B.	$18°N$	$106°42'E$	010400H
C.	$19°N$	$105°53'E$	011800H
D.	$19°47'N$	$106°8'E$	021100H
E.	$20°22'N$	$107°E$	022400H
F.	$20°42'N$	$107°47'E$	031400H

---

[13]Msg, COMUSMACV 030307Z Jul 1964. The information on the Swatow deployments was soon disputed, but North Vietnamese naval movements remained a concern. See also msgs, COMUSMACV 252331Z Jun 1964; 010015Z Jul.
[14]Msg, CP 100342Z Jul 1964.

G.	21° 19'N	108° 24'E	040600H
H.	[2]1° 17'N	108° 49'E	042000H
I.	20° 47'N	107° 40'E	050200H
J.	20° 8'N	106° 45'E	051500H
K.	19° [3]7'N	106° 1'E	060300H
L.	19° 9'N	106° 19'E	061800H
M.	18° 41'N	105° 58'E	061800H
N.	18°N	106° 50'E	071100H
O.	17° 33'N	106° 45'E	071300H
P.	17° 15'N	107° 20'E	080400H[15]

As established during *John R. Craig*'s patrol, the closest point of approach to the North Vietnamese littoral remained eight nautical miles and four miles to the offshore islands. Captain Herrick was authorized to delay his departure for up to twenty-four hours from the various points if he expected intelligence collection there to be especially productive. At the same time, *Picking* was allowed to quickly pass through those areas deemed sterile. In either case, the patrol commander had orders to alert Commander Seventh Fleet of changes to the schedule. Captain Herrick, however, retained considerable discretion in the length of time allowed in the various areas:

Point	Approximate Duration of Orbit (hours)
A.	10
B.	8
C.	14
D.	8
E.	10
F.	12
G.	12
I.	8
J.	8

---

[15] As most histories of the Tonkin Gulf incidents have revealed, determining the correct sequence of events has been complicated by the fact that Washington, Honolulu, Taiwan, the gulf itself, and often ships underway were located in different time zones. To simplify the time conversion process, throughout Chapters XIV-XVII local time in the waters off mainland Southeast Asia is considered Hotel (H) Time. South Vietnam adhered to H Time while North Vietnam operated on Golf (G) Time (i.e., 1 hour earlier than H Time). Local time in Washington (on Eastern Daylight Time (EDT) in August 1964) was exactly 12 hours behind H Time. Thus, 0100 on 5 August in the gulf would correspond to 1300 on 4 August in Washington. Zulu (Z) Time (Greenwich Mean Time), used in the Navy's message traffic, is 8 hours behind H Time and 4 hours ahead of Washington time.

Point	Approximate Duration of Orbit (hours) continued
K.	10
M.	12
O.	12
P.	12

In addition, Admiral Johnson specifically called for the Desoto Patrol ship to locate North Vietnamese radar transmitters and to estimate their range capabilities; chart navigational lights, landmarks, and buoys; obtain current, tide, and other information near river mouths; photograph all prominent landmarks and islands in the same areas and near built-up locations; conduct radarscope photography along the coast; and monitor junk traffic that might be infiltrating into South Vietnam. A communications van embarked in *George K. MacKenzie* would be transferred to *Picking* just prior to the latter ship's departure from Taiwan.[16]

By mid-July, however, General Westmoreland expressed doubts that the Desoto Patrol could provide the 34A program with adequate intelligence. Because of inclement weather during *John R. Craig*'s cruise, the actual intelligence return had been minimal. Further, COMUSMACV observed that the "Desoto Patrol is regarded as a potentially useful method of collecting DRV intelligence needed here" but that "it is questionable that the relatively brief Desoto [electronic intelligence] and sea intel samplings would produce results which are as accurately representative of long term events as regularly recurring" maritime air patrols. He added that "perhaps the ultimate answer to more complete DRV [electronic intelligence] and sea intel of the type needed here would be development of a mix of regularly recurring patrols/recon conducted by high altitude aircraft, maritime aircraft, destroyers and possibly submarines."[17] Perhaps reflecting his lower estimation of the value of the Desoto Patrol to the 34A program, General Westmoreland decided that, in contrast to the March mission, a MACV liaison officer need not accompany the July-August patrol.[18]

---

[16] Msgs, COM7FLT 110652Z Jul 1964; 170531Z.
[17] Msg, COMUSMACV 192241Z Jul 1964. See also msgs, CP 090528Z May 1964; COMUSMACV 111205Z Jul; ADMINO CP 152123Z.
[18] Msgs, COM7FLT 170531Z Jul 1964; 260955Z.

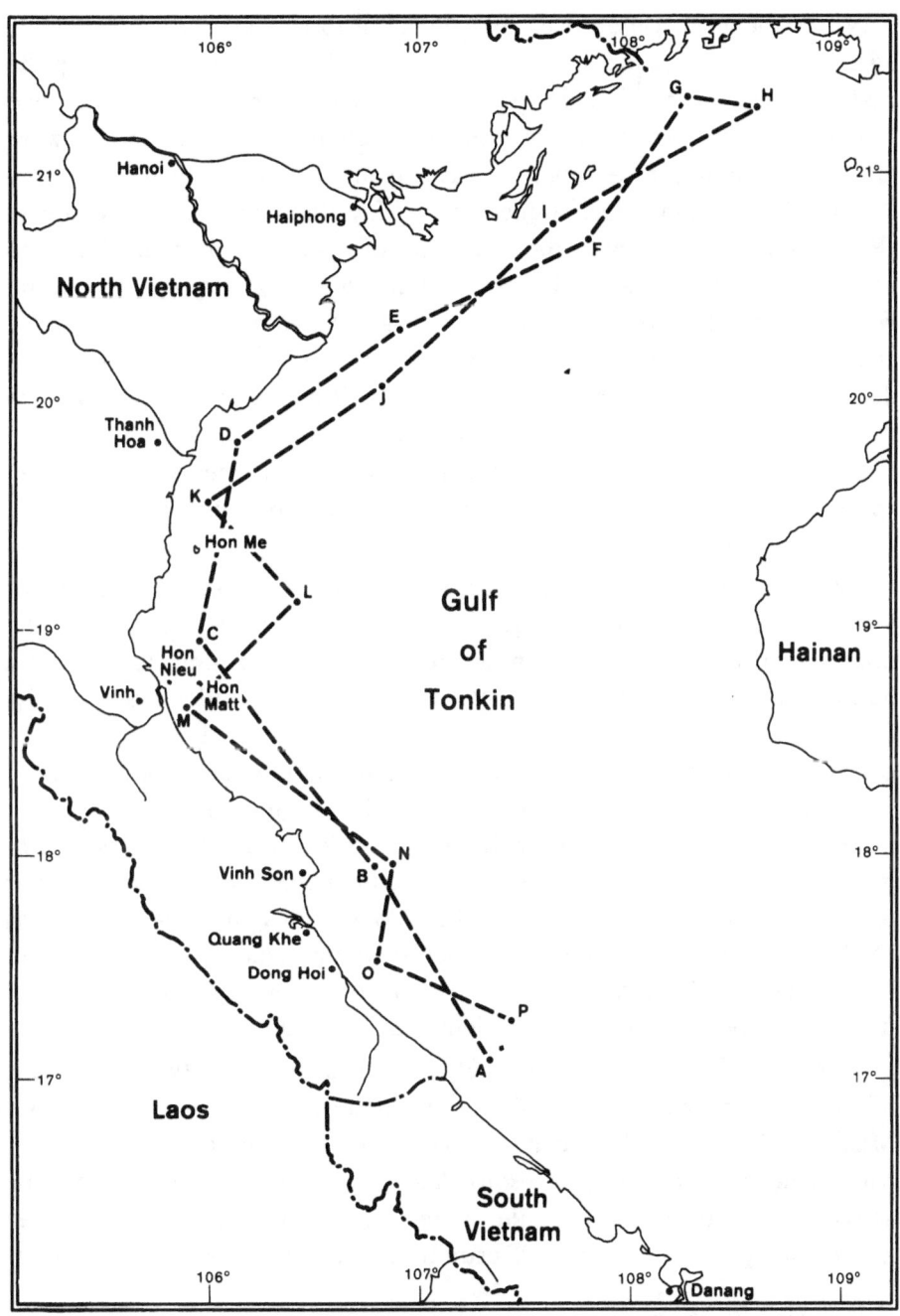

Intended Track of the Desoto Patrol

No connection, other than that detailed above, existed between the 34A maritime operation and the Desoto Patrol. To be sure, earlier in the year Pacific commanders proposed combined operations of these two forces. Since it was known that North Vietnamese coastal radars were turned off when U.S. equipment was activated, Admiral Sharp, then the Pacific Fleet commander, suggested in May that "we could coordinate [PTF] raids in NVN with the operation of a shipboard radar to reduce possibility of NVN radar detection of the delivery vehicle."[19] Admiral Felt endorsed this proposal, stating that "a U.S. destroyer could be made available for this purpose."[20] CINCPAC also expanded on the concept, detailing a scenario whereby a PTF and a Swift boat would be vectored to the target area by the destroyer. A U.S. naval officer would be carried in the Swift to monitor the vector commands. If an enemy naval vessel appeared on the scene, the escorting PTF could be guided by the U.S. ship to engage the contact.

By the time COMUSMACV considered these proposals at the end of June, the situation had changed. The maritime force was then fully operational, the South Vietnamese crews were performing better, and a number of missions in North Vietnam were concluded successfully. Further, General Westmoreland felt that the complex problem of coordinating combined actions exceeded the competence of the South Vietnamese crews. He observed that "in theory such levels could ultimately be attained, however the present orientation of effort is toward more modest 34A goals." The general added that "any activity on our part immediately preceding a [maritime operations] mission such as [a] DD's appearance would tend to be self defeating since the enemy would be alerted."[21] Thereafter, consideration of operating Desoto Patrol destroyers and 34A craft in tandem was dropped.

Indeed, CINCPACFLT raised the concern that the two operations might interfere with one another during the July-August mission. COMUSMACV assured the naval commander that as long as *Maddox*, which had replaced *Picking* as the Desoto Patrol ship, did not deviate from the assigned time and route schedule, there would be no problem. And given at least thirty-six hours notice, Westmoreland could adjust 34A operations

---

[19]Msg, CPFLT 190259Z May 1964.
[20]Msg, CP 272258Z May 1964. Even earlier CINCPAC had alluded to the possibility of combined operations. See CP 090528Z May 1964.
[21]Msg, COMUSMACV 250741Z Jun 1964.

Destroyer Maddox (DD-731) several months before her famous cruise in the Gulf of Tonkin.

to allow *Maddox* greater latitude in the patrol area. Admiral Moorer responded that it might not always be possible to provide the proposed changes thirty-six hours in advance. The general accepted the difficulties involved in this coordination, but stated that as long as the Special Operations Group in Saigon was given expeditious notice of course or time changes, "34A operations will be adjusted to prevent interference."[22] In accordance with this concept, Admiral Moorer authorized Admiral Johnson to effect liaison with MACV "to assure all feasible measures are taken to avoid interference with 34A operations."[23]

As instructed, Seventh Fleet representatives met with MACV staff officers during the fourth week in July and exchanged information. Based on his knowledge of past patrols, Admiral Johnson doubted that the destroyer would have to remain in one area longer than scheduled. Nevertheless, he advised Commander Taiwan Patrol Force to inform Captain Herrick, the Desoto Patrol commander, of the special nature of operations in the Gulf of Tonkin. Commander Seventh Fleet stipulated:

A. That patrol ship should carefully assess collection requirement opportunity with an 'eye on the clock' and keep [all concerned] informed of intentions in most expeditious manner possible.

B. That most coordination problems are resolved by timely and complete [situation reports], and that due to sensitivity of the area, what...may have been common occurrence (E.G. being shadowed by patrol...craft, overflown by aircraft or subject [of] unusual radar interest) may be, in this case, a significant event and worthy of a special [situation report].[24]

Even as COMUSMACV deemphasized the importance of the Desoto Patrol to his operations against North Vietnam, other U.S. leaders questioned the need for any destroyer surveillance effort along the Communist periphery. In July, the Chief of Naval Operations called for an analysis of the Desoto Patrol program's value. Admiral McDonald specifically wanted to ensure that the Navy was not just "DeSoto

---

[22]Msg, COMUSMACV 250705Z Jul 1964. See also msgs, CPFLT 150157Z Jul 1964; COMUSMACV 192241Z; CPFLT 222224Z.
[23]Msg, CPFLT 222224Z Jul 1964. See also Johnson, Interview, p. 237.
[24]Msg, COM7FLT 260955Z Jul 1964.

patrolling once a quarter because it has been going on for some time."[25] At the end of the month, Admiral Moorer responded that the advantages gained from the operation outweighed the disadvantages. The chief benefit was the realistic training provided officers and men in close proximity to unfriendly forces. Almost as important was the opportunity provided "to assert our traditional belief in the right of free use of international waters...the importance of [which] has been emphasized [time] and again [but] is particularly worthy of repetition at this time."[26] To emphasize this point, Admiral Moorer requested permission to sail a destroyer during August or September, into the Sea of Okhotsk, a body of water near the Soviet Union not entered by a U.S. naval vessel in eleven years. A third advantage of the patrols was the operational intelligence derived from the Communist powers. CINCPACFLT believed that close observation by these nations of U.S. ships was the only meaningful disadvantage of the patrol program.[27]

In addition, Admiral Sharp provided further justification for the Desoto Patrol in the Gulf of Tonkin. CINCPAC observed that visual intelligence of the North Vietnamese coast had not been obtained since March. Also, with the continuation of the Yankee Team carrier air operations in Laos and the possibility of overt action against North Vietnam, current intelligence became all the more essential. Lastly, an increase in 34A operations required more recent information of the target area.[28]

Preparations for the Desoto Patrol mission for July-August proceeded as scheduled. The detailed guidelines issued by Commander Seventh Fleet on 11 and 17 July, however, reflected a greater awareness of the risks involved than was evident earlier in the year. While the air protection of *John R. Craig* was deemed to be unnecessary, air cover for *Maddox* was on alert and close at hand. *Ticonderoga*, engaged in Yankee Team operations, specifically was directed to provide the Desoto Patrol ship with on-call air support against naval vessels and aircraft. Communications from *Maddox* were maintained through the Naval Communications Station, Philippines. During the patrol, that facility closely monitored operational messages from the ship and from Captain Herrick, and expeditiously passed them to

---

[25] Quoted in memo, OP-002 to OP-03/OP-06/OP-92, ser 00197-64 of 18 Jul 1964.
[26] Msg, CPFLT 302237Z Jul 1964.
[27] *Ibid*. The deployment of antisubmarine carriers in the Sea of Japan was also considered in this reply to the CNO.
[28] Msg, ADMINO CP 152123Z Jul 1964.

all concerned. If under attack or "harassment which clearly indicates imminent danger to the lives and/or safety of ship," *Maddox* was directed to send a "flash" precedence message to CINCPACFLT, COMUSMACV, and Commander Taiwan Patrol Force. At the same time, *Maddox* or Captain Herrick would alert *Ticonderoga* through the High Command communication circuit without delaying to encode the message. Further, *Maddox* had orders to undertake radio checks every four hours, send periodic situation reports, and transmit daily operational summaries.[29]

With preparations virtually complete, Pacific naval commanders awaited the final JCS order to execute the Desoto Patrol. That directive came on 22 July, when the Joint Chiefs of Staff instructed CINCPAC to undertake the long-planned reconnaissance mission into the Gulf of Tonkin.[30]

34A Operations in North Vietnam

While *Maddox* made ready to get underway, U.S. leaders instituted last-minute changes to the 34A program. Enemy coastal defenses were becoming harder and more dangerous to penetrate. As early as April, CINCPAC concluded that, with 30,000 Viet Cong and twice as many supporters in South Vietnam, the enemy was aware of the 34A base at Danang. Communist observers could monitor the arrival and departure of the PTFs and PCFs and personnel in training. CINCPAC also considered it possible that enemy agents were among the South Vietnamese LDNN and boat personnel and were "reporting details of operations to Hanoi."[31]

The increased activity of North Vietnam's coastal fleet in July posed another problem. In this connection, an attack by the South Vietnamese-manned boats, against targets on the offshore islands and Vinh Son, scheduled for the 22nd, was postponed when intelligence detected two North Vietnamese Swatows off Hon Nieu and three others near Hon Me. Fearing that these 34A activities were compromised, COMUSMACV dispatched PTF-3, PTF-4, PTF-5, and PTF-6 on the same day to

---

[29]Msg, COM7FLT 170531Z Jul 1964; See also CPFLT 140203Z Jul 1964.
[30]Msgs, JCS 171456Z Jul 1964; ADMINO CP 182057Z; CPFLT 191937Z; JCS 221930Z; CP 222159Z; CPFLT 252132Z.
[31]Msg, CP 012205Z Apr 1964.

reconnoiter the coastal area. The boats brought back intelligence of little value. Five days later, while engaged in a junk seizure southeast of Vinh Son, two PTFs and two Swift boats were attacked unsuccessfully by North Vietnamese patrol craft.[32]

Although a rather modest threat to the United States Navy, the North Vietnamese Navy in August 1964 posed a great danger to the 34A operation. The first-line combatants of the enemy fleet were twenty-four "Swatow" motor gunboats acquired from the Chinese between 1958 and 1962. The 83-foot vessels had crews of about thirty men and carried two or three 37-millimeter guns, two twin 14.5-millimeter guns, and six to eight depth charges. The Swatows had a designed speed of 28 knots and the craft carried surface-search radar. The North Vietnamese Navy also operated twelve Soviet-built P-4 motor torpedo boats delivered to Haiphong in late 1961. These craft had crews of eleven men and were armed with one twin 14.5-millimeter gun mount aft and two torpedo tubes amidship. The range of the torpedoes carried was 4,500 yards. The PTs were capable of 52-knot speeds. The North Vietnamese naval arm, essentially a coastal defensive force, also consisted of four Soviet "S.0.1" class submarine chasers, four minesweeping boats, and forty district patrol craft.[33]

Decisionmakers in Washington were concerned that "improved and alerted coastal defenses make shore raids extremely difficult." In addition to this factor, the Secretary of Defense was troubled that the "tempo of attack was not building up in consonance with improving capabilities." McNamara asked his military advisors whether the conduct of "standoff gunfire or rocket attack" might be more advantageous than operations ashore.[34] Westmoreland responded that the maritime force was testing the use of 81-millimeter mortars and intending to experiment with 4.5-inch rockets and recoilless rifles. The general assumed that the long-standing

---

[32] Msgs, COMUSMACV 240915Z Jul 1964; 271035Z; 301031Z.
[33] CIA, National Intelligence Survey, North Vietnam, of Jul 1964, p. 62; ONI, Naval Vessels of the Sino-Soviet Bloc, ONI 32-8, Change No. 1, of 13 Oct 1960; ONI, Naval Ships of the Sino-Soviet Bloc, ONI 32-8A, of 22 Dec 1961; ONI, "The Far East Communist Bloc Navies in 1961," *ONI Review* (Apr 1962), p. 149; DIA, "The Far East Communist Bloc Navies in 1962," *DIA Naval Intelligence Review* (Apr 1963), p. 33; CIA, National Intelligence Survey, North Vietnam, of Jan 1972, pp. 108-09; COM7FLT, "NVN PT Boat Exploitation Team Report," of July 1966; CNO, North-Vietnam Navy Order of Battle, of 24 Jul 1964; CNO, Characteristics/Armament of PT Boats and Motor Gunboats.
[34] Msg, JCS 260003Z Jul 1964.

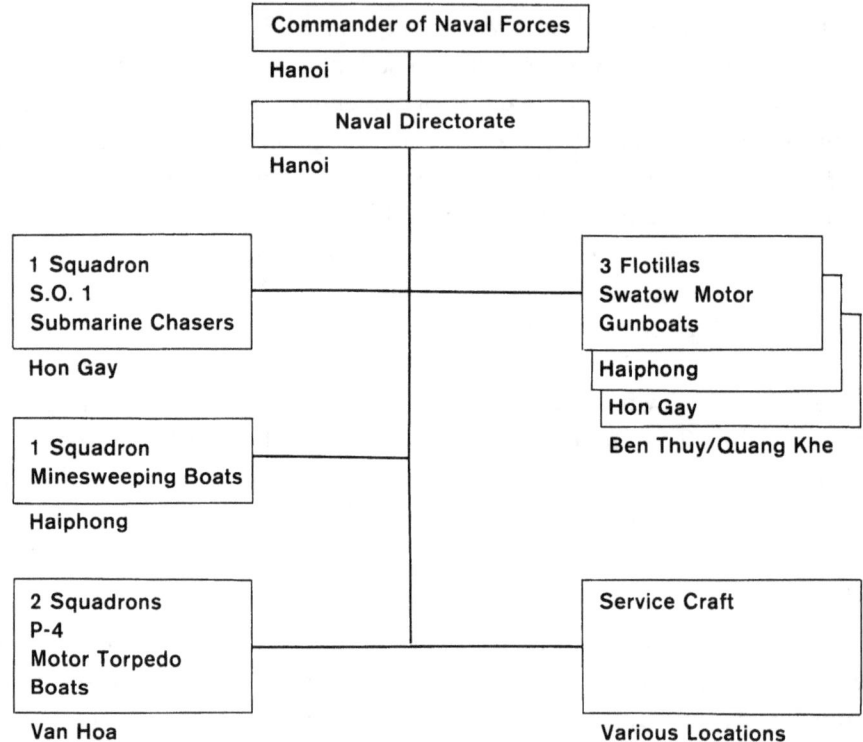

restriction on firing from a vessel offshore would be removed. COMUSMACV, however, concurred with Admiral Sharp that authorizing the South Vietnamese Air Force to bomb selected targets in North Vietnam was the most effective way to increase pressure on the Hanoi regime.[35]

On 30 July, the day PTF-2, PTF-3, PTF-5, and PTF-6 departed Danang for their missions against the Hon Me and Hon Nieu targets, General Westmoreland issued his plan of action for the August 34A program based on the "assumption that off-shore bombardment will be approved." The new schedule provided for an increase in operations, most of which included shore bombardment or sabotage, "of 283 percent over the July

---

[35]Msgs, COMUSMACV 291233Z Jul 1964; CP 291345Z.

program and 566 percent over June." COMUSMACV added that the "tempo of operations and pressure on the DRV will be further increased as more boats become operationally ready."[36]

Although the PTF force sailed for North Vietnamese waters prepared to execute a bombardment of enemy targets if operations ashore proved infeasible, COMUSMACV still exhibited some doubt as to his authority to order offshore shelling. On 1 August he requested "ASAP, policy reading on stand off bombardment of DRV coastal targets." He added that unless he was directed otherwise, the maritime force would bombard the Vinh Son radar station and the enemy security post on the south bank of the Ron River on 3 August.[37] He was not directed otherwise.

The 30 July foray north by the South Vietnamese-manned PTFs proceeded as scheduled. By 2315H the four boats reached a point southeast of Hon Me at 19°N 106° 16'E. Here, they parted company, with PTF-3 and PTF-6 heading for Hon Me and PTF-5 and PTF-2 for Hon Nieu.

The first two boats arrived off the southern end of their island at 0021H on 31 July. During the approach run to the target, a water tower and associated military structures, the boats spotted one North Vietnamese craft. About the same time, the enemy opened fire with 30 and 50-caliber machine guns, wounding four South Vietnamese on board PTF-6. That the North Vietnamese were not surprised came as no revelation to the maritime force. Both boat groups received intelligence beforehand that the enemy would be aware of their presence. With a landing to set demolition charges now out of the question, the South Vietnamese commander ordered the targets hit from offshore. Aided by moonlight and illumination rounds, the PTFs poured in 40-millimeter, 20-millimeter, and 57-millimeter recoilless rifle fire. In this attack, the first standoff bombardment conducted during the 34A campaign, the two boats destroyed a gun emplacement and a number of buildings. They retired from the area at 0048H. Although unaware of its presence, the boat force was pursued by a North Vietnamese Swatow motor gunboat, T-142. Later, the commander of T-142 reported his inability to catch up with the departing South Vietnamese units.

---

[36]Msg, COMUSMACV 301107Z Jul 1964.
[37]Msg, COMUSMACV 010717Z Aug 1964. See also msg, CP 011840Z.

The other boat section, consisting of PTF-2 and PTF-5, reached a point 800 yards northeast of their target, a communications station on Hon Nieu, at 0037H on 31 July. As at Hon Me, the South Vietnamese mission commander decided against landing a sabotage team. With the target in sight, both boats shelled the area, scoring hits on a communication tower. Fire then was shifted to other targets on the island, which generated ineffective enemy counterfire. At 0113H both craft withdrew from the area, having accomplished their task.

The Hon Me Nastys returned on a direct route to Danang, arriving there at 0955H and 1055H on 31 July. PTF-2 and PTF-5 left the vicinity of Hon Nieu and retraced the route followed when they entered North Vietnamese waters the previous evening. PTF-5 reached Danang at 1045H and PTF-2 closed the South Vietnamese port at 1120H after being delayed nearby with engine trouble.[38]

The *Maddox* Patrol

Three days earlier, at 0800H on 28 July, *Maddox*, under Commander Herbert L. Ogier, put to sea from Keelung, Taiwan, bound for the South China Sea. On board was Captain John J. Herrick, Commander Destroyer Division 192 and Commander Task Group 72.1, plus personnel temporarily assigned from various shore stations to man the electronic collection van secured to the deck prior to sailing.[39] In addition, a petty officer was embarked to accomplish conventional photography. Another man, trained in radarscope photography, subsequently transferred to *Maddox* from *Ticonderoga*.

On the morning of 31 July, the destroyer rendezvoused with oiler *Ashtabula* (AO-51) for underway refueling due east of the Demilitarized Zone at 17° 1.5'N 108° 29.5'E. While steaming alongside *Ashtabula*, at approximately 0820H, *Maddox* sighted two unidentified craft, which

---

[38]Msgs, CPFLT 261859Z Jan 1964; COMUSMACV 230715Z Jul; COMUSMACV 010321Z Aug; 070231Z; 070253Z; Special Operations Division, SACSA, Talking Paper, "Operation Plan 34A Maritime Operations in the Gulf of Tonkin, July/August;" SACSA, "Description of South Vietnamese Operations on 30/31 July 1964;" SACSA, Chart of 30/31 July 1964 34A operation; MACV, Command History, 1964, Ann. A, pp. IV-2—IV-4; Krisel, "Special Maritime Operations in Vietnam," pp. 120-21; *U.S.-V.N. Relations*, bk. 4, pt. IVC.2(b), pp. 5, 11; Bucklew, Interview with Mason, pp. 366-79; Mulford, Interview.

[39]Captain Herrick's task designation initially was Commander Task Unit 72.1.2.

appeared to Captain Herrick to be similar to Nasty class PT boats, passing five miles ahead on a southerly course. Within the next half hour, two more vessels passed astern, also heading south. Of the latter group, one appeared to observers to be a Soviet P-6 class boat but actually was the older American-built PTF-2. While no communications were exchanged with the vessels sighted, it now is clear they were the four South Vietnamese-manned PTFs returning to Danang.[40]

At 0845H, with underway replenishment completed, *Maddox* activated her radars and other electronic equipment and steamed for Point Alpha. At 1320H, the Desoto Patrol ship reached her destination and began an orbit of the area. In addition to sixty to eighty fishing junks, *Maddox* personnel sighted an observation post and what was believed to be a radio facility on Gio Island. Although no electronic activity was identified as emanating from this station, the monitoring personnel on board picked up Communist early warning emissions while in the area. The ship then headed for Point Bravo.[41] Early the following morning, 1 August, U.S. intelligence sources noted what was believed to have been the first reaction by the North Vietnamese to the presence of the July-August Desoto Patrol.

As yet unaware of this information, the ship remained in the vicinity of Point Bravo, a little over eight miles from the mainland, during most of the morning of 1 August and then sailed for Point Charlie without incident. As before, North Vietnamese fishing craft plied their trade along the coast, but no enemy naval vessels appeared. During the late afternoon, the destroyer passed five miles to the northeast of Hon Matt. After reaching Point Charlie at 1800H, *Maddox* reported the existence of a number of communications antennae along the beach, which Captain Herrick guessed were being used to relay a fix on the ship. Intelligence later revealed that the American ship was tracked all day. At 2115H, the vessel reached a position five miles southeast of Hon Vat, a small islet close to Hon Me. At no time during the August patrol did any American ship come closer to North Vietnamese soil.

The uneventful nature of the patrol soon changed. In the early morning hours of Sunday, 2 August, North Vietnamese naval headquarters

---

[40]Msg, CTU72.1.2 310135Z Jul 1964; *Maddox*, Patrol Report, ser 002 of 24 Aug; *Maddox*, Deck Log, 1-31 Jul.

[41]Msgs, CTU72.1.2 311320Z Jul 1964; 011200Z Aug; *Maddox*, Deck Log, 1-31 Jul 1964; *Maddox*, Patrol Report, ser 002 of 24 Aug.

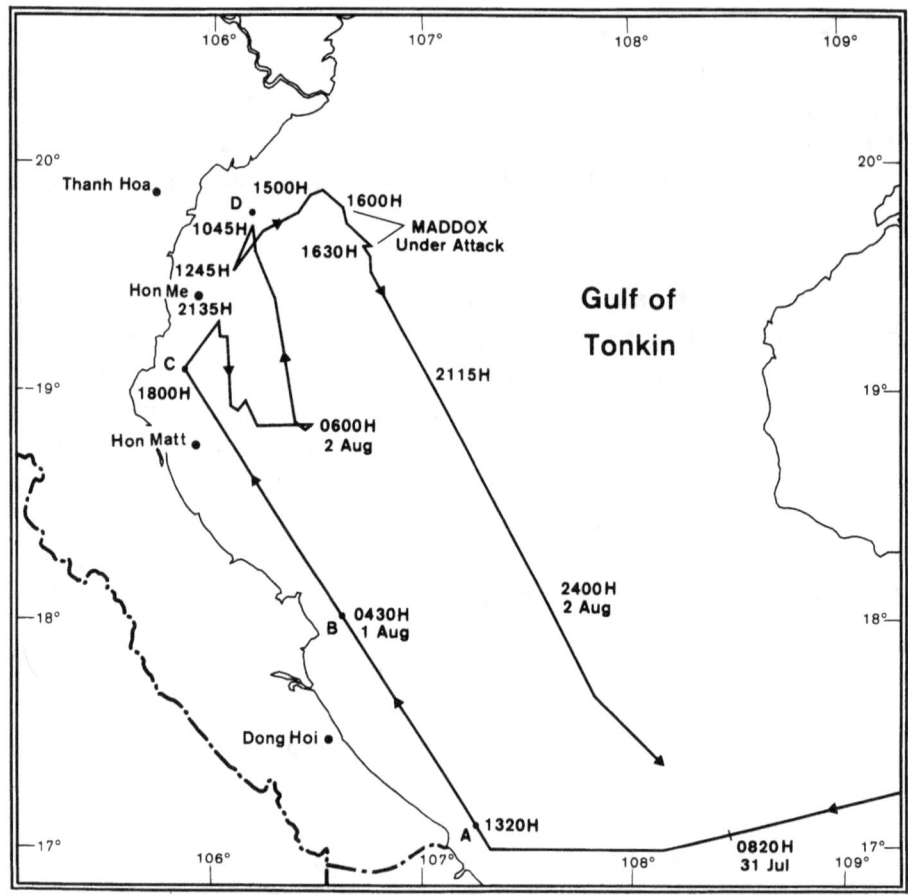

Track of Maddox, *31 July-2 August 1964*

ordered coastal forces to prepare for battle that night. Soon afterward, the Northern Fleet headquarters at Van Hoa (Port Wallut) dispatched as reinforcements for the three Swatows already in the Hon Me-Hon Nieu area, Division 3 of PT Squadron 135. The three P-4s of this unit were due to arrive at Hon Me around 0400H.

At 0324H on 2 August, Captain Herrick was informed by American intelligence of the imminent danger. Thirty minutes later, he sent a "flash" precedence message stating "contemplate serious reaction my movements [vicinity] Pt Charlie in near future. Received info indicating

KN-9907

Captain John J. Herrick, Commander Destroyer Division 192, and Commander Herbert L. Ogier, Commanding Officer of Maddox *(DD-731), shortly after the naval engagement in the Gulf of Tonkin.*

possible hostile action."[42] Shortly afterward, *Maddox* ended the orbit at Point Charlie and steamed due east for the open sea at an unhurried 10 knots. Captain Herrick planned to remain there until daylight when it would be safer to return to coastal waters.[43] At 0645H, Captain Herrick

---

[42]Msg, CTU72.1.2 011954Z Aug 1964. See also McNamara in *Hearings on the Gulf of Tonkin*, p. 10; Sharp, *Strategy For Defeat*, p. 40; Johnson, *Vantage Point*, p. 114.
[43]Msg, CTU72.1.2 012048Z Aug 1964.

reported that unless otherwise directed he would proceed back toward the coast and Point Delta. But, he added that "if info received concerning hostile intent by DRV is accurate, and have no reason to believe it is not, consider continuance of patrol presents an unacceptable risk."[44] Admiral Johnson "noted" Captain Herrick's concern but directed the Desoto Patrol commander to resume the operation. The admiral reminded Herrick, however, that he was authorized to "deviate from itinerary at any time you consider unacceptable risk to exist."[45] *Maddox* reached the vicinity of Point Delta about 1045H on 2 August and turned south on the first leg of a planned eight-hour orbit off Thanh Hoa. A number of junks sailed in the area, but *Maddox* adjusted her track to avoid passing through any concentrations. Captain Herrick reported that "no further evidence of hostile intent" had been received.[46] About the same time, however, CINCPAC and Commander Seventh Fleet received a new intelligence evaluation that indicated the North Vietnamese were preparing to repulse further attacks on Hon Me and as a result of this heightened sensitivity might attack the Desoto Patrol ship.

About thirty-five minutes after noon on 2 August, lookouts and radar in *Maddox* picked up three naval craft, identified as P-4 torpedo boats, ten miles north of Hon Me and heading south at 20 knots. The American destroyer reversed course and headed northeastward toward Point Delta. Soon afterward, *Maddox* personnel observed two Swatows, north of the island, heading south at 10 to 15 knots. Both groups entered a cove on Hon Me.[47] As it soon became clear, these North Vietnamese forces were preparing to attack. The group gathered around Hon Me consisted of Swatows T-142 and T-146 and Division 3 of PT Squadron 135, comprising P-4s T-333, T-336, and T-339. About 1400H, the force was ordered to carry out a torpedo attack on the "enemy."[48]

---

[44] Msg, CTU72.1.2 012245Z Aug 1964.
[45] Msg, COM7FLT 020100Z Aug 1964. See also U.S.G. Sharp, transcript of interview with Ella Belle Kitchen, U.S. Naval Institute, in San Diego, CA, 1969-1970, Vol. II, p. 220.
[46] Msg, CTG72.1 020315Z Aug 1964.
[47] The sources slightly vary as to the actual time of the sightings and radar contacts. See msg, CTG72.1 020531Z Aug 1964; *Maddox*, Patrol Report, ser 002 of 24 Aug; *Maddox*, Deck Log, 1-31 Aug 1964.
[48] The North Vietnamese, in their history of the war, have corraborated the evidence that they ordered the PT unit to attack *Maddox*. See Socialist Republic of Vietnam, *Vietnam: The Anti-U.S. Resistance War*, p. 60.

After departing the Hon Me area, *Maddox* steamed toward Point Delta. By 1500H the ship was twelve miles east of that reference point and headed in a northeasterly direction. At that time and for the next two hours the sky was overcast but visibility extended ten miles. A 10-knot wind did not disturb the relatively calm sea.

At 1500H, the surface radar in *Maddox* picked up a contact thirty miles to the southwest near Hon Me. Radar operators tracked the contact, evaluated as a patrol boat because of its 30-knot speed, on a course of 50°, almost parallel to that of the destroyer. During the next forty-five minutes, the Desoto Patrol ship increased speed from 10 to 25 knots, headed east briefly, and then made to the southeast as more enemy boats were identified. These maneuvers were intended to open the contacts, which were also increasing their speed and closing. At 1530H Commander Ogier sounded General Quarters. Ten minutes later Captain Herrick sent an uncoded "flash" precedence message to Commander Seventh Fleet and the carrier task group stating that *Maddox* was "being approached by high speed craft with apparent intention of torpedo attack. Intend to open fire if necessary self defense."[49] The task group commander then requested that *Ticonderoga* provide his ship with air support. Steaming 280 miles to the southeast of the Desoto Patrol destroyer, *Ticonderoga* already had four F-8E Crusaders airborne. These aircraft, armed with Sidewinder missiles, Zuni rockets, and 20-millimeter cannon, immediately were vectored to the scene. *Turner Joy* (DD-951), serving as a forward radar picket ship for the carrier group, also received orders to steam toward *Maddox* at best possible speed.

Before these reinforcements arrived, Captain Herrick reported the three torpedo boats closing his ship at 50 knots. They were then eleven and one-half nautical miles distant. By 1600H the destroyer was twenty-five miles from the North Vietnamese coast and steaming to the southeast at 27 knots. The enemy vessels, then identified positively as three P-4s in column, closed to 9,800 yards off the starboard quarter. Five minutes after the hour, *Maddox* fired three 5-inch/38-caliber warning shots to deter further approach. The North Vietnamese craft continued closing fast. They made no attempt with signal flags, lights, pyrotechnics, radio, or other means to clarify their threatening maneuver.

---

[49]Msg, CTG77.5 021008Z Aug 1964. See also *Maddox*, Action Report, ser 003 of 24 Aug; *Maddox*, Patrol Report, ser 002 of 24 Aug; *Maddox*, Deck Log, 1-31 Aug.

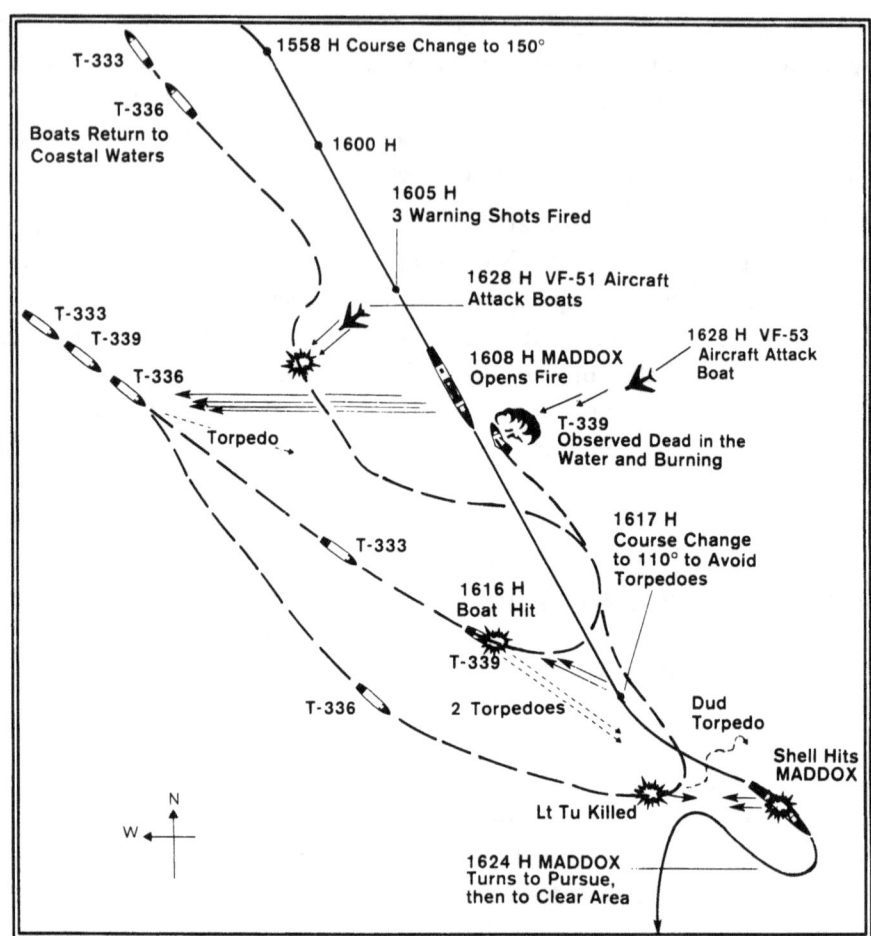

Naval Engagement of 2 August

At 1608H *Maddox* opened fire on the enemy, then 9,000 yards from the ship, with her 5-inch and 3-inch guns.[50] Unobserved by *Maddox*, the first boat in the enemy formation, T-336, launched one of her two torpedoes at a range of between 9,000 and 5,000 yards. Then, either because her torpedo was launched or because of heavy fire from the American destroyer, the lead boat temporarily turned away to the south. But, the second and third vessels, T-339 and T-333, pressed the attack.

---

[50] During the subsequent action, the ship's six twin-mounted 5-inch/38-caliber guns and four twin-mounted 3-inch/50-caliber guns fired 283 rounds.

Within 3,000 yards of *Maddox*, T-339 launched two torpedoes, just as 5-inch fire hit the craft. The damaged boat retired from the battle with difficulty. At this point, *Maddox* changed course to 110° to avoid two torpedoes, which passed by 200 yards to starboard. Meanwhile, T-333, with North Vietnamese squadron commander Captain Le Du Khoai on board, passed astern of the ship without launching torpedoes. At that point, T-336 returned to the scene of action, falling in behind Khoai's boat on the approach. Closing to 2,000 yards, T-336 launched one torpedo and fired her 14.5-millimeter guns at the U.S. ship. A round from this craft hit the Mark 56 fire director pedestal on *Maddox* and lodged in an ammunition handling compartment below.[51] But, the enemy boat commander, Lieutenant Tu, paid with his life for this accomplishment. *Maddox* gunfire raked T-336 as she passed astern, killing the officer at this battle station near the helm. Recognizing the enemy's daring, Commander Ogier later stated that the "attacking boats were aggressive and showed no tendency to abort their torpedo run even though they were confronted with a heavy barrage of fire."[52]

By 1630H the surface action was over. The enemy boats put about and made for shore. Captain Herrick pursued them for a short while until it was clear that the North Vietnamese craft were outdistancing the destroyer and that there was a danger of hitting unexploded torpedoes in the area. At the same time, the *Ticonderoga* aircraft, led by Commander James B. Stockdale, arrived overhead. After directing the aircraft to the enemy, *Maddox* retired to the southeast at best speed. The F-8s discovered T-339 only five miles from *Maddox* while the other boats had covered several additional miles. The two Crusaders from VF 51 unsuccessfully attacked the northerly pair with Zuni rockets and cannon fire. Antiaircraft fire from the boats hit one of the aircraft, forcing the pilot to make an emergency landing at Danang. At the same time, two F-8s of VF 53 concentrated on T-339, first expending their Zuni rockets and then strafing with their guns. On each run, hits were observed on the vessel, which stopped dead in the water and began to burn near the stern. Running low on fuel, the three remaining Crusaders returned to *Ticonderoga*.

---

[51] The round now is in the custody of the Navy Memorial Museum in Washington, D.C.
[52] *Maddox*, Action Report, ser 003 of 24 Aug 1964, p. 10. See also *Maddox*, Deck Log, 1-31 Aug; msgs, CTG72.1 020807Z; 020808Z; 020949Z; CTG77.5 021008Z; *Cavalier* 131115Z Jul 1966; SSO MACV 031107Z Mar 1968.

NH-95611

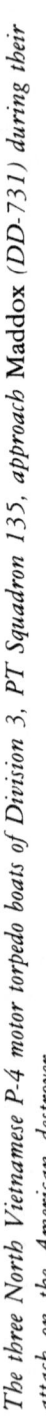

The three North Vietnamese P-4 motor torpedo boats of Division 3, PT Squadron 135, approach Maddox *(DD-731) during their attack on the American destroyer.*

Intelligence sources indicated that T-339 sank in the vicinity of 19° 47'N 106° 31'E.[53] In addition, T-336 was heavily damaged, requiring a tow from T-333 to reach shore. The latter craft received damage to her auxiliary engine, but with the exception of a low lubrication oil-pressure reading, was ready for further action. Both boats beached just south of the Lach Chao Estuary. The boat group remained there for the next three days.[54]

As soon as *Maddox* was out of immediate danger, Admiral Johnson took steps to limit the consequences of the action. A second flight of F-8 Crusaders, that relieved the first group over *Maddox*, was ordered not to pursue the enemy boats. Captain Herrick was directed to "retire from area until situation clears and further advised." He also was instructed to "not pursue attacking craft" but to "fire as necessary in self defense."[55] No further action took place, however, and by the early morning hours of 3 August, *Maddox* was approaching the mouth of the gulf.

Interlude Between Engagements

A little more than two hours after the close of the combat action in the Gulf of Tonkin, Admiral Moorer ordered continuation of the Desoto Patrol. The Pacific Fleet commander stated that "in view *Maddox* incident consider it in our best interest that we assert right of freedom of the seas and resume Gulf of Tonkin patrol earliest."[56] To enhance the credibility of this demonstration of resolve, *Maddox* now was joined by *Turner Joy*, a *Forrest Sherman* class destroyer carrying three rapid-fire, 5-inch/54-caliber guns, four twin-mounted, 3-inch/50-caliber guns, and advanced fire control systems. CINCPACFLT altered the previous operational schedule. He now ordered *Maddox* and *Turner Joy* to proceed to Point Charlie, close by Hon Me, and then move northward toward Point Delta off Thanh

---

[53]A North Vietnamese naval officer captured in 1966, who purportedly prepared the action report of the 2 August action, claimed that T-339 only sustained a hit in its after smoke generator and limped safely back to shore. But numerous contradictions appear in his rendition of events and the intelligence available at the time reported the loss of the boat. See msg, *Cavalier* 131115Z Jul 1966. See also Windchy, *Tonkin Gulf*, pp. 147-48.

[54]Msgs, CTG77.5 021008Z Aug 1964; COM7FLT 020859Z; CTG77.5 021506Z; *Cavalier* 131115Z Jul 1966; ltr, Moore to Eller, of 17 Sep 1969; *Maddox*, Action Report, ser 003 of 24 Aug 1964; *Maddox*, Patrol Report, ser 002 of 24 Aug; Stockdales, *In Love and War*, pp. 4-10, 449-52.

[55]Msg, COM7FLT 020859Z Aug 1964. See also msg, CTG77.5 021008Z.

[56]Msg, CPFLT 021104Z Aug 1964.

Hoa. On 4 August, the destroyers were to retrace their track to Point Charlie. During the next three days, the patrol ships were scheduled to steam through points L, M, N, O, and P before ending the mission. Each night, the ships had orders to retire to the east for safety. CINCPACFLT stated that the closest point of approach to North Vietnam remained eight nautical miles to the mainland and four nautical miles from the offshore islands.[57] Admiral Sharp concurred with CINCPACFLT's resumption of the patrol and with the changes to the schedule. But he directed his naval component commander to delay implementation until the JCS gave approval.

At this point, Captain Herrick expressed concerns about reentry into the Gulf of Tonkin, noting:

> It is apparent that DRV has cut [*sic.*] down the gauntlet and now considers itself at war with U.S. It is felt that they will attack U.S. forces on sight with no regard for cost. U.S. ships in the Gulf of Tonkin can no longer assume that they will be considered neutrals exercising the right of free transit. They will be treated as belligerents from first detection and must consider themselves as such.[58]

He also observed that tactical considerations weighed against *Maddox* undertaking a renewed patrol:

> DRV PTs have advantage especially at night of being able to hide in junk concentrations all across the Gulf of Tonkin. This would allow attack from short range with little or no warning. Present USS-gunnery suit not too well fitted for anti-PT even in daylight. Short hull DD such as *Maddox* too shortlegged [limited fuel capacity] for long patrol where high speeds are required as in PT evasion. Consider resumption of patrol can only be safely undertaken by DD, CL/CA [cruiser] team and with continuous air cover.[59]

About the same time, the Defense Intelligence Agency concluded that information collected revealed that since March the North Vietnamese had become "increasingly sensitive to incursions from the South and to the threat of extension of the war and bombing." The agency further observed that the "torpedo attempt on *Maddox* indicates North Vietnam-

---

[57]*Ibid*; *Maddox*, Patrol Report, ser 002 of 24 Aug.
[58]Msg, CTG72.1 021443Z Aug 1964.
[59]*Ibid*. See also msgs, ADMINO CP 021255Z Aug 1964; COM7FLT 021255Z; CPFLT 021407Z.

ese intent and readiness to take aggressive action if they consider their territory immediately threatened."[60]

U.S. leaders in Washington, however, did not share this interpretation. The President met with Secretary of State Rusk, Secretary of Defense McNamara, Chairman of the Joint Chiefs of Staff General Wheeler, and other senior officials of the administration late in the morning on 2 August. They concluded that the attack might have resulted from the unilateral actions of an aggressive North Vietnamese boat commander or a local shore command. President Johnson observed later that "we were determined not to be provocative, nor were we going to run away. We would give Hanoi the benefit of the doubt — this time — and assume the unprovoked attack had been a mistake."[61] As the patrol was resumed, North Vietnam was informed that U.S. ships would continue to steam where they pleased in international waters. Further, the North Vietnamese were warned to be "under no misapprehension as to the grave consequences which would inevitably result from any further unprovoked offensive military action against United States forces."[62]

As directed by the President, at 1225 Eastern Daylight Time on 2 August, the Joint Chiefs of Staff ordered completion of the interrupted Desoto Patrol. Admiral Moorer's route and time changes were accepted. But, CINCPAC was advised that the ships now could approach no closer than twelve nautical miles to the North Vietnamese mainland. Continuous daylight air cover was provided for, but the aircraft were stationed east of the two destroyers to avoid the possibility of overflying Communist territory. Reflecting concern with the Defense Intelligence Agency's conclusions, Admiral Sharp also was directed to ensure that the patrol avoided approaching the North Vietnamese coast during the period of the next 34A maritime mission.[63] In accordance with these instructions, Commander Seventh Fleet, at 0822H on 3 August, requested that COMUSMACV provide him with information on the timing of the next 34A mission to preclude interference with the Desoto Patrol. General Westmoreland responded that the Seventh Fleet destroyers should remain

---

[60] DIA, report, of August 1964.
[61] Johnson, *Vantage Point*, p. 113.
[62] Quoted in *Ibid.*
[63] Msg, JCS 021725Z Aug 1964; "Statement by the President Upon Instructing the Navy to Take Retaliatory Action in the Gulf of Tonkin, August 3, 1964" in *Public Papers of the Presidents of the United States, Lyndon B. Johnson: 1963-64* (Washington: GPO, 1965), bk. II, pp. 926-27.

clear of the waters generally between the 17th and 18th parallels and stay east of 108° 20'E during 3 and 4 August.

At this time, there was concern in the Washington intelligence community that the North Vietnamese considered the 34A and Desoto Patrol operations as one. Hence, the CNO advised CINCPACFLT that intelligence revealed that the "heightened sensitivity and resultant attack by the DRV [on *Maddox*] possibly was aftermath of a [reported] attack on Hon Me Island." He added that "following this attack, [intelligence] indicated DRV intentions and preparations to repulse further such attacks."[64] A short while later, intelligence units in the Pacific were informed that on 1 August the New China News Agency reported that the North Vietnamese had protested to the International Control Commission that at about 2340H on 30 July "the U.S. and the South Vietnamese administration sent two naval vessels to shell Hon Ngu Island [and] Hon Me Island." The conclusion was drawn, therefore, that the tracking and subsequent attack on *Maddox* could have been provoked by "enemy" incursions into the Gulf of Tonkin a day or two before the arrival of *Maddox* in the area. A bulletin of the CIA issued on 3 August affirmed that "Hanoi's naval units have displayed increasing sensitivity to U.S. and South Vietnamese naval activity in the Gulf of Tonkin during the past few months."[65]

Maddox and *Turner Joy*, both under the operational control of Captain Herrick as Commander Task Group 72.1, got underway from a position between Hainan and the Demilitarized Zone about 0900H on 3 August and headed into the gulf. Captain Herrick received additional guidance with regard to enemy hostilities. He was instructed to destroy any enemy vessels that attacked *Maddox* or *Turner Joy*. Admiral Moore in *Ticonderoga* was told that in the event of "another unprovoked attack...on Desoto Patrol, it is mandatory maximum effort be made achieve complete destruction attacking units."[66] U.S. ships and aircraft were authorized to maintain fire on enemy vessels which were within the eleven-mile coastal zone, if the latter craft attacked from those waters or retired there after the action. However, U.S. ships were not allowed to undertake hot pursuit into the eleven-mile zone.

---

[64]Msg, CNO, of 2 Aug 1964.
[65]CIA, Bulletin, of 3 Aug 1964.
[66]Msg, COM7FLT 030553Z Aug 1964. See also msg, JCS 022349Z Aug.

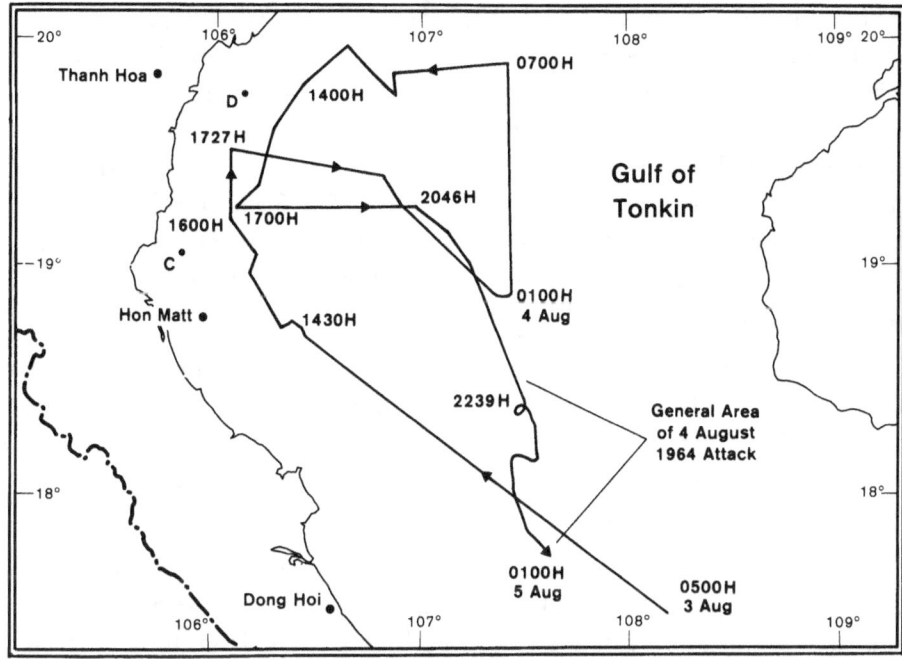

Track of Maddox and Turner Joy, 3-5 August 1964

During the morning and early afternoon of 3 August, the ships steered a northwesterly course toward Point Charlie. The passage was uneventful until 1420H when one of the ships detected apparent radar emissions from a surface vessel, indicating that the pair of ships was under surveillance. A little more than an hour later, the destroyers reached the vicinity of Point Charlie, where they turned north toward Point Delta. In fact, from at least 1637H on, the North Vietnamese tracked the Desoto Patrol ships. Swatow T-142 shadowed the destroyers on the sortie north, periodically reporting to shore stations. Upon reaching the Point Delta area at 1727H, *Maddox* and *Turner Joy* turned to the east and made for the relative safety of a nighttime orbit in the open sea.[67]

At this time, the South Vietnamese maritime force had been at sea for one hour and seventeen minutes. The four-boat group, PTF-1, PTF-5,

---

[67]Msgs, COM7FLT 022225Z Aug 1964; CTG72.1 022330Z; COMUSMACV 030022Z; 030335Z; COM7FLT 030552Z; CTG72.1 030745Z; COM7FLT 031010Z; CTG72.1 031403Z; *Maddox*, Patrol Report, ser 002 of 24 Aug.

PTF-2, and PTF-6, was scheduled to bombard a North Vietnamese radar installation at Vinh Son and a security post on the south bank of the Ron River. The force departed Danang at 1610H on the evening of 3 August. Each of the boats carried an eighteen-man South Vietnamese crew and a portable 57-millimeter recoilless rifle, in addition to other weapons. The trip north was uneventful until 1845H, when PTF-2 suffered a mechanical failure seventy miles east of the DMZ, forcing her to return to Danang. The remaining vessels proceeded to a point east of Vinh Son, where they separated and made for their respective targets.

At midnight on 3 August, PTF-1 and PTF-5 opened fire on the radar facility near Vinh Son. For twenty-five minutes, the South Vietnamese poured 770 rounds of 57-millimeter and 40-millimeter fire into the target area. The boats then withdrew and headed for Danang, reaching that port about 0715H on 4 August.

Operating alone, PTF-6 took up station off the mouth of the Ron River. At 2352H the boat began illuminating and shelling the security post in this area with her 57-millimeter, 40-millimeter, and 20-millimeter weapons, which ignited several fires. Here, the enemy responded with small arms fire, which failed to hit the craft. Shortly after the boat's retirement from the action at 0020H on 4 August, PTF-6 was pursued by an enemy vessel, which approached at 25 knots. Easily outdistancing the enemy boat, PTF-6 sped south, arriving in Danang at 0625H that morning.[68]

In the meantime, while awaiting daylight at a position approximately 100 miles from the coast, the Desoto Patrol ships made radar contact with another vessel which closely paralleled their course for over an hour around midnight. Captain Herrick strongly suspected that the shadower was a Communist bloc patrol craft. The suspected shadower, probably the Swatow T-142, broke contact at 0100H.[69]

During the night of 3-4 August, Admiral Johnson, Commander Seventh Fleet, suggested that after the following day's mission the Desoto Patrol be ended. With their radius of action restricted to the sixty-mile track between Point Delta and Point Charlie, he noted that the ships would be

---

[68]Joint Staff, JCS, 34A Chronology of Events; Joint Staff, JCS, "Description of South Vietnamese Operations on 3/4 August 1964;" msg, COMUSMACV 040955Z Aug 1964; JRC (JCS), "Chronology of Events Relating to the Gulf of Tonkin Incidents," of 10 Aug 1964 in Porter, *Vietnam: The Definitive Documentation*, Vol. II, pp. 313-14.
[69]Msgs, CTU72.1.2 031546Z Aug 1964; CTG72.1 040511Z.

easy to locate.[70] Admiral Moorer, commander of the Pacific Fleet, did not concur. He apprised the Seventh Fleet commander that "termination of Desoto Patrol after two days of patrol OPS [subsequent] to *Maddox* incident...does not in my view adequately demonstrate U.S. resolve to assert our legitimate rights in these international waters."[71] Admiral Moorer added that the ships should patrol the Charlie to Delta track for the next two days, proceed to another point to the north on the third day, and return to the Charlie-Delta track on the fourth day, before departing the gulf. He believed that these sorties would demonstrate the U.S. determination to continue the patrols, possibly draw the enemy away from the 34A activities, and preclude interference between the two operations. The JCS agreed with the revised schedule.

At the same time, Admiral Sharp raised objection to the JCS directives that prohibited the destroyers from approaching closer than twelve miles to the North Vietnamese coastline, even in hot pursuit. Noting his dissatisfaction with the rules of engagement, the Pacific commander observed:

> A United States ship has been attacked on the high seas off North Vietnam. The *Maddox* quite properly repulsed the attackers and one of the attacking boats was destroyed. Now, our friends and enemies alike will await what additional moves the United States will take. [The JCS directives] appear to be a retreat at a time when aggressive measures are necessary.[72]

In response, the JCS reaffirmed the decision that the Desoto Patrol ships were barred from entry into the eleven-mile zone, even in hot pursuit. However, in the event of an attack on the patrol, aircraft could retaliate against the attackers in waters up to three miles of the enemy coastline.[73]

As his ships returned to the patrol track on the morning of Tuesday, 4 August, Captain Herrick again expressed his concern for the safety of the U.S. force. The task group commander concluded that the "evaluation of info from various sources indicates that DRV considers patrol directly involved with 34-A OPs. DRV considers U.S. ships present as enemies because of these OPs and have already indicated their readiness to treat us

---

[70] Msgs, COM7FLT 031712Z Aug 1964; COM7FLT 031134Z Aug; COMUSMACV 031231Z.
[71] Msg, CPFLT 032259Z Aug 1964. See also Sharp, Interview, pp. 222-23, 226.
[72] Msg, CP 032353Z Aug 1964. See also msgs, CPFLT 032259Z Aug; JCS 032351Z; 040331Z.
[73] Msg, JCS 041433Z Aug 1964.

in that category."[74] Herrick believed that the enemy was especially sensitive about the area around Hon Me because of his concentration of coastal patrol forces there. The captain felt that his ships would be most vulnerable to the enemy at that point. The North Vietnamese could hide behind the island and then launch a sudden attack that would be difficult to detect or repulse because of the short distance to the Desoto Patrol track.[75]

Night Action in the Gulf of Tonkin

At 0700H on the morning of 4 August, almost seven hours after the PTF force departed their target area off Vinh Son, *Maddox* and *Turner Joy* turned west toward the North Vietnamese coast, arriving in the vicinity of Point Delta around 1400H. The ships then proceeded to the southwest toward Point Charlie with *Ticonderoga* aircraft circling overhead or nearby. At 1435H Captain Herrick reported having been shadowed for the past four hours from a distance of fifteen miles by a vessel he believed to be a motor gunboat. About 1700H, the Desoto Patrol force reached a position to the northeast of Point Charlie, changed course to the east, and headed out to sea. At no time did the patrol sail closer than sixteen miles to the coast.

The North Vietnamese were fully aware of the passage of the American ships. Late in the afternoon of 4 August, Swatows T-142 and T-146 received orders from the naval headquarters in Haiphong to prepare for military operations that night. T-333, one of the P-4s involved in the action on 2 August, also was scheduled to participate in the operation. But, due to an inability to repair her lubricating oil casualty, this unit was not able to deploy. Based on the subsequent U.S. contact with a number of enemy vessels, it is clear that other unidentified units were alerted as well.[76] Learning that another attack was planned, at 2040H Captain Herrick sent a "flash" precedence message stating that he had received information "indicating attack by PGM/P-4 imminent" and that the

---

[74]Msg, CTG72.1 040140Z Aug 1964.
[75]*Ibid.*
[76]*Hearings on the Gulf of Tonkin, the 1964 Incidents*, pp. 17, 92.

patrol force was "proceeding southeast at best speed."[77] By then, the ships were more than sixty nautical miles southeast of Hon Me at 19° 10.7'N 107°E on a heading of 90° and at a speed of 20 knots.

Maddox, using her surface radar for long-range search, was 1,000 yards ahead of *Turner Joy*. Subsequent to the engagement on the night of 4 August, Commander Ogier reported that the contacts detected on his destroyer's radar were bona fide. Weather and wake contacts were quickly identified as such. And meteorological conditions that night were particularly good for radar operations. No North Vietnamese junks or fishing craft sailed that far out to sea after dark, and none was detected that night. With their scopes free of clutter, the experienced naval radarmen could clearly distinguish the enemy fast craft.[78] Weather conditions in the Gulf of Tonkin that night included a 10 to 20-knot wind from the southeast and intermittent thunderstorms. Because of the cloud cover, with a ceiling at about 2,000 feet, the night was moonless and dark. The sea was moderate with 2 to 6-foot waves.

At 2041H on 4 August, *Maddox* picked up a surface contact forty-two miles to the northeast in the area where both ships had intended to cruise during the night. This was the same position used by the Desoto Patrol destroyers the previous night. During the next hour, first *Maddox* and then *Turner Joy* established clear radar contact with three surface vessels that Captain Herrick determined were patrol craft because of their speeds in excess of 30 knots. The unidentified craft attempted to close with the Desoto Patrol ships.[79]

At that point, Captain Herrick ordered both U.S. destroyers to change course to the southeast (130° and then 140°) at maximum speed. Fearing a

---

[77]Msg, CTG72.1 041240Z Aug 1964. The turn to the southeast actually was not ordered until 2046H. See also msgs, 040635Z Aug; 042158Z; JRC (JCS), "Chronology of Events Relating to the Gulf of Tonkin Incidents," p. 314; Sharp, *Strategy For Defeat*, p. 43.

[78]For instance, Seaman Dennis P. Plzak, who manned *Turner Joy*'s surface search radar, stated after the attack: "I have spent many hours on the surface search and I evaluate them as definite contacts. It appeared to me that there was a definite plan used by the craft. At one time I held clearly three contacts, one directly astern of us and two moving in and out." Dennis P. Plzak, Statement of 7 Aug 1964. See also Robert E. Johnson, and Marshall L. Hakala, Statements, of 7 Aug; DESDIV 192, Chronology, ser 002 of 13 Aug; *Maddox*, Patrol Report, ser 002 of 24 Aug; *Maddox*, Action Report, ser 004 of 25 Aug; *Turner Joy*, Action Report, ser 004 of 11 Sep.

[79]Another contact, possibly equipped with radar, was detected as close as twenty miles to the east and paralleling the American ships' passage south but made no attempt to close with them. This was perhaps the Swatow motor gunboat that Captain Herrick and Commander Barnhart believed used its radar to vector the P-4s toward the destroyers. See *Turner Joy*, Action Report, ser 004 of 11 Sep 1964, p. vi-2; DESDIV 192, Chronology, ser 002 of 13 Aug 1964, p. 2.

American destroyer Turner Joy (DD-951) as she looked in the spring of 1964.

trap, the task group commander attempted to open the threatening contacts. However, the latter vessels turned as well to intersect the course of the American ships. At 2107H, radar on *Maddox* determined that the three surface craft had joined in close formation about thirty-two miles from the ship. With both U.S. destroyers now proceeding at 30-knot speed, Herrick changed their heading more to the southeast (160°). By 2145H, the radar contacts had drifted out of range and disappeared aft.

Almost one-half hour later, both *Maddox* and *Turner Joy* picked up three or four contacts in close formation only thirteen miles behind and approaching at 30 knots. The fire control radars of both ships locked on these contacts. The threatening surface craft closed to 23,200 yards. At this point, *Maddox* and *Turner Joy* radars identified another contact only 9,800 yards due east and approaching at 35 to 40 knots. When this latter craft (shown as contact V1 on page 430 chart) closed to 7,000 yards, at 2239H, *Turner Joy* opened fire. *Maddox* immediately followed suit. The ships then were at 18° 17'N 107° 32'E.[80]

Almost at the same time, the single contact to the east turned to the left and opened range. Lieutenant (j.g.) Frederick M. Frick, the watch officer in the *Maddox* combat information center (CIC), evaluated this maneuver, plotted and recorded on his dead reckoning tracer, as a torpedo launch. In short order, sonar on *Maddox* reported torpedo noises.[81] Commander Ogier ordered full right rudder to comb the track of the suspected torpedo and warned *Turner Joy*.[82] The latter destroyer immediately came right on course 210° just as crewmen spotted a torpedo wake. Lieutenant (j.g.) John J. Barry, USNR, the officer in charge of Fire Control Director

---

[80]*Turner Joy*'s Deck Log and Quartermaster Log state that fire was opened at 2235H but this is not supported by the ship's CIC Log or other sources.

[81]The reports of sonar contacts were less reliable than those of radar. The sonarmen in *Maddox* had not trained with their equipment while the ship steamed at 30 knots. Thus, engine, aircraft, ship propeller, and other noises could be misinterpreted as torpedo noises. Still, this first reported torpedo was considered valid, as were two others, by a number of sources, including Captain Herrick. He overheard the sound of the torpedo running on the bridge speaker system when sonar reported. See John J. Herrick, Statement, of 7 Aug 1964. See also Frederick M. Frick, Statement, of 7 Aug; *Maddox*, Action Report, ser 004 of 25 Aug; *Maddox*, Patrol Report, ser 002 of 24 Aug; COM7FLT, "NVN PT Boat Exploitation Team Report," p. IV.I.1.

[82]At no time during the night engagement did *Turner Joy*'s sonar detect torpedo noises. However, the particular type of sonar carried by the destroyer was noted for its poor performance. During previous peacetime exercises, dummy torpedoes passed *Turner Joy* close aboard without being detected. Indeed, at the time when the first torpedo was sighted, *Turner Joy*'s sonar could not hear the screws of *Maddox*, only 1,000 yards ahead, because of the turbulence of her wake. See *Turner Joy*, Action Report, ser 004 of 11 Sep 1964.

430 United States Navy and Vietnam Conflict

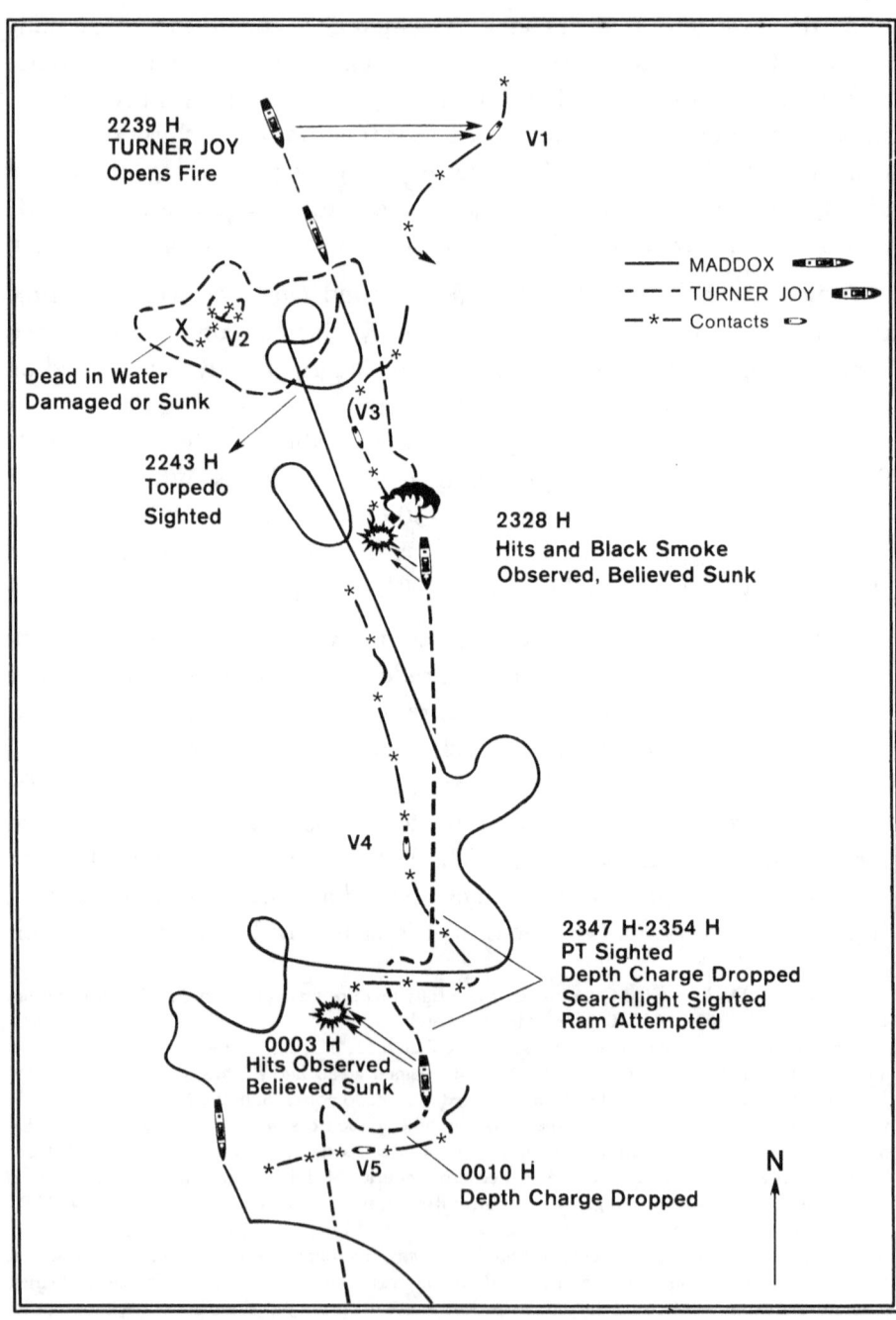

Naval Action on the Night of 4 August

51 located high in the ship's superstructure, spied "a distinct wake...on the port side about five hundred feet from the ship...moving from aft forward on a parallel course to this ship." He added that the "wake itself appeared light in color and more just below the surface than anything cutting the water on the surface" and that it "formed a definite vee in the water." Barry, an experienced ASW officer, had seen many actual torpedo wakes prior to the August incidents.[83] This sighting of a torpedo wake 100 to 500 feet to port was corroborated by one of Barry's subordinates, Seaman Larry O. Litton, by Seaman Rodger N. Bergland positioned in Fire Control Director 52, and by the port side lookout, Seaman Edwin R. Sentel, the latter of whom reported the information to the bridge.[84] When the hostile craft returned at 50 knots on an intercept course, two 5-inch mounts on *Turner Joy* again took it under fire. Fire control radar indicated that hits were scored.

At 2210H, one F-8 Crusader and two A-4D Skyhawks arrived overhead to provide a combat air patrol. Although aircraft overflew the Desoto Patrol ships all day, they had retired to *Ticonderoga* at dusk. When Rear Admiral Robert B. Moore, Commander Task Force 77, received Captain Herrick's request for air support at 2125H, he immediately launched the three-plane alert force. Fifteen minutes later, four A-1H Skyraiders were sent aloft. Additional planes later were launched from *Constellation*, making a total of sixteen aircraft providing protection overhead. But, the effectiveness of this air cover was limited due to the darkness of the night, cloudy sky, and unsatisfactory illumination devices.[85] The aircraft strafed waters where the enemy boats were believed to be, but most of the pilots, including future Vice Admiral and Medal of Honor recipient Commander James Stockdale, did not see any hostile craft. Nonetheless, the pilots of two *Ticonderoga* A-1s, Commander George H. Edmondson, commanding officer of VA 58, and his wingman,

---

[83]John J. Barry, Statement, of 7 Aug 1964.

[84]Larry O. Litton, Statement, of 7 Aug 1964; Rodger N. Bergland Statement of 7 Aug; Edwin R. Sentel, Statement, of 7 Aug; DESDIV 192, Chronology, ser 002 of 13 Aug; *Maddox*, Action Report, ser 004 of 25 Aug; *Turner Joy*, Action Report, ser 004 of 11 Sep. Seven years later, Lieutenant (j.g.) Barry and Seaman Bergland maintained the accuracy of their torpedo wake sighting. See Windchy, *Tonkin Gulf*, pp.271-73.

[85]In fact, while the various flares and star shells proved of little assistance in locating the small enemy boats in the inky night, Commander Ogier believed that they did help the North Vietnamese maintain contact with the larger destroyers. See *Maddox*, Action Report, ser 004 of 25 Aug 1964, p. 11.

Lieutenant Jere A. Barton, both experienced at night search, reported significant information. Flying between 700 and 1,500 feet above the water, the aviators sighted gun flashes as well as bursts of light at their altitude that they attributed to an enemy vessel's antiaircraft fire. On one pass over the destroyers, Commander Edmondson identified a "snakey," high-speed wake a mile and a half ahead of *Maddox*, the lead ship. Lieutenant Barton on another pass spotted a dark object, in the wake midway between the two destroyers, that soon moved away from the ships and out of sight.[86]

At 2242H all surface contacts were gone from the radars of *Maddox* and *Turner Joy*, now steaming independently. For the next ten minutes, both ships maneuvered to avoid possible torpedoes reported by sonar. Then at 2301H, *Turner Joy* picked up several contacts between 2,000 to 6,000 yards to the west. At 2310H and 2318H, the ship briefly opened fire on the fleeting targets. One contact (V2) was plotted dead in the water and subsequently presumed damaged or sunk, but verification was not possible.

Heading south again at 2321H, *Turner Joy* tracked another surface craft (V3) 3,600 yards aft of her and closing at 48 knots. When the hostile contact reached 2,500 yards, the ship's guns opened up with a heavy volume of fire. Crewmen observed numerous explosions.[87] Radarmen also witnessed many hits on the target, which disappeared from all screens at 2328H.[88] Commander Robert C. Barnhart, *Turner Joy*'s commanding officer, and others saw a thick column of black smoke rise from the target area. This boat was presumed sunk.

Soon afterward, another high-speed contact (V4) approached from the north following *Turner Joy*. The ship changed course to starboard several

---

[86]Msg, CTF77 070252Z Aug 1964. Admiral Stockdale's account appears in *Love and War*, pp. 11-24, 453-55. In 1971, after his retirement, Commander Edmonson reconfirmed these visual observations. See Windchy, *Tonkin Gulf*, p. 279.

[87]Throughout the engagement that night, a number of sailors witnessed the damage or destruction of enemy vessels. Topside personnel observed explosions on plotted targets followed by fire. *Turner Joy* Seaman Patrick C. McWeeney, for instance, "saw what appeared to be a small craft burning off the starboard bow about 30° on the horizon" and "watched it burn for about 20 seconds and then go out, like the craft sunk." Patrick C. McWeeney, Statement, of 8 Aug 1964. See also Rodger N. Bergland, Dean L. Abney, Charles D. Reed, Statements, of 8 Aug.

[88]Although unspecific as to time, Chief Radarman Robert E. Johnson reported one contact that night "saturated by shell fire on the scope" and when "firing ceased, the contact remained for...approximately fifteen seconds, then disappeared," which he evaluated as indicating that the boat was sunk. Robert E. Johnson, Statement, of 7 Aug 1964. See also Dennis P. Plzak, Marshall L. Hakala, Statements, of 7 Aug.

times and the contact overshot the destroyer's wake. In the light of star shells fired by *Maddox* and flares dropped by aircraft, *Turner Joy* crewmen identified this target as an enemy PT boat. Boatswain's Mate 3rd Class Donald V. Sharkey, Seaman Kenneth E. Garrison, and Gunner's Mate Delner Jones all observed the craft from their station at the 3-inch/50-caliber Gun Mount 32. Sharkey stated that the "outline of this contact was clearly seen by me and was definitely a PT boat."[89] Garrison corroborated this sighting and added that "I saw it long enough to make sure what it was."[90] The day after the battle, 5 August, Jones sketched the craft, which he had seen for the first time the previous night, for Radarman 1st Class John B. Spanka. Garrison agreed with the accuracy of this visual representation. Then Spanka compared the drawing with an intelligence photograph of a P-4 PT boat. He found that the "two were very similar in nature" and "particularly noteworthy was the elongated bow." Spanka added, "I had no trouble identifying his sketch as the P-4."[91]

At 2347H *Turner Joy* dropped a depth charge astern in an attempt to shake the enemy pursuer. Throughout the latter part of the action, several enemy craft appeared to guide on the wakes of the two destroyers. Commander Ogier believed the North Vietnamese used this tactic because they lacked on board radar.[92] Around this time a seaman amidships and sailors manning Gun Mount 31 in *Turner Joy* observed machine gun fire hit the water from aft forward, about 40 or 50 yards to port. It is possible, however, that what they were seeing was the splash of American shell fragments.[93] At 2354H Commander Barnhart turned his ship hard left and attempted to ram the craft, but without success. The enemy boat, now 1,500 yards on the starboard side of the U.S. destroyer, was taken under fire exactly at midnight. At 0003H on 5 August, after radarmen observed four bursts on target, the contact disappeared from the screen.

---

[89]Donald V. Sharkey, Statement, of 7 Aug 1964.
[90]Kenneth E. Garrison, Statement, of 7 Aug 1964. See also Dean L. Abney, Statement, of 8 Aug 1964; DESDIV 192, Chronology, ser 002 of 13 Aug; *Turner Joy*, Action Report, ser 004 of 11 Sep.
[91]John B. Spanka, Statement, of 9 Aug 1964. See also Delner Jones, Statement, of 7 Aug 1964; Arthur B. Anderson, Statement, of 7 Aug.
[92]*Turner Joy* and *Maddox* detected no seaborne radar emissions during the engagement. It should be noted, however, that the ECM equipment in both ships was found to be inadequate for the task. See *Maddox*, Patrol Report, ser 002 of 24 Aug 1964, p. 4. See also *Maddox*, Action Report, ser 004 of 25 Aug; *Turner Joy*, Action Report, ser 004 of 11 Sep.
[93]Harvey A. Headley, Jr., Thomas Contreras, Donald L. Vance, and Anthony J. Rosenbaum, Statements, of 8 Aug 1964.

During the last attack, all of *Turner Joy*'s bridge personnel, including Commander Barnhart, sighted a searchlight to the north in the general vicinity of the trailing enemy boats. Senior Chief Quartermaster Walter L. Shishim related that he observed the light "by eye and its beam...by binoculars" and that it "remained at constant brightness and the beam was an elongated fan shape pointing up."[94] Signalman 3rd Class Gary D. Carroll added that "the light was moving around and at times skyward. It made a couple of swoops at us before going out."[95] His shipmate, Signalman 2nd Class Richard M. Bacino, concluded that "as a Signalman, I feel I can tell a searchlight from any other light that could possibly be mistaken for such."[96] Several of the men verified through the CIC the current position of *Maddox*, which ruled out that ship as the source of the light. When American aircraft were dispatched to investigate what was perhaps a North Vietnamese boat-to-boat signalling attempt, the light was extinguished.[97]

Meanwhile, *Maddox*, almost ten miles to the west of *Turner Joy*, dropped a depth charge and fired in the general vicinity of a contact reported astern. No results were observed. At 0010H *Turner Joy* took similar actions to ward off a contact (V5) trailing her. For the next forty minutes, the U.S. destroyers dropped depth charges or fired their guns at contacts. At the same time, *Turner Joy* returned to her position 4,000 yards astern of *Maddox*. The Desoto Patrol ships then steamed for the mouth of the gulf and a rendezvous with destroyer *Samuel N. Moore*. There were no further sightings of the enemy.

The entire engagement lasted about four hours. Throughout the melee, *Maddox* and *Turner Joy* fired 249 5-inch shells, including 24 star shells, and 123 3-inch rounds. The two destroyers also dropped four or five depth charges, one of which failed to detonate, against boats following in their wakes.[98]

---

[94] Walter L. Shishim, Statement, of 7 Aug 1964.
[95] Gary D. Carroll, Statement, of 7 Aug 1964.
[96] Richard M. Bacino, Statement, of 7 Aug 1964.
[97] Richard M. Bacino, Gary D. Carroll, Richard B. Johnson, Walter L. Shishim, Richard D. Nooks, Statements, of 7 Aug 1964; DESDIV 192, Chronology, ser 002 of 13 Aug 1964.
[98] DESDIV 192, Chronology, ser 002 of 13 Aug; *Maddox*, Patrol Report, ser 002 of 24 Aug 1964; *Maddox*, Action Report, ser 004 of 25 Aug; *Turner Joy*, Action Report, ser 004 of 11 Sep; *Maddox*, Deck Log, CIC Log, Sonar Log, Quartermaster Log; *Turner Joy*, Deck Log, CIC Log, Quartermaster Log; John J. Herrick, Statement, of 7 Aug 1964; Herbert L. Ogier, Statement, of 7 Aug; "Chronology of Events Relating to DESOTO Patrol Incidents in the Gulf of Tonkin on 2 and 4 August 1964," of 10 Aug; Joint Staff, JCS, "Tonkin Gulf Incidents, 2-4 Aug 1964;" msgs, CTG77.5 041336Z Aug

In August 1964, the U.S. and North Vietnamese armed forces fought in open combat for the first time in the long Vietnam conflict when Communist naval units attacked American ships in the Gulf of Tonkin. Ironically, these attacks, as the available evidence now suggests, were in response to U.S. efforts to moderate North Vietnamese actions in Southeast Asia. The 34A program and the Desoto Patrol, which appeared to be the catalysts for the assaults, were key elements of the American campaign of pressure mounted against North Vietnam during 1964. The 34A coastal boat force, increasingly effective by August, was directed, trained, and supplied by American military personnel, although manned by South Vietnamese sailors. U.S. involvement, in all probability, was known to the Communists. The Desoto Patrol was an operation entirely distinct from the 34A program in terms of command, forces involved, and mission, which was primarily to collect intelligence. But the destroyers did contribute to the growing U.S. military presence on the borders of North Vietnam and intelligence gathered for the 34A effort was an important responsibility of the Desoto Patrol.

Nonetheless, American leaders did not seek to provoke a North Vietnamese reaction in order to secure a *casus belli*, as often has been alleged. Naval officers, especially, were confident that the Communists were unable, unwilling, and unlikely to challenge the U.S. Navy at sea. Acquiescence to American power rather than military opposition, was expected. When it became evident, through intelligence sources, that the enemy did intend to attack, halting the Desoto Patrol was vetoed because fleet commanders then felt it imperative to stand up to the military threat and to reassert the traditional American support for freedom of the sea. Because North Vietnam did not publicly acknowledge a twelve-mile territorial limit until after the August incidents, the previously established three-mile limit was valid under international law. Thus, *Maddox* and *Turner Joy* sailed outside of North Vietnam's territorial waters at all times.

Contrary to previous assertions, the North Vietnamese could not confuse the Desoto Patrol with 34A operations. *Maddox* was clearly distinguishable from the South Vietnamese fast craft on 2 August. The four PTFs cleared the gulf before the start of the destroyer's patrol and the

---

1964; 041434Z; CTG72.1 042158Z; *Turner Joy* 050511Z; 062331Z; CTG77.6 070046Z; CTF77 070252Z; CPFLT 071101Z; JRC (JCS), "Chronology of Events Relating to the Gulf of Tonkin Incidents," pp. 314-15.

ship did not reach the area of the South Vietnamese maritime attack until almost forty-two hours later. *Maddox* and *Turner Joy* were far out to sea in the early morning hours of 4 August when the maritime force struck targets near Vinh Son. In addition, almost from the beginning of the patrol in the gulf, the ships were tracked visually and on radar by the North Vietnamese. The first attack took place in relatively clear weather and in broad daylight. Neither were the actions initiated by over-zealous North Vietnamese boat commanders. Intelligence unmistakably revealed that the naval headquarters in Ben Thuy and Van Hoa issued the orders. Available information suggests that the North Vietnamese, increasingly sensitive to the South Vietnamese incursions into their coastal regions, consciously struck at the U.S. destroyers in retaliation.

That an attack occurred on 2 August is beyond contention. Physical evidence, including a spent Communist round taken from the destroyer's superstructure and photographs of the enemy naval craft, complement the wealth of other extant information. In addition, the North Vietnamese subsequently acknowledged attacking *Maddox*. As the succeeding chapter will show, the validity of the 4 August attack also was established, thus convincing American leaders that a strong reaction was warranted.

CHAPTER XV

The American Response to the Tonkin Gulf Attacks

Shortly after 0900 EDT on 4 August 1964, Secretary of Defense McNamara notified President Johnson and other officials about the developing crisis in the Gulf of Tonkin. Soon thereafter, General Wheeler, Chairman of the Joint Chiefs of Staff, telephoned Admiral Sharp at his CINCPAC headquarters in Hawaii to ensure that the carrier task force commander, Admiral Moore, was aware of the danger to the destroyers and that he would take "positive aggressive measures to seek and destroy attacking forces if the attack should occur."[1] At 1000 EDT, the Secretary of Defense assembled a group in his Pentagon office to discuss possible retaliatory measures should an attack materialize. In addition to McNamara, the group included the Deputy Secretary of Defense, Cyrus Vance; the Director of the Joint Staff, Lieutenant General David A. Burchinal, USAF; and several members of the Office of the Director of Operations, Joint Staff, the latter of whom were familiar with targets in North Vietnam. In the next hour, the group considered counterattacks on the enemy boats themselves, on four of their bases, and on the fuel dumps which supported the bases. The mining of ports also was discussed.

Shortly after 1100 EDT, the Washington command post received word that the American destroyers were under attack and reporting numerous enemy torpedoes. Secretary McNamara then convened a meeting with Secretary of State Rusk, Deputy Secretary of Defense Vance, the Special Assistant to the President for National Security Affairs, McGeorge Bundy, and the Joint Chiefs of Staff. At 1240 EDT, while the JCS continued their deliberations, McNamara briefed President Johnson, Secretary Rusk, and

---

[1] Joint Staff, JCS, Tonkin Gulf Composite Diary.

the National Security Council on the latest developments in Southeast Asia.

In the meantime, Pacific military commanders took immediate steps to reaffirm the U.S. position. At 2354H, acting on previous instructions, Admiral Sharp ordered CINCPACFLT to initiate aerial and surface pursuit and destruction of the attacking craft up to three miles from offshore islands and eleven miles from the enemy coast. Even as *Maddox* and *Turner Joy* maneuvered to avoid reported torpedoes, Admiral Johnson advised Captain Herrick not to proceed too far to the southeast because the patrol was scheduled to resume on 5 August. The admiral "emphasized that patrols will be continued" and if the destroyers were "confronted with attack [they were to] use all means available to destroy enemy including aggressive pursuit."[2]

Other commanders prepared their forces for retaliatory action. Admiral Moorer advised his Seventh Fleet commander that reprisal attacks against the enemy craft and their bases was a strong possibility. In that regard, CINCPAC called for "punitive U.S. air strikes...in increasing stages of severity" against enemy craft near Hon Me and Hon Ne and in the Lach Chao Estuary; against the naval facilities at Quang Khe, Ben Thuy, and Hon Me; and against the oil storage complex at Ben Thuy, which held 10 percent of the North Vietnamese fuel supply and was the sole source for the patrol craft based nearby. He further recommended that U.S. ships be allowed to approach as close as three miles to North Vietnam and that aircraft be authorized hot pursuit into North Vietnamese air space.[3] Admiral Sharp also requested permission to consider hostile, and to attack, any North Vietnamese or Chinese Communist aircraft "whose actions and behavior indicate within reasonable certainty that air attack on U.S. forces is intended."[4]

In Washington, the JCS completed their deliberation on the afternoon of 4 August and suggested three possible courses of action that were similar to the options previously suggested by Admiral Sharp. The Joint Chiefs of Staff proposed air strikes against the PT base at Ben Thuy and the fuel facilities there and at Vinh; against the bases at Ben Thuy and

---

[2]Msg, COM7FLT 041540Z Aug 1964. See also msgs, CP 041554Z; COM7FLT 041606Z; CPFLT 041644Z; COM7FLT 041830Z.
[3]Msg, CP 041657Z Aug 1964. See also msgs, CPFLT 041509Z Aug; COM7FLT 041645Z; 041830Z; CPFLT 042014Z; CP 042035Z; CINCPAC, Command History, 1964, p. 371.
[4]Msg, CP 041718Z Aug 1964.

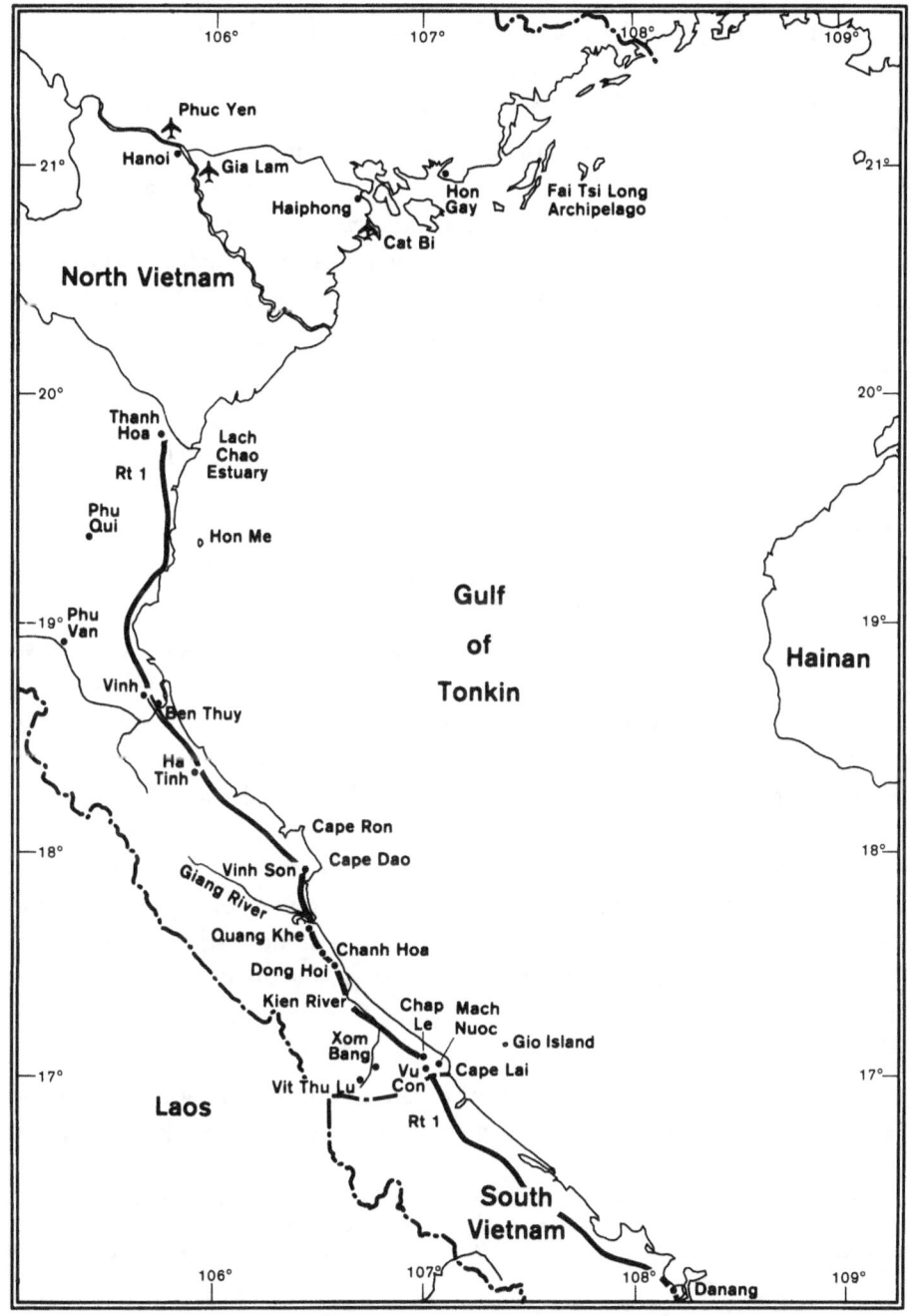

Area of U.S. Naval Operations in North Vietnam, 1964-1965

Quang Khe, the patrol boat staging area in the Lach Chao Estuary, and the fuel depots at Ben Thuy and Vinh; or against all five coastal naval bases, the petroleum storage sites, and the naval base at Haiphong.[5]

While taking these proposals under advisement, the Secretary of Defense took particular interest in mining contingencies as well. At McNamara's specific direction, preparations were made to conduct aerial minelaying operations against the five naval bases in North Vietnam. He ordered the airlift of 100 Mark 50 mines to fleet carriers. Although mines subsequently were flown to *Ticonderoga* and *Constellation*, this preparatory action was overtaken by the course of events.[6]

On 4 August, at 1300 EDT, the President asked McNamara, Rusk, Vance, Bundy, and John McCone, Director of the Central Intelligence Agency, to lunch with him at the White House. President Johnson's highest officials unanimously agreed that this second attack against U.S. naval vessels required retaliatory action. The President concurred and ordered execution of the reprisal.[7]

At almost the same time, however, Captain Herrick sent a message which cast doubt on the 4 August incident. He told Admiral Moorer: "Review of action makes many reported contacts and torpedoes fired appear [doubtful]. Freak weather effects on radar and overeager sonarmen may have accounted for many reports. No actual visual sightings by *Maddox*. Suggest complete evaluation before any further action taken."[8] A short while later he added that the "entire action leaves many doubts except for apparent ambush at beginning."[9] Nevertheless, in the same message, Captain Herrick reported information he had received from *Turner Joy* indicating that the ship was fired on by small caliber guns and illuminated by searchlight. Further, *Turner Joy* concluded that at least one of the attacking craft was hit by her gunfire.

The task group commander's doubts caused concern in Washington and in the Pacific Command. Upon receipt of Captain Herrick's messages,

---

[5]Joint Staff, JCS, Tonkin Gulf Composite Diary; Outline Chronology of Washington Actions, tab B.
[6]Msgs, CP 041547Z Aug 1964; 051840Z; CPFLT 130059Z; CP 280350Z Oct; CPFLT 140403Z Nov; CP 240042Z; COM7FLT 311102Z Mar 1965; memo, OP-601 to CNO, ser BM0001780-64 of 15 Dec 1964.
[7]Joint Staff, JCS, Tonkin Gulf Composite Diary; Johnson, *Vantage Point*, p. 114; David C. Humphrey, "Tuesday Lunch at the Johnson White House: A Preliminary Assessment," *Diplomatic History*, Vol. 8 (Winter 1984), pp. 84-85.
[8]Msg, CTG72.1 041727Z Aug 1964.
[9]Msg, CTG72.1 041754Z Aug 1964.

General Burchinal, Director of the Joint Staff, telephoned Admiral Sharp for clarification. CINCPAC stated that, regardless of Herrick's uncertainty, intelligence information revealed the enemy's hostile intentions. Further, Admiral Sharp received another evaluation by Captain Herrick, based on new information about an hour and twenty minutes after his first report, which stated that he was "certain that original ambush was bonafide." Although the captain discounted a number of the torpedo reports, some of which he attributed to the noise of the destroyers' own screws or to the screws of the attacking craft, he referred to positive sightings by crewmen of *Turner Joy* of enemy boats and torpedoes as evidence for the attacks.[10] Despite this message, Admiral Sharp was less confident than he had been earlier. When Secretary of Defense McNamara called him around 1600 EDT on 4 August, CINCPAC suggested that the order for the retaliatory strike be delayed until he received more definitive information. The attack then was scheduled for 1900 EDT (0700H on 5 August), only three hours away. McNamara decided that preparations would continue uninterrupted but that confirmation of the attack was essential. He told the Pacific commander that "we obviously don't want to do it (the strike) unless we are damned sure what happened."[11]

Soon afterward, Admiral Sharp received confirmation through intelligence sources than an attack on the American ships had taken place. These reports indicated that during the 4 August action the North Vietnamese observed an enemy aircraft falling into the sea and claimed possible damage to an enemy vessel. A short while later, the North Vietnamese also reported that two enemy airplanes were shot down and at least one more was damaged. Since no American aircraft were lost during the engagement, this report can be attributed to common battlefield exaggeration regarding enemy casualties or to misinterpretation of the many falling flares and other pyrotechnics. Yet another intelligence source indicated that on 4 August two North Vietnamese vessels were lost but the remainder were alright. This information coincided with the report of a senior captain in the North Vietnamese Navy, captured trying to infiltrate into South Vietnam in 1967, who related that three torpedo boats were

---

[10]Msg, CTG72.1 041848Z Aug 1964. See also msg, CTG72.1 041754Z Aug.
[11]Joint Staff, JCS, Tonkin Gulf Composite Diary. See also Outline Chronology of Washington Actions, tab B; JCS, *History*, pt. 1, pp. 11-22.

sunk before 5 August 1964, which would include the one lost on 2 August and two lost during the night action on 4 August.[12] Finally, yet another report indicated that a Captain Khoai had met the foe. This was clearly a reference to Captain Le Du Khoai, commander of North Vietnamese PT Squadron 135.[13]

The commanders involved in the Gulf of Tonkin incident agreed that hostile action had been taken against their ships on 4 August. While preparations were underway for the strikes, Admiral Moorer asked the commanding officers of *Maddox* and *Turner Joy*, "can you confirm absolutely that you were attacked?"[14] Commander Barnhart replied that he could "confirm being attacked by 2 PT craft" and cited as evidence the sighting of the torpedo by a number of his crewmen, the black smoke from one target, the silhouette of several boats, and the radar tracks of high-speed contacts. He rated the chance any one of the enemy boats had been sunk as "only highly probable."[15] Commander Ogier initially reported that he could "not confirm was attacked by PTs or Swatows or that any PT or Swatow sunk."[16] But, on 6 August, Commander Ogier stated that he "believed [at] the time that the *Maddox* was under attack by PT boats. Later I doubted that so many torpedoes could have been fired and have missed. I am now convinced that...torpedo attacks did take place." On the same date, Captain Herrick stated that "certainly a PT boat action did take place."[17] Based on these conclusions, Admiral Johnson reported that he was "convinced beyond any doubt that *Maddox* and *Turner Joy* were subjected to an unprovoked surface torpedo attack on the night of 4 August." That view was shared by Admirals Sharp and Moorer.[18]

---

[12]*Hearings on the Gulf of Tonkin*, pp. 92, 9-11, 17-18, 59-62, 75, 77; Johnson, *Vantage Point*, p. 114. For different interpretations of the intelligence referred to in these sources, see Stockdale, *In Love and War*, pp. 453-55; "The 'Phantom Battle' that led to War." *U.S. News and World Report* (23 Jul 1984), pp. 56-67.

[13]Khoai's identity and position were established in 1967 when U.S. naval personnel interrogated captured North Vietnamese PT boat officers and men. See McNamara in *Hearings on the Gulf of Tonkin*, p. 18.

[14]Msg, CPFLT 042134Z Aug 1964.

[15]Msg, *Turner Joy* 042310Z Aug 1964.

[16]Msg, *Maddox* 050226Z Aug 1964.

[17]Msg, CTG72.1 062355Z Aug 1964.

[18]Ltr, COM7FLT to CINCPACFLT, ser N13-00141 of 14 Aug 1964. See also ltr, SECNAV to Fulbright, of 18 Dec 1967; Sharp, Interview, Vol. II, p. 230; Sharp, *Strategy For Defeat*, p. 44; Johnson, Interview, pp. 237-38; Senate Armed Services Committee, *Nomination of Admiral Thomas H. Moorer*, pp. 23, 33, 35-37.

Investigations that were carried out during the next several weeks also supported the reality of the enemy's attack. General Burchinal's review of the messages held in Washington convinced him of the action's validity. Captain Alex A. Kerr, a representative of Commander Seventh Fleet, was flown on board the two destroyers shortly after the battle. Following a thorough study of all the evidence available, he too was convinced that a torpedo attack had occurred. In addition, a Defense Department team, which included Commander Andrew Serrell and Captain Ralph S. Wentworth, Jr., flew to the Western Pacific to interview participants, examine statements, reports, charts, messages, and other pertinent materials. The group concluded that the attack was genuine, primarily because of the visual confirmation by *Turner Joy* personnel of the torpedo picked up on *Maddox*'s sonar, the sightings of the enemy craft, and the similarity of the tracks recorded by both ships' radar.[19]

These findings, however, only substantiated the information available to national leaders at 1719 EDT on 4 August, about five hours after the attack, when they ordered the reprisal strikes.[20] The formal order to execute the operation, soon named Pierce Arrow, directed CINCPAC to employ carrier aircraft to "conduct a one-time maximum effort attack" by 0800H on 5 August "with objective of maximum assurance of high level of target destruction."[21] The targets were the Swatows and PT boats located at Van Hoa, Hon Gay, Ben Thuy, Quang Khe, and in the Lach Chao Estuary. Initially, carrier-based aircraft also could attack enemy naval craft outside the three-mile territorial limit. Later than night, the Secretary of Defense, with the concurrence of Cyrus Vance and General Wheeler, modified this last instruction by allowing strikes against enemy naval vessels "wherever they find them," but only during the first of two strikes planned for the overall operation.[22] In addition, the fuel storage facilities at Vinh were targeted. Finally, the JCS ordered resumption of the Desoto Patrol.

---

[19]Alex A. Kerr, transcript of interview with Paul Stillwell, U.S. Naval Institute, in Annapolis, MD, 1984, pp. 459-60; Serrell, memo for record, of 14 Aug 1964; memo, Director Joint Staff to SECDEF of 7 Aug; memo, Friedman to Fitzwater, of 19 Aug.

[20]Shortly afterward, at 1725 EDT, Secretary of Defense McNamara, who then was conferring with Deputy Secretary of Defense Vance and the Joint Chiefs of Staff, received word from Admiral Sharp that, based on Captain Herrick's latest messages and the intelligence reports, he was convinced the North Vietnamese had attacked the destroyers. See Joint Staff, JCS, Outline Chronology of Washington Actions, tab B; Sharp, Interview, pp. 230, 250-51; Sharp, *Strategy for Defeat*, p. 44; Johnson, *Vantage Point*, p. 115; JCS *History*, pt. 1, p. 11-22.

[21]Msg, JCS 042119Z Aug 1964. See also Sharp, Interview, pp. 230, 250-51.

[22]Joint Staff, JCS, Outline Chronology of Washington Actions, tab B.

In order to lessen the chances of a Chinese reaction, these attacks were aimed solely at enemy craft, as opposed to their bases. CINCPAC also had orders to ensure that all naval aircraft flew clear of Hainan Island and approached no closer than fifty miles from the Chinese Communist border. As President Johnson observed to a number of congressmen later that evening, "I did not want the leaders in Peking to misunderstand the reason our planes were over the Tonkin Gulf. They had to understand that the retaliation was aimed only at North Vietnam, not Red China, and that the objective was limited."[23]

Pierce Arrow

At 0455H on 5 August, Commander Task Force 77, Rear Admiral Robert B. Moore, received orders from Commander Seventh Fleet to prepare his forces, including carriers *Constellation* and *Ticonderoga*, for the attack on the North Vietnamese targets.[24] The strikes were scheduled for 0800H that morning, leaving just over three hours for planning, briefing of the pilots, and coordinating the actions of both carrier wings. Further, both carriers were already undertaking intensive air operations associated with reconnaissance flights in Laos and other missions. In *Ticonderoga*'s case, her aviators and crewmen had conducted uninterrupted operations for more than twenty-four hours prior to the receipt of Seventh Fleet's orders. Under these circumstances, it is not surprising that Task Force 77 was several hours late in initiating the air strikes against North Vietnam.

Ticonderoga launched her first group of attack aircraft at 1043H. This vanguard flight, composed of 4 A-1 Skyraiders, orbited the carrier until 1135H, when they departed for the highest priority target, the Vinh oil complex. With a head start, the slower A-1s were scheduled to reach the target at 1325H, about the same time as the 6 F-8s, 6 A-4s, and 1 RF-8A which *Ticonderoga* launched between 1216H and 1223H. At 1234H, 6 more F-8s and 1 RF-8 of Carrier Air Wing 5 took off from the carrier to

---

[23]Johnson, *Vantage Point*, p. 117. See also msgs, JCS 042119Z Aug 1964; CP 042153Z; JCS 042157Z.

[24]It appears that Admiral Moore had not received a copy of the message from CINCPACFLT to COM7FLT (041509Z) alerting naval commanders to the strong possibility that an air strike soon would be ordered. See COM7FLT, Pierce Arrow Chronology, ser 10010 of 6 May 1967. See also Execute Message Chronology, of 4 Aug 1964.

The American Response to the Tonkin Gulf Attacks 445

An A-4 Skyhawk attack aircraft is launched from aircraft carrier Ticonderoga *during August 1964 operations off North Vietnam.*

attack the enemy craft at the Quang Khe base. Another 6 tankers and 2 Skyraiders for search and rescue supported the *Ticonderoga* force.

At 1300H, *Constellation* began to launch Skyraiders of Carrier Air Wing 14. Of these 8 A-1s, 4 were assigned to the North Vietnamese boats at Hon Gay and the remaining 4 to Lach Chao.[25] This launch was followed by another at 1430H, when 10 Skyhawks headed for Hon Gay and 5 A-4s made for Lach Chao. Several F-4s and 1 RF-8A provided combat air patrol and post-strike photographic support over Hon Gay while 2 F-4 Phantoms and 1 RF-8A did the same about Lach Chao.

At 2336 EDT (1136H), President Johnson announced to the nation, over radio and television, that the North Vietnamese attacks against ships of the United States Navy demanded a positive response: "That reply is being given as I speak to you tonight. Air action is now in execution against gunboats and certain supporting facilities in North Viet-Nam which have been used in these hostile operations."[26] However, the strike group from *Ticonderoga* did not attack the fuel facilities at Vinh until 1330H, almost two hours after the President's announcement. *Constellation*'s aircraft reached their first target at 1540H.

The North Vietnamese paid a heavy price for the attack against *Maddox* and *Turner Joy*. *Ticonderoga* aircraft struck the Vinh petroleum depot in two separate attacks, leaving an estimated 90 percent of the facility in flames. In the first mission, four Skyhawks of Commander Wesley L. McDonald's VA 56 and the Crusaders of Commander Stockdale's VF 51 approached simultaneously from two directions and strafed enemy antiaircraft sites around the POL facility. Although flak suppression generally was achieved, one F-8 was hit and the pilot was forced to land his damaged plane at Danang. The following A-1s of VA 52 and other A-4s then dove on the target, dropping their general purpose bombs and firing rockets precisely on individual storage tanks. Post-strike reconnaissance photographs revealed that the attack on Vinh was a success. Thereafter, the formation flew on to the nearby Ben Thuy naval base, where the *Ticonderoga* aircraft sank one boat and damaged three others. About three hours later, eight Skyhawks returned from the ship for a second strike. The flight set the remaining fuel tanks ablaze and sank two of the three previously damaged craft at Ben Thuy.

---

[25] Because of foul weather, Van Hoa was dropped as a target.
[26] *Public Papers of the Presidents of the United States: Lyndon B. Johnson, 1963-1964*, bk. II, p. 927. See also Joint Staff, JCS, Tonkin Gulf Composite Diary.

Ticonderoga's strike on Quang Khe also produced good results. The Crusaders of VF 53 made repeated runs against North Vietnamese naval craft at anchor or trying to flee the harbor. At least one boat was sunk and five others were damaged. Several more F-8s flew overhead cover, prepared to deal with aerial intruders.

In the meantime, aircraft from *Constellation* arrived at Hon Gay, their assigned target, about 1540H. Making a fast approach from the southeast, the A-4Cs of VA 144 attacked the North Vietnamese naval craft in the inner harbor. The enemy gunners on board immediately responded with intense antiaircraft fire. Soon afterward, shore batteries joined the defense. On his second pass over the enemy boats, Lieutenant (j.g.) Everett Alvarez, Jr., reported that his aircraft was hit. The officer bailed out near Hon Gay before his Skyhawk splashed. When his survival transmitter signalled from the ground that the pilot was alive, the Air Force dispatched an HU-16 SAR aircraft from Danang. However, returning pilots reported that rough terrain and the proximity of North Vietnamese troops made a successful rescue unlikely. The aircraft was recalled. Lieutenant Alvarez, soon captured by the enemy, became the first American aviator interned in North Vietnam. He resisted the physical and mental abuse of his captors for eight and one-half long years before his release in 1973.

Even as Alvarez went down, the Skyhawks from *Constellation* continued to strafe the North Vietnamese antiaircraft defenses with 2.75-inch rocket and 20-millimeter cannon fire. Then, the A-1s of VA 145 swooped in to rake the disabled or fleeing Communist craft. Although the enemy was not surprised at Hon Gay, the naval air units inflicted great damage on the boats. Photo reconnaissance after the initial strike recorded one Swatow gunboat aground and burning in the harbor, another Swatow burning but underway, and one P-4 burning and slowly circling to starboard. The Skyraiders damaged or sank at least three additional vessels. The attack flight turned and made for the sea about 1600H, ending the brief but effective action.

A second flight from *Constellation* headed for a suspected concentration of North Vietnamese P-4s and Swatows in the Lach Chao Estuary. Enroute to the target area, however, the nine attack aircraft found five enemy naval craft about two miles off the coast between the estuary and Hon Ne, a nearby island. When the naval aircraft closed on these vessels, the Communist gunners opened up. The five Skyhawks dived on three craft to

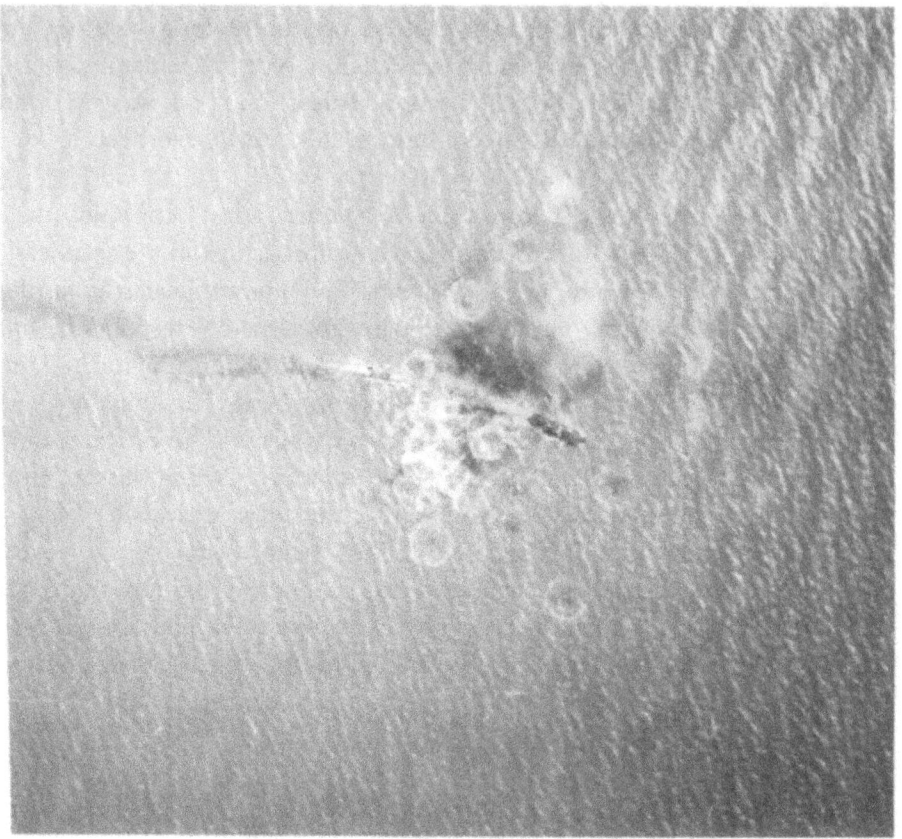

NH-95612

A North Vietnamese Swatow gunboat, followed by a P-4 motor torpedo boat, under attack by Constellation *(CVA-64) aircraft off the Lach Chao Estuary on 5 August 1964.*

the north while the four Skyraiders attacked the other two. On his first run, Lieutenant James S. Hardie's A-1 received three hits. Before retiring from the battle, however, the young officer completed his mission. The pilot later made an emergency landing on board *Constellation* with his badly damaged plane. His fellow pilots of VA 145 continued the attack. But, as he dived on the enemy for the third time, Lieutenant (j.g.) Richard C. Sather was shot down. Lieutenant Sather was the first of many naval aviators to die in the line of duty over Southeast Asia. His remaining comrades pressed the attack, leaving the two vessels dead in the water and smoking. The Skyhawks also disabled or destroyed the other three enemy naval craft. By 1600H this action was over.

Completing the day's combat, six *Ticonderoga* aircraft flying armed reconnaissance along the coast sank another PT boat. Of the 34 PTs or Swatows estimated to comprise the Communist coastal fleet on 5 August, naval air units hit 33 of them with rocket and cannon fire. The American pilots destroyed 7 North Vietnamese vessels, severely damaged 10 ten more, and inflicted lesser damage to the other 16.[27] On the American side, four of the sixty-seven aircraft engaged were damaged or destroyed and two naval aviators were lost. Another casualty occurred when Petty Officer Joe Lee Williams, after working for eighteen continuous hours on deck arming *Ticonderoga* aircraft, fell into the propeller of an E-1B and was killed.[28]

The Desoto Patrol Continues

At 0044H on 5 August, even before these air strikes began, CINC-PACFLT directed the immediate resumption of the Desoto Patrol in the Gulf of Tonkin. He further ordered naval aircraft to attack and destroy any North Vietnamese patrol boats found in the area of the patrol. Captain Herrick subsequently advised the Seventh Fleet commander that he considered *Maddox* unsuitable for this task due to equipment failures experienced in the previous actions and her low ammunition stocks. Further, the captain pointed out that "*Maddox* considered to be [prime] target after evasion of several attempts at destruction. Believe DRV Navy will go to any lengths to achieve destruction of *Maddox* to save face."

---

[27]The exact figures on boats sighted and boats destroyed vary somewhat because of incomplete photo reconnaissance after the attacks. For example, CINCPAC, Command History, 1964, p. 372, lists eight boats destroyed and twenty-one damaged. The figures cited in the text were collected by the Seventh Fleet staff, which evaluated the relevant information in 1967. See COM7FLT, Pierce Arrow Chronology and Post Operation Questions, ser 1001 of 6 May 1967.

[28]JCS, NMCC OPSUMS, of 5 and 6 Aug 1964; COM7FLT, "NVN PT Boat Exploitation Team Report," July 1966, p. IV-B-1; OP-333E, Summary of Briefing Items, of 3, 5, 12 Aug 1964; msgs, CP 042227Z Aug 1964; CTG77.5 050414Z; 050450Z 050520Z; 051310Z; CPFLT 051428Z; CP 052000Z; CTF77 061140Z; CPFLT 140059Z; CTG77.6 140952Z; CTF77 141052Z; 141128Z; CPFLT 150207Z; CTG77.6 151235Z; 151237Z; CPFLT 151933Z; CTG77.6 160354Z; CTF77 160448Z; 160518Z; CTG77.5 161008Z; 161407Z; 041829Z Nov; ltr, CINCPACFLT to CINCPA-CAF, ser 21/00050 of 29 Oct 1964; memos, Haering to OP-05W, ser 00673-64 of 1 Sep 1964; ser 00881 of 10 Dec; Historical Summaries of CVW-14; VF-51, VF-53, VF-142, VF-143, VA-52, VA-55, VA-56, VA-144, VA-145, VA-146; CNO, Personnel Losses; Stockdales, *In Love and War*, pp. 25-33.

An enemy Swatow gunboat burns near Hon Ne following attack by naval aircraft during the Pierce Arrow strike on 5 August 1964.

Turner Joy was in a better condition of readiness, although Herrick observed that at one point in the action on 4 August all of the ship's 5-inch/54-caliber guns were out of commission. The captain reported that all of these factors "caused concern."[29] Nevertheless, at 0405H on 5

---

[29]Msg, CTG72.1 042002Z Aug 1964.

August, Admiral Johnson directed that both ships reenter the Gulf of Tonkin to resume operations. In accordance with his orders, ten aircraft from *Ticonderoga* and *Constellation* orbited in the area from one hour before sunrise to one hour after sunset during the three-day patrol. Skyraiders provided an aerial barrier between the destroyers and the coast while Phantoms and Crusaders flew overhead cover. To ensure the proper use of the aerial resource, Commander Task Force 77 was assigned operational control of the Desoto Patrol.

After searching the area of the previous night's action for debris or other evidence, the two destroyers shaped a course shortly after 1200H on 5 August for the North Vietnamese coast, to which they were authorized to approach no closer than eleven miles. Several hours later, while moving toward the patrol track between points Charlie and Delta, *Maddox* reported nine rapidly approaching contacts on her radar. The destroyers prepared to open fire. However, the contacts disappeared. Two of *Constellation*'s Phantoms sent to investigate sighted several small junks near the U.S. ships. After reaching the patrol line, *Maddox* and *Turner Joy* turned south toward Point Charlie before retiring at sunset to the mouth of the gulf. The next day the ships took on fuel from *Kennebec* (AO-36) and ammunition from *Edson* (DD-946) and *Samuel N. Moore*. During daylight hours on 7 and 8 August, the ships continued to patrol off the North Vietnamese littoral, without incident. Finally, at 1400H on 8 August, *Maddox* and *Turner Joy* steamed for the open sea, completing the last phase of a momentous Desoto Patrol.[30]

Further U.S. Reactions

While *Maddox* and *Turner Joy* undertook these operations, an extremely important political event occurred in Washington that exerted long-term influence on the role of the United States in Southeast Asia. On 7 August, the Tonkin Gulf Resolution, as proposed by the Johnson administration, was passed unanimously in the House of Representatives and approved in the Senate by an eighty-eight to two margin. Based upon the recent events in the Gulf of Tonkin, this measure specifically stated that the United

---

[30]Msgs, CPFLT 041644Z Aug 1964; COM7FLT 042005Z; CTG72.1 042041Z; COM7FLT 042256Z; CTF77 071142Z; 071458Z; 080148Z; 080630Z; 080730Z; 090748Z; *Maddox*, Deck Log, 1-31 Aug.

States was prepared "as the President determines, to take all necessary steps, including the use of armed force, to assist any member or protocol state of the Southeast Asia Collective Defense Treaty requesting assistance in defense of its freedom."[31] This resolution served as the legal basis for the armed support provided by the United States to South Vietnam throughout the Southeast Asian conflict.

In the meantime, U.S. forces concentrated in the South China Sea to support Task Force 77 and to deter a possible North Vietnamese or Chinese military reaction. During the week following the Pierce Arrow strikes, *Bon Homme Richard*'s scheduled deployment to the United States was postponed, and *Ranger* was ordered from the Eastern Pacific to Southeast Asian waters. Following JCS direction, on 7 August CINCPAC ordered his naval component commander to maintain four attack carriers in the Western Pacific, two of them in the South China Sea. During the same week, Admiral Johnson sailed from Japan on board his flagship, *Oklahoma City*, to coordinate the operations of the Seventh Fleet. *Topeka* (CLG-8) and her cruiser-destroyer group also steered a southerly course. Further, steps were taken to ensure the safety of naval forces from Communist submarines. The antisubmarine carrier *Kearsarge* and her escorts steamed from Yokosuka for Yankee Station, while seaplane tender *Pine Island* headed for Danang to establish a base there for the P5 Marlin squadron then at Sangley Point. The Seventh Fleet Patrol Force established an antisubmarine barrier with shore-based aircraft between the Chinese mainland, Taiwan, and Luzon to detect and track any Communist submarines moving toward Southeast Asia. Finally, the Seventh Fleet's Amphibious Ready Group, composed of *Valley Forge*, *Alamo* (LSD-33), and *Cavalier* (APA-37), and embarking the Marine Special Landing Force, sortied from Subic on the evening on 5 August for a point off the coast of central South Vietnam.

As extra insurance in case the Pierce Arrow retaliation led to an outright Communist attack, the 9th Marine Expeditionary Force began loading in Okinawa on board the ships of Rear Admiral John M. Lee's Amphibious Force, Seventh Fleet. The Marine air group on the island and the 1st Marine Brigade in Hawaii also were alerted for deployment to the operating area. In addition, CINCPAC readied for possible movement to

---

[31]Public Law 88-408 (78 Stat. 384).

Southeast Asia two Army infantry brigades, sizeable Pacific Air Force units, and the Floating Forward Depot ships in Subic.

Between 5 and 12 August, U.S. Pacific forces converged on the scene. By the end of the week, *Ticonderoga*, *Constellation*, *Kearsarge*, *Oklahoma City*, *Topeka*, 25 destroyers, 4 submarines, 10 minesweepers, and the land-based planes of the Seventh Fleet Patrol Force formed a powerful fleet concentration. In addition, on board 15 amphibious ships were three Marine battalions prepared for immediate landing.[32]

Another consequence of the Tonkin Gulf crisis was a CINCPAC recommendation of 8 August to undertake an additional destroyer patrol in the area starting four days later. Admiral Sharp observed that the "primary purpose of patrol is to assert U.S. rights in the international waters off NVN and to ascertain through NVN reaction whether they intend to continue attacks on [the] high seas."[33] On 17 August, the admiral called for a concerted follow-up to the Pierce Arrow actions, including a resumption of the Desoto Patrol and the deployment to South Vietnam of U.S. air base defense forces. CINCPAC stressed that "pressures against the other side once instituted should not be relaxed by any actions or lack of them."[34] He felt that the shock effect of the Pierce Arrow strike and the U.S. military presence in Laos of the Yankee Team effort should not be dissipated. Indeed, the admiral warned that a fall off of activity "could easily be interpreted as period of second thoughts about Pierce Arrow and events leading thereto as well as sign of weakness and lack of resolve."[35] Nevertheless, due to continuing concern in Washington that these operations might stimulate a Communist reaction, none of Admiral Sharp's proposals was approved at the time.

The September Incident

On 9 September 1964, however, national authorities approved the recommendations of CINCPAC and CINCPACFLT for another Desoto

---

[32]OP-333E, Summary of Briefing Items, August 1964; CINCPAC, Command History, 1964, pp. 371-73; msgs, CPFLT 041653Z Aug 1964; COM7FLT 041750Z; 042040Z; 042321Z; JCS 050043Z; CPFLT 050158Z; 052323Z; 052324Z; 060841Z; 061514Z; CP 070422Z; CPFLT 070521Z; COM7FLT 071430Z; CPFLT 080417Z; COM7FLT 122130Z; 181031Z; Sharp, Interview, pp. 232-33.
[33]Msg, CP 080155Z Aug 1964. See also msg, JCS 101403Z.
[34]Msg, CP 170530Z Aug 1964.
[35]*Ibid.* See also Johnson, Interview, p. 240.

Patrol in the Gulf of Tonkin. During this three-day mission, scheduled to start in mid-September, patrol ships were allowed to sail no closer than twenty miles to the North Vietnamese mainland and no closer than twelve miles to Communist islands. The destroyers, however, could approach the three-mile limit if in hot pursuit of attackers. U.S. aircraft providing cover were permitted to enter North Vietnamese air space in hot pursuit of enemy surface vessels or aircraft.[36] In order to provide coordination between surface and air elements, Commander Carrier Task Group 77.6, Rear Admiral William S. Guest in *Constellation*, exercised operational control of the Desoto Patrol. The on-scene commander was Captain Ernest E. Hollyfield, Jr., Commander Destroyer Division 52. He flew his flag in *Morton* (DD-948) which, along with *Richard S. Edwards*, was selected to conduct the September patrol.

On 13 September, *Morton*, commanded by Commander John C. McGill, Jr., embarked a communications van and Naval Security Group personnel at Subic and sortied for a rendezvous with Commander Jack Evans's *Richard S. Edwards* at the mouth of the Gulf of Tonkin. The destroyers spent the next two days cruising the area waiting for final authorization and for the weather to clear. One hour after dawn on 17 September, *Morton* and *Richard S. Edwards* entered the gulf and began their patrol. The ships spent the next two days cruising along the North Vietnamese coast, retiring to seaward at sunset for their night steaming area. It became evident on 18 September that the ships were being tracked both by unidentified surface craft and the North Vietnamese radar station at Vinh Son. Captain Hollyfield later stated, "I knew that we were being very closely watched, and that if we were to have any trouble it would probably be that night."[37]

On the night of 18 September, the darkened destroyers steered a southeasterly course, with *Morton* in the van and *Richard S. Edwards* 2,000 yards astern. The sea was calm. Under a 50 percent cloud cover, the light of a half-moon allowed visibility up to four miles. Then, at 1929H, about forty-five miles off the North Vietnamese coast, *Morton*'s radar picked up a fast-closing surface contact about 20,000 yards to the east. When the

---

[36] CINCPAC, Command History, 1964, p. 375; msgs, CPFLT 090916Z Sep 1964; 120203Z; COM7FLT 120633Z.

[37] E. E. Hollyfield, Statement, of 22 Sep 1964 encl. in Naval Investigating Team, "Incident in the Gulf of Tonkin on 18 September 1964 Involving USS *Morton* (DD-948) and USS *Edwards* (DD-950)," of 29 Sep 1964 (hereafter Barton Report).

contact maneuvered to intercept the American destroyers, both ships sounded General Quarters and increased speed to 30 knots. Soon afterward, *Morton* and *Richard S. Edwards* picked up a second radar contact 13,700 yards to the northwest and closing fast. With thoughts of the August attacks in his mind, and confronted with two high-speed surface vessels converging on his ships in the same general area as the earlier actions, Captain Hollyfield concluded that he was maneuvering into a trap. He immediately requested air support from carriers in the area. *Bon Homme Richard* promptly launched two F-8C Crusaders.[38]

At 2016H Captain Hollyfield ordered *Morton* to fire a warning round at the first contact. Soon afterward, *Richard S. Edwards* did the same with the second contact. The patrol ships then were about fifty miles east of Vinh at 18°45'N 106°46'E. The gunfire elicited no response from the ever-approaching contacts. Captain Hollyfield later observed that at this point he "was fully aware of the most serious national and international implications of opening fire." He added, "I was equally aware of the most serious national and international effects of loss or damage to one of our ships at this time in this area."[39]

Between 2022H and 2026H, the captain directed his ships to commence fire on the hostile craft. *Morton* targeted the first contact, then 7,000 yards to port. The 5-inch and 3-inch guns in *Richard S. Edwards* locked on the second target, now 12,000 yards to starboard. Having studied reports of the August incidents thoroughly, Captain Hollyfield already had made up his mind to open fire well before the enemy closed to the effective range of his torpedoes (4,500 yards). At 2023H the patrol commander reported that his forces were "under attack" by surface craft and that he was maneuvering to evade torpedoes.[40] Shortly afterward, he requested additional air support. During the next hour, 2 F-4s, 4 A-4s, 2 E-1Bs, and 1 A-1 flew to the scene. Although the two leading Crusaders lacked sufficient illumination ordnance, one of the pilots, Lieutenant Warren A. Woodrow of VF 194, spotted two wakes close by *Richard S. Edwards*.[41]

---

[38] E. E. Hollyfield, Statement, of 22 Sep 1964 encl. in Barton Report; COMDESDIV 52, report, ser 003 of 24 Sep 1964; ltr, Hollyfield to Eller, of 24 Jul 1969; msg, CTU77.6.6 181542Z Sep 1964.
[39] Msg, CTU77.6.6 181824Z Sep 1964.
[40] Msg, CTU77.6.6 181223Z Sep 1964.
[41] Msg, CTG77.6 181251Z Sep 1964; Barton Report.

During the next ninety minutes, both ships fired on at least four radar contacts, several of which disappeared from radar screens after receiving apparent hits. At no time in the night's action did the destroyers receive return fire. Sonarmen on both ships picked up a number of what the operators thought were torpedo noises, but these sounds were later evaluated as the return from the destroyers' own screws. Captain Hollyfield subsequently concluded that no torpedoes were fired at his ships. At 2130H both ships shelled another contact which had pulled abeam. *Richard S. Edwards* reported the craft sunk by five hits. The action ended at 2136H when the American destroyers ceased fire.[42] The entire action, during which *Morton* and *Richard S. Edwards* fired 170 5-inch and 129 3-inch projectiles, lasted a little over two hours.[43]

When Captain Hollyfield reported that his ships were under attack, CINCPAC prepared to launch another retaliatory air strike on North Vietnam. In taking this step, Admiral Sharp bore in mind a JCS alerting order stating that "if we can establish that an intentional attack has in fact been made on DeSoto Patrol, our response must be substantial."[44] Specifically, the Joint Chiefs envisaged air attacks against the enemy patrol craft and their bases and other military targets, such as the fuel facilities in Haiphong, and aerial mining of major ports. In addition, the military chiefs wanted CINCPAC to consider a preliminary night attack by American B-57 bombers and carrier aircraft against Phuc Yen airfield, where newly delivered Chinese MiG aircraft were stationed. Under the detailed plan drawn up by CINCPAC, targets assigned to carrier aircraft included the army supply depot at Vinh and the PT boat facilities at Ben Thuy. Air Force planes based in South Vietnam were to hit the enemy barracks at Vit Thu Lu and Chap Le and the ammunition depot at Xom Bang. Admiral Sharp informed the JCS that it would take nine hours to adequately prepare his forces for the daylight strikes and even longer for nighttime operations.[45]

---

[42]Barton Report; COMDESDIV 52, report, ser 003 of 24 Sep 1964; CINCPAC, Command History, 1964, pp. 376-77; msgs, CTU77.6.6 181542Z Sep 1964; CTG77.7 181722Z; CTU77.6.6 181824Z; CTU77.6.6 190138Z.

[43]COMDESDIV 52, report, ser 003 of 24 Sep 1964; Barton Report; msg, CTU77.6.6 190138Z Sep 1964.

[44]Msg, JCS 181508Z Sep 1964.

[45]Secretary of Defense McNamara was displeased that the reprisal could not be meted out sooner. See Barton Report; CINCPAC, Command History, 1964, pp. 376-77; msgs, JCS 181508Z Sep 1964; 182035Z; CP 182240Z.

In any case, the operation could not be carried out until it was confirmed that the enemy actually had attacked the Desoto Patrol. During the morning of 19 September, *Constellation* aircraft and the two destroyers, now joined by *Rupertus* (DD-851), searched the area for oil or debris. No physical evidence of an attack was discovered.[46] *Morton* and *Richard S. Edwards* then resumed their patrol off North Vietnam, without incident. That night, the Desoto Patrol ships received air cover from a P-2 Neptune patrol plane, based at Tan Son Nhut, which could illuminate the sea with its searchlights and flares. The destroyers prepared to resume their mission at sunrise on the 20th. At that point, however, the JCS postponed the cruise, and the destroyers departed the gulf.[47]

During the search for battle debris and the patrol's tense passage along the North Vietnamese coast, Captain Hollyfield was inundated with "flash" precedence messages requiring information about the incidents that would allow U.S. leaders to make a decision on retaliation. Four days after the incident, the task group commander wrote: "More faith must be put in the on-scene commander to do his duty fully and make reports on his actions as quickly as is humanly possible. But accomplishment of his mission must come first." He observed that, "this cannot be done when he is pummeled by FLASH precedence questions from all levels of superior echelons."[48] Some five years later, however, the captain concluded:

> Commencing with the 2 August attack on *Maddox*, the Navy for the first time in warfare found itself required to feed near real-time details of the action into the complex international politico-military play in Washington.... In order for the U.S. to play the game to national advantage, our Navy had to feed accurate, detailed information to Washington at flash precedence.[49]

In contrast to the Gulf of Tonkin incidents in August, intelligence revealed no positive intention by the North Vietnamese to attack Captain Hollyfield's ships. Nor were reports available showing that Communist naval vessels had participated in an engagement at sea. Instead, through-

---

[46]COMDESDIV 52, report, ser 003 of 24 Sep 1964; msgs, 182000Z Sep 1964; 190155Z.
[47]COMDESDIV 52, report, ser 003 of 24 Sep 1964; msgs, JCS 182037Z Sep 1964; CP 182205Z; CPFLT 190749Z; CTG77.6 192135Z.
[48]Hollyfield, Statement, of 22 Sep 1964. See also COMDESDIV 52, report, ser 003 of 24 Sep; memo, CNO to SECNAV, ser 0037P33 of 30 Sep; ltr, CINCPACFLT to CNO, ser 33/001473 of 20 Dec 1967; msgs, JCS 181550Z Sep 1964; CPFLT 190234Z.
[49]Ltr, Hollyfield to Eller, 24 Jul 1969. See also msg, CTG77.6 230530Z Sep 1964.

A flight of A-4 Skyhawks of Attack Squadron 146 fly over aircraft carrier Constellation *(CVA-64), steaming in the Gulf of Tonkin during the late summer of 1964.*

out 18 September, there were indications that the North Vietnamese dispersed their naval craft to conceal their locations. The Communist naval forces were ordered to avoid provocations. CINCPAC expressed the view, shared by CINCPACFLT, that while the U.S destroyers had probably engaged the enemy vessels, there was no verification of the enemy's intention to attack.[50] Contrary to their open admission of involvement in the attack on 2 August, the North Vietnamese vehemently

---

[50]McNamara testified in 1968 that the 18 September incident "was not preceded by, nor accompanied by, nor followed by intelligence reports of the kind that we had available to us on both the August 2 and August 4 incident." *Hearings on the Gulf of Tonkin*, pp. 17, 62-63.

denied any connection with the September incident. On 19 September, taking all of these factors into consideration, the JCS ordered CINCPAC to cancel the proposed air strike against North Vietnamese targets.[51]

To make a comprehensive study of the September incident, on 21 September the Navy dispatched an investigating team to Southeast Asia headed by Acting Assistant Chief of Naval Operations (Fleet Operations) Captain Harry H. Barton. The team interviewed crewmen from *Morton* and *Richard S. Edwards*, studied the performance of surface and fire control radars, communications, and sonar during the action, and reconstructed the tracks of both the American destroyers and the contacts. When the group completed their study, Captain Barton concluded that he was 90 percent certain of the presence of one small, high-speed craft near the American patrol and 50 percent sure of two others. But, the investigation produced no concrete evidence that surface fire or torpedoes had been directed against the Desoto Patrol ships.

On 23 September, in a preliminary report to Washington, Captain Barton stated that although Captain Hollyfield acted prudently and "within the frame work of his guidance" in attacking the enemy before they were able to close the range, "hostile intent was not established and fire was opened prematurely."[52] However, in the final report, issued one week later, Captain Barton concluded that the tactical commander acted correctly in opening fire when he did because "a high speed (20 knots or greater) radar contact without lights in a hostile environment as the Gulf of Tonkin is suspect and may be subject to attack."[53] In addition, he noted that Captain Hollyfield acted in conformance with his orders since the Navy's regulations clearly directed commanders "to destroy...hostile forces prior to their reaching attack positions."[54] The specific operation orders of the Seventh Fleet which governed Captain Hollyfield reiterated the right of self-defense and clearly permitted firing on threatening vessels. The American ships did not have to be hit or sunk before their commanders could take defensive steps.[55]

---

[51]Msgs, JCS 190004Z Sep 1964; CP 190010Z; 191803Z; *Washington Star*, 20 Sep; *New York Times*, 21 Sep; *Washington Post*, 21 Sep.
[52]Msg, CTG77.6 230530Z Sep 1964.
[53]Barton Report, p. 7.
[54]*Navy Regulations*, Sections 611, 613, 614. On 19 September Admiral McDonald fully supported Hollyfield's decision to fire first; Barton Report.
[55]COM7FLT, OPORD 201-64, of 11 Feb 1964, Ann. D, app. XI, tab A. See also Barton Report; msgs, CTU77.6.6 191411Z Sep 1964; 191412Z; 191505Z; CPFLT 192207Z; NASCUBIPT

The Crisis Subsides

By the time Captain Barton submitted his first report, the crisis that began on 2 August with the North Vietnamese attack on *Maddox* had abated. As a result, on 26 September, the JCS ordered a relaxation of Seventh Fleet readiness. While *Bon Homme Richard* remained at Yankee Station to conduct reconnaissance operations over Laos, *Constellation* sailed for Japan and *Ticonderoga* put into Subic. The antisubmarine warfare group formed around *Kearsarge* steamed for Hong Kong. In addition, naval authorities ended the antisubmarine barrier in Luzon Strait and the air patrols along the Communist periphery. Task Force 76, with the embarked 9th Marine Expeditionary Force, sailed for ports in the Philippines, Okinawa, and Japan. Only one amphibious ready group remained on station off South Vietnam.[56]

Almost immediately after *Morton* and *Richard S. Edwards* ended their mission on 19 September, the Joint Chiefs of Staff gave preliminary consideration to another Desoto Patrol. Yet, at the same time, the JCS directed CINCPAC and other Pacific officials to prepare a justification for the possible resumption of this program. Admiral Sharp responded on 21 September that intelligence collection was the primary military factor, while the political justification was "our right to go anyplace we desire on the high seas which is a right we must never give up." The admiral observed that "if they can keep us out of the Gulf of Tonkin what do we do when they try to stop us using the straits of Malacca."[57] General Westmoreland felt that the patrols were necessary to reestablish an American presence off the North Vietnamese coast, to tie down the enemy's forces in static defenses, and to "provide provocation to Commie if he chooses to take bait for retaliatory actions." The general also believed that the patrols should not be kept separate from 34A operations. He observed that the "best tactics would seem to be mixed timing of MAROPS and Desoto to achieve max harassment and confusion of DRV/CHICOM defenses and max prospects of 34A successes."[58]

220125Z; 221143Z; CTG77.6 230530Z; Horacio Rivero, Jr., transcript of interview with John T. Mason, Jr., U.S. Naval Institute, in Newport, RI, and Coronado, CA, May-Nov 1975, pp. 439-40.
[56] Msgs, CP 280001Z Sep 1964; COM7FLT 010115Z Oct; 061630Z.
[57] Msg, CP 210025Z Sep 1964. See also JCS 201845Z Sep.
[58] Msg, COMUSMACV 211422Z Sep 1964.

The Pacific Fleet commander, Admiral Moorer, concluded that the military value of the patrols was significant. They provided intelligence on the North Vietnamese coastal forces, defenses, and maritime infiltration into South Vietnam; enabled U.S. naval forces to gain operational experience in unfriendly waters; diverted enemy attention from the 34A activities; and denied the Asian Communist powers claim to the Gulf of Tonkin as a *mare nostrum*. The admiral believed the Desoto operations also could determine the "attitude of DRV toward USN maritime patrols by measuring their response to the patrol, i.e., establish the degree and success of delivering the 'message to Hanoi.'" Further, CINCPACFLT agreed with Admiral Sharp that "we must continue to assert our right for the free use of international waters" because "any obvious withdrawal of our surface patrols could be interpreted in other world [capitals] (such as Djakarta, Peiping and Moscow, together with the Free World), as indicating a lack of resolve on our part to attain this basic national objective." Admiral Moorer concluded that "if the patrol were not to be resumed, the CHICOMS could claim that the United States stood down to their threat and is in fact a paper tiger."[59] Although these views were taken into consideration in Washington, in September President Johnson ordered the Desoto Patrols in Southeast Asia suspended. They were never resumed.[60]

The night action of 4 August 1964 in the Gulf of Tonkin dramatically influenced the American approach to the conflict in Southeast Asia. Based upon actual sightings, sonar and radar reports, intelligence on enemy activities, and other pertinent information, indicating that North Vietnamese fast craft attacked *Maddox* and *Turner Joy* on the night of 4 August, U.S. leaders initiated a prompt and forceful response. The Pierce Arrow strikes, which inflicted serious damage on the North Vietnamese Navy, demonstrated the determination of American civilian and military leaders to maintain a naval presence in the Gulf of Tonkin and to deter perceived Communist expansion in Southeast Asia. This purpose was reaffirmed with the resumption of the destroyer patrols from 5 to 8 August and 17 to

---

[59] Msg, CPFLT 230639Z Sep 1964.
[60] Msgs, JCS 201845Z Sep 1964; CP 210025Z; COMUSMACV 211422Z; CP 230550Z; CPFLT 230639Z; CP 260756Z; COM7FLT 061639Z Oct; *U.S.-V.N. Relations*, bk. 4, pt. IVC.2(b), p. 28; CINCPAC, Command History, 1964, p. 385.

19 September. Pacific commanders continually urged that the pressure on North Vietnam to desist from its militant policies not be lessened.

At the same time, however, concern grew in Washington that U.S. actions in the gulf might escalate the conflict. As a result, the administration cancelled the patrol proposed for mid-August. The September cruise of *Morton* and *Richard S. Edwards* was authorized, but the ships had orders to sail farther from the hostile coast than before. The confusing results of that patrol fostered greater caution. No additional Desoto Patrols were approved, and during the remainder of the year the strength of the U.S. naval presence off North Vietnam diminished markedly. Thus, from a military standpoint, the naval actions in August and September proved anticlimactic. Their real significance was to inspire the Tonkin Gulf Resolution, which to many Americans marked the beginning of the war in Southeast Asia.

CHAPTER XVI

Preparations for an Expanded Conflict

Throughout the latter months of 1964, as the Navy improved the combat readiness of its Pacific Fleet forces, U.S. policymakers considered the direction of American policy in Southeast Asia. Despite the North Vietnamese naval attacks in the Gulf of Tonkin and the American retaliation, the basic American approaches to ending North Vietnamese support of the war in South Vietnam and Laos did not change. These events merely intensified the debate between those who believed that the problem could be resolved by placing the primary focus on actions within South Vietnam as opposed to leaders, such as Ambassador Taylor, the Joint Chiefs of Staff, CINCPAC, and CINCPACFLT, who inclined toward increasing military pressures against the North. Despite this difference in emphasis, there was general agreement among American leaders of the need for an overall increase in the nation's military efforts in Southeast Asia.

By the fall of 1964, the various measures to deter North Vietnam were embodied in CINCPAC Operation Plan 37-65.[1] Among the documents used as a basis for the new strategic guide was Admiral Felt's Operation Plan 33, promulgated in 1963, and his Operation Plan 37-64. Also integrated into the new plan was COMUSMACV's Operation Plan 34A, which detailed the maritime and other covert activities against North Vietnam. The refined strategic appreciation, which was entitled "Military Actions to Stabilize the Situation in RVN and/or Laos," embraced "all actions and force options designed to cause the Democratic Republic of Vietnam (DRV) to cease and desist in its support of communist insurgency in Laos and RVN."[2] The JCS approved the plan on 7 August 1964.

---

[1] CINCPAC, Command History, 1964, p. 53.
[2] *Ibid.*

As in the earlier Operation Plan 37-64, three increasingly severe phases of military action were outlined. They were (1) border control operations in the South Vietnam-Cambodia-Laos border areas, which entailed activities to interdict enemy infiltration; (2) "tit-for-tat" reprisals against targets in North Vietnam in the form of one-time bombing strikes, commando raids, and aerial mining of major ports; and (3) a systematic air campaign against North Vietnamese military and industrial resources. In this latter stage, the objective was not just to diminish the enemy's will to fight, but also his physical capability to support the war in the South.

Appended to Operation Plan 37 was a comprehensive list of ninety-four targets in North Vietnam considered to be crucial to the enemy's war-making ability and his sustenance of the insurgencies in South Vietnam and Laos. Grouped into five categories, the targets included airfields, transportation assets, military installations and logistic facilities, industrial plants, and targets of opportunity along lines of communication. The Pierce Arrow strikes of August 1964 already made use of the information developed in the "94 target list" to locate and hit the North Vietnamese coastal flotilla. Operation Plan 37, with its targeting annex, eventually became the vehicle by which U.S. naval forces conducted the bombing campaign against North Vietnam in early 1965.

Several other actions that were not listed in Operation Plan 37, but which were intended to exert subtle pressure on the North Vietnamese, were recommended within two weeks of the Tonkin incidents. At that time, Admiral Sharp proposed a landing exercise in South Vietnam by the 9th Marine Expeditionary Brigade. In addition to its possible psychological influence on Hanoi, CINCPAC felt that this landing would offer excellent training for naval and Marine Corps amphibious forces. Secondly, the admiral suggested the creation of a major U.S. base in South Vietnam that "would provide one more indication of our intent to remain in [Southeast Asia] until our objectives are achieved . . . . By an acknowledged concrete U.S. commitment, beyond the advisory effort, it informs the communists that an overt attack on the RVN would be regarded as a threat to U.S. forces."[3] Because of its accessibility from the air and sea, port facilities, and strategic location, Admiral Sharp saw Danang as the optimum location for that base. Although neither of these proposals was approved at the time, the use of an expanded American military presence

---

[3] Msg, CP 170530Z Aug 1964.

on South Vietnamese soil to deter or counter Communist actions was adopted in early 1965.[4]

At the end of September 1964, CINCPACFLT forwarded his overall appraisal of the alternatives available to the United States in resolving the Vietnam conflict. Admiral Moorer viewed a total disengagement from South Vietnam as unlikely unless there was a greater deterioration of the internal situation. The more probable course of action envisioned by the admiral had the United States exerting greater influence over the South Vietnamese government and war effort, increasing U.S. military participation in the counterinsurgency struggle, and taking offensive measures against North Vietnam. Anticipating that some measure of increased military effort would be approved, the naval leader recommended the reinforcement of U.S. ground, air, and naval forces in the Western Pacific and the buildup of logistic resources in Thailand, the Philippines, and Okinawa. He endorsed CINCPAC's concept for the establishment of a major base and port complex at Danang, including the construction of piers, magazines for ammunition storage, and fuel dump facilities; the widening of the existing airfield runway; and the completion of a parallel runway. In addition, he called for the construction of a jet-capable airfield at Chu Lai. Admiral Moorer also proposed the development of a fleet anchorage and small advanced naval base at Cam Ranh Bay, an operational and supply base near Vung Tau, and a naval and air complex at Phu Quoc. Of even greater significance, the Pacific Fleet commander recommended the deployment to these sites of strong American air defense and ground combat units to provide security. While calling for these unilateral U.S. steps, however, Admiral Moorer observed that

> without a solid government, based on popular support, the military effort against the VC in the RVN has little chance of success as is rather conclusively borne out by the events and deteriorating situation which have been evidenced over the past year. The strategic concept required for success in the RVN calls for a careful coordination of military operations with the governmental development of a national improvement program aimed at urban and rural development to influence and

---

[4]Memo, OP-60 to CNO, ser BM00945-64 of 19 Jun 1964; CINCPAC, Command History, 1964, pp. 52-54; MACV, Command History, 1964, pp. 160-65; Sharp, *Strategy For Defeat*, pp. 46-48; Westmoreland, *A Soldier Reports*, pp. 87-109, 112; *U.S.-V.N. Relations*, bk. 4, pt. IVC.2(b), pp. 4, 16-24; JCS Papers 2343/326-6, 332, 383, 426, 441, 446, 450, 477; msg, CPFLT 160137Z Aug 1964; JCS, *History*, pt. 1, pp. 10-38—10-40, 11-18—11-19, 11-34—12-20, 13-5—13-9.

benefit the masses. While it seems we (and the RVN) have given this considerable lip service, this concept has really never been meaningfully applied.[5]

For this purpose, CINCPACFLT stressed the need to expand the role of U.S. military personnel in the advisory effort, and especially their work to promote control of the population by the government. In addition, he called for greater use of U.S. material assistance as a means of influencing South Vietnamese policies.

The admiral stressed, however, that merely maintaining the status quo in South Vietnam was an unacceptable strategy. He felt it "plain that if we are really serious about Vietnam we should stop treading water in midstream and take positive action against NVN." The admiral added that U.S. actions "may well involve direct confrontation with the CHICOMS," but he accepted it "as a necessary risk" if the whole of Southeast Asia were not to be lost. CINCPACFLT concluded his appraisal by emphasizing that "time is running out on us and unless some drastic action is taken now" the only recourse would be the total implementation of military measures planned against North Vietnam, including an all-out bombing campaign, aerial mining of ports, and a maritime blockade.[6]

The 34A Maritime Campaign

The drastic action against North Vietnam sought by Admiral Moorer was not provided by the 34A maritime operation, which lost momentum in the latter months of 1964. In fact, on 4 August, during the Tonkin Gulf crisis, the boat force moved from Danang to Cam Ranh Bay, due to the possibility of North Vietnamese retaliation for the Pierce Arrow strikes. The force remained there for five days while U.S. leaders awaited the possible Communist response. With none forthcoming, the Danang establishment soon resumed routine functions, but operations into North Vietnamese waters did not begin again until the fall of 1964.[7]

---

[5]Msg, CPFLT 290418Z Sep 1964.
[6]*Ibid.*
[7]Msgs, COM7FLT 041537Z Aug 1964; CP 041607Z; COMUSMACV 041911Z; JCS 042119Z; COMUSMACV 070231Z.

In the meantime, planning was underway to resume a campaign in the North that might include not only the PT boats, but also submarine-launched raiding parties. COMUSMACV advanced the latter idea on 11 August when he proposed the use of transport submarines to infiltrate an eighty-man team into the islands of the Fai Tsi Long Archipelago, at the northern end of the Gulf of Tonkin, well beyond the range of the PTFs and PCFs. After CINCPAC requested his view, Admiral Moorer stated that with proper training of personnel, and the establishment of absolute security, the operation was technically feasible. However, Admiral Moorer recommended that "this type of operation should not be approved for implementation until the U.S. is willing to overtly participate in operations against NVN."[8] Based on his naval component commander's views, Admiral Sharp disapproved COMUSMACV's proposal.

Also in August, Secretary of Defense McNamara explored the need for more boats to conduct 34A operations in Southeast Asia. The Navy concluded that more PTFs were indeed essential, especially since the old American-built PTF-1 and PTF-2 were unsatisfactory. Accordingly, on 7 August U.S. representatives received authority to enter into urgent negotiations with the Norwegian government for the purchase and priority delivery of eight boats. The new Nastys incorporated important design improvements resulting from operational experience in the Southeast Asian environment. For example, the noise level of the Napier-Deltic engines was reduced by 50 percent and the boats' range was extended to 900 miles at 35 knots with the installation of larger fuel tanks. On 27 August, negotiations with the Norwegians were finalized. The first four new PTFs were scheduled for delivery to Subic Bay from March to June 1965.[9]

Steps also were taken to limit even further the U.S. connection with the maritime operation. Each PTF was under the charge of an American naval

---

[8] Msg, CPFLT 150339Z Aug 1964. See also JCS Paper 2343/529-1.

[9] Memos, OP-60 to SECNAV, of 11 Jan 1964; VCNO to SECNAV, ser 00034 of 22 Jan; SECNAV to SECDEF, ser 00034 of 27 Jan; SECDEF to SECNAV, of 20 Feb; CNO, memo for record, No. 0046-64 of 28 Feb; OP-343E3, memo for record, of 9 Apr; OP-03 to CNO, ser 00434-64 of 19 Aug; OP-03 to OP-343, of 20 Aug; CNO, memo for record, ser 0048P09 of 20 Aug; OP-60 to OP-34, ser 000713-64 of 27 Aug; OP-343E memo, of 4 Sep; SECNAV to SECDEF, ser 00167P34 of 16 Sep; ltrs, CNO to CHBUSHIPS, ser 0027P43 of 7 Aug 1964; CHBUSHIPS to CHBUSANDA, ser 526-004558 of 15 Sep; OP-343E slide presentation, "PTF Program," of Aug; msgs, CLFLT 201812Z Aug 1964; ADMINO CP 302128Z Dec; *U.S.-V.N. Relations*, bk. 4, pt. IVC.2(b), p. 27.

officer of the Boat Training Team while in Danang, although only South Vietnamese personnel officered and crewed the boats during actual operations in North Vietnamese waters. To make the supporting nature of the U.S. role clearer, Admiral McDonald had proposed in May 1964 that the PTFs be transferred from the U.S. Navy to the South Vietnamese Navy under a leasing arrangement. The dramatic events in the Gulf of Tonkin in August reemphasized the necessity to disassociate the United States from the operations against North Vietnam. Accordingly, on 16 November the Secretary of the Navy authorized the CNO to sign a five-year lease of the PTFs to South Vietnam.[10]

In the meantime, the maritime program resumed. On 3 October 1964 South Vietnamese-crewed boats probed off Vinh Son in the first operation north of the 17th parallel in two months. The mission was aborted because of rough seas. Several nights later the boats successfully completed their task, although plans to seize a junk on the 14th were dropped when authorization from higher authority arrived too late. The weather again forced cancellation of a mission on the 25th. Three days later PTFs 3, 5, and 7 bombarded enemy installations near Vinh Son and Cape Dao. On this occasion the enemy responded with automatic weapons fire and unsuccessfully attempted to intercept the force with junks, PTs, and night-flying aircraft. Foul weather again caused postponement of the few missions scheduled for November. Finally, on 25 November, six boats of the maritime force poured 57-millimeter recoilless rifle, 81-millimeter mortar, and automatic weapons fire into targets on Gio Island just north of the 17th parallel. Two days later the fast craft shelled enemy installations on Cape Ron. The final maritime operation of the year was conducted on 8 December, when four of the boats bombarded the Mach Nuoc radar facility. In general, operational restrictions and the northeast monsoon limited the effectiveness of the 34A boat force during October and November 1964.[11]

---

[10]Msgs, CNO 071517Z May 1964; ADMINO CP 021013Z Oct; 010036Z Nov; 010058Z; OP-343, memos, "Progress on PTF Readiness," of 22 Jun 1964; "Documentary Summary," of 6 Nov; ltr, SECNAV to CNO, ser 2677P43 of 16 Nov, 1st Endorsement of CNO to SECNAV, ser 2676P43 of 12 Nov.

[11]MACV, Command History, 1964, Ann. A, pp. A-2, IV-4—IV-7; Krisel, "Special Maritime Operations in Vietnam," pp. 122-32; U.S.-V.N. Relations, bk. 4, pt. IVC.2(b), pp. 27, 37-42; msgs, COMUSMACV 151044Z Oct 1964; 290855Z; 290955Z; 260415Z Nov; JCS Papers 2343/457-1, 458, 460, 466, 472-1, 489-1; JCS, History, pt. I, pp. 11-23, 11-26, 12-19—12-23.

Following the December mission, planning continued for a later resumption of the 34A program. Specifically, CINCPAC and COMUSMACV defined a program which consisted of PTF bombardment of selected sites in North Vietnam and coastal sweeps in search of targets of opportunity below the 19th parallel. In keeping with current U.S. policy, primary consideration was given to the psychological effect of the attacks rather than their military success. Secondary missions included capture of North Vietnamese naval craft and the seizure and destruction of junks. Provision also was made for eight U.S. aircraft to give direct support to the Nastys, when they operated south of the 19th parallel.

Following his visit to Vietnam, between 8 and 12 December 1964, the Army Chief of Staff, General Harold K. Johnson, concluded that the maritime program tied down North Vietnamese resources, diverted the attention of the enemy leadership, and produced anxiety among the coastal population. Based on this conclusion and the recommendations of the Saigon command, the general proposed that the maritime operations not only be continued but increased. Although Deputy Secretary of Defense Vance approved execution of the new program on 14 December, he authorized only secondary operations and bombardment of four specific targets. The Deputy Secretary of Defense did not approve coastal sweeps, which gave the boat commanders some latitude to choose their targets. Action on the remainder of the program was deferred until the enemy's response to the first phase could be analyzed.

At the same time, COMUSMACV was given more flexibility in the conduct of 34A operations. On 19 December McGeorge Bundy concurred with General Westmoreland's proposal that missions be approved in monthly increments in Washington, after which COMUSMACV could implement a particular operation based on his knowledge of local weather and sea conditions and the operational readiness of boats and crews. By the end of January 1965, other controls also were relaxed. The South Vietnamese Air Force now was allowed to cover 34A operations south of the 18th parallel. And CINCPAC could order junk seizures without Washington approval. Subsequently, this same authority was extended to psychological warfare and intelligence collection operations. Nevertheless, of the four missions authorized in mid-December, only three were carried out by the South Vietnamese officers and men of the maritime force by the end of January. Thus, despite some relaxation of operational control, the full potential of the naval operation had not yet been realized.[12]

The Strengthening of North Vietnamese Sea and Air Defenses

An unwanted consequence of the limited U.S. and South Vietnamese actions taken against the North during 1964 was to alert the enemy to the relative weakness of their coastal and air defenses. Apparently as a result of the Desoto Patrols, the Pierce Arrow strikes, and the maritime raids, the North Vietnamese began to upgrade their defensive capabilities. At the end of August, CINCPACFLT concluded that these defensive measures virtually ruled out amphibious raids by company-size forces, as provided for in contingency plans, along the North Vietnamese coast. Admiral Moorer advised that nothing smaller than battalion-size operations be mounted, and then only against Gio, the southernmost island in North Vietnam. On 21 October he reiterated this conclusion and called for the planning of air strikes against coastal targets, which promised to be less hazardous.[13]

As late as mid-1964, the enemy's air defense network was still relatively modest. North Vietnam's air force consisted of 30 trainers, 50 transports, and 4 helicopters, none capable of combating U.S. jet aircraft. Hanoi possessed no surface-to-air missiles and only 700 antiaircraft guns of various calibers. Only twenty simple early warning radars complemented the air defense weapons. As a result, U.S. aircraft were fairly safe when operating above 20,000 feet. But, in the latter part of 1964, this situation began to change. On 6 August, seventeen MiG-15s and MiG-17s were received from China. These aircraft were augmented with another thirty-six interceptors by December. The Communist powers also supplied North Vietnam with more capable radars. At the end of February 1965, the Communists possessed an early warning and radar defense system that

---

[12]Krisel, "Special Maritime Operations in Vietnam," pp. 133-50; msgs, COMUSMACV 040900Z Dec 1964; CPFLT 102342Z; 070453Z Jan 1965; 140032Z; CP 190512Z; 231816Z; COMUSMACV 110359Z Mar; JCS 200019Z; CPFLT 252217Z; CP 270317Z; 070119Z Apr; JCS Papers 2339/166; 2343/502, 508, 516, 529, 553, 555.
[13]Msg, CPFLT 210317Z Oct 1964.

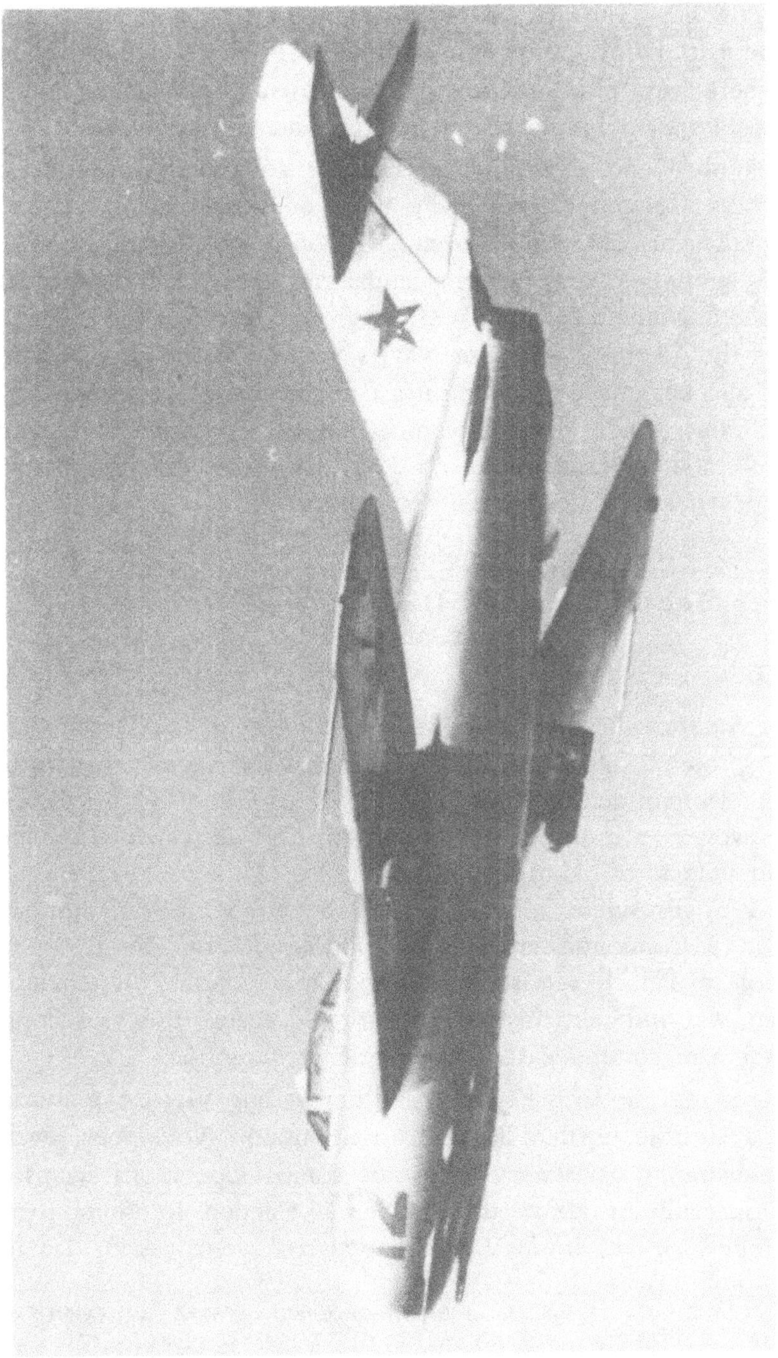

USN-1169274

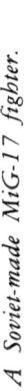

A Soviet-made MiG-17 fighter.

extended over the Gulf of Tonkin, Laos, northeast Thailand, and northern South Vietnam. During the next month, CINCPAC intelligence concluded that there were nine confirmed and seven suspected antiaircraft fire control radars sited in the coastal regions and around Hanoi.

The number and capability of Hanoi's antiaircraft weapons also increased as Communist merchant ships delivered more and more munitions. The arsenal in mid-March 1965 consisted of 816 medium, 350 light, 321 automatic, and 27 other antiaircraft guns. This total did not include the uncounted small arms of the ground forces or those weapons on board the North Vietnamese Navy's Swatow gunboats. Ominously, evidence also began to grow that surface-to-air missiles were entering the country. Thus, when naval air forces began the intensive bombing campaign in the beginning months of 1965, they faced defenses that were a good deal more lethal than a year earlier.[14]

The United States Defers Stronger Actions Against the North

While American leaders restrained the conduct of the Desoto Patrol and 34A programs after the Tonkin Gulf crisis of August, they entirely ruled out stronger actions against North Vietnam in 1964. At the same time, however, planning and preparation for an expanded conflict increased dramatically during the last months of the year. NSAM 314, approved by President Johnson on 10 September 1964, authorized retaliation for Communist attacks on U.S. forces, in principle. But specific permission to launch reprisal strikes, not to mention a systematic air campaign, was withheld. Instead, the struggle against the Viet Cong in South Vietnam continued to receive primary attention.

The U.S. reaction to the sudden and devastating Viet Cong attack on Bien Hoa Air Base, north of Saigon, carried out on 1 November, revealed the administration's hesitancy to initiate combat operations against the North, especially just before the presidential election. In addition to the twenty-four U.S. and South Vietnamese aircraft destroyed or damaged,

---

[14]Msgs, COMUSMACV 112345Z Jun 1964; ADMINCPFLT 250347Z Aug; COMUSMACV 290955Z Oct; 210152Z Nov; 190920Z Jan 1965; CPFLT 152334Z Feb; CINCPAC, "Weekly Intelligence Digest," No. 9-65 of 26 Feb 1965; No. 14-65 of 2 Apr; CINCPAC/COMUSMACV, *Report on the War in Vietnam* (Washington: GPO, 1969), p. 13; JCS Paper 2343/432.

four Americans were killed and seventy-two wounded in the barracks area. This was the first large-scale assault against an American installation in South Vietnam.[15] In the aftermath of the Bien Hoa incident, Ambassador Taylor, General Westmoreland, Admiral Sharp, and Admiral Moorer called for reprisal air strikes, and CINCPAC recommended a target list that included the North Vietnamese barracks at Dong Hoi, Vit Thu Lu, and Chanh Hoa, as well as the MiG base at Phuc Yen, near Hanoi. Admiral Moorer observed that the Viet Cong had long possessed the capability to attack airfields or other installations in South Vietnam at which Americans were based. He concluded that the mortaring of Bien Hoa represented a major change of course by the Asian Communist powers. CINCPACFLT stated that "if the U.S. is to maintain her position and prestige in the RVN and SEASIA, it is necessary to conduct an immediate and heavy reprisal" against North Vietnam.[16] But he added that the "objective of the reprisal must be to eliminate NVN strength" to support the insurgency in the South, rather than "tit-for-tat operations [which] are not sufficient."[17]

At the same time, the JCS went further and urged the initiation of a progressive air campaign against Communist targets in Laos and North Vietnam, including B-52 attacks on Phuc Yen airfield and carrier strikes on Hanoi's Gia Lam and Haiphong's Cat Bi airfields. Just before the Bien Hoa attack, Admiral McDonald, the Chief of Naval Operations, stressed the need for such a step in the event of an enemy attack on U.S. forces. Although CINCPAC did not press for this option then, Admiral Sharp later stated that "such attacks would have had a major effect upon North Vietnam and might well have been the very thing needed to stop North Vietnamese aggression in the south and to bring Southeast Asia back to a peaceful, stabilized situation."[18]

---

[15] Of related significance, it appears that after September 1964, the North Vietnamese dropped serious consideration of negotiating a U.S. withdrawal of support for the South Vietnamese regime through the third-party channel afforded by the Seaborn Mission. See Herring, *The Secret Diplomacy of the Vietnam War*, pp. 5, 12-13, 37-44.

[16] Msg, CPFLT 012131Z Nov 1964. Ironically, what might have been a Communist effort to deter greater U.S. involvement in the conflict resulted instead in a hardening of American attitudes. See Dave Richard Palmer, *Summons of the Trumpet: U.S.-Vietnam in Perspective* (San Rafael, CA: Presidio Press, 1978), p. 50.

[17] Msg, CPFLT 012131Z Nov 1964.

[18] Sharp, *Strategy For Defeat*, p. 49. See also memo, Executive Assistant, CNO to OP-09, OP-06, OP-03, OP-05, of 26 Oct 1964.

To prepare for the execution of any contingency, CINCPAC marshaled his forces in Southeast Asia. *Ticonderoga*, already in Subic Bay, left that port for the operating area off Danang on 1 November. She joined *Constellation*, and both carriers came under the command of Rear Admiral Henry L. Miller, Commander Task Force 77. *Bon Homme Richard* and her escorts sortied from Yokosuka, Japan, for the South China Sea. *Kearsarge* and her antisubmarine warfare task group sailed for Southeast Asian waters at the same time. *Mount McKinley* (AGC-7), with Rear Admiral John M. Lee, Commander Amphibious Force, Seventh Fleet on board, steamed from Subic Bay to control forces slated for possible amphibious landings. The Amphibious Ready Group, with *Princeton*, *Alamo*, and *Cavalier*, stood ready off the South Vietnamese coast to land its embarked Marine Special Landing Force. Six Task Force 76 ships embarked two Marine infantry battalions in Okinawa and Hong Kong, and two more Marine battalions prepared for airlift from Okinawa. With other U.S. forces, the Seventh Fleet was soon prepared to take any steps required. But the Johnson administration decided against further action. Accordingly, on 5 November, CINCPAC ordered a relaxation of the alert.[19]

Although the JCS, CINCPAC, and CINCPACFLT, and a number of prominent civilian policymakers continued to urge strong actions against the North, the administration again emphasized winning the conflict in the South. Neither the Tonkin Gulf incidents of August nor that of September significantly altered this policy, which had been decided upon at the Honolulu conference in June. This position was reinforced by Buddhist and student riots in Hue and Saigon, frequent government reorganizations, and Byzantine power struggles among the South Vietnamese military and political elite, which created havoc with the counterinsurgency campaign. The longevity of the South Vietnamese government, and indeed of the country as a whole, was in question. In addition, the Communists made serious inroads at this time into formerly

---

[19]Msgs, CPFLT 312149Z Oct 1964; CP 010501Z Nov; COM7FLT 010640Z; CPFLT 011541Z; 020017Z; 020225Z; 032233Z; 042057Z; memo, OP-33, of 1 Nov 1964; CINCPAC, Command History, 1964, pp. 381-83; Sharp, *Strategy For Defeat*, pp. 48-49, 51-54; Westmoreland, *A Soldier Reports*, p. 111; *U.S.-V.N. Relations*, bk. 4, pt. IVC.2(b), pp. ii-v, 25-42; JCS, *History*, pt. I, pp. 12-20— 12-24, 13-10; JCS Papers 2339/149, 153, 154; 2343/457, 462, 470, 492; Roger Fox, *Air Base Defense in the Republic of Vietnam, 1961-1973* (Washington: Office of Air Force History, 1979), pp. 14-16; Johnson, *Vantage Point*, 121.

government controlled areas. As Admiral Sharp later observed, "the United States courses of action were severely inhibited by the persistent danger that the GVN would simply dissolve."[20]

While concern over South Vietnam's stability influenced the American decision not to expand hostilities into the North, the situation also led to defensive measures, including the deployment to South Vietnam of 502 military policemen and security troops from the armed services. A reinforced Marine company of 153 men reached Danang on 5 December to provide security for the vital airfield there. In addition, plans called for the deployment to Danang of a Marine light antiaircraft missile battalion armed with Hawk missiles. But, at the last moment, the ships carrying this battalion, *Vancouver* and *Union* (AKA-106), were redirected to Okinawa.

In the meantime, efforts were underway to upgrade existing facilities at Danang airfield where a Marine medium helicopter squadron of Operation Shufly had been based since 1962. In September 1964, Detachment A of Naval Mobile Construction Battalion 9 was airlifted from Okinawa to Danang to improve the Marine unit's water supply. After forty-one days of arduous well drilling, Chief Equipment Operator R. W. Thomas's SEABEE detachment struck an adequate supply of water at 403 feet. Similarly, in mid-December, *Thomaston* transported a dredge from Saigon to Danang in order to improve conditions at the port for deep-draft ships.

In the same period, Admiral Sharp pressed for the construction at Danang of a second runway capable of accommodating jet aircraft. He also endorsed Admiral Moorer's request for the establishment of a jet airfield at Chu Lai, fifty miles south of Danang, in order to prepare for the possible deployment of a Marine expeditionary force with its assigned air wing. The admiral asserted that the "changing situation in Southeast Asia, the now contemplated offensive air actions against the DRV, and the possibilities of VC/DRV/CHICOM counteraction have underscored the importance" of the proposed construction.[21] Because the Navy had military construction responsibility for Southeast Asia, CINCPACFLT quickly drew up project cost estimates and engineering requirements for the 10,000-foot, parallel runway at Danang and the 10,000-foot runway and related facilities at Chu Lai. Both programs were placed at the top of the Pacific Command's priority construction list. In December the

---

[20]CINCPAC, Command History, 1964, pp. 305, 374. See also Sharp, Interview, p. 241.
[21]Msg, CP 260536Z Nov 1964.

Secretary of Defense gave final approval to both of the airfield construction projects.[22]

Throughout the latter months of the year anxiety over possible Chinese Communist intervention was a constant theme in American policy discussions. The unexpected decision of the Chinese to provide the North Vietnamese with MiG aircraft in August increased these apprehensions. At the same time, reports were received that Communist submarines were enroute to the South China Sea. The fact that China became a nuclear power, with the detonation of an atomic device in October 1964, added to American concern. Many military leaders, however, continued to be confident that strong actions against North Vietnam would not lead to a Chinese role in the conflict. This appreciation was bolstered by a Special National Intelligence Estimate, issued on 9 October, which downplayed the risk of a major Chinese reaction. In general, the JCS expressed greater optimism regarding Chinese intentions than their civilian superiors in Washington or key commanders in the operational theater. In one instance, in October 1964, the Joint Chiefs briefly considered a U.S. Navy-Marine lodgement along the littoral of North Vietnam at one or more points between Haiphong and Vinh. The intended purpose of the action was to increase pressure on Hanoi to end its support of insurgency. After consultation with Admiral Moorer, Admiral Sharp recommended that any operation be conducted at the southern-most site near Vinh in order to minimize the effect on the Chinese.[23]

Admiral Sharp also advised restraint on other measures proposed by the JCS. In November, the Joint Chiefs renewed their call for strong actions against the North, including a short but devastating air campaign, aerial

---

[22]Msgs, CINCPAC, JCS, CPFLT, COMUSMACV, COM7FLT, 3 Aug-23 Dec 1964; Flag Plot Briefers, of 19 Nov, 7 Dec, 9 Dec; ltr, CINCPACFLT to CINCPAC, ser 45/00937 of 4 Dec; COM7FLT, Annual Report, 1964, p. 8; MACV, Command History, 1964, pp. 110-11; 1965, p. 123; CINCPAC, Command History, 1964, p. 340; Sharp, *Strategy For Defeat*, pp. 47-49; Tregaskis, *Southeast Asia: Building the Bases*, pp. 42-43; Westmoreland, *A Soldier Reports*, pp. 87, 105, 109, 112-13; JCS, *History*, pt. I, pp. 13-23—13-30, 16-37—16-40; JCS Papers 2054/644-6; 2339/157, 161, 162; 2343/488, 493, 497, 501; Momyer, *Air Power in Three Wars*, p. 17; Fox, *Air Base Defense in the Republic of Vietnam*, pp. 16-18; Cooper, *Lost Crusade*, p. 245; Jack Shulimson and Charles M. Johnson, *U.S. Marines in Vietnam: The Landing and the Buildup, 1965* (Washington: History and Museums Division, Headquarters, USMC, 1978), pp. 4-5.

[23]Ltrs, CINCPACFLT to CINCPAC, ser 62/000257 of 18 Oct 1964; ser 62/000268 of 29 Oct; CINCPAC, Command History, 1964, pp. 383-84; msg, CNO 071359Z Aug 1964; DNI 071543Z; CNO 071545Z; JCS 052237Z Oct; William C. Westmoreland, "Vietnam in Perspective," *Military Review* (Jan 1979), p. 37; Johnson, *Vantage Point*, p. 119; Rivero, Interview, pp. 450-51; Humphrey, "Tuesday Lunch at the Johnson White House," p. 83.

mining of ports, and a coastal blockade. The admiral cautioned that these steps should be seen as a last resort and that they had a "high probability of provoking CHICOM reaction."[24] Alternatively, CINCPAC proposed, at the end of November, the initiation of a campaign of graduated pressures against the North Vietnamese in order to lessen the threat of intervention. Specifically, he proposed a three-phase program composed of: (1) progressively intensified strikes against three Viet Cong infiltration routes in the panhandle of Laos; (2) strikes against infiltration-associated targets in North Vietnam; and (3) ultimately a gradual expansion of air operations to other important targets further north. Because of their distance from the Chinese border and limited severity, Admiral Sharp believed these aerial assaults would not provoke the Communist power. Instead, he envisaged a pattern of attack that would

> feature systematic and progressive attacks of ever-increasing intensity and severity, but sufficient time was to be allowed between strikes so the DRV and Chinese Communist reaction could be assessed. If it was determined that the action was not achieving the objective, the campaign was to resume its inexorable and increasingly destructive march toward Hanoi.[25]

Admiral Sharp concluded that these measures, which were similar to those actually undertaken early in 1965, "should convince the DRV to cease aiding Viet Cong and Pathet Lao [and indeed] might also cause him to recall his insurgents."[26]

At the time CINCPAC was formulating a possible plan of action, other U.S. civilian and military policymakers engaged in an intensive effort to achieve a consensus on future measures in Southeast Asia. Following the Bien Hoa attack, in early November 1964, the President directed the

---

[24] Msg, CP 230555Z Nov 1964.
[25] CINCPAC, Command History, 1964, p. 384-85.
[26] Msg, CP 230515Z Nov 1964. See also msg, CP 230555Z; CINCPAC, Command History, 1964, p. 385; Maxwell Taylor, *Responsibility and Response* (New York: Harper and Row, 1967), pp. 27-28, 32-36; msgs, CP 250810Z Jul 1964; 011707Z Aug; 110340Z; COMUSMACV 150123Z; CP 290335Z; 010246Z Nov; CINCPAC, Command History, 1964, p. 373; Sharp, Interview, p. 254; *U.S.-V.N. Relations*, bk. 4, pt. IVC.2(b), pp. 40-42; Sharp, *Strategy For Defeat*, pp. 33, 48, 58; JCS, *History*, pt. I, pp. 12-37—12-39, 12-43, 13-9—13-13, 13-22; JCS Papers 2054/635-6, 644-6; 2118/223; 2339/144, 152, 153, 157; 2343/383; Momyer, *Air Power in Three Wars*, pp. 20, 22; Curtis E. LeMay and Dale O. Smith, *America Is In Danger* (New York: Funk and Wagnalls, 1968), pp. 248-52, 260; John Barr Colwell, transcript of interview with John T. Mason, Jr., U.S. Naval Institute, in Washington, D.C., 1973-1974, pp. 319, 322.

establishment of an NSC working group to study the alternatives open to the United States. The JCS in Washington, and Ambassador Taylor, General Westmoreland, and other officials in South Vietnam also provided their views. Consistent with past recommendations, the JCS called for a short, sharp air campaign against the North. At the other end of the policy spectrum, however, General Westmoreland inclined toward support for increased efforts in South Vietnam and a continuation of covert maritime operations. Ambassador Taylor proposed measures similar in many respects to those specified by Admiral Sharp. The final report of the working group to the President was a compromise solution representing the desire of some officials to limit additional escalatory actions until the South Vietnamese government had stabilized, as opposed to the emphasis by other leaders on increasing military pressure in the North.

The directive promulgated by the President on 1 December 1964 basically reflected the final report of the working group and detailed a two-phase program of action in Southeast Asia. During the thirty-day Phase I, to begin on 15 December, the South Vietnamese and U.S. governments would press with renewed vigor existing measures, such as the 34A maritime program. Additionally, major Communist attacks against U.S. personnel or installations or against the South Vietnamese could be answered by allied air retaliation on specific targets in the North. Although the term was no longer used, these reprisals were akin to the old "tit-for-tat" strikes. U.S. leaders also planned to initiate the bombing of infiltration routes, key bridges, and other targets in the Ho Chi Minh Trail and adjoining areas of eastern Laos, as a further means of deterring North Vietnam.

If the Communists showed no signs of relenting in their support of the southern insurgency, and there was improved cohesion of the South Vietnamese government, Phase II would be implemented. This stage of the program also could be triggered if it was determined that South Vietnam could be preserved only by U.S. military action. The second phase, lasting from two to six months, entailed the gradually increasing and systematically applied air strike campaign laid out by Admiral Sharp and others. The bombing program consisted of increasingly serious air attacks, adjusted according to circumstances, first against infiltration-associated targets south of the 19th parallel and later against sites farther north. Eventually, the campaign could consist of air strikes on all military-related targets, aerial mining of North Vietnamese ports, and a U.S. coastal blockade. As stated in the planning document,

> the whole sequence of military actions would be designed to give the impression of a steady, deliberate approach, and to give the U.S. the option at any time (subject to enemy reaction) to proceed or not, to escalate or not, and to quicken the pace or not.[27]

Barrel Roll Armed Reconnaissance in Laos

In accordance with Phase I of the new program, U.S. Navy and Air Force units were alerted on 11 December for armed reconnaissance and strike missions along the infiltration routes into eastern Laos. This move followed word from the new U.S. Ambassador in Laos, William H. Sullivan, that Laotian Premier Souvanna Phouma approved the initiation of U.S. combat air operations in his country. His one condition was that, to avoid international criticism, the actions not be publicized. The JCS directed CINCPAC to conduct two strikes, each by four aircraft, at least three days apart (later reduced to forty-eight hours), during the week beginning 14 December. The first mission selected by the Joint Chiefs entailed a search for targets of opportunity along Laotian Route 8, two miles from the North Vietnamese border to its junction with Route 12. If none was found, the aircraft had orders to bomb a military staging area on this infiltration route into South Vietnam. The second mission called for armed reconnaissance of Route 12, between the North Vietnamese border and Ban Na Kok, and Route 121. Strike aircraft were to hit a chosen military strongpoint if they had not expended their ordnance already. Operational restrictions were explicit; risk to participating aircraft was to be minimized, the use of napalm was prohibited, and North Vietnamese airspace could not be entered. However, Admiral Sharp was authorized to select the conventional ordnance and aircraft he felt best suited to the mission. CINCPAC also was directed to provide the flight

---

[27] Quoted in JCS, *History*, pt. 1, p. 14-27. See also U.S.G. Sharp, "Strategic Direction of the Armed Forces," Naval War College Lecture, 1977, pp. 13-15; James Clay Thompson, *Rolling Thunder: Understanding Policy and Program Failure* (Chapel Hill, NC: Univ. of North Carolina Press, 1980), pp. 24-27; Robert L. Gallucci, *Neither Peace Nor Honor: The Politics of American Military Policy in Viet-Nam* (Baltimore: Johns Hopkins Univ. Press, 1975), pp. 39-45; Robert F. Futrell and Martin Blumenson, *The Advisory Years to 1965*, in series *The United States Air Force in Southeast Asia* (Washington: Office of Air Force History, 1981), pp. 255-56.

with air cover, conduct aerial photography after the strike, and prepare for search and rescue operations. The Assistant Secretary of Defense for International Security Affairs, John T. McNaughton, emphasized to the JCS that the "purpose of the missions was to send a signal of deeper U.S. involvement, the signal to be more psychological in nature than of pure military effectiveness."[28]

The President personally approved the two missions, under the overall Barrel Roll program, on 12 December 1964. Two days later, U.S. Air Force aircraft successfully undertook the first of the operations. The initial Barrel Roll mission assigned to the Navy was scheduled for 17 December and involved units of Carrier Air Wing 9 embarked in *Ranger*, which previously had been flying Yankee Team reconnaissance operations. The naval aircraft were 4 propeller-driven A-1H Skyraiders escorted by 4 F-4B Phantoms and followed by 2 RF-8A photo reconnaissance aircraft. After searching prescribed routes and finding no Communist road movement, the four "Spads" struck a military staging area with rocket and cannon fire, severely damaging or destroying ten buildings. The flight also attacked a highway bridge, as a target of opportunity, with 500-pound and 250-pound bombs, almost half of which failed to explode due to an arming malfunction. Although the bridge approach was cut and eight nearby buildings destroyed, the bridge itself sustained no major damage.

The attack on the bridge resulted in the establishment of operational procedures and command relationships that remained in effect for the rest of the Barrel Roll operation. Ambassador Sullivan complained to CINCPAC that the naval aircraft might have interfered with an attack on the bridge by Laotian air forces, to which that target also was assigned. As a result, Admiral Sharp advised CINCPACFLT that "targets of opportunity are confined to unmistakably military activity of a transient or mobile nature," and that "fixed installations will be struck only in connection with attacks on clearly identified military convoys and military personnel or when prebriefed as a secondary target."[29] CINCPACFLT also was instructed to coordinate his operations with the Vientiane embassy through COMUSMACV, following procedures similar to those used in Yankee Team, because that arrangement had been "well understood...and effective over past seven months."[30]

---

[28]Quoted in JCS, *History*, pt. 1, p. 15-12.
[29]Msg, CP 190156Z Dec 1964. See also msg, CP 190052Z Dec.
[30]Msg, CP 190156Z Dec 1964.

Ranger (CVA-61) ordnancemen load 250-pound bombs on an A-1 Skyraider being readied for Barrel Roll operations in Laos during early March 1965.

Although JCS and CIA representatives doubted that the North Vietnamese recognized these strikes as an escalation of American resolve, four additional missions were planned for the rest of December. The first two were conducted with minor results by Air Force F-105 Thunderchiefs from the 2nd Air Division, based in South Vietnam, on 21 and 25 December. The Seventh Fleet undertook the final two missions of the approved package. On 30 December Skyraiders from *Hancock* searched for military activity along Route 9. Finding none, the naval aircraft bombed and left burning six buildings near Ban Keng Khan Kao. Three days later, another flight of Task Force 77 aircraft, composed for the first time of A-4E Skyhawks, bombed and strafed their secondary target, a military camp, destroying three buildings and heavily damaging others.

To discuss Barrel Roll and other matters, the Coordinating Committee for U.S. Missions in Southeast Asia, established in late 1964 to enhance the unity of efforts by U.S. officials in the area, met in Saigon during the first week in January 1965. The U.S. ambassadors to South Vietnam, Laos, and Thailand, and a CINCPAC representative concluded that it "seemed probable that such minor scale air operations were unrecognized by Hanoi and Peiping as increments of pressure designed to influence the (North Vietnamese) will to continue aggression."[31] The conferees found that the missions had enhanced Thai and Laotian morale, promoted operational proficiency by U.S. aviators, forced the dispersal of enemy logistic staging areas, and discouraged daytime road movement by Communist supply vehicles or personnel. On balance, however, it was concluded that the effect on infiltration into South Vietnam was negligible.

The Brink BOQ Sabotage

The Johnson administration's continuing reluctance to expand the war also was revealed on Christmas Eve, when Communist saboteurs detonated a powerful explosive device in Saigon's Brink Hotel, where U.S. officers were quartered, killing 2 men and injuring over 100 Americans, Australians, and Vietnamese. Many of the wounded were rushed to the Saigon Station Hospital, where the naval medical staff, several of whom also were injured in the blast, carried out their duties with professional

---

[31]CINCPAC, Command History, 1965, p. 393.

dedication and self-sacrifice.³²

The 1 December presidential directive specifically provided for an appropriate U.S. response in these circumstances and identified the Vit Thu Lu military barracks in North Vietnam as a suitable target for air retaliation. The JCS, CINCPAC, COMUSMACV, and Ambassador Taylor called for just such an action by aircraft embarked in *Hancock* and *Ranger*, then steaming near Yankee Station, and by Air Force units based in South Vietnam. Fully loaded naval air squadrons awaited the order to execute the mission. State and Defense Department officials, however, were reluctant to take the step at this time due to the continuing weakness of the South Vietnamese government. President Johnson also feared Communist reprisals against U.S. dependents. On 29 December he ruled against retaliation for the Brink Hotel bombing.³³

Nevertheless, steps were taken to protect American lives in the event of additional attacks or the fall of General Khanh's government. Most notably, Admiral Sharp ordered CINCPACFLT to deploy naval forces off Vung Tau for the possible protection or evacuation of U.S. dependents and other non-combatants. Admiral Moorer implemented this directive by concentrating two amphibious task groups in the area. One of these, commanded by Captain Adrian V. Lorentson and composed of *Lenawee*, *Washburn*, and *Gunston Hall* (LSD-5), proceeded from its previous operating area off Cape Ke Ga. At the same time, *Princeton*, *Bexar*, and *Thomaston* departed Subic Bay under the command of Captain Paul J. Knapp. Between 26 and 27 December, both amphibious formations arrived off Vung Tau, with two battalions of the 9th Marines and HMM 162 embarked. Commander Task Force 76, Rear Admiral Lee, and the Commanding General, 9th MEB, Brigadier General John P. Coursey, USMC, arrived in *Mount McKinley* prepared to exercise command of any evacuation from Saigon. A third amphibious task group, composed of *Vancouver*, *Henrico*, and *Union* and carrying another Marine BLT, remained in Subic Bay on twelve-hours notice. For the next two weeks the

---

³²Ltr, Head Medical Dept. to CO HSAS, of 17 Nov 1965.

³³CTF77, report, ser 0014-65 of 29 Mar 1965, encl. 5; CINCPAC, Command History, 1964, pp. 116-21; 1965, pp. 389-401; MACV, Command History, 1964, pp. 113-14; JCS, *History*, pt. I, pp. 15-11—15-14; 15-18—15-24; Westmoreland, *A Soldier Reports*, pp. 111-14; MACV, Command History, 1965, pp. 209-10; Fox, *Air Base Defense in the Republic of Vietnam*, pp. 18-19; "Intelligence Assessment on the Situation in Vietnam by a National Security Council Working Group on Vietnam, November 13, 1964," in Porter, *Vietnam*, Vol. II, pp. 326-31; Futrell and Blumenson, *The Advisory Years to 1965*, pp. 256-57.

assembled forces maintained their readiness for contingency operations. By 8 January 1965, however, the tension in the South Vietnamese capital abated and, on that date, all but Captain Knapp's amphibious task group was returned to routine duty.[34]

Thus ended another of the crises that characterized 1964 and the early months of 1965. Admiral Johnson reflected on the changing nature of his fleet's duties in these words:

> It was apparent that the norm for SEVENTH Fleet operations was no longer training, port visits and fleet exercises, but a level not experienced since the early 1950's. Protracted periods at sea, sensitive operations, and the danger of enemy action had become common and the general milieu in which the SEVENTH Fleet operates gave no indications that the coming year would bring respite.[35]

Barrel Roll Continues

As 1965 opened, the Barrel Roll armed reconnaissance flights into Laos were carried out in much the same manner as during the previous month. As approved during the first week in January, on the 10th Skyraiders from *Hancock* overflew Route 23, strafing the only traffic sighted — three motorcycles and an oxcart. The naval aviators then attacked an enemy staging area, destroying seven buildings. After receiving antiaircraft fire, the A-1Hs were joined by four escorting F-8Es in suppressing the flak. Three days later Air Force jets struck the first significant target of the Barrel Roll campaign, the Ban Ken Bridge on Route 7, a primary infiltration route from North Vietnam to the Plain of Jars. The attacking aircraft collapsed the bridge, causing enemy logistic traffic to back up at this critical "choke point." However, permission to follow up this strike with attacks on the concentrated enemy vehicles was denied because of the restriction mandated by Washington that missions be no less than forty-eight hours apart.

On 15 January, naval aircraft launched the first night armed reconnaissance of the Barrel Roll program. Barrel Roll 10 entailed a search for enemy movement along Route 23, a main artery of the Ho Chi Minh

---

[34] COM7FLT, Weekly Summaries, 23 Dec 1964-12 Jan 1965; CINCPAC, Command History, 1964, p. 386; CINCPACFLT, Annual Report, FY1965, pp. 17-18; Johnson, *Vantage Point*, p. 121.
[35] COM7FLT, Command History, 1964, p. 11.

Trail. No secondary target was assigned. About 2200, the first of three echelons in the six-plane flight sighted and attacked a five-vehicle convoy. But, the difficulty of operating at night was highlighted soon afterward when several of the pilots lost contact with one another. In an effort to regroup, the flight leader became disoriented and strayed off course. Coming upon a village that he believed contained enemy supply vehicles, the flight leader and his wingman dropped their 250-pound bombs on target. Unfortunately, the village, Ban Tang Vai, was held by Laotian government troops. Although casualties and damage were minor, Laotian government officials understandably lodged protests and Barrel Roll operations were suspended for the time being. On 17 January CINCPACFLT formally expressed his regrets to General Thao Ma, head of the Royal Laotian Air Force. To reassure the Laotians that the incident was an aberration, CINCPAC and CINCPACFLT also invited General Ma to observe operations from *Ranger*. This and other measures allayed the concerns of the Laotians and, after a lapse of eight days, Barrel Roll operations were authorized once again.

As a result of Barrel Roll 10, CINCPACFLT ordered that the rules of engagement be strictly observed in order to minimize further accidents. But night armed reconnaissance would continue. The JCS felt these operations provided "at minimum risk from enemy combat action, signals to Hanoi readily distinguishable from extensive other air operations Laos," even though they expected "that these missions will find targets of opportunity only by random chance, with odds less than even and probably diminishing."[36]

Increased Combat Readiness

Although the Tonkin Gulf engagement did not result in the outbreak of large-scale conflict in Southeast Asia, many naval leaders were convinced that this event was imminent. The perception began to grow that rather than exhibiting restraint, as a result of the U.S. military pressures applied during the previous year, the Communists were determined to pursue a more aggressive course. Admiral Sharp expressed this conclusion in March 1965, noting that there had "been a shift of communist tactics

---

[36]Msg, JCS 231809Z Jan 1965.

during the past year," the primary objective of which was to "bring about the disengagement of the U.S. in South Vietnam." He believed that the enemy felt that "if they can kill Americans, harass U.S. personnel, and destroy U.S. facilities the American public will, in time, become so tired of the war that we will abandon our efforts there."[37]

In response to Admiral McDonald's request for an "honest, hard NON-EQUIVOCAL assessment" of enemy intentions, Vice Admiral Rufus L. Taylor, the Director of Naval Intelligence, submitted an appraisal which concluded that the Chinese and the North Vietnamese were encouraged by the destabilization in South Vietnam and the limited U.S. counteractions. He believed the Chinese now were determined to push Viet Cong and Pathet Lao efforts to a successful conclusion. Admiral Taylor reasoned that the recent buildup of military strength in the southern part of China and the provision of arms and munitions to the North Vietnamese revealed Chinese intentions. He observed that, "if we think it is important to us, as I do, to keep Southeast Asia out of Chinese Communist hands, we must commit ourselves to extensive hostilities in that area." Finally, Admiral Taylor recommended that "we should be prepared at an early date to either commit U.S. forces in sufficient strength to insure victory for our side or get out before it is too late."[38]

The fleet was already making preparations to fight the limited conventional war that national strategists had long studied as the logical response to localized aggression. During late 1964 and early 1965, the Seventh Fleet was augmented by units from the First Fleet in the Eastern Pacific and the Atlantic Fleet. In all, the fleet received 15 additional ships, including 1 attack carrier, 3 submarines, 10 destroyer types, and 1 LST. There also were plans to add 10 more ships. To increase air strength, another attack carrier and a patrol squadron, equipped with P-3 Orion aircraft, were scheduled to deploy to the Western Pacific and there was a doubling in the number of aircraft in the fleet replacement pool.

The prospect of hostilities also spurred the delivery of new weapon systems and equipment. As related earlier, the advanced design RA-5C reconnaissance aircraft joined the Pacific Fleet at the end of 1964. At the same time, the F-4 Phantom II brought improved Sidewinder and Sparrow air-to-air missiles to the Western Pacific. The Navy scheduled the

---

[37]CINCPAC, "Statement before the House Foreign Affairs Committee," of 23 Mar 1965, p. 9.
[38]Memo, OP-92 to CNO, of 27 Jan 1965.

introduction into the Seventh Fleet of the all-weather A-6A Intruder for May 1965. Strike aircraft were modified to carry most conventional ordnance, including 250-pound and 500-pound bombs configured with a special tail, labeled Snakeye, which allowed lower bombing runs, and the new family of CBU anti-personnel bombs. Gladeye and Sadeye, dispensers that scattered various conventional munitions over wide areas, also were readied for fleet use by the Naval Ordnance Test Station, China Lake, California. And development of the Walleye and advanced Bullpup air-to-surface weapons was expedited. A new 20-millimeter cannon and its Mark 4 pod were rushed to the fleet for use with A-4 and F-4 aircraft. The Shrike missile system, designed to home in on enemy radars, joined the operating forces in March 1965. Stocks of many of these ordnance items were ordered on an emergency basis.

Steps additionally were taken to replenish ordnance stocks. The Pacific Fleet was critically short of such essential items as 250-pound and 500-pound bombs, 500-pound fire bombs, and Bullpup missiles. To streamline the management of aerial ordnance, CINCPACFLT charged Commander Service Force, U.S. Pacific Fleet with sole responsibility for this task. To meet immediate needs, the reserve stocks of units not engaged in operations were distributed as was ordnance left over from World War II and the Korean conflict. Although some problems persisted, by early April 1965 the CINCPACFLT Logistics Division concluded that there were "sufficient in-theater stocks to meet the current Navy/Marine Corps requirements in Southeast Asia" and that "the resupply system is adequate and the procurement programs are generally adequate."[39]

Naval communications were improved during this period with the introduction of new systems and procedures. The latest equipment was installed on a priority basis in flagships, aircraft carriers, and cruisers. The number of ships with an automatic encryption capability increased. Steps also were taken to provide additional frequencies, transmitters, and antenna arrays and to assure better coordination of transmitting procedures between ship-based and shore-based facilities. In February 1965 the Pacific Fleet Message Center was able to process 44,571 messages, as compared with 30,047 the previous February.

Operations conducted during the latter part of 1964 and early 1965 also revealed a number of tactical problems that demanded solution

---

[39] Memo, Deputy CINCPACFLT to SECNAV Naval Aide, of 13 Apr 1965.

before the fleet could be prepared for full-scale combat. Commander Seventh Fleet reported in December that "arising, undoubtedly from an undue emphasis on nuclear warfare in the last few years, the art of conventional warfare has been misplaced if not lost."[40] For example, CINCPACFLT reported that the North Vietnamese attacks against *Maddox* and *Turner Joy* "graphically portrayed a general deterioration in surface gunnery and coordinated air/surface operational capabilities."[41] Recognition of this deficiency provided the stimulus for intensive training of Seventh Fleet units in gunnery.

While the number and types of surface combatants committed to the Southeast Asian conflict were more than adequate to sustain operations, the recurring problems of ship obsolescence and material shortages remained. Because of the fleet's advancing age and past lack of scheduled maintenance and overhaul, the "deterioration of hulls, piping systems, and cabling had become an increasing problem."[42] The condition of the fleet's material supply was generally satisfactory, but aeronautical material and equipment and construction equipment and spare parts inventories were less than 50 percent of the required total.

National leaders long had expressed concern over the sufficiency of sealift resources to support a war in Southeast Asia. These fears were realized when the MSTS nucleus fleet, which consisted of eighty-nine ships in January 1965, experienced difficulty transporting helicopters, light aircraft, other outsized cargo, and supplies both to and within Southeast Asia. To meet the increasing demand, the Navy shifted MSTS passenger, cargo, and tanker ships from other routes. Further, MSTS reactivated numerous ships of the National Defense Reserve Fleet, even though many of these were in poor material condition. It also became necessary to charter U.S. and foreign merchantmen. Through these extraordinary measures, the logistic pipeline at sea to the combat theater was maintained.

The subject of conventional warfare deficiencies was addressed by naval commanders at a conference on air strike ordnance convened at CINC-

---

[40]COM7FLT, "Lessons Learned, Southeast Asia Operations, 1964," ser N3-00223 of 19 Dec 1964, p. B-1. Admiral McDonald expressed the same view earlier. See McDonald, "Address to Commandant's Conference, Wash., DC, 29 Sep 1964."

[41]CINCPACFLT, Annual Report, FY1965, p. 24.

[42]DOD, Joint Logistics Review Board, *Logistic Support in the Vietnam Era*, (hereafter JLRB), (Washington: The Board, ca. 1971), Vol. II, p. 47.

PACFLT headquarters during the third week in November 1964. Among the major concerns discussed at the meeting and in subsequent fleet reports was the lack of proficiency in handling, loading, and delivering conventional ordnance. To rectify the problem, the Seventh Fleet introduced new instructional materials and conducted exercises with live ordnance.

The extended deployment in Southeast Asian waters also revealed the need for greater information on the enemy and the operating area. Seventh Fleet aviation units found that although they were called upon to conduct air strikes within range of a variety of antiaircraft weapons, they often lacked detailed information on enemy defenses. This was especially the case since existing intelligence publications on antiaircraft order of battle "have become oriented almost exclusively toward support of nuclear operations."[43] Other target intelligence was available, but was too imprecise or not current. Similarly, naval commanders concluded that there were gaps in the maps and charts, beach surveys, and oceanographic studies of Southeast Asia produced during previous years. Commander Seventh Fleet especially noted the need for data on climatological and weather conditions, particularly over coastal waters. While existing maps of Southeast Asian land areas were more satisfactory, few fleet units possessed copies. To correct these deficiencies, Admiral Johnson requested that the Fleet Intelligence Center, Pacific, whose workload already had increased 400 percent since 1959, the Fleet Weather Center on Guam, relevant naval offices in Washington, and other U.S. agencies provide his forces with accurate and current informational materials. These aids began reaching the combat theater in the spring of 1965, just when the need became acute.

Events following the Tonkin Gulf actions also tested the adequacy of sea-based support forces. Admiral Johnson found that "when the tempo of operations increases and the ratio of time at sea to time in port changes, mobile support resources are not adequate and are improperly located to support sustained operations at sea during a period of crisis."[44] The Joint Logistics Review Board, formed in 1969 to evaluate the support effort, came to the same conclusion and added that the "World War II underway replenishment ships were inefficient and hard pressed to meet the

---

[43]COM7FLT, "Lessons Learned," p. C-2.
[44]*Ibid.* p. E-1. See also msg, CPFLT 112014Z Nov 1964.

demands imposed on them because of slow transit speeds, low transfer rates, and unreliable and obsolete equipment."[45] In the last quarter of 1964 the Seventh Fleet's Mobile Logistic Support Force (Task Force 73) delivered 1,300 short tons above the average issue of provisions. In January 1965 underway replenishments averaged 300 a month, but by the end of February the number rose to 429. It became increasingly evident that not nearly enough ships were available to accommodate this surge. For example, not all deployed combatants received adequate fresh provisions. And because general stores were resupplied from Yokosuka, Japan, 2,000 miles from the South China Sea, a number of Seventh Fleet ships had shortages of clothing, aviation lubrication oil, and other items.

The diminished capability of the underway replenishment force during this period of extended operations highlighted the Seventh Fleet's dependence on facilities ashore. The installations in the Philippines, and especially those in the Subic Bay-Sangley Point area, were of critical importance in sustaining the forward deployment of the Pacific naval forces. By the end of March 1965, there was a four-fold increase in ships entering the bay for resupply and refueling. Similarly, the Naval Magazine at Subic became the most active ammunition supply activity in the Western Pacific.[46] In addition to supporting the fleet in late 1964, the Naval Magazine handled 3,000 short tons of Air Force munitions each month. The Naval Supply Depot at Subic also experienced a dramatic increase in its workload. During and just after the Tonkin Gulf actions the facility issued 300 percent more material to the fleet than it had during previous comparable periods.

Although the logistic support provided the Seventh Fleet by shore-based facilities was adequate to sustain current operations, the concentration of naval forces in the South China Sea severely strained the bases in the Philippines. CINCPACFLT observed, for example, that the fuel oil storage capacity at Subic barely met requirements, and that an interruption of tanker traffic to the fuel facility at one point had reduced fuel on hand to a four-day supply. Demands on Subic were increased further by the necessity to provide a reserve supply of POL, in the event the enemy destroyed storage facilities in South Vietnam. Admiral Moorer stressed that to meet all requirements, the fleet needed an additional storage

---

[45]JLRB, Vol. II, p. 209.
[46]Memo, Deputy CINCPACFLT to SECNAV Naval Aide, of 13 Apr 1965.

capacity of 265,000 barrels. As a result of his recommendations, the construction of new storage tanks, capable of containing 350,000 barrels, was added to the Fiscal Year 1965 budget and construction begun immediately. Further plans to build tanks for another 240,000 barrels were expedited. And to provide an immediate reserve supply of POL for U.S. forces in South Vietnam, MSTS stationed two tankers in the bay.

The Naval Magazine at Subic faced similar problems. It held a total of 16,200 short tons of ammunition, but requirements in contingency plans and for current operations or training exceeded 35,000 tons. CINCPACFLT requested the priority construction of magazines in anticipation of greater hostilities. Similarly, the Naval Supply Depot at Subic, which was inundated with requests for material from the operating theater at the end of 1964, was unable to satisfy the total demand. With stocks based on a normal tempo of operations, shortages of ship and aircraft spare parts quickly developed. For example, photographic equipment for the RA-3B, weapons system parts for the SP-2, and maps and charts for aircraft were unavailable. In the period following Tonkin Gulf, 75 percent of the requisitions for spare parts had to be referred by the Naval Supply Depot to other facilities. But, to prepare for future contingencies, material stocks soon were concentrated at Subic from throughout the Western Pacific and construction of additional warehouses was accelerated. To improve conditions at Sangley Point, CINCPACFLT took steps to speed up construction of additional hangars and maintenance and berthing facilities. All of these measures to ready the fleet for extended combat soon proved their value when full-scale hostilities began in the early months of 1965.[47]

Although Desoto Patrol, Pierce Arrow, Yankee Team, and Barrel Roll were in many ways limited or short-term applications of naval power, Pacific Fleet personnel received considerable long-term benefit from these operations. Fleet chaplains reported, for example, that the morale of

---

[47] Ltrs, CINCPACFLT to CNO, ser 4200816 of 20 Oct 1964; CINCPACFLT to CNO, ser 31/001004 of 29 Dec; OP-406, memo, of 3 Mar 1965; memo, Deputy CINCPACFLT to SECNAV Naval Aide, of 13 Apr 1965; CINCPACFLT, Annual Report, FY1965; CINCPAC, Command History, 1964, pp. 110-12; 1965, Vol. II, pp. 568-71; msgs, CPFLT 112014Z Nov 1964; CP 052323Z Jan 1965; CPFLT 082227Z Feb; COMUSMACV 220615Z; CPFLT 221847Z; COM7FLT, "Lessons Learned;" memo, Executive Assistant to CNO to Special Assistant to Chairman JCS, of 8 Feb 1965; Paul Van Leunen, Jr., "Naval Weapons Today," *U.S. Naval Institute Naval Review 1965* (1964), pp. 47-53; JLRB, Vol. I, p. 9; Vol. II, pp. 45-49, 59-63, 156, 197, 202-06, 209-10, 294; Naval Historical Division, "History of U.S. Naval Operations in the Vietnam Conflict, 1965-1967," pt. II, pp. 745-46; William D. Irvin, transcript of interview with John T. Mason, Jr., U.S. Naval Institute, in Washington, DC, 1978, pp. 582-83, 587, 594-96, 604-23.

officers and men alike was high, especially after the Tonkin Gulf actions. The extended deployments, long working hours, and the tropical heat taxed endurance, but the importance of the collective task invigorated the crews of the Seventh Fleet ships in Southeast Asian waters. One ship-hopping chaplain, Commander Thomas D. Parham (CHC), reported: "I preached in one of the destroyers involved in the Gulf of Tonkin incident the Sunday after it happened. I remember the feeling of exhilaration on board and the hope of getting back into action again."[48]

These actions also provided naval personnel with invaluable operational experience. Commanders received first-hand knowledge of the control and coordination necessary for combat operations and the logistic support needed by units in the theater over an extended period of time. Ammunition and other supply requirements could be determined better under realistic conditions. Similarly, the procedures for collecting, processing, and disseminating tactical intelligence gained from aerial reconnaissance were well defined by early 1965. Surface sailors were exposed to enemy fire for the first time in many years, highlighting the value of improving shipboard radar and gunnery techniques. Further, naval officers became familiar with the composition of friendly and enemy forces, the nature of the physical environment, and the objectives of U.S. policy. Rear Admiral Donald W. Wulzen, Commander Amphibious Force, Seventh Fleet, later noted that "when the decision to commit the Marines in the northern area...of the Republic of Vietnam finally came, the Navy-Marine Team was prepared and planning was complete. The forces were in all respects ready for action."[49]

During the period from August 1964 through January 1965, the Navy prepared for the wider war that many of its leaders saw approaching. The fleet deployed additional surface and air units, sealift ships, aircraft, and weapons in the Western Pacific; built more storage and handling facilities at its logistic installations; and increased stocks of ordnance, equipment, and general supplies. Further, naval commanders developed plans for major combat actions.

---

[48]Moore, *et al.*, "Chaplains With U.S. Naval Units in Vietnam," p. 90.
[49]COMPHIBFOR7FLT, "History of Amphibious Operations in South Vietnam, March 1965-December 1966," p. 4. See also CINCPACFLT, Annual Report, FY1965; *Constellation*, Intelligence Report, ser 0026 of 7 May 1965; *Coral Sea*, Intelligence Report, ser 0013 of 23 May 1966; *Ranger*, Intelligence Report, ser 0080 of 28 May; memo, DNI to SECNAV, ser 00411P92 of 19 Mar 1965.

Throughout these months, the American government considered initiating large-scale bombing, mining, and blockading operations in North Vietnam to deter that country's support of the insurgencies in Southeast Asia. Naval leaders were prominent among those strategists who favored stronger measures to restrain the Communists. Top officials of the Johnson administration and a number of military commanders, however, were concerned that this step might bring about overt Chinese and North Vietnamese intervention into the conflict. Another cause for caution was the fear that the South Vietnamese government and war effort might collapse, regardless of U.S. actions. Hence, the United States did not retaliate against North Vietnam when the Viet Cong shelled Bien Hoa Air Base in November 1964 and sabotaged the Brink BOQ the following month. As alternatives to striking directly at the North Vietnamese, the administration continued the Desoto Patrols, Yankee Team reconnaissance flights, and covert 34A campaign and launched the Barrel Roll armed reconnaissance in Laos, operations in which the Pacific Fleet played a large part.

Concern for the possible consequences of these programs, however, also influenced their conduct. Operational restrictions, in addition to other problems at the tactical level, limited the effectiveness of these measures in deterring the aggressive behavior of the North Vietnamese in the region. Conversely, North Vietnam's strengthening of antiaircraft and coastal defenses, diplomatic intransigence, and attacks on U.S. personnel and installations in South Vietnam appeared to signal the enemy's intent to prosecute the war on an expanded scale.

CHAPTER XVII

The Navy Begins Extended Combat Operations in Southeast Asia, 1965

Even as the United States demonstrated continued reluctance to widen the conflict, early in 1965 North Vietnam launched additional attacks against American personnel and installations in South Vietnam, compelling the Johnson administration to make critical decisions on future strategy in Southeast Asia.

One example of American caution was the delayed and limited reinstitution of the Desoto Patrols, approved by presidential action in December 1964 as a facet of the Phase I program. On 28 January 1965, the JCS called for the initiation on 3 February of such a patrol, which would approach no closer than thirty miles from North Vietnam and remain south of the 20th parallel. Pacific Fleet commanders designated *George K. Mackenzie* and *Ernest G. Small* (DDR-838) to undertake this operation.

During the four-month hiatus in the Desoto Patrols, the Pacific Fleet continued to prepare for these missions. Due to the possibility that the North Vietnamese might resume their attacks on American ships in the Gulf of Tonkin, selected surface units conducted exercises in gunnery, target acquisition, night illumination, alert procedures, and communications. PTFs from Danang simulated high-speed attacks on fleet destroyers. Although Admiral Moorer reported to Admiral McDonald on 2 February that *George K. Mackenzie* and *Ernest G. Small* were fully ready, the patrol was postponed when U.S. officials realized it coincided with the Tet holiday. Fears also were expressed that the patrol might be seen as provocative at a time when Soviet Premier Aleksei Kosygin was visiting Hanoi.

Conversely, the North Vietnamese showed little concern over taking direct hostile action against the United States. Following the Bien Hoa and Brink Hotel incidents in November and December 1964, neither of which brought a U.S. response, the Communists launched their most spectacular attack yet on U.S. forces in South Vietnam. On 7 February 1965, Viet Cong mortars shelled the American advisors compound at Pleiku, killing eight men and wounding 109 others.

A clear consensus quickly developed among civilian and military leaders of the Johnson administration that the Pleiku attack was a direct provocation demanding an immediate and forceful response. As a result, President Johnson authorized reprisal strikes, named Flaming Dart I, against pre-selected targets in North Vietnam, ordered the evacuation of American dependents from South Vietnam, and directed the deployment to Danang of a Marine Hawk surface-to-air missile battalion standing by in Okinawa. Elements of the unit were airlifted to South Vietnam on the 8th and the remainder of the air defense battalion and supporting elements followed soon afterward by sea on board *Gunston Hall*, *Washburn* (AKA-108), and *Vernon County*.

In the same week, CINCPAC alerted his forces in the Western Pacific. The 173rd Airborne Brigade on Okinawa had orders to stand by for possible deployment to the Saigon area. Even before receiving a directive to do so, CINCPACFLT ordered the concentration of Seventh Fleet forces in the South China Sea. This was quickly accomplished, since *Ranger* and her escorts were already at Yankee Station engaged in Barrel Roll and Yankee Team operations, and *Hancock* and *Coral Sea* had just departed the area for Subic Bay after standing down from the cancelled Desoto Patrol operation. Reversing course, the two carriers steamed at 27 knots into the Gulf of Tonkin and soon joined *Ranger*.

At this point, due to the growing tension in the area and the possibility of a response by Communist powers to the Flaming Dart reprisals, naval leaders considered the establishment of a seaplane base at Danang. On 11 February, Vice Admiral William I. Martin, the Assistant Chief of Naval Operations (Air), suggested that a detachment or squadron of SP-5B Marlin aircraft, supported by a tender, be stationed at this port in order to improve surveillance of both submarines and shipping in the area. A secondary advantage of this deployment would be relief of airfield congestion in the Philippines and elsewhere. The admiral also suggested that the opportunity be seized to demonstrate the value of seaplanes, lest the aircraft be stricken from the Navy's inventory by Secretary of Defense McNamara. Accordingly, that same day CINCPACFLT stationed a detachment of aircraft and seaplane tender *Salisbury Sound* (AV-13) at Danang, under the command of Rear Admiral Richard L. Fowler, commander of the Seventh Fleet patrol force. From this location, over the next five days, the eleven SP-5Bs of Patrol Squadron 47 supported the ASW patrol of the South China Sea. However, this operation was short-lived, especially because of concern by the Pacific Fleet commander that Viet Cong saboteurs might attack the Danang seadrome. As a result, on 16 February the Danang activity was deactivated and the naval patrol forces relocated to Sangley Point in the Philippines.[1]

In the meantime, the Washington command designated U.S. Navy, Air Force, and Vietnamese Air Force units to carry out the Flaming Dart I reprisal strike, a mission which came under the overall coordination of the Air Force's 2nd Air Division. The targets assigned to *Ranger* were the military barracks at Vit Thu Lu while *Coral Sea* and *Hancock* focused on the barracks at Dong Hoi. Soon after *Ranger* launched her A-1H Skyraiders on 7 February, problems of command and control began to emerge. In order to avoid possible interference with nearby targets assigned to South Vietnamese and U.S. Air Force units, the 2nd Air Division commander requested that the naval aviators from *Ranger* delay their strike for thirty minutes. Admiral Miller, Commander Task Force 77, readily acceded to the request, ordering the Skyraiders to orbit *Ranger* while further launches were stopped. Following this hold, the 2nd Air Division called for another delay. This time Admiral Miller denied the request since his aircraft were approaching their targets and reports indicated that the weather was favorable for the air attacks. However, once they arrived over the target area, *Ranger*'s aviators encountered low-lying clouds which obscured the Vit Thu Lu barracks. Hence, they were compelled to cancel the mission.

The naval air squadrons from *Hancock* and *Coral Sea* also met adverse weather conditions, but these were not severe enough to halt their attack on the Dong Hoi army compound, located twenty miles north of the

---

[1] Future events indicated that this anxiety was justified, for on 27 March 1965, USNS LST-550, carrying general cargo, was mined while beaching in Danang harbor. Although damage to the ship was not severe, the LST required assistance from tug *Lipan* and salvage ship *Reclaimer* to make her seaworthy. Flag Plot Briefers, Feb 1965; msg, CPFLT 160952Z Feb; VP 47, Command History, of 29 Apr; PATFOR7THFLT, Command History, FY1965; memo, OP-502 to CNO, ser 002001P50 of 11 Feb 1965.

DMZ. The camp consisted of over 275 barracks and administrative buildings spread over a large area. Streaking in at 500 knots under a low cloud ceiling, the attack squadrons, with twenty-nine aircraft, crossed the coast south of Dong Hoi and followed Route 1 north into the target area. At 1502, attack squadrons from *Coral Sea*'s Carrier Air Wing 15 dropped their 250-pound bombs and fired 2.75-inch rockets into the building complex. Unfortunately, the enemy was not surprised. Intense small arms, automatic weapons, and 37-millimeter antiaircraft fire, some coming from two Swatows in the Kien River, hit the Skyhawk of Lieutenant Edward A. Dickson, USNR, of VA 155. Commander Peter Mongilardi, Jr., the commanding officer of VA 153, heard Dickson radio that, despite the damage to his plane, he was pressing the attack. But, with his aircraft on fire, the young officer soon was forced to eject and he was lost when his parachute failed to open. Lieutenant Dickson was the second naval aviator killed in the hostile North Vietnamese sky.

The attack squadrons from *Hancock*'s Carrier Air Wing 21 then rolled in for the second phase of the strike on Dong Hoi. After expending their ordnance, the seventeen Skyhawks of VA 212 and VA 216 headed out to the safety of the sea. They were followed into the target area by RF-8A poststrike photographic aircraft of VFP 63. By 1535 the attack on Dong Hoi was over. Although seven other aircraft from the carrier task force were hit, none was lost, partly due to the effective flak suppression provided by F-8 Crusaders from the *Coral Sea* and *Hancock* fighter squadrons. Aerial photographs revealed that sixteen buildings had been destroyed and six others damaged. Unsatisfied with the result, CINCPACFLT characterized Flaming Dart I as "at best a qualified and inadequate reprisal."[2]

The South Vietnamese aircraft carried out their attack on Chap Le on 8 February, but authorization for an additional strike on Vit Thu Lu was denied by the State and Defense Departments, in order to avoid the appearance of a systematic air campaign. The President also publicly proclaimed that the United States wanted no wider war. With the desired political message apparently sent to Hanoi, Task Force 77 prepared for a return to normal operations. *Hancock* departed Yankee Station for upkeep at Subic Bay on 10 February 1965.

---

[2]CINCPACFLT, "The United States Navy in the Pacific, 1965," ser 1/00847 of 18 Jul 1967, p. 21.

The Communist response to Flaming Dart I came that same day when Viet Cong saboteurs detonated an explosive device at the American billet in Qui Nhon that killed or wounded forty-four Americans. As was true after the Pleiku attack, U.S. policymakers called for retaliatory strikes and President Johnson authorized air attacks on pre-selected targets in the North. In this operation, known as Flaming Dart II, the South Vietnamese and U.S. air forces were assigned Vu Con barracks as their primary target with Chap Le as an alternate. The Navy's primary objective was the barracks at Chanh Hoa. In the event of foul weather, Dong Hoi would be attacked instead.

Hancock immediately returned to Yankee Station and by 0430 on 11 February, all three Task Force 77 carriers were prepared to launch their strikes. Difficulties in coordinating the South Vietnamese participation resulted in what CINCPACFLT described as an "irritating delay" in the operation.[3] But, at 1232 the slower, propeller-driven Skyraiders from *Ranger* took off for the North Vietnamese coast as the first increment of the three-carrier, ninety-nine plane strike. Weather conditions were only marginally better over Chanh Hoa than they had been on the 7th at nearby Dong Hoi. As a result, the attacking formations had to make their approach under the cloud cover at lower than the optimum level for target acquisition and bomb release. By 1400 lead elements arrived over the target, which consisted of seventy-six barracks and support buildings spread over a one-square-mile area. Led by attack squadrons from *Ranger*, the strike force unloaded 250-pound and 1,000-pound bombs and fired over 850 rockets at military structures in the enemy's cantonment at Chanh Hoa. At the same time, F-8E Crusaders and F-4B Phantoms attacked antiaircraft positions with their Zuni rockets and 20-millimeter guns. A total of 6 Crusaders, 2 Phantoms, and 25 Skyraiders provided air cover and reconnaissance escort. Coordinating the whole operation from aloft was Commander Warren H. Sells, who commanded *Hancock*'s Carrier Air Wing 21. Later assessments revealed that the Navy destroyed or damaged twenty-three of the seventy-six buildings in the camp.

The cost of this mission was high, especially for *Coral Sea*. One A-4C, damaged by enemy flak, diverted to Danang airfield, where the aircraft's unexpended ordnance exploded during landing. The pilot escaped uninjured but his plane was destroyed. A second Skyhawk lost power over

---

[3] *Ibid.*, p. 20.

An armed A-1 Skyraider launches from Ranger (CVA-61) for a bombing mission in Southeast Asia during the spring of 1965.

the Gulf of Tonkin, forcing the aviator, Lieutenant William T. Majors of VA 153, to eject. He was successfully recovered by an Air Force HU-16 amphibian aircraft from the SAR group. A third aircraft, this time a Crusader on flak suppression, was hit by North Vietnamese antiaircraft fire. Losing control of his aircraft, Lieutenant Commander Robert H. Shumaker of VF 154 bailed out over enemy territory and soon joined Lieutenant Alvarez in captivity.

Following this mission, American leaders evaluated the overall conduct of the Flaming Dart reprisal strikes. General Westmoreland complained that the command arrangement for Flaming Dart II, with CINCPAC exercising operational control through CINCPACAF of U.S Air Force units in South Vietnam, while COMUSMACV controlled only South Vietnamese Air Force units, resulted in confusion at the Saigon command post. Admiral Sharp responded that the information available to him was passed on to the Air Force command expeditiously and that his directives were clear. The admiral further observed that "the Navy's carrier forces, operating under similar instructions and orders, were not confused and had carried out their preparations and strikes smoothly and with a minimum of fuss in accordance with the basic operations order."[4] In the end, the command arrangement for the bombing campaign remained basically unchanged.

Assessing the actual attacks, Secretary of Defense McNamara, on 17 February, stated that "although the four missions left...operations at the targets relatively unimpaired, I am quite satisfied with the results" because "our primary objective, of course, was to communicate our political resolve [which] I believe we did." The secretary, however, also noted that 267 sorties resulted in the damage or destruction of only 69 buildings out of a total of 491. He added:

> Future communications of resolve...will carry a hollow ring unless we accomplish more military damage than we have to date. Can we not better meet our military objectives by choosing different types of targets, directing different weights of effort against them, or changing the composition of the force? Surely we cannot continue for months accomplishing no more with 267 sorties than we did on these four missions.[5]

---

[4]Msg, CP 130356Z Feb 1965. Thompson, in *Rolling Thunder*, pp. 73-77, discusses the effect of command arrangements on the Rolling Thunder program.

[5]Memo, SECDEF to Chairman JCS, of 17 Feb 1965.

The Chief of Naval Operations defended the results of the Flaming Dart strikes by calling attention to the fact that under optimum operational conditions planners only expected to achieve a 30 percent damage rate using 1,700 bombs. With the relatively moderate weather on 11 February, the naval aviators actually accomplished that requirement with a limited number of aircraft and only 483 bombs. The converse was true on 7 February at Dong Hoi when poor flying conditions precluded a significant attack. The CNO concluded that improved results under those conditions would not come until all-weather attack aircraft, such as the A-6A Intruder, entered combat.

Naval leaders also recommended, once again, that operational commanders be given flexibility to select weapons, aircraft, and the timing of strikes based on their knowledge of the target, enemy defenses, and environmental conditions. Addressing the cause behind the loss of seven naval aircraft from June 1964 to the end of February 1965, the Pacific Fleet commander stated that air operations in Southeast Asia "have been oriented directly toward the accomplishment of political objectives [while] operational considerations have been secondary." Admiral Moorer detailed the tactical difficulties in these words:

> Three of the aircraft were lost in attacks on targets under very poor weather conditions which forced the employment of low altitude delivery tactics. With greater tactical freedom, these strikes might have been postponed or alternate targets struck. Adequate target flexibility was not available. In the case of Flaming Dart II, the weather alternate was separated from the primary target by less than five miles.[6]

The naval leader observed that these relatively high losses would not occur in a sustained air campaign in which the operational commander made the basic tactical decisions. A subsequent evaluation by the Defense Department of the effectiveness of the National Military Command System during the Vietnam War echoed the admiral's views when it concluded that "Washington certainly was too deeply involved in the details of actually running the war, particularly the air war in the north."[7]

---

[6] Msg, CPFLT 031912Z Mar 1965. See also Rivero, Interview, p. 452.

[7] DOD, *Report to the Secretary of Defense on the National Military Command Structure* (Washington: GPO, 1978), p. 25. A similar discussion of the Defense Department's role in the air war is found in Palmer, *The McNamara Strategy*, pp. 121-22. See also memos, Executive Assistant to the CNO to Special Assistant to the Chairman JCS, of 8 Feb 1965; Admin Aide to VCNO, ser 0047P09 of 8 Feb;

Rolling Thunder Gets Underway

Following the dramatic Communist attacks on American facilities and personnel in South Vietnam, many U.S. leaders called again for a sustained air offensive against North Vietnam. On 7 February, presidential advisor McGeorge Bundy, in Saigon on an informational visit, advocated the implementation of Phase II of the program developed in December. He made this proposal despite his recognition that South Vietnamese cohesion remained uncertain and the possibility that the campaign might bring on conflict with China. Ambassador Taylor, Admiral Sharp, and the JCS soon endorsed his recommendation for a series of air attacks against North Vietnam by U.S. and South Vietnamese forces.

The Joint Chiefs quickly drew up a suitable campaign program, having used the previous months to compile target lists, force deployment schedules, and logistic requirements. The JCS plan for an eight-week campaign was based on the ninety-four-target list drawn up in the fall of 1964, which specified fixed targets south of the 19th parallel and armed reconnaissance of Route 7, a vital infiltration roadway. The JCS also called for shore bombardment by naval warships, a resumption of Desoto Patrols, and ground actions in Laos, but none of these latter operations was approved. The Joint Chiefs, influenced by General Johnson's growing concern over Chinese intentions, were less confident than before that the Asian Communist power would not intervene. Indeed, they now deemed it probable that Chinese "volunteers" would enter North Vietnam, much as they had in Korea in 1950. And the Joint Chiefs felt that the Soviets would provide North Vietnam with antiaircraft weapons and radars, possibly including SA-2 surface-to-air missiles. The JCS, however, believed the enemy threat manageable. The military heads advised the

---

ser 00087P09 of 19 Feb; Executive Assistant to the CNO to OP-03, ser 00052-65 of 26 Feb; Acting DCNO (Air) to CNO, ser 00204P05 of 3 Mar; OP-342 to OP-34, ser 00105-65 of 28 Apr; reports, CO VA 153, ser 010/65 of 15 Feb 1965; CO *Ranger*, ser 349 of 18 Feb; CARDIV3 (TF77), ser 0014 of 29 Mar; CO *Reclaimer*, ser 016 of 2 May; CO *Hancock*, ser 0144 of 28 May; CO *Coral Sea*, ser 0306 of 1 Nov; msgs, CPFLT, COM7FLT, CTF79 28 Oct 1964-3 Mar 1965; CTF77/COMCARDIV3, OPORD 302-65; CNO, "Vietnam Chronicle, Flaming Dart;" CINCPACFLT, "Naval Operations against North Vietnam, August 1964-May 1968," p. 5; CINCPAC, Command History, 1965, Vol. II, pp. 317-24; JCS, *History*, pt. II, pp. 17-12—17-25; Miller, Interview, pp. 359-63; Sharp, Interview, Vol. I, pp. 257, 263-64; *U.S.-V.N. Relations*, bk. 4, pt. IVC.3, pp. 23-30; Westmoreland, *A Soldier Reports*, pp. 115-16; Gallucci, *Neither Peace Nor Honor*, pp. 45-46; Johnson, *Vantage Point*, pp. 122-26; Futrell and Blumenson, *The Advisory Years to 1965*, pp. 265-66.

Command Arrangements for the ROLLING THUNDER Bombing Campaign

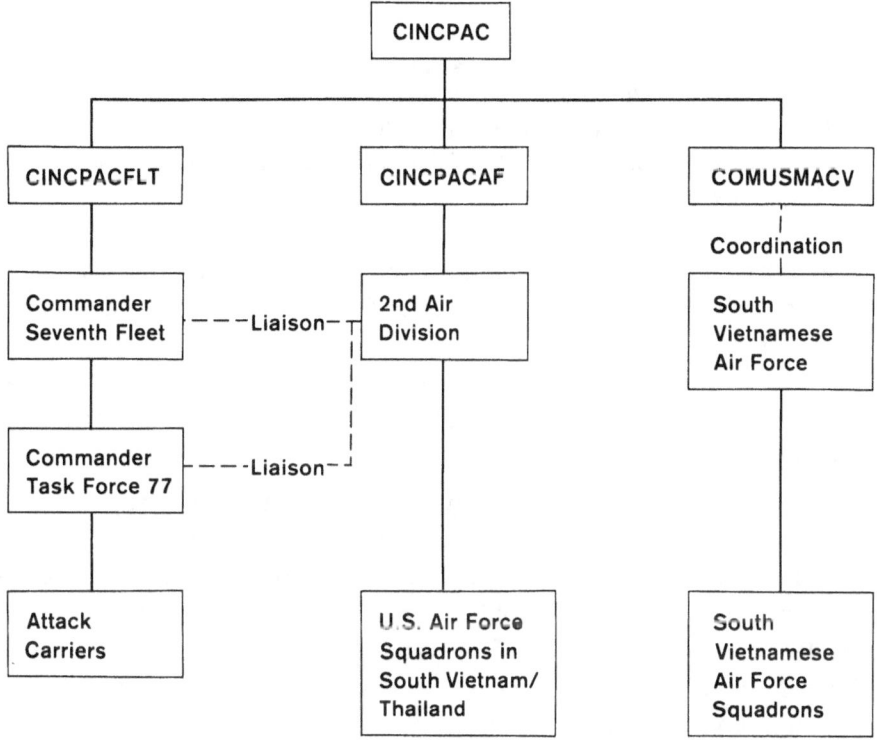

Secretary of Defense that the strikes should not be tied directly to specific Communist acts in South Vietnam. They wanted to avoid any semblance of "tit-for-tat," but instead desired a coordinated campaign against the enemy's lines of communication — a distinctly military objective.

Admiral Sharp now agreed that Ho Chi Minh, who "has never doubted ultimate victory," would not be deterred by selective attacks on targets in the North. The admiral stated that the new U.S. objective should aim to assure that the "spectre of his eventual defeat *in SVN* [italics added] would be the message we should convey, and would be the one most likely to bring him to the conference table on our terms."[8] To achieve this

---

[8] Msg, CP 271945Z Feb 1965. Thompson in *Rolling Thunder*, p. 29, discusses the continual search for a break in the enemy's resolve. See also Cooper, *Lost Crusade*, pp. 258-61; memo, Bundy to

aim, CINCPAC proposed the use of U.S. air power in Laos, South Vietnam, and North Vietnam south of the 19th parallel to interdict the Viet Cong supply line with attacks on depots, military barracks, headquarters, and transportation resources and routes. Admiral Sharp concluded:

> We should make use of our abundant air power to increase the destruction of VC supplies and manpower at the far end of the line,...making it more and more difficult to get men and materials into the pipeline in southern DRV. The combination of the two should slowly strangle the VC.[9]

Nonetheless, the President and his chief civilian advisors planned to launch a more limited air campaign against two or three selected targets in North Vietnam. In consideration of JCS advice, the start of the program was not to be keyed to a Viet Cong provocation. On 13 February 1965, the President gave final approval to the campaign, identified as Rolling Thunder.

The first operation, Rolling Thunder 1, was a strike planned for 20 February by U.S. aircraft against the Quang Khe naval base and by South Vietnamese units against the Vu Con barracks. However, the old obstacle to stronger U.S. actions, political turmoil in South Vietnam, again intruded upon the conduct of operations. On 19 February, dissidents within the South Vietnamese armed forces launched a *coup d'etat* aimed at toppling General Khanh. Although short-lived, the coup attempt forced postponement of Rolling Thunder 1.

Subsequent attempts to carry out Rolling Thunder strikes were foiled either by the domestic situation in South Vietnam or by bad weather. An additional delay resulted when the administration decided against conducting a strike, by now designated Rolling Thunder 4, on the same day that an important Communist meeting convened in Moscow. General Wheeler referred to this and other constraints by observing that there were "sizable and vexing domestic and international political problems inherent in U.S. military operations against NVN." He noted that the administration was trying to "steer a careful course which would lead to the greatest possible effect on the enemy both in and out of RVN while

---

President, of 7 Feb 1965 in Porter, *Vietnam: The Definitive Documentation on Human Decisions*, Vol. 2, pp. 349-57.
[9]Msg, CP 271945Z Feb 1965.

keeping at a minimum the chances of bringing the Chinese Communist[s] into open battle."[10]

Two weeks later, on 2 March 1965, Rolling Thunder 5, the initial mission, was conducted and a campaign that lasted for more than three years finally was underway. The U.S. Air Force and South Vietnamese aircraft which carried out this attack caused heavy damage to North Vietnamese facilities at Xom Bang and Quang Khe and also sank two gunboats at the latter location. But the increasingly effective air defenses of North Vietnam shot down one South Vietnamese and five U.S. Air Force planes. Three of the downed pilots were rescued by search and rescue forces that included naval aircraft, destroyers, and a submarine. Starting on 2 March, the Navy also began providing support for later Rolling Thunder missions by employing aerial reconnaissance planes from *Ranger* and *Coral Sea* to collect intelligence on the enemy. These flights received the designation Blue Tree.

While almost three weeks elapsed between Flaming Dart II and Rolling Thunder 5, another twelve days passed before Rolling Thunder 6 was launched. Aside from difficulties with South Vietnamese Air Force readiness and the ubiquitous heavy weather, command and control problems again became a problem. With planning, authorizing, and coordinating responsibility split between U.S. organizations in Washington, Honolulu, and Saigon, and between U.S. and South Vietnamese commands in Saigon, coordination of the Rolling Thunder program proved troublesome. Somewhat offsetting this negative factor was the speed with which operational commanders adapted to the system, partly as a result of their experience with the Yankee Team and Barrel Roll programs. Nonetheless, those U.S. officials who viewed Rolling Thunder as a means to influence the North Vietnamese through increasing military coercion were dissatisfied with the limited amount of force actually applied against the enemy.

On 15 March 1965 the U.S. Navy entered the Rolling Thunder campaign. On that day, Admiral Miller's Task Force 77 carriers *Hancock* and *Ranger* launched their squadrons for an attack on the Phu Qui ammunition depot, located halfway between Vinh and Thanh Hoa. Crossing the coastline near Hon Me, sixty-four Skyhawks and Skyraiders reached the target at 1300. Fortuitously, it was free of the cloud cover which blanketed the surrounding area. The attack aircraft were preceded

---
[10]Quoted in JCS, *History*, pt. II, p. 18-16.

by eight F-8Cs, whose pilots sought out enemy antiaircraft defenses, and followed by two RF-8A reconnaissance aircraft. Approaching through intense and sustained 37-millimeter, automatic weapons, and small arms fire, the strike aircraft dropped their 250-pound bombs and fired rockets and 20-millimeter cannons at the depot complex. And, for the first time, napalm bombs were used in the North. When the naval strike group headed out to sea, they left behind twenty-one destroyed or severely damaged buildings. One hour and forty-five minutes later, the U.S. Air Force also struck the target.

Although enemy aircraft did not contest the skies, 8 Phantoms, 10 Crusaders, and 2 Skyraiders flying combat air patrol were prepared for this contingency. Except for damage to 4 of the slower A-1Hs, all 94 planes reached the safety of the sea. Once over the water, however, Lieutenant (j.g.) Charles F. Clydesdale of *Ranger* was forced to ditch his damaged and smoking Skyraider. *Wiltsie* (DD-716), one of two plane guards, quickly dispatched a helicopter to the site of the crash. Tragically, the young pilot was unable to swim free of his sinking plane before it went down.

Rolling Thunder 6 was considered a limited success. Still, few U.S. leaders believed that a message of American resolve to prevail in Southeast Asia was being sent to the Communists. Military commanders again recommended a relaxation of operational restrictions to enable them to apply their resources with greater efficiency. For example, Admiral Moorer observed that Blue Tree reconnaissance flights during the four days prior to the attack gave advance notice to the North Vietnamese. He asked again that commanders be allowed to choose from a number of preselected targets based on their knowledge of weather conditions, enemy defenses, and other local conditions.

By mid-March 1965, many American policymakers and military commanders were convinced that the goal of deterring North Vietnam from its support of insurgency in Southeast Asia through military pressure had not been achieved. These leaders now pressed for a transformation of Rolling Thunder operations from retaliation against single targets of politically symbolic value to aerial interdiction of the enemy's logistic pipeline through Laos and southern North Vietnam. The object was to isolate enemy forces in the South from their rear base. On 15 March 1965, at a seminal meeting of the U.S. national security establishment, President Johnson endorsed this appreciation of the situation and mandated a reemphasis on the war in South Vietnam. The President recognized the diminished value of the Rolling Thunder program as a diplomatic tool. At the same time, he took steps to increase the military effectiveness of the operation. This represented a key shift in American strategic policy toward the war in Southeast Asia.

During the meeting, President Johnson relaxed some of the previous restrictions on aerial operations. It no longer was necessary that each strike be a combined U.S.-South Vietnamese venture, that only one primary target be assigned U.S. units, that the targets be confined to a limited geographic area, or that Washington approve a switch to alternate targets when the local situation demanded. Nonetheless, the President cautioned that no actions be taken that might engage the MiGs in the Hanoi area. To limit this risk, air strikes and Blue Tree reconnaissance were prohibited north of the 20th parallel. Should the aerial photographic aircraft or their fighter escorts encounter MiGs in that area, they were directed to withdraw.

The operational instructions for Rolling Thunder 7 reflected these changed procedures. The JCS assigned U.S. air and naval forces two targets and two alternates that could be struck during the day, at any time in a seven-day period from 19 to 25 March. Another new feature was authorization for armed reconnaissance along a segment of Route 1 between Vinh Son and Ha Tinh. On 19 March, shortly after Air Force units bombed the ammunition depot at Phu Van, ninety-three naval aircraft from *Coral Sea* and *Hancock* struck supply depots and barracks at Phu Van and Vinh Son. At both locations, nearly half the structures were destroyed or damaged. Thus, when Rear Admiral Henry L. Miller relinquished command of Task Force 77 to Rear Admiral Edward C. Outlaw on 17 March 1965, Rolling Thunder already was evolving into the major military campaign it became in the next three years.[11]

---

[11]OP-34, memo, ser 00175-65 of 16 Mar 1965; memo, OP-342 to OP-34, ser 00105-65 of 28 Apr; CINCPAC, Command History, 1965, Vol. II, pp. 324-28; CNO, "Vietnam Chronicle," Vol. I, 2 Feb-20 Apr 1965; COMCARDIV3, report, ser 0014 of 29 Mar 1965; CINCPACFLT, "Naval Operations against North Vietnam, August 1964-May 1968;" MACV, Command History, 1965, pp. 199-201, 206; Westmoreland, *A Soldier Reports*, pp. 116-19, 122; msgs, COMUSMACV 050834Z Nov 1964; 070445Z Mar 1965; 091449Z; CPFLT 142001Z; 170301Z; JCS 200019Z; JCS, *History*, pt. II, pp. 18-2—18-26; Sharp, *Strategy For Defeat*, pp. 63-80; *U.S.-V.N. Relations*, bk. 4, pt. IVC.3, pp. i-xviii, xxiv-xxv, 31-73; Miller, Interview, pp. 365-70; Sharp, Interview, Vol. I, pp. 268-70, 295-96; Vol. II, pp. 332-34; JCS Paper 2339/169; Momyer, *Air Power in Three Wars*, pp. 18-20; Sharp, "Strategic Direction of the Armed Forces," pp. 15-19; John B. McPherson, "Vietnam: The Perspective of a Former Vice-Director of the Joint Staff" in A.F. Hurley and R.C. Ehrhart, eds., *Air Power and Warfare:*

The Seventh Fleet's Attack Carrier Striking Force (Task Force 77) steaming at Yankee Station in the Gulf of Tonkin on 19 March 1965. The aircraft carriers shown are Coral Sea (CVA-43), Hancock (CVA-19), Ranger (CVA-61), and Midway (CVA-41).

The Transformation of Barrel Roll

While the Rolling Thunder campaign developed in North Vietnam, American air forces continued their Barrel Roll attacks against enemy infiltration routes running through Laos. After a ten-day interruption, these missions resumed on 25 January 1965, when four Skyraiders from *Ranger* overflew roads in the panhandle. Finding no enemy activity, the aircraft attacked their secondary target, a highway bridge at Tchepone, with 500 and 250-pound bombs, and dropped an entire span. For the next several weeks, Navy and Air Force Barrel Roll aircraft flew route reconnaissance missions along the roads of eastern and southern Laos and conducted strikes on secondary military targets. On 10 February, four Skyraiders from *Ranger*, on night reconnaissance over Route 23, discovered twenty-three enemy trucks proceeding in convoy and destroyed eleven of the vehicles.

Nevertheless, operational commanders were not satisfied with the overall results of the Barrel Roll program. In early February Admiral Sharp concluded that the armed surveillance was "disappointing in that only a trickle of vehicular traffic" was detected. And because many of the secondary targets "had been destroyed or damaged by [the Laotian air force] or dismantled and abandoned [by the Communists] prior to U.S. strikes," the Barrel Roll "effects achieved have been negligible compared to [the] effort expended."[12]

As was the case with Rolling Thunder, much of the problem was ascribed to the tight control of missions exercised from Washington. Admiral Sharp observed that "there was profound uncertainty at nearly all command levels regarding the authority to execute a particular mission" and that "attempting to clarify the situation took valuable time of higher ranking staff officers and imposed additional burdens on the overloaded communications circuits."[13] Admiral Miller, Commander Task Force 77, also commented that he

---

The Proceedings of the 8th Military History Symposium, United States Air Force Academy, 18-20 October 1978 (Washington: U.S. Air Force, 1979), pp. 337-40; Thompson, *Rolling Thunder*, pp. 28-82; U.S.G. Sharp, "Air Power Could Have Won in Vietnam," *Air Force* (Sep 1971), pp. 82-83; U.S.G. Sharp, "Vietnam Strategy -Then and Now," *Congressional Record* (Aug 1972); Gallucci, *Neither Peace Nor Honor*, pp. 46-56; Johnson, *Vantage Point*, pp. 127-32, 140; John Morrocco, *Thunder From Above: Air War, 1941-1968* in series *The Vietnam Experience* (Boston: Boston Publishing Co., 1984), pp. 32-57.

[12] Msg, CP 050207Z Feb 1965. See also CINCPAC, Command History, 1965, p. 399.
[13] CINCPAC, Command History, 1965, Vol. II, p. 395.

received many directives out in that area [Pacific] after we became involved [there] in making attacks, on what bombs to use, what ammunition to use, what fuses to use. There were many, many detailed instructions that confused everybody and caused a great deal of unnecessary work and unnecessary involvement.[14]

CINCPACFLT complained that the established time delay between missions allowed only several hours in the late afternoon to complete search and rescue and aerial photographic operations. Obtaining good photographic coverage was hampered further by the presence of late afternoon shadows. Coordination of target selection between Washington, Pacific military commands, and the U.S. Embassy in Vientiane posed additional problems.

In an effort to make the Barrel Roll program more effective, Admiral Sharp and General Westmoreland recommended massive air attacks on three key transportation bottlenecks, or "choke points," followed by periodic seeding of these target areas with delayed-action ordnance and armed reconnaissance of approach routes to destroy the resulting concentration of enemy vehicles. The three critical targets selected were Nape Pass and Mu Gia Pass, both astride roads into Laos from North Vietnam, and a ford on Route 23, the main road south toward the border of South Vietnam. On 15 February, the JCS approved the proposed strikes.

The Navy carried out the first choke point interdiction mission on 28 February 1965. On that day, 14 Skyhawks and 10 Skyraiders, accompanied by 2 Crusader photographic reconnaissance aircraft, were launched from *Coral Sea* to open a new phase of Barrel Roll. All 10 A-1Hs and 6 of the A-4C strike aircraft pounded Mu Gia Pass with 117 500 to 2,000-pound bombs, some set to explode six days after impact. When no antiaircraft fire was encountered, the 8 Skyhawks, primarily assigned for flak suppression, added their cluster bomb units (CBU), air-to-surface rockets, and 20-millimeter cannon fire to the strike. The attacking aircraft cratered and cut the road in many places and buried a 140-foot section with landslides.

Admiral Moorer informed Admiral McDonald that the mission, planned and executed on short notice because it was initially assigned to the Air Force, was "an outstanding operation." CINCPACFLT added that "a comparison of this short-fuzed operation to the many small claps of

---

[14]Miller, Interview, Vol. II, pp. 344, 357.

rolling thunder minus lightning over the past several days proves our point." Admiral Moorer was especially gratified that the Deputy Assistant Secretary of Defense, Alain C. Enthoven, was on board to observe the Barrel Roll strike. The admiral felt that "this operation was worth a thousand words in explaining to him our capabilities and emphasizing the fact that the carrier task forces have all the components of such operations in one package and, hence, experience little or no coordination problems."[15]

On 3 March the Air Force carried out the second choke point attack, this time on Nape Pass, rendering Route 8 impassable to logistic vehicles. On 21 March twenty-one *Hancock* aircraft again struck the approaches to Mu Gia Pass, which had replaced the ford as a target, with conventional ordnance and delayed-action bombs. Approaches to the area were heavily cratered and a landslide covered part of Route 23. Although one plane received damage from small arms fire, all of the naval aircraft on the strike returned safely to the carrier. By 23 March the Navy had carried out twenty-one of the forty-three Barrel Roll missions. The 275 sorties flown by Seventh Fleet aircraft, based in *Ranger*, *Coral Sea*, and *Hancock*, consisted of 134 strike, 28 flak suppression, 56 combat air patrol, 32 aerial photographic, and 25 escort operations. This total did not include the supporting weather reconnaissance, aerial refueling, search and rescue, and electronic intelligence flights, which also engaged the fleet's resources.

Notwithstanding the effort expended, William Sullivan, the U.S. Ambassador to Laos, expressed his "feeling that we have not...as yet conveyed steady signal because we have been jumping around too much in our [tactical military] objectives."[16] Admiral Sharp agreed with his evaluation. Characterizing Barrel Roll as "part of the integrated actions designed to impress Hanoi and Peking of the extent of U.S. resolve," CINCPAC observed that after the first month of operation the program "did not have degree of intensity that would make it distinguishable from Yankee Team."[17] He added that except for the Mu Gia Pass and Nape Pass choke point strikes and one other successful mission, there had been little improvement in the situation. As a result, Admiral Sharp called for a major air campaign against the North Vietnamese logistic complex in

---

[15] Msg, CPFLT 010109Z Mar 1965.
[16] Msg, AMEMBVT 061215Z Mar 1965.
[17] Msg, CP 050253Z Mar 1965.

Laos, a recommendation that was approved by national authorities at their White House conference on 15 March. Hence, as was the case with Rolling Thunder, Barrel Roll increasingly was seen less as a political tool to demonstrate American determination and more as a military operation aimed at the interdiction of enemy lines of communication.

In the case of Laos, however, there were two separate operational zones. One of these was in the north, around the Plain of Jars, where the struggle was essentially between the Laotian government and the Communist Pathet Lao. Combat and logistic support to the Pathet Lao flowed across North Vietnam's western border. In the south, where Laotian government forces were confined to the Mekong valley population centers, over 100 miles west of the border with South Vietnam, the fight between the contending Laotian factions was secondary to the struggle for Vietnam. Here, the corridor through southern Laos served as the main logistical pipeline of North Vietnam's military push into South Vietnam. As a consequence, in March the JCS directed that the armed reconnaissance operation in Laos be divided between the two areas. The Joint Chiefs especially wanted a concentration of effort on the Ho Chi Minh Trail in southern Laos in order to reduce the growing volume of enemy forces, munitions, and supplies entering South Vietnam. On 3 April the JCS created a new operational sector, thereafter identified as Steel Tiger, which included the Communist infiltration routes from Nape Pass south. The Barrel Roll area then comprised the infiltration routes north of Nape Pass, primarily Routes 6 and 7, which extended from North Vietnam into the Plain of Jars. Operational restrictions were relaxed in both areas, allowing commanders much greater flexibility.[18]

Seventh Fleet Operations off South Vietnam

Accompanying the transformation of the Rolling Thunder and Barrel Roll campaigns was an increased effort to halt seaborne infiltration.

---

[18]OP-33, memo, "Barrel Roll 10 Chronology," of 18 Jan 1965; CC *Constellation*, report, ser 057 of 1 Feb; COMCARDIV3 (TF77), report, ser 0014 of 29 Mar; memo, Mullenix to Director, Operations Evaluation Group, ser 00241-65 of 1 Apr; OP-33, tabulation, "Barrel Roll Mission and Date Flown, as of 1500 14 April;" msgs, CP 050253Z Mar 1965; 170410Z; 190037Z; JCS 192332Z; 200019Z; 231549Z; 231953Z; Miller, Interview, pp. 352-54; CINCPAC, Command History, 1965, Vol. II, pp. 393-401; MACV, Command History, 1965, pp. 209-10; CINCPACFLT, study, ser 301/00658 of 15 Jun 1965, pp. 7, 11.

Navy Begins Extended Combat Operations in Southeast Asia

During 1964 the North Vietnamese greatly stepped up their infiltration by sea into South Vietnam but this surge remained unsubstantiated until early 1965. Then, on the morning of 16 February, a U.S. Army helicopter pilot made a discovery that had a profound effect on this situation. Flying several hundred feet above the coast south of Qui Nhon, the officer sighted a camouflaged ship close to the shore in Vung Ro, a bay in central Vietnam. He reported his finding to the 2nd Coastal District Senior Advisor at Nha Trang, Lieutenant Commander Harvey P. Rodgers, who immediately notified Lieutenant Commander Ho Van Ky Thoai, the South Vietnamese coastal district commander. South Vietnamese Skyraiders soon were dispatched to the bay, where they capsized and sank the enemy trawler. Nonetheless, a substantial amount of the ship's cargo already was unloaded and stacked at various points on shore.

To destroy the contraband and scour the area for the enemy, the South Vietnamese command ordered a search by ground troops, salvage of the ship's cargo by Vietnamese LDNN commandos, and additional air strikes for that night. However, the local province chief temporarily disapproved use of his troops, fearing that the enemy was too strong around the bay. And the requested air force planes never arrived overhead. The next day, however, air strikes were carried out against supply caches ashore. South Vietnamese escort *Chi Lang II* and LSM *Tien Giang* (HQ-405), the latter with a paramilitary regional force company on board, also made several attempts to enter the bay, but the Viet Cong drove them back with small arms fire. Further delays on the part of the South Vietnamese resulted in inaction on the 18th.

Finally, after three days and nights, during which time the enemy was free to secure many of the supplies already ashore, the South Vietnamese landed in the bay. Early on the morning of the 19th, following a largely inaccurate napalm air strike on suspected enemy positions, submarine chaser *Tuy Dong*, *Chi Lang II*, and *Tien Giang* closed the beach, only to meet heavy machine gun and small arms fire, 500 to 800 yards offshore, that forced a withdrawal. The flotilla tried again at 1035 but withdrew after pouring 3-inch and 20-millimeter fire into the Viet Cong positions. A third attempt was successful. The troops in this operation landed at 1100 and by 1515 were able to secure the area around the ship and to evaluate the extent of the enemy's supply cache. Then, fifteen LDNN and their SEAL advisor, Lieutenant Franklin W. Anderson, retrieved supplies from the sunken wreck.

These forces found the largest concentration of Viet Cong munitions and supplies discovered to date. The 130-foot ship and a jungle area the size of three football fields contained 100 tons of Russian and Chinese-made weapons, ammunition, explosives, and medical supplies.[19] From papers retrieved by the divers, it was clear that the trawler was North Vietnamese. There also were indications that previous deliveries had been made to the bay.

The discovery of the enemy trawler in Vung Ro made a significant impression on senior officers. Vice Admiral Paul P. Blackburn, Jr., only recently assigned as Commander Seventh Fleet, observed:

> Although there have been numerous unconfirmed reports of sea infiltration in the past, none of these have been verified. The event at Vung Ro Bay, however, is considered to be positive proof that sea infiltration is occurring and raises the strong possibility that at least a portion of the unconfirmed reports of the past were, in fact, true. Sea infiltration into RVN is now proved.[20]

General Westmoreland fully shared the admiral's views, and he pressed for the reinstitution of a U.S. anti-infiltration patrol in conjunction with the South Vietnamese, who as yet were unable to mount an effective effort. Indeed, their poor showing at Vung Ro reaffirmed previous observations by U.S. naval advisors that the South Vietnamese coastal operation was inadequate.

Although the Vung Ro incident had a definite influence on the decision to undertake a combined U.S.-South Vietnamese coastal patrol, other stimuli also were at work. One of these was the new stress on isolating the southern battleground from outside sources of support. Additionally, Admiral Moorer observed that "it seems clear that our national policy

---

[19] The total included 1 million rounds of small arms ammunition, 3,500 to 4,000 rifles and submachine guns, 500 pounds of TNT, 2,000 mortar rounds, 1,500 grenades, 1,500 rounds of recoilless rifle ammunition, 1 57-millimeter recoilless rifle, and 17 machine guns of various caliber.

[20] Msg, COM7FLT 141500Z Mar 1965. This conclusion, however, still was not universally accepted. Even in March 1965, for example, the Secretary of the Navy and CNO continued to express skepticism that coastal infiltration was substantial. See CNO, "Vietnam Chronicle," Vol. I, "Sea Surveillance, Market Time," 1965.

towards SVN is shifting from one in which we attempted to maintain an 'advisory' image in SVN to one of active and overt U.S. participation." He advised Admiral McDonald that the fleet was "on the scene with the capability and if our efforts are needed we are ready to go."[21] In addition to using naval forces for coastal patrol, Admiral Moorer noted that his Pacific Fleet units could take strong action to aid the South Vietnamese with shore bombardment, aerial mining, UDT inshore activities, over-the-beach logistic support, amphibious lift for South Vietnamese troops, submarine reconnaissance, and naval air strikes against the Viet Cong. Admiral Moorer wanted to "confirm the President's reported belief that the Navy offers the most effective and uncomplicated means to bring pressure to bear in the [Southeast Asian] area." He informed Admiral McDonald, "unless you feel to the contrary, I will push in this direction."[22]

On 9 March, one day before Admiral Moorer forwarded his recommendations to Washington, General Westmoreland and Rear Admiral Roger W. Mehle, Director of the Strike Warfare Division in the Office of the Chief of Naval Operations, arrived on board *Ranger*, Commander Task Force 77's flagship, to discuss naval participation in the war with Admiral Miller. The general suggested that carrier aircraft operating from Yankee Station conduct aerial reconnaissance of suspected enemy ammunition and supply caches in Quang Ngai Province. Once the Viet Cong were found, attack aircraft could immediately be directed to strike the targets. On the following day, the Seventh Fleet received approval to use its carrier-based air units against enemy forces in South Vietnam. Reflecting the change in direction of the Southeast Asian war, air operations in the South then were given priority over those in Laos and North Vietnam. The actual commitment of Seventh Fleet aircraft, however, was delayed until the land-based air forces under COMUSMACV proved unable to handle the growing number of combat missions and until a fourth aircraft carrier was deployed to the Western Pacific at the end of the month. In April, for the first time, the fleet lent its air support to the war in the South with a strike by *Midway*, *Coral Sea*, and *Yorktown* (CVS-10) aircraft on Viet Cong positions northwest of Saigon. For the next sixteen months, similar in-country operations were launched

---

[21]Msg, CPFLT 100023Z Mar 1965.
[22]*Ibid.*

An F-4 Phantom II from aircraft carrier Midway *(CVA-41), deployed at Dixie Station, bombs Viet Cong positions in South Vietnam.*

from a new operating area southeast of Cam Ranh Bay, at 11°N 110°E, known as Dixie Station.[23]

Another purpose of the meeting on board *Ranger* was to complete planning for the U.S.-South Vietnamese coastal patrol. General Westmoreland informed the naval officers present that "he needed help from all the resources in the...area in order to beat the VC military machine and to inspire or shame the Vietnamese, particularly the [navy], into doing a better job, since they were about the worst of the three services in VN."[24]

---

[23]CINCPACFLT, "Naval Operations against North Vietnam, August 1964-May 1968," p. 7; CINCPAC, Command History, 1965, Vol. II, pp. 325, 414, 420-21; msg, CPFLT 100023Z Mar 1965.

[24]Msg, CPFLT 100023Z Mar 1965.

By this time, representatives of the Naval Advisory Group, the Seventh Fleet, and the Vietnamese Navy had developed an overall concept of operations for the coastal patrol, including command relationships, rules of engagement, division of operational areas and responsibilities, and a myriad of other details. Initially, the U.S. Navy planned to implement its new coastal surveillance role in stages. However, General Johnson, the Army Chief of Staff, who was undertaking an important fact-finding mission to Saigon for the President, voiced criticism of this incremental approach. As a result, the Navy elected on 11 March to begin a full program immediately.

As finally established, the Seventh Fleet conducted the coastal patrol with 3 or 4 destroyers, 6 minesweepers, 3 to 5 shore-based SP-2H Neptune reconnaissance aircraft, and 3 carrier-based A-1Hs. Carrier photographic reconnaissance planes also overflew coastal areas. In conjunction with 16 South Vietnamese coastal patrol craft and 100 junks, the U.S. units established a barrier at the 17th parallel and eight patrol areas along the entire coast. The area covered extended forty miles out to sea. The SP-2s carried out a daily patrol from Tan Son Nhut Airfield on the outskirts of Saigon. The A-1Hs scanned the coast between Cape Ke Ga and the DMZ. Both groups of naval aircraft gave special attention to ten likely enemy landing spots.

U.S. patrol ships and aircraft used visual search, their radar, and other electronic equipment to detect and track suspicious contacts of trawler size and vector South Vietnamese ships to them. But, only South Vietnamese personnel were authorized to board, search, or seize suspected infiltrating vessels, and then only within the three-mile territorial limit (later changed to twelve miles). To enhance coordination and radio communication, Vietnamese naval personnel accompanied U.S. ships and land-based aircraft. At the same time, U.S. naval advisors sailed with South Vietnamese units.

U.S. naval units, both surface and air, were organized as the Seventh Fleet's Vietnam Patrol Force. To coordinate that force with COMUS-MACV's efforts, U.S. naval officers responsible for tactical control in an operating area established liaison with the Saigon headquarters and the Vietnamese Navy through the Naval Advisory Group and five Coastal Surveillance Centers at Danang, Qui Nhon, Nha Trang, Vung Tau, and An Thoi. This command relationship was influenced by guidance from the Vice Chief of Naval Operations, Admiral Horacio Rivero, who advised

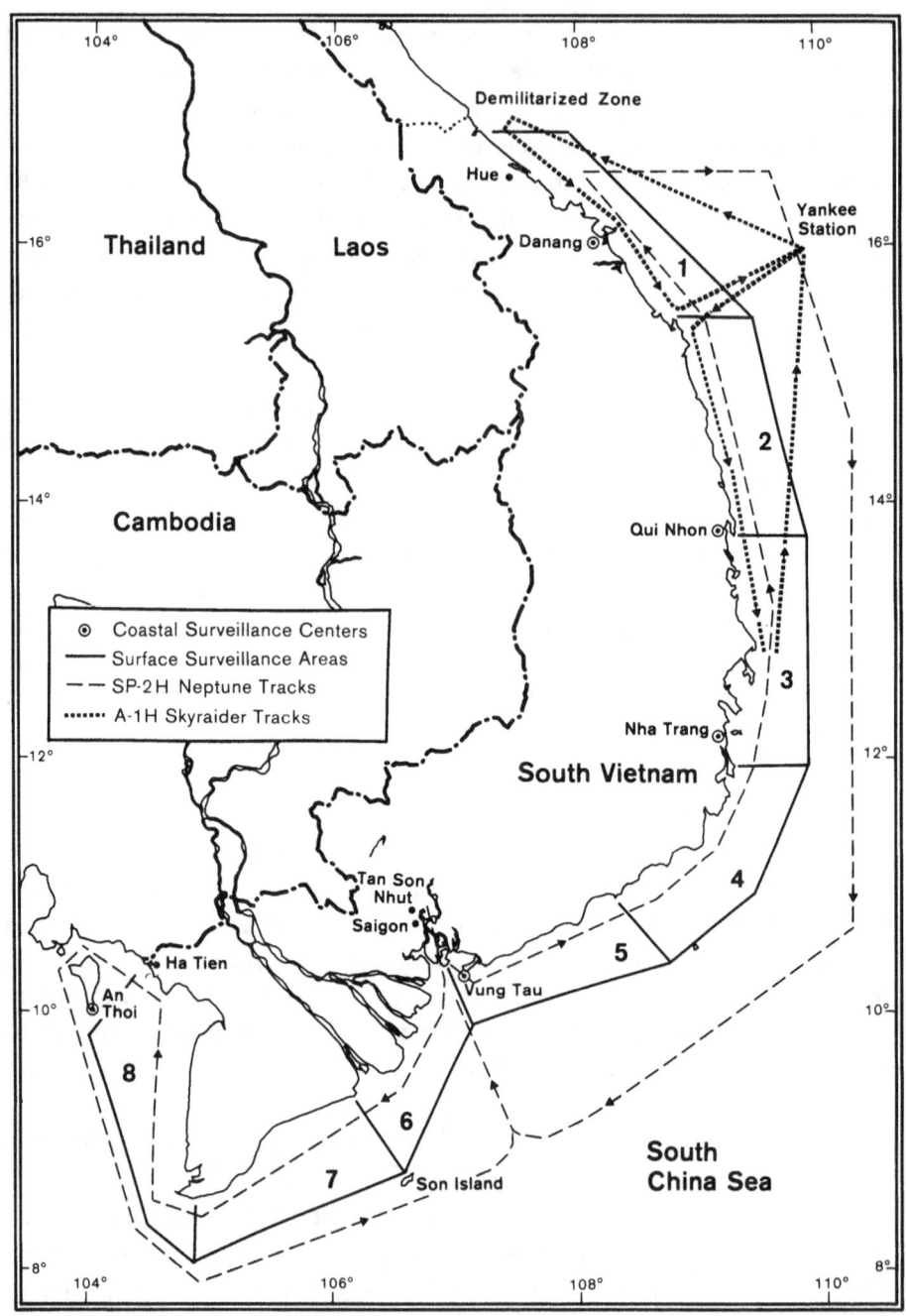

Market Time Patrol Areas

that "any preparatory actions for additional Navy participation in South Vietnam action be taken with the objective of having this Naval activity remain under control of CINCPACFLT rather than having it transferred to some other command, such as COMUSMACV."[25]

On 11 March 1965 Commander Seventh Fleet inaugurated the U.S.-South Vietnamese coastal patrol operation, soon designated Market Time, when he directed Admiral Miller to dispatch two of his destroyers to the coastal surveillance zone. *Higbee* (DD-806) and *Black* (DD-666) proceeded to the South Vietnamese coast between Hue and Nha Trang to monitor maritime traffic. SP-2Hs from Patrol Squadron 2, based at Tan Son Nhut, also began their daily flights over the coast. On the 15th, President Johnson gave formal approval to the U.S.-South Vietnamese anti-infiltration operation in the waters off South Vietnam. That same day, Admiral Blackburn activated the Vietnam Patrol Force (Task Force 71). By the end of March, ten Seventh Fleet ships patrolled the coastal waters in conjunction with five SP-2Hs and five A-1Hs.[26]

During this period, the combined U.S.-Vietnamese coastal surveillance force experienced both the satisfactions and frustrations that characterized Market Time operations in succeeding years. Early in March, units of South Vietnamese Coastal Division 11 intercepted a thirty-two-foot junk unloading cargo just south of the DMZ. The surprised crew quickly scuttled their vessel. After interrogating the captured crewmen and salvaging the junk's cargo, the South Vietnamese determined that this boat was part of North Vietnam's infiltration effort. Contraband recovered included Chinese rifles, ammunition, explosives, grenades, and other supplies. On the 18th, *Higbee* sighted another suspicious trawler. This contact was reported to the Naval Advisory Group, which immediately passed the communication to Vietnamese naval headquarters. Within ten minutes the captain of *Higbee* learned that the ship was cleared of suspicion by the South Vietnamese. The following day an RA-3B from *Hancock*, on an aerial photographic mission, spotted a coastal freighter near Cape Ke Ga, but the South Vietnamese refused to investigate since their patrol craft already had passed through the area and seen nothing. Nearby, on the 20th, other U.S. aircraft were fired on from two junks near Trau Island. South Vietnamese Skyraiders attacked the vessels as *Buck* (DD-761) and

---

[25]OP-09A, memo, ser 000120P09 of 9 Mar 1965.
[26]*Higbee*, *Buck* (DD-761), *Pluck* (MSO-464), *Pivot* (MSO-463), *Radford* (DD-446), *Nicholas* (DDE-449), *Phoebe* (MSC-199), *Peacock* (MSC-198), *Widgeon* (MSC-208), and *Vireo* (MSC-205).

An SP-2 Neptune patrol plane of Operation Market Time visually inspects a junk in the South Vietnamese coastal waters off Vung Tau.

two South Vietnamese units converged on the scene. When friendly forces reached one of the heavily damaged junks, they found that twenty-one of the thirty-four persons on board were dead as a result of the attack. Three of them were South Vietnamese troops, indicating the difficulty of differentiating between friends and enemies. On the 28th, Coastal Division 33 approached a large, black, steel-hulled ship in the Dai River and the suspicious vessel immediately departed the area at high speed. Although *Radford*, *Nicholas* (DDE-449), and several other Market Time ships searched for the unidentified vessel, it was not located.

From this modest beginning, the U.S.-South Vietnamese Market Time program burgeoned in succeeding years, becoming a highly sophisticated anti-infiltration operation. The U.S. surface force eventually comprised destroyers, destroyer escorts, minesweepers, Swift boats, patrol gunboats, LSTs, and Coast Guard ships. SP-2s, P-5B Marlin seaplanes, and P-3A Orions flying from South Vietnam and the Philippines provided air surveillance. Coordination and tactical control was enhanced by a refined system of radar and communications-equipped coastal surveillance centers located at key sites along the South Vietnamese littoral. In addition, beginning in April, the coastal patrol received support from the PTFs of the 34A maritime force, based in Danang, which now were reoriented toward a greater emphasis on anti-infiltration and intelligence actions above and below the 17th parallel.[27]

The Seventh Fleet Lands the Marines at Danang

Even as the Market Time patrol took shape, steps were taken by the Navy and Marines to establish a major presence ashore of combat forces.

---

[27]Erdheim, *Market Time*, pp. 4-6, 8-9; CINCPACFLT, "The United States Navy in the Pacific, 1965," pp. 26-30; COM7FLT, Command History, 1965, pp. 1-2; CINCPACFLT, Annual Report, FY1965, p. 19; CINCPAC, Command History, 1965, Vol. II, pp. 435-37; JCS, *History*, pt. II, pp. 17-15, 24-16—24-35; R.L. Schreadley, "The Naval War in Vietnam, 1950-1970," USNIP, Vol. 97 (May 1971), pp. 186-91; COM7FLT, Weekly Summaries, 181722Z Mar 1965; 250124Z; 311240Z; Flag Plot, "Summary of Briefing Items," Mar 1965; OP-09A, memo, ser 000120P09 of 9 Mar; OP-34, memo, ser 00175-65 of 16 Mar; MACV, Command History, 1965, pp. 12-14, 54-55, 88, 149, 172-73; CNO, "Vietnam Chronicle," Vol. I, "Sea Surveillance, Market Time," 1965; Department of State, "Aggression From the North," pp. 15-19; Sharp, *Strategy For Defeat*, p. 140; msgs, COM7FLT, COMUSMACV, CPFLT 22 Feb-31 Mar 1965; Assistant Chief of Staff for Intelligence, Department of the Army, "The Role of Cambodia in the NVN-VC War Effort, 1964-1970," Overview, pp. 39, 50; Krisel, "Special Maritime Operations in Vietnam," pp. 133-50; Ho Van Ky Thoai, Interview, pp. 23-31.

Behind this decision in March 1965 was a complex series of policy discussions. As early as August 1964, military commanders considered the deployment of ground troops to defend American installations in South Vietnam. That action was not taken, however, due in part to the assurances of CINCPAC and CINCPACFLT that the Marine Special Landing Force and airborne forces on Okinawa could rush to the defense of Danang, Bien Hoa, and Tan Son Nhut airfields should the need arise.

After the Bien Hoa attack in November 1964, the issue reappeared. At that time the JCS gave consideration to landing units of the Special Landing Force at Danang and another force near Saigon. Admiral Sharp cautioned, however, that while U.S. troops "would enhance security [at South Vietnamese airfields] they will not solve the problem" of the worsening internal military situation.[28] In the fall of 1964, Admiral Sharp and Admiral Moorer concurred in the need for enhanced defensive measures, but they were less concerned with the actions of local guerrillas than by the North Vietnamese and Chinese threat. Intent as they were on prosecuting the war against North Vietnam, these naval leaders were especially anxious to protect Danang, long considered in contingency plans as a strategic site and the base from which many actions against the North Vietnamese were launched. From that port and airfield complex, U.S. Air Force and Marine aircraft provided the Yankee Team and Barrel Roll operations in Laos with fighter, SAR, and other support and from there the South Vietnamese-manned 34A maritime force set out on their missions to the North. Although a company-size Marine security detachment reached the area in December 1964 and were joined there by the Marine Hawk missile battalion two months later, by early 1965 Danang remained a visible and vulnerable symbol of the U.S. commitment to defend South Vietnam.

While the two admirals realized the strategic importance of the base and sought to ensure its defense, they were reluctant to introduce large American ground forces into South Vietnam. For example, in October 1964, when the JCS proposed the use of the SLF to counter a suspected but never attempted Viet Cong offensive against Quang Ngai city, seventy-five miles southeast of Danang, Admiral Moorer cautioned that "prior to any landing of U.S. Marines, every effort should be made to

---

[28]Msg, CP 020400Z Nov 1964. See also Shulimson and Johnson, *U.S. Marines in Vietnam*, p. xii; Sharp, Interview, Vol. I, pp. 234, 235, 242; msgs, CP 170530Z Aug 1964; COMUSMACV 150123Z; 021114Z Nov.

undertake this operation with RVN resources." The Pacific Fleet commander elaborated on the significance of the contemplated action and also noted an operational problem that hindered future U.S. ground combat actions:

> If landing of U.S. ground troops is ordered, it should be borne in mind that this will be the first such landing by U.S. forces in Southeast Asia in a potentially imminent combat situation. Prior to any such landing, determination should be made as to length of time U.S. forces will be maintained ashore and also the method of withdrawal. In the event Viet Cong attack on Quang Ngai becomes evident counteraction must be initiated immediately. Removal of the Viet Cong once they are in Quang Ngai City will entail extensive destruction of life and property of friendly Vietnamese.[29]

Several developments at the end of the year prompted renewed discussion of the possible role of U.S. ground forces in South Vietnam. The sabotage of the Brink Hotel on Christmas Eve reemphasized the point made by the Bien Hoa attack that U.S. personnel and facilities were vulnerable to Communist military action. Three days later Viet Cong forces, for the first time formed into a divisional-size unit, stood and fought a pitched battle with South Vietnamese regular units at Binh Gia near Saigon. Before they withdrew after four days of combat, the enemy virtually destroyed two government battalions. U.S. leaders feared that the battle of Binh Gia heralded a transition by the Communists from guerrilla warfare to more conventional operations. Finally, U.S. intelligence began to ascertain that North Vietnamese regular units of regimental size were infiltrating into the South. The threat of major North Vietnamese participation in the southern conflict and the disintegration of the South Vietnamese defensive effort convinced many U.S. strategists during the next several months that American ground units were required to redress the growing imbalance of forces.

Soon after the Brink Hotel disaster, President Johnson intimated to top officials in Saigon that bombing the North, and by implication other military pressures, would not reverse the situation. Instead, he suggested the use of U.S. troops to strengthen the resolve of the South Vietnamese armed forces. But alternatives to the unilateral commitment of U.S. forces still were sought. In line with the President's "more flags" program, the

---

[29] Msg, CPFLT 070647Z Oct 1964.

JCS studied the deployment of an international force to South Vietnam as a deterrent and symbol of "Free World" solidarity. Asked for his views, CINCPACFLT concluded that the concept "falls short of the political, military and logistic realities of the current situation" in Southeast Asia. Admiral Moorer observed that "in the case of SEATO, most military planners firmly believe that the U.S. would have to take unilateral action before any agreement would be reached in the SEATO organization."[30] The Pacific Fleet commander also felt that landing a multi-national contingent near the DMZ was unwise from a tactical point of view and that his amphibious lift and logistic support resources would be strained to the utmost to deploy and maintain the force. Because of these and other objections, the proposed creation of an international force was deferred, although the armed forces of a number of U.S. allies subsequently participated in the conflict.

The Viet Cong attack on Pleiku on 7 February 1965 proved to be the catalyst for the dispatch of ground units to Danang. The U.S. response to that event and to the Qui Nhon incident soon afterward focused on air actions against North Vietnam. But President Johnson and other U.S. leaders were concerned that the strong measures planned might in turn trigger a violent Communist reaction. To deter enemy attacks, or failing that, to defend against them, the JCS on 11 and 20 February recommended the deployment to Danang of a Marine expeditionary brigade (MEB) consisting of approximately 5,000 officers and men to serve under the operational control of MACV. CINCPAC agreed that this step was essential for the protection of the base.

On 17 February CINCPACFLT informed Admiral Sharp that two Marine BLTs currently afloat off South Vietnam could be landed in six and forty-four hours respectively. By marshaling available ships, including the vessels that had just been used to transport the Hawk missile battalion and two BLTs, an entire MEB could complete the deployment to Danang by D-Day plus fifteen. At the same time, the small security detachment in Danang could be reinforced to BLT strength in nine hours by airlift from Okinawa. Supporting air elements would consist of the Shufly helicopter squadron, already at the airfield, and the helicopter squadron afloat. Additionally, headquarters of the Marine aircraft group, an F-4 squadron, and several smaller detachments could deploy to the airfield. An A-4

---

[30]Msg, CPFLT 242318Z Dec 1964.

squadron would fly to the site once facilities were adequate. To provide further backup for the MEB, Admiral Moorer cancelled participation of the Hawaii-based 1st Marine Brigade in Exercise Silver Lance and ordered the embarkation at Pearl Harbor of lead elements. He anticipated moving the unit forward to Okinawa.

The following day CINCPAC observed that the enemy was fully capable of sabotaging the airfield, hitting it with mortar or recoilless rifle fire, and launching a battalion-size assault. Admiral Sharp reiterated the need for Marine ground forces to provide a deterrent to such attacks. He stated that "in view of the vulnerability of Danang, consider it important that we act rather than react" and that with the deployment of a full MEB "believe the likelihood of VC/DRV attack of the Danang complex would be greatly reduced."[31] The JCS concurred in the need for the full MEB at Danang and its replacement on Okinawa by the 1st Marine Brigade.

Troubled that the United States was charting an unknown course with the proposed Marine deployment, Ambassador Taylor in Saigon at first objected to the move. However, agreeing with General Westmoreland that Danang needed some additional protection, he recommended that one BLT be landed for base defense, rather than the entire MEB. COMUSMACV accommodated the ambassador's reservations by limiting his immediate request to two battalions for Danang, although the general preferred a larger force. Additional units would be deployed at a later date. He did not ask for tactical air units.

On 24 February, CINCPAC reiterated his earlier recommendations that the whole MEB and its supporting air units, with the exception of the A-4 squadron which could follow later, be deployed as "an act of prudence which we should take before and not after another tragedy occurs."[32] At the same time, Admiral Sharp concurred with COMUS-MACV's proposal that the brigade's components be landed incrementally. He also repeated the recommendation that the 1st Marine Brigade in Hawaii be transported by amphibious ships to the Western Pacific and the Special Landing Force be reconstituted in the South China Sea for quick reaction contingencies. The JCS endorsed CINCPAC's course of action and reinstated earlier plans to deploy an A-4 squadron.

---

[31] Msg, CP 180210Z Feb 1965. See also msg, CPFLT 172201Z Feb 1965.
[32] Msg, CP 240315Z Feb 1965.

Two days later, on 26 February, President Johnson authorized the landing, again revising the composition of the force by restricting it to two BLTs and one helicopter squadron. With the exception of the 1st Marine Brigade move, the other deployments recommended were deferred for later decision. In implementing the President's order, the JCS instructed CINCPAC that the mission of the Marine forces would be to secure the airfield, port facilities, landing beaches, and U.S. installations against enemy attack. It was stressed that the "U.S. Marine Force will not repeat not engage in day to day actions against the Viet Cong."[33] Soon after Admiral Sharp passed these directives to CINCPACFLT, Admiral Moorer ordered the concentration of forces at Danang.

Seventh Fleet commanders had already taken steps to prepare for the landing. On 3 March officers of the Amphibious Force, Seventh Fleet (TF 76) met with 9th MEB and MACV representatives in Danang to discuss the tactical details of the operation. Following standard amphibious practice, Commander Task Force 76, Rear Admiral Wulzen, commanded both naval and Marine units until the landing force was established ashore, at which point the Commanding General 9th MEB, Brigadier General Frederick J. Karch, USMC, was to assume this responsibility. Also on 3 March, the task force flagship, *Mount McKinley*, sortied from Subic Bay with Rear Admiral Wulzen and the Headquarters, 9th MEB embarked. The ship shaped course for Danang to join *Henrico*, *Union*, and *Vancouver*, which carried the 3rd Battalion, 9th Marines. *Higbee* remained close by to provide antisubmarine warfare and gunfire support, while the carrier *Hancock*, escorted by *England* (DLG-22), *Gurke* (DD-783), *Leonard F. Mason* (DD-852), and *Rogers* (DD-876), provided air cover. Soon after *Mount McKinley*'s arrival off Danang on the 6th, Admiral Wulzen and General Karch coordinated their plans. The next day *Princeton*, *Bexar*, and *Thomaston*, with the Seventh Fleet's Special Landing Force on board, sailed from Subic for South Vietnamese waters. *Princeton*, with HMM 365, was ordered to make the best possible speed to Danang. Soon afterward, the 2nd Battalion, 3rd Marines was loaded on board the Amphibious Squadron 1 task group of *Lenawee*, *Washburn*, and *Gunston Hall* in the Philippine port. Several Marine BLT's of the 3rd Marines stood ready on Okinawa for airlift to South Vietnam. And Landing Ship Squadron 9, with another Marine BLT on board, remained on alert. In the meantime, all

---

[33]Msg, JCS 070001Z Mar 1965.

Seventh Fleet forces in the South China Sea maintained a high state of readiness.

The command to execute the landing at Danang was received in the Western Pacific on 7 March and H-Hour was established as 0800 Danang time on the next day. As U.S. naval forces converged on the South Vietnamese port, Vice Admiral Paul P. Blackburn, Commander Seventh Fleet, ordered the landing to proceed. At 0545 on 8 March 1965, *Mount McKinley*, *Henrico*, *Union*, and *Vancouver* entered the harbor and anchored 4,000 yards from shore. At 0600 Admiral Wulzen gave the traditional amphibious command to "land the landing force." Initially, the weather was relatively favorable. Shortly after Admiral Wulzen ordered the landing, however, the wind picked up to between 20 to 25 knots and a six to eight-foot surf was reported at Red Beach II, the designated landing area northwest of the city, forcing him to set the new landing time as 0900. By that time weather conditions had improved. Even so, only amphibious tractors (LVTP) and larger landing craft (chiefly LCMs) were used in the ship to shore movement, while the small LCVPs were not allowed to participate. At 0842 the first wave headed for shore. Between 0902 and 0918 the LVTPs and LCMs landed the 3rd Battalion, 9th Marines, the first battalion-size U.S. ground combat unit deployed to South Vietnam. Included in the forces landed at Danang were Commander Herbert S. Tilley's Naval Beach Group 1, Western Pacific Detachment, and more than 200 naval corpsmen, dentists, doctors, and chaplains. Despite the heavy seas, the operation was carried out without loss of life. Early in the afternoon, General Karch assumed operational control of the 9th MEB as a naval component commander under COMUSMACV.

With ground troops ashore, the landing craft then proceeded to ferry cargo between the ships and the landing area. This tedious and at times dangerous work continued well into the night. A total of twelve LCMs from *Henrico* and *Union*, assisted by LCUs and landing vehicles, tracked (LVT), engaged in this task. The physical exhaustion of the crews caused by the rough seas and long hours finally began to exact a toll. It took up to one hour to load LVTPs in the surging swell and beaching was equally difficult. When one LCU broached in the surf, cargo unloading activities halted for two hours. Although this craft was pulled free, four LCMs broached or became stranded on the sand. Another boat lost its bow ramp.

Utility landing craft 1476 transports Marine vehicles and equipment ashore at Danang's Red Beach II on 8 March 1965 as Naval Beach Group 1 personnel prepare to assist. Three ships of the amphibious task group can be seen anchored out in the harbor.

Once ashore, however, the supplies and equipment were moved expeditiously by the naval beach group.

As this operation took place, the U.S. Air Force airlifted elements of the 1st Battalion, 3rd Marines from Naha, Okinawa, to Danang. Although traffic congestion at the Danang airfield delayed this operation, by the end of the day one BLT was landed by air to bolster the defense of the port city. On the following day, 9 March, the air strength at Danang was augmented when *Princeton* arrived with twenty-three UH-34 helicopters of HMM 365 on board. Shortly after arrival at 0620, squadron personnel began ferrying the aircraft, sometimes under small arms fire, to the airfield. Once there, the helicopters were turned over to pilots and crews of HMM 162, who had arrived by aircraft from Okinawa that morning. At that point, *Princeton* proceeded to Okinawa to take on another complement of helicopters. On the 14th, the amphibious assault ship rejoined *Bexar* and *Thomaston* in the South China Sea and the Seventh Fleet Amphibious Ready Group was fully reconstituted.

Meanwhile, meteorological conditions at Danang did not improve. The four to five-foot plunging surf caused another four LCMs providing supplies for the troops ashore to broach and swamp. Cargo ferrying operations slowed as the available craft were used to pull the boats off the beach. Another complication at Red Beach II arose when it was learned by Admiral Wulzen that the South Vietnamese troops being used to defend the beachhead were scheduled to be withdrawn on the afternoon of 9 March. This factor, plus the weather conditions, led the admiral to shift logistic operations to the Danang Museum Ramp. Although that facility was relatively constricted, it afforded landing craft a partially protected approach up the Han River. To shorten transit time for the boats, Admiral Wulzen ordered four of his ships to shift their anchor to the eastern area of the harbor, which was accomplished by 1300. Further assistance was provided when *Thomaston* and *Bexar* entered the harbor late in the afternoon. The four LCMs and one LCU from those ships gave a welcome boost to the operation. By midnight, 9 March, all troops, vehicles, and combat loaded cargo were ashore.

During the next two days landing craft continued around-the-clock offloading of general cargo and equipment, despite the foul sea conditions. Difficulties were eased considerably when an LST ramp on Tiensha Peninsula, near the harbor entrance, began to receive supplies. By 0610 on 12 March 1965, all cargos were ashore. After backloading boats and

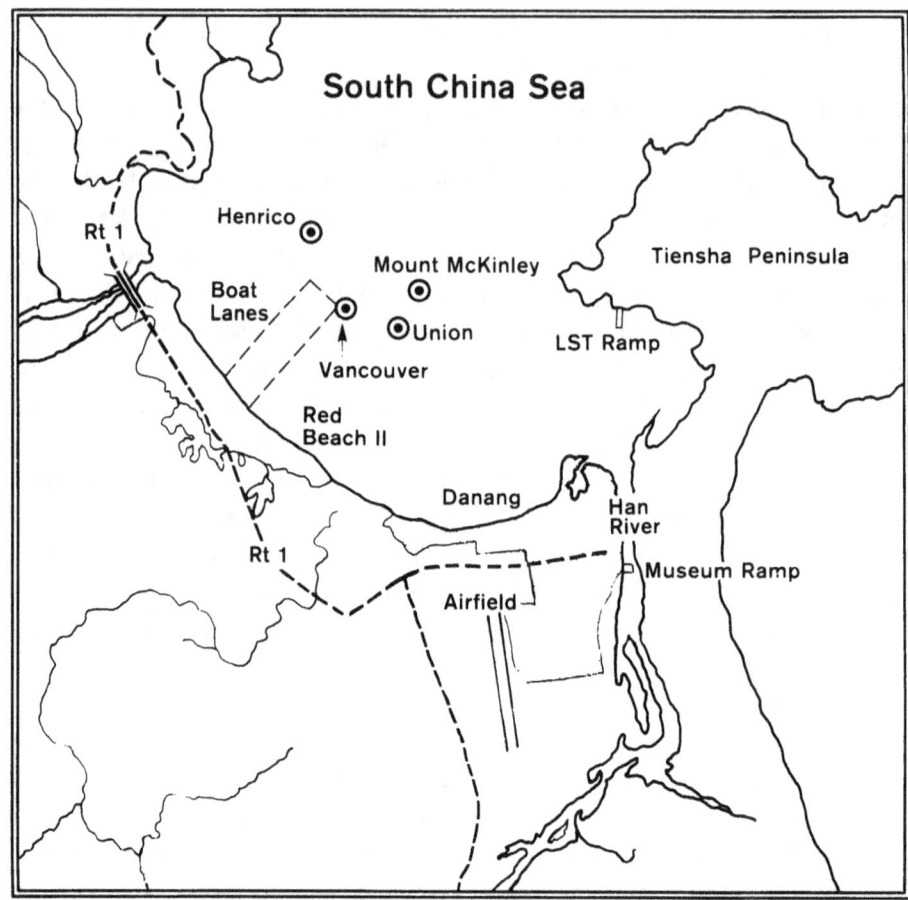

Landing the Marines at Danang, 8 March 1965

loading equipment, the assembled ships of the amphibious task force sortied from Danang harbor and stood out to sea. During the four-day operation, 1,461 troops, 222 vehicles, and 1,858 tons of ammunition and supplies were landed. Admiral Wulzen concluded that the ability of the participating naval personnel to "conduct a successful landing in spite of a heavy harbor swell, marginal surf conditions, rain and — most dangerous of all — fatigue, reflects their excellent training and skill and the judgment required by this extremely arduous and exacting assignment."[34]

---

[34] CTF76, report, "History of Amphibious Operations in South Vietnam, March 1965-December 1966," p. 8.

During the remainder of March the Marine defense force at Danang continued to swell. The remaining Marine ground elements and MAG 16 arrived in Danang on 16 March on board LST *Terrell County*. And, on the 22nd, another five LSTs delivered essential equipment and supplies to the South Vietnamese port. This supply effort was critical, since it was still unclear whether the MEB would remain in South Vietnam on an extended deployment, and MACV had not yet begun full-scale logistic support for the unit. In the following month, Admiral Moorer and Admiral Sharp endorsed the request of COMUSMACV and the Commanding General, 9th MEB for the addition of a third BLT, a regimental headquarters, and the A-4 and F-4 squadrons. Following these deployments, the 9th MEB and attached units reached a strength of 8,878 officers and men by the end of April 1965.

Even as Marine strength for Southeast Asian contingencies was increasing, national leaders considered a change in the mission for U.S. ground forces, which reflected a new turn in the course of the Vietnam conflict. Following a White House meeting on the evening of 26 February, Army Chief of Staff Johnson was dispatched to Southeast Asia to make recommendations on the future direction of U.S. strategy. During his visit to South Vietnam, from 5 to 12 March, the general conferred with Ambassador Taylor, Admiral Sharp, General Westmoreland, and other top U.S. officials. Ambassador Taylor continued to emphasize the application of military pressures against North Vietnam to resolve the southern problem. General Westmoreland, however, observed that the rapid disintegration of the South Vietnamese defensive effort and the corresponding Communist surge required a direct U.S. military commitment to the southern war. It was at this time that the general called for using U.S. air units in South Vietnam and for American counter-infiltration patrols along the coast. Westmoreland also suggested that ground forces be prepared to prevent threatened areas from falling to the enemy. General Johnson agreed that the time had come to deploy U.S. Army combat units to South Vietnam. Their proposed areas of operation, whether in the coastal and population centers or in the sparsely inhabited Central Highlands, would inevitably bring them into action against the Viet Cong.

On 15 March 1965, in his critical meeting with Secretary of Defense McNamara and the JCS, President Johnson reaffirmed his determination to preserve the existence of South Vietnam with whatever resources were required, including U.S. ground troops. The JCS and General Westmoreland favored employing an Army division in the high plateau area of Pleiku and Kontum Provinces, a center of enemy strength, as well as troop deployments to the Saigon area. Admiral Sharp and Ambassador Taylor, who previously communicated their views, however, preferred the establishment of firm lodgements along the coast before U.S. troops were deployed to the more exposed and logistically difficult border areas. On 29 March, at a meeting of the Secretary of Defense, Ambassador Taylor, and the JCS, these conflicting concepts received a hearing. The Secretary of Defense tentatively decided on the creation of defended enclaves on the coast from which combat forces might extend into the interior once a logistic base was assured and operational experience gained.

Whatever differences existed regarding zones of operation, it was significant that these government officials and military leaders now accepted the premise that U.S. troops would be engaged in direct operations against the enemy. On 1 April, after meeting with the National Security Council, the President approved the dispatch to northern South Vietnam of two additional Marine BLTs. Of greater portent, however, he authorized reorientation of the MEB mission from defense to one which the JCS understood to be counterinsurgency combat operations against Viet Cong and North Vietnamese forces. Lyndon Johnson's decision became U.S. policy with the issuance, on 6 April 1965, of National Security Action Memorandum 328. That directive laid the basis for a ground war in South Vietnam that soon overshadowed all other aspects of the Southeast Asian conflict.[35]

On 30 March 1965, shortly before these decisions were made, Admiral Moorer turned over command of the Pacific Fleet to Vice Admiral Roy L. Johnson. In his closing remarks during the ceremony on board *Bennington*, Admiral Moorer expressed the perception held by many naval officers that

---

[35]*Ibid.*; Shulimson and Johnson, *U.S. Marines in Vietnam*, pp. 3-27; COM7FLT, Command History, 1965; CINCPACFLT, "The United States Navy in the Pacific, 1965," pp. 23-25; memo, OP-06 to Director Joint Staff, JCS, ser 0005P60 of 7 Jan 1965; CINCPAC, Command History, 1965, Vol. II, pp. 277-84, 452-53; MACV, Command History, 1965, pp. 30-32, 99; msgs, CP, CPFLT, COMUSMACV, CTF76 16 Feb-20 Mar 1965; JCS, NMCC Operational Summaries, of 8-13 Mar; COM7FLT, Weekly Summaries, of 2, 10, 18, 25, and 31 Mar; JCS Papers 2339/162; 2343/493; JCS, History, pt. I, p. 13-30; pt. II, pp. 18-7, 19-1—19-17, 20-14—20-15, 21-1—21-20; Westmoreland, *A Soldier Reports*, pp. 113-14, 123-31; Sharp, *Strategy For Defeat*, pp. 69-74; *U.S.-V.N. Relations*, bk. 4, pt. IVC.4, pp. i-xvi, 1-25; IVC.5, pp. 1-17, 41-62, 66-71, 91-93, 124-26; Sharp, Interview, Vol. I, pp. 258-61, 272-73; Fox, *Air Base Defense in the Republic of Vietnam*, pp. 19-20; Cooper, *Lost Crusade*, pp. 259, 270-71; Johnson, *Vantage Point*, pp. 138-41.

momentous events were about to unfold in Southeast Asia. The departing CINCPACFLT observed that he felt "like a fire chief that leaves a roaring fire just when he gets the hoses hooked up and is ready to turn on the water."[36]

As the admiral suggested, the early months of 1965 witnessed a dramatic change in U.S. strategy toward Southeast Asia. Actions against North Vietnam swiftly progressed from the one-time Flaming Dart reprisal strikes to the systematic Rolling Thunder bombing program. But the evident failure of these and previous measures in the pressure campaign shifted the focus of the war back to South Vietnam. The Rolling Thunder, Yankee Team, and Barrel Roll programs, and the newly created Market Time operation, now emphasized the interdiction of enemy support for the Viet Cong. With the deployment of Pacific Fleet Marine forces to Danang, the United States signaled even greater commitment to the survival of South Vietnam. Although not clearly recognized at the time, this landing represented the end of the "limited partnership" that had characterized American policy in Southeast Asia. From this point on, the unilateral application of U.S. military power would be the predominant factor in an expanding war.

---

[36]Quoted in CINCPACFLT, "The United States Navy in the Pacific, 1965," p. 57.

APPENDIX I

Key U.S. Naval Leaders 1959-1965

SECRETARIES OF THE NAVY

William B. Franke	8 Jun 1959–20 Jan 1961
John B. Connally, Jr.	23 Jan 1961–20 Dec 1962
Fred H. Korth	3 Jan 1962–1 Nov 1963
Paul H. Nitze	27 Nov 1963–30 Jun 1967

CHIEFS OF NAVAL OPERATIONS

Admiral Arleigh A. Burke	17 Aug 1955–1 Aug 1961
Admiral George W. Anderson, Jr.	1 Aug 1961–1 Aug 1963
Admiral David L. McDonald	1 Aug 1963–1 Aug 1967

COMMANDERS IN CHIEF, PACIFIC

Admiral Harry D. Felt	31 Jul 1958–30 Jun 1964
Admiral Ulysses S.G. Sharp	30 Jun 1964–31 Jul 1968

COMMANDERS IN CHIEF, U.S. PACIFIC FLEET

Admiral Herbert G. Hopwood	1 Feb 1958–31 Aug 1960
Admiral John H. Sides	31 Aug 1960–30 Sep 1963
Admiral Ulysses S.G. Sharp	30 Sep 1963–26 Jun 1964
Admiral Thomas H. Moorer	26 Jun 1964–30 Mar 1965
Admiral Roy L. Johnson	30 Mar 1965–30 Nov 1967

COMMANDERS SEVENTH FLEET

Vice Admiral Frederick N. Kivette	30 Sep 1958–7 Mar 1960
Vice Admiral Charles D. Griffin	7 Mar 1960–28 Oct 1961
Vice Admiral William A. Schoech	28 Oct 1961–13 Oct 1962
Vice Admiral Thomas H. Moorer	13 Oct 1962–11 Jun 1964
Vice Admiral Roy L. Johnson	11 Jun 1964–1 Mar 1965
Vice Admiral Paul P. Blackburn, Jr.	1 Mar 1965–7 Oct 1965

CHIEFS OF THE NAVY SECTION, MILITARY ASSISTANCE ADVISORY GROUP, VIETNAM/NAVAL ADVISORY GROUP, VIETNAM

Captain John J. Flachsenhar	Jan 1958–Jul 1960
Captain Henry M. Easterling	Jul 1960–Dec 1961
Captain Joseph B. Drachnik	Dec 1961–Jan 1964
Captain William H. Hardcastle	Jan 1964–Apr 1965

APPENDIX II

Glossary of Abbreviations and Terms

ACNO	Assistant Chief of Naval Operations
AD	Destroyer Tender
ADG	Degaussing Ship
AE	Ammunition Ship
AF	Stores Ship
AFS	Combat Stores Ship
AG	Miscellaneous Ship
AGC	Amphibious Force Flagship
AGS	Surveying Ship
AID	Agency for International Development
AK	Cargo Ship
AKA	Attack Cargo Ship
AKD	Cargo Ship, Dock
AKL	Light Cargo Ship
AKS	Stores Issue Ship
AKV	Aircraft Ferry
ALUSNA	American Legation, U.S. Naval Attache
AMCONSUL	American Consul
AMEMB	American Embassy
AMEMBVT	American Embassy, Vientiane
AO	Oiler
AOE	Fast Combat Support Ship
APA	Attack Transport
APD	High-speed Transport
APSS	Transport Submarine
ARG	Internal Combustion Engine Repair Shop
ARL	Landing Craft Repair Ship
ARPA	Advanced Research Projects Agency
ARS	Salvage Ship
ARSD	Salvage Lifting Ship
ARST	Salvage Craft Tender
ARVN	Army of Vietnam

ASD	Assistant Secretary of Defense
ASW	Antisubmarine Warfare
ATF	Fleet Ocean Tug
AV	Seaplane Tender
AVS	Aviation Supply Ship
BEQ	Bachelor Enlisted Quarters
BJU	Beach Jumper Unit
BLT	Battalion Landing Team
BOQ	Bachelor Officers Quarters
BSU	Boat Support Unit
BUMED	Bureau of Medicine and Surgery
BUPERS	Bureau of Naval Personnel
BUSANDA	Bureau of Supplies and Accounts
BUSHIPS	Bureau of Ships
BUWEPS	Bureau of Naval Weapons
CA	Heavy Cruiser
CARDIV	Carrier Division
CB	Construction Battalion
CBPAC	Naval Construction Battalions, U.S. Pacific Fleet
CBU	Cluster Bomb Unit
CD	Coastal District
CDADV	Coastal District Advisor
CDTCVN	Combat Development and Test Center, Vietnam
CEC	Civil Engineer Corps
CG	Commanding General
CH	Chief
CHC	Chaplain Corps
CHICOM	Chinese Communists
CHINFO	Naval Office of Information
CHJCS	Chairman of the Joint Chiefs of Staff
CIA	Central Intelligence Agency
CIC	Combat Information Center
CICV	Combined Intelligence Center, Vietnam
CIDG	Civilian Irregular Defense Group
CINC	Commander in Chief
CINCLANTFLT	Commander in Chief, U.S. Atlantic Fleet
CINCNAVEUR	Commander in Chief, U.S. Naval Forces, Europe
CINCPAC(CP)	Commander in Chief, Pacific
CINCPACFLT(CPFLT)	Commander in Chief, U.S. Pacific Fleet
CINCUSARPAC	Commander in Chief, U.S. Army, Pacific
CJCS	Chairman of the Joint Chiefs of Staff
CL	Light Cruiser
CLG	Light Guided Missile Cruiser
CMC	Commandant of the Marine Corps

CNA	Center for Naval Analyses
CNO	Chief of Naval Operations
CO	Commanding Officer
COM	Commander
COM1FLT	Commander First Fleet
COM7FLT	Commander Seventh Fleet
COMUSMACV	Commander U.S. Military Assistance Command, Vietnam
CPADMINO	Commander in Chief, Pacific, Administrative Officer
CRUDIV	Cruiser Division
CTF	Commander Task Force
CTG	Commander Task Group
CTU	Commander Task Unit
CV	Aircraft Carrier
CVA	Attack Aircraft Carrier
CVE	Escort Aircraft Carrier
CVS	Antisubmarine Warfare Aircraft Carrier
CVW	Attack Carrier Air Wing
CY	Calendar Year
DCIA	Director Central Intelligence Agency
DCNO	Deputy Chief of Naval Operations
DD	Destroyer
DDE	Antisubmarine Destroyer
DDG	Guided Missile Destroyer
DDR	Radar Picket Destroyer
DE	Destroyer Escort
DEPCOMUSMACV	Deputy Commander U.S. Military Assistance Command, Vietnam
DEPSECDEF	Deputy Secretary of Defense
DER	Radar Picket Escort Ship
DESDIV	Destroyer Division
DESRON	Destroyer Squadron
DIA	Defense Intelligence Agency
DIRPACDOCS	Director, Bureau of Yards and Docks, Pacific Division
DL	Frigate
DLG	Guided Missile Frigate
DMZ	Demilitarized Zone
DNI	Director of Naval Intelligence
DOD	Department of Defense
DRV	Democratic Republic of Vietnam
ECM	Electronic Countermeasures
EDT	Eastern Daylight Time
E&E	Evasion and Escape

FAR	Laotian Armed Forces (derived from the French *Force Armee Royaume*)
Flag Plot	Naval Command Center, Washington
FMFPAC	Fleet Marine Force, U.S. Pacific Fleet
FPB	Fast Patrol Boat
FRAM	Fleet Rehabilitation and Modernization
FY	Fiscal Year
GPO	Government Printing Office
GVN	Government of South Vietnam
HMM	Marine Medium Helicopter Squadron
HMR	Marine Transport Helicopter Squadron
HQ	Headquarters
HQ	Vietnamese Navy (derived from the Vietnamese *Hai Quan*)
HSAS	Headquarters Support Activity, Saigon
ICC	International Control Commission
INTEL	Intelligence
ISA	International Security Affairs
JCS	Joint Chiefs of Staff
JFADV	Junk Force Advisor
JLRB	Joint Logistics Review Board
JRC	Joint Reconnaissance Center
JTF	Joint Task Force
JUSMAG	Joint U.S. Military Advisory Group
LCM	Landing Craft, Mechanized
LCPL	Landing Craft, Personnel, Large
LCU	Landing Craft, Utility
LCVP	Landing Craft, Vehicle and Personnel
LDNN	South Vietnamese Naval Commandos (derived from the Vietnamese *Lien Doc Nguoi Nhia*)
LPD	Amphibious Transport Dock
LPH	Amphibious Assault Ship
LSD	Landing Ship, Dock
LSIL	Landing Ship, Infantry, Large
LSM	Landing Ship, Medium
LSMR	Landing Ship, Medium, Rocket
LSSL	Landing Support Ship, Large
LST	Landing Ship, Tank
LVT	Landing Vehicle, Tracked
LVTP	Landing Vehicle, Tracked, Personnel
MAAG	Military Assistance Advisory Group
MAAGCAM	Military Assistance Advisory Group, Cambodia
MAAGVN	Military Assistance Advisory Group, Vietnam
MABS	Marine Air Base Squadron

Glossary of Abbreviations

MACSOG	Military Assistance Command, Vietnam Special Operations Group (Studies and Observation Group)
MACV	Military Assistance Command, Vietnam
MAG	Marine Aircraft Group
MAP	Military Assistance Program
MARDIV	Marine Division
MAROPS	Maritime Operations
MAW	Marine Aircraft Wing
MCS	Marine Countermeasures Support Ship
MEB	Marine Expeditionary Brigade
MiG	Russian-made Fighter Aircraft
MINDIV	Minesweeping Division
MLMS	Minesweeping Launch
MSC	Minesweeper, Coastal
MSF	Minesweeper, Fleet
MSO	Minesweeper, Ocean
MSTS	Military Sea Transportation Service
MSTSFE	Military Sea Transportation Service, Far East
MTT	Mobile Training Team
NA	Naval Attache
NAD	Naval Advisory Detachment
NAG	Naval Advisory Group
NAS	Naval Air Station
NAVAIRLANT	Naval Air Force, U.S. Atlantic Fleet
NAVAIRPAC	Naval Air Force, U.S. Pacific Fleet
NAVCOMSTA	Naval Communication Station
NAVFORV	Naval Forces, Vietnam
NAVPHIL	Naval Forces, Philippines
NAVSEC	Navy Section
NCFPAC	Naval Construction Forces, Pacific
NHC	Naval Historical Center
NLF	National Liberation Front
NMCB	Naval Mobile Construction Battalion
NMCC	National Military Command Center
NOSGPAC	Naval Operations Support Group, U.S. Pacific Fleet
NSAM	National Security Action Memorandum
NSC	National Security Council
NVA	North Vietnamese Army
NVN	North Vietnam
NWIP	Naval Warfare Information Publication
OIC	Officer in Charge
ONI	Office of Naval Intelligence

OP	Subordinate Office in Office of the Chief of Naval Operations
OPLAN	Operation Plan
OPNAV	Office of the Chief of Naval Operations
OPORD	Operation Order
OPSUMS	Operation Summaries
OSD	Office of the Secretary of Defense
PACAF	Pacific Air Forces (USAF)
PACFLT	U.S. Pacific Fleet
PATFOR7FLT	Patrol Force, Seventh Fleet
PC	Submarine Chaser
PCE	Escort
PCF	Fast Patrol Craft
PEO	Programs Evaluation Office
PG	Gunboat
PGM(100-foot)	Motor Gunboat
PGM(165-foot)	Motor Gunboat
PHIBFOR	Amphibious Force
PHIBFORPACFLT	Amphibious Force, U.S. Pacific Fleet
PHIBFOR7FLT	Amphibious Force, Seventh Fleet
PHIBGRU	Amphibious Group
PHIBPAC	Amphibious Force, U.S. Pacific Fleet
PHIBRON	Amphibious Squadron
PHIBTRACOM	Amphibious Training Command
POL	Petroleum, Oil, Lubricants
POW	Prisoner of War
PPBS	Planning Programming Budgeting System
PRES	President of the United States
PSYWAR	Psychological Warfare
PT	Motor Torpedo Boat
PTF	Fast Patrol Boat
PX	Post Exchange
RAG	River Assault Group
RDT&E	Research, Development, Test, and Evaluation
RLT	Regimental Landing Team
RPC	River Patrol Craft
R and R	Rest and Recuperation
RVAH	Reconnaissance Attack Squadron
RVN	Republic of Vietnam
RVNAF	Republic of Vietnam Armed Forces
SACSA	Special Assistant for Counterinsurgency and Special Activities
SAR	Search and Rescue
SC	Submarine Chaser

SC	Supply Corps
SCB	Ship Characteristics Board
SCUBA	Self-contained Underwater Breathing Apparatus
SEABEE	Naval Construction Battalion Personnel
SEAL	Naval Commando
SEASIA	Southeast Asia
SEATO	Southeast Asia Treaty Organization
SECAF	Secretary of the Air Force
SECARM	Secretary of the Army
SECDEF	Secretary of Defense
SECNAV	Secretary of the Navy
SECSTATE	Secretary of State
SELF	Short Expeditionary Landing Field
SERE	Survival, Evasion, Resistance, and Escape
SERVPAC	Service Force, U.S. Pacific Fleet
SITREPS	Situation Reports
SLF	Special Landing Force
SNIE	Special National Intelligence Estimate
SS	Steamship
SS	Submarine
SSBN	Nuclear Powered Fleet Ballistic Missile Submarine
SSG	Guided Missile Submarine
SSGN	Nuclear Powered Guided Missile Submarine
SSN	Nuclear Powered Attack Submarine
STAT	SEABEE Technical Assistance Team
STCAN	French-designed River Patrol Craft
SUBFLOT	Submarine Flotilla
SVN	South Vietnam
TERM	Temporary Equipment Recovery Mission
TF	Task Force
UDT	Underwater Demolition Team
UN	United Nations
USA	U.S. Army
USAF	U.S. Air Force
USAIRA	U.S. Air Force Attache
USARMA	U.S. Army Attache
USARMVT	U.S. Army Attache, Vientiane
USMC	U.S. Marine Corps
USN	U.S. Navy
USNIP	*U.S. Naval Institute Proceedings*
USNR	U.S. Naval Reserve
USNS	U.S. Naval Ship
USO	United Services Organization
USOM	U.S. Operations Mission

USS	United States Ship
VA	Attack Squadron
VAP	Heavy Photographic Squadron
VAW	Carrier Airborne Early Warning Squadron
VC	Viet Cong
VCNO	Vice Chief of Naval Operations
VCP	Composite Photographic Squadron
VF	Fighter Squadron
VFP	Light Photographic Squadron
VMA	Marine Attack Squadron
VMF	Marine Fighter Squadron
VNAF	Vietnamese Air Force
VNN	Vietnamese Navy
VP	Patrol Squadron
VQ	Fleet Air Reconnaissance Squadron
WESTPAC	Western Pacific
YMS	Auxiliary Motor Minesweeper
YOG	Gasoline Barge, Self-propelled

APPENDIX III

Larger Vessels Of The South Vietnamese Navy 1959-1965

Submarine Chaser (PC)

Chi Lang (HQ-01)   (Inactivated 1962)
Van Hiep (HQ-02)
Dong Da (HQ-03)   (Inactivated 1961)
Tuy Dong (HQ-04)
Tay Ket (HQ-05)
Van Don (HQ-06)   (Transferred to VNN 1960)

Submarine Chaser (SC)

Unnamed (HQ-601)   (Inactivated 1960)
Unnamed (HQ-602)   (″   )

Escort (PCE)

Dong Da II (HQ-07)   (Transferred to VNN 1961)
Chi Lang II (HQ-08)   (″   1962)
Ky Hoa (HQ-09)   (″   1962)
Chi Linh (HQ-10)   (″   1964)
Nhut Tao (HQ-11)   (″   1964)

Motor Gunboat (PGM)

Phu Du (HQ-600)	(Transferred to VNN 1963)
Tien Moi (HQ-601)	(")
Minh Hoa (HQ-602)	(Transferred to VNN 1963)
Kien Vang (HQ-603)	(")
Keo Ngua (HQ-604)	(")
Kim Quy (HQ-605)	(")
May Rut (HQ-606)	(")
Nam Du (HQ-607)	(")
Hao Lu (HQ-608)	(")
To Yen (HQ-609)	(")
Dienh Hai (HQ-610)	(" 1964)
Truong Sa (HQ-611)	(" 1964)

Auxiliary Motor Minesweeper (YMS)

Ham Tu (HQ-111)	(Inactivated 1960)
Chuong Duong (HQ-112)	(")
Bach Dang (HQ-113)	(")

Minesweeper, Coastal (MSC)

Ham Tu II (HQ-114)	(Transferred to VNN 1959)
Chuong Duong II (HQ-115)	(")
Bach Dang II (HQ-116)	(" 1960)

Landing Support Ship, Large (LSSL)

No Than (HQ-225)
Linh Kiem (HQ-226)

Landing Ship, Infantry, Large (LSIL)

Long Dao (HQ-327)
Than Tien (HQ-328)
Thien Kich (HQ-329)
Loi Cong (HQ-330)
Tam Xet (HQ-331)

Larger Vessels Of the South Vietnamese Navy 547

Landing Ship, Tank (LST)

Cam Ranh (HQ-500)   (Transferred to VNN 1962)
Da Nang (HQ-501)   ("   )
Thi Nai (HQ-502)   ("   1963)

Landing Ship, Medium (LSM)

Hat Giang (HQ-400)
Han Giang (HQ-401)
Lam Giang (HQ-402)
Ninh Giang (HQ-403)
Huong Giang (HQ-404)   (Transferred to VNN 1961)
Tien Giang (HQ-405)   ("   1962)
Hau Giang (HQ-406)   ("   1963)

Light Cargo Ship (AKL)

Hoa Giang (HQ-451)

Gasoline Barge, Self-propelled (YOG)

HQ-470
HQ-471   (Transferred to VNN 1963)

Landing Craft, Utility (LCU)

HQ-533
HQ-534
HQ-535
HQ-536
HQ-537
HQ-538
HQ-539

Minesweeping Launch (MLMS)

HQ-150   (Transferred to VNN 1963)

HQ-151	(Transferred to VNN 1963)
HQ-152	,,
HQ-153	,,
HQ-154	,,
HQ-155	,,
HQ-156	,,
HQ-157	,,
HQ-158	,,
HQ-159	,,
HQ-160	,,
HQ-161	,,

Primary Source: Naval Ship Systems Command, "MAP Ship and Craft Summary."

Bibliographic Note

Official Records

Unless otherwise indicated, all documents cited in this work are located in the Operational Archives of the Naval Historical Center. As stated in the foreword a number of these sources retain a security classification at the time of publication.

Within the Operational Archives, the Post 1946 Command, Report, and Plan files are lucrative resources for the naval history of the war. Arranged by their originating command, and thereunder chronologically, these record groups contain pertinent documents originated by the Office of the Secretary of Defense, Defense Intelligence Agency, JCS, and unified commands, such as CINCPAC and MACV, and other government agencies. By far the largest portions of these groups are materials generated by the Office of the Chief of Naval Operations, the Atlantic and Pacific Fleets, the numbered fleets, other naval operating forces, shore-based commands, and individual ships. The records include yearly command histories, annual reports, cruise reports, action reports, operation plans and orders, combat studies, and statistical compilations.

Of particular worth are separate collections in the Archives accessioned from the Navy Secretariat of the JCS, the Office of the Chief of Naval Operations, Seventh Fleet, Naval Forces, Vietnam, and the Naval Advisory Group, Vietnam. The last group contains information that is especially valuable for study of the Vietnamese Navy. This documentation is supported by the microfilmed message traffic of the Pacific Command, the Pacific Fleet, and Naval Forces, Vietnam. Additional records created by naval combat and support units, ships, training centers, and research organizations are housed at the Washington National Records Center in Suitland, Maryland, but remain under the cognizance of the Naval Historical Center.

Executive and Congressional Documents

Among the most important sources for study of American strategy and policy-making during the Vietnam era are the twelve-volume Pentagon Papers series, more formally identified as Department of Defense, *United States-Vietnam Relations: 1945-1967* (Washington: GPO, 1971); and the companion *Senator Gravel Edition of the Pentagon Papers* (Boston: Beacon Press, 1971). Equally rich is the Joint Chiefs of Staff, *History of the Joint Chiefs of Staff: The Joint Chiefs of Staff and the War in Vietnam, 1960-1968* (Washington: Historical Division, Joint Secretariat, JCS, 1970). Pertinent information also is found in the Department of Defense, *Annual Report of the Secretary of Defense* (Washington: GPO, 1960-1965) for the fiscal years from 1959 to 1964. Decisionmaking at the theater level is well treated in the yearly CINCPAC Command History series, completed during the period; the MACV Command History volumes, issued in 1964 and thereafter; and the Commander in Chief, Pacific-Commander U.S. Military Assistance Command, Vietnam, *Report on the War in Vietnam* (Washington: GPO, 1969). The historical offices associated with the Armed Services have produced a number of works that provide a wealth of detail on various aspects of the war. They include the following naval titles:

Hooper, Edwin B. *Mobility, Support, Endurance: A Story of Naval Operational Logistics in the Vietnam War, 1965-1968.* Washington: Naval History Division/GPO, 1972.

Moore, Withers M., Bergsma, Herbert L., and Demy, Timothy J. *Chaplains With U.S. Naval Units in Vietnam, 1954-1975.* Washington: History Branch, Office of Chief of Chaplains, 1985.

Tregaskis, Richard. *Southeast Asia: Building the Bases: The History of Construction in Southeast Asia.* Washington: Naval Facilities Engineering Command/GPO, 1975.

Naval History Division. *Dictionary of American Naval Fighting Ships.* Washington: Naval History Division/GPO, 1959-1981. 8 vols.

_____. "History of Naval Operations in Vietnam, 1946-1963." Unpublished history in Naval Historical Center, 1964.

_____. "History of U.S. Naval Operations Vietnam, 1964." Unpublished history in Naval Historical Center, 1970.

Marine Corps, Army, and Air Force works on the Southeast Asian conflict that were of particular value to this history included:

Fails, William R. *Marines and Helicopters, 1962-1973.* Washington: History and Museums Division, Headquarters USMC, 1978.

Fox, Roger. *Air Base Defense in the Republic of Vietnam, 1961-1973.* Washington: Office of Air Force History, 1979.

Futrell, Robert F. and Blumenson, Martin. *The Advisory Years to 1965* in series *The United States Air Force in Southeast Asia.* Washington: Office of Air Force History, 1981.

Futrell, Robert F. *Ideas, Concepts, Doctrine: A History of Basic Thinking in the United States Air Force, 1907-1964.* Maxwell AFB, AL: Air Univ., 1971.

Kelley, Francis J. *U.S. Army Special Forces, 1961-1971* in series *Vietnam Studies*. Washington: Department of the Army/GPO, 1973.

Momyer, William. *Airpower in Three Wars*. Washington: USAF, 1978.

Rawlins, Eugene W. and Sambito, William J. *Marines and Helicopters, 1946-1962*. Washington: History and Museums Division, Headquarters USMC, 1976.

Shulimson, Jack and Johnson, Charles M. *U.S. Marines in Vietnam: The Landing and the Buildup, 1965*. Washington: History and Museums Division, Headquarters, USMC, 1978.

Spector, Ronald H. *Advice and Support: The Early Years, 1941-1960* in series *United States Army in Vietnam*. Washington: Center of Military History, U.S. Army, 1983.

Whitlow, Robert H. *U.S. Marines in Vietnam: The Advisory and Combat Assistance Era, 1954-1964*. Washington: History and Museums Division, Headquarters, USMC, 1977.

Research organizations, working under Defense Department contract, compiled a number of excellent studies of specific aspects of the war, including:

Erdheim, Judith. *"Market Time."* Study CRC 280. Washington: Center for Naval Analyses, 1975.

Halpern, A.M. and Fredman, H.B. *Communist Strategy in Laos*. Santa Monica, CA: Rand Corp., 1960.

Hickey, G.C. and Davison, W.P. *The American Military Advisor and His Foreign Counterpart: The Case of Vietnam*. Santa Monica, CA: Rand Corp., 1965.

Johnson, James W. *River and Canal Ambush Problems, Republic of Vietnam, 1962*. Washington: Research Analysis Corp., 1963.

Lauve, Anita. *The Origins and Operations of the International Control Commission in Laos and Vietnam*. Rand Study RM-2967. Santa Monica, CA: Rand Corp., 1962.

Rand Corporation. *The Sierra Project: A Study of Limited Wars*. Report No. R-317. Santa Monica, CA: Rand Corp., 1958.

Weiner, M.G., Brom, J.R., and Koon, R.E. *Infiltration of Personnel from North Vietnam: 1959-1967*. Santa Monica, CA: Rand Corp., 1968.

Other useful works prepared by departments of the Executive Branch of the U.S. goverment include:

Department of Defense, Joint Logistics Review Board. *Logistic Support in the Vietnam Era*. Washington: The Board, 1971.

_____. *Report to the Secretary of Defense on the National Military Command Structure.* Washington: GPO, 1978.

_____. *Semiannual Report of the Secretary of Defense.* 1 Jan-30 Jun 1957. Washington: GPO, 1958.

_____. *Semiannual Report of the Secretary of Defense.* 1 Jan-30 Jun 1958. Washington: GPO, 1959.

Department of State. "Aggression from the North: The Record of North Vietnam's Campaign to Conquer South Vietnam." *The Department of State Bulletin.* (22 Mar 1965).

_____. *A Threat to the Peace: North Vietnam's Effort to Conquer South Vietnam.* Washington: GPO, 1961.

Public Papers of the Presidents of the United States: John F. Kennedy, 1961. Washington: GPO, 1962.

Public Papers of the Presidents of the United States: Lyndon B. Johnson: 1963-64. Washington: GPO, 1965.

U.S., Congress, Senate, Committee on Armed Services. *Nomination of Admiral Thomas H. Moorer, USN, to be Chairman, Joint Chiefs of Staff.* 91st Cong., 2nd sess. Washington: GPO, 1970.

U.S., Congress, Senate, Committee on Foreign Relations. *Hearings on the Gulf of Tonkin, the 1964 Incidents.* 90th Cong., 2nd sess. Washington: GPO, 1968.

The U.S. President's Committee to Study the United States Military Assistance Program. *Composite Report.* Washington: the Committee, 1959.

Papers of Individual Officers

Also held in the Operational Archives are the papers of a number of key naval leaders. The letters, memoranda, and public pronouncements of Admirals Arleigh Burke, George W. Anderson, and David L. McDonald, successive Chiefs of Naval Operations during the period of this book, shed light on high-level policymaking. Equally useful are the materials preserved by Admirals Claude Ricketts and Horacio Rivero, successive Vice Chiefs of Naval Operations, and Admirals H.L. Miller, W. M. Beakley, and W.D. Irvin. Information on the naval assistance and advisory program can be found in the papers of Captain J.B. Drachnik, head of the MAAG's Navy Section from 1961 to 1964. In addition, the documentary collection of Captain J.P. Sylva elucidates the Navy's role in Laos during the height of the international crisis there.

Bibliographic Note 553

Oral Histories

To supplement the written record, the authors conducted taped interviews with a number of naval officers who participated in the Southeast Asian Conflict. The recollections of Brigadier General E.J. Bronars; Captains J.B. Drachnik, M.C. Friedman, and W.H. Hardcastle; Lieutenant Commander T.F. Wooten; and Lieutenant T.M. Browne regarding the advisory and assistance program are particularly helpful. The interviews with William Colby, P.H. Bucklew, M.L. Mulford, W.H. Hamilton, and R. Marcinko provide essential background to the counterinsurgency and special operations story while that with Captain Sylva details his unique experiences in Laos. The war, from the perspective of the Vietnamese Navy, is described in detail by nine of its top officers, who were interviewed by representatives of the Naval Historical Center in 1975, following their immigration to the United States. A second major group of oral histories used in this volume consists of the interviews by the U.S. Naval Institute with CNO Arleigh Burke; Commanders in Chief, Pacific, H.D. Felt and U.S.G. Sharp; fleet commander R.L. Johnson; Admirals J.B. Colwell, J.W. Cooper, C.D. Griffin, E.B. Hooper, H.L. Miller, H. Rivero, and A.G. Ward; and Captain Bucklew. Interviews with Admiral Burke by the John F. Kennedy Library and Princeton University; with Admiral Hooper by the U.S. Marine Corps Historical Center; and with Captain Drachnik by the John F. Kennedy Library provide additional information on the naval aspects of the war.

Memoirs and Autobiographies

Colby, William. *Honorable Men: My Life in the CIA*. New York: Simon and Schuster, 1978.

Cooper, Chester L. *The Lost Crusade, America in Vietnam* . New York: Dodd, Mead and Co., 1970.

Eisenhower, Dwight D. *The White House Years: Waging Peace, 1956-1961*. New York: Doubleday and Co., 1965.

Halpern, Samuel E. *WEST PAC 64*. Boston: Brandeis Press, 1975.

Hilsman, Roger. *To Move a Nation: The Politics of Foreign Policy in the Administration of John F. Kennedy*. Garden City, NY: Doubleday, 1967.

Johnson, Lyndon B. *The Vantage Point: Perspectives of the Presidency, 1963-1969*. New York: Holt, Rinehart and Winston, 1971.

McNamara, Robert S. *The Essence of Security: Reflections in Office*. New York: Harper and Row, 1968.

Ridgway, Matthew B. *Soldier: The Memoirs of Matthew B. Ridgway*. New York: Harper and Brothers, 1956.

Schlesinger, Arthur M., Jr. *A Thousand Days: John F. Kennedy in the White House*. Boston: Houghton Mifflin, 1965.

Sharp, U.S.G. *Strategy For Defeat: Vietnam in Retrospect*. San Rafael, CA: Presidio Press, 1978.

Sorensen, Theodore C. *Kennedy*. New York: Harper and Row, 1965.

Stockdale, Jim and Sybil. *In Love and War: The Story of a Family's Ordeal and Sacrifice During the Vietnam Years*. New York: Harper and Row, 1984.

Taylor, Maxwell D. *Responsibiity and Response*. New York: Harper and Row, 1967.

_____. *The Uncertain Trumpet*. New York: Harper, 1960.

Tran Van Don. *Our Endless War: Inside Vietnam*. San Rafael, CA: Presidio Press, 1978.

Westmoreland, William C. *A Soldier Reports*. New York: Doubleday and Co., 1976.

Secondary Works

Aliano, Richard A. *American Defense Policy from Eisenhower to Kennedy: The Politics of Changing Military Requirements, 1957-1961*. Athens, OH: Ohio Univ. Press, 1975.

Austin, Anthony. *The President's War*. New York: Lippincott, 1972.

Blaufarb, Douglas S. *The Counterinsurgency Era: U.S. Doctrine and Performance, 1950 to the Present*. New York: The Free Press, 1977.

Browne, Malcolm. *The New Face of War*. New York: Bobbs-Merrill, 1965.

Chae-Jin Lee. *Communist China's Policy Toward Laos: A Case Study 1954-67*. Manhatten, KS: Center for East Asian Studies, Univ. of Kansas, 1970.

Charlton, Michael and Moncrieff, Anthony. *Many Reasons Why: The American Involvement in Vietnam*. New York: Hill and Wang, 1978.

Coletta, Paolo E. *United States Navy and Marine Corps Bases, Overseas*. Westport, CT: Greenwood Press, 1985.

Democratic Republic of Vietnam. *Facts and Figures Concerning U.S. and U.S. Agents' Sabotage Activities in North Vietnam*. Hanoi: Ministry of Foreign Affairs, 1963.

Dommen, Arthur J. *Conflict in Laos: The Politics of Neutralization.* New York: Praeger, 1971.

Enthoven, Alain C. and Smith, K. Wayne. *How Much Is Enough?* New York: Evanston, 1971.

Fall, Bernard B. *Anatomy of a Crisis: The Laotian Crisis of 1960-1961.* Garden City, NY: Doubleday, 1961.

_____. "The Pathet Lao: A 'Liberation Party' " in Robert A. Scalapino, ed. *The Communist Revolution in Asia: Tactics, Goals, and Achievements.* Englewood Cliffs, NJ: Prentice Hall, 1965.

_____. *Street Without Joy.* Harrisburg, PA: Stackpole Co., 1951.

Fitzgerald, Oscar P. "U.S. Naval Forces in the Vietnam War: the Advisory Mission, 1961-1965" in Robert W. Love, Jr. *Changing Interpretations and New Sources in Naval History.* New York: Garland Publishing, 1980.

Galloway, John. *The Gulf of Tonkin Resolution.* Rutherford, NJ: Farleigh Dickinson Univ. Press, 1970.

Galucci, Robert L. *Neither Peace Nor Honor: The Politics of American Military Policy in Viet-Nam.* Baltimore: Johns Hopkins Univ. Press, 1975.

Gettleman, Marvin *et al.*, eds. *Conflict in Indo-China: A Reader on the Widening War in Laos and Cambodia.* New York: Random House, 1970.

Goldstein, Martin E. *American Policy Toward Laos.* Cranbury, NJ: Associated University Presses, 1973.

Goulden, Joseph C. *Truth is the First Casualty: The Gulf of Tonkin Affair — Illusion and Reality.* New York: Rand McNally, 1969.

Hall, David K. "The Laos Crisis, 1960-61" in Alexander L. George, David K. Hall, and William E. Simons. *The Limits of Coercive Diplomacy; Laos, Cuba, Vietnam.* Boston: Little, Brown and Co., 1971.

_____. "The Laotian War of 1962 and the Indo-Pakistani War of 1971" in Barry M. Blechman and Stephen S. Kaplan, eds. *The Use of the Armed Forces as a Political Instrument.* Washington: Brookings Institution, 1976.

Herring, George C., ed. *The Secret Diplomacy of the Vietnam War: The Negotiating Volumes of the Pentagon Papers.* Austin: Univ. of Texas Press, 1983.

Hovey, Harold A. *United States Military Assistance: A Study of Policies and Practices.* New York: Frederick A. Praeger, 1965.

Jane's Fighting Ships, 1968-1969. Raymond V.B. Blackman, ed. London: McGraw-Hill, 1970.

Jordan, Amos A., Jr. *Foreign Aid and the Defense of Southeast Asia.* New York: Frederick A. Praeger, 1962.

Kahan, Jerome. *Security in the Nuclear Age: Developing U.S. Strategic Weapons Policy.* Washington: Brookings Institution, 1975.

Kaufman, William W. *The McNamara Strategy.* New York: Harper and Row, 1964.

Kennedy, John F. *Strategy of Peace.* New York: Harper and Brothers, 1960.

Kissinger, Henry. *Nuclear Weapons and Foreign Policy.* New York: Harper and Brothers, 1957.

Kolodziej, Edward A. *The Uncommon Defense and Congress, 1945-1963.* Athens: Ohio Univ. Press, 1966.

Langer, Paul F. and Zasloff, Joseph J. *North Vietnam and the Pathet Lao: Partners in the Struggle for Laos.* Cambridge, MA: Harvard Univ. Press, 1970.

Le May, Curtis E. and Smith, Dale O. *America Is in Danger.* New York: Funk and Wagnalls, 1968.

Lewy, Guenter. *America in Vietnam.* New York: Oxford Univ. Press, 1978.

McPherson, John B. "Vietnam: The Perspective of a Former Vice-Director of the Joint Staff" in A.F. Hurley and R.C. Ehrhart, eds. *Air Power and Warfare: The Proceedings of the 8th Military History Symposium, United States Air Force Academy, 18-20 October 1978.* Washington: USAF, 1979.

Marek Thee. *Notes of a Witness: Laos and the Second Indochinese War.* New York: Random House, 1973.

Mecklin, John. *Mission in Torment.* Garden City, NY: Doubleday and Co., 1965.

Morrocco, John. *Thunder From Above: Air War, 1941-1968* in series *The Vietnam Experience.* Boston: Boston Publishing Co., 1984.

Nuechterlein, Donald E. *Thailand and the Struggle for Southeast Asia.* Ithaca, NY: Cornell Univ. Press, 1965.

Palmer, Dave Richard. *Summons of the Trumpet: U.S.-Vietnam in Perspective.* San Rafael, CA: Presidio Press, 1978.

Palmer, Gregory. *The McNamara Strategy and the Vietnam War: Program Budgeting in the Pentagon, 1960-1968.* Westport, CT: Greenwood Press, 1978.

Pike, Douglas. *Viet Cong: The Organization and Techniques of the National Liberation Front of South Vietnam.* Cambridge, MA: MIT Press, 1966.

Polmar, Norman. *Aircraft Carriers: A Graphic History of Carrier Aviation and Its Influence on World Events.* Garden City, NY: Doubleday and Co., 1969.

Porter, Gareth, ed. *Vietnam: The Definitive Documentation of Human Decisions.* Stanfordville, NY: Earl M. Coleman Enterprises, Inc., 1979.

Rowe, John S. and Morison, Samuel L. *The Ships and Aircraft of the U.S. Fleet.* Annapolis: Naval Institute Press, 1972.

Schratz, Paul R. "The Military Services and the New Look, 1953-1961: The Navy" in David H. White, ed. *Proceedings of the Conference on War and Diplomacy.* Charleston, SC: The Citadel, 1976.

Sisouk Na Champassak. *Storm Over Laos: A Contemporary History.* New York: Praeger, 1961.

Stevenson, Charles A. *The End of Nowhere: American Policy Toward Laos Since 1954.* Boston: Beacon Press, 1972.

Thompson, James Clay. *Rolling Thunder: Understanding Policy and Program Failure.* Chapel Hill, NC: Univ. of North Carolina Press, 1980.

Toye, Hugh. *Laos: Buffer State or Battleground.* New York: Oxford Univ. Press, 1968.

Turner, Gordon B. "Air and Sea Power in Relation to National Power" in Gordon B. Turner and Richard D. Challener, eds. *National Security in the Nuclear Age: Basic Facts and Theories.* New York: Frederick A. Praeger, 1960.

Windchy, Eugene G. *Tonkin Gulf.* Garden City, NY: Doubleday, 1971.

Yarmolinsky, Adam. *The Military Establishment: Its Impacts on American Society.* New York: Harper and Row, 1971.

Articles

Burke, Arleigh. "The Sea Carries Security on Its Back." *Navy — Magazine of Seapower.* Vol. 1, No. 1 (May 1958).

Cagle, Malcolm W. "Sea Power and Limited War." *U.S. Naval Institute Proceedings.* Vol. 84, No. 7 (Jul 1958).

Case, William. "USS Sacramento (AOE-1)." *U.S. Naval Institute Proceedings.* Vol. 93, No. 12 (Dec 1967).

Chen, King C. "Hanoi's Three Decisions and the Escalation of the Vietnam War." *Political Science Quarterly.* Vol. 90, No. 2 (Summer 1975).

Clapp, Archie J. "Shu-Fly Diary." *U.S. Naval Institute Proceedings.* Vol. 89, No. 10 (Oct 1963).

Defense Intelligence Agency. "The Far East Communist Bloc Navies in 1962." *DIA Naval Intelligence Review.* (Apr 1963).

Dommen, Arthur J. "The Future of North Vietnam." *Current History*. (Apr 1970).

Dulles, John Foster. "Challenge and Response in United States Policy." *Foreign Affairs*. Vol. 36, No. 1 (Oct 1957).

Geneste, Marc E. "Danger from Below." *U.S. Naval Institute Proceedings*. Vol. 86, No. 11 (Nov 1960).

Hilsman, Roger and Pelz, Stephen E. "When is a Document not a Document -And Other Thoughts." *Diplomatic History*. Vol. 3, No. 3 (Summer 1979).

Humphrey, David C. "Tuesday Lunch at the Johnson White House: A Preliminary Assessment." *Diplomatic History*. Vol. 8 (Winter 1984).

Kerby, Robert L. "American Military Airlift During the Laotian Civil War, 1958-1963." *Aerospace Historian*. Vol. 24 (Spring 1977).

Leunen, Paul Van, Jr. "Naval Weapons Today." *U.S. Naval Institue Naval Review, 1965.* (1964)

'Limited War: Where do they Stand." *Army, Navy, Air Force Register*. Vol. 80, No. 4146 (May 1959).

McClendon, F.O., Jr. "Doctors and Dentists, Nurses and Corpsmen in Vietnam." *U.S. Naval Institute Naval Review*. (May 1970).

Marolda, Edward J. "The Influence of Burke's Boys on Limited War." *U.S. Naval Institute Proceedings*. Vol. 107, No. 7 (Aug 1981).

Merdinger, Charles J. "Civil Engineers, Seabees, and Bases in Vietnam." *U.S. Naval Institute Naval Review*. (May 1970).

Miller, George H. "Not for the Timid." *U.S. Naval Institute Proceedings*. Vol. 85, No. 5 (May 1959).

Murphy, R.P.W. and Black, E.F. "The South Vietnamese Navy." *U.S. Naval Institute Proceedings*. Vol. 90, No. 1 (Jan 1964).

New York Times. 2 Feb; 21 Sep 1964.

Office of Naval Intelligence. "The Far East Communist Bloc Navies in 1961." *The ONI Review*. (Apr 1962).

_____. "Major Political/Economic Developments in the Sino-Soviet Bloc, 1959." *The ONI Review*. Vol. 15, No. 4 (Apr 1960).

_____. "Report from Vietnam." *The ONI Review*. (Oct 1962).

_____ "Status of the Cold War in Southeast Asia." *The ONI Review*. Vol. 15, No. 1 (Jan 1960).

Parke, Everett A. "Report From Vietnam." *The ONI Review* . (Oct 1962).

Paul, Roland A. "Laos: Anatomy of an American Involvement." *Foreign Affairs*. (Apr 1971).

Pelz, Stephen E. "When Do I have time to Think?' John F. Kennedy, Roger Hilsman, and the Laotian Crisis of 1962." *Diplomatic History*. Vol. 3, No. 2 (Spring 1979).

"The 'Phantom Battle' That Led to War." *U.S. News and World Report*. (23 Jul 1984).

Schreadley, R.L. "The Naval War in Vietnam, 1950-1970." *U.S. Naval Institute Proceedings*. Vol. 97, No. 819 (May 1971).

Sharp, U.S.G. "Air Power Could Have Won in Vietnam." *Air Force*. (Sep 1971).

_____. "Vietnam Strategy — Then and Now." *Congressional Record*. (Aug 1972).

Simmons, K.W. "National Security in the Nuclear Age." *U.S. Naval Institute Proceedings*. Vol. 86, No. 6 (Jun 1960).

Sokol, Anthony E. "Sword and Shield in our Power Structure." *U.S. Naval Institute Proceedings*. Vol. 85, No. 4 (Apr 1959).

Taylor, Brown. "The Lesser Deterrent." *U.S. Naval Institute Proceedings*. Vol. 85, No. 8 (Aug 1959).

Taylor, LeRoy. "Naval Operations in Confined Waters and Narrow Seas." *U.S. Naval Institute Proceedings*. Vol. 86, No. 6 (Jun 1960).

Tilford, Earl H., Jr. "Two Scorpions in a Cup: America and the Soviet Airlift to Laos." *Aerospace Historian*. (Fall/Sep 1980).

Westmoreland, William C. "Vietnam in Perspective." *Military Review*. (Jan 1979).

Index

Unless otherwise indicated, all military personnel are USN and all ships are USS.

A

A and J Mid-America, SS, 356
Abing, Lieutenant (j.g.) James H., 197
"Actions to Stabilize the Situation in the Republic of Vietnam," 372
Advanced Research Projects Agency, 139, 233, 317
Advisors, 24, 127, 134-35, 166, 201, 211, 219, 348, 353, 357, 513-14, 517; see also Military Assistance Advisory Group, Vietnam
  to Vietnamese Navy, 1959-1961, 137, 143, 145-48, 150-51, 157, 160-63
  to Vietnamese Navy, 1961-1963, 220-21, 223-25, 227-34, 236, 240, 242-44, 247, 262, 267
  to Vietnamese Navy, 1964, 299, 303, 304-06, 308-14, 317-18, 322, 324-26, 329-30, 332-33
Africa, 7, 55, 106
Agency for International Development, 198, 346
Agerholm (DD-826), 394
Air America, 52
Air and Naval Gunfire Liaison Company, 286
Air cover, 50, 179, 270, 381, 405, 420-21, 431, 457, 480, 498, 526; see also combat air patrol
Aircraft types
  attack
    A-1 Skyraider, 296, 310, 444, 446-48, 451, 455, 482, 498, 499 (photo), 505, 509, 513
    A-1H Skyraider, 251, 273, 311, 314, 385, 431, 480, 484, 496, 506, 510, 517, 519
    AD-6 Skyraider, 56, 250-51, 272
    A-3 Skywarrior, 291, 296
    A3D Skywarrior, 51, 216
    A-4 Skyhawk, 296, 444, 445 (photo), 446, 449, 455, 458 (photo), 487, 497, 505, 510, 525, 531
    A-4C Skyhawk, 447, 498, 510
    A4D Skyhawk, 80, 85, 431
    A-4E Skyhawk, 482
    A-5 Vigilante, 291
    A-6 Intruder, 279, 296
    A-6A Intruder, 487, 500
    A-7 Corsair II, 279
  bombers, 9
    B-52 (Air Force), 473
    B-57 (Air Force), 372, 456
  electronic countermeasures/air early warning
    AD-5Q Skyraider, 183-85
    E-1B Tracer, 449, 455
    EA-1F Skyraider, 184-85, 186 (photo), 187
    EA-3B Skywarrior, 379, 385, 394
    EC-121 Warning Star, 126, 296, 394
  fighters
    F-4 Phantom II, 279, 291, 296 (photo), 385-86, 446, 451, 455, 486-87, 506, 516 (photo), 524, 531
    F-4B Phantom II, 480, 498
    F-8 Crusader, 296, 417-19, 431, 444, 446-47, 451, 455, 497, 500, 510
    F-8C Crusader, 455, 506
    F-8D Crusader, 385-86
    F-8E Crusader, 415, 484, 498
    F8F Bearcat, 250
    F8U Crusader, 51, 61, 78
    F-100 (Air Force), 387
    F-102 (Air Force), 184-85, 187
    F-105 (Air Force), 182
  helicopters, 11, 27, 31, 33, 37-38, 42, 52, 61, 73, 80, 85, 125, 165, 178, 216, 288, 317, 330, 377, 470, 506
    CH-46 Sea Knight, 279-80
    CH-53 Sea Stallion, 279
    H-19A, 52
    H-21 (Army), 178
    HUS, 12 (photo)
    SH-3A Sea King, 279, 297
    UH-1B Iroquois (Army), 214
    UH-2A Seasprite, 279, 297
    UH-34 Seahorse, 52, 60, 78, 126, 179, 297, 385, 529
    UH-46A Sea Knight, 281
  HU-16 Albatross (Air Force), 447, 500
  L-19 Cessna, 330
  MiGs, 386, 456, 507
    MiG-15, 389, 470
    MiG-17, 389, 470, 471 (photo)
  patrol, 123
    P-2 Neptune, 279, 297, 457
    P-2V Neptune, 216
    P-3 Orion, 279, 296, 486, 521
    P-5M Marlin, 52, 169, 216, 297, 452
    SP-2 Neptune, 320, 491, 520 (photo), 521
    SP-2H Neptune, 517, 519
    SP-5B Marlin, 495, 496, 521
  reconnaissance, 62, 169, 291, 378, 385-86
    RA-3B Skywarrior, 187, 376, 379, 389, 491, 519

RA-5C Vigilante, 391, 486
RF-8A Crusader, 379, 381, 385, 389, 390 (photo), 444, 446, 480, 497, 506
RF-101 (Air Force), 379-80
S-2 Tracker, 296
tankers, 446
  A-3B, 380
trainers, 470
  T-28 Trojan, 250-51, 311
  T-28B Nomad, 250
transports, 31, 165, 270, 288, 291, 378, 470
  C-123 (Army), 350, 352
  C-130, 272, 287
Air defenses, 184, 395, 465, 470, 505
Air Early Warning Squadron 1, 68
Air Early Warning Squadron 13, 183
Air Early Warning Squadron 13, Detachment 1, 183-87
Airfields, 61, 284
  in Laos, 24-25, 51, 64
  in South Vietnam, 197, 251, 352, 363, 465, 475-76, 498, 522, 524-26, 529
  in North Vietnam, 366, 464, 473
Air Force units, 72, 79, 97, 169, 288, 293, 447, 453, 479-80, 483-84, 500, 507, 509
  2nd Air Division, 260, 379-80, 384, 482, 496
  315th Air Division, 5
Air Force, U.S., 7, 9, 168, 490, 500, 529
  air interception in South Vietnam, 183-85, 187
  training of Vietnamese Air Force, 250-52
  in HSAS, 254-58, 261
  operations in Laos, 387, 389, 510-11, 522
  operations in North Vietnam, 456, 498, 505
Air interception, 184-87
Airlift, 260, 275, 287, 524, 526-27; see also sealift
  U.S. capability, 14, 27, 99, 277, 293
  in Laos crises, 33-34, 51-52, 64, 69, 72, 79-80, 85
  Soviet, 49, 53-54, 57, 60
Air operations, 293, 375
  in Laos, 56, 366, 405, 479, 482, 485, 515
  in South Vietnam, 183, 186, 515
  in North Vietnam, 444, 515
Air patrol, 119, 158, 169, 171-73, 187, 460
Air strikes, 489
  in Laos, 82-83, 387-88
  in South Vietnam, 273, 323, 513, 515
  in North Vietnam, 366, 368, 438, 449, 459, 470, 473, 478, 507
Airstrips, 38, 179, 196-99, 287, 348, 350, 352, 354
Alamo (LSD-33), 452, 474
Allendorfer, Commander Harry C., Jr., 73n
Allies, U.S., 2, 7, 30, 36, 91, 98, 106, 278
Alvarez, Lieutenant (j.g.) Everett, 447, 500
Alvin C. Cockrell (DE-366), 176

Ambush, 247, 249, 260, 312, 317, 348, 353, 440, 441
American Consul General, Hong Kong, 356
American Society of Newspaper Editors, 100
Amphibious Construction Battalion 1, 338
Amphibious forces, 11, 13, 41-42, 51, 73, 103, 280-82
Amphibious Force, Seventh Fleet, 8, 452, 526
Amphibious Force, U.S. Atlantic Fleet, 115, 211
Amphibious Force, U.S. Pacific Fleet, 8, 115, 211, 339
Amphibious Group 1, 205
Amphibious Group, Western Pacific, 68
Amphibious Objective Studies Program, 42, 283
Amphibious operations, 112, 178, 242-43, 366
Amphibious Ready Group, Seventh Fleet, 8, 42, 282, 284, 474, 529
  deployment for Laos crisis, 47, 52, 54, 62, 68, 74, 77, 80
  deployment for Diem coup, 269-70, 272, 274
  deployment for Tonkin Gulf crisis, 452, 460
Amphibious Squadron 1, 286, 526
Amphibious Squadron 7, 61, 286
Amphibious task forces, 42, 77, 286, 530
Amphibious task groups, 42, 77, 281, 483-84
Amphibious Warfare Readiness Branch, 114, 116, 121, 213
Anderson, Admiral George W., Jr., 165, 189, 202, 205, 219, 225
  Laos crises, 78, 82-83
  STATs, 120-21, 192
  coastal patrol, 123-24, 171, 173
  counterinsurgency, 208-10, 212, 215
  HSAS, 253-54, 258
  on the war, 265-66, 268, 276, 367
Anderson, Lieutenant Commander Richard E., (CEC), 113
Anderson, Lieutenant Franklin W., 310, 514
An Khe, 198
Annam, 199
An Thoi, 137, 230, 319, 321, 517
Antiguerrilla warfare, 88n, 89, 94, 210, 431
Antisubmarine warfare, 64, 77-78, 130, 180, 241, 288, 296, 474, 496, 526
An Xuyen Province, 150, 320, 322, 324, 330, 333
An Xuyen Quarantine, 320, 322-24
Ap Bac battle, 267-68, 276
Armed Forces Policy Council, 2
Armed Forces Radio Service, 257
Armed Forces Staff College, 210
Army units, 14, 28, 41-42, 79, 82, 85, 107, 288, 293, 363-65, 453, 531, 532
  Army Support Command, 359
  1st Special Forces Group, 97
  2nd Airborne Battle Group, 51
  Army Support Group, 363
  173rd Airborne Brigade, 495

Index

8th Transportation Company (Light Helicopter), 165-66
57th Transportation Company (Light Helicopter), 165-66
93rd Transportation Company (Light Helicopter), 178
Engineers, 346
Special Forces, 24, 27, 90, 104, 113, 194, 197-98, 348, 350, 352
Army, U.S., 7, 20, 187, 214, 221, 234, 243, 304, 513
   Laos crises, 60, 72
   guerrilla warfare, 99, 112, 114-16
   helicopters to South Vietnam, 165, 179
   HSAS, 252-55, 257, 260-61, 361
A Ro, 352
Arp, Lieutenant Commander Philip S., 251
Ashcroft, Commander Jerome L., 233
Asheville (PGM-84), 290 (photo)
Ashtabula (AO-51), 410
Asia, 15, 21, 49, 55, 98, 106, 241, 369
Asian mainland, 7, 78
Askland, Lieutenant Jon A., 244
Assistant Chief of Staff for Operations, 108
Assistant Chief of Staff for Plans, 268, 370
Assistant Chiefs of Naval Operations
   Air, 495
   Fleet Operations and Readiness, 190, 459
   Plans and Policy, 209
Assistant Director for Rural Affairs, 198
Assistant Division Commander, 3rd Marine Division, 79
Assistant for Naval Aspects of Special Operations, 121
Assistant Secretary of Defense (International Security Affairs), 24, 123, 480
Assistant Secretary of Defense (Office of Special Operations), 96, 98, 204
Atlantic Fleet, U.S., 7, 104, 112, 189, 337, 486
Atomic weapons, 6, 14, 55, 476; see also nuclear weapons
Atsugi, Japan, 61, 78
Attack Carrier Striking Force, Seventh Fleet, 8, 294
Attack squadrons
   52, 446
   56, 446
   58, 431
   144, 447
   145, 447-48
   152, 311
   153, 497, 500
   155, 497
   212, 497
   216, 497
Attopeu, 25
Attorney General, U.S., 101
Aubert, Commander George A., 118, 119 (photo)
Austin (LPD-4), 280
Australia, 7, 147, 286

B

Bachelor enlisted men's quarters, 255, 258
Bachelor officers quarters, 255, 493
Bacino, Signalman 2nd Class Richard M., 434
Bac Lieu, 150, 182
Baldwin, Chief Radarman Elden, 224
Balua Island, 323
Ban Ban, 57, 381
Ban Don, 197
Bang Cao Thang, Lieutenant Commander (South Vietnamese), 146
Bangkok, Thailand, 24, 28, 52, 62-63, 68, 72, 79-80, 85, 257, 261
Ban Ken Bridge, 484
Ban Keng Khan Kao, 482
Ban Me Thuot, 197
Ban Na Kok, 479
Ban Tang Vai, 485
Ban Ti Srenh, 196
Barnhart, Commander Robert C., 427n, 432-34, 442
Barry, Lieutenant (j.g.) John J., USNR, 429, 431
Barton, Captain Harry H., 459-60
Barton, Lieutenant Jere A., 432
Bases, 14-15, 22, 73, 214
   U.S., 111, 283-84, 490
   in South Vietnam, 159, 168, 208, 224, 230, 237, 309, 314, 319, 329, 338, 340, 376, 406, 452, 464-65, 495, 522, 524, 532
   in North Vietnam, 160, 202, 341, 343, 437-38, 440, 444-46, 456, 504
Bassac River, 234
Ba Xuyen Province, 179, 326
Bay of Pigs, 100-01, 128, 201, 334
Beach jumper units, 96, 209, 217
Beach surveys, 178, 182
Beakley, Admiral Wallace M., 96, 104, 112
Beef-up reports, 265
Begley, Commander Robert E., 260
Belle Grove (LSD-2), 80, 85
Ben Goi, 376-77
Ben Luc, 347
Ben Nghe Canal, 357
Ben Nhi Canal, 323
Bennington (CVS-20), 50, 52, 54, 61-62, 64, 78-79, 286, 532
Ben Thuy, 343, 436, 438, 440, 443, 446, 456
Bergen, Norway, 340
Bergland, Seaman Rodger N., 431
Berkeley (DDG-15), 320, 379
Berlin, 7, 29, 118
Berlin crisis, 106, 120, 128, 171
Bexar (APA-237), 345, 483, 526, 529
Bien Hoa Airbase, 311, 472-73, 477, 493, 495, 522-23

Biet Hai commandos, 190, 238; see also commandos
Binh Dinh Province, 237
Binh Duong Province, 310
Binh Gia, 523
Binh Thanh Thon, 350
Blackburn, Vice Admiral Paul P., Jr., 77, 287, 514, 519, 527
Black (DD-666), 519
Blockade, 119-20, 289, 325-26, 366, 368, 370, 466, 477, 479, 493
Bluegill (SS-242), 180, 241
Board of Inspection and Survey, 10
Boat and craft construction, 158, 161, 227-30, 233, 312-13, 332
Boat and craft types
  amphibious landing craft and vehicles, 4, 14, 31, 215
    amphibious tractors, 527
    landing craft, mechanized, 13, 43-44, 146, 149-51, 227, 245, 248-49, 280, 316, 327, 329, 527, 529
    landing craft, personnel, large, 13, 314, 316
    landing craft, utility, 151, 245, 280, 527, 529
    landing craft, vehicle and personnel, 13, 43-45, 149-51, 182, 214, 227, 245, 247-49, 310, 329, 527
    landing vehicles, tracked, 527
  fuel-oil barges, 168, 240
  gasoline barges, self-propelled, 173, 320
  junks, 155-61, 169-71, 201-03, 228-34, 237-39, 247, 262, 304, 309, 311-14, 319-24, 326-27, 329-30, 332, 342-43, 395, 400, 411, 414, 424, 451, 468-69, 517, 519, 521
  minesweeping
    auxiliary motor minesweepers, 153
    minesweeping boats, 407
    minesweeping launches, 239-41, 329
  motor torpedo boats, 90-91, 93, 189, 203-04, 206, 209, 340, 407, 414-15, 420, 432-33, 441-43, 449, 456, 467-68
  patrol, 90-91, 109, 116, 415, 449
    fast patrol boats, 90-91, 205-06, 208, 218, 334-35, 337, 339-41, 343, 397, 402, 406-09, 411, 426, 435, 467-69, 494, 521
    fast patrol craft, 339, 406, 467, 521
  river, 43, 161-62
    air boats, 139, 317
    armored motor launches, 329
    commandaments, 149, 151, 316
    FOM, 149n
    marsh screws, 317
    monitors, 149, 151, 245, 316, 329-30, 331 (photo)
    rescue boats, 139
    river patrol craft, 316
    STCAN, 149-50, 247-48, 316, 327, 329-30, 331 (photo)
    swimmer support boats, 140, 214, 227
    turbo-powered boats, 139
    vedettes, 149n, 150, 237, 356
    Wizard boats, 139-40
    Zodiac boats, 140
  sampans, 138, 234, 323, 330, 343
Boat Support Unit 1, 339
Boat Training Team, Danang, 338, 342, 468
Bo De River, 243, 322
Bombing campaign, 464, 466, 472, 500; see also air operations, air strikes
Bon Homme Richard (CVA-31), 68, 74, 379, 452, 455, 460, 474
Bon Sar Pa, 197
Booby traps, 198, 238
Borneo, 68
Bouam Long, 382
Boum Oum, 49
Bowers, Petty Officer R.L., 353
Boxer (CVS-21), 11
Boyle, Brigadier General Andrew J., USA, 77, 84
Boyum, Captain John, 269-70
Bradway, Captain William S., 344
Brady, Commander Donald B., 187
Braine (DD-630), 61
Breton, SS, 250
Bridges, Styles, 71
Bringle, Rear Admiral William F., 379
Brink Hotel attack, 482-83, 493, 495, 523
British, 3, 96, 242, 284-85
Bronars, Major Edward J., USMC, 329
Bronze Star, 196
Brown, Equipment Operator 3rd Class W.T., 348
Brown, Winthrop, 66, 77, 83
Brushfire war, 4, 98
Bryer, Lieutenant Commander Bruce A., 228
Buchanan (DDG-14), 275
Buck (DD-761), 519
Bucklew, Captain Phillip H., 303-05, 340
Bucklew Report, 303-04, 313, 318, 320, 322, 325-26, 330
Buckner Bay, Okinawa, 31, 33, 46, 51, 54, 62, 77, 80, 179, 286
Buddhists, 196, 268-70, 276, 474
Bugara (SS-331), 122
Bu Gia Map, 350
Bundy, McGeorge, 437, 440, 469, 502
Buon Mi Ga, 196
Bu Prang, 197
Burchinal, Lieutenant General David A., USAF, 437, 441, 443
Bureau of Naval Personnel, 116, 209-11, 267
Bureau of Ships, 116-17, 138-39, 240, 316, 319, 337
Bureau of Weapons, 116-17, 294

Bureau of Yards and Docks, 113, 116, 361
Burke, Admiral Arleigh A., 5 (photo), 43, 48 (photo), 70 (photo), 91, 92 (photo), 96-97, 106, 130, 139, 280, 291, 293
  on U.S. strategy, 3, 6, 11, 15, 17, 20
  Laos crises, 30, 37, 40, 47, 50, 53, 55-56, 66, 71-72, 75
  on guerrilla warfare, 99-102, 111, 113-16
  intervention in South Vietnam, 104, 108
Burma, 17, 240
Byng, Rear Admiral John W., 50, 61

C

Cai Lon River, 323
California, 61, 140, 147, 189, 193, 339, 346, 359, 487
Calvert (APA-32), 62, 64
Camau, 150
Camau Peninsula, 172, 230, 237, 242-43, 302, 320, 322, 325
Cambodia, 43, 118, 172-73, 175, 248, 261, 302-03, 311, 325, 371-72
Cambodian border area, 75, 150, 196-97, 234, 247, 320, 326, 350, 352, 464
Cambodian government, 44
Cambodian Navy, 44n
Cam Ranh Bay, 178, 230, 234, 242, 245, 310, 375-77, 465-66, 516
Cam Ranh (HQ-500), 273, 327
Canada, 147
Cang; see Chung Tan Cang
Can Tho, 149, 227, 232, 245
Cao Lanh, 326
Cape Camau, 68, 167, 173, 175
Cape Dao, 468
Cape Ke Ga, 283, 483, 517, 519
Cape Lai, 375
Cape Ron, 341, 343, 468
Cape Vung Tau, 180, 283
Capitaine (AGSS-336), 242
Capital Kin Do Theater, Saigon, 358
Card (T-AKV-40), USNS, 178, 355-56
Cargo Handling Battalion 2, 359
Carpenter, Captain William M., 66n
Carrier air wings
  5, 444
  9, 480
  14, 446
  15, 497
  21, 497-98
Carrier task forces, 61, 281, 385, 437, 497, 511
Carrier task groups
  Laos crises deployments, 28, 31, 34, 46, 50, 61, 67-68, 77
  Diem coup deployments, 270, 272, 275
  Laos air operations, 379, 385, 389
  off North Vietnam, 391, 415, 460
Carroll, Signalman 3rd Class Gary D., 434

Carter Hall (LSD-3), 85, 340
Catamount (LSD-71), 64
Cat Bi Airfield, 473
Catfish (SS-339), 202-03
Cat Lo, 232, 308, 348
Cavalier (APA-37), 452, 474
Ceasefire in Laos, 63, 66, 72-75, 81-82, 84, 106, 109
Central Committee of the Vietnam Workers' Party, 299, 301
Central Highlands, 25, 183, 197, 350, 531
Central Intelligence Agency, 96, 201
  and Laos, 49, 52, 60, 63, 86, 373
  and Vietnam, 203, 335, 338, 422, 482
Certeza Surveying Company, 154
Chairman, Joint Chiefs of Staff, 4n, 131, 342, 421, 437
Chairman, Ship Characteristics Board, 116
Chanh Hoa, 473, 498
Chaplains, 259, 263, 491-92, 527
Chap Le, 456, 497-98
Charles, Constructionman Thomas M., 348
Charles E. Brannon (DE-446), 176
Chau Doc, 150
Chau Doc Province, 196
Cheyenne (T-AG-174), USNS, 293
Chief, Bureau of Ships, 203
Chief, Military Assistance Advisory Group, Laos, 77
Chief, Military Assistance Advisory Group, Vietnam, 44, 93, 122, 152, 169, 179, 190, 239
Chief, Naval Advisory Group, 327
Chief, Navy Section, Military Assistance Advisory Group, Vietnam, 89, 166, 193, 214
Chief of Far Eastern Operations, Central Intelligence Agency, 335
Chief of Naval Operations, 3, 42, 165, 202, 337, 382, 405n, 473, 501
  Laos crises, 15, 30, 52, 55, 69, 71, 78, 83
  unconventional warfare, 96-97, 101
  conflict in South Vietnam, 106, 108, 219, 253-54, 264-66, 268
  guerrilla warfare, 111-12, 114, 116-17, 120
  infiltration, 123-24, 514n
  development of counterinsurgency capability, 189, 205-06, 209-10, 212, 215, 217
  fleet readiness, 289, 291-93
  Tonkin Gulf incidents, 404, 422, 468
Chief of Naval Operations (South Vietnamese), 305, 321, 332, 342
Chief of Staff, Royal Navy, 3
Chief of Staff, U.S. Army, 69, 342, 469, 531
Chief of Staff, U.S. Pacific Fleet, 93, 193, 282-83
Chief of Staff, Vietnamese Navy, 137, 142, 327
Chief of the Advanced Research Projects Agency Vietnam field unit, 314
Chief of the General Staff (South Vietnamese), 136

Chief, Programs Evaluation Office, Laos, 23, 93
Chi Lang (HQ-01), 146
Chi Lang II (HQ-08), 323, 513
China, 15, 21, 37, 217, 396, 444; see also Peoples Republic of China
  Laos crises, 36, 56, 83
  deterrence of, 107, 109, 127
  military aid supplied by, 301, 390, 470
  intervention into Southeast Asia, 368, 476, 486, 502
China Lake, California, 487
Chinese border area, 36n, 444, 477
Chinese Communists, 155, 237, 241, 286, 438, 461, 466
  militancy, 15, 17, 278
  Laos crises, 55, 69
  intervention, 337, 368, 371, 475-77, 486
  Desoto Patrol, 393-94, 396, 460
Chinese Nationalist Marines, 109n
Choke points, 484, 510-11
Cholera, 199, 344
Chon; see Tran Van Chon
Cho Quan Infectious Disease Hospital, Saigon, 344
Cho Ray Hospital, Saigon, 259
Christensen, Lieutenant Keith L., 330
Chuc; see Nguyen Chuc
Chu Lai, 465, 475
Chung Tan Cang, Rear Admiral (South Vietnamese), 143, 298-99, 305, 313, 342
Chuong Thien Province, 332
Cigainero, Chief Utilityman James W., 198
Civic action, 88, 101, 212, 324, 344, 355; see also nation-building, pacification
  by STATs, 194, 198-99, 348-50, 352, 354
  by HSAS, 258-59, 345
Civil affairs, 27, 211
Civil Engineer Corps, 192
Civil Engineer Corps Officer School, 211
Civil Guard Boat Operation Training Center, 249
Civil Guard (South Vietnamese), 159, 238, 243, 249, 262; see also paramilitary forces
Civilian Irregular Defense Group, 194, 198
Clandestine operations, 115, 121, 192, 200; see also covert operations
Clay, Captain Donald N., 215, 266
Clydesdale, Lieutenant (j.g.) Charles F., 506
Coastal defenses, 91, 406-07, 461, 470, 493
Coastal districts (South Vietnamese), 137, 158, 225, 308, 319, 321
  1st, 137, 230, 232-33, 236, 314
  2nd, 230, 232, 234, 513
  3rd, 229-30, 232, 308
  4th, 137, 229-30, 232, 308, 322, 324
Coastal Force (South Vietnamese); see South Vietnamese Navy units
Coastal patrol, 130, 138, 162, 240, 295, 320, 323, 325, 398

early plans for, 94, 104, 107, 109, 120, 125
  by Coastal Force, 232-33, 304, 309
  by combined forces, 165-67, 171, 177, 239, 289
  by Sea Force, 154, 242, 304
  Market Time, 514-17, 519, 521
Coastal Patrol Plan, 239
Coastal surveillance centers, 224, 230, 262, 517, 521
Coast Guard, U.S., 521
Coast watcher system, 94
Co Chien River, 326
Code of Conduct, 382, 384
Coedes, Capitaine de Fregate Pierre (French), 44
Cofat factory, 255
Cogswell (DD-651), 61
Colby, William, 335
Cold War, 15, 22, 96-98, 209-10, 214-15, 218, 280, 393
Combat air patrol, 185, 431, 446, 506, 511; see also air cover
Combat information center, 429, 434
Combined exercises, 79n, 241, 284, 286
Combined operations, 123, 169, 173, 175-76, 239, 402
Commandant of the Cambodian Navy, 44
Commandant of the Marine Corps, 69, 293
Commandant of the Marine Corps (South Vietnamese), 273
Commander Amphibious Force, Seventh Fleet, 182, 265n, 281, 286, 474, 492
Commander Amphibious Force, U.S. Atlantic Fleet, 103, 204
Commander Amphibious Force, U.S. Pacific Fleet, 103, 189, 205-06, 212
Commander Amphibious Group 1, 281
Commander Amphibious Training Command, U.S. Pacific Fleet, 303
Commander Carrier Division 3, 287
Commander Carrier Division 7, 379
Commander Carrier Task Group 77.6, 454
Commander Construction Battalions, U.S. Pacific Fleet, 193-94, 200, 347
Commander Destroyer Division 12, 396
Commander Destroyer Division 32, 397
Commander Destroyer Division 52, 454
Commander Destroyer Division 192, 398, 410
Commander First Fleet, 8, 62
Commander Fleet Marine Force, Seventh Fleet, 286
Commander in Chief, Pacific, 6-7, 24-25, 100, 117, 122, 376, 465, 472, 474; see also Felt, Sharp
  capability of forces, 13, 281, 292
  Laos crises, 1959-1960, 28, 31, 34, 36-37, 39, 42-43, 50-51, 54-55, 58
  Laos crises, 1961-1962, 60-61, 67, 74, 77, 79, 84

counterinsurgency, 88-89, 95
intervention in South Vietnam, 107-09, 119
military assistance, 132, 150, 164, 219-20, 229, 253, 258, 313, 361-62
coastal patrol, 166, 169, 172-73, 176
fleet assistance to South Vietnam, 178-79, 184-85, 187
SEABEEs, 194, 198, 346, 349
actions against North Vietnam, 201-03, 334-35, 337, 341, 370, 372, 406, 463-64, 467-69
Diem coup, 264-65, 268-70, 275
air operations in Laos, 378, 380, 388, 479-80, 485, 511
Desoto Patrol, 393, 395, 397-98, 402, 405, 414, 421, 441, 452-53, 458, 460
air operations in North Vietnam, 438, 443-44, 456, 459, 473, 477, 483, 495, 500, 504
deployment of Marine forces to South Vietnam, 522, 524-26
Commander in Chief, Pacific Air Force, 500
Commander in Chief, U.S. Atlantic Fleet, 205, 210-11, 213, 337
Commander in Chief, U.S. Pacific Fleet, 7-8, 15, 18, 90-91, 269-70, 302, 376-77, 382, 470, 474-75, 483, 495, 533; see also Hopwood, Sides, Sharp, Moorer, R.L. Johnson
capability of forces, 14, 40, 283, 289, 291, 292, 295, 487-88, 490-91
Laos crises, 28, 31, 33, 37-38, 64-66, 68
unconventional and guerrilla warfare, 97, 117, 205-06, 208, 210-11, 213, 216
military assistance, 130, 145
coastal patrol, 167-69, 172, 176-77, 519
fleet support to South Vietnam, 178-80, 183, 344, 357
SEABEEs, 192, 199-200, 349
logistic support in South Vietnam, 252-54, 261
actions against North Vietnam, 335, 342, 463, 465-66
air operations in Laos, 380, 480, 485, 510
Desoto Patrol, 396, 398, 402, 405-06, 419-20, 422, 425, 438, 449, 453, 458, 461
air operations in North Vietnam, 444n, 473, 496-98
ground forces for South Vietnam, 522-23, 524, 526
Commander Joint Task Force 116, 27-28, 79
Commander Minesweeping Division 73, 168
Commander Naval Air Force, U.S. Pacific Fleet, 384
Commander Naval Construction Battalions, U.S. Pacific Fleet Detachment, Republic of Vietnam, 200
Commander Naval Construction Forces, Pacific, 24
Commander Naval Forces, Philippines, 254, 339

Commander Naval Operations Support Group, U.S. Pacific Fleet, 340
Commander Naval Stations and Schools (South Vietnamese), 137
Commander Pacific Division, Bureau of Yards and Docks, 361
Commander Patrol Force, Seventh Fleet, 169, 172
Commander Service Force, U.S. Pacific Fleet, 200, 283, 487
Commander Service Squadron 3, 355
Commander Seventh Fleet, 8, 90, 165, 268, 273, 275, 287n, 355, 377, 380, 386, 438, 443-44, 488- 89, 527
Laos crises, 33, 46, 51, 61, 68, 74, 77-78
on fleet readiness, 40-42
coastal patrol, 173, 175, 514, 519
surface and air support to South Vietnam, 180, 182-83, 185-87, 344
part in Desoto Patrol, 393-95, 398-99, 404-05, 414-15, 421, 424-25, 449
Commander Taiwan Patrol Force, 398, 404, 406
Commander Task Force 76, 64, 68, 483, 526
Commander Task Force 77, 431, 444, 474, 496, 509, 515
Commander Task Group 72.1, 410, 422
Commander Task Unit 72.1.2, 410n
Commander Training Force, U.S. Pacific Fleet, 294
Commander U.S. Military Assistance Command, Vietnam, 269, 305-06, 313, 335, 371, 467, 469, 480, 517, 519
naval support to South Vietnam, 182, 184, 187, 196, 198, 200, 254, 346, 349
part in Desoto Patrol, 395, 397, 400, 402, 404, 406, 408-09, 421
air operations in Southeast Asia, 483, 500, 515
on U.S. ground forces in South Vietnam, 525, 527, 531
Commander U.S. Taiwan Defense Command, 18
Commanding General, 1st Marine Aircraft Wing, 27
Commanding General, 9th Marine Expeditionary Brigade, 483, 526, 531
Commanding General, 3rd Marine Division, 74
Command Junk 471, 323-24
Commandos, 190, 238, 310, 327, 339, 513; see also LDNN, SEALs
Command relationships, 253-54, 335, 480, 517
Commissaries, 252, 260, 359
Communism, 15, 47, 49, 71, 73n, 75, 109
Communist bloc, 15, 21, 36, 53, 98-99, 278, 394, 424
Communist Party of North Vietnam, 156
Composite Photographic Squadron 61, 51
Composite Photographic Squadron 63, 51
Compton, Captain Oliver D., 54
Comstock (LSD-19), 31
Condon, Major General John P., USMC, 286-87

Conferences, 18, 169, 335, 346, 488, 512; see also meetings
 diplomatic, 62-63, 66
 military assistance, 139, 164-65, 179
 on conflict in South Vietnam, 264-65, 474
Conflict (MSO-426), 176
Congo crisis, 7
Congress, 17, 69, 71, 90, 131, 134, 278, 354
Connally, John B., Jr., 291
Conquest (MSO-488), 169
Constellation (CVA-64), 279, 453, 458 (photo), 460, 474
 in Yankee Team reconnaissance, 379, 385, 388-89, 391
 Tonkin Gulf incidents, 431, 440, 451, 454, 457
 in Pierce Arrow strikes, 444, 446-48
Construction, 113, 192, 198, 258, 284, 359, 364, 377, 465, 475-76, 491
 in Laos, 24-25, 64, 192
 by STATs, 199, 348-50, 352-53
Construction Battalion Base Unit, 193
Construction Battalion Center, Port Hueneme, California, 346
Conventional forces, 102, 213; see also general purpose forces
 requirement for, 3-4, 6, 8, 20, 104, 118, 278, 366
 diminished strength of, 13, 277, 288
Conventional war, 6, 11, 14, 27, 93, 277-79, 281, 288, 486, 488; see also limited war
Convoy escort, 64, 150, 326
Conway, Lieutenant Commander Thomas J., 251
Cook (APD-130), 178, 188
Coontz (DLG-9), 122
Coordinating Committee for U.S. Missions in Southeast Asia, 482
Coral Sea (CVA-43), 183, 505, 507, 515
 deployment for Laos crises, 54, 64, 67-68, 74
 in Flaming Dart strikes, 495-98
 in Barrel Roll operations, 510-11
Core (T-AKV-41), USNS, 146, 165, 219
Coronado, California, 189, 339
Corps areas (South Vietnamese), 225
 I Corps, 286
 III Corps, 249
 IV Corps, 242, 249
Counterespionage, 225
Counterguerrilla forces, 100, 121, 211-12
Counterguerrilla operations, 57, 99, 103, 112, 116
Counterguerrilla warfare, 99, 100, 102, 104, 111, 115
Counterinsurgency, 288, 305, 334, 346, 349, 373, 465, 532; see also civic action, nation-building
 development of doctrine, 88, 98, 110-11, 128
 naval application, 90, 104, 112, 129, 158, 160
 Navy adopts, 189, 192, 194, 200, 208-12, 215-18
 results in South Vietnam, 265, 269, 298, 301, 355, 366, 371, 474
Counterinsurgency Education and Training Program, 210
Counterinsurgency operations, 27, 36, 123, 130, 210, 212, 214, 249
"Counterinsurgency Operations in South Vietnam and Laos," 93
Counterinsurgency Plan, 93, 158, 164
Counterintelligence, 225
Coups, 142, 298, 375, 504
 by Kong Le, 45-47
 against Diem, 264, 269, 272-73, 275-76, 299, 319, 332
Coursey, Brigadier General John P., USMC, 483
Covert operations; see also clandestine operations
 naval preparation for, 96-97, 112, 206
 against North Vietnam, 200-01, 203, 334-35, 338, 344, 365, 371, 373, 463, 478
Croston, Calvin J., (CHC), 259
Cruiser-Destroyer Force, U.S. Pacific Fleet, 8
Cruiser-Destroyer Group, Seventh Fleet, 8
Cua Lon River, 243
Cua Viet, 159
Cua Viet River, 159
Cuba, 7, 106
Cuban Missile Crisis, 214, 292, 367
Cubi Point, Philippines, 43, 284, 287
 support in Laos crises, 51, 54, 61, 67, 69, 78, 80, 85
 VAW 13 deployment to, 183-84
 support for Southeast Asia operations, 187, 281-82, 379
Curfews, 326
Current (ARS-22), 377
Currituck (AV-7), 377
Cushman, Major General Robert E., USMC, 287
Customs service (South Vietnamese), 232, 304
Cuu Long, 227, 319

D

Dai River, 521
Dalat, 309
Dalby, Lieutenant Colonel Marion C., USMC, 233
Dam Pau, 195
Danang, 38, 52, 155, 162, 178, 188, 241, 245, 260-61, 311, 345, 356, 417, 446-47, 498
 Vietnamese Navy facilities in, 137, 159-60, 230-32, 308, 319
 base for coastal patrol, 168, 170-72, 517
 base for 34A maritime operations, 190, 203, 208, 310, 319, 335, 339-43, 395, 406, 408, 410-11, 424

deployment of U.S. forces to, 375, 475, 495-96, 521-22, 524-27, 529-31, 533
development of U.S. base, 452, 464-65
Danang Coastal District, 157
Danang Museum Ramp, 529
Darlac Province, 196-97
Darnell, Lieutenant Commander Donald P., 396
Davis, Rear Admiral James R., 361
Decker, General George H., USA, 69, 70 (photo)
Defense Department, U.S., 8, 20, 66n, 101, 266, 294, 380, 443, 501
  Laos crises, 28, 30, 37, 54, 56, 60, 63, 74
  intervention in South Vietnam, 106, 118, 124
  provision of military aid, 131-32, 139
  on counterinsurgency, 201, 212, 346
  actions against North Vietnam, 483, 497
Defense Department Special Survey Team in Laos, 45
Defense Intelligence Agency, 420-21
De Haven (DD-727), 269, 393
Delaware River, 204
Del Giudice, Lieutenant David, 44, 189
Demilitarized Zone, 156, 159-60, 187, 236, 410, 422, 497, 517, 519, 524
Democratic Republic of Vietnam (North Vietnam), 135, 241, 400, 461, 504
  Laos crises, 39, 55-56
  U.S. actions against, 201-02, 337, 372, 409, 463, 475, 477
  defenses, 397-98, 460
  hostility, 414, 422, 425, 525
Department of State for National Defense (South Vietnamese), 148, 158, 161, 228, 238
Department of the Army, 363
Deputy Assistant Secretary of Defense, 511
Deputy Assistant Secretary of Defense for Installations and Logistics, 364
Deputy Chief of Naval Operations for Operations (South Vietnamese), 310
Deputy Chief of Staff for Military Assistance Affairs, 161
Deputy Chief of Staff for the Navy (South Vietnamese), 136
Deputy Chief of Staff, U.S. Pacific Fleet, 193-94
Deputy Chiefs of Naval Operations
  Air, 216
  Fleet Operations and Readiness, 96, 112, 182, 209, 284
  Logistics, 116, 120-21
  Manpower and Naval Reserve, 114
  Plans and Policy, 97, 102, 209, 216, 366
Deputy Commander in Chief, U.S. Army, Pacific, 63
Deputy Commander U.S. Military Assistance Command, Vietnam, 338
Deputy Officer in Charge of Construction, 200
Deputy Secretary of Defense, 107, 203, 364, 437, 443n, 469
Deputy Special Assistant to the President for National Security Affairs, 101
Deputy Under Secretary of State, 124
Desertion, 231, 262, 308, 333
Desoto Patrol, 443, 472, 491, 493-95, 502
  early patrols, 393-97
  preparation for August 1964 patrol, 398, 400, 402, 404-06
  August 1964 patrol, 411, 414-15, 419, 421-27, 431, 434-35, 449, 451
  September 1964 patrol, 453-54, 456-57, 459
  aftermath of Tonkin Gulf incidents, 460-62, 470
Destroyer divisions, 64
  11, 33
  152, 46
  171, 50
  212, 50
  251, 50
Deterrence, 4, 7
Dewey (DLG-7), 9
Dickson, Lieutenant Edward A., USNR, 497
Diem; see Ngo Dinh Diem
Dinh Manh Hung, Lieutenant Commander (South Vietnamese), 242, 273
Dinh Tuong Province, 151
Director, Central Intelligence Agency, 440
Director, Joint Staff, Joint Chiefs of Staff, 437, 441
Director, Logistic Plans Division, 113
Director, Long Range Objectives Group, 293
Director of Central Intelligence, 101
Director of Communications, Plans and Policy Division, 217
Director of Military Assistance, 132
Director of Naval Intelligence, 486
Director, Politico-Military Policy Division, 40, 84, 165, 209
Director, Strategic Plans Division, 103, 113-14, 214
Director, Strike Warfare Division, 515
Dirksen, Everett M., 71
Dispensaries, 199, 252, 258; see also hospitals
Dixie Station, 516
Djakarta, Indonesia, 461
Don; see Tran Van Don
Don Chau, 196
Dong, 237-38
Dong Ba Thin, 348, 352
Dong Ha, 202
Dong Hoi, 283, 398, 473, 496-98, 500
Dong Tien Canal, 152
Douglas Aircraft Corporation, 250
Doyle, Commander James H., 396
Drachnik, Captain Joseph B., 193, 220-21, 223, 225, 229, 238, 240-41, 265-67, 299, 300 (photo), 306

coastal patrol, 166, 168, 170, 172-73, 242
  on river warfare, 214-15, 247, 316
  on infiltration, 236, 302
Draper Committee, 131-32
Draper, William H., 131
Drydocks, 145, 208, 338
Duc Pho, 199
Duc Pho District, 199
Dulles, Allen W., 101
Dulles, John Foster, 1-3
Duncan (DDR-874), 379
Duncan Island, 155
Duong Dong, 232
Duong Dong Light, 154
Duong Van Minh, General (South Vietnamese), 138, 275, 298
Dupuis, Capitaine de Corvette Serge (French), 45
Durbrow, Eldridge, 135
Dynamic (MSO-432), 176

E

"E & E/Survival in South Vietnam," 384
East Coast, U.S., 204-05
Easterling, Captain Henry M., 134, 139-40, 240
Eastern Pacific, 7, 281, 452, 486
Eastern Repair Facility (South Vietnamese), 227, 308, 319
Economic assistance, 23, 47, 49, 164; see also military aid and assistance
Edmonds (DE-406), 172
Edmondson, Commander George H., 431-32
Edson (DD-946), 451
Eisenhower administration, 1, 8, 15, 21-24, 46-47, 58, 281, 283
Eisenhower, Dwight D., 1, 7, 14, 31, 47, 56, 94, 97-98, 131
Egypt, 15
Eldorado (AGC-11), 286
Electronic countermeasures, 183, 185, 433n
Enclaves, 532
Endurance (MSO-435), 176
Engage (MSO-433), 177
Engineering School (South Vietnamese), 310
England (DLG-22), 526
Enterprise (CVAN-65), 279
Enthoven, Alain C., 511
Epping Forest (MCS-7), 377
Ernest G. Small (DDR-838), 494
Escort Division 72, 176
Escort Squadron 7, 176
Esteem (MSO-438), 169
Estes (AGC-12), 64, 68
Europe, 118, 128, 147
Evacuations, 270, 273, 483, 495
Evasion and escape, 190, 206, 211, 382, 384; see also survival, evasion, resistance, and escape

Excel (MSO-439), 118
Exercise Director, Tulungan exercise, 286
Exercises, 7, 11, 31, 86, 97, 147, 167, 205, 212, 217, 241-42, 244, 270, 309, 322, 326, 330, 464, 484, 489, 494
  Air Cobra, 285
  Experience IV, 284
  Green Light, 61
  Jungle Drum, 284
  Pony Express, 64-65, 68, 73-74
  Sea Devil, 284
  Silver Lance, 525
  Tulungan, 179, 284-87
  Yellow Bird, 272
Explosive ordnance disposal, 377

F

Fai Tsi Long Archipelago, 467
Far East, 7, 29, 155, 220, 278
Far Eastern Fleet (French), 145
Felt, Admiral Harry D., 43, 99, 100, 110 (photo), 132, 220, 223, 228, 253, 258, 261, 268, 305-06, 322
  on Pacific strategy, 6, 14, 18, 241
  in Laos crises of 1959-1960, 26-28, 29n, 30-31, 34, 36, 39, 46-47, 50, 52-55, 57
  in Laos crises of 1961-1962, 60-62, 67, 72, 75, 77, 82, 84, 86
  counterinsurgency advocate, 88-90, 93-95, 158
  intervention in South Vietnam, 107-08, 109n, 119-20, 122, 124, 126
  Vietnamese Navy, 138, 150, 157, 161-62, 164, 316, 325
  on coastal patrol, 166, 168-69, 171, 173, 176-77
  U.S. Navy support to South Vietnam, 179-80, 184, 186-87, 199, 302-04
  Diem coup, 269-70, 275-76
  actions against North Vietnam, 200, 202-03, 334, 337, 370-72, 375-76, 397, 402, 463
Ferriter, Lieutenant (j.g.) Robert L., 195
Fighter squadrons
  51, 417, 446
  53, 417, 447
  111, 385
  154, 500
  194, 455
Fire Control Director 51 (*Turner Joy*), 429, 431
Fire Control Director 52 (*Turner Joy*), 431
Fire-control systems, 322, 419, 429, 431, 459, 472
Firedrake (AE-14), 51
First Fleet, 7, 292, 303, 486
1st Philippines Battalion Combat Team, 286
First Sea Lord (British), 3, 96
Fitzgibbons Bachelor Enlisted Men's Quarters, 258

Flachsenhar, Captain John J., 134
Flag Plot Branch, 73n, 114
Flak suppression, 446, 497, 500, 510-11
Fleet Air Reconnaissance Squadron 1, 379
Fleet anchorage, 376-77, 465
Fleet Intelligence Center, Pacific, 489
Fleet Rehabilitation and Modernization, 10, 292
Fleet Weather Center, Guam, 489
Flexible response, 1, 3-4, 8, 20, 128, 201, 277; see also graduated military response, military pressure
Floating Forward Depot, 293-94, 453
Flood relief task force, 126
Florida, 317
Florida Everglades, 139
Foley, Rear Admiral Francis D., 46
Force Objective Plan, 241
Foreign Military Assistance Act of 1961, 132
Foreign policy, 18, 20-21, 40, 95, 338n
Forrest Sherman class destroyer, 419
Fortify (MSO-446), 177
Fort Marion (LSD-22), 51, 64, 67-68
Fowler, Rear Admiral Richard L., 496
France, 22, 75, 145
Franke, William B., 9-11, 13
Frauenfelder, Lieutenant (j.g.) Henry, 350, 352
Freedom of the seas, 419, 435
Free-fire zones, 322, 330
Free world, 3, 15, 36-37, 94, 98, 101, 106, 228, 461, 524
French, 22-23, 36, 84, 116n, 134, 140, 158, 396
French Indochina War, 22, 36, 130, 134, 139, 143, 151, 158, 249
French training mission in Laos, 24
Frick, Lieutenant (j.g.) Frederick M., 429
Friedman, Captain Malcolm C., 252-55, 258, 261, 355, 358, 364
Fuji, Japan, 77
Futema Air Facility, Okinawa, 43, 60

G

Gallant (MSO-448), 170
Garbe, Lieutenant (j.g.) Warren M., 199, 350
Gardner, Hospital Corpsman 1st Class T.G., 199
Garrison, Seaman Kenneth E., 433
Gates, Thomas S., Jr., 5 (photo)
Gay, Captain Jesse B., Jr., 193-94
Gayety (MSF-239), 240
General Line and Naval Science School, 211
General Line School, 140
General purpose forces, 215, 218, 278, 295; see also conventional forces
General Staff College (South Vietnamese), 309
General war, 2-4, 9, 14, 28, 41, 88, 209, 213-14, 278
Geneva Agreement, 22-23, 58, 134-35, 137, 219

Geneva Conference on Laos, 63, 66n, 83-86, 106-07, 109, 118
"General Declaration and Protocol on Neutrality of Laos", 84, 373
Gentner, Rear Admiral William E., Jr., 103, 114-15, 165
George K. MacKenzie (DD-836), 397, 400, 494
George Washington (SSBN-598), 4
Germany, 55
Gia Lam Airfield, 473
Giang River, 202
Gibson, Glen, 364
Gillette, Captain Norman C., Jr., 37-38
Gilpatric, Roswell, 107, 126, 203
Gio Island, 160, 411, 468, 470
Gipson, Chief Equipment Operator Willie, 346
Go Cong Province, 329
Godel, William H., 139
Graduated military response, 1, 56, 338; see also flexible response, military pressure
Graham, Commander Ralph E., 168-69
Graham, Lieutenant (j.g.) John R., 205
Gray diesel engines, 229
Great Britain, 66, 75, 84, 286
Greece, 131
Griffin, Admiral Charles D., 46, 49, 51, 53-54, 58, 61-62, 68, 74, 182-83, 284
Group 559 (North Vietnamese), 57, 85
Group 759 (North Vietnamese), 156n, 236
Growler (SSG-577), 9
Guadalcanal (LPH-7), 280
Guam, 28, 39, 46, 187, 282-83
Guam (LPH-9), 280
Guano fertilizer, 155
Guerrilla warfare, 24, 88n, 90, 96-104, 111-18, 120-21, 189-90, 201, 211, 285, 303, 523
Guest, Rear Admiral William S., 454
Gulf of Siam, 42, 137, 154, 167, 172-73, 259, 312
  deployments into for Laos crises, 52, 61-62, 68, 74, 77
  coastal patrol in, 157, 174, 176, 187, 320, 323-24
Gulf of Tonkin, 368, 397, 460-61, 472
  destroyer patrols in, 394, 396, 398, 404-06, 419-20, 422, 427, 449, 451, 454, 459
  fleet operations in, 444, 467, 494-95, 500
Gulf of Tonkin incidents, 393, 399n, 426, 435, 437, 442, 457
  effect on fleet operations, 389, 391, 489-92
  effect on U.S. policies, 451, 453, 463-64, 466, 468, 472, 474, 485
Gun Mount 31 (*Turner Joy*), 433
Gun Mount 32 (*Turner Joy*), 433
Gunnery, 147, 176, 294, 309, 488, 492, 494
Gunston Hall (LSD-5), 483, 495, 526
Gurke (DD-783), 526

H

Hai Muoi Tam Canal, 151
Hainan Island, 33, 68, 375, 394, 422, 443
Haiphong, 366, 370, 407, 426, 440, 456, 473
Halibut (SSGN-587), 9
Halsey Powell (DD-686), 53
Ham Luong River, 323
Hammarskjold, Dag, 38
Ham Tu II (HQ-114), 143
Hancock (CVA-19), 179, 183, 271 (photo), 287, 483, 495, 519, 526
  in Laos crises, 33, 46-47, 77-79
  Diem coup, 270, 272, 274-75
  air operations in Laos, 391, 482, 484, 511
  air operations in North Vietnam, 496-98, 505, 507
Handclasp, Project, 259, 344
Hanks, Lieutenant Commander William E., 229
Hanoi, 17, 202, 371, 472-73, 494, 507
Han River, 529
Hanson (DDR-832), 275, 348
Hanson, Utilitiesman 2nd Class L.W., 348
Hao Mon Dong, 343
Harbor defense, 130
Hardcastle, Captain William H., 221, 300 (photo), 306, 308, 312-14, 324-25, 327, 329
Hardie, Lieutenant James S., 448
Harkins, General Paul D., USA, 79, 187, 199-200, 220, 229, 247, 304, 306, 316
  Laos crises, 63, 67, 75
  on insurgency in South Vietnam, 164, 264-67, 269, 276
  HSAS, 258, 260-61
  on actions against North Vietnam, 334-35, 338, 395-96
Ha Tien, 174, 322
Ha Tinh, 507
Hau Giang (HQ-406), 330
Hau My, 151
Hawaii, 7, 117, 132, 138, 437
  naval and Marine forces in, 41, 61-62, 206, 217, 292, 452, 525
  meetings and conferences in, 164-65, 169, 171, 179, 228, 364, 370
Hays, Commander Lyle R., 356
Headquarters, Commandant, U.S. Marine Corps, 116, 209
Headquarters Support Activity, Saigon, 255, 257-62, 339, 345-46, 357-59, 361, 363-65
  Billeting Division, 257
  Fiscal Department, 359
  Operations Department, 260
  Port Terminal Division, 358
  Public Works Department, 257, 359
  Real Estate Division, 255
  Supply Department, 359
Head, Special Operations Section, 215
Heavy Photographic Squadron 61, 187
Heavy Photographic Squadron 61, Detachment Alpha, 282
Hedgepeth, Lieutenant Commander Charles H., 217
Heintges, Brigadier General John H., USA, 23, 29, 57
Heintges Plan, 24
Heinz, Rear Admiral Luther C., 66n
Henrico (APA-45), 31, 483, 526-27
Herrick, Captain John J., 413 (photo), 438, 449
  Desoto Patrol preparations, 398-99, 404-06
  2 August patrol, 410-15, 417, 419
  between patrols, 420, 422, 424
  4 August patrol, 425-27, 429, 431
  action reports, 440-42, 443n, 450
Herter, Christian, 38
Higbee (DD-806), 519, 526
High Command communication circuit, 406
Ho Chi Minh, 22, 201, 503
Ho Chi Minh Trail, 378
  early use of, 57, 73, 75, 85
  surge through in 1964, 301, 303, 375
  U.S. air operations over, 391, 478, 484-85, 512
Hoch, Lieutenant Wesley A., 232, 300 (photo), 324
Hoi An, 159
Hollister (DD-788), 393
Hollyfield, Captain Ernest E., Jr., 454-57, 459
Holmes, Vice Admiral Ephraim P., 206
Holts, Lieutenant (j.g.) Philip P., 190
Hon Dat Hill, 323
Hon Gay, 443, 446-47
Hong Kong, 38, 53, 178, 257, 272, 274, 345, 356, 460, 474
Hon Matt, 398, 411
Hon Me, 398, 406, 408-12, 414-15, 419, 422, 426-27, 438, 505
Hon Ne, 438, 447
Hon Nieu (also Hon Ngu), 398, 408-10, 412, 422
Honolulu, Hawaii, 335, 371, 399n, 474, 505
Hon Vat, 411
Hooper, Rear Admiral Edwin B., 77, 79, 85, 265n, 281, 286, 288n
Hopwood, Admiral Herbert G., 15, 28, 33, 37-38, 41-42, 46, 90-91, 130; see also Commander in Chief, U.S. Pacific Fleet
Hornet (CVS-12), 46-47
Hoskins, Equipment Operator Constructionman E.J., 348
Hospitals, 194, 199, 234, 258, 344; see also dispensaries
Hostvedt, Admiral Erling (Norwegian), 92 (photo)
Ho Tan Quyen, Commander (South Vietnamese), 141 (photo), 147-48, 150, 179-80, 225, 242, 249, 268, 305

Index

command of Vietnamese Navy, 140, 142
coastal patrol, 157, 168, 176, 228, 231, 239
Diem coup, 272-73, 298-99
Hot pursuit, 390, 422, 425, 438, 454
House of Representatives, U.S., 451
Ho Van Ky Thoai, Lieutenant Commander (South Vietnamese), 145, 513
Howley, Lieutenant Thomas, 222 (photo)
Hue, 38, 159, 180, 199, 234, 275, 283, 352, 474
Hue Vietnamese Church, 259
Humphrey, Hubert H., 71, 354
Hung; see Dinh Manh Hung
Hunter-Killer Group, Seventh Fleet, 8, 50, 53, 67, 78-79
Huong Giang (HQ-404), 273, 330
Huttig, Lieutenant (j.g.) Ray B., 225
Hydrography, 147, 377, 395

I

Ia Drang Valley battle, 197
Illusive (MSO-448), 170
Ilo Ilo Island, 327
Impervious (MSO-449), 177
Implicit (MSO-455), 176
Independence (CVA-62), 9
Independence Day (South Vietnamese), 49, 122, 180, 269
India, 240
Indian border, 15, 368
Indochinese peninsula, 69, 281, 369
Indonesia, 7, 17, 240, 394
Indonesian Archipelago, 283
Infiltration, 91, 94, 111, 113, 119, 123, 130, 155-57, 166, 247, 332, 350, 461, 513-14, 519; see also smuggling
  through Laos, 25, 58, 71, 85, 124, 236, 301, 366, 373, 375, 464, 477-79, 482, 484, 509, 512
  into Mekong Delta, 104, 173, 175-76, 236, 248, 302-04, 310, 322, 325, 333
  into northern South Vietnam, 158, 160, 169, 171-73, 175-77, 236
Infrared sniper scopes, 317
Ingersoll (DD-652), 396
Insecticides, 117
Intelligence, 29, 53, 89, 158, 177, 180, 182-83, 188, 192, 216, 245, 282, 296, 303, 378, 382, 384, 388, 393, 489, 492, 511
  organizations, 17, 161, 224-25, 236, 262, 299
  training, 115, 211, 230, 309
  on infiltration, 156, 169, 171, 247-48, 310, 320, 379, 391, 521
  on North Vietnam, 338, 342-43, 389, 394-400, 405-07, 409, 411-12, 414, 419, 422, 433, 435-36, 441, 443n, 457, 458n, 460-61, 469, 472, 505, 523
Interdepartmental task forces, 104, 110, 125
Interdiction, 155, 158, 246-47, 506, 510, 512

International Control Commission, 135, 371, 422
International Security Affairs, Office of, 66n, 131-32, 134
Intracoastal movement, 234, 236, 247
Iraq, 15
Iwakuni, Japan, 28, 31, 80, 272, 286
Iwo Jima (LPH-2), 272, 280

J

Jackson, Captain Henry S., 77, 80
James, Captain Daniel V., 217
Jamming devices, 117
Japan, 7, 147, 155, 252, 284, 460
  U.S. amphibious forces in, 31, 42, 46, 62, 77
  U.S. air units in, 68, 270, 379
John R. Craig (DD-885), 396, 399-400, 405
Johnson administration, 1, 338, 365, 368, 371-73, 392, 451, 474, 482, 493-95
Johnson, Chief Radarman Robert E., 432n
Johnson, Commander Ivar A., 181 (photo)
Johnson, General Harold K., USA, 469, 505, 517, 531
Johnson, Lyndon B., 71n, 73n, 110 (photo)
  on U.S. support for South Vietnam, 109, 316, 365
  pressure against North Vietnam, 334-35, 337-38
  response to Tonkin Gulf incidents, 421, 437, 440, 444, 446, 461
  actions on eve of war, 472, 483, 495, 498, 506-07, 519, 523-24, 526, 531-32
Johnson, U. Alexis, 52, 124
Johnson, Vice Admiral Roy L., 383 (photo), 452, 484, 489, 532
  visits to South Vietnam, 345, 377
  and Desoto Patrol, 398, 400, 404, 414, 419, 424, 438, 442, 451
Joint Chiefs of Staff, 6, 219-20, 265, 267, 270, 272, 275, 305-06, 452
  Laos crises, 31, 37, 41, 52, 54-55, 64, 69, 74, 79, 80, 82
  counterinsurgency and counterguerrilla warfare, 90, 93, 99, 201
  intervention in South Vietnam, 102, 107-08, 120, 123, 125-26, 128
  military aid, 131-32, 134
  naval support to South Vietnam, 183-84, 231, 239, 253, 304
  HSAS, 362-65
  actions against North Vietnam, 334, 367-69, 437-38, 456, 459, 463, 473-74, 476, 478, 483, 502, 504, 507
  air operations in Laos, 386, 388, 479, 482, 485, 510, 512
  Desoto Patrol, 393, 395, 406, 420-21, 425, 443, 457, 460, 494

deployment of U.S. forces to South Vietnam, 522, 524-26, 531-32
Joint General Staff (South Vietnamese), 136, 161, 224-25, 273, 305, 309, 325, 332
Joint Logistics Review Board, 489
Joint operations, 150, 152, 238, 330, 380
Joint operations centers, 27
Joint Research and Test Activity, 317
Joint Staff, Joint Chiefs of Staff, 125
Joint Task Force 116, 27
 in 1959-1960 Laos crises, 28, 31, 33-34, 38-39, 46, 50-51, 54
 in 1961-1962 Laos crises, 61, 63, 77, 81, 84-85
Jones, Gunner's Mate Delner, 433
"Junk Blue Book", 233
Junk Division Commanders School (South Vietnamese), 310
Junk force (South Vietnamese), 104, 111, 124-25, 157-60, 220, 228, 230-31, 236; see also South Vietnamese Navy units, Coastal Force
Junk Skippers School (South Vietnamese), 310

K

Kannack, 352
Karch, Brigadier General Frederick J., USMC, 526-27
Kearsarge (CVS-33), 39, 67 (photo), 68, 452-53, 460, 474
Keelung, Taiwan, 394, 396, 398, 410
Kefauver, Rear Admiral Russell, 355
Kennebec (AO-36), 451
Kennedy administration, 4n, 9n, 188, 195, 269-70, 277, 281, 288, 292-93, 306
 actions in Laos crises, 59, 63, 73, 76, 78, 81
 counterinsurgency and counterguerrilla measures, 97, 99, 100, 110, 128, 201
 support for South Vietnam, 95, 122, 137, 165, 228
Kennedy, John F., 1, 101, 277
 and Laos crises, 60, 72, 79, 81
 adoption of counterinsurgency and counterguerrilla warfare, 98-100, 113-14, 210n, 213, 217
 support for South Vietnam, 95, 118, 124-25, 127-28, 160, 164, 220
Kennedy, Robert F., 101
Kerr, Captain Alex A., 443
Khang Khay, 381, 387
Khang; see Le Nguyen Khang
Khanh Hoa Province, 237
Khanh; see Nguyen Khanh
Khoai; see Le Du Khoai
Khrushchev, Nikita, 15, 98
Kien Giang Province, 320
Kien Phong Province, 152
Kien River (North Vietnam), 343, 497

Kien River (South Vietnam), 322
Kim; see Le Van Kim
King (DLG-10), 275
King, Lieutenant John R., 224
King of Laos, 47, 49
Kirkpatrick, Rear Admiral Charles C., 42
Kitty Hawk (CVA-63), 279, 375, 379-81, 384-85, 387-88
Kivette, Vice Admiral Frederick N., 34, 38, 41-42, 90-91
Klusmann, Lieutenant Charles F., 381-82, 383 (photo), 384-85
Knapp, Captain Paul J., 347 (photo), 483
Knight, Lieutenant Burton L., 339
Koelper, Captain Donald E., USMC, 358
Kong Le, 45-47, 49-50, 53-55, 57, 373, 375
Kontny, Lieutenant (j.g.) Vincent L., 199
Kontum, 25
Kontum Province, 532
Korea, 55, 252, 368, 502
Korean conflict, 18, 78, 96, 107, 367, 384, 487
Kosygin, Aleksei, 494
Kronstadt patrol vessel, 396
Kuechmann, Lieutenant Jerry, 381
Kuntze, Captain Archie C., 346, 362 (photo)

L

Lach Chao Estuary, 419, 438, 440, 443, 446-47
Lam Nguon Tanh, Commander (South Vietnamese), 140
Landing Craft, Amphibious Boats Section, 138
Landing Ship Squadron 9, 286, 526
Language training, 193, 223
Lansdale, Brigadier General Edward G., USAF, 98-99, 106, 204, 338
Lao Cham Island, 342
Lao Dong Party, 156
Lao Kay, 202
Laotian air force, 378, 389, 480, 509
Laotian Armed Forces, 22-24, 29, 39, 43, 47, 60, 63, 66, 73, 78
Laotian army, 23, 76
Laotian border area, 39, 45, 53, 73, 464
Laotian government, 22-23, 26, 29, 43, 56, 66, 74, 375, 485; see also Royal Laotian Government
Laotian National Assembly, 46
Laotian panhandle, 378, 389, 477, 509
La Salle (LPD-3), 280
Latin America, 7, 55, 106
Lazarchick, Lieutenant Frank T., 299
LCU-1476, 528 (photo)
LDNN commandos (South Vietnamese), 148, 238, 310, 327, 339, 341-42, 355, 406, 513-14; see also commandos
Leader (MSO-490), 118
Leadership, 140, 143, 146, 175, 233, 262, 265, 298-99, 311, 342

Lebanon crisis, 6, 10, 22, 40, 86, 367
Le Du Khoai, Captain (North Vietnamese), 417, 442
Lee, Rear Admiral John M., 40, 452, 474, 483
Lemnitzer, General Lyman L., USA, 48 (photo), 70 (photo)
Lenawee (APA-195), 46, 270, 483, 526
Le Nguyen Khang, Lieutenant Colonel (South Vietnamese), 273
Leonard F. Mason (DD-852), 526
Le Van Kim, 298
Lewis, Commander John B., 172
Lexington (CVA-16), 31, 32 (photo), 50-51, 53-54, 61-62, 68, 183
Light Photographic Squadron 63, 379, 497
Light Photographic Squadron 63, Detachment C, 381
Limited partnership, 127-28, 164, 166, 187, 201, 533
Limited war, 88, 297, 301, 486; see also flexible response, conventional war
  concept, 1, 4
  forces, 7, 13-14, 20, 41, 280
  in Southeast Asia, 15, 17-18, 21, 36
  readiness for, 209, 213-14, 217-18, 253, 277-78, 281, 293
Lindenmayer, Lieutenant Commander Louie L., 231
Lines of communication, 24-25, 367, 369, 464, 503, 512
Linh Kiem (HQ-226), 243, 244 (photo)
Lipan (ATF-85), 154, 496
Lippman, Walter, 369
Little Creek, Virginia, 204
Litton, Seaman Larry O., 431
Lodge, Henry Cabot, 341, 356, 370, 376
Logistics, 112, 154, 159, 162-63, 192, 206, 211, 219, 240, 261, 281, 291, 337, 339, 374, 492, 512, 515, 524, 531
  facilities, 14, 172, 377, 490
  forces, 31, 33, 62, 80, 168, 280
  HSAS, 252-54, 262, 358, 361-65
Logistics Division, U.S. Pacific Fleet headquarters, 487
Long An Province, 329
Long Dao (HQ-327), 143, 144 (photo), 154
Long Range Objectives Group, 90, 294
Long Tau River, 328-29
Long Xuyen, 149
Lon Nol (Cambodian), 119 (photo)
Lorentson, Captain Adrian V., 483
LST-550, USNS, 496n
LST-629, 178
LST-630, 178
Luang Prabang, 38, 53, 56, 66, 73
Luckey, Major General Robert B., USMC, 46
Luther, Captain Roger W., 42
Luzon, Philippines, 31, 452
Luzon Strait, 460

Lyman K. Swenson (DD-729), 270, 275, 320, 356
Ly Nhon, 329
Lynn, Commander Doyle W., 385-86

Mc

McAlister, Lieutenant (j.g.) John, 44
McCone, John, 440
McDonald, Admiral David L., 217, 293, 380, 468, 486, 494, 510, 515
  actions against North Vietnam, 337, 367, 369, 473
  Desoto Patrol, 404, 459n
McDonald, Commander Wesley L., 446
McElroy, Neil, 2
McGarr, Lieutenant General Lionel C., USA, 122, 124, 126, 134, 152, 156, 161, 168, 179, 190
McGill, Commander John C., Jr., 454
McGinty (DE-365), 176
McInerby, Lieutenant (j.g.) Dennis, 241
McNamara, Robert S., 102, 108, 213, 221, 247, 338n, 386, 388, 467, 496, 500, 531
  Laos crises, 60, 69, 72, 82
  military support to South Vietnam, 127, 164-66, 169, 171, 173-74, 179, 224, 228, 308, 311, 316, 349
  organization of commands, 219-20, 305-06
  infiltration, 236, 302
  Diem coup, 265, 267, 276
  conventional war readiness, 277, 289, 293
  actions against North Vietnam, 335, 337, 340, 342, 368, 370-71, 407
  in Tonkin Gulf crises, 421, 437, 440-41, 443n, 456n, 458n
McNaughton, John T., 480
MacPherson, Rear Admiral Robert A., 398
McWeeney, Seaman Patrick C., 432n

M

Mach Nuoc, 468
Maddox (DD-731), 379, 403 (photo), 438, 440, 442-43, 446, 449, 451, 457, 461, 488
  preparations for Desoto Patrol, 402, 404-06, 410
  2 August 1964 patrol, 411, 413-17, 419, 435
  between patrols, 420, 422-23, 425
  4 August 1964 patrol, 426-27, 429, 432-34, 436
Magoffin (APA-199), 51, 64, 67-68
Mahan (DLG-11), 180, 275
Majors, Lieutenant William T., 500
Malaya, 7, 94
Mang Yang Pass, 198
Manila Pact, 82
Manila, Philippines, 50, 64, 203, 286
Mansfield, Mike J., 71
Mapping, 187, 282

Marine Corps units, 4, 14, 28, 104, 214, 217, 280, 288, 293, 379, 453, 464, 475, 533
Fleet Marine Force, U.S. Pacific Fleet, 8, 13, 41
Fleet Marine Force, Seventh Fleet, 8
3rd Marine Division, 41, 79, 286-87
9th Marine Expeditionary Force, 286-87, 452, 460
1st Marine Brigade, 61, 292, 452, 525-26
Expeditionary Brigade, 107, 524-25, 532
3rd Marine Expeditionary Brigade, 79
9th Marine Expeditionary Brigade, 464, 526-27, 531
3rd Marine Expeditionary Unit, 79-80, 85
Special Landing Force, 77, 80, 269, 284, 452, 474, 522, 525-26
regimental landing teams, 27, 41, 51
battalion landing teams, 13, 27, 42, 50, 62, 64, 69, 72, 74, 270, 272, 275, 280, 282, 483, 524- 27, 531-32
3rd Marines, 80, 287
   1st Battalion, 68, 529
   2nd Battalion, 31, 62, 67, 527
4th Marines, 62
5th Marines
   1st Battalion, 69
7th Marines
   1st Battalion, 50, 54
9th Marines, 80, 483
   1st Battalion, 80
   2nd Battalion, 74, 286
   3rd Battalion, 67, 74, 77, 80, 85, 287, 526-27
12th Marines, 80
Marine reconnaissance units, 96, 121, 217
   3rd Marine Reconnaissance Battalion, 182
   Marine Reconnaissance Team, Danang, 339
   Marine Pathfinders, 121
Hawk surface-to-air missile battalion, 495, 522, 524
1st Marine Aircraft Wing, 41, 69, 272, 286
Marine aircraft groups, 27, 41, 67, 80, 452, 524
   13, 62
   16, 31, 531
Marine air base squadrons
   12, 31, 80, 287
   16, 60
Marine Air Control Squadron 4, 80
Marine attack squadrons, 291
   211, 31
   212, 61
   332, 80, 85, 287
Marine fighter squadrons, 291
   154, 61
   312, 61
   451, 78
Marine medium helicopter squadrons
   162, 85, 483, 529
   261, 77, 80, 85
   361, 475
   362, 179
   363, 78
   365, 526, 529
Marine Observation Squadron 2, 31
Marine Transport helicopter squadrons
   162, 46, 64
   163, 50
Marine Corps, U.S., 11, 13, 42, 209, 220, 278-79, 284, 296, 384, 487
Marine railways, 146, 227, 232
Market Time; see operations
Mark 56 fire director, 417
Mars (AFS-1), 281
Marshall (DD-676), 275
Marsh (DE-699), 176
Martin, Vice Admiral William I., 495
Mason, Lieutenant Ruth A., (NC), 362 (photo)
Mason, Rear Admiral Redfield, 283
Massive retaliation, 1, 2
Material Division, 91
Material Improvement Plan, 10
Material readiness, 10, 39, 117, 143, 145, 175, 292, 318
Mathews (AKA-96), 81
Maury (AGS-16), 42, 52
Medal of Honor, 431
Medical and dental care, 252, 263, 284, 309, 364, 482
   by SEABEEs, 197, 199, 352-54
   training, 211, 310
   facilities, 258, 344
Mediterranean, 7
Meetings; see also conferences
   on Laos crises, 60, 63, 66, 72
   guerrilla warfare, 99, 102
   conflict in South Vietnam, 122, 124, 169, 171, 173-74, 228, 265-66, 506-07, 531-32
   communist, 299, 504
   on fleet operations, 377, 489, 516
Mehle, Rear Admiral Roger W., 515
Mekong Boat Flotilla, 43-45
Mekong Delta, 125-26, 138, 179, 182, 272
   infiltration into, 104, 172, 236, 302-03, 310, 320, 332-33
   naval operations in, 149-50, 154, 245, 248, 316
   communists in, 196, 304-05, 324, 328, 330
   coastal patrol of, 230, 320, 325
Mekong River, 26, 152, 229
   U.S. naval operations on, 43, 45, 104, 118
   Vietnamese Navy patrol of, 111, 326-27, 333
   enemy movement on, 234, 237, 248
Mekong River Valley, 22, 55, 66, 512
Melson, Vice Admiral Charles L., 62
Meo, 86, 373, 382
Mercedes Benz engines, 240, 319
Merchant ships, 155, 292, 356, 395, 472, 488

Message Center, U.S. Pacific Fleet, 487
Meteorology, 395; see also monsoons, typhoons, weather
Metropole Hotel, Saigon, 258
Middle East, 7
Midway (CVA-41), 33, 61-62, 68, 515
Miles, Rear Admiral Milton, 303
"Military Actions to Stabilize the Situation in RVN and/or Laos", 463
Military aid and assistance, 49, 116, 131-32, 221, 253
  to Laos, 23, 40, 43, 58-60, 63, 86
  to South Vietnam, 118, 130, 137, 162, 164-65, 219, 312, 332
Military Assistance Advisory Group, Laos, 73, 84-85
Military Assistance Advisory Group, Republic of China, 253
Military assistance advisory groups, 114-15, 132, 134-35, 211
Military Assistance Advisory Group, Vietnam, 44, 90, 134, 147, 149, 161, 169, 172, 189, 208, 247, 267; see also advisors
  mission, 130-31
  military assistance, 139, 240
  advisors, 201, 219-21, 223
  HSAS, 252-55, 257-60
Military Assistance Program, 89, 91, 111, 134, 208, 212, 241, 253, 261, 305-06
  in Laos, 24, 43
  provision of boats and craft, 139, 228, 239, 247, 311, 313-14, 316
  training, 147, 251
Military police, 126, 254, 258, 358, 474
Military pressure, 372, 463, 478, 485, 506, 523, 531; see also graduated military response, flexible response
Military Sea Transportation Service, 31, 260, 292, 488, 491
  aircraft ferries, 165, 178, 355
  LSTs, 240, 281, 356, 359
  Victory ships, 293
Military Security Service (South Vietnamese), 225
Miller, Lieutenant Commander Harry R., (CHC), 259
Miller, Rear Admiral Frank B., 61
Miller, Rear Admiral George H., 293
Miller, Rear Admiral Henry L., 78, 108, 269, 370, 474, 496, 505, 507-09, 515, 519
Mindoro, Philippines, 286
Mine Defense Laboratory, Panama City, Florida, 317
Mine detection, clearance, and destruction devices, 117
Mine divisions, 64
  31, 377
  32, 377
  33, 377

93, 118
Mine Flotilla 1, 377
Mine Force, U.S. Pacific Fleet, 8
Mine Group, Seventh Fleet, 8
Mines; see ordnance
Minesweeping divisions
  71, 177
  73, 167-69, 172
  91, 176
Minh; see Duong Van Minh
Minh Hoa Island, 324
Minh Thanh, 350
Minings, 202, 440, 493, 515
  river, 130, 151, 249, 317, 357
  harbor, 355, 366, 368, 437, 456, 464, 466, 477, 479
Missiles; see ordnance
Mobile air control team, 380
Mobile Logistic Support Force, Seventh Fleet, 8, 168, 377, 490
Mobile Support Team, Danang, 208, 335, 338-39, 342
Mobile training teams, 52, 162, 206, 211, 225, 250, 252, 332
  7, 189
  7A, 227
  3-62, 224
  10-62, 190
  3-63, 241
  4-63, 190
  8-63, 251
  1-64, 251
  2-64, 319
  7-64, 318
  1-65, 309
  2-65, 318
  3-65, 309
  4-65, 311
Moc Hoa, 350
M113 armored personnel carriers, 314, 316
Mongilardi, Commander Peter, Jr., 497
Mongols, 231
Monsoons, 187, 320, 350, 353, 389, 468; see also meteorology, typhoons, weather
Montagnards, 194, 197, 350
Monterey, California, 140, 147
Monticello (LSD-35), 50, 54, 68, 74
Moore, Rear Admiral Robert B., 389, 391, 422, 431, 437, 444
Moorer, Vice Admiral Thomas H., 274 (photo), 292, 384, 440, 442, 465, 483, 490, 532
  fleet support to South Vietnam, 185, 344, 355-57, 514-15, 522
  air operations in Laos, 380, 510-11
  Desoto Patrol, 395, 398, 404-05, 419, 421, 425, 461, 494
  actions against North Vietnam, 466-67, 473, 476, 501, 506
  deployment of ground forces, 475, 524-26

Morale, 40, 107, 125, 177, 179-80, 263, 344, 391
"More flags" program, 523
Morgan, Commander Robert L., 177
Morton (DD-948), 454-57, 459-60, 462
Moscow, 461, 504
Mountbatten, Lord Louis (British), 3, 96
Mount McKinley (AGC-7), 474, 483, 526-27
Mu Gia Pass, 510-11
Muskingum(T-AK-198), USNS, 356
Mutual Security Act of 1947, 131
My An District, 152
My Qui, 152
My Tho, 149, 327
My Tho River, 327

N

Naha, Okinawa, 529
Nam Can, 150, 243
Nam Dong, 353
Nam Du (HQ-607), 234
Nam Tha, 76-78
Nape Pass, 510-12
Napier-Deltic engines, 467
Nasty fast patrol boats, 92 (photo), 93, 204-05, 207 (photo), 337, 340-41, 410-11, 467, 469
National Campaign Plan, 225
National Defense Reserve Fleet, 488
National Liberation Front of South Vietnam, 17
National Military Command Center, 380
National Military Command System, 380, 501
National Public Service Decree, 308
National security action memoranda
　111, 127
　288, 371-72, 378
　314, 472
　328, 532
National Security Council, 69, 72, 124, 371, 438, 478, 532
National War College, Washington, 210
Nation-building, 113, 195, 332, 349; see also civic action, counterinsurgency
Naval Academy, U.S., Annapolis, Maryland, 210-11
Naval Advanced Training Center (South Vietnamese), 309-10
Naval Advisory Detachment, Danang, 338-39
Naval Advisory Group, U.S. Military Assistance Command, Vietnam, 306, 313, 317, 517, 519
Naval Air Force, U.S. Pacific Fleet, 8, 296
Naval Air Stations
　Agana, Guam, 51
　Atsugi, Japan, 61
　Barbers Point, Hawaii, 384
　Cubi Point, Philippines, 51
　North Island, San Diego, California, 384
　Whidbey Island, Washington, 384
Naval Attache, Saigon, 138, 140, 142, 147-48, 157, 180, 182, 187, 266
Naval attaches, U.S., 210
Naval Beach Group 1, 44
Naval Beach Group 1, Western Pacific Detachment, 527
Naval Communications Station, Philippines, 405
Naval Component Commander, Joint Task Force 116, 79
Naval component commanders, 184, 275, 420, 452, 467, 527
Naval Construction Battalions, U.S. Pacific Fleet Detachment, Republic of Vietnam, 347
Naval construction forces, 24, 101, 113, 121
Naval Deputy to the Chief of Staff of the Armed Forces (South Vietnamese), 137, 140, 158, 239, 272-73, 275, 298, 305
Naval Exchange, Subic Bay, Philippines, 252
Naval Group China, 303
Naval gunfire support, 103, 149, 243, 320, 323, 326, 526
Naval headquarters (South Vietnamese), 224, 228, 273, 299, 329, 519
Naval Inspector General, 283
Naval Magazine, Subic Bay, Philippines, 490-91
Naval Medical Research Unit 2, 344
Naval mobile construction battalions, 126, 192-93, 286; see also SEABEEs
　3, 197, 282
　5, 39, 195
　9, 346, 475
　10, 80, 199
Naval operations command center, 248
Naval Operations Support Group, U.S. Atlantic Fleet, 209, 218
Naval Operations Support Group, U.S. Pacific Fleet, 209, 218, 303, 339
Naval Ordnance Test Station, China Lake, California, 487
Naval Postgraduate School, Monterey, California, 147
Naval regulations, 459
Naval Reserve Training Fleet, 295
Naval Reserve, U.S., 171
Naval School, Nha Trang (South Vietnamese), 134, 154
Naval Security Group, 454
Naval Ship Repair Facility, Subic Bay, Philippines, 146
Naval Stations and Schools (South Vietnamese), 137
Naval Supply Center, Oakland, California, 359
Naval Supply Center, Saigon (South Vietnamese), 137, 162, 227
Naval supply depots
　Guam, 28
　Oakland, California, 61
　Sangley Point, Philippines, 359

Subic Bay, Philippines, 284, 359, 490-91
Yokosuka, Japan, 28, 44, 61, 359
Naval support activities, 253-54
Naval Support Activity, Taipei, 253-54
Naval War College, U.S., Newport, Rhode Island, 88n, 140, 147, 210-11
"Naval Warfare Information Publication 29-1," 190-91
Naval zone commands (South Vietnamese), 225, 248, 262, 321-22
Navarro (APA-215), 77, 80
Navigational aids, 42
Navy Liaison Officer, Fort Bragg, North Carolina, 121
Navy-Marine Corps Cold War Advisory Panel, 208
Navy Medical Corps, 211
Navy Plans Branch, 114, 213
Navy Purchasing Office, London, 319
Navy Section, Military Assistance Advisory Group, Vietnam, 130, 134, 161, 215n, 220, 229, 247, 267, 303, 306, 312
Navy Supply Corps School, 211
Necas, Hospital Corpsman 2nd Class Roger C., 352
Needham, Rear Admiral Ray C., 193, 282
Negotiations, diplomatic, 63, 66, 73-74, 81, 106-07, 109, 118, 128, 467
Nelson, Lieutenant Mark V., 307 (photo)
Neutralism, 49
Neutralists (in Laos), 75, 84, 373-74, 378
New China News Agency, 422
New Life Hamlet, 353-54
New Look, 1
Newport, Rhode Island, 140, 147
New Year Offensive, 53, 57
New York, New York, 240
New Zealand, 286
Ngo Dinh Diem (South Vietnamese), 17, 95, 149, 181 (photo), 304, 334
  Communist infiltration, 25, 29n, 75
  Laos crises, 40, 76, 86, 106-08
  U.S. ship visits to Saigon, 49, 180
  U.S. intervention, 109, 120, 122, 125-26
  U.S. military assistance, 111, 127, 134, 137, 164-65
  Vietnamese Navy, 136, 142, 150, 157-58, 228-29
  coup against, 264, 266-70, 272-73, 275-76, 298-99, 302, 319, 332, 375
Ngo Dinh Nhu, Madame (South Vietnamese), 319
Ngo Dinh Nhu (South Vietnamese), 275
Nguyen Chanh Thi, Lieutenant Colonel (South Vietnamese), 142
Nguyen Chuc, 156
Nguyen Dinh Thuan (South Vietnamese), 138-39, 228

Nguyen Khanh, General (South Vietnamese), 298, 308, 328, 371-72, 376, 483, 504
Nguyen Van Thieu, General (South Vietnamese), 298
Nguyen Van Thong, Lieutenant (South Vietnamese), 159
Nha Be, 329
Nha Trang, 137, 241, 245, 251, 260-61, 266, 352, 376-77, 513, 517
  naval schools, 134, 146, 162, 224, 230, 310
  Vietnamese Naval Academy, 146-47, 224
  repair facilities, 232, 308, 319
Nhu; see Ngo Dinh Nhu
Nicholas (DDE-449), 519n, 521
Night image intensifiers, 317
Night operations, 205, 247
94 target list, 464, 502
Ninh Giang (HQ-403), 143
Ninh Thuan Province, 353
Nitze, Paul H., 70 (photo), 369, 386
Noble (APA-218), 269, 272
Nolting, Frederick E., Jr., 109, 122, 127, 156, 164, 181 (photo), 264-65
Nong Het, 57
Norfolk, Virginia, 18, 217, 340
Norodom Sihanouk (Cambodian), 175, 311
North Atlantic Treaty Organization, 7
North Borneo, 64
North Korea, 7, 284, 393
North Vietnamese air force, 470
North Vietnamese border area, 26, 36n, 39, 53, 479, 512
North Vietnamese General Staff, 156n
North Vietnamese government, 372
North Vietnamese naval headquarters, 411-12, 426, 436
North Vietnamese Navy, 236, 407, 441, 449, 461, 472
North Vietnamese Navy Units
  Northern Fleet, 412
  125th Sea Transportation Unit, 236
  PT Squadron 135, 442
  Division 3, PT Squadron 135, 412, 414
  T-142, 409, 414, 423-24, 426
  T-146, 414, 426
  T-333, 414, 416-17, 419, 426
  T-336, 414, 417, 419
  T-339, 414, 416-17, 419
North Vietnamese People's Army, 155-56, 170
Norway, 204, 339-40
Norwegian government, 337, 340, 467
Norwegian Navy, 204
No Than (HQ-225), 155
Nuclear-powered ships, 9
Nuclear warfare, 1, 3, 9, 294, 380, 488
Nuclear weapons, 1-4, 14, 20, 71, 279; see also atomic weapons
Nucleus port crews, 28

O

Oakland, California, 61, 359
Obsolescence of ships, 9, 13
Office of Information, 206
Office of Naval Intelligence, 17
Office of Naval Research, 117
Office of Special Operations, 96-97, 338
Office of the Assistant Secretary of Defense for International Security Affairs, 132
Office of the Chief of Naval Operations, 40, 66n, 73n, 91, 253, 260, 266, 515
  unconventional and counterguerrilla warfare, 97, 102-03, 113-14, 116-17
  counterinsurgency, 209-10, 213
Office of the Deputy Chief of Naval Operations (Fleet Operations and Readiness), 114
Office of the Deputy Secretary of Defense for International Security Affairs, 131
Office of the Director of Operations, Joint Staff, Joint Chiefs of Staff, 437
Office of the Secretary of Defense, 125
Office of the Special Assistant for Counterinsurgency and Special Activities, 338
Officer Candidate School, 211
Officer in Charge, Naval Construction Battalions, U.S. Pacific Fleet Detachment, Republic of Vietnam, 348
Officer in Charge of Construction, Southeast Asia, 63
Officer in Charge of Construction, Thailand, 24
Ogier, Commander Herbert L., 410, 413 (photo), 414, 417, 427, 429, 431, 433, 442
Okanogan (APA-220), 44
Okinawa, 43, 179, 252, 282, 283, 286, 465
  support during Laos crises, 27, 31, 33, 39, 41-42, 51, 60, 62-64, 68-69, 77, 79, 82
  support during Diem coup, 270, 272, 275
  support during 1964-1965 fleet deployments, 452, 460, 474, 495, 522, 525-26
Okinawa (LPH-3), 280
Oklahoma City (CLG-5), 345 (photo), 377, 452-53
Olsen, Lieutenant (j.g.) Allen N., 352
Ong Doc River, 175
Ong Trang, 243-44
Operational restrictions, 479, 493, 506, 512
Operation plans; see also plans
  CINCPAC 32, 292
  CINCPAC 32-59, 26, 82, 88
  CINCPAC 32(L)-59, 26, 28, 31, 34, 36, 39, 50, 54
  CINCPAC 33, 463
  CINCPAC 34, 334
  CINCPAC 37-64, 372, 378, 463-64
  CINCPAC 37-65, 463
  CINCPAC 46-56, 6
  CINCPACFLT 75-61, 169
  CINCPACFLT 75-62, 172
  COMUSMACV 34A, 335, 337-38, 371, 395, 397, 463
Operations
  Barrel Roll, 479-80, 482, 484-85, 491, 493, 495, 505, 509-12, 522, 533
  Blue Tree, 505-07
  Dong Tien, 152
  Flaming Dart I, 495-98, 533
  Flaming Dart II, 498, 500-01, 505, 533
  Market Time, 519, 521, 533
  Pierce Arrow, 443-44, 452-53, 461, 464, 466, 470, 491
  Rolling Thunder, 502, 504-07, 509, 512, 533
  Sea Dog, 327
  Shufly, 179, 475, 524
  Steel Tiger, 512
  Waterglass, 183, 185, 187
  Wise Tiger, 202
  Yankee Team, 378-81, 389-92, 405, 453, 480, 491, 493, 495, 505, 511, 522, 533
Ordnance, 229, 295, 386
  automatic weapons, 301, 323, 514n
    Browning automatic rifles, 229
    30-caliber machine guns, 229, 314, 329, 409
    50-caliber machine guns, 149, 229, 289, 314, 329, 341, 409
  bombs and munitions dispensers, 14, 117, 279, 446
    250-pound, 295, 480, 481 (photo), 485, 487, 497-98, 506, 509
    500-pound, 295, 480, 487, 509-10
    750-pound, 387
    1,000-pound, 498
    2,000-pound, 295, 510
    cluster bomb units, 487, 510
    delayed action, 511
    Gladeye, 487
    Lazy Dog antipersonnel, 282
    napalm, 295, 479, 506, 513
    Sadeye, 487
    Snakeye, 487
    Walleye, 279, 487
  depth charges, 14, 407, 433-34
  flamethrowers, 205, 249
  45-caliber pistols, 229
  guns, 294, 297, 301, 407
    3-inch, 244, 329-30, 416, 434, 455-56
    3-inch/50-caliber, 154, 289, 322, 416n, 419, 433
    5-inch, 294, 416, 431, 434, 455-56
    5-inch/38 caliber, 415, 416n
    5-inch/54 caliber, 419, 450
    6-inch, 294
    8-inch, 294
    16-inch, 294
    14.5-millimeter, 407, 417

20-millimeter, 149, 151, 154, 185, 203, 205, 244, 343, 409, 415, 424, 447, 487, 498, 506, 510
37-millimeter, 381, 407, 497, 506
40-millimeter, 149, 154, 203, 205, 244, 289, 335, 340-41, 343, 409, 424
57-millimeter recoilless rifle, 343, 409, 424, 468, 514n
grenade launchers, 301, 317
grenades, 514n
mines, 198, 327, 377
  anti-tank, 301
  Claymore, 317
  Mark 50, 440
  river, 117, 150-51, 240, 249, 316-17, 355, 357
missiles, 9, 100, 117, 180, 217, 278-79, 294, 470, 472
  Bullpup, 279, 295, 487
  Hawk, 475, 495, 522, 524
  Polaris, 4, 228
  Redeye, 289
  SA-2, 502
  Shrike, 279, 487
  Sidewinder, 279, 386, 415, 486
  Sparrow, 279, 296 (photo), 486
  Talos, 295
  Tartar, 295
  Terrier, 295
mortars, 301, 495, 514n
  60-millimeter, 154, 343
  81-millimeter, 149, 289, 323, 327, 340, 407, 468
multiple bomb racks, 279
pyrotechnics
  flares, 431n, 433, 441, 457
  star shells, 431n, 433-34
rifles, 159, 229, 514n
rockets, 279, 387, 446, 506, 510
  2.75-inch, 447, 497
  3.5-inch, 205
  4.5-inch, 407
  Zuni, 415, 417, 498
submachine guns, 159, 514n
Thompson submachine guns, 229
torpedoes, 14, 295, 407, 416-17, 438, 440-43, 455-56, 459
Oregon Mail, SS, 44
Oriskany (CVA-34), 272, 275
Osterhoudt, Captain Raymond S., 213
Outlaw, Rear Admiral Edward C., 507
Overhauls, 10, 40, 145-46, 153, 206, 227, 292, 318, 338, 488
Oxley, Lieutenant (j.g.) Francis M., 350

P

Pacific Architects and Engineers Corporation, 364

Pacification, 199, 344, 348, 371; see also civic action
Pacific Command, U.S., 14, 107, 109, 169, 241, 253, 440, 475
  readiness during Laos crises, 26-27, 30, 39, 55, 75
  readiness during Diem coup, 272
Pacific Fleet, U.S., 50, 97, 104, 212, 303, 493-94, 532-33
  mission, 7, 27, 130
  conventional war capability, 18, 41, 93, 277, 281, 284, 292, 294-97, 463, 486-87, 491, 515
  deployments for Laos crises, 46, 52
  operations in South Vietnamese waters, 177, 180
  SEAL and STAT units, 189, 192-93, 349
Pacific Ocean, 28, 30, 117, 171, 285, 297, 510
  U.S. military units, 14, 61, 252, 281, 422
  U.S. military leaders, 93, 220
Pacific theater, 79, 91, 126, 132, 302
Pakse, 45, 51
Panama Canal, 205, 292
Panama City, Florida, 317
Panjang Island, 320
Paracel Islands, 33, 119, 154-55, 168-69
Paramilitary forces, 28, 94-95, 197, 238, 267, 308-09, 325, 329, 330, 513; see also Civil Guard, Self Defense Corps
Paramilitary operations, 101, 121, 205
Paratroops, 46, 50, 142, 152
Parham, Commander Thomas D., (CHC), 492
Parke, Commander Everett A., 119 (photo), 180, 266
Parsons (DDG-33), 53
Pathet Lao, 22, 98, 109, 373, 375, 382, 477, 486, 512
  1959 crisis in Laos, 26, 29, 36, 40
  Kong Le coup, 45, 47, 53-55, 57
  1961-1962 crisis in Laos, 60, 66, 73-78, 82-83
  U.S. air operations against, 378, 381, 388
Patrol Force, Seventh Fleet, 452-53, 496
Patrol squadrons
  2, 519
  40, 52, 77, 169
  47, 496
Pattle Island, 155
Paul Revere (APA-248), 50, 54, 68, 74, 344
Peace Corps, 354
Peacock (MSC-198), 519n
Pearl Harbor, Hawaii, 68, 206
Peking (also Peiping), 17, 52, 444, 461
Pentagon, 380, 437
Peoples Republic of China, 7, 393; see also China
Perch (APSS-313), 217
Perkins, Lieutenant Robert C., 314
Pershing Field, Saigon, 358
Persistent (MSO-491), 176

Persons, Rear Admiral Henry S., 161-62
P-4 motor torpedo boats (North Vietnamese), 407, 414-15, 418 (photo), 426-27, 433, 447, 448 (photo)
Phan Rang, 353
Phan Thiet, 50, 54, 283
Philadelphia Naval Shipyard, 203-04
Philco Corporation, 364
Philip (DD-498), 320
Philippine Navy, 240
Philippines, 7, 73, 94, 185, 240, 242, 286, 358, 521
  air facilities in, 43, 51, 61, 77, 495
  naval support facilities in, 206, 283-84, 340, 465, 490
Phillips, Captain Robert A., 344
Phnom Penh, 43-44, 49, 118, 261
Phoebe (MSC-199), 519n
Phoenix (T-AG-172), USNS, 293
Phong, Commander (South Vietnamese), 307 (photo)
Phong Saly Province, 22
Photographic interpretation, 282
Photography, 51, 187, 233, 376, 395-96, 400, 410, 480
Phoui Sanikone (Laotian), 23
Phoumi Nosavan (Laotian), 23, 65 (photo)
  Kong Le coup, 46-47, 49-50, 52-53, 55, 57-58
  1961-1962 crises in Laos, 59-61, 63, 75-76, 84, 86
Phuc Yen airfield, 456, 473
Phu Du (HQ-600), 327
Phuoc Hoa, 239
Phuoc Tuy Province, 238-39
Phu Qui, 505
Phu Quoc Island, 154, 167, 173-75, 230, 245, 259, 320, 322, 323, 465
Phu Van, 507
Phu Yen Province, 237
Picking (DD-685), 398-400, 402
Piedmont (AD-17), 356
Pierce Arrow; see operations
Pine Island (AV-12), 52, 172, 452
Pioneer Myth, SS, 340
Pirate Islands, 324
Pirie, Admiral Robert B., 216
Pitcher, Lieutenant (j.g.) William F., 352
Pivot (MSO-463), 519n
Plain of Jars, 54-55, 57, 60, 75, 375, 378-79, 385, 388-89, 484, 512
Plain of Reeds, 138, 151, 350
Planning Programming Budgeting System, 338n
Plans, 6, 24, 43, 84, 102, 114, 121, 148, 192, 198, 208, 219, 224, 289, 309, 363-64, 398, 491; see also operation plans
  defense of Laos, 26, 28, 64
  defense of Southeast Asia, 26, 88
  defense of South Vietnam, 104, 107, 361
  counterinsurgency, 93-95, 269, 304, 326, 371

  coastal patrol, 158-59, 161, 169, 239
  actions against North Vietnam, 334-35, 337, 372, 463, 470, 492, 502, 522
  Marine deployments to South Vietnam, 475, 526
Pledge (MSO-492), 169, 170 (photo)
Pleiku city, 183-84, 197-98, 350, 495, 498, 524
Pleiku Leprosarium, 259
Pleiku Province, 532
Plei Me, 197
Plei Mrong, 197
Plei Ta Nangle, 198
Pluck (MSO-464), 519n
Plzak, Seaman Dennis P., 427n
Point Barrow (AKD-1), 340
Point Defiance (LSD-31), 17, 80, 206, 208, 272
Point Yankee, 376; see also Yankee Station
Polaris submarine, 4, 278, 288
Polei Krong, 197
Politico-Military Policy Division, 66n, 76, 209
Pollux (AKS-4), 51
Popowich, Lieutenant Clyde V., 196
Port calls, 7, 38, 49, 53, 118, 122, 212, 269
Port Hueneme, California, 193, 346
Port operations, 28, 359
Port services, 260, 263
Potomac River, 205
Preble (DLG-15), 9
Presgrove, Commander Charles K., 231
Presidential directives, 483
Presidential Palace (South Vietnamese), 142, 272
Presidential Program, 110, 118, 135, 137, 160, 164
Princeton (CVS-37), 11
Princeton (LPH-5), 12 (photo), 178-79, 188, 269, 286-87, 345, 474, 483, 526, 529
Prisoners of war, 39, 154-55, 234, 241, 244, 301, 382, 384
Procurement of material, 291, 294-95
Programs Evaluation Office, Laos, 23-24
Projection of power ashore, 7, 62, 69, 277-78, 288, 295
Propaganda, 29, 180
Protestant Chapel Fund, 259
Providence (CLG-6), 269, 344
Provo (T-AG-173), USNS, 293
P-6 patrol craft (North Vietnamese), 411
Psychological warfare, 114, 158, 306, 329
  training, 115, 202, 211, 230
  execution, 202, 236, 327, 338, 343, 469
PT-810, 203-04
PT-811, 203-04
PTF-1, 204, 337, 340-41, 423-24, 467
PTF-2, 204, 337, 340-41, 408-11, 424, 467
PTF-3, 204-06, 207 (photo), 340, 406, 408-09, 468
PTF-4, 204-06, 207 (photo), 340, 406
PTF-5, 340, 343, 406, 408-10, 423-24, 468

PTF-6, 340, 343, 406, 408-09, 424
PTF-7, 340, 468
PTF-8, 340

Q

Quang Khe, 156, 202, 341, 343, 398, 438, 440, 443, 446-47, 504-05
Quang Nam Province, 159
Quang Ngai city, 199, 345, 352-53, 522-23
Quang Ngai Province, 158, 515
Quang Tri, 38, 178, 283, 352-53
Quang Tri Province, 160
Queenfish (SS-393), 241
Quemoy-Matsu crisis, 22, 29
Qui Nhon, 178, 180, 182, 241, 260-61, 283, 352, 498, 517, 524
Quyen; see Ho Tan Quyen

R

Rach Gia, 150, 228, 232, 308, 319, 322-23
Radford, Admiral Arthur W., 131
Radford (DD-446), 395-96, 519n, 521
Radios, 117, 156, 159-60, 193, 202, 363, 386, 406, 415, 517
Raids, 91, 112, 202, 237, 366, 407, 464, 470
Railroads, 162, 192, 201-02, 240
Raleigh (LPD-1), 280
Ramsey, Rear Admiral Paul H., 93
Ranger (CVA-61), 9, 452, 483, 515-16
  air operations in Laos, 391, 480, 485, 495, 509, 511
  air operations in North Vietnam, 496, 498, 505-06
Rayburn, Sam, 71
Reclaimer (ARS-42), 154, 355, 496n
Reconnaissance, 51, 126, 168, 187, 216, 284, 296, 394, 406, 492, 515
  coastal and river, 44, 91, 103, 182, 190, 192
  over Laos, 74, 86, 368, 378-81, 385, 387-89, 391-92, 444, 460, 479-80, 484-85, 493, 509-12
  over North Vietnam, 366, 368, 372, 446-47, 449, 498, 502, 505-07
Recruiting, 231, 262, 308-09, 333
Red Beach II, Danang, 527, 529
Reed, Rear Admiral Allan L., 190
Renville (APA-227), 69
Repair and Maintenance Team, Danang, 338, 342
Republic of China, 7; see also Taiwan
Republic of Vietnam Armed Forces, 89, 135, 152, 184, 366, 504
  U.S. assistance to, 95, 104, 111, 118, 130, 137, 177, 264, 523
  improvement of, 265, 268, 275
  under attack, 299, 332
Republic of Vietnam (South Vietnam), 130, 184-85, 272, 349, 465-66, 514, 523

U.S. support of, 275, 337, 464, 473
enemy in, 332, 504
U.S. logistic organization in, 362-63
Research and development, 117, 278, 297
Research and Development Field Unit, 233
Reserve Fleet, 171, 240, 292
Resident Officer in Charge of Construction, Vientiane, 64
Rest and recuperation flights, 257
Restricted waters, 91, 103, 111, 115, 190-91, 213, 215n, 339
Reynolds, Lieutenant (j.g.) Ann P., (NC), 362 (photo)
Rhade tribesmen, 196
Rhode Island, 140, 147
Richard S. Edwards (DD-950), 394, 454-57, 459-60, 462
Richardson, Lieutenant General James L., USA, 79
Ricketts, Admiral Claude V., 83n, 302, 340, 349, 367-69
Rightists (in Laos), 23, 53, 58, 76, 373, 375
River assault groups (South Vietnamese); see South Vietnamese Navy units
River Force (South Vietnamese); see South Vietnamese Navy units
Rivero, Admiral Horacio, 517
River patrol, 94, 111-12, 130, 149, 316, 325, 327
River Transport Escort Group (South Vietnamese); see South Vietnamese Navy units
River Warfare Force, 214-15
Roberts, Major General Carson, USMC, 27-28, 39
Roche, Lieutenant (j.g.) William H., 353
Rodgers, Lieutenant Commander Harvey P., 513
Roeder, Rear Admiral Bernard F., 68
Rogers (DD-876), 526
Rogers (DDR-876), 46
Rolling Thunder operation; see operations
Ron River, 409, 424
Rostow, Walt W., 101
Routes
  1 (North Vietnam), 341, 343, 497, 507
  15 (South Vietnam), 239
  19 (South Vietnam), 198
  4 (Laos), 379
  6 (Laos), 379, 512
  7 (Laos), 379, 484, 502, 512
  8 (Laos), 479, 511
  9 (Laos), 482
  12 (Laos), 479
  23 (Laos), 484, 509-11
  121 (Laos), 479
Routh, Lieutenant (j.g.) Alan C., 190
Royal Laotian Government, 22, 25, 29, 33, 36, 59, 77; see also Laotian government
Ruff, Lieutenant Lowell H., 353

Rules of engagement, 425, 485, 517; see also standard operating procedures
Rung Sat Special Zone, 329-30, 333
Rung Sat Swamp, 150, 240, 245, 317, 328
Rupertus (DD-851), 457
Rural Rehabilitation Program, 198
Rusk, Dean, 81, 95, 107, 126-27, 278, 285, 375, 421, 437, 440
Russell, Admiral James S., 115
Russell, Richard B., 71
Ryan, Lieutenant (j.g.) Bruce, 233

S

Sabotage, 121, 191, 356, 523
　training, 99, 190
　planning, 202, 338, 366, 397-98, 408
　execution, 341, 343, 410
Sacramento (AOE-1), 280-81
Saigon, 44, 134-35, 142, 150, 157, 165, 179, 183, 190, 197, 203, 219, 223, 245, 253, 270, 272, 350, 353, 355, 357, 370, 376, 380, 474, 483
　visits, 49, 122, 161, 167-68, 178, 180, 241, 266, 269, 305, 311, 335, 344, 356, 375, 377, 502, 517
　Vietnamese naval headquarters, 137, 149, 153, 224, 329
　Vietnamese training, construction, repair, and supply facilities, 137, 140, 145-46, 149, 161, 227, 230, 249, 309-10
　Vietnamese naval forces in, 227, 238, 326
　U.S. headquarters, 193, 200, 255, 268, 338, 341, 404, 500, 505
　U.S. logistic facilities, 252, 254-55, 257-62, 358-59, 361, 363, 482
Saigon Arsenal (French), 145
Saigon Naval Shipyard, 139, 145-46, 161-62, 227-29, 245, 272-73, 313, 318
Saigon River, 49, 180, 245, 249, 269, 272-74, 355
Saigon shipping channel, 327, 330, 355-57
Saigon Station Hospital, 258-59, 361, 482
Saint Paul (CA-73), 33, 49, 64, 294
Sakhalin Island, 397
Salamis battle, 314
Salisbury Sound (AV-13), 496
Salvage, 310, 355, 513
Sambor Rapids, 45
Sam Neua Province, 22, 26, 29-30, 38
Samuel N. Moore (DD-747), 379, 434, 451
San Diego, California, 205-06
Sangley Point, Philippines, 33, 43, 61, 242, 283-84, 452, 490-91, 496
San Jose, Philippines, 287
Sasebo, Japan, 67
Sather, Lieutenant (j.g.) Richard C., 448
Savannakhet, 57
Savidge, Rear Admiral Paul, 303

Schade, Rear Admiral Arnold F., 76, 84, 165
Schneider, Captain Frederick H., 49
Schoech, Vice Admiral William A., 78, 85, 167, 169, 175, 177, 179, 183, 393
Schools, 102, 114-15, 146-47, 162, 210-11, 249-50, 262, 309-10, 318, 332
Schroder, Lieutenant Donald C., 324
SEABEEs, 113, 287
　in Laos crises, 24-25, 27, 80
　in South Vietnam, 196-98, 346, 348-50, 352-54, 365, 475
SEABEE technical assistance teams, 113, 115, 120-21, 129, 189, 192-95, 198-200, 211-12, 218, 348-49, 354-55
　0301, 197-98
　0302, 197-98
　0501, 194-96, 198
　0502, 194, 196-98
　0503, 350
　0504, 350, 352
　0505, 353
　0506, 353
　0903, 352
　0904, 352-53
　1001, 199-200
　1002, 199-200
　1003, 350
　1004, 352
SEABEE well drilling teams, 346, 349, 354
　1, 347
　2, 347
　3, 348
　4, 348
　5, 348
Seaborn, J. Blair (Canadian), 371
Seaborn Mission, 473n
Sea control, 288
Sea Force (South Vietnamese); see South Vietnamese Navy units
Sealift, 80, 492; see also airlift
　capability, 14, 41, 99, 277-78, 291, 293, 297, 488
　in Laos crises, 27, 33, 85
Sea lines of communication, 7, 27; see also lines of communication
Sealion (APSS-315), 217
SEALs, 191 (photo), 342, 514
　development of, 103, 112, 115, 121, 129, 211, 212, 217, 218
　tactics, 190, 192
　and fast patrol boats, 203, 205-06
　command of, 209, 213
SEAL Team 1, 189-90, 303, 339
"SEAL Teams in Naval Special Warfare," 190
SEAL Team 2, 190
SEAL Training Team, Danang, 339
Sea of Japan, 7, 397, 405n
Sea of Okhotsk, 405
Sea patrol, 119, 158, 172-73, 177, 323

Search and rescue, 216-17, 391, 446-47, 480, 500, 505, 510-11, 522
Searchlights, 434, 440, 457
Secretary of State for National Defense (South Vietnamese), 138, 228
Secretary of the Navy, 9-11, 13, 205, 217, 291, 294, 369, 386, 468, 514n
Self Defense Corps (South Vietnamese), 239, 247
Sells, Commander Warren H., 498
Seminole (AKA-104), 51, 85
Senate Armed Services Committee, 15
Senate, U.S., 451
Senior Advisor, 2nd Coastal District, 513
Senior Junk Force Advisor, 231, 233
Seno, 27, 38, 51
Sentel, Seaman Edwin R., 431
Sentry (MSF-299), 240
Serene (MSF-300), 312
Serrell, Commander Andrew, 443
Service Force, U.S. Pacific Fleet, 8, 193, 288n, 355, 359
Seven Mountains, 196
17th parallel, 119, 157, 160, 168-69, 171-73, 176-77, 187, 468, 517, 521
Seventh Fleet, 7-8, 118, 122, 126, 146-47, 164, 180, 183, 185, 187, 189, 282, 287, 292, 309, 335, 344, 376-77, 444, 452, 474, 484, 495, 515, 521, 526-27
   deployments for Laos crises, 1959-1960, 31, 34, 38-42, 46, 49-51, 53-54, 58
   deployments for Laos crises, 1961-1962, 61-62, 64, 69, 73-74, 77,86
   coastal patrol, 123-25, 168-69, 176-77, 187, 512, 517, 519
   coup deployments, 142, 269, 272, 276
   air operations in Laos, 380-81, 389, 391-92, 482, 511
   Desoto Patrol, 393-94, 404, 421, 459-60
   preparations for war, 486-90, 492
Shangri La (CVA-38), 33
Sharkey, Boatswain's Mate 3rd Class Donald V., 433
Sharp, Admiral Ulysses S.G., Jr., 102, 208, 216, 274 (photo), 302, 341, 349, 357, 408, 467, 483, 485
   logistic support in South Vietnam, 361-64
   bases in South Vietnam, 377, 464, 475
   Desoto Patrol, 396, 398, 402, 405, 420-21, 425, 453, 460-61
   air operations against North Vietnam, 437-38, 456, 473, 476-78, 500, 502-04, 509
   Tonkin Gulf attacks, 441-42, 443n
   air operations in Laos, 479-80, 510-11
   troop deployments to South Vietnam, 522, 524-26, 531-32
Shawkey, Lieutenant Dallas W., 234
Shell Oil Company, 208
Shelter (MSF-301), 312
Shelton (DD-790), 393
Shelton, Lieutenant Wallace A., 184
Shepard, Lieutenant Commander Philip B., 225
Ship and boat yards, 145-46, 227-29, 236, 239, 318
Ship construction and modernization, 9, 10, 13, 90, 125, 137, 236, 278, 280-81, 288-89
Ship Repair Facility, Subic Bay, Philippines, 340
Ship Repair Facility, Yokosuka, Japan, 44
Ship types
   aircraft carriers, 4, 9, 11, 14, 40-41, 62, 78, 93, 97, 183, 214, 278, 297, 375, 379, 389, 391, 440, 444, 455, 487, 495, 498, 505, 511, 515, 526
   aircraft ferries, 165, 178, 355
   antisubmarine warfare, 50, 62, 295, 405n, 452
   attack, 50, 68, 279, 295, 452, 486
   escort, 11
   amphibious, 4, 11, 31, 41, 77, 93, 214, 242, 278, 291-92, 294, 453, 525
   amphibious assault ships, 11, 50, 77, 216, 280, 289, 291, 295, 297, 529
   amphibious force flagships, 295
   amphibious transport docks, 214, 280, 289, 291, 295, 297
   landing ships, dock, 11, 31, 42, 62, 68, 214, 280, 295
   landing ships, infantry, large, 44, 143, 151, 153-54, 243, 247, 320, 323, 327, 329
   landing ships, medium, 137, 143, 153, 162, 214, 240-41, 243, 273, 309, 319, 330, 513
   landing ships, medium, rocket, 294
   landing ships, tank, 11, 31, 33, 51, 62, 68, 162, 240, 243, 273, 281, 295, 327, 352, 356, 359, 486, 521, 531
   landing support ships, large, 153-55, 243-44, 247
   cruisers, 93, 294-95, 420, 452, 487
   guided missile, 180
   light guided missile, 344
   destroyer types, 180, 295, 486
   destroyer escorts, 68, 171-74, 176-77, 289, 295, 521
   destroyers, 33, 62, 68, 93, 123, 179, 270, 286, 320, 356, 393-96, 398, 400, 402, 404-05, 410-11, 414-17, 419-21, 423, 425, 427, 429, 432-38, 441, 443, 451-59, 492, 494, 505, 512, 517, 521
   escorts, 103, 137, 240-42, 295, 312, 320, 323, 513
   guided missile frigates, 180
   radar picket escort ships, 295
   submarine chasers, 136-37, 143, 145-47, 153-54, 168, 170, 173, 241-42, 394, 407, 513

gunboats, 90, 93, 125, 234, 237, 239-40, 289, 299, 311-12, 319-20, 323, 327, 339, 521; see also Swatow gunboats
minesweepers, 453, 517, 521
   coastal, 104, 137, 143, 242, 295, 394
   fleet, 240, 312
   ocean, 167-68, 171, 176, 289, 295
submarines, 9, 64, 68, 180, 202-03, 214, 241, 295, 400, 453, 486, 505
   ballistic missile-firing, 4, 278, 288
   communist, 124, 179, 302, 394, 452
   transport, 192, 216-17, 281, 467
support
   ammunition ships, 33, 62, 280, 295
   attack cargo ships, 31, 42, 62, 68, 126, 281
   attack transports, 31, 44, 62, 68, 214, 270, 344
   aviation supply ships, 281
   cargo ships, 41, 68, 173, 281, 295, 488
   combat stores ships, 281, 289, 297
   fast combat support ships, 289, 297
   fleet ocean tugs, 355-56
   fleet tugs, 295
   high-speed transports, 281
   hospital ships, 361
   landing craft repair ships, 126
   light cargo ships, 153, 208, 320
   oilers, 33, 62, 280-81, 295, 410
   repair ships, 62, 146, 295
   salvage craft tenders, 357
   salvage lifting ships, 357
   salvage ships, 355
   seaplane tenders, 52, 172, 295, 377, 452, 495-96
   stores issue ships, 281
   stores ships, 62, 281, 295
   surveying ships, 42, 52, 295
   tankers, 295, 488
   transports, 33, 41, 51, 54, 62, 68, 278, 295
   Victory ships, 293
Shishim, Senior Chief Quartermaster Walter L., 434
Shore bombardment, 244, 294, 297, 322, 330, 408-09, 469, 502, 515
Short Expeditionary Landing Field, 287
Shoup, General David M., USMC, 48 (photo), 69, 70 (photo)
Shows of force, 33-34, 78, 87, 212, 366, 379, 392; see also military pressure
Shumaker, Lieutenant Commander Robert H., 500
Siberia, 7
Sides, Admiral John H., 97, 179, 184-85, 192-93, 205
   fleet readiness, 14, 50, 282-83, 292, 294
   Laos crises, 62, 64, 67, 77, 97
   coastal patrol, 167-68, 171-72, 177
   beach surveys, 178, 182-83

   logistic support in South Vietnam, 252-54, 258-59, 261
Sihanouk; see Norodom Sihanouk
Simpson, Brigadier General Ormand, USMC, 79, 85, 287
Singapore, 145, 302
Sixth Fleet, 7
Skagit (AKA-105), 64
Skate (SSN-578), 9
Skates, T.M., 24-25
Skipjack (SSN-585), 9
Smedberg, Vice Admiral William R., III, 114
Smith, Horace, 28-30, 38
Smith, Rear Admiral Daniel F., 270
Smoot, Vice Admiral Roland N., 18
Smuggling, 155, 158, 247, 304; see also infiltration
Soc Trang, 78, 179, 188, 266
Soirap River, 237, 239, 330, 357
Sonar, 317, 429, 432, 440, 443, 459, 461
Song Ong Doc, 232
Son Island, 154, 173
Sonnenshein, Captain Nathan, 145
S.O.1 submarine chasers (Soviet), 407
Souphanouvong (Laotian), 22, 26, 75
South Asia, 15
South China Sea, 7, 25, 80, 179, 270, 282, 284-85, 377
   fleet deployments in 1959-1960, 28, 31, 33-34, 37, 46, 50-52, 54, 58
   fleet deployments in 1961-1962, 61-63, 67-68, 73-74, 86
   fleet deployments in 1964-1965, 375, 385, 392, 452, 490, 495-96, 527
Southeast Asia Collective Defense Treaty, 452
Southeast Asian mainland, 24, 42, 55, 61, 69, 282, 286-87
Southeast Asian nations, 7, 22, 40, 59, 72, 113, 128
Southeast Asia Treaty Organization, 29-31, 55-56, 59, 62, 64, 69, 72, 107, 130, 284-87, 361, 524
   Council, 100
   Field Forces, 73
   Military Advisors Council, 285
Southeast Asia Treaty Organization Military Advisors Fourteenth Conference, 62
Southerland (DDR-743), 275
South Korea, 7
South Vietnamese Air Force, 56, 161, 272, 310, 314, 356
   U.S. naval assistance to, 250-52, 311
   air operations, 330, 408, 469, 496, 498, 500, 505
South Vietnamese armed forces; see Republic of Vietnam Armed Forces
South Vietnamese Army, 265, 269, 299, 301, 309-10, 314, 316, 332-33
   relationships with navy, 136, 225, 304

river craft, 138-39, 227
joint operations, 150-52, 238, 242, 325-28, 330
coastal patrol, 159-61
navy support of, 240-41, 245, 248
South Vietnamese Army units
   Field Command, 138
   5th Division, 142
   21st Division, 142
   Rangers, 238-39
South Vietnamese border area, 25, 73, 123, 464, 510
South Vietnamese government, 38
   under Diem, 17, 52, 75, 111, 122, 124, 127-28, 135, 164, 172, 180, 269-70, 298, 304, 326
   under Khanh, 337, 349, 357, 370, 375, 392, 465, 474-75, 478, 583, 593
South Vietnamese Marine Corps, 136-37, 142, 148, 150, 154-55, 224, 230, 304, 325
South Vietnamese Naval Academy, 146-47, 224, 242, 309
South Vietnamese Naval Staff, 137, 224-25, 228, 321
South Vietnamese Navy, 44, 130, 134, 140, 142, 161-63, 193, 219-20, 225, 250-62, 266, 305, 327-28, 332-33, 468
   coastal patrol, 94, 109, 157-59, 166, 169, 172-73, 175, 304, 320, 516-17
   river operations, 94, 304, 325-26, 329-30
   personnel, 118, 135-37, 224, 308
   material readiness, 143, 145-46, 226, 318
   training, 146-48, 180, 308-09, 311
   River Force, 148-50, 245-49
   Sea Force, 154-55, 157-59, 239-42
   Coastal Force, 228, 230, 232, 234, 237, 239
   Diem coup, 272-73, 298-99, 302
South Vietnamese Navy units
   Coastal Force, 135, 157-58, 160-61, 190, 225, 228-32, 234, 238-39, 262, 304, 308-10, 312-16, 316, 319-21, 324, 327, 332-33
   Coastal divisions, 220, 230, 238, 320
      11th, 159, 519
      15th, 233-34
      16th, 233-34
      24th, 231
      33rd, 233, 237, 327, 329, 521
      34th, 308, 323
      37th, 233
      43rd, 323
      44th, 323
   River Force, 136-37, 143, 147-52, 154, 189, 215, 220-25, 227, 237, 245, 247-49, 262, 298, 304, 306, 316-18, 325-27, 329-30, 333
   River assault groups, 149-50, 220, 243, 245, 247-48, 250, 306, 316-17, 325, 329-30, 332

River Transport Escort Group, 150, 248, 308, 316
Sea Force, 136-37, 143, 147-48, 153-55, 157, 159, 166, 173, 175-77, 220, 225, 230, 232, 234, 239-40, 242-43, 247, 262, 273, 299, 304, 306, 312, 317, 319-24, 326-27, 329-30, 333, 356
Underway Training Group, 149, 154
Souvanna Phouma (Laotian), 22-23, 46-47, 49, 75-76, 78, 373-75, 377, 387-88, 479
Soviet Union, 2, 4, 185, 405; see also Union of Soviet Socialist Republics
   threat from, 7, 15, 37, 98, 107, 109
   in Laos crises, 49, 56, 84
Spanka, Radarman 1st Class John B., 433
Special Assistant to the President for National Security Affairs, 437
Special Forces camps, 195-98, 348, 350, 352-54
Special Forces; see Army, U.S., units
Special Group (Counterinsurgency), 201
Special Group (5412), 203
Special Military Representative to the President, 4n
Special MSO Patrol Group, 176
Special National Intelligence Estimate, 476
Special operations, 112, 114, 148, 205-06, 209, 217, 310, 339
Special operations group, 213, 215
Special Operations Group, U.S. Military Assistance Command, Vietnam, 338, 341, 404
Special Operations Section, 116, 266
Special operations teams, 112, 115
Special Warfare Center, U.S. Army, 122, 210-11
Sputnik, 2, 98
Standard operating procedures, 389; see also rules of engagement
State Department, U.S., 20, 175, 179, 396
   in Laos crises, 28, 30, 37, 54, 56, 60, 63, 74
   insurgency in South Vietnam, 106, 122, 201
   foreign aid, 131-32, 134
Stockdale, Vice Admiral James B., 417, 431, 446
Story, Lieutenant (j.g.) Douglas E., 311
Strait of Malacca, 460
Strategic Hamlet Program, 198, 243, 299, 304, 353
Strategic Plans Division, 112, 165, 209
Strategists, 3, 4, 55, 75, 334, 486, 493, 523
Strategy, 1-4, 18-20, 98, 166, 301, 328, 388, 466, 531, 533
Stratton, Samuel S., 30
Strean, Rear Admiral Bernard M., 172
Strike Warfare Division, 209
Stroh, Rear Admiral Robert J., 43
Strong, Captain Stockton B., 50
Studies and Observation Group, 338; see also Special Operations Group
Stump, Admiral Felix B., 13-14
Subic Bay Naval Base, 178, 335, 339

Subic Bay, Philippines, 168, 172, 282, 357, 454, 467
  fleet concentrations, 33, 38, 46, 50, 53, 64, 77, 80, 178, 208, 217, 269, 281, 293, 337, 379, 452-53, 460, 474, 483
  logistic support facilities, 145, 206, 283, 319, 338, 340, 490
Sublimited warfare, 213
Submarine Force, U.S. Pacific Fleet, 8
Submarine Group, Seventh Fleet, 8
Subversion, 25, 84, 88-89, 96, 98-99, 128, 160, 285
Sugg, Commander Howard A.I., 215n
Sullivan, William H., 479-80, 511
Supply, 206, 211, 227, 262, 318-19, 332, 363
Surfbird (ADG-383), 242
Survey teams, 146, 253, 303, 312, 376
Survival, evasion, resistance, and escape, 382, 384, 391; see also evasion and escape
Survival kits, 102, 117
Swatow gunboats (North Vietnamese), 472, 497, 505
  maritime operations in North Vietnam, 202-03, 341, 343, 398, 406-07, 409
  Tonkin Gulf incidents, 414, 423-24, 426, 427n, 442-43
  Pierce Arrow strikes, 446-47, 448 (photo), 449, 450 (photo)
Swift fast patrol craft, 314, 337, 339-40, 397, 402, 407
Swimmers, 341, 343
Sylva, Lieutenant John P., (CEC), 64, 65 (photo)
Syria, 15

T

Tactics, 89, 101, 151-52, 210, 322, 325, 433, 460, 465
  guerrilla warfare, 24, 103, 115, 190, 192
  river warfare, 215, 339
Tac Van, 348
Tahimik, 285-87
Taiwan, 33, 46, 148, 253, 344, 394, 396-97, 399n, 400, 410; see also Republic of China
Taiwan Defense Command, U.S., 253
Taiwan Patrol Force, Seventh Fleet, 8
Taiwan Strait, 7, 68, 286
Taiwan Strait crisis, 6, 10, 15, 40, 54, 86, 367
Talladega (APA-208), 80
Tam Xet (HQ-331), 44
Tan An, 243
Tanh; see Lam Nguon Tanh
Tan Hiep, 347
Tan Son Nhut Airfield, 184-85, 187, 258, 274, 320, 352, 380, 457, 517, 519, 522
Task elements, 8
Task forces, 8, 27, 86, 270
  71, 519
  72, 8
  73, 8, 33, 62, 168, 377, 490
  76, 8, 51, 54, 62, 74, 182, 292, 460, 474, 526
  77, 8, 61, 179, 391, 444, 452, 482, 497-98, 505, 507, 508 (photo)
  79, 8
Task groups, 8, 28, 31, 54, 80
Task units, 8
Tawakoni (ATF-114), 356
Tawasa (ATF-92), 356
Taylor, General Maxwell D., 4, 4n
  as Kennedy advisor, 101, 125
  Chairman, Joint Chiefs of Staff, 342, 376
  as U.S. Ambassador, Saigon, 364, 463, 473, 478, 483, 502, 525, 531-32
Taylor mission to South Vietnam, 76, 124-25, 127, 164, 201
Taylor, Vice Admiral Rufus L., 486
Tay Ninh, 151, 352
Tchepone, 73, 509
Temporary Equipment Recovery Mission, 134-35
Teredo worms, 312
Terrell County (LST-1157), 85, 531
Terrorists, 255-58
Tet (Vietnamese holiday), 494
Thailand, 240, 349, 386, 390, 465, 472, 482
  Laos crises, 22, 29, 38, 47, 52, 55, 60, 72-73, 75, 78
  deployment of U.S. forces, 79-87, 176, 293
Thang; see Bang Cao Thang
Thanh Hoa, 283, 444, 420, 505
Than Tien (HQ-328), 327
Thao Ma, General (Laotian), 485
Thap Muoi Canal, 152, 248
Thede, Commander William L., 233
Thetis Bay (CVE-90), 11
Thetis Bay (LPH-6), 28, 31, 33, 36-39, 42, 62, 64, 67-68, 74
Thi; see Nguyen Chanh Thi
Thieu; see Nguyen Van Thieu
34A maritime operations, 190, 463, 522
  inception and early operations, 200, 203, 338-39, 341-42
  Desoto Patrol, 395, 397-98, 402, 404-07, 422, 425, 435, 460
  post Tonkin Gulf, 466-69, 478
Thoai; see Ho Van Ky Thoai
Thomas, Chief Equipment Operator R.W., 475
Thomaston (LSD-28), 46, 269, 475, 483, 526, 529
Thong; see Nguyen Van Thong
Thuan; see Nguyen Dinh Thuan
Thu Duc, 273
Tibbets, Rear Admiral Joseph B., 78-79
Tibet, 15, 43
Ticonderoga (CVA-14), 389, 390 (photo), 391, 453, 460, 474

Index

Tonkin Gulf incidents, 405-06, 410, 415, 417, 422, 426, 431, 440
  Pierce Arrow strikes, 444, 446-47, 449, 451
Tien Giang (HQ-405), 513
Tiensha Peninsula, 529
Tilley, Commander Herbert S., 527
Time zones, 399n
"Tit-for-tat" air strikes, 372, 464, 473, 478, 503
Toledo (CA-133), 33
Tonkin Gulf Resolution, 451, 462
Topeka (CLG-8), 452-53
Torpedo attack, 414-15, 417, 420, 429, 431-32, 437, 442-43, 455
Training Command, U.S. Pacific Fleet, 8
Tranh Dong River, 150
Tran Hung Dao, 231
Tran Hung Dao Street, 255, 258
Transportation of troops and supplies, 41, 49, 103, 112, 149, 303, 326
Tran Van Chon, Commander (South Vietnamese), 136, 140
Tran Van Don, Major General (South Vietnamese), 159-60, 275, 298
Trau Island, 519
Trawlers, 170, 236-37, 301, 319, 513-14, 519; see also infiltration
Triebel, Rear Admiral Charles O., 113, 121
Tripoli (LPH-10), 280
Tri Ton, 196
Triton (SSN-586), 9
Trottno, Steelworker 2nd Class William W., 348
Tuan Bien, 238
Tu, Lieutenant (North Vietnamese), 417
Tu Moi Canal, 152
Turkey, 131
Turner Joy (DD-951), 415, 419, 422-23, 426-27, 428 (photo), 429, 431-38, 440-43, 446, 450-51, 461, 488
Tuy Dong (HQ-04), 143, 513
Tuyen Doc Province, 195
Tuy Hoa, 266
Twining, General Nathan F., 48 (photo)
Type commanders, 8, 116
Type commands, 8, 384
Typhoons, 39, 46; see also meteorology, monsoons, weather

U

Udorn, Thailand, 60, 73, 80-81, 85, 385
U Minh Forest, 138
The Uncertain Trumpet, 4
Unconventional Activities Committee, 103
Unconventional Activities Working Group, 97, 103
Unconventional warfare, 95-97, 99, 103, 113-16, 121-22, 190, 200, 205, 209-10, 228

Unconventional Warfare Equipment Coordinator, 116
Under Secretary of the Navy, 205
Underwater demolition teams, 95-96, 99, 112, 115, 121, 148, 178, 182, 202, 205, 209, 217, 342, 377, 515
  11, 189
  12, 44, 182, 189
  21, 121-22
Underwater swimmer propulsion devices, 102, 117
Underway replenishment, 398, 410-11, 489-90; see also vertical replenishment
Underway Training Group (South Vietnamese); see South Vietnamese Navy units
Unification of Vietnam, 17, 29, 58, 75
Unified commanders, 7, 18, 124, 132
Unified commands, 219-20, 252-53
Union (AKA-106), 475, 483, 526-27
Union of Soviet Socialist Republics, 66; see also Soviet Union
United Nations, 29-30, 34, 37-40, 72
United Service Organization, 257
United States, 259, 317, 370, 384
  forces in, 20, 109, 204
  Vietnamese training in, 140, 147, 223, 241, 250
Urquhart, Commander Lennus B., (SC), 359
U.S. Armed Forces, 2, 81, 100, 128, 165, 276, 377, 435
U.S. country team, Laos, 37, 39, 50
U.S. country team, Vietnam, 89
U.S. embassies
  Saigon, 232, 261
  Vientiane, 480, 510
U.S. Fleet, 221, 277, 279
U.S. Government, 14, 23, 66, 180, 208, 245, 269, 275, 293, 357, 478
U.S. Military Assistance Command, Thailand, 79
U.S. Military Assistance Command, Vietnam, 266-68, 303, 308, 317, 355, 524, 526, 531
  establishment, 30, 220
  STATS, 193, 199
  intelligence, 236, 247
  command structure, 225, 305-06
  logistic support, 252-55, 261, 362-64
  actions against North Vietnam, 335, 338, 395-96, 400, 404
U.S. Naval School, Pre-Flight, 211
U.S. Operations Mission, South Vietnam, 23, 198, 232, 346, 348-49, 352, 354

V

Valley Forge (LPH-8), 77, 80, 85, 452
Vam Lang, 237
Vammen (DE-644), 176
Vance, Cyrus, 364, 437, 440, 443, 469

Vancouver (LPD-2), 205, 280, 475, 483, 526-27
Van Don (HQ-06), 241
Vang Pao, Colonel (Laotian), 373
Van Hoa (also Port Wallut), 412, 436, 443, 446n
Veatch, Hospital Corpsman T.L., 197
Vernon County (LST-1161), 62, 80, 495
Vertical envelopment, 11
Vertical replenishment, 281; see also underway replenishment
Vice Chief of Naval Operations, 83n, 115, 302, 340, 349, 369, 517
Vice President, 71n, 73n, 109
Victory Plan, 304, 320
Vientiane, 25, 27, 38, 46, 49-53, 55, 64, 66, 69, 71-73
Viet Cong, 17, 127, 139, 148, 150, 152, 164, 179, 198, 202, 216, 229, 238, 241, 243-44, 255, 265, 267, 287, 312, 322, 324-30, 350, 357, 366, 369-70, 465, 475, 486, 515-16, 522, 526, 531-32
   infiltration, 75, 111, 124, 156-58, 160, 172, 183, 187, 236, 247-48, 301-02, 320, 325, 395, 477, 504, 513-14, 533
   strength, 89, 122, 128, 332, 406
   attacks, 125, 138, 151, 182, 196-97, 234, 249, 260, 264, 266, 268, 317, 323, 348, 353, 361, 472, 493, 495, 523-25
   sabotage, 240, 355, 358, 495-96
Viet Cong units
   502nd Battalion, 152
   504th Battalion, 152
   206th Company, 237
Viet Minh, 22, 78, 82-83, 201, 388
Vietnam conflict, 169, 188, 198, 287n, 304, 391, 435; see also Vietnam War
Vietnam Delta Infiltration Study Group, 303; see also Bucklew Report
Vietnamese Air Force; see South Vietnamese Air Force
Vietnamese armed forces; see Republic of Vietnam Armed Forces
Vietnamese Army; see South Vietnamese Army
Vietnamese Marine Corps; see South Vietnamese Marine Corps
Vietnamese Navy; see South Vietnamese Navy
Vietnam Patrol Force, Seventh Fleet, 517, 519
Vietnam War, 62, 191, 218, 501; see also Vietnam conflict
Vinh, 283, 386n, 438, 440, 443-44, 446, 455-56, 476, 505
Vinh Binh Province, 196, 326
Vinh Chau, 182
Vinh Hy, 234
Vinh Long, 149
Vinh Son, 398, 406-07, 409, 424, 426, 436, 454, 468, 507
Vinnell Corporation, 364
Vinson, Carl, 71

Vireo (MSC-205), 519n
Virginia, 18, 204
Visits
   by officials, 7, 106, 109, 138-39, 150, 161, 178, 224, 265, 308, 311, 316, 344-45, 370-71, 375, 469, 502, 531
   by ships and craft, 205, 269, 344-45
   by teams, 45, 76, 117, 201
Vit Thu Lu, 456, 473, 483, 496-97
Vladivostok, 397
Voun Khom, 45
Vu Con, 498, 504
Vung Ro, 513-14
Vung Tau, 147, 241, 245, 320, 328-29, 465
   Vietnamese Navy facilities, 137, 230, 310, 319, 517
   forces assembled off, 270, 272, 275
Vung Tau Peninsula, 274

W

Walton (DE-361), 172, 174
Ward, Vice Admiral Alfred G., 141 (photo), 366-68
Warren, Captain Harry S., 116, 213
Wars of national liberation, 98, 110, 113
War Zone C, 350
Washburn (AKA-108), 483, 495, 526
Washington, 139, 205, 380, 437, 443, 451, 457, 489, 505
Washington Navy Yard, 205
Washtenaw County (LST-1166), 80
Wattay Airfield, 25
Wear, Lieutenant Commander John R., (CEC), 348
Weather, 42, 296, 527; see also meteorology, monsoons, typhoons
   in Laos, 381, 388-89, 391
   in Gulf of Tonkin, 427, 454
   in North Vietnam, 496, 498, 504-05
Weiss (APD-135), 180-83, 188
Weller, Major General Donald M., USMC, 61, 74
Wendt, Rear Admiral Waldemar F.A., 214
Wentworth, Captain Ralph S., Jr., 443
Westchester County (LST-1167), 85
West Coast, U.S., 217, 292
Westergaard, Commander Clarence W., 44
Western Pacific, 15, 212, 334
   U.S. forces in, 7, 33, 40-43, 64, 78, 80, 183, 185, 452, 465, 495, 515
   bases, 283-84, 490, 492
   strategy, 278, 282
Western Repair Facility (South Vietnamese), 227, 232, 308
Westmoreland, General William C., USA, 313, 347 (photo), 380, 514, 516
   34A maritime operations, 338, 397-98, 400, 402, 407-08, 421, 460, 469

Index

HSAS, 361-63
  air operations, 473, 478, 500, 510, 515
  deployment of forces to South Vietnam, 525, 531-32
Wheeler, General Earl, USA, 342, 421, 437, 443, 504
White, General Thomas D., USAF, 48 (photo), 70 (photo)
White House, 60, 63, 66, 95, 102, 106, 201, 440, 512, 531
Whitehurst (DE-634), 176
Whitfield County (LST-1169), 80
Widgeon (MSC-208), 519n
Wiedmer, Lieutenant (j.g.) Roger E., 352
Williams, Captain Edward A., 396
Williams, Major General Samuel T., USA, 44, 89, 134-35, 158
Williams, Ogden, 198
Williams, Petty Officer Joe Lee, 449
Williams, Rear Admiral Joseph W., Jr., 377
Wiltsie (DD-716), 506
Windham County (LST-1170), 80
Winston (AKA-94), 345
Wiseman (DE-667), 174, 176

Wisenbaker, Lieutenant (j.g.) Richard, 197
Wood, Lieutenant (j.g.) S.E., 73n
Woodrow, Lieutenant Warren A., 455
Woody Island, 155
Wooster, Lieutenant Barbara, (NC), 362 (photo)
Wooten, Lieutenant Commander Thomas F., 317
World War II, 8, 11, 96, 137, 303, 384, 487
Wright, Lieutenant Commander John A., 200
Wulzen, Rear Admiral Donald W., 492, 526-27, 529-30
Wycliff Bible Translators, 259

XYZ

Xieng Khouang, 379, 381, 385, 387
Xom Bang, 456, 505
Yabuta, Mr. (Japanese), 313-14, 332
Yankee Station, 376, 379, 388-89, 392, 452, 460, 483, 495, 497-98, 515
Yankee Team; see operations
Yokosuka, Japan, 28, 31, 44, 61, 68, 286, 356, 452, 474, 490
Yorktown (CVS-10), 515

☆U.S. GOVERNMENT PRINTING OFFICE: 1986-486-587

www.ingramcontent.com/pod-product-compliance
Lightning Source LLC
Chambersburg PA
CBHW080719300426
44114CB00019B/2419